Robert Duncan
The Ambassador from Venus

The publisher gratefully acknowledges the generous support of the Humanities Endowment Fund of the University of California Press Foundation.

The publisher also gratefully acknowledges the generous support of Jamie Rosenthal Wolf, David Wolf, Rick Rosenthal, and Nancy Stephens as members of the Publisher's Circle of the University of California Press Foundation.

Robert Duncan

THE AMBASSADOR FROM VENUS
A BIOGRAPHY

Lisa Jarnot

Foreword by Michael Davidson

UNIVERSITY OF CALIFORNIA PRESS

BERKELEY LOS ANGELES LONDON

University of California Press, one of the most distinguished university presses in the United States, enriches lives around the world by advancing scholarship in the humanities, social sciences, and natural sciences. Its activities are supported by the UC Press Foundation and by philanthropic contributions from individuals and institutions. For more information, visit www.ucpress.edu.

University of California Press
Berkeley and Los Angeles, California

University of California Press, Ltd.
London, England

For acknowledgment of previous publication, please see credits, page 511.

Library of Congress Cataloging-in-Publication Data

Jarnot, Lisa, 1967–
    Robert Duncan, the Ambassador from Venus : a biography / Lisa Jarnot.
        p.   cm.
    Includes bibliographical references and index.
    ISBN 978-0-520-23416-1 (cloth. : alk. paper)
    1. Duncan, Robert, 1919–1988.   2. Poets, American—20th century—
Biography.   3. Modernism (Literature)—United States.   4. San Francisco
(Calif.)—Intellectual life—20th century.   5. Art and literature—United
States—History—20th century.   6. Gay men—United
States—Biography.   I. Title.
    PS3507.U629Z72   2012
    811'.54—dc23
[B]   2012015163

Manufactured in the United States of America

20   19   18   17   16   15   14   13   12   11
10   9   8   7   6   5   4   3   2   1

This book is printed on Natures Book, which contains 50% post-consumer
waste and meets the minimum requirements of ANSI/NISO Z39.48–1992
(R 1997) (*Permanence of Paper*).

For Thomas

Harvey Brown recalls Olson's story of walking around and around the block near Duncan's house before building up the courage to actually ring the bell. "Well how would *you* feel," he asked Brown, "if you were about to meet the Ambassador from Venus?"

BOB CALLAHAN, introduction to "The Correspondences: Charles Olson and Carl Sauer"

CONTENTS

FOREWORD

Michael Davidson

grand collage, I name It, having only the immediate event of
words to speak for It.   ROBERT DUNCAN, *Bending the Bow*

Robert Duncan's life offers a particular challenge for the biographer. He was
a widely respected, if determinedly controversial, poet associated with the
Black Mountain school, but his early career is marked by involvement in a
number of significant literary communities. He participated in the Anaïs
Nin and Henry Miller circle in the 1940s, the surrealist movement around
View magazine during the same period, anarcho-pacifist political move-
ments in New York and the Bay Area, and the Berkeley Renaissance of the
late 1940s. He maintained close friendships with the objectivists, initially
with Louis Zukofsky on the East Coast and then with George Oppen and
Carl Rakosi in San Francisco. Although he retained his loyalty to Black
Mountain peers, his oeuvre—which includes ballads, children's rhymes,
masques, and imitations of Edith Sitwell—often seems at odds with the
more self-consciously avant-garde work of his contemporaries. Following the
success of his 1960 book, *The Opening of the Field,* and his powerful antiwar
poems in *Bending the Bow* in 1968, Duncan's reputation expanded interna-
tionally: his work was translated into many languages, and his publications
extended to mainstream literary journals, academic conferences, and presses.
Reading Duncan's life under the narrow mantle of Black Mountain poetics
misses the more erratic trajectory of his career and the eclectic nature of his
poetics. Lisa Jarnot's biography offers a useful corrective.

If Duncan's literary career occupied multiple sites, his self-mythologizing defies attempts to create a consistent narrative. Duncan thought of his life as an allegory in which everyday events held cosmic and mythic potential. In the theosophical household where he was raised, quotidian reality was regarded as a spiritual revelation. One's reading of Shakespeare or the circumstances of one's birth or world-historical events such as wars or natural disasters were clues to cosmic mysteries, and reading became an act of spiritual hermeneutics. For Duncan's adoptive parents—as for his poetics—the work of poetry was "to arouse in a contemporary consciousness reverberations of old myth, to prepare the ground so that when we return to read we will see our modern texts charged with a plot that had already begun before the first signs and signatures . . . were worked upon the walls of Altamira or Pech-Merle."[1] Such attitudes are components of the romantic imagination, to be sure, but Duncan *lived* the mythopoeic in ways that would have thoroughly perplexed Emerson or Stevens.

Duncan's mythopoeic imaginary helped produce the vatic voice that reached its most profound articulation in "A Poem Beginning with a Line by Pindar" or the later *Passages* series, but it also gave him an impish permission to adopt multiple roles and postures. By regarding his life as story, he distanced himself from received traditions and codes of behavior, making it difficult for the literary genealogist to create a coherent narrative. He liked to refer to himself as a "derivative poet" who poached from anything he might be reading, whether it was an article in *Scientific American* or a linguistic textbook or the metaphysical poets. Notoriously eclectic in his readings, Duncan could chat as knowledgeably about the Oz books, E. Nesbit, and Krazy Kat as he could about Schopenhauer or Stravinsky (he had no difficulty talking about writers he'd never read as well). His conversation was legendary for its brilliance and paratactic brio. He tended to suit his address to his interlocutor, and since, due to an ocular condition, he was unable to synchronize his vision, it was often difficult to tell which eye was looking at you and which was looking at something over your shoulder. When he became stimulated by the conversation and the rush of his own ideas, he often confused dates and personalities. I once invited him to give a lecture on Ezra Pound as modernist at which he proceeded to talk about aerial bombardment during World War II, the DNA code, his Jewish ancestry (he had none), his grandmother's life on the frontier, art glass, what is wrong with pop art, the Waite tarot deck, and various sexual experiences during the late 1940s—all without mentioning Pound. If this was disconcerting for the audience, it was for me a brilliant demonstration of

Pound's collage method. And if his "seizure of talk" was exasperating to the source-hunting student, it was also magical, carrying the listener along in a kind of verbal trance. Pound's *logopoeia,* the "dance of the intellect among words," could not have been more vividly realized. Lisa Jarnot has patiently sorted out the facts from what Duncan, in a telling oxymoron, called his "fictive certainties" and has provided us with an invaluable base for reading his poems. At the same time, Jarnot respects the generative force of Duncan's self-mythologizing and treats it as a crucial dimension of his poetics.

That poetics—what Charles Olson called "open field" or "projective" verse—is indebted to modernists like Pound and Williams and was forged among conversations with Duncan's contemporaries: Olson, Robert Creeley, Denise Levertov, Robin Blaser, and Jack Spicer. We are fortunate that he lived at some distance from his peers, thereby necessitating extensive correspondence and providing the biographer with an invaluable record. "Open form" casts poetry as a participant in, not a container for, realms of value that lie obscured from view. Where Pound hoped to erect a dynastic edifice against social decay or Eliot sought an objective correlative against solipsism, Duncan's peers emphasized the role of the body, perception, and cognition in re-engaging art with the human and natural world. Duncan's favorite metaphor for this embodied relationship to that larger world is the children's circle dance, which appears centrally in *The Opening of the Field,* albeit linked to a recurring "Atlantis" dream.[2] The dance, like the poem, is a "place of first permission" where one returns to biological and cultural origins—the lost continent of Atlantis or the lost mother of the birth trauma—through the physical act of responding to music. If this dance of discovery is innocent, its origins are heretical—sexually polyvalent, polytheistic, communalist—threatening the holy family and the capitalist state. For Duncan, in the dance and the dream, we become "creatures without imagination, as if moved by a plot or myth told by a story-teller who is not ourselves. Wandering and wondering in a foreign land or struggling in the meshes of a nightmare, we cannot escape the compelling terms of the dream unless we wake, any more than we can escape the terms of our living reality unless we die."[3] The open field is both an imperative about poetry's unfettered exploration of image, sound, and logos and a stance toward the organic unfolding of biological and social life. Unlike the work of many postwar poets, Duncan's is not self-expressive or confessionalist but rather a "structure of rime" that repeats in its architectonics the history of mimetic acts. "I create in return," Duncan says, suggesting that his art achieves novelty by responding to what surrounds him.

In developing his poetics during the 1950s and early 1960s, at the height of the cold war and the New Criticism, Duncan rejected the era's belief that modernism was a return to the "hard dry verse" of neoclassicism (Hulme, Babbitt) or that it needed to be purged of its avant-garde excesses (Clement Greenberg, the New Critics) or, indeed, that it needed to serve as a buttress against ideology. Duncan saw modernism as a much longer and more eclectic tradition. His work reads the contributions of Pound, Eliot, H. D., Stein, and Williams as an expansion of romanticism that predates its European, post-Enlightenment version and claims heritage with pre-Socratic and mystical traditions. Much of his great, unfinished poetic memoir, *The H. D. Book,* testifies to modernism's evolution from Pound's "spirit of romance" and shows how the syncretic religions and philosophical traditions of preclassical Greece and Egypt were carried forward in Apuleius, the Provençal poets, Dante, and the British romantics, culminating in Victorian writers (Lewis Carroll, Browning, Rossetti) and the era of Yeats and the Golden Dawn. No less heretical is *The H. D. Book*'s reading of a gynocentric modernism, the product of powerful women writers, editors, and activists: Virginia Woolf, Laura Riding, Marianne Moore, Gertrude Stein, Mina Loy, Mary Butts, Dorothy Richardson, and Edith Sitwell. Significant women mentors in Duncan's life—Miss Keough in Bakersfield, his theosophical Aunt Fay, and subsequent friends such as Mary Fabilli, Denise Levertov, Virginia Admiral, and Helen Adam—reinforced the centrality, for Duncan, of a female modernist tradition while allowing him to write his autobiography through their example.

Duncan's learning and erudition could be intimidating, and his interest in the occult and theosophical caused Olson to speak somewhat dismissively of the poet's Bay Area scene as "an *école des sages ou mages.*"[4] Yet this almost medieval sense of poetic coterie is the animating force in many of his poems. Adapting Dante, Duncan apostrophized his poet colleagues in "Sonnet 3":

> Robin, it would be a great thing if you, me, and Jack Spicer
> Were taken up in a sorcery with our mortal heads so turnd
> That life dimd in the light of that fairy ship
> *The Golden Vanity* or *The Revolving Lure.*[5]

If Duncan was esoteric and cosmopolitan in his cultural interests, he was also—proudly—a Western regionalist who linked the anarchic, independent spirit of a new poetry to his Western forebears.

Jarnot renders California's rich and colorful history of alternative communities and political movements as well as the landscapes in which Duncan lived—from the hot Central Valley where he grew up and the windy landscape of Morro Bay where his family spent holidays, to the cultural richness of the Mission District and the rugged beauty of Western Marin County where he and Jess established households. In doing so, she not only chronicles the life of a major U.S. poet but contributes to western cultural history.

Jarnot's account of the San Francisco Renaissance of the 1950s is particularly vivid, reminding us of the importance of community in forging a new art. But "community" by no means implies "consensus," and the period was marked as much by animadversions and sectarian conflicts as by efforts to find a common aesthetic. Contentions around issues of gay community, political activism, literary censorship, racism, alternative religious practices, and popular culture were generative in challenging the consensus model of intellectual life, linking politics and aesthetics in ways that were anathema to most Cold War intellectuals. Jarnot provides an excellent account of the sites where the San Francisco Renaissance took place: the King Ubu Gallery, which Duncan co-organized with Jess and other artists (and where, renamed the Six Gallery, Allen Ginsberg gave his first reading of "Howl"); Jack Spicer's Magic Workshop at the San Francisco Public Library; the East-West House, where Joanne Kyger gave Sunday readings; Kenneth Rexroth's house on Scott Street; and Duncan and Jess's De Haro Street home. Supplementing the more private events at these locations were public occasions in North Beach bars like The Place or Gino and Carlo's, and formal readings by out-of-town visitors at San Francisco State University's nascent Poetry Center, where Duncan coordinated readings. Except for the latter, these venues—and the many little magazines and publishing ventures that extended haphazardly from them—were unaffiliated with academic or civic art institutions.

At the same time that Duncan participated in the formation of the poetry community, he maintained a domestic distance from it through his long relationship with Jess, an artist and collagist whom he met in 1950 and with whom he shared a household until his death. That household provided a beacon for many younger gay friends and poets, who, in a pre-Stonewall world, sought alternative models for a synthesis of domestic and artistic life. "Willingly I'll say there's been a sweet marriage," begins Duncan's *Passages* 10, yet quickly he equivocates: "In the beginning there was weeping, / an inconsolable grief."[6] If there were tempests in their domestic life, their love for each other provided a stable center and safe haven amid literary contentions and controversies. For all of Duncan's extensive travels, readings, and lecturing, he valued the rituals of the household—shopping and cooking, working on jigsaw puzzles, entertaining visitors, watching television (*Hogan's Heroes* and *Upstairs, Downstairs* were favorites), listening to records, and collaborating on art projects. The incomplete jigsaw puzzle that was a fixture in the couple's various households is a metaphor for the "grand collage" that the two men pieced together daily out of art and affection.

Throughout his multiple lives, Duncan remained a political poet whose work—from the early, courageous essay "The Homosexual in Society" of 1944 to his late *Passages* poem against the Viet Nam war—confronted social oppression and state-sponsored terror. The Viet Nam war, to which he, like most American poets, was opposed, became a test of loyalties between Duncan and his old friend Denise Levertov, who partook of a more overt social activism. At the heart of their disagreement was the extent to which poetry could be the vehicle for political views. Although Duncan's antiwar poems of the 1960s—"Up Rising," "The Multiversity"—are strident and even didactic, subsequent *Passages* poems treat the war in Viet Nam in mythic terms, as a sign of cosmic disorder. Duncan saw the war as a national allegory, the return of America's "unacknowledged, unrepented crimes" (the persecution of antinomians, Indian genocide, slavery) in present history. To record these seismic changes, poetry must be a place where the war, in all its contradictory power and confusion, can be experienced: "the poet's role is not to oppose evil, but to imagine it: what if Shakespeare had opposed Iago, or Dostoevsky opposed Raskalnikov [sic]—the vital thing is that they *created* Iago and Raskalnikov."[7] Speaking of "Uprising," Duncan says, "[It is] not that the war was or was not important to me, but how come it was of import to the poem."[8] To contemporary ears, these remarks may seem an overly aestheticized response to human pain and suffering, but for Duncan, they were a way to yoke his aesthetics of responsibility to an ethics of witness and testimony. He had a distinctly postmodern understanding of the discursive character of moral and ethical claims, but his stance created a barrier between himself and more activist friends, a stance that became hard to sustain in the early 1970s.[9]

Jarnot's account of Duncan's last years is a moving testimony to his intellectual vitality despite increasing physical weakness and pain:

> When I come to Death's customs,
>   to the surrender of my nativities,

> that office of the dark too I picture
> as if there were a crossing over,
> a going thru a door,   in obliteration
> —at last, my destination Time will not undo—[10]

His coming to "Death's customs," imagined in a poem for Baudelaire, became fact when he experienced massive kidney failure in 1984. Although he continued to teach, travel, and give readings, his body was severely weakened, and his busy schedule was invaded by a regular regime of dialysis and visits to hospitals for tests. A group of young friends in the community formed a support system to take him for walks, read to him, and transport him to his doctors' appointments. The poet who had gleefully anticipated his creative "late period" was not to enjoy that status. The poems that he wrote for his last collection, *Ground Work II,* are especially moving as he revisits his favorite themes—the old mysteries of light and dark, soul and body, truth and war—now experiencing them through his ailing body as lived realities. In his last poem, "After a Long Illness," he describes in graphic detail "the failure of systems" and the "break-down of ratios" that finally claimed him in February 1988.[11] At the same time, he turns to Jess, recognizing that the fear "of not seeing you again" is more powerful than the fear of Death—whom he regards as a power of poetry, "Lord of a Passage that unites us." These final poems are resilient, reflective pieces in which the poet, who had always seen "the underside turning," faces the full implications of the permission he describes in *The Opening of the Field.*

Permission, for Duncan, was the trust that the world of the poem would yield significant form. Writing was a form of reading the book of the world for what "It" had to tell us—the capitalization of "It" indicating a second order of creation, the event raised to sacrament or epiphany yet necessarily bound to language. "Working in words I am an escapist; as if I could step out of my clothes and move naked as the wind in a world of words. But I want every part of the actual world involved in my escape. I bring the laws that bound me into an aerial structure in which they are unbound as outlines of a prison unfolding."[12] Unlike the orthodox religious believer, Duncan was not much interested in transcendence but, rather, in the intensification of the moment, "everlasting omen of what is," as he concluded in "Often I Am Permitted to Return to a Meadow."[13] And unlike the orthodox formalist, Duncan was an "escapist" into language, not its jailer. That the open field provides access to limits or boundaries that commit him to the "structure of rime" is a persistent paradox in his poetics. The error, as he made clear in his antiwar poems, was to mistake limits for barriers to be overcome—to view war as a test of who has more power or see God as a somewhat bigger version of ourselves. To read the book of the world for its meaning, Duncan lived as though he would be its subject, the prodigal son who recovers the lost continent and family, Childe Duncan to the dark tower comes.

I remember seeing a photograph of Duncan at age two looking seriously at the camera as he stands in the yard of his family home in Alameda. It is an uncanny photograph, showing the steady stare and intensity of concentration that characterized the grown man. He appears already aware of his own story, the romance of the child chosen to be, as Jarnot subtitles her book, "the ambassador from Venus." If Duncan read his life as myth, Jarnot patiently unweaves the dense skein of that myth to show the multiple strands of which it is made. It is a testimony to her diligence and scholarly rigor that Jarnot is able to keep the multiple stories alive in *her* story, so that we may live in the passages that Robert Duncan has laid out for us.

PREFACE

Robert Duncan stands out as a curious figure in the landscape of contemporary American poetry. He defined himself as a derivative poet fond of the aesthetics of the Victorian age, yet he was also deeply rooted in the twentieth-century influences of surrealism, Ezra Pound, Hilda Doolittle, James Joyce, and Gertrude Stein. He was recognized as a member of the Black Mountain school, yet he was loyal to a regional San Francisco poetics. He was an experimental writer, yet he can as easily be described as a metaphysical poet and a master of the lyric. He possessed a voracious appetite for the ideas of modern science and psychology, yet also gleefully claimed kinship with those who "practiced the seasons" and adhered to a "practice of the gods."

Perhaps most importantly, Robert Duncan reveled in the world of the story—the story of Frank Baum's Oz, or the story of the worship of the Minoan bull god in early Greece, or the story of order and chaos that unfolded in the United States and abroad during the 1960s. No subject was too far afield to enter his work, and no piece of information lacked the potential to generate a story. That Duncan titled his first major collection of essays *Fictive Certainties* is no accident: he lived his life with a respect for the certainties to be found in the "fictive" landscape of the imagination and with a belief that truths about the universe could be mined from the very structure of language. His devotion to the creative imagination was absolute.

For those who received him into the world in 1919, Robert Duncan came as a messenger from another time and place. Though he sought to debunk the expectations that his theosophist parents held for him, in the process he came to define himself on equally formidable terms. One fact stands clear throughout the testimonies of his friends and lovers and his volumes of poetry composed over fifty years: when Robert Duncan died at the age of sixty-nine, he was mourned for accomplishments not unlike those predicted by his parents. While his frantic habits of speech often exhausted his companions and he was subject to the rages and tantrums of an overactive metabolism, Duncan's life suggests something more. To his audiences, he was a great teacher; to his students, he was a generous mind; and to an international community, he was one of the most important avant-garde poets of the mid-twentieth century. It is not possible to pull together all of the threads that made Robert Duncan who he was. What follows is a sketch of his life, a story drawn from the many bright weavings that he left in his work and in his relationships.

ACKNOWLEDGMENTS

In the course of my research, Robert Duncan's friends, without exception, granted me a share in the generosity, goodwill, and love for life that so characterized his being.

Two people made a special effort to help me understand Robert Duncan's "dailiness," and their insights were key factors in the making of this book. Jess Collins agreed that it was an appropriate time for a biography of Duncan to be written, and he welcomed me into his life for a little bit over a decade, allowing me to experience the rituals of household that he had shared with Duncan. Barbara Jones and her family in Bakersfield, California, extended me great hospitality. Barbara's memories of her brother as a child and of their life in the San Joaquin Valley were in all ways illuminating. Their insights were key factors in the making of this book.

This book was also made possible through the ongoing tireless support of my husband, Thomas Evans. His own studies of Jess, Duncan, and the West Coast assemblage artists contributed at every turn to the thoroughness of this book. His companionship allows me to live in a household as rich as Jess and Duncan's.

I am grateful to Robert Duncan's friends, family, students and acquaintances:

Gerald Ackerman, Robert Adamson, the late Virginia Admiral, Charles Alexander, the late Donald Allen, Michael Anania, Bruce Andrews, Norman Austin, Todd Baron, Dawn Michelle Baude, Tosh Berman, Charles Bernstein, Robert Bertholf, the late Robin Blaser, Richard Blevins, George Bowering, the late Stan Brakhage, the late David Bromige, the late James Broughton, the late Norman O. Brown, Leo Brumm, David Burton, the late Hilde Burton, Pauline Butling, Reed Bye, Don Byrd, Janine Canan, Brian Caraher,

Larry Casalino, Tom Clark, Norma Cole, Jack Collom, Julia Connor, William Corbett, Cheryl Creatrix, Penelope Highton Creeley, the late Robert Creeley, Frank Davey, Michael Davidson, the late Fielding Dawson, the late Alberto de Lacerda, Diane di Prima, Paul Dolan, Jennifer Dorn, Chris Edwards, Edward Eigner, Lewis Ellingham, Ekbert Faas, the late Lillian Fabilli Osborne, Mary Fabilli, Larry Fagin, Alice Fahs, Mimi Fahs, John Felstiner, Jack Foley, Raymond Foye, Michael Franco, David Franks, Stephen Fredman, Susan Friedland, Susan Gardner, Philip Garrison, Karl Gartung, Albert Gelpi, Paula Giannini, David Gitin, Albert Glover, Robert Glück, Carl Grundberg, the late Thom Gunn, Linda Hamalian, Mitch Harris, Bobbie Louise Hawkins, Lyn Hejinian, Patricia Hill, Maria Hindmarch, Ida Hodes, Robert Hogg, Eric Homberger, David Howard, Joyce Jenkins, Pierre Joris, Rodger Kamenetz, Robert Kelly, Carolyn Kemp, the late Gladys Kennard, Kevin Killian, Sean Killian, Anne Kingsbury, R. B. Kitaj, Michael Kronebusch, Joanne Kyger, the late Jackson Mac Low, David Matlin, John Matthias, Bernadette Mayer, Tolbert McCarroll, Michael McClure, the late Marjorie McKee, Duncan McNaughton, William McPheron, David Meltzer, Peter Michelson, Noreen Norton, Alice Notley, the late Liam O'Gallagher, Pauline Oliveros, Michael Palmer, Louis Patler, Ian Patterson, Bob Perelman, Larry Price, Ilya Prokopoff, the late Stephen Prokopoff, Odyssia Quadrani, George Quasha, Susan Quasha, Jed Rasula, Tom Raworth, Leslie Reagan, Peter Riley, Judith Roche, Steven Rodefer, Bob Rose, Diane Rothenberg, Jerome Rothenberg, Michael Rumaker, Edward Sanders, Tom Savage, David Schaff, Harris Schiff, Alvin Schwartz, the late Armand Schwerner, Robert Sheldon, Aaron Shurin, Ron Silliman, Joseph Simas, Joel Singer, Mary Margaret Sloan, George Stanley, Chuck Stein, Tony Stoneburner, David Levi Strauss, William Sylvester, John Taggart, Susan Thackrey, John Tranter, Christopher Wagstaff, Fred Wah, Keith Waldrop, Rosmarie Waldrop, Anne Waldman, Lewis Warsh, Barrett Watten, Heloise Wilson, the late Keith Wilson, Robert A. Wilson, Paul Zukofsky.

To my peers who assisted me with this project:

James Boaden, Lee Ann Brown, Miles Champion, Stephen Cope, Tim Davis, Benjamin Friedlander, Michael Friedman, Peter Gizzi, Devin Johnston, Daniel Kane, James Maynard, Ben Mazer, Peter O'Leary, Kristin Prevallet, Patrick Pritchett, Tae-Wol Stanley, Brandon Stosuy, Stacy Szymaszek, Elizabeth Willis.

To the libraries and librarians who assisted me in my research:

Michael Basinski, James Maynard, and Susan Michel at the Poetry/Rare Books Collection at the State University of New York at Buffalo; Anthony Bliss at the Bancroft Library at the University of California, Berkeley; Jeanne Sommers at Kent State University; Rutherford Witthus and Melissa Watterworth at the Dodds Collection at the University of Connecticut, Storrs; John Skarstad at the University of California, Davis; Bradley Westbrook at the University of California, San Diego; Ken Hooper at Bakersfield High School; Barry Bunch at the University of Kansas, Lawrence; Angie Kindig at the University of Notre Dame Archives; Tom Hyry and Patricia Willis at the Yale University Beinecke Library; F. Jason Torre at Stony Brook University, State University of New York; Tony Power at Simon Fraser University; New Directions Publishers, which granted me access to its Robert Duncan author files.

To my research assistants and students:

Joshua Baldwin, J. P. Craig, Alan Felsenthal, Geoffrey Gatza, Whit Griffin, Kaplan Page Harris, Evan Kennedy, Paul Klinger, Mark Molnar, Michael Nicoloff, Albert Onello, Annette Roberts, Christian Roess, Clelia Scalia, Ken Walker, John Wieja, Amy Wright. Thanks to the Naropa students who attended my 1998 graduate seminar on Robert Duncan, accompanying me on a journey through many of Duncan's favorite books and offering rigorous insights into all of his work: Jennifer Asteris, Jeff Carmack, John Chinworth, the late kari edwards, Yoko Eishima, Derek Fenner, Ryan Gallager, Christopher Luna, Amy McCarrel, Jeni Olin, Dylan Patterson, Cedar Sigo, Lisa Trank, Saskia Wolsak.

To my teachers:

This work is the result of my studies with the late John Clarke and the late Robert Creeley. The seeds of this work (and my Duncan-related research efforts) were sown by the late Harvey Brown, editor of Frontier Press. I would also like to thank Edward Sanders, whose lecture on Olsonian book-length research projects, given at the Naropa Institute during the summer of 1997, inspired me to continue my studies of Robert Duncan's work and to write this biography. This book would not exist without his encouragement and friendship.

To my editors and the estate of Robert Duncan:

Mary Margaret Sloan and Christopher Wagstaff of the Jess Collins Trust were committed to making this book a reality and helped me to clear many hurdles along the way. University of California Press editor Linda Norton took an interest in this book when it was still in its preliminary stages. Laura Cerruti and Rachel Berchten saw the manuscript through its many drafts. My copy editor, Adrienne Harris, worked closely with me for nearly a year to arrive at the final manuscript.

To my family:

And finally, much gratitude to my parents, Mary Jane and Joseph Jarnot, who welcomed me home during my many research trips to Buffalo, New York.

***

Chapters of this book appeared in *Abacus, Blaze, Boxkite,* the *Chicago Review, Drunken Boat, Fascicle, Jacket, No,* the *Poetry Project Newsletter,* and *Xanthippe.*

TEXTUAL NOTES

Throughout the text I refer to the subject as Robert Duncan, though at various points his legal name was Edward Howe Duncan, Robert Edward Symmes, and Robert Edward Duncan. Duncan's companion Jess Collins is referred to by his chosen name, Jess.

· · ·

A note on Duncan's spelling: in letters to friends, journal entries, and poems, Duncan often dropped the *e* from past-tense verbs ("learnd") or shortened common words ("though" to "tho" or "could" to "cld"). Two of Duncan's early mentors, Ezra Pound and Jaime de Angulo, also used abbreviation and disregarded spelling conventions in their correspondence. Duncan may have inherited this idiosyncrasy when he worked as de Angulo's secretary. In poems, Duncan's omission of the *e* from the past tense was a metrical cue, indicating the syllable count ("learnd," one syllable; "learned," two syllables). The quotes herein preserve all such spellings and eschew the use of *[sic]* in the interest of preserving Duncan's style.

· · ·

Several texts preceding the publication of this volume also provide important information about Robert Duncan's life and work. Ekbert Faas's *Young Robert Duncan* gives a view into Duncan's early life (1919–52). I have in this biography noted points at which Faas's information was incorrect as well as points at which the reader may want to refer to Faas for more detailed information. Kevin Killian and Lewis Ellingham's biography of Jack Spicer, *Poet*

Be Like God, includes a good deal of information about Duncan's relationship with Spicer and about the larger constellations of community around the Berkeley and San Francisco Renaissance. Michael Davidson's *The San Francisco Renaissance: Poetics and Community at Mid-Century, Ghostlier Demarcations: Modern Poetry and the Material Word,* and *Guys Like Us: Citing Masculinity in Cold War Poetics* are all important works. Two of my peers, Devin Johnston and Peter O'Leary, have written books that also explore Duncan's work from a critical angle: Johnston's *Precipitations* and O'Leary's *Gnostic Contagion.*

While I have attempted here to give readers a good view into the source materials and personal circumstances surrounding Duncan's poems, I have refrained from deeper interpretations of the work in my interest to shape the book as biography rather than criticism. This book is the culmination of almost twenty-five years of research. I hope that my work will open the gate to a deeper understanding of Duncan's life and poetry and his relationships with the writers and artists whose work intersected with his.

ONE

Childhood's Retreat

The Antediluvian World

At dawn in Oakland in the cold of the year I was born, January
7th, with the sun before rising or just below the horizon in the
false dawn and Saturn in his own house, in Capricorn. But that
is according to the old astrological convention. Actually, the sun
has advanced; the winter solstice has progresst to the sign of
Sagittarius. I was born in the head of the archer. ROBERT
DUNCAN, "A Sequence of Poems for H. D.'s Birthday"

HE WAS CASE NUMBER 27,436 at the Children's Home Society. Though
he would later be known as Robert Symmes, and later still as Robert Dun-
can, at birth he was given the name Edward Howe Duncan in honor of his
father, a railroad engineer on the Southern Pacific line.[1] What evidence re-
mains of the elder Edward Duncan is his careful rounded signature on his
wife's interment papers in Oakland, California's Mountain View Cemetery,
dated February 23, 1919. Marguerite Duncan hadn't intended to deliver her
tenth child at home, but she had been ill, and a local hospital refused to ad-
mit her, fearing that she was infected with the Spanish influenza, which had
reached epidemic proportions since its onset in spring 1918 and would kill
nearly 20 million people worldwide by the winter of 1919. The 1919 flu strain
killed pregnant women in unusually high numbers, but other factors prob-
ably contributed to Marguerite's death some hours after her son's birth on
January 7. She was a small woman in her late thirties who had already given
birth to nine children, two of whom had been stillborn.[2] Though accounts
of the morning vary, the home delivery was probably overseen by a Dr. Woods,
aided by the older Duncan girls and one of Marguerite's nieces. Duncan's
sister Anne conjured the scene some sixty years later: "I stood at the foot of
my mother's bed and watched Robert being born. I was two years old, and I
remember a great deal of blood and water. He was born at six o'clock in the
morning and mother died, I think, at four o'clock the same afternoon."[3]

The Duncans then lived at 2532 Twelfth Avenue, in the San Antonio
neighborhood of Oakland, a landscape steeped in literary lore. During the
1880s, the young Gertrude Stein had lived here, where houses stood on lots

once owned by Spanish rancher Luis Peralta.[4] With a steep triangular roof that loomed above the properties on either side, 2532 Twelfth Avenue had been built during the first wave of the neighborhood's development. The residence had probably once been the main house of a dairy estate, and the property still included a flat-roofed barn. While the house was sizable by city standards, it likely provided cramped quarters for the nine Duncans. From the front porch, its tenants entered a high-ceilinged foyer with a stairwell and adjoining living room. Behind the living room was a dining room, and beside it, a narrow brick kitchen with a wood-burning stove. The second floor contained two bedrooms, the larger to the back and the smaller to the front. After Robert's birth, the house had to accommodate not only the Duncans but also a woman named Mae, who apparently consoled Edward Duncan after the loss of his wife and who brought two children of her own.[5] The two oldest Duncan daughters, Edna and Marguerite, cared for their newborn brother, but before long, eighteen-year-old Edna fled the crowded household. Family legend held that the elder Edward Duncan "went into shock that lasted for months" after Marguerite died.[6] Ultimately, he could no longer manage the children's care, and the entire Duncan brood was effectively orphaned by late 1919 or 1920.[7] Duncan later heard pieces of the story from his adoptive parents: "For six months my father, the other Edward Howard Duncan, might have kept me and my two older sisters cared for me. But my father was poor, a common day-laborer. He could not afford it. Then, there must have been a period in a hospital, awaiting adoption."[8]

Edward Duncan's tenuous relationship with his wife's family seemed to play a role in the abandonment as well. Marguerite's brother Wesley Carpenter and his wife, Myrtle, offered to take responsibility for the three youngest Duncan children. Welsey, a meter reader for the Pacific Gas and Electric Company, had the financial resources to take on his sister's children. With little explanation, Edward Duncan refused their offer. As one of Robert Duncan's biological sisters later explained to him, "All four of Momma's sisters had wanted to adopt any of us that Dad wasn't going to keep, so that we would not be separated. Dad's edict was that we were not to go to anyone that was a relative."[9] Relations between the Carpenters and the Duncans had been uneasy from the beginning. Edward had married Marguerite in San Francisco on September 21, 1900, without the blessing of her family, which was perhaps protective of its youngest child.

Born in the spring of 1883 in Oakland, Marguerite Pearl Carpenter was nicknamed Daisy. Endowed with a mischievous grin and sharp gray eyes, she was the family gem. Her father, Lewis Carpenter, a native of Kentucky, and her mother, Isabelle McIntee, the daughter of Irish immigrants, passed on to Marguerite the distinct Anglo-Irish Carpenter characteristics that she would in turn pass on to her eight children. They were stocky people with unruly chestnut-brown hair and broad faces, proud to be part of a lineage dubbed by genealogists "the family of heroes."[10] The first Carpenters to come to America—both named William—arrived in the colonies in the early seventeenth century. One landed in Providence, Rhode Island, in 1636; the other sailed into a Massachusetts harbor on the *Bevis* two years later. Robert Duncan was a descendant of the latter, though at various points in his auto-biographical writings he claimed descent from both. The William Carpenter of Duncan's lineage was born in England in 1605 and arrived in America at the age of thirty-three with his wife, Abigal. He settled in Weymouth, where he served as a representative to Massachusetts's general court in Boston. His children, grandchildren, and great-grandchildren eventually scattered throughout Massachusetts, Rhode Island, Missouri, and Kentucky, where, in 1833, Robert Duncan's maternal grandfather, Lewis Whipple Carpenter, was born to Whipple Carpenter and Elizabeth True. After the death of their mother in 1850, the teenaged Lewis and his brother Milton made their way west from Savannah, Missouri, to San Francisco. Lewis Carpenter, who later garnered a reputation as an eccentric naturalist, set off without horse or wagon, trekking across the Great Plains on foot.[11]

Some years after Lewis Carpenter's arrival in San Francisco and his marriage to Isabelle McIntee, he and his family moved to a house on Ninth Avenue in East Oakland, just above the Lake Merritt district. Carpenter spent the next several years working at various trades and moving his family from neighborhood to neighborhood as the boundaries of Oakland expanded. He and Milton worked for several years in a broom-making factory. Later, he ran a dairy with his sons Lewis and Wesley, and still later he worked as a house painter. When he died in 1924 at ninety-one, he was buried next to his wife and their daughter Marguerite in Oakland's Mountain View Cemetery.

TWO

Native Son of the Golden West

> The soul, my mother's sister, Aunt Fay, told me . . . was like a
> swarm of bees, and, at night, certain entities of that swarm left
> the body-hive and went to feed in fields of helium—was it in the
> upper atmosphere of the Earth or in the fire-clouds of the Sun?
> The 'higher' ascended nightly, and in its absence, the 'lower'
> dreamed, flooding the mind with versions of the Underworld.
> ROBERT DUNCAN, *The H. D. Book*

FAYETTA HARRIS PHILIP TURNED thirty-seven during the summer of
1919. On most days she could be found at Philip & Philip, the corner drug-
store on Fruitvale Avenue in East Oakland that she managed alongside her
husband, Bruce. Each morning she rose at dawn, pinned her red-brown hair
into a bun, and made breakfast for her children, Mercedes and Harold, be-
fore opening the store. When the children were visiting their grandmother,
Fayetta spent the early hours in her treasured library, pulling books from the
shelves and composing lengthy pseudoscientific treatises, which she referred
to as her "discoveries." With her mother's encouragement, Fayetta had been
attending occult reading groups since she was a teenager, and by her early
adult years, she was not only a member of one of Oakland's burgeoning her-
metic brotherhoods, she was also a self-proclaimed expert on all matters meta-
physical. Her authority, she told friends, was owed to her meticulous study
of the phenomenon of light in the Egyptian pyramid of Giza during a previ-
ous incarnation. In her present human form—when she was not filling pre-
scriptions, writing poems, and theorizing about the gaseous composition of
the soul—she was searching for the key to light's great secrets.[1]

Oakland's Fruitvale neighborhood during the early 1900s was, in many
ways, still a part of the American frontier. At Philip & Philip, customers
stopped in to buy Fayetta Philip's special black-salve horse liniment, a cure-
all for ailments from appendicitis to cancer. Farms, dairies, and logging set-
tlements dotted the Oakland Hills, and downtown storefronts took on a car-
nival atmosphere, with gold rush pawnshops and saloons in restless
cohabitation with dusty-curtained shops advertising palm readings by

6

Egyptian gypsy clairvoyants and world-renowned spiritual mediums. The town's Anglo immigrants were progeny of pioneer families that had come from the northern territories of the Oregon Trail and from the east, across the Great Plains and through the Sierra Nevada:

> This land, where I stand, was all legend
> in my grandfather's time: cattle raiders,
>   animal tribes, priests, gold.
> It was the West. Its vistas painters saw
>   in diffuse light, in melancholy,
> in abysses left by glaciers as if they had been the sun
>   primordial carving empty enormities
>   out of the rock.[2]

The Oakland Hills that Fayetta looked upon in 1919 had long ago been home to the Ohlone Indians, and much later, in 1775, European explorers had arrived and gradually handed over the land to cattle ranchers. The area known as Encinal to the Spanish became the city of Oakland in the early 1850s, when a young lawyer and real estate speculator from New York City, Horace Carpentier, purchased the land, established a charter, and became the city's first mayor. Since then, Oakland had expanded a great deal, attracting many refugees as well as transplants from neighboring San Francisco after the 1906 earthquake, nearly doubling its population between 1900 and 1910. By 1919, downtown Oakland was a central hub of the Southern Pacific Railroad, providing connections to Los Angeles, New Orleans, Denver, and Portland.

Managing a drugstore during the First World War was a full-time activity for the Philip family. Fayetta spent long days assisting customers, unpacking stock in the backroom, and attending to her two children, who played in the enclosed yard behind the store. During lulls, she gossiped with customers and passersby, outtalking her listeners at every turn. Acquaintances described her as "a real character"—the lady pharmacist of Fruitvale who collected rocks and believed that Shakespeare's plays had been written by philosopher Francis Bacon.[3] One of the first women to graduate from the University of California's pharmacy program, she had given up her aspirations to become a doctor like her sister Dee, instead studying English literature, geology, and physics. That summer in the aftermath of the First World War, the talk in the drugstore was about the soldiers coming home and the town's recovery from the deadly influenza epidemic of the previous winter.

But a more peculiar topic dominated the conversation one August afternoon when Myrtle Carpenter walked into Philip & Philip and heard Fayetta telling a customer about her younger sister, Minnehaha, who was eager to adopt a child. An astrologer had told Minne and her husband, Edwin, both devout hermeticists, that their destiny was to adopt a boy born at dawn on January 7 that year, under an unusual alignment of the stars. Though Minne had secured a job at the local Children's Home Society of California and enlisted the help of the fraternal association of the Native Sons of the Golden West, she had not found this baby.[4] Myrtle Carpenter excitedly chimed in that her sister-in-law, Marguerite Duncan, had given birth to a boy on January 7—around dawn, she thought—and died shortly thereafter. The baby was now up for adoption.[5]

Robert Duncan came to know the story well. Before his birth, his adoptive parents, the Symmeses, had participated in a theosophical group in the Bay Area, a hermetic brotherhood modeled after late nineteenth-century occult groups such as London's Hermetic Order of the Golden Dawn and Madame Blavatsky's Theosophical Society of New York and India. The Symmeses told Robert that he had been sent to them. His astrological chart indicated that he, in a past life, had been an inventor on the mythological continent of Atlantis. He was of the ancient generation that had recklessly destroyed its own world. Born under the sign of Capricorn, with the moon in Pisces, his ascendant was in Sagittarius, and the presence of Gemini in his sixth house suggested that he had acted as a messenger in a previous incarnation.[6] According to hermetic doctrine, his mother had simply been the "vehicle" of his birth, an agent of his reincarnation; she had died so that he might be handed over to his rightful parents. The Symmeses had formulated their requirements for their adoptive child some time before 1919: the baby would be born at the time and place appointed by the astrologers, the natural mother would die shortly thereafter, and the child would be of Anglo-Saxon Protestant descent.[7]

In Celtic tradition, August 1 marks the Lammas Tide, a celebration of the first harvest of the autumn. This date fascinated Robert Duncan, and it appeared in several of his poems. On this date in 1919, Fayetta Philip told her sister Minnehaha of Myrtle Carpenter's strange and hopeful news.[8] The Symmeses arranged to see the Duncan child immediately, and on August 4, they assumed custody of six-month-old Edward Howe Duncan through an agreement between Edward Duncan Sr. and the Native Sons and Daughters Central Committee on Homeless Children of San Francisco. Minnehaha and Edwin took the baby home to their apartment in Oakland at 914 Taylor Avenue, soon renaming him Robert Edward Symmes in honor of a family friend.[9] Seven months later, California's Superior Court designated the Symmeses as the child's legal parents. In October 1920, the couple adopted a second child, a baby girl they named Barbara Eleanor Symmes. Born in Oakland almost exactly a year after Robert, Barbara had come to her adoptive parents in a similar way, through a reading of her astrological chart. Her role was to introduce "good karma" into the household to balance her older brother's dark side.

Outside of their interests in the occult, the Symmeses were in most ways a typical middle-class couple. Conservative in their political views, Edwin and Minnehaha would be remembered as principled California citizens—he as a prominent public works architect and she as a busy socialite who served on committees, chaired community council meetings, and volunteered her time to a range of organizations, from the Children's Home Society to the Kern County Council of Campfire Girls.[10] Writing of his adoptive father's family in *The H. D. Book,* Robert Duncan reported that the Symmeses "had moved West . . . first into Ohio at the beginning of the nineteenth century, and then on, at the frontier or beyond the frontier of America, into California."[11] Symmes and its variation Semmes are Anglo-Saxon names. Several members of the clan emigrated to St. George's, Maryland, from England in the mid-1600s and continued into Ohio to make their livelihoods as potters and farmers.[12] In recounting the family history, Duncan occasionally merged those Symmeses of Ohio with another branch of the family that came to the Massachusetts Bay Colony during the early 1600s and slowly migrated westward. In an apparent embellishment of his adoptive father's lineage, he once wrote, "In my father's line American origins went back to the Calvinism of the Massachusetts Colony where the ancestral patriarch oldest son to oldest son to my stepfather had been Reverend Zackariah Symmes."[13]

If this version of the story is true, then Edwin Symmes's ancestors were not linked to the Symmeses of Maryland and Ohio. Instead, they arrived in Boston on the *Griffin* on September 18, 1634. The ship's passenger list includes not only the Reverend Zackariah Symmes but also the religious dissenter Anne Hutchinson.[14] Symmes, upon arriving in the colonies, became known for his testimony against Hutchinson in her trials for sedition and heresy. Duncan could not resist incorporating this colorful story into early sketches for an autobiographical novel he composed in 1941: "We are descended from witches and burners of witches. How my ancestors gave witness that she,

Anne Hutchinson, had talked on deck at night with a Dark Stranger who had a covenant between them, and by the Governor of Massachusetts given birth of two monsters out of wedlock."[15]

Edwin Symmes was a frail and studious man with an obsessive work ethic. Born on February 14, 1883, in Livermore, California, to Charles O. Symmes and Elizabeth Johnson, he spent part of his youth in Oakland, where his father was a railroad engineer on the Southern Pacific line. Symmes's later ill health was foreshadowed on more than one occasion during his youth, first by a foot injury that interrupted his education and later by unspecified illnesses in 1904 and 1905.[16] Around 1904, he met his future wife, Minnehaha Harris, and in 1905, at the age of twenty-two, he registered at the University of California at Berkeley, receiving a joint degree in architecture and engineering four years later. He soon found work in San Francisco as a draftsman and, beginning in January 1913, he helped design San Francisco's Palace of Fine Arts under the direction of the master architect Bernard Maybeck. This project, one of the wonders of the 1915 Panama-Pacific International Exposition, brought Edwin Symmes his first public recognition.[17]

Duncan's adoptive parents married on July 9, 1913, in Oakland, some nine years after their first meeting and four months after their engagement. Their partnership was neither difficult nor extraordinary, despite the fact that the two had carefully arranged the date, time, and location of their union for a favorable astrological alignment.[18] Their lengthy premarital flirtations had been interrupted on several occasions, such as in 1906 when Minnehaha moved to Oregon in the aftermath of the San Francisco earthquake to teach in a one-room schoolhouse. She was thin "like a sparrow," her friends said. Robert wrote of her, "She was a beautiful woman I suppose. She had black hair that was wild and naturally waving about her head and a fine delicate nose, nostrilled like a nervous horse . . . but we could see her irrational angers in those eyes. . . . She was perhaps in this even a magnificent creature, tyrannical with the beauty of will that the tyrant has."[19] Duncan's ambivalence toward her and his fascination with her authority surfaced openly in his later poetry, most famously in "My Mother Would Be a Falconress":

> I tear at her wrist with my beak to draw blood,
> and her eye holds me, anguisht, terrifying.
> She draws a limit to my flight.
> Never beyond my sight, she says.[20]

Abandoned by her father when she was two and raised by several strong-minded women, Minnehaha Harris was by early adulthood willful, resourceful, and controlling. The youngest of three daughters, she was often the peacemaker between her equally willful older sisters, Fayetta and Dee. When she met Edwin Symmes in 1904, she was attracted to his shy manner and professional ambitions; he was a mate she could depend on. In photographs, he posed with the rigid stance of a prep school cadet, but his lanky, awkward figure and his boyish face countered any authoritarian resolve. He had a basic gentleness, evidenced by the inscriptions he left in the Symmes children's books, including short rhymed couplets for his wife and "the kiddies."[21]

Between their marriage in 1913 and Robert's adoption in 1919, Edwin and Minnehaha Symmes lived in San Francisco, Oakland, Yosemite, and Alameda, California, staying close to relatives on both sides of the family. Edwin's siblings, Charles and Alvie, lived in Oakland, as did Minnehaha's mother, Mary, and sister Fayetta. In the first months that Duncan was with them, Edwin and Minnehaha took him to Yosemite, where Edwin, then a novice architect, had found work with the Yosemite National Park Company designing the park's first tourist hotels and drafting plans for a network of highways built in and around the park during the early 1920s. Despite their relative isolation, the Symmeses fared well in Yosemite. Between the spring of 1921 and the summer of 1923, they lived there periodically while a house was being constructed for them in Alameda. In the wintry seclusion of Yosemite's employee camps, the Symmeses had limited access to the news of the day. The United States, ostensibly on the road to a postwar "return to normalcy" under the Republican administrations of Warren G. Harding, and later Calvin Coolidge, faced a backlash of social unrest. Prohibition laws had prompted an active trade in bootleg alcohol, and labor and communist movements had formed in response to domestic turbulence. The murder convictions of Italian anarchists Nicola Sacco and Bartolomeo Vanzetti in the summer of 1921 were a focal point for this unrest. Their trial, imprisonment, and 1927 executions, built on dubious charges arising from antiradical paranoia, attracted international attention. For Duncan, an anarcho-pacifist throughout his adult life, the case helped shape his political beliefs.

While he took his first baby steps on the remote peaks of Yosemite, the texts that would later so clearly inform Duncan's poetics were coming into print: 1922 marked the publication of James Joyce's *Ulysses,* followed in 1923 by Sigmund Freud's *The Ego and the Id,* and in 1924 by André Breton's

Manifesto of Surrealism. Especially important to the Symmeses, who believed in an ancient Egyptian homeland, was the news in November 1922 of the discovery of Tutankhamen's tomb at Luxor in the Valley of the Kings.

In the unstable interbellum era, the Symmes children enjoyed the comforts of a stable middle-class household. They later remembered little of their sojourns in Yosemite, though both could reconstruct essential facts with the help of the many photographs their parents took between 1920 and 1923. In these photographs, the two youngsters appear thoroughly entertained, sharing toys, perching on rocks between the sequoias, and, in one image, riding in the back of a car with a petting-zoo donkey. The closeness of their ages facilitated an intimate companionship. Sandy-haired, bright-eyed Robert posed with his toddler sister, Barbara, clutching him around the waist, her brown curls all but obscuring her grin.

For Duncan, this period brought a traumatic event that left a lifelong mark, though he had little memory of it. During the winters in Yosemite, his parents sent him outdoors wearing sunglasses because of his susceptibility to snow blindness. While running through the snow one winter morning in 1922, he fell, shattering the sunglasses and injuring his left eye. Despite a doctor's efforts to reverse the damage through a regimen of stereopticon exercises and prescription eyeglasses, Duncan was left permanently cross-eyed at the age of three.[22] He alluded to the flaw in his vision sporadically throughout his work, as in "A Sequence of Poems for H. D.'s Birthday": "I had the double reminder always, the vertical and horizontal displacements in vision that later became separated, specialized into a near and a far sight. One image to the right and above the other. Reach out and touch. Point to the one that is really there."[23] After the accident, Duncan wore corrective eyeglasses for the remainder of his childhood, finally discarding them during his first year of college, when doctors informed him that he was unlikely to regain normal sight.

THREE

The Architecture

It must have recesses. There is a great charm in a room broken up in plan, where that slight feeling of mystery is given to it which arises when you cannot see the whole room from any one place . . . when there is always something around the corner.   GUSTAV STICKLEY, *Craftsman Homes,* quoted in Robert Duncan's "The Architecture, *Passages* 9"

One-half of the world is looking for something nasty and one-half of the world is looking for something gnostic.   ROBERT DUNCAN, New College of California lecture, 1986

WHEN NOT SECLUDED IN YOSEMITE, the Symmeses began the transition to their new home in Alameda, which would be Robert Duncan's main residence for the first seven years of his life. A sleepy island town appended to the southernmost part of Oakland, Alameda had once been a peach orchard, cultivated by Spanish settlers. The house that Edwin Symmes designed and had built there in 1922 was at 1700 Pearl Street, some blocks from a narrow sandy beach with a view of the San Francisco skyline across the bay. In Alameda's mild coastal climate, the foliage on the city's palm and fruit trees changed little with the seasons, their green tones paling in the dry summers and deepening in the winter rains. The blocks of pink and beige adobe houses interspersed with lemon trees and flowering plants made for a tidy suburban atmosphere. Behind the walls surrounding the property, the Symmes house was an architectural anomaly, resembling a Spanish Mission building from the outside but offering its greatest surprises inside. Its main foyer opened onto a room modeled after a theosophical chapel. High wooden crossbeams formed a cathedral ceiling, and a stairwell at the room's center led to an interior curtained balcony that was a memorable part of the house for the Symmes children, who crept up there to spy on their parents' dinner parties. Robert Duncan never separated the architecture of that household from the mysteries of his family's religious practices. Excluded from the hermetic rituals because of his age, he was never sure what would appear from behind doors or out of the darkened alcoves as he made his way through the large, angular rooms:

> In the inner chamber, the adults, talking on, wove for me in my childish overhearing, Egypt, a land of spells and secret knowledge, a background drift of things close to dreaming—spirit communications, reincarnation memories, clairvoyant journeys into a realm of astral phantasy where all times and places were seen in a new light, of Plato's illustrations of the nature of the soul's life, of most real Osiris and Isis, of the lost Atlantis and Lemuria, and of the god or teacher my parents had taken as theirs, the Hermetic Christos.[1]

While the eccentric interior of the house was a haven for Edwin and Minnehaha Symmes, the grounds of the property had been planned for the children. Enclosed by a maze of high white stucco walls, the yard had tall ferns that created shadows around an ornamental pond and fountain. Stone paths radiated from the fountain toward a studio at the back of the property. Duncan and his sister spent their days chasing each other among the foliage, holding tea parties in a sandbox and exploring a fallen tree that had been left in the yard for their amusement.[2] When Edwin's sister Alvie Symmes Brumm and her husband, Leo, moved into a house nearby, Robert and Barbara raced bicycles up and down the long driveway on Pearl Street with their younger cousins, Leo Jr. and Carol, and ran through the spray from a garden hose on summer days. In early 1923, the family again retreated to Yosemite, but after Duncan and his sister contracted measles that spring, the Symmeses returned to Alameda permanently. Duncan, then four years old, began his formal education that September at the Everett School in Alameda, where he remained until he was eight. Meanwhile, Minnehaha resumed her work with local orphanages, and Edwin disengaged himself from the National Park Service, finding work at an architecture firm in San Francisco in 1924.

With a new home and a middle-class income came a sense of leisure. Minnehaha and the children left the Bay Area during the summer of 1925, vacationing in Santa Barbara, where Duncan and his sister became acquainted with their mother's cousins. The following summer, the destination was Bracken Brae, near Big Sur, and during subsequent years, the family rented a trailer at Morro Beach, midway down the California coast near San Luis Obispo. From season to season, Duncan became familiar with the contrasts of light and dark, the visible and the invisible. Each autumn he was pulled from the radiance of the shoreline back to the shady house where the elders of the hermetic brotherhood met.

If there was anything unusual about Duncan during those years, it was a certain distance and sullen affect. Though he and his sister were the center of attention in the household, this attention was a mixed blessing. They were not only singled out as "the adopted children" at family gatherings but also stood out because of the roles their parents had assigned them in their theosophical cosmic drama. Throughout their childhoods, they puzzled over these roles, uncertain of how to process and respond to their parents' mysticism. Duncan also knew that his natural mother's death and the months he had spent in the care of his teenaged sisters had left him with certain deficits: "only that period can account in my mind for the acute feelings of deprivation . . . that are in my poems."[3] In his 1970 poem "Santa Cruz Propositions," he reflected on his ambivalence toward mother figures:

> And under Her wingspread, fascinated,
> the boy plays with his building blocks
> —sad, deep, absorbd, utter solitude—as if
> the element that surrounds him *cared*.[4]

Compensation for early losses came via his adoptive mother's family. If Duncan, as he later claimed, was a derivative poet, his first sources of imaginative inspiration were the Harris family women: his adoptive mother, Minnehaha Harris Symmes; his aunt Fayetta Harris Philip; and his grandmother Mary Cooley Harris. As he said in 1985, "There's one real grandmother for me, and that's my mother's mother. The family was a matriarchy."[5] The Harrises were, by Duncan's description, "mountain people," and he took pride in the novelty of their backwoods beginnings. Born on October 20, 1855, to Oregon Trail pioneers Elizabeth Hill and Miller Cooley, Mary Cooley was raised in the eastern part of what would later be the state of Oregon, not far from the California border. These Northwest Territories had been explored by Lewis and Clark during the early 1800s: a wilderness of diverse terrains from hilly vistas surrounding the Columbia River to valleys of conifers and acres of rolling, flat wheat fields. Newcomers lived in uneasy proximity to indigenous tribes, and violent skirmishes were common.

As a teenager, Duncan's grandmother met and married a curly-haired schoolteacher named Gamaliel Fullenwider Harris and moved with him to Alturas, California. Gamaliel was a colorful character in Modoc County, a small, blustery southerner who liked to be the center of attention. During the Modoc War of 1872, he conspired with the native leader Captain Jack, whose negotiations with the United States Army to establish reservation land for the local tribes ended badly. After the army routed the Modocs, Gamaliel redirected his energies, joining the California state legislature and later becoming a Superior Court judge. Partly as a tribute to Captain Jack and partly in response to Longfellow's "Song of Hiawatha," he named his youngest daughter Minnehaha. Fayetta Harris Philip mused in her autobiography that her younger sister's name seemed appropriate: "She loved to play in the water . . . around in the lakes, and the horses would trot, and she would bounce up and down. If there was a pan of water anyplace, she would love to play in it, so she was called Minne Ha Ha, play in the water."[6]

Mary Cooley had five daughters with Gamaliel Harris, two of whom perished in a diphtheria epidemic in 1878. Fayetta was born in 1881, Dee in 1883, and Minnehaha in 1887. In 1889, Mary left the hard-drinking Harris, first seeking refuge with her father's kin in Curry County, Oregon, and later with relatives in Santa Barbara. In 1891, she moved the family to a boarding house in San Francisco, remaining there until the earthquake of 1906. With long hours of work and support from her extended family, Mary Harris ushered her children into the twentieth century. Fayetta Harris became a pharmacist, Dee became a physician, and Minnehaha completed a degree in education at San Francisco State College in 1909. But the Harris girls were equally witness to a culture that had disappeared by the time of Robert Duncan's childhood. Fayetta's autobiographical writings focus extensively on her grandfather's cattle ranch, where she made mud pies in Curry County's Rowdy Creek and tiptoed through the woods in fear of Modocs. In a single generation, the family transitioned from the log cabins, smokehouses, and chicken coops of eastern Oregon to the gold rush city of San Francisco, where Mary Harris worked at the federal mint on Mission Street and where her daughters completed college, married, and began families.

Duncan rendered his adoptive grandmother as a mythological figure in *The H. D. Book:* "Close to the wood-lore of her origins in frontier life, she had some natural witch-craft perhaps. But then it may be too that all Grandmothers, as in fairytales, are Wise Women or Priestesses of Mother Nature. I was but a boy when she died, and with her death, my family's tie with the old wisdom-way was broken."[7] Barbara Jones, in contrast, remembered Mary Harris as "a regular old grandma."[8] During the family's frequent visits to Howe Street, Barbara and Robert played in a greenhouse filled with ornamental flowers and ferns, images that conjured another memory for Duncan: "I would be put to bed among the potted plants by the wall that was all windows of a sunroom or herbarium . . . , and as my elders talked in the inner chamber, I, outside, could gaze at the night sky where some star was 'mine' and watched over me, stars were eyes, or the first star seen was a wish or would grant a wish."[9]

What the elders spoke of in that inner chamber was a mystery to the children in the house. As Robert and Barbara heard the voices drift through the halls, they understood they were not to rehearse what they heard in front of the uninitiated, and grasped that the adults "speaking in hushed or deepened voices, or speaking in voices that were not their own, regarded myth as they regarded certain poems and pictures as speaking from the realm of lost or hidden truth."[10] Fayetta later described a time around 1893 when her mother encountered an acquaintance from Oregon who relayed the message "My wife has something to tell you." Intrigued, Mary Harris agreed to meet with the woman and a medium, through whom Harris communicated with her deceased infant daughters.[11] Deeply affected by this message from the spirit world, Harris joined several friends in forming a hermetic brotherhood, a makeshift "initiatory order" of students of theosophy who began meeting regularly, conducting séances, and waiting for instruction from the astral plane.

Tea-leaf divination, séances, numerology, and palm reading were apparently the core of Duncan's grandmother's religious practices. The finer details are lost, but it is clear that Mary Harris's interest in the occult fit into a pattern in the culture. The Bay Area's turn-of-the-century hermetic brotherhoods were part of the western world's growing preoccupation with unconventional forms of theurgy. During the late 1800s, hermetic societies sprang up in Europe so quickly that even the most ardent enthusiast had difficulty keeping track of their activities. In 1912, Aleister Crowley described his own enigmatic Order of the Temple of the East as an amalgam of the knowledge of twenty theosophical and Masonic societies, including the Gnostic Catholic Church, the Order of the Knights of Malta, the Hidden Church of the Holy Grail, the Ancient and Accepted Scottish Rite of Masonry, the Swedenborgian Rite of Masonry, and the Rosicrucian Order.[12] Two of the more influential organizations of the day were the Hermetic Order of the Golden Dawn, founded in England in 1888, and Helena Petrovna Blavatsky's Theosophical Society, established in New York in 1875.[13] The voluminous mystical literature generated by these groups prompted a flurry of do-it-yourself living room rituals, which laid the groundwork for the phenomenon known today as the Western esoteric tradition. Duncan later found inspiration in the writings of Golden Dawn initiates such as William Butler Yeats, G. R. S. Mead, and Jessie Weston; that these post-Victorian theosophies held a relation to modernist poetries was the key to his continued interest in them as an adult. In a 1972 lecture on T. S. Eliot's "The Waste Land" and the early twentieth-century revival of gnosticism in poetry, Duncan reflected, "The end of the nineteenth century is filled with a new genre—from under earth, from dried tubers, those things you thought you had buried came schlepping up the cellar stairs."[14] His curiosity about "that-which-had-been-buried" fueled his intellectual and creative pursuits throughout his life. From Sigmund Freud's excavations of the human mind to H. D.'s interest in palimpsestic language, to the more literal archaeological discovery of the Nag Hammadi manuscripts of the New Testament in 1945, psychology, science, and the paranormal informed the narratives of Duncan's poems. Where Eliot, Pound, and H. D. occupied themselves with little-known occult testimonies during the 1920s, the same "pot and pantheism" of Neoplatonic and heretical Christian writings defined the Harris and Symmes clans' religion.[15]

Traditionally, hermetic brotherhoods—organized around the teachings of the figure the Greeks knew as Hermes Trismegistus—assimilate a broad range of spiritual tenets, objectives, and sacred writings. Duncan described the religious interests in his childhood household as similar to those of the "popular cults of the Hellenic period," and he reported that his parents read the major texts of Egyptian, Greek, and Christian religions "in light of second century theosophies."[16] Equally venerated were the gnostic writings of Valentinus, the teachings of the Roman Empire's Mithraic mystery cults, and the rich field of early Neoplatonic texts such as the works of Plotinus, Plutarch, and Proclus. Spiritual instruction was also gathered from more recent sources: A. P. Sinnett's *Esoteric Buddhism,* MacGregor Mathers's *The Qubalah Unveiled,* and G. R. S. Mead's *Fragments of a Faith Forgotten.* The less literary minded could take alternative routes to the land of Ibis-headed Thoth. During the 1920s, archaeological excavations in Egypt's Valley of the Kings opened the gates to a new orientalism. Rumors of a mummy's curse soon inundated popular culture, and the ancient boy king Tutankhamen was a figure of high interest. Within the decade, Hollywood had produced several tales of the mysterious and monstrous, including Carl Freund's *The Mummy,* starring Boris Karloff, which opened in 1931 when Duncan was twelve years old. The new spirituality was highly compatible with the entertainment industry, and California became a natural hotbed of occult activity. When theosophical teachings arrived from Europe, American followers infused them with folklore and moneymaking schemes, readily mixing the carnival aspects of P. T. Barnum with a neoshamanism borrowed from the indigenous tribes of the Pacific Northwest.[17] By 1927, a major Rosicrucian order had set up camp in San Jose, opening its Egyptian Museum there in 1932. Farther down the coast, an offshoot of Blavatsky's Theosophical Society opened an institute in Ojai during the mid-1920s, with Annie Besant at its helm, later to flourish under the direction of her protégé, the Indian guru Jiddu Krishnamurti.[18] Duncan never embraced the theosophy of Ojai but acknowledged its influence. When East Coast poet Charles Olson chastised him and other Bay Area writers for their interest in magic and ritual, proclaiming the state of affairs in San Francisco to be as "ominous as Ojai," Duncan in turn remarked of Olson, "He suspects, and rightly, that I indulge myself in pretentious fictions."[19]

Those pretentious fictions defined Duncan's early experiences of the narrative world. The dignified figures of Christ and Lao Tse were central to his grandmother's pantheon, alongside an array of tabloid literature. Prominent were *Azoth: The Occult Magazine of America,* "An Inspirational, Helpful, Philosophical and Progressive Magazine of Constructive Thought"; and *The All Seeing Eye,* which kept its readership up to date on the latest discoveries in the ancient world while also providing speculative accounts of the Druids and Stonehenge. Duncan kept the August 1921 issue of *Azoth*—with its articles "The Occult Side of Einstein's Theories," "Leaves from a Kabbalist's Notebook," "Fate and Freewill," and "Interior Stars"—as a keepsake of his childhood. In turn, his Aunt Fay typed and illustrated a series of tracts about her own mystical discoveries, distributing them to relatives as annual Christmas newsletters.[20]

Writing had found a place and a purpose in the Symmes and Harris households, though Duncan's earliest forays into this creative realm were but an anticipated aspect of his character. He later told his friend Helen Adam about his Aunt Fay's response to one of his childhood poems: "This is very lazy of you. You have been a poet already in so many lives."[21] Unfazed, Duncan wrote throughout his childhood, and, knowingly or not, the adults around him granted him the permission to indulge in a pot and pantheism of his own. Despite his skepticism about his family's pseudo-orthodoxies, he eventually turned to many of its hallowed texts for creative inspiration when constructing his poems. At the center of his library were a large number of books out of which he fashioned a poetics paying tribute to both his mother's theosophical interests and his father's profession as an architect. Duncan's "The Architecture, *Passages* 9" with its collage of quotations from Gustave Stickley's 1909 *Craftsman Homes* and an inventory of his own bookshelves, illustrates this inclination:

> from the bookcases   the glimmering titles arrayd   keys
>
> Hesiod   ·   Heraklitus   ·   *The Secret Books of the Egyptian Gnostics* . . .
>
> "Take a house planned in this way, with a big living room, its
> great fireplace, open staircase, casement windows, built-in seats,
> cupboards, bookcases . . . and perhaps French doors opening out
> upon a porch" . . .
>
> > *La Révélation d'Hermès Trismégiste*
> > *Plutarch's Morals: Theosophical Essays*
> > *Avicenna*
> > *The Zohar*
> > *The Aurora*[22]

The household of his early years radiated a rare creative splendor. Though he incorporated new flourishes with each retelling, his stories of his childhood always returned to the same assertion: family gatherings had provided him with all the material he needed to kindle his imagination. He had been a regular spectator of animated and sometimes heated conversations about the business of Plato, Shakespeare, and *The Egyptian Book of the Dead*. He later shaped his own household to provide analogous intellectual comforts, and he often informed his audiences of the debt he owed his adoptive family: "They were spinning a tale beyond belief and I wanted to go into that tale."[23]

FOUR

A Part in the Fabulous

My parents thought that I was inflicted on them, and that
I was something considerably more than they were.
ROBERT DUNCAN, Vancouver Conference, 1963

In the family I grew up in they always had great talkers at the
table. They disappeared later because I took over.   ROBERT
DUNCAN, Berkeley Conference, 1965

THERE WAS TO BE A CATASTROPHE: the first world would be de-
stroyed by water, the present world incinerated in a fiery apocalypse. Dun-
can heard the tale from his parents, his grandmother, and his Aunt Fay, and
he and his cousins talked about it as they splashed in the waves on summer
outings. The notion consumed his imagination, and his sleep was haunted
by its images:

> Taller than Morro Rock ... the breakers of that catastrophe must be. I would
> try to picture the flood enormous enough to crash upon the mountains ... as
> if they were but banks of sand, a wave to drown the San Joaquin. Or I would
> listen, curled up on the ledge back of the seat in the coupe, as Mother drove
> us home from the movies ..., for the sea-roar. Now it will come, now it is
> coming, pouring in from the coast to meet and overwhelm us.[1]

The myth of Atlantis was an enduring inspiration for Duncan's poems,
starting with a recurring childhood dream:

> A field appeared ... unbroken by rock or tree, a rise to the horizon of the
> ripe-headed grass bending toward the east where there was no wind blowing.
> There a ring of children danced so that I was in the center, crownd, a game of
> imminent disaster. ... In the dream, the disaster was a great Deluge, in in-
> ward bursting doors under the pressure of overwhelming waters.[2]

Minnehaha and Edwin Symmes interpreted the dream for their son: "the
disaster was an old memory, a wound in time, never forgotten by its chil-
dren, which was the death-throe of Atlantis."[3]

In 1880, Ignatius Donnelly's pop geological tract *Atlantis: The Antediluvian World* drew on the connections between cultures on opposite sides of the Atlantic to prove the existence of an ancient midocean civilization, submerged beneath the muddy shallows of the Great Sargasso Sea off the coast of Spain. Plato's dialogues, the *Timaeus* and *Critias,* were also esteemed texts for the Symmeses. The *Timaeus* described the undersea realm in detail: "in this island of Atlantis there was a great and wonderful empire which had rule over the whole island and several others, and over parts of the continent, and, furthermore, the men of Atlantis had subjected the parts of Libya within the columns of Hercules as far as Egypt, and of Europe as far as Tyrrhenia."[4]

Duncan's early perception of himself was fused with his parents' devotion to Plato's dialogues and to the texts of the Neoplatonic mystics of the second century A.D. Noting that his family was drawn "toward the fabulous in Plato," Duncan wrote, "I have never shed this disposition toward the fabulous: it has been kept as a pole of tensions in . . . my imagination."[5] Moreover, his parents told him that this mysterious place had been his ancient home. "I belonged, too, to the generation that had been destroyed in a cataclysm before the world we lived in began. I had a part in the fabulous."[6]

What began as a childhood anxiety dream evolved into a poet's life's work. In "Often I Am Permitted to Return to a Meadow," the first poem in his 1960 book *The Opening of the Field,* he synthesized the hermetic influences of his youth and clarified the role that theosophy would have in his life. Never initiated into the hermetic brotherhood, he sought passage from his parents' world of middle-class "coffee table" hermeticism to his own place in the fabulous—not a religion, but a poetics. Within that meadow, he embedded his childhood memory:

> It is only a dream of the grass blowing
> east against the source of the sun
> in an hour before the sun's going down
>
> whose secret we see in a children's game
> of ring a round of roses told.[7]

Through the composition of poems, Duncan came to reconfigure a practice of magic, seeking in language what his parents had sought in their dreams, in the instruction of their spirit guides, and in the alignments of the stars. Family enthusiasm for locating the gnosis hidden in myth awoke Duncan to the notion that his life would be charted not at the séance table but through a bibliomancy of his own design.[8] If fairy tales held numinous truths, so might the books he read and subsequently so would his poetry.

That Duncan became a self-described "bookish poet" is of little surprise given the importance of storytelling in his formative years. In 1965, he said, "My involvement with myth comes from the fact that before I could read myself, my parents read me fairy tales and . . . myths. And so they belonged to . . . the very first world that seemed to be the world that might be poetry."[9] Some years after Minnehaha's death, Duncan's Aunt Fay reminded him of his earliest bond with his adoptive mother: "Looking backward to your early childhood, I see her sitting in a small rocker holding you on her lap, and reading Japanese poems to you. . . . No doubt in my mind that you chose her for a mother."[10] The volume *Little Pictures of Japan* invited children to enter the world of poetry and perhaps also the world of carnal desire. Duncan was mesmerized by the colorful illustration of the poet asleep beneath a quilt with two friends: "what comes immediately . . . is my sitting with my sister, my mother between us, looking at the pictures . . . as my mother reads aloud. The picture I am looking at is of three young men sleeping on a mat. One of them, the poet Basho, has awakened."[11]

Much of the essential reading material of Duncan's childhood was ushered into print by editor Olive Beaupre Miller. Her multivolume collection, *My Bookhouse,* was published in 1920; *Little Pictures of Japan* soon followed. While Miller sought to publish works that enforced an ethical lifestyle for the young, in the Symmes household, the experience of reading and being read to was more complex. In the act of listening to a poem or fairy tale, Duncan and his sister were initiated into revelations far more extraordinary than the rules of manners and morals. Miller's anthologies promised their young readers that they might discover long-hidden information about the structure of the universe. "My parents felt there was a truth in fairy tales. . . . Very early I must have gotten the information that something within you could feel that certain fairy tales were very true, others were just stories."[12]

Another immediate pleasure came from the stories of the Greeks. In *The H.D. Book,* Duncan mused, "In the dawn of intelligence, before I could read or write, there was a story or fairytale told of Cupid and Psyche. In the beginning I heard of this god Eros and of the drama of loss and search. I understood only that there was a wonder in this tale."[13] Part of the wonder was the shock of Psyche's awakening. Spying on Cupid to ascertain his true physical form, she was thrown, unprepared, into a world of knowledge.

Duncan identified with the "awakenings" of Basho and Psyche because he too had come into the world awakened from a long sleep. During this cycle of his journey, he would bear witness to the horrors unleashed by humanity's misuse of its knowledge. As Psyche had burned Cupid with the oil of her lamp, so modern humanity would immolate itself in a catastrophic fire. Into his adulthood, Duncan confronted the threat of nuclear holocaust with scientific curiosity rather than fear; he saw it as a logical potentiality of the world he lived in.[14]

Humanity's recurring loving and destructive instincts are sketched out in Duncan's "A Poem Beginning with a Line by Pindar":

> Scientia
> holding the lamp, driven by doubt;
> Eros naked in foreknowledge
> smiling in his sleep;
> . . . .
> Psyche travels
> life after life, my life, station
> after station,
> to be tried
>
> without break . . .[15]

Science and myth were twin tracks for Duncan from the beginning of his intellectual life. During his teens, he "read avidly about dinosaurs and geological epochs," as a cousin later reminded him: "My last remembrance of you was in the back seat of Uncle Ed and Aunt Minne's car on our way to . . . Morro Bay . . . Remember? You were impressing me with all the technical knowledge you had about animals."[16]

A final and clearly instrumental inspiration in Duncan's early imaginative life was L. Frank Baum's world of Oz. The straightforward message of the Oz series later served as a grid for Duncan's beliefs about poetry: "in the Land of Oz, an-y-thing is poss-i-ble. For it is a won-der-ful fair-y coun-try."[17] When the series was continued by other writers after Baum's death in 1919, Duncan collected each new volume as part of his own hermetic metaphysical territory. When he reached adolescence and his parents decided "to throw out all of those keys of childhood," Duncan clung to Baum's work, eventually enshrining it in the bedroom he shared with his partner, Jess, in San Francisco.[18]

The fantastical yarns of childhood primed Duncan for the vocation of storytelling. He picked the forms of sentences and narrative fragments out of the air, waiting for an appropriate moment to enter conversations. Enveloped in a rush of voices, at first he struggled with the language, and, according to family legend, he began speaking later than most children.[19] The trouble of talk was twofold for Duncan: at first there was too little of it; later there would be too much. His elementary-school writing exercises contain hints of dyslexia, and one of his unfinished and unpublished poems mythologized those early labors: "At ten Don Juan could not spell. / The alphabet betrayed his hell."[20] As his mastery of language increased, he found a way to participate in the household antics. He sometimes joked that he learned early that he could engage everyone's attention by announcing at breakfast, "I had a really funny dream last night."[21] Invoking his powers as the lost messenger of Atlantis, he could compel his parents to drop their forks and listen with rapt attention.

The encouragement and inclination to talk were a mixed blessing. Barbara remembered spending summer evenings on the porch listening to her preadolescent brother spin macabre tales while she and other neighborhood children sat transfixed in terror and delight.[22] His ability to mesmerize his listeners shaped his reputation as a writer. But by the time he entered the community beyond his family, his endurance as a speaker exhausted his private and public audiences alike.[23] Duncan implied that he suffered as much from his logorrhea as those upon whom it was unleashed. Yet his anxious relation to speech seemed part of his destiny, both as the abandoned child of his biological family and as the chosen Atlantean of the Symmes clan.

FIVE

The Wasteland

Your resemblances and "recognitions" may mark you as a
Symmes on the broad canvas of Duncan.   EDNA KEOUGH
TO ROBERT DUNCAN, undated letter

IN LATE 1927, Edwin and Minnehaha Symmes again relied on an astro-
logical forecast by the elders of the hermetic brotherhood to guide a major
decision—the last time that cosmic imperatives took precedence over prag-
matic household decision making. The family would move to the nascent
town of Bakersfield, where Edwin saw the promise of a professional practice
all his own. Not long after the family's arrival in October, he found employ-
ment as a public works architect. The transition was not as effortless as the
stars had foretold: the family had landed in a desert valley three hundred
miles from friends, relatives, and the urban sophistication of the Bay Area.
The Symmeses moved into a cramped, one-story adobe cottage at 1908 Verde
Street, not far from a row of tar-covered thoroughfares classified as down-
town. The children, uprooted from the indulgences of their grandmother
and aunts, now turned to Minnehaha for attention. When she suffered an
allergic reaction to the San Joaquin Valley's foliage during the summer of
1928, she retreated to bed, sipping medicinal lemon water. The following
year, her condition burgeoned into an incapacitating hay fever that confined
her to a darkened back room of the house.

Meanwhile, eight-year-old Robert and his younger sister explored Verde
Street, pedaling their bicycles past the low, flat cottages and palm trees and
around the nearby Roosevelt Elementary School, which they would attend
that fall. In this era before air conditioning, they took refuge at night on the
enclosed sleeping porch at the front of the house, perfecting their storytell-
ing skills amid the din of field crickets. Duncan rarely admitted to fond
memories of Bakersfield, but the locale seeped into his creative life in deli-
cate reveries. Decades later, he remembered the place he had sometimes
characterized as a suburban hell:

the wilderness beyond the edge of town, the riverbottom road,
the lingering, the wandering, the going astray,
to find some wanton promise the derelict landscape most portrayd in me,
the fog's sad density of cold,
in me, the solitary and deserted paths,
in me, the marshy wastes, the levee road
where day after day as if driven by the wind
I impatiently strode . . .[1]

Within the derelict landscape was a contrary force of growth. The city's namesake, Colonel Thomas Baker, had transformed the valley's southern swamplands into alfalfa fields during the 1860s. From this start, a town grew up in 1898, along with an active grape and cotton-farming industry. From the flat city streets in the valley rose the Temblor range to the west, the Tehachapi to the south, and the Sierra Nevada to the east. Along the foothills grazed sheep and cattle, and with the surrounding oil-rich land, Bakersfield's population swelled throughout the early twentieth century.

As members of the middle class in the postwar quiet of the early 1920s, Edwin and Minnehaha Symmes maintained an economically stable and politically conservative household and raised their children accordingly. Duncan noted in 1976, "When I was a child I was always wanting to play household and house."[2] In the late 1930s when he had his first experience of an itinerant bohemian lifestyle, he longed for the material comforts of home. Indeed, money was a constant theme in Duncan's life, arising first in battles with his mother over his allowance and trust fund and later in his obsessive financial record keeping during his reading and lecture tours. While he occupied the counterculture, he rejected its economic and emotional instability.

The Symmeses shared their neighbors' political views and biases and socialized primarily within white Protestant circles. Bakersfield's Chinese and Japanese immigrants had to settle for jobs as gardeners and cooks, and many of the Japanese students at Duncan's high school were subsequently interred in American prison camps during the Second World War. Basque farmers from the Pyrenees also came to the Central Valley during the gold rush era, soon to dominate Bakersfield's shepherding industry. On a national level, Congress met this deluge of newcomers with immigration restrictions, and Ku Klux Klan activity spiked, peaking with a membership of nearly five million in 1924.

Duncan occasionally mentioned his family's anti-Semitism and also noted that his parents "thought they were very adventuresome when they had some Catholic friends."[3] He once unkindly deemed his mother "a Ku Klux Klan democrat," though Barbara preferred to characterize her mother more benignly as a community activist tending to the needy. Edwin Symmes embraced traditional Republican politics, as evinced by his daughter's memory of waking up on a November morning in 1928 to find a cheerful handwritten message pasted on her wall: "Hoover Wins—Hurray!"[4]

In a small town in an era of social discretion, Edwin and Minnehaha Symmes developed a certain prudence about their public activities:

> They were isolated from their Brotherhood, their studies changed to studies that were respected by the community . . . By the time I was adolescent, my father was involved in the study of botany and local historical sites. After his death, Mother was relieved, I think, that [the Brotherhood's] way of studying things might be dismissed. New friends did not share her belief—that was part of it—but then, though her belief may have lasted, her interest did not last.[5]

The Symmeses also briefly sent Robert and Barbara to a Congregational Sunday school, and Edwin joined the Masons, ascending the local ranks with ease.[6] Almost overnight Duncan lost his status as a phantom from an underwater kingdom; he was now the eldest son of middle-class professionals. His parents' social standing spawned apprehensions that Duncan carried into adulthood:

> Last night in a dream I sat with my family at a dinner—a political discussion arose and my hatred of this world of adults surged up—the boy who had sat trying to perform within the adult salon broke wild—I threw a plate of soup at my aunt, I broke a tureen of hot vegetables over my mother's head—I hate their world—yet always it intrudes—my duties in their world destroy my inner world of childhood— . . . I upset the dinner table and walkd from the room.[7]

While his parents were shifting their focus from the metaphysical to the physical, their uninitiated child carved out a compromise, becoming the poet-archivist of the Symmeses' theosophical history: "What was left me from the talk of the elders in that antechamber of my childhood was now all my own. My parents, living far from the center of things, were concerned with security and status . . . : our religion became something we did not talk about to everybody. I talked to myself about it."[8]

In the late 1920s, he also wrote his first poems. One enduring keepsake of this era is a Bell-Wether Invincibles cigar box decorated with colored construction paper, inside which he safeguarded "Poems by Robert E. Symmes" dedicated to "the bestest grandma in the world from her grandson."[9] The collection includes "occasional" poems transcribed by the nine-year-old for "Thanksgiving," "Roosevelt's Birthday," and "Spring":

> Baby life in fields does play
> Cherries are ripe, birds are gay,
> Between them all they raise a cheer,
> Sweet cherries are ripe, spring is here.[10]

The box's multihued paper decorations, cut into geometric shapes and glued at odd angles, have the look of a cubist castle with tinfoil spires.

Barbara remembered being coerced into sketching portraits of her enthusiastic older brother. When she attempted to opt out of such art lessons— citing a lack of confidence in her abilities—Duncan prodded her to "just keep drawing."[11] When the tomboyish Barbara managed to escape his grip, Duncan retreated to the dusty volumes on his parents' bookshelves and to the Beale Memorial children's library downtown. In addition to the Oz series, Kipling's *Jungle Books,* Grimm's *Fairy Tales,* and Swift's *Gulliver's Travels* kept him occupied into his teens. Reading was an integral activity for all the Symmeses, but Duncan's reading habits took on a new distinction: he seemed able to recite the contents of a book before opening it.[12]

With the two-year anniversary of the Symmeses's move to Bakersfield came bad news. Minnehaha fell ill again in the fall of 1929, and on October 19, the family matriarch, Mary Cooley Harris, died, one day short of her seventy-fourth birthday. The Symmeses departed for the Bay Area, where, at 10 A.M. on October 22, Harris's ashes were interred at the Chapel of the Chimes Mausoleum in Oakland, and the hermetic brotherhood conducted a religious service. Six days later, the stock market crashed, and the American economy that had seemed so stable came to a standstill.

In the aftermath of these events, during March 1930, Minnehaha noticed that eleven-year-old Robert was "extremely nervous."[13] At the end of the year, he faced another stressful transition, transferring to Bakersfield's William Penn School in the middle of sixth grade. The following autumn he moved on to Emerson Junior High, where he was placed in an advanced class supervised by one of the school system's most respected teachers, Mrs. Millie Munsey. Nervousness aside, he excelled academically, to the puzzlement of his sister, who rarely saw him study. He also had his first taste of extracurricular activity, signing on as a reporter for the school newspaper, the *Emersonian,* and later becoming its editor.[14]

The beginning of the Depression years saw the Symmeses' economic status waver, but they adapted better than most. In April 1931, they moved to a larger house at 2330 Truxton Avenue. The property was nearer to downtown, parallel to the Southern Pacific tracks, and two blocks from the tree-lined Jastro Park where the children played after school. In addition to affording the near-pubescent children separate bedrooms for the first time, the house included a second-floor den where Edwin Symmes entertained his friends and sometimes challenged his children to a game of pool.[15] The gap that had opened between the upper and working classes over the previous decade left the Symmeses on the comfortable side of the poverty line, as did President Roosevelt's 1933 allocation of money to public works projects. At times when Edwin had difficulty finding work, he kept the family afloat by drawing off his life insurance policy and by renting rooms in the new house to a kindergarten teacher, Mary Tyson, and her brother Royal.

Throughout those years, the family took trips to the ocean and to the Bay Area. The usual summer venue was Morro Beach, but in August 1931, the Symmeses also visited Hollywood Beach, and in December, they celebrated Christmas with Fayetta in Berkeley. The annual forays to the ocean made their way into Duncan's later poems. In the shadow of Morro Rock's inactive volcano, the Pacific became an Atlantis in Duncan's imagination. He recalled that he would "lie awake before going off to sleep at the summer cottage at Morro Beach, letting the crash of the surf take over and grow enormous."[16] Reveling in his fantasies of apocalypse, he allowed the summer trips to claim a less sinister place in his memory. In "A Glimpse," he wrote:

> Come, yellow broom
> and lavender in bloom,
> . . . .
> hot and dreaming in the morning sun,
> I ever from where I am return,
> as if from this boyhood privacy
> my life burnd on in a smoke of me,
>
> mixt with sage in the summer air
>   and lavender,
> and the stream from its shade
> runs down to the bay and beyond to the sea.[17]

Entering adolescence and "boyhood privacy," Duncan negotiated his way through a series of vague taboos relating to the carnal world. He lacked the vocabulary to describe or acknowledge his early masturbation experiences. The enlightened visions of European psychoanalysis and the sexual revolution of the Roaring Twenties had stopped short of the Symmeses' door. In a 1963 lecture, Duncan reported, "I had no picture of what a sexual act would be. The most reference that would ever be made to my sexual organs would be my aunt saying 'now you know you never take all your clothes off at the same time. You take your shirt off and you put the top of your pajamas on. . . .' You kept this secret that was going to come out of this egg at some point; you kept it beautifully in a shell."[18]

While he was later happy to imagine himself a gigolo, he could not escape the Victorian prohibitions of childhood. Unlike his sexually liberated Beat Generation counterpart Allen Ginsberg, Duncan leaned toward the proscribed sexuality that he had first encountered in the myth of Cupid and Psyche: "I understand what Lawrence says when he says 'Do not touch me, for touch is charged and not familiar.' That whole world of the Greek gods was the world of do-not-touch-me."[19] "Crushes" and flirtation were Duncan's specialty, and the poems of his adult years typically veiled the act of sexualizing in complex metaphor.[20]

Duncan's earliest poems were his most explicit. He mischievously noted that his first writings adopted variations of iambic pentameter, comforting in their repetitive, masturbatory beat:[21]

> Now pale as magnolia and blue in the starlight
> The flesh of the thigh 'gainst the dark of his pubes
> Stood stark and alive, and his body clear shining
> Translucent—a light in the void of the darkness
> Above his pale forehead the dark hair ran gleaming
> And sharp from the cold, his dark eyes shown yet darker
> His dark eyes, so frightened, so huge in the shadows
> And bracing his hands to the cool of her shoulder
> He poised as if listening and swayed scarcely moving.[22]

The waters of sexual awakening were further muddied by Duncan's gravitation toward men. He sought out both heterosexual and homosexual experiences during his adolescent years, but the parameters of "normal" sexual pleasure were left ill defined and unarticulated. Even when he arrived in liberal Berkeley in 1936, his new acquaintances did not understand his description of himself as a homosexual. As one friend mused, "Who knew what it meant?"[23] By Duncan's account, his mother knew what it meant, as did his high school classmates, who called him "Sissie Symmes." One peer remembered, "He was certainly not an athlete and at that time knew he was probably homosexual."[24] Describing himself as his adoptive mother's "gay" falcon, Duncan even viewed his homosexuality as an unspoken part of his parents' wishes—a sign of his karmic deviance—and he speculated that Minnehaha fostered that identification. He told his friend Robert Kelly that his mother had dressed him in girl's clothing as a child and that, when he entered puberty, she kept him home from school once a month on a regular cycle.[25]

By midadolescence, Duncan's sexual identity took form through two complementary Oedipal dramas. As much as he disliked Minnehaha's domineering, he found something to admire in her feminine wiles. Meanwhile, his adoptive father's aloofness challenged his own skills of seduction.[26] Edwin was a nervous, balding chain smoker who spent long days at the office and retreated to the garage on weekends to tinker with a newfangled ham radio. Barbara remembered a remoteness in her adoptive father, sensing that he was conflicted about involving himself emotionally in his children's activities.[27] Duncan recorded a similar thought:

> My father . . . never did what he did not want to do—[he] always was doing what was like a hobby for him—at the office his architecture—at home architecture, photography, stamps, astrology, flower slides. . . . My mother would call me from my own hobbies—she would consider my drawing, writing, reading as criminal—as it interfered with my changing the hose on the lawns in the summer. I understand now that she hated me—because it was my father she hated—it was my father who did nothing, who never could be disturbed to do these tedious little errands that laid the weight on me. It was my father . . . who left his desk in a disorder of many objects, who left his socks on the floor.[28]

Despite Edwin Symmes's self-involvement, Duncan experienced him as a benign, if not affectionate, male role model. He sometimes characterized his adoptive father as an intellectual versed in Masonic lore and other times as a stodgy but successful public works architect. He may have exaggerated Edwin's interest in the occult, but the elder Symmes at least cared about affairs of the imagination. Though Minnehaha was the one who read to the children at night, it was her husband who brought home Robert Louis Stevenson's *Treasury of Children's Stories* and who designed the Symmes family bookplates—complete with a sketch of their former abode in Alameda and a shield with the family motto, "Droit Et Loyal" ("right and loyal")—which were carefully pasted in the household's books.

Edwin Symmes tutored his son in architectural drafting, and Duncan remembered being groomed to follow in his father's footsteps: "I was praised in the very beginning for drawing and for every sign . . . They expected an architect. And they trained me for an architect."[29] Through Symmes's encouragement, Duncan developed an interest in mathematics early on, and he later embedded a punning image of the crossroads of Eros and Intellect in the love poem "Circulations of the Song": "I will take up geometry again. / The mysteries of here and there, above and below, / now and then, demand new / figures of me."[30] Where architecture occurred in Duncan's poems, it was linked to homoerotic longing. And though he quickly lost interest in his adoptive father's profession, he found a way to internalize this early influence, as he told an interviewer in 1985:

> What I notice is that I architect my poems. . . . Rooms are not just square boxes. You design how people move through them and so that's [a] projected imagination already of how you're not going to live in a room, but how you're going to go from one passageway to another. So, it's very natural that I would eventually have a long poem called "Passages."[31]

SIX

The Fathering Dream

> Ghosts and lovers of my sixteenth year, old themes
> and changing keys of a persisting music,
> here, the colors face, I cannot recall the face, there,
> some pattern revivifies the scheme. What
> was the accurate contour of the fathering dream?
>
> ROBERT DUNCAN, "Marginalia from
> Thom Gunn's *Moly*"

> I was a poet who started without talent. ROBERT DUNCAN,
> Vancouver Conference, 1963

IN THE SUMMER OF 1935, the Symmeses rented a bungalow on the Santa Barbara beachfront. Sixteen-year-old Robert Duncan slept in a courtyard patio under mosquito nets, surrounded by citrus trees and lush, big-eared palms. Just before the school year began, on September 10, Edwin Symmes died after suffering a massive heart attack alone in the house on Truxton Avenue, where he had gone to recuperate from an earlier attack. Symmes had been in failing health for some time; his heavy smoking contributed to his death at fifty-two, as did the stress of supporting his family during the Depression years. Duncan wrote in 1941, "My father had a different way of aging, of being old in the beginning like a tree—there was no death in him—all of him burned thin and furious inside—He . . . had no hate for us, no passion yet you felt all the hatred and passion and sex was there hurrying inside of him like a great redwood or a mountain burning forever until there was only ash."[1]

Symmes's death was a headline that week with the *Bakersfield Californian* reporting, "So greatly beloved was Mr. Symmes in civic life, many organizations have passed resolutions of sorrow at his death."[2] The Masonic rites in his honor on September 13 were presided over by the Bakersfield Commandery of Knights Templar and a local Boy Scout troop. One of the pallbearers, Lewis A. Burtch, would marry Minnehaha three years later.

Symmes's body was then transported to the California Crematorium Columbarium in Oakland, where another service took place on September 14, after which his ashes were interred in the Guidance Garden of the Chapel of the Chimes Mausoleum. Within the week, Minnehaha and the children returned to Bakersfield, and Duncan began his final year of high school. Duncan processed his grief through writing, incorporating the theme of his adoptive father's death into several stories. A short piece variously titled "The Meek One" and "Transit" features a widower with Edwin Symmes's middle name, Joseph: "When it was dark outside and cold, he sat in the shadow inside staring at the fire. He felt that death was a flame, burning clear and blue and at its rim gold. The empty night was peace, and the empty flame was peace. He felt that death was peace and dreamed of death."[3]

Duncan began spending more time alone, escaping to the movie theater and to Michener's hamburger stand on 18th Street. He also took long walks along the Kern River, edged by yellow poppies. The river was a substantial hike from the residential area of town, but he was drawn there day and night, sometimes missing classes: "I was just emerging from the mythosexual dream-world of my junior and senior years at high school—a world so associated with the tule fogs of winter Bakersfield and the Kern River country beyond our house and with the late spring heats of that Mojave/San Joaquin Valley."[4] The feelings within this adolescent dream-world found their focus in Edwin Symmes's death. Duncan wrote, in "Poems from the Margins of Thom Gunn's *Moly*":

> The year my father died died into me and dyed
> anew the green of green, the gold gold shone from,
> the blue that colors seas and skies to speak
> of sadness innocence most knew,   and into Man
> a mystery to take the place of fatherhood he grew
> in me, a ghostly bridegroom fathering his bride in me,
> . . . .
>   It was a fiery ghost,
> a burning substitution darkening all the sexual ways,
> striving in those urgencies to speak,   to speak,
> to heal unutterable injuries . . .[5]

Fascinated with the Greek myth of Psyche, Duncan was likewise intrigued by the underbelly of Bakersfield: the banks of the Kern and the edges of public parks, where he could meet other young men in search of intimacy.

Despite its conservative surface, Bakersfield possessed an oil-town toughness, and Duncan experienced two violent episodes there that he associated with his transition out of childhood: one, a high school thrill ride that went wrong; the other, an incident he described variously as a beating or a rape by a deranged teenager.[6] Duncan spoke about the latter incident in a *Gay Sunshine* magazine interview in the 1970s. At the age of sixteen, after a sexual encounter with another boy in the park, the boy flew into a rage and pummeled Duncan, opening large gashes on his chin and temples. Sliding out of his attacker's grip, Duncan ran home and collapsed on the doorstep of the Truxton Avenue house. He woke up on a hospital stretcher, his mother and police officers hovering over him, seeking a description of the boy, who was later named a suspect in a murder.[7] Duncan's renderings of this significant event emphasized the intrigue rather than the trauma and cast his assailant as a mythological creature: "His eyes looked like moon stars look—beautiful and exciting! And all the time I'm trying to look beautiful and exciting, trying to look like him, because I feel my face change. I'm entranced but so is he. . . . So I answer entrancement with being entranced."[8] The tone of this retelling masks any deeper psychological distress Duncan may have felt, although ambivalent feelings about his sexuality remain in his later writing. In one of his first major works, "The Venice Poem," he was to write "cock sucking breeds self-humiliation."[9]

Throughout high school, Duncan had struggled to balance his sexual and creative desires against the threat of social humiliation. An A student, except in "Military," he signed on for activities that allowed him to show off his prowess as a speaker and writer, including the Debate Luncheon Club and the dramatics club Props and Paints. He took part in the senior play, was an assistant editor of the yearbook, and worked on the school newspaper, the *Blue and White*.[10] With his hair cropped short, he was a square-headed kid, and his thick glasses exaggerated the drift of his wayward eye. Despite his looks and a certain girlish posture, he made friends easily. His sister later remarked, "Everyone was his friend," but she also admitted that he was treated with an admixture of deference and teasing that could border on contempt.[11] He gained some respect from his peers as a writer, composing substantial narratives that often returned to an early childhood theme:

> Thousands of years ago there lived on the island of Atlantis an ancient and noble family, the House of Bird-of-Gold. It was one of this illustrious house who in the latter era of the Empire lead *[sic]* the third expedition against the barbarians of the Australian wastes. The legend of the family was that Marc

one of the sons of Adam had brought from the Garden a Bird of Gold. The family of Marc lived in the mountains of Persia for seven to the seventh generation and then it came to pass that Noom who was of that house stole the sacred bird from the family ark and fled into Atlantis.[12]

This four-page account of the last days of Atlantis, with its lavish accents, bears the hallmarks of his early writing. The characters' melodrama of gossip and bickering seems a thinly veiled critique of the Symmes household:

> The mother of Hadius was the lovely Cretan actress Meme who in the dance of the Tapirs before the King of the Western World had brought his proposal of marriage and it was rumored . . . that he had no claim to the name of the House of the Bird-of-Gold, but was the bastard of . . . his mother and the Emperor Cronos himself. . . . "Did you hear . . ." Meme spoke across the table as soon as the servant carried out the soups. "Did you hear that Madlyn of the House of the Silver Horn was left?"
> "Left?" Alise was suddenly interested.
> "It was terribel [sic] . . ." Meme gloated. "She had a quarrel with her husband and he slipped out of port without her. Set sail and left her at the dock screaming and beating against the railings. . . ."
> "The royal family left two days ago." Caldus said.
> "It was so noble of them to have stayed so long to keep up the spirit of the common people." . . .
> Now Lydia spoke. . . . "We are going to the mountain fortress where we shall await the last Day. . . . The Sacred Orders have sealed themselves with the archives of the Empire and await the Catastrophe. The stars move even now and the caravan shall set out at dawn for the mountains north."[13]

During his freshman year at Kern County Union High School, Duncan enrolled in English composition, English literature, algebra, French, history, and physical education. In the following two years, his study of French, Latin, and history led him to consider poetry as a vocation. On a trip to the library, he "found out that the most any poet had made that year was $400."[14] The poet was Ogden Nash, a staff writer for the *New Yorker,* whose odd rhyming off-color portraits inspired Duncan to attempt his own rhymes in the mid-1930s:

> O once I was gay, Lilly would simmer.
> I've still got my bust, and nothing is primmer
> Than my 22 waist. But I've got this damn liver
> Along with my bust and my model T flivver.
> O I was once gay but I've still got my liver
> As such I drink tea (see her lips quiver).[15]

Beyond Nash loomed the more substantial influence of his high school teacher Edna Keough. An amateur poet who had published in provincial magazines such as the *San Franciscan,* the *Lyric West,* and the *Carmel Pine Cone Cymbal,* she had the unusual academic specialty of twentieth-century modernist literature. Her class gave the sixteen-year-old Duncan the impetus for his "conversion to poetry": "I was to find anew the world of Romance that I had known in earliest childhood in fairy tale and daydream and in the romantic fictions of the household in which I grew up. Now it seems my soul first set out on its journey in my falling in love with my teacher, with some intimation of spirit in her, that reappeared later disguised in the foolish even vain presentation of a taste for the modern."[16]

The thirty-five-year-old Keough reciprocated Duncan's affections, discussing literature with him after school, reading his poems, and giving him books, including D. H. Lawrence's *The Man Who Died.*[17] Duncan later joked that Keough had been the perfect audience for his early narcissistic performances: "I fell in love with her because every single day really was molded around . . . getting to the classroom and having that hour, and then I very rapidly discovered that I could also go to her house and pour out bad poetry at her by the hour and she would look enthralled."[18]

When Duncan told Keough of his plans to study English literature at the University of California at Berkeley, she expressed skepticism about his fate in academia, a piece of news that distressed Minnehaha Symmes. Already forced to accept that her son had little interest in a career in architecture, she issued a warning tinged by jealousy: the spinster English teacher with the dark searching eyes belonged to a category of "thwarted women." When Duncan entered college the following year, Minnehaha further berated him: "Poets write about things like you were having with your teacher and this would be disgraceful."[19]

For Duncan, the crush on his teacher seemed like a divine intervention. Her classroom was "the place of the numen," a monumental discovery for a young man trying to put his own stamp on his parents' theosophical ideas.[20] Another key to this discovery was the poetry of Hilda Doolittle, which Edna Keough read aloud to her students. The memory filled the opening pages of Duncan's comprehensive study of modernism, *The H. D. Book,* where he described his first encounters with H. D.'s early imagist poem "Heat":

> The path of H. D.'s work, between that poem and the many levels of consciousness mastered in the *War Trilogy,* and the path of my own recognitions

in poetry and life, between that classroom where I had resolved to devote my life to poetry and the first formative crises when I began to see what that poetry was to be, had their coordinations.

A classroom had been a meeting room. I had come at the appointed hour with a lover's joy in her company . . . : these things she loved she gave me to love. Books were the bodies of thought and feeling that could not be otherwise shared . . . : certain writers so revealed what human being had been that each of us had a share in that being. Love and Poetry were so mixed in the alembic that they coinhered in a new experience.[21]

From that high school classroom, Duncan was propelled into his life's work, and Keough later reported the satisfaction of nurturing this student of high promise: "You don't understand that in thirty years of teaching, you were the only poet I had."[22] His childhood had been bookended by two major wars, and he would build his early career around a study of the writers who inhabited the war-torn space of Europe: the surrealists, the imagists, the expatriates Gertrude Stein, H. D., Ezra Pound, and T. S. Eliot. Two dominant characteristics of Duncan's personality—his ferocious intellectual appetite and equally ferocious narcissism—facilitated his early successes. When he left Bakersfield to attend the University of California in 1936, he was a talkative, enthusiastic teenager intent upon becoming a writer, and while he had never been initiated into his parents' religion, he was soon to mature into a poet who circled back to the myths, books, and secrets of his family.

TWO

————

Toward the Shaman

SEVEN

The Little Freshman Yes

I am liable in the late afternoon
lingering to remember in the various cities
the familiar streets, clock-towers, magnolias,
to remember, reconstructing yet not
faultlessly as then, for the singular vision
has departed, reconstructing the cities
in sand, not faultlessly, roughly,
impatiently—indicating only a shadow . . .

ROBERT DUNCAN, "Fragment, 1940"

THE SAN FRANCISCO–OAKLAND BAY BRIDGE was completed in the fall of 1936, creating the first direct route for automobile traffic between San Francisco and the Oakland East Bay. From the span, one could view the blue-green waters of San Francisco Bay, separated from the Pacific by the Golden Gate headlands and Marin County. The massive waterway, inspiring the imagination of all who lived near it, had served as a stopping point for Gold Rush treasure seekers and by 1930 was the center of the Pacific Coast maritime industry.

Freshman class member Robert Duncan arrived at the Berkeley campus of the University of California that September, revisiting the locales of his early childhood and wandering amid the school's damp eucalyptus groves. Founded in 1868 as a merger of the College of California and the Agriculture, Mining, and Mechanical Arts College of Oakland, Berkeley had evolved into a successful research university. Its curriculum was modeled after that of Yale and Harvard, but its prestige rested on its scientific leadership. During the 1930s, Ernest Lawrence built ion accelerators and atom smashers—cyclotrons—in the campus's radiation lab, for which he won the 1939 Nobel Prize in science. The university's soon-to-be-named Lawrence Livermore National Laboratory quickly became a nerve center for atomic research.

Among classmates, Duncan was known as the lanky effeminate freshman named Symmes. He registered for entry-level courses in geology, history, English, and philosophy, adding German during his second semester, and reluctantly meeting his mandatory military requirement. He quickly found his place in Berkeley, pursuing both politics and poetry, and with his mother's encouragement, pledging to the Acacia Fraternity, a Masonic order that took inspiration from Pythagoras. Indifferent to the obligatory fraternizing, Duncan later claimed he joined Acacia because it had the most dilapidated house on campus and was most in need of Minnehaha's financial support.[1] He also assumed that this humble fraternity would be more tolerant of his homosexuality than would more prestigious organizations on campus.[2]

His economic and emotional bond to Minnehaha remained strong, evidenced by his frequent candid letters to her throughout his late teens and early twenties. The letters reveal the difficulties he faced during his first year away from home. September marked the first anniversary of Edwin Symmes's death, and Duncan contracted pneumonia during the fall.[3] In a note to his mother in spring 1937, he wrote:

> Where I could never have weathered this season last year without your protection directly—my personality is safe this year. While the same problems confront me . . . (it is my basic nature and nothing external) last semester being fall season was no threat at all. I did not even have to regard emotional adjustments which [are] a great factor this semester. My House adjustments—the protection of a strong institution and my opportunity in developing a cultural side which takes interest and pursuit all are factors which lead me to say that I am at last safe.[4]

Duncan's "cultural side" quickly took priority over his academic pursuits. While he reported to his mother that his scholarship was "tragic"—earning mostly Bs and Cs —he immersed himself in extracurricular activities, working for the campus literary magazine, the *Occident;* becoming a fixture in a local poetry club; and making frequent trips across the bay to the San Francisco opera house.[5] He wrote Minnehaha about his plan for cultural advancement outside the classroom:

> Music well under way—Beethoven, Bach, Brahms, Tchaikovsky, Stravinsky, Debussy, Ravel, Strauss, Sibelius, Wagner etc. etc.—
>
> read: Steinbeck's Mice and Men
> Whitman's Leaves of Grass
> Jeffers' Solstice
>
> art: El Greco discovered Courvoisier
> galleries—

Federal art exhibit

Ella Young's Celtic lectures[6]

Absorbed in the intellectual opportunities on campus and in San Francisco, Duncan set out to find the persona of the poet. In his introduction to *The Years As Catches* in 1966, he wrote, "By my eighteenth year, I recognized in poetry my sole and ruling vocation. Only in this art—at once a dramatic projection and . . . a magic ritual in which the poet comes into being— . . . it seemd to me, could my inner nature unfold."[7]

His devotion to poetry was soon tested at the *Occident*.[8] While other staff members were loyal to a traditional closed-verse poetics, Duncan wanted to solicit more ambitious pieces of writing. He later told an audience that his persistence in this editorial faceoff was a sign that writing was to be his craft:

> While there were some twenty poets who were ruling the whole scene at the University of California, and they all knew what poetry was, it was Auden and Spender, and I couldn't see this, and so when we were looking at student poems they would be "no, no, no, no, no, no, no," and a little freshman "yes" . . . and I had a stubbornness that should've told me I was going to be able to hold out for the rest of my life. . . . What I didn't know of course is that I would be the only one to survive at the age of fifty . . . to actually be a poet.[9]

Through his work at the *Occident,* Duncan met two novice writers, Robert Haas and Louise Antoinette Krause. He reported the news to his mother: "I have met this boy at the I[nternational] House and a girl who writes beautifully, Louise Krause. . . . Both of them encourage me to read Eliot, read Beaudilier *[sic]* (the one who wrote "Flowers of Evil"). . . . Both warn me to stay away from Stein. I told them that I was easily influenced by other people's cadences."[10] In lectures thirty years later, he revised this tale, recalling that Krause insisted his writing was too "lurid." She steered him away from Eliot with a pronouncement that changed his life: "He must read Pound."[11] Whether it was Krause or another source that turned him toward Pound, the immense scale of the *Cantos* opened a breathtaking landscape for the young writer. To his pantheon of early modernist masterpieces in painting, music, and literature, Duncan added Pound's epic: "I went trembling and running to a bookstore on Telegraph Avenue and found there the *XXX Cantos*. And I opened the page and read 'And then went down to the ship' and I said—I can't bear it, this is too much. For a whole week I went around with 'And then went down to the ship.' It was a poem that opened up exactly like an Oz book."[12]

With its Oz book opening, the *Cantos* shook the foundations of avant-garde verse, proceeding like a great Homeric adventure and creating a historical collage of multiple languages and colorful villains and heroes. Pound's work, begun in 1915, four years before Duncan's birth, drove the aspiring poet to consider unconventional possibilities for the form and content of poetry. In 1912, with H. D. and Richard Aldington, Pound had circulated the precepts of a new movement called imagism. Duncan later integrated imagist ideas into his own poetics and into his study of modernism, *The H. D. Book*. And despite Krause's warnings, another modernist, Gertrude Stein, soon became Duncan's "patron saint." Robert Haas, then exchanging letters with Stein, lent Duncan recordings of the poet reading her work.[13] An early piece of Duncan's, "A Bone Only for Jenniver," opened with the Stein-influenced lines

> Only and ever for Jenniver lightly. And that to for Jenniver
> only lightly. And ever and only. Ever and only. Ever and
> only. Ever and only for Jenniver lightly.
> Lightly for Jenniver Jenniver only. Lightly for Jenniver
> lightly for Jenniver lightly for Jenniver only . . .[14]

While H. D., Virginia Woolf, and D. H. Lawrence had provided openings to modernist writing for Duncan, his peers at Berkeley introduced him to artists who promoted other sorts of aesthetic propositions. His expanding canon became a regular topic in his letters home:

> If while I am sweeping I murmer [sic] Stravinsky a couple of times I am in absolute ectasy [sic]. Dos Passos, Dostoyevsky and Dickens I would say to myself . . . write it down . . . On and on . . . in the night and over flowers and in spare time talking, writing to myself . . . Cabell, Colette, Cummings . . . Shakespeare, Shelley, Sherwood, Sheridan, Shaw, Sophocles, Stein, Synge, Schiller, Four Saints in Three Acts . . . Fall of a City . . . and Murder in the Cathedral . . . and Ezra Pound's Cantos XXX–XLV.[15]

Duncan's Stein derivations continued into the mid-1950s, and Pound's influence resonated throughout his life's work. In the 1965 essay "The Lasting Contribution of Ezra Pound," he described Pound's role as "the carrier of a tradition or lore in poetry, that flowered in the Renaissance after Gemistos Plethon, in the Provence of the twelfth century that gave rise to Albigensian gnosis, the trobar clus, and the Kabbalah, in the Hellenistic world that furnished the ground for orientalizing-greek mystery cults, Christianity, and neo-Platonism."[16] From Pound's sense of poetic melody and "the tone leading of vowels," Duncan needed to take only a short step to Igor Stravinsky's theories of sound in musical compositions: "In the Norton Lectures of 1939–40 on *Poetics of Music,* published in 1947, Stravinsky defined melody as 'the intonation of the melos, which signifies fragment, a part of a phrase. It is these parts that strike the ear in such a way to mark certain accentuations.' From the unit of the musical phrases, music and poetry too seemed to be turning to the articulation of the immediate particle—the melos or syllable."[17] The confluence of those two ideas in poetry and music provided an early cornerstone for Duncan's method of composition: he resolved that repeated vowel phrases would work together to form melodies throughout his poems.

EIGHT

A Company of Women

> All of us poets need women to listen to us. And Robert Graves is right about the muse. You're way ahead when you have a circle of them around looking enthralled. ROBERT DUNCAN, Vancouver Conference, 1963

> At Berkeley ... we'd go and sit and listen to records. There were about five, maybe ten people who would do that.... And I'd see Robert and Mary and Lili and then Cecily there. And they were always having a wonderful time, so that I expected that he would be very witty. And he was, fantastically. VIRGINIA ADMIRAL in interview, 1998

SIX MONTHS INTO COLLEGE Duncan met two women crucial to the development of his ideas about art and politics, Lillian Fabilli and Cecily Kramer. He paid homage to them in the opening chapter of *The H. D. Book,* where they appear as Lilli and Athalie. Fabilli, raised in a large, close-knit Italian Catholic family primarily in the San Joaquin Valley town of Visalia, supported herself in Berkeley by keeping house for a well-to-do couple. A lonely teenager with little money, Fabilli met fellow student Cecily Kramer after a few weeks, and the two became fast friends. The outgoing Kramer, a San Francisco native whom Duncan later described as "a jewess," was the first to befriend Duncan, and she introduced him to Fabilli. From this start, the group of women around Duncan expanded quickly to include Fabilli's older sister Mary, Virginia Admiral, Ida Bear, Pauline Kael, and Janet Thurman. Key early mentors to him, the women became the core of his social and domestic life—he often referred to them as his sisters—and shaped his unofficial education. The Fabillis' combination of working-class ideals and sophisticated grassroots intellectualism intrigued Duncan. When he met Lili Fabilli in 1937, she was a painter, a writer, and a self-declared anarchist who also dabbled in Trotskyism. Through her—and soon through Virginia Admiral's—example, Duncan was able to carve an unusual place in chaotic prewar politics. Admiral later commented on Duncan's way of formulating his ideas: "when Robert came across new people, he was very open. Almost as though he said to himself 'I want to learn everything I can from this person.'"[1] Berkeley was teeming with idiosyncratic political sects. Duncan subsequently recalled, "We know about Stalinists and Trotskyites but in those days you had to know what a Lovestonite [was] and it went on and on. It was fascinating and it was wonderful, like knowing all the medieval heresies."[2]

Duncan was quick to jump into the fray. He had graduated from high school while German troops were on the march in Rhineland, and Spanish Loyalist forces were battling General Franco's fascist Nationalist front. By fall 1937, nearly three thousand Americans had joined a brigade of international volunteers in Spain to aid the Loyalist troops. Discussions of the political situation in Europe dominated the discourse at Berkeley, where the administration had begun implementing anticommunist legislation, thereby launching three decades of political conflict throughout the University of California system. Duncan was one of those "looking around at politics and feeling where we were in it—the Spanish Civil War was the thing."[3]

Removed from the conservatism of his Bakersfield household, Duncan found a new political consciousness: "Now I come to the certain realization that no poet or writer today is going to progress without a certain consciousness of the social problems and movements."[4] He wrote his mother about his exploration of leftist groups, ranging from church organizations to the YMCA and the "only too wishy-washy Young Communist League [YCL]." In the end he joined the American Student Union (ASU) on campus, explaining, "I had more friends there, friends who were leaders (tho I have quite a few among the YCL) and because I couldn't really be sincere in the YCL."[5] At his first ASU meeting, Duncan was named director of publications, "sitting on an executive council with three young communists and five moderate socialist students from cooperative houses, [and] student heads of student labor unions."[6] The formation of the ASU heralded the beginning of the student movement in the United States and laid the foundation for the youth activism of the 1960s. A coalition of the former National Student League and the Student League for Industrial Democracy, the movement peaked between spring 1936 and spring 1939, mobilizing some half a million students in annual antiwar protests. The students also sought numerous reforms, including "federal aid to education, government job programs for youth, abolition of the compulsory Reserve Officers' Training Corps (ROTC), academic freedom, racial equality, and collective bargaining rights."[7]

The eastern border of the Berkeley campus then touched on the architectural landmark Sather Gate. In the "Sather Gate tradition," students gathered at the gate's perimeter, observing the administration's restrictions on political meetings on university grounds while remaining conspicuously within sight and earshot of those inside the boundaries of the campus. Sociologist Max Heirich wrote of this tradition in *The Beginning: Berkeley 1964:*

> This compromise . . . allowed proselyters *[sic]* access to a voluntary audience of university personnel but without the overt concurrence of the administration or faculty. . . . University President Robert Gordon Sproul made it clear that students had a right to attend meetings at Sather Gate . . . , but that the university was not involved. . . . After 1938, when collection of funds was added to the list of prohibited political activities (to counter a student attempt to raise funds for medical relief in the Spanish Civil War), fund raising also became assigned to the Sather Gate area.[8]

In his sophomore year, Duncan's growing political activism incited a fraternity house controversy. In October 1937 he wrote to his mother that the "anti-neoculture and the upper rotc boys" took offense at his involvement in the ASU: "Their contention was that . . . it was not for the good of the house that I should be associated with the leftist front. They insisted . . . that I shouldn't be seen with friends . . . who were even more prominent leaders in the field. 'WE will be labeled reds' they cried."[9] Rather than discontinue his association with the ASU, Duncan dropped the fraternity and deepened his engagement with activities outside the strictures of the university.

In the first chapter of *The H. D. Book,* Duncan wrote of these Berkeley politics and his education by his new female companions. He recalled afternoons spent outdoors reading James Joyce's poetry with Cecily Kramer and Lili Fabilli. Like his fellow male students, Duncan was required to participate in ROTC drills twice a week, a prelude to the impending U.S. involvement in the Second World War:

> In the jostling streams, lower classmen, some in uniform, some still to change into uniform, went . . . toward the gymnasium. It was the hour for R.O.T.C. classes that impended. . . .
> "You don't have to go," Lili commanded, raising her hand in a dramatic gesture that had been delegated its powers by the conspiracy of our company. "Stay with Joyce." . . .
> Turning from the authority that the requirements and grades of the university or the approval of my teachers had once had over me to a new authority in the immediacy of what I had come to love, I came into a new fate.[10]

This new fate may have been opened to Duncan by Edna Keough in Bakersfield, but it took root through the influence of the women he was closest to in Berkeley. In conversations with them, he came to believe that his own work as a poet was an inherently political act and that the freedom of humanity as a whole transcended that of any separatist group. Amid the many left-wing fronts, Duncan eventually positioned himself as an anarchist, and his later writings and public statements remained true to anarchist politics, espousing distrust for governments and doctrines. As he wrote in "The Homosexual in Society" in 1944, "Only one devotion can be held by a human being seeking a creative life and expression, and that is a devotion to human freedom, toward the liberation of human love, human conflicts, human aspirations. To do this one must disown all the special groups (nations, religions, sexes, races) that would claim allegiance."[11] With poetry as a ruling vocation, he folded the field of the political into his life's work. Anarchism became a metaphor for the existence of a spiritual order superior to the realm of manmade law.

From the convergence of Duncan, Cecily Kramer, and Lili Fabilli emerged a community. The friends' adolescent enthusiasm soon attracted others to their company. In January 1937, twenty-three-year-old Mary Fabilli arrived in Berkeley, leaving Visalia at the urging of her sister Lili. Raven-haired, with a stern, square face, Mary entered the budding literary scene with an air of authority. She first roomed with Lili and then lived with Virginia Admiral, sleeping on the sofa in the large room that Admiral rented in a Bancroft Avenue boarding house.

Her initial meeting with Duncan occurred on campus in the fall of 1937. Cecily Kramer had told her about "a wonderful young man" who was interested in the arts and writing. Fabilli and Duncan had read each other's poetry in the March and April 1937 issues of the *Occident,* Fabilli publishing under the pen name Aurora Bligh. Duncan was eighteen years old, and as Mary Fabilli later recalled, he was already an obsessive monologist.[12] Like others, she was also struck by his physical appearance, his large head and "unruly straight black hair, a conventional hair cut, with dark eyes, one of which looked at you and the other roamed elsewhere into space.... His shoulders were broad enough but his hips very narrow, his hands large and expressive in the wrists."[13]

The two sat side by side in American literature and philosophy classes, fending off boredom by exchanging notes and comical sketches.[14] Throughout his life, Duncan considered Fabilli to be one of his three central peers in poetry, alongside Sanders Russell and Jack Spicer. Given his wide-ranging associations with writers over several decades, such a statement testifies to the degree of Fabilli's influence. In turn, Fabilli wrote in the introduction to her 1968 collection *Aurora Bligh,* "Robert seemed to be a magician of the marvelous, arriving at the most unexpected times to show us his discoveries whether of records (music and poetry), books, or reproductions of paintings. His enthusiasm was unfettered and often contagious, his devotion to poetry religious and his pen prolific."[15]

The intimate Berkeley circle gained another new member during 1938, an art student from Chicago named Virginia Admiral. Admiral had completed a degree at the university in February but had remained in Berkeley to attend graduate classes in art. Lili Fabilli remembered a day in 1937 or 1938 when Admiral approached her and her friends at a restaurant, asking to share their table. Admiral had a different memory of this first contact:

> Just before I met them, I had a tachycardia that put me in the hospital, and nobody knew what caused it and it went on for what seemed like weeks. I finally figured out it was because my boyfriend had died the previous fall.... I had moved from the top floor of this rooming house to ... the ground floor and I was spending most of my time in bed, and I had sort of dropped out of the university ... and I saw Lillian turned away by the landlady.... I assumed she had applied for a room, and [the landlady] said there are none. So I went out ... and said, "You can share my room" because I thought I'd like to know them.... At that point, I began to take interest in life.[16]

Not long after Admiral's meeting with the Fabilli sisters, Duncan also entered her world:

> I was sharing a room I think with Mary at the time. A garret . . . on Bancroft. It had these windows that opened out, and it was on the top floor. We had a mimeograph machine. Robert was up there. He was reading a poem. I think it was probably "Ritual," and he was squirming around. He said later he had crabs.[17]

As their friendship developed, their conversations meandered into politics, and Admiral attempted to set the younger Duncan on an improved path:

> He was in the ASU, . . . which was a blanket group . . . supporting collective security, . . . a dilution of the Communist Party line. . . . Whereas the group I was associated with (I wasn't actually a member at that time but became later) was Trotskyites. There were about seven Trotskyites and about thirty YCLers, and by that time they had stopped speaking to each other. . . . We congregated by [the storefront headquarters of] an education group. . . . And one person or another would talk. And . . . outsiders could come. . . . At that time I didn't go to internal meetings. I was just what you'd call a sympathizer. But I was doing leaflets and . . . a lot of stuff. Robert was in the ASU, and I explained to him how terrible it was to be in the ASU and all the . . . problems . . . —that it was wrong-headed and all of that stuff. And he went along with it. So he was similarly a sympathizer with the Trotskyite youth group.[18]

Duncan also joined Admiral in editing a mimeographed magazine called *Epitaph*. The first and only issue was published in spring 1938, with cover art by Mary Fabilli and writing and artwork by Duncan, Fabilli, Admiral, Ida Bear, Louise Antoinette Krause, and James Fitzgerald. Duncan contributed three poems—"Ritual," "Relativity, A Love Letter, and Relative to What; A Love Letter," and "Self Portrait at 90"—and three drawings. The poems had hints of T. S. Eliot and Ogden Nash, but Duncan showed his true prowess in the Stein derivation "Relativity, A Love Letter":

> Dark leads into the streets and dark leads into the streets and a shut door. Partly only into being and a shut door. Partly only in being and a shut door. Being as in being nowhere. Being as to come into being in partly only and outside. Dark leads into the streets and a shut door.
>
> To come suddenly upon something. Suddenly upon something and partly only in being. To be outside and partly in being in by the inside. Suddenly inside to come suddenly partly only to being. Being only as for one partly understanding and a shut door.[19]

Duncan also began sharing his poems with Admiral, and she became a meticulous critic of his early writing:

> I'd actually go over his poetry word for word, line for line, and I was a fanatical punctuator.... I'd say, "Now what does this line mean?" ... There was one poem, something about the monkey on his back in a park, and I said, "Now what does that mean? Tell me where you got it," and he was trying to explain it. I would say, "That's too personal an allusion. An allusion has to be related to by the person who's reading the poem.... That's incomprehensible."[20]

By 1938, the pull of creative life had begun to overshadow any vague academic aspirations Duncan may have had. He was spending more time with his friends and less time in the classroom, relishing the opportunity to share his interests in art and politics. Duncan's real education came through that bohemia, remembered fondly by Virginia Admiral: "Robert and Lili loved to cook. We listened to Robert's records: Stravinsky, Hindemith, Bach cantatas, Edith Sitwell, T. S. Eliot. In the evenings Mary and I would be doing watercolors or drawing, and Lili had developed a way of making crayon designs on cloth, then fixing them with a hot iron. Robert would be typing, listening to music, talking, none of it interfering with the poem he was working on."[21]

NINE

The Dance

For my Other is not a woman but a man
the King upon whose bosom let me lie.
ROBERT DUNCAN, "The Torso"

DESPITE HIS TALKATIVE NATURE, Duncan didn't reveal many details about his sexuality to his female admirers. Virginia Admiral noted that he sometimes acted "campy," and Mary Fabilli recalled that when Duncan first mentioned his sexual preference to them, "none of us were interested because we didn't think of him as a boyfriend."[1] But Cecily Kramer did seem to take issue with her friend's sexuality, as did Mary Fabilli later in life when she became more committed to the Catholic Church. Virginia Admiral remembered, "Cecily was very concerned with philosophical and spiritual aspects of something she felt to be a terrible mistake. . . . In those days there was a lot of feeling against homosexuality, and I didn't have it, but I know Mary did . . . She wasn't trying to turn Robert away from his choice. But basically he could assume that all three of his friends . . . wanted him to become heterosexual."[2]

Duncan briefly shared an apartment with Virginia Admiral and Mary Fabilli, sometimes giving mixed messages to his female companions. He often entered their bedrooms in the middle of the night to recite new poems to them, and he clung to them for emotional support. In a 1940 letter to Lili Fabilli, he wrote, "From the time Cecily, Mary and you and I talked together it was a world in which people were kind to me, in which there were people of love and peace. Yet I know how my need was one to be loved more than to love. I have not helped you as you have rescued me so many times."[3] Mary Fabilli also was frustrated that Duncan treated her as "another Robert," oblivious to her individuality.[4] While Fabilli reciprocated her younger friend's familial feelings, Duncan's demands for attention came to tear at their relationship.

Into his twenties, Duncan remedied such situations by descending on new households, starting a fresh cycle of monologuing and helping himself to the contents of kitchen cupboards. In addition to his stay with Fabilli and Admiral, he lived in a boarding house north of campus at 1542 Hawthorne Terrace, and also with the Fabilli sisters' friend Vincent Elgrin, who offered a bridge between the worlds of Duncan's female friends and that of the gay community in Berkeley—known to inhabit a small cluster of streets in north Berkeley.[5] In a *Gay Sunshine* interview, Duncan also spoke of his fraternity as a place of sexual exploration:

> I began to see this wasn't like high school. . . . We'd go to a place where you could dance, where they'd drink quite a bit, and I began to be aware. All frat houses took their pledges to Finochio's just to give 'em this shock of what they'd never seen before. . . . Finochio's had imported from Japan this great youth, he was probably 18, and they also had another 20 year old gorgeous, bewildering male presence in women's clothes yet. Well, I saw there were pleasure boys.[6]

Whether the expeditions to Finochio's were meant to shock the young pledges or to encourage a lifestyle, the fraternity quietly accepted homosexuality among its members. "I remember the sophistication of the frat house 'cause they said: 'Well, we know why that guy's taking you to the opera all the time and when he stops taking you to the opera we'll know ya came across.'"[7]

During his second year at Berkeley, in the spring of 1938, Duncan became smitten by a graduate student named Ned Fahs whom he met at a dance on campus. Before long, the two were dating. A PhD candidate in romance philology, Fahs charmed Duncan with both his looks and his erudition. Virginia Admiral remembered Ned as "the only important one" of the men Duncan met in Berkeley.[8] Thereafter, whenever Duncan reflected on a force he called the Eros, he cited his relationship with Fahs as its cardinal example. A symbol of desire, Fahs continued to enter Duncan's poems some twenty years after the relationship ended. In "The Structure of Rime XI," Fahs is a ghost who stands at the cusp of Duncan's creative life:

> There are memories everywhere then. Rememberd, we go out, as in the first poem, upon the sea at night—to the drifting.
>
> Of my first lover there is a boat drifting. The oars have been cast down into the shell. As if this were no water but a wall, there is a repeated knock as of hollow against hollow, wood against wood. Stooping to knock on wood against the traps of the night-fishers, I hear before my knocking the sound of a knock drifting.[9]

From its beginning, the relationship with Fahs was tied to Duncan's childhood fantasies, and it allowed him to identify further with Minnehaha, who was still his closest confidant during his late teens:

> My ideal, my strong picture like with N., with whom I did fall in love, was of someone ten years older than me. In that way I think I was replicating my mother's and father's relationship in which I was my mother falling in love with my father.... So I set my cap for N. who was a wolf playing the scene. I ... had heard about him first and then snared him and so on. It was Jane Austen all over again, getting my man like ... in the movies.[10]

The relationship launched an adventure that would take Duncan away from his comrades in Berkeley. Fahs, near the completion of his studies, was soon to move to Delaware, where he had secured a job teaching French.

Meanwhile, Duncan finished his sophomore year in May 1938 and enrolled in two summer classes, zoology and English. When not studying or spending time with Ned, he visited at the cottage the Fabilli sisters and Virginia Admiral were renting from their friend Ida Bear. Admiral remembered the season as a turning point: "At Ida's we would talk about coming to New York. We felt [in] exile [from] New York or Paris or London or someplace, so that I think Robert and I and . . . Janet [Thurman] were all convinced that we had to go to New York. It was just a question of when."[11]

It became clear that Duncan would be the first to leave for the East Coast. During the first week of September, Ned Fahs completed his PhD examinations and celebrated with Duncan and other friends before leaving to begin his new job. Duncan described the difficult parting to his mother: "Miss Rosenberry (a friend of Ned's) drove us to the station. Then he was gone; I knew that I should have been going with him. All the things I was staying for seemd so very small when weighed against the emptiness of that moment. Rosie (Miss Rosenberry) lent me a handkerchief, there could be no pretense at that moment . . . ; and then we went and had a beer and some steamed clams."[12]

Having said their good-byes, Fahs traveled east and Duncan moved back to his fraternity house, bringing along a dog named Haille. Heartsick, he fell back upon the comforts of family, spending time in Oakland with his Aunt Fay and with his father's sister Alvie Brumm. On September 11, 1938, he wrote his mother to congratulate her on her recent marriage to an old family friend, Lewis Andrew Burtch.

Duncan made a vague attempt to return to his studies, enrolling in three English classes and an introductory French course that fall and ending the semester with a string of Cs. When plans to edit a second issue of *Epitaph* with Admiral fell through, he struggled to finish his academic work so that he could travel east in December to visit Fahs. He told his mother of his loneliness and also described his emotional state to his new friend Sanders Russell, a young poet he had met through Fahs: "I'm all illogical and impractical about it but I'm in love and there's little to remedy that now—no I haven't started writing again, I'm trying frantically to crawl thru this semester—my mind has become less acute, less habited in misuse."[13]

When Duncan left Berkeley in December, his future in academia was in question, and his transcripts showed below-average grades. Nine years would pass before he returned to the university, not to complete his undergraduate degree but to study medieval history with scholar Ernst Kantorowicz.

During the Second World War, Duncan hopscotched between the West Coast and New York, making stops in Chicago, Provincetown, Boston, Kansas City, and the Deep South. His intimate relationships during that time were as complicated as his travel routes, and his early and mid-twenties brought experiments with heterosexuality, marriage, and prostitution. As the United States made its way into the Second World War, Duncan made his way into an emotional war, undertaking a quest to find his adult identity via shamanistic rituals and makeshift Freudian self-analysis. Though he later rejected the stereotype of the emotionally tortured creative genius, his days as a young writer were marked by considerable drama.[14]

Before heading east in December 1938, Duncan returned to Bakersfield briefly to spend the holidays with his mother, who agreed to send him one hundred dollars a month if he would finish his education by December 1941.[15] Duncan at times acknowledged the special privilege of his mother's support as he watched his friends scramble to make ends meet. Virginia Admiral found employment as a senior artist with the Works Progress Administration (WPA), and the Fabillis also registered with the WPA in Oakland with the help of an art professor from Berkeley.[16] Duncan confided to Sanders Russell that he did not want such a commitment:

> I recognize only too well that I hate the bourgeois class and at the same time that I am limited by being a member of that class. Now I am inclined to believe that my rebellion is no proletariat consciousness, but a rebellion of any worker in art, a sort of furious snobbery. . . . At the same time I believe blindly that the overthrowing of the bourgeois class and the epic of proletariat civilization is the life of the movement today, that the glorious bourgeois are indeed the hollow men, the stuffed men.[17]

With a financial advance from his mother, Duncan moved to Philadelphia to live with Ned Fahs in an apartment at 4521 Chester Avenue. As part of a vague plan to continue college, he had his high school and college transcripts sent to Philadelphia's Temple University. More keenly on his mind was the short distance between Philadelphia and Manhattan, where he could test the waters of a new artistic and political community. At the age of twenty and far from home, he was nervous about making his way in a new metropolis: "I must tho try and break in—I am stamped—the social registar [sic] does me no good—any cities [sic] social registar [sic] has a minus percent of the people I want to know—I thot of going to the socialist headquarters—but I have been too timid so far—as I am not a party member and I don't know too much about the organization of the party."[18]

New York was a noisy city, busy with activity beyond Duncan's expectations. His timidity about breaking into East Coast circles was shared by another newcomer, Anaïs Nin, who returned to the United States from Paris in 1939 and would soon befriend Duncan: "In Paris, when entering a room, everyone pays attention, seeks to make you feel welcome, to enter into conversation. . . . Here it seems everyone is pretending not to see, hear, or look too intently. The faces reveal no interest, no responsiveness."[19]

The cross-country move left Duncan both disoriented and excited. To friends in Berkeley, he sent homesick missives throughout early 1939: "My Lili—I want so to come back—it is only the prospect of New York that keeps me here and this summer with Ned—I love him if possible even more—but I love you too and when you write why aren't you here—and *when Virginia writes*—I am so homesick—I want to jump the next train and come back."[20]

Nonetheless, Duncan began to explore the culture of New York, which was becoming a haven for artists forced out of Europe by the Second World War. Duncan reported to Lili Fabilli: "I saw a rug by Joan Miro and another rug by Hans Arp and one by Kandinsky and I saw little tea trays by Paul Klee and I went to the Dali show and in the window of one of the galleries was a wonderful Rouault . . . and then Ned and I went to a Russian Tea Room like the one in San Francisco and there in a front booth was Salvador Dali that strange beautiful little man with the huge sick eyes like a child's."[21] Duncan had arrived in Manhattan at the tail end of the surrealist movement, which had begun with Breton's *Manifesto of Surrealism* in 1924 and by 1939 had matured in its new habitat. The Julien Levy Gallery on East 57th Street showed the works of Max Ernst and Salvador Dalí regularly throughout the early 1940s, and the Museum of Modern Art, established a decade earlier, showcased works in its permanent home in midtown Manhattan. Those influences not only came into Duncan's early writing but also inspired him to experiment with visual works. His notebook sketches show attention to Cocteau's sensuous lines and to the styles of Kandinsky and Miró. In a letter to friends in Berkeley, Duncan catalogued the works, mostly "cut out from magazines," that graced his walls: Rouault, Matisse, Picasso, Admiral, Dufy, Kandinsky, Miró, Symmes, Rousseau, Giotto, and Braque.[22]

The poetry scene in Manhattan was also expanding during the war years. James Laughlin's *New Directions in Prose and Poetry* magazine launched in 1936, and the following year the *Partisan Review* began publication. The first issue of *New Directions* included works by Wallace Stevens, Gertrude Stein, Lorine Niedecker, Louis Zukofsky, and other luminous figures of the modernist movement. In the preface, Laughlin explained the anthology's calling: "Experimental writing has a real social value, apart from any other."[23] In 1940, *View,* a major surrealist-influenced publication edited by Charles

Henri Ford and Parker Tyler, entered the New York literary landscape. When André Breton arrived in New York the following year, he brought European surrealism to the American avant-garde with *VVV,* a magazine he coedited with David Hare, Marcel Duchamp, and Max Ernst.[24]

After nearly six months of domestic life with Fahs, both in Philadelphia and in a New York apartment on Bedford Street, Duncan traveled to the West Coast briefly to visit the Fabilli sisters and Virginia Admiral. In September, he returned east, boarding a cross-country train and taking delight in the Rocky Mountains and the vistas of the Midwest. The trip was his first chance to survey the middle of the country at a leisurely pace, and he wrote about it with naïve excitement: "The mountains are really thrilling and then the little towns and lakes in the green wooded valley. . . . The Cumberland with the winding green clear river and the forests covering the hills. . . . As we pass I populate the woods with Cooper Indians, and around Baltimore there are many little woods of sunlight and green and dark shadows where Indians lurk too constantly."[25]

The autumn offered some clarity and optimism. He looked forward to moving into a new apartment with Ned, this time at 239 Prince George Street in Annapolis, Maryland. Fahs had accepted a teaching job in the foreign languages department at the Naval Academy, and Duncan had been offered a scholarship to study at an experimental arts school in North Carolina, Black Mountain College.[26] However, when he arrived at Black Mountain that September and was interviewed by the faculty, he was immediately turned away. Duncan recorded his humiliation in a letter to his mother: "I want to say again that altho the college would not say why they decided against me—they did say that they were not influenced by the financial statement. You and Ned and Aunt Faye all of you want to pretend that finances had something to do with it and not that they didn't believe in me."[27]

Duncan later told variant stories about his experience at Black Mountain, sometimes saying that his anarchist ideas had been the problem, other times saying that there had been questions about his mental state. In either case, he quickly regrouped and began two new ventures: a novel and a new magazine project called *Ritual.* The novel, never completed, kept him occupied during his time on the East Coast. As he reported to his mother in one of his monthly letters, "I am starting work on a new opus. . . . It may be that I will not be able to work it out for I find that writing prose for me is very often like trying to carve marble with a butcher knife."[28] Variously titled *The Shaman, Toward the Shaman,* and *The Shaman as Priest and Prophet,* the book was cobbled together out of the self-reflective journal entries that filled several of his early notebooks.

Still disappointed about the Black Mountain rejection, Duncan made preliminary plans to continue his education elsewhere, at New York University or at a Baltimore-area school. He also temporarily retreated from his relationship with Fahs to seek some emotional and financial independence. From late September 1939 through the end of the year, Duncan lived with his friends Jeff and Connie Rall in New York City, at 35 Ridge Street on the Lower East Side. He explained to his mother that he hoped to get a job rather than rely on support from her or Ned, and he reflected upon his passage into adulthood:

> At first in Berkeley I realized that the drive to write came into conflict with my university career (not you notice with study at the university—but with a career at the university). I began to realize that I wanted achievement rather than success. Then I met Ned and he is all mixed up with my being in life and I realized that there are responsibilities in loving—that one does not just love but one must solve all those responsibilities of understanding and believing and sacrificing that are part of love.[29]

Duncan's exile to the Lower East Side offered diversions that sidetracked his job search:

> That part of New York is a foreign world running east of the Bowery and south of Delancey and the bridge sticking out into the dark and disappearing. England disappears entirely and Roumania [sic], Poland & Russia have complete control. Everything . . . is kosher, knishes & borscht. . . . Delancey Street [at night] is a wonderful street with vendors of sweet potatoes, chestnuts, . . . imported halvah from Turkey, from Russia, from Brooklyn, vendors of ties and handkerchiefs, of clothespins and little white dishes, hags selling papers, old men sitting like Rabbis talking in circles about problems of metaphysics.[30]

Jeff Rall also provided inspiration toward a bohemian lifestyle. Duncan wrote to Pauline Kael about the new friendship:

> Jeff was a theater usher—about twenty-five or six—His father was a big boy in the I.W.W. and Jeff at 15 left home—gone on the bum—at 16 was a Communist—joined the Trotskyist group way back when. . . . He knew his left movement inside out—outside of Hal Draper's library—I haven't seen a better one than his. . . . Also Jeff paints— . . . in earnest—(I am amazed at

the way some of these people blossom under a little encouragement). He is one of the boldest people in his use of color and form that I have yet met.[31]

Casting aside his ambitions for economic self-reliance, Duncan made frequent visits that autumn to the Museum of Modern Art and its library, where he pursued a self-designed study program and began "working on an essay on modern art . . . typified by [the] surrealism of Dali, Tchelitchew and the decadent American school of Benton and Wood."[32] He mailed home progress reports about his jobhunting, occasionally also outlining fantastic plans to apply to various colleges in the East.

TEN

From Romance to Ritual

DUNCAN'S RELATIONSHIP WITH NED FAHS CONTINUED from a distance throughout the fall of 1939, with Fahs making a weekend trip to New York in October, during which the two attended the Ballet Russes and strolled through the Museum of Modern Art. Over Christmas weekend, Fahs again came to the city to view a Picasso show and to share a late night preholiday celebration with Duncan and Jeff and Connie Rall. As Duncan wistfully noted in a letter to his mother, it was his first Christmas away from home, but his anxiety was pacified by a Christmas Eve train trip through the Hudson Valley to visit Phoenix Press editors James and Blanche Cooney in Woodstock, New York.

Duncan had first announced himself to the Cooneys in a spring 1939 letter to the couple explaining, with some flourish, his relation to the craft of poetry: "All my current works are narratives and prophecies—all that I aspire to do is communicate somehow my psychic experiences as the poets of the pre-moralist age—as the young druid poets and those who wore the cloak of blue feathers in Ireland and as all poets must do . . . —speak not the conscious but the subterranean contact with elemental forces.[1]

The Cooneys were at the center of the Maverick Art Colony, editing *Phoenix* magazine and running the Phoenix Press. The Colony, founded in

1904 by writer Hervey White, was an offshoot of Woodstock's original art-ists' commune, Byrdcliffe, established at the turn of the century. Hosting artisans and musicians throughout the summer, Byrdcliffe consisted of stu-dios dotting the Catskill Mountains. Hervey White's dedication to music, and the concert hall and theater he built, attracted musicians from around the world. The Cooneys had opened their print shop with White's help and had begun publishing the works of internationally known poets and novel-ists such as Anaïs Nin, Lawrence Durrell, and Henry Miller. Nin, an occa-sional visitor to the Cooneys' home, described the tenor of the place in her diaries: "James Cooney, red-haired, Irish, with his hair falling over ingenu-ous green eyes, humorous and romantic, emotional and generous. They live in a log cabin in the woods. They wanted to go back to the earth, to live a Lawrencian life, but a community one, gathering together people with the same interests."[2] Duncan and Fahs met Anaïs Nin on this Christmas visit in 1939, and Duncan was fascinated with her, a petite woman with fine fea-tures and dark hair and eyes like his adoptive mother. He reported home to Bakersfield: "She was just over from France—a refugee from the war dictatorship—Her writings with those of such people as Charles Henri Ford and Lawrence Durrell ... are among the most important in the interna-tional advance-guard."[3] Nin, though still shell-shocked from her recent re-turn from Paris, also took special note of the meeting. After a meal in front of the fireplace, Duncan read a poem to the group, and the guests took a tour of the Phoenix's printing press and workshop. In her diary entry about that night, Nin described Duncan as "a strikingly beautiful boy ... with . . . a faunish expression and a slight deviation in one eye, which made him seem to be looking always beyond and around you."[4] She also noted that he "talked obsessionally, overintently, overwillfully" and that it seemed to be his nature to "maintain a monologue, not a dialogue."[5]

Returning to Annapolis after the holiday, Duncan and Fahs resumed their life together, welcoming a puppy they named Admiral Togo into the household. While Fahs continued teaching at the Naval Academy, Duncan celebrated his twenty-first birthday and started work on *Ritual* magazine. In the new year, Virginia Admiral and Janet Thurman moved east, giving Dun-can more reason to make hitchhiking forays from Annapolis to New York. Admiral and Thurman first lived in a loft at 30 East 14th Street overlooking Union Square. It became a home away from home for Duncan and also at-tracted visitors like Nin, who described the place in her diaries:

The first floor houses a shop, a hamburger bar, a shoe shop and a synthetic orange juice bar. . . . The place is cold, but the hallways and lofts are big and high-ceilinged and the only place possible and available to a painter. . . . The enormous windows which give on the deafening traffic noise of Fourteenth Street have to be kept closed. There are nails on the walls for clothes, a sterno burner for making coffee. We drink sour wine out of paper cups. There Virginia and Janet [Thurman] paint, study acting and dancing, type when they need money.[6]

Once settled in the city, Admiral worked to establish a career, beginning studies with painter Hans Hofmann at the Art Students League in the early 1940s.[7] She also kept a foothold in the literary community, coediting *Ritual* magazine with Duncan. The first order of business was to publish work by Anaïs Nin. Duncan and Admiral showed up on her doorstep at the George Washington Hotel in Greenwich Village, as Nin reported in her diaries: "He is shy. He enters obliquely, as if to avoid collision. He talks as if under hypnosis. He invites me to contribute to a magazine called Ritual. . . . They are both children out of *Les Enfants Terribles*. But they are children."[8]

Duncan wasted little time getting to know Nin better, and despite her initially ambivalent feelings toward him, she too was drawn into the relationship. The two were dangerously matched: Nin, with her interest in sexual intrigue and the romance of creative life, fed Duncan's already narcissistic vision of himself as a lover and writer. Supporting each other's new projects and jointly exploring Freudian and surrealist theories of the psyche, Nin and Duncan became inseparable. Nin was a critical reader of Duncan's poetry as well as a clever, if not entirely conventional, analyst. Born in 1903 in Paris, she had spent her childhood battered by the whims of her creative parents. In Europe before the war, she began her diaries, recording with pride a number of affairs she carried out under the nose of her husband, a wealthy banker named Hugh Guiler. Beyond the enticement of such dramas, Duncan was drawn to the sensuous, dreamlike images in Nin's writing. Her *House of Incest*, published in 1936, opened his imagination to new directions for his own work and inspired him to return to his novel in progress, *Toward the Shaman*.

Duncan also began his career as a published poet in earnest during 1940, when the Cooneys published two of his poems, "We Have Forgotten Venus" and "Persephone," in *Phoenix* magazine. This early writing still had a hint of Eliot and an ongoing preoccupation with the war in Europe. "Persephone" closed with

We remember in symbols such violence:
the splintering of rock, the shock of the trauma,
in which she was taken from us. Shade
falls under the shadow ... shade upon shade.
Spotted with bonewhite, splinter of driftwood,
the bark wet with terror, no sleep,
only waiting. Only we wait, our wounds barely heald
for the counterattack before sunrise.[9]

Duncan told his mother that his interest in ritual and shamanism had made its way into the poems and that "Persephone" was tied to his novel as "a fragment of the movement of simulations and prayers and visions—the Shaman as Priest and Prophet."[10] To Pauline Kael he noted another influence: "After several severe doses of Joyce's latest opus I have deserted the phrase and turned my attention upon the individual word—yet in a poem such as PERSEPHONE or in the short lyric 'Birds drifting thru the haze of soot'— where I was working ... on word transitions—the phrasing stands up—I feel confident of that now."[11] Joyce's *Finnegans Wake* had further attuned him to the melodies of language, but the interchange between poetry and music in his work also had antecedents in his studies of Pound and Stravinsky. He explained to Kael that his composition process was evolving to account for such melodies: "The poem 'Birds drifting thru the haze of soot' ... is—at least in the first part[—]built around word sounds. Birds to Brides, haze to tryst, soot to set, haze to wait—roof to reef."[12]

Meanwhile, the first and only issue of *Ritual* was published in spring 1940 with two names on its masthead: Virginia Admiral in New York and Robert Symmes in Annapolis, Maryland. From the beginning, Duncan had wanted the magazine to showcase writing of friends from Berkeley:

There will be so much to print—work by Ida Bear—her sharp, clinical prose uncovering the ritual of the daily act—the divinity of the commonplace— and Mary Fabilli weaving death and the collapse of this civilization ... —into wreaths of flowers—ploughing the clean earth over it all— ... and Lillian and myself and Sanders Russell moving within the circles of the new sainthead.[13]

Ritual reconvened those who had appeared in *Epitaph* during the spring of 1938. It also added two new contributors, Sanders Russell and Anaïs Nin. Duncan published his own "Passage over Water," as well as the play excerpt "Hamlet: A Draft of the Prologue." Sanders Russell's "Ten Poems" appeared, as did a prose piece by Ida Bear, Mary Fabilli's poem "Cecily," an excerpt of Nin's *The House of Incest,* and the prose piece "Dreams" by Virginia Admiral.

As the war took a grim turn in early 1940, with the German army cutting a swath through northern Europe, Duncan faced his own crisis: by May, his relationship with Ned Fahs was drawing to a close. "Passage over Water," written during the early spring, commented on the deterioration of the relationship:

> Let the oars be idle, my love, and forget at this time
> our love like a knife between us
> defining the boundaries that we can never cross
> nor destroy as we drift into the heart of our dream,
> cutting the silence, slyly, the bitter rain in our mouths
> and the dark wound closed in behind us.[14]

Duncan confessed to his mother, "I have ended it with Ned. It was not a quarrel at all but just that at this time of separation I felt that it was not right to . . . think of coming together again. His mother coming East furnished the immediate cause; but it has been clear to me for a long time that the . . . direction that seems to be open for me . . . would only confuse him."[15] Fahs's desire to stay at the Naval Academy had contributed to the split, as had his decision to take in his mother after she suffered a nervous breakdown, leaving him little room to continue an intimacy with another man. Duncan also recognized his own role in the breakup: "Love for me paranoic *[sic]*, devouring, always to be torn with disbelief that it would continue, driven at last in my fear to read his letters, to listen, to find in every attention he gave to anyone a desertion, a sudden loss of love."[16] He understood that Fahs had satisfied his need to revisit a drama from his childhood:

> When I talk about Ned—it is easily apparent to me . . . that in many ways he is my father—the burdens Ned seemd to bear, the way he was so tired with them, the guilts over money owed, the consuming myth of the debt he had to pay—and his body itself—then when I come to this—to my father and I realize that I am conscious of living out all he rejected—for I have the feeling that he refused to love, [that he refused] to become the artist rather than the success.[17]

Duncan turned for comfort to Virginia Admiral, Anaïs Nin, and two new friends, the poet and novelist Kenneth Patchen and his wife, Miriam.

The Patchens had moved to Greenwich Village in January 1940, and through his meeting with them, Duncan was inspired to focus again on his career, telling Sanders Russell, "We (V[irginia] and I) visited with Anaïs and spent three of the evenings with Kenneth Patchen . . . and his wife. He liked the first section of Shaman very much . . . and he is going to try to get it in New Directions 1940."[18]

That summer, Duncan also sought solace in the Cooney household on Maverick Road. There he became as concerned about the war in Europe as he was about the loss of Ned. On June 14, 1940, Nazi forces had taken Paris, and Duncan thought about leaving the United States. He reported to Sanders Russell,

> We sit here, Jimmy and Blanche and the children and I—planning the time of migrations; Mexico, . . . some refuge beyond this hysteria for there is work to be done in a quiet time. We set type, pump water, empty the buckets, sit in the outhouse at night hearing the frogs sing and the late spring rains run from the shingled roof. Or during the day we dig in the garden, stir roots, and pile a little wall of stones between pine trunks. Knowing that these flowers must be left behind, that walls will be broken thru and the quiet grass spring up behind us.[19]

Duncan's friendship with the Cooneys brought a new sense of family, and by the middle of 1940, he was a full-time resident of the Maverick Colony. Blanche Cooney provided the pleasure of female companionship that had been so critical in his Berkeley life. Cooney remembered her own deep attachment to Duncan:

> Robert was in my real life. My androgynous friend. Jimmy and I both loved him but he was my pal, my constant companion. Hanging diapers on the clothesline, getting a meal for a crowd . . . he was there for me, dependably helpful, and dependably crazy. We were twenty-one, twenty-two years old, on the same wave length, struck at the same time by the risible, the ridiculous. Dark, slim, his right eye off center did not detract from his beautiful faun look; it kept him surprising.[20]

Duncan wrote his mother in August that he had taken to herb gardening and was "drinking a quart of milk a day, eating two well rounded meals." He also added a more detailed psychodramatic report for her approval:

> I weigh around 145, do not smoke, drink a beer occasionally, at times eat immoderately, but I can still fast. I am given to mumbling my words so that no

one can hear them; I am quiet in my movements. . . . I am bearded—I will send you a photograph one of these days. . . . Teeth are bad, eyes give no trouble tho at times vision at a distance is blurred, ears are all right tho its [sic] a wonder since they never seem to get washed.[21]

While living on Maverick Road, he began planning an ambitious "reading series," for which he wrote "sermons" to deliver to the Woodstock community. Blanche Cooney remembered,

> Robert at twenty-one had the audacity to ask Hervey for the use of the Maverick Concert Hall on Sunday morning. . . . He wished to deliver a sermon. Not as a priest, minister, guru, but as a Shaman, in touch with the unseen world of gods, demons, and ancestral spirits. Hervey said yes. He couldn't resist audacity. Robert stood at the lectern, an Indian poncho over his clean shirt and jeans, and with perfect composure spoke to the assembled group.[22]

The first sermon, "Where this is veneration even a dog's tooth emits light," was infused with the ambitious idealism of Duncan's early prose:

> This return to speaking aloud among you is significant. Poetry has strayed far from its origins in time and now to gain strength, to know what it is all for, we must go back. It is because of this that speeches, Vanzetti's speech in court . . . comes to my mind, are greater, more real poetry than the poetry written, than the centuries of Keatses and Shelleys we have passed thru whispering their poetry in corners. It is a good thing to speak of love; I do not frown upon . . . the Keatses and Shelleys, for there is no pettiness in their dark groves, there is no hate among their fauns. But this is a slight thing. Today we cannot be slight—and needing to encompass more, sensing the duty and responsibility of our work, there comes a need to speak and it is natural that the love poem becomes the epic conception and that the epic conception establishes certain compulsions that must be actualized and then the form of the sermon is used.[23]

The "audacity" of Duncan's sermon project seemed partly the by-product of his privileged childhood role as a messenger from another world. His Aunt Fay's theosophical essays were almost certainly a model for Duncan's prose, as were Anaïs Nin's journals and fiction.

But as the summer drew to a close, Duncan faced more serious questions about his future. In mid-October, he decided to register for the draft. Fearing imprisonment if he did not register, he made a compromise, explaining to Minnehaha, "I will make the second best—that is protest against the service itself—that it is a human indignity that is too great to bear."[24] Increasingly,

Duncan's letters to his mother seemed designed to antagonize her as much as to rehearse his political stances: "If my conscientious objection to the draft is recognized I will next year probably save money to go either 1) to the West Indies or 2) to India. . . . In the meantime I worry a lot about you, my chere mama, how you rationalize this man-killing machinery, and . . . no longer a simple psychic question but one of good taste—voting for President. Your focus and mine are so vastly different."[25]

His communications with the local draft board were equally provocative. Using lingo from his readings of eastern religion and Freudian psychoanalysis, Duncan argued against participating in the war. Replying to a draft survey question "On what grounds do you object to military service?" he wrote,

> The illusion of possession is a manifestation of the ego. Possession of a body, a name, an honor, a person, an object, a country, a law. In so far as we defend or seek to secure these, then we yield to this illusion, we dwell in the ego separation and we are at error.[26]

In reply to another question about his beliefs, Duncan wrote,

> It is only in our own direct contact with reality, with a human being, a tree, a river, a mountain, with movement through space and time, only within ourselves, in our own revelation that we may discover the essential, the meaning and the way of our own life.[27]

In the end, his maneuvers were not convincing to the United States Army, and the following spring he was called to service.

ELEVEN

Queen of the Whores

To arrive at the unknown through the disordering of *all the senses,* that's the point.   ARTHUR RIMBAUD TO GEORGE IZAMBARD, 1871

DURING THE FALL AND WINTER OF 1940, Duncan remained in Woodstock to finish the second issue of *Ritual,* now renamed the *Experimental Review.* He also briefly took the helm of the Phoenix Press when the Cooneys went to investigate a new farming venture in Georgia. Needing to provide for himself emotionally and financially through the cold Catskills winter, Duncan recruited a group of younger writers and artists to Maverick Road, including Alvin and Marguerite Schwartz, Jack Johnson, and New York comrade Jeff Rall.[1] In September, another kindred spirit, Sanders Russell, arrived, having been invited by Duncan to live with him that winter. Duncan had been intrigued by Russell's writing since their first meeting: "Sanders was . . . already a mature poet. In the small company of poets I have known who have been and remain for me real poets, he was the first one. He had his own language, derived from Jeffers and from Eliot and Auden along another line but having undergone a creative change in Sanders' intense meditation and speculations upon the nature of consciousness and the landscape as an object and mirror of being."[2] There was a personal attraction as well. For Duncan, Russell was a "mature idol" with "deep set luminous eyes and the figure, nose and the mouth chiseled after a Greek mode in the material of a certain kind of Irish stock—not red haird, not small and dark, but impassive, white fleshd and tall."[3]

Russell's somewhat eccentric interests in Native American shamanistic practices, eastern religions, and yoga sparked the curiosity of the small Woodstock community. Alvin Schwartz, a fledgling playwright and future writer for the *Superman* comic book series, remembered that Russell seemed particularly sophisticated to the younger people at the Colony. He recalled watching the newcomer practice yogic breathing seated in a field, melting a patch of snow around his body.[4]

While Sanders Russell shared Duncan's preference for men, the two were not fated to enter into a sexual relationship. Duncan tried to explain this new friendship to his mother, perhaps masking his disappointment in Russell's inattention to his advances:

> We are both Shaman, conscious of the powers our sexual nature endows us with—I do not know yet if two of equal powers can exist together so. . . . The, shall we say, karma laws of the SHAMAN—tend to produce a noli me tangere—a necessity of isolation even in sex which I have transgresst against. It is a law which I respect now tho—and I fear that if it were forgotten evolution would run off into a swamp.[5]

Russell's passion for the spiritual was contagious, and it inspired Duncan to improvise magic practices, playing surrealist games and conducting séances with friends. He had returned to his parents' hermeticism, in one journal entry describing a conjuring party:

> Last night was another interlude of terror. After descending from a session in the attic in which Sanders [Russell], Jeff [Rall], [Marguerite Schwartz], Alvin [Schwartz] and I tried once more to open the doors of fear—we have a desire to go into the world on the other side of those doors—I said; "I wish there would be a knocking at the door—and I don't mean that door," I said pointing to the front door. "I mean that one," pointing to the attic trapdoor. At that moment there was a loud knock (as if the attic door had actually been lifted and dropped). Alvin was so terrified that his face actually turned white. Sanders and I immediately ascended to the attic again—the others followed. . . . Nothing. But then after ten minutes or so we relaxed—as we laughed and talked—I lay back on the floor—a growing presence came over us. As it reached a speedy peak [Marguerite] remarked on this change. Everyone had felt it—and Jeff, [Marguerite] and Alvin went downstairs. . . . There was another minor crest of fear which those downstairs felt also—but it passed and left us quite dispossessed.[6]

With a meditative attentiveness to his surroundings, Duncan began to approach poetry as a place to record physical and physiological phenomena. Sanders Russell taught him to "tune up" into a poem, to begin writing in moments of heightened sensory stimulation. Duncan hinted at this early training in his Woodstock notebooks:

> In the middle of the night both Billy [Wright] and I awoke. The snow was evidently melting from the roof in some odd way—there was the terrible sense we have had in this house of being surrounded—the hostile one

walking—this time up and down the back porch. I . . . had a sense of some-
one crouching at the back window—someone running off the porch across
the snow. I called for Sanders—to have the reassurance that he was there—
talking between rooms in the dark we decided it had been the snow
dropping.[7]

When, on the following day, Russell wrote a poem with the line "invisible
footfalls / surround us," Duncan committed the image to memory. Nearly
twenty years later, he resuscitated it in "A Poem Beginning with a Line by
Pindar":

> Oh yes!   Bless the footfall where
> step by step   the boundary walker
> (in Maverick Road   the snow
> thud by thud   from the roof
> circling the house—another tread)[8]

When he was not engaged in rituals such as "sitting naked all night
in the late autumn . . . on a rock" and "trying to talk to trees," Duncan re-
turned to the *Experimental Review*.[9] On December 1, 1940, he assembled
and bound copies of the new issue with the help of Fanny Secord, Sanders
Russell, and Marguerite Schwartz.[10] The publication named Russell and
Admiral as associate editors, and its gray cover bore a drawing by Duncan
called "Improvisation on the Method of Miro." The magazine included re-
views of the work of Henry Miller, Franz Kafka, and Dylan Thomas, as well
as excerpts of Duncan's "Toward the Shaman" and of Anaïs Nin's *House of
Incest*. Other early contributors to the magazine included Lawrence Durrell,
Thomas Merton, Harvey Breit, and Jack Johnson, and its editorial statement
read, "The experiment is not to foster an eccentricity or a novelty of lan-
guage, nor to create a new literature: it is to . . . bring everything into con-
sciousness, to develop the artist's awareness in the field of observation—in
the world of objects, values, dreams, in tensions within the social and eco-
nomic order as well as in more involved states of consciousness—the way of
the primitive, the saint, or the mystic."[11]

Excited that the project was finished and eager to be the center of atten-
tion, Duncan turned the floor of the December 1 sewing party into a stage.
"We put on the Swahili female dance. I danced—the music let me cut
loose forget every thing in the room, become the idiot—I found myself
crawling jerking my head, shoulders—the whole body twitching, making

faces, dancing on my shoulders. . . . this is part of the awakening possibilities of the SHAMAN."[12]

With his eye on a teenaged sculptor named Nicholas De Vol, Duncan used his newfound shamanistic powers as a tool of seduction. Despite his autumn vow of chastity, that winter he began a number of brief affairs, one of which—a relationship with Anaïs Nin's cousin Eduardo Sanchez that began in early 1940—propelled him away from the Woodstock community. The two had been apart through the autumn, but on December 3, Sanchez invited Duncan to visit him in North Carolina:

> Why do I want you here? Obviously because as a lover I want you. But if this were all, I would have you stay in Woodstock, and I would curb my impatience for one month, and then come to you . . . in January. But there is the father in me too. . . . He wants you and Virginia [Admiral] to have a change, rest, not to have to worry about food, cleaning, etc.; to have plenty of time and plenty of room to work.[13]

Duncan described his new lover to Blanche Cooney as "a pleasantly handsome blond Spanish mildish man in appearance—with nice exotic eyes (like little almonds) . . . given to biting, buggering, and being over enthusiastic."[14] Sanchez, then staying in Asheville with his sister and her two young children, was a renaissance man of sorts—an astrologer and writer who had lived in Florence during the 1930s and had published a novel called *The Round* as Eduardo Santiago. Anaïs Nin had experienced her own teenaged crush on her cousin, whose Spanish blood and Harvard education had made him a captivating visitor to her childhood household.

Boarding a bus on December 23, Duncan took Virginia Admiral with him on the trek south. Arriving in Asheville on Christmas Eve, he was eager to engage with Sanchez yet nervous about the physical relationship: "He slides toward some terrible sadism in his sex—the original biting becomes a biting that stands like a fragile door to tearing the body to pieces furiously."[15] The wealthy Sanchez had also extended an offer to provide for him financially—and suggested that Duncan begin psychoanalysis upon his return to New York. For Duncan, the proposal was overwhelming: "I want to be untouched—every time my life is tied to anything—the press, these people, I want to rebel, to get loose."[16] But after a long, bleak bus ride back to New York, Duncan had a change of heart. Abandoning Woodstock and the Phoenix Press, he accepted Eduardo Sanchez's offer to fund his psychoanalytic treatment. Virginia Admiral recalled that she helped Duncan toward this decision:

> My psychoanalyst at that time was Dr. Ernest Schweitzer. I had sent all my friends to him. He was caught in England during the war and came over here without his family. And then had to intern at Bellevue free for a year before he could practice here. So he took us, for a dollar, two dollars, whatever we could afford to pay. And we'd go up five flights to this little room, midtown. I sent Robert to him, and he turned him down. He said there's no reason for him to be psychoanalyzed. He doesn't want to be different than he is.[17]

Duncan in fact lasted for four weeks after beginning treatment with Schweitzer on January 3, 1941. On February 6, the analyst terminated the sessions. While Duncan's friends recalled various reasons for the short-lived analysis, he described his final session in his notebook: "'You are not unhappy'—he said. 'Only when one is unhappy is one willing to go thru the death that is necessary here for rebirth.'"[18]

Duncan did have reasons to be unhappy at the beginning of 1941. The unfinished business of the draft loomed in his mind, and Ned Fahs returned to his thoughts as well. Duncan tried to contact Fahs more than once during the early part of the year, though his phone calls were intercepted by Fahs's mother. Perhaps out of those confusions, Duncan considered returning to the Bay Area to attend college. In a New Year letter, he confided to Minnehaha Symmes that he hoped at last to achieve some financial independence: "Everyone has been saying for centuries that the artist must suffer but I am going to try in this coming year to get to a place where my suffering can go on at a little different level from that of . . . being cold and eating just off and on."[19] Short on money, Duncan frequented Anaïs Nin's apartment, bringing his journals for her to read and seeking free meals from her kitchen. The center of an active literary scene, Nin's West Village quarters drew the likes of the Patchens, Louise and Edgar Varèse, George Barker, and Henry Miller.[20] When not there, Duncan stayed with Virginia Admiral, gazing out the loft's windows toward the midtown skyline as he worked on his novel: "I sit in an island of a lamp in this great studio of Virginia's. A car outside pulls away from the curb, sirens— the lost floating sounds in the streets that lead so far away. I sit in the huge city, in an island of light, small, infinitesimal. Look down from a great height, move down into the canyons of the city. In one window, I sit bent over this book of my life. Tonight I am the magician, the priest."[21]

That winter, Duncan roamed the neighborhood south of Union Square, which Anaïs Nin described in her diary: "The houses are old, the shops small. In [Washington] Square old Italians play chess on stone tables. There are trees, patios, back yards. It has a history. The university was built by the Dutch. I love the ginkgo trees, the studio windows, the small theaters, Bleecker Street with its vegetable carts, fish shops, cheese shops. It is human. People stroll about. They sit in the park."[22] Duncan's own impressions of the neighborhood filled his journals alongside writings of a more pornographic nature. Under the category of "whoring stories," he began a series of narratives that opened with statements such as "I walked into McDougal's Saturday night like the Queen of the Whores." Recording encounters with businessmen, transvestites, and cripples, Duncan tried a permutation of his *Toward the Shaman* novel:

> From the dark, forbidden, lower center of him, from the pit below his belly where the tabooed legs twisted came the penis that belonged to his magnificent body, a cock like a God's. I felt with my hand around its base then knowing the strength and fullness of the penis and we entered the subterranean blind male-male copulation of the Lemurian world, turning upon each other, like plants, like mammoth early animals coming together with two penises between them.[23]

The stories, true or imagined, were inspired by Anaïs Nin, who, alongside Henry Miller, had been commissioned to write obscene narratives for a wealthy patron. Nin in turn recruited Duncan and other friends to help, and she kept records of the group's activities:

> Everyone is writing up their sexual experiences. Invented, overheard, researched from Krafft-Ebbing and medical books. We have comical conversations. We tell a story and the rest of us have to decide whether it is true or false. Or plausible. . . . Robert would offer to experiment, to test our inventions, to confirm or negate our fantasies.[24]

Duncan later enjoyed recalling such moments of sexual prowess, in 1976 telling his younger friend Chris Edwards about his exploits. According to Edwards, Duncan

> mentioned that a group of them used to meet with Anaïs Nin to tell stories and guess which were true or not (he figured they'd never believe he'd actually found a one-legged dwarf, let alone seduced him in a stairwell). . . . I took the dwarf story with a grain of salt, as a signifier of extreme behavior, not a

recounting of literal fact. There was no such qualification in the way it was told, however. I do remember RD saying that his main job, as AN's [Anaïs Nin's] "secretary" or "assistant," was to get the 3pm lover down the back stairs before the 4pm lover came up the front.[25]

Throughout the winter and spring of 1941, Duncan followed Nin's example, stumbling into a number of confusing intimate relationships. Carrying on his long-distance love affair with Eduardo Sanchez, he also briefly became enamored of another acquaintance of Nin's, Nicolas Calas, a recent arrival from Paris's surrealist circles.[26] An even more significant drama was brewing in his friendship with Virginia Admiral. Mary Fabilli's recent marriage to Griff Borgeson in Berkeley put the idea of matrimony into Duncan's head, and Admiral became a plausible candidate for the partnership.[27] To complicate the matter, Admiral was joined in New York that winter by Marjorie McKee, a painter who had been her roommate in Chicago. Admiral remembered when the diminutive, enthusiastic thirty-year-old McKee met Duncan: "It wasn't a question of introducing [them]. . . . I'd be crashing at Margie's and he'd need a place, so he'd be crashing there. Our lives were intertwined. And whoever was intertwined with me would be intertwined with Robert and whoever else was around that we were involved with."[28] Duncan was happy to call upon McKee when he needed housing, but there was more to the relationship as well. In mid-January 1941, he wrote in his journal, "Now I am staying at Marjorie's—we slept together last night like babes in the wood and talked about life and love problems."[29]

Anaïs Nin's published diary also pointed to an ongoing flirtation she had with Duncan. Throughout January and February, he was a frequent visitor to her apartment, joining her in journal-writing marathons. Duncan's *Toward the Shaman* now filled his notebooks, and Nin scrawled her comments in the margins.[30] In these journals reside the most substantial traces of Duncan's feelings about his relationships with his parents, with Ned Fahs, and with the young women central to his early life. The often candid, detached, and analytical language gives a perspective on Duncan's grasp of psychoanalysis. At the same time, he possessed an untamed energy that Anaïs Nin compared to that of a pet monkey she had brought home that winter: "Robert is emerging as a poet. His talks are like bonfires. His hair falls over his eyes as he writes as if he were an eager child drawing. His fingers are always stained with carbon paper or typewriter ribbon and he leaves his fingertips on my pages, as the monkey left paw marks on my bathroom walls."[31]

Amused and repulsed by Duncan's energy, Nin included several sketches of him in her ongoing diary project:

> Robert came with a recording by Edgar Varèse. He danced for us. It was a creation. He invented a nonhuman, abstract dance, a war of elements, torn, resoldered, percussion gestures to the percussion sounds of Varèse. His face was like a mask. . . .
>
> I love his humor, his trickeries, and language. It is the fecund labyrinth again, with so many rooms, cells, vibrations, percussions, repercussions. . . . Even when he dances and his eyes are glazed, expressionless, as in an Egyptian fresco, or even when he plays the idiot and no longer recognizes me, or the beast towering over me with grimaces and lines out of Saint-John Perse, or Cocteau, we laugh.[32]

On February 19, 1941, Duncan's bohemian reveries were cut short by a letter from the draft board rejecting his request for conscientious objector status. In a panic, he withdrew from the romantic entanglements of New York, fleeing south to visit Jeff Rall in his hometown of Kansas City. Variously traveling by bus and hitchhiking, Duncan spent part of February and March on the road seeking a reprieve from the anxiety of conscription. Met instead by snowy weather and a shortage of cash, he quickly turned back from his "insane journey," along the way spending an "early morning unloading pork in South Chicago" and near Pittsburgh waiting for a ride "in the cold wind at a rubbish heap called Breezewood."[33] By the middle of March, he was back in New York seeking temporary refuge with his new friend Marjorie McKee.

TWELVE

Enlisted

> We are strangely
> innocent killers. Gonzales,
> Daniel Garcia and I talk idly, lying on our bunks
> before mess-call. We say that in September
> there will be fiestas and dances in the bordertowns.
> We do not talk of killing.
>
> ROBERT DUNCAN, "A Spring Memorandum:
> Fort Knox"

ON MARCH 26, 1941, Duncan began his compulsory service in the United States Army, just as American forces were mobilizing toward action. He was sent to Fort Knox, Kentucky, for training and became a member of Company C of the 8th Battalion. Duncan later said that he had refused a career as an officer, abiding by a Taoist ideal that one should "go to the bottom."[1] He wrote the Cooneys about his first impressions of army life: "We have been consigned to the Armored Force Replacement Center.... In six weeks we will be drivers of tanks and motorcycles. There is a death a day by accident here ... we were told. I wonder ... where the pin dropped out from under my world—how I have landed here in this bog."[2]

Anaïs Nin and Kenneth and Miriam Patchen encouraged Duncan to leave the army. The Patchens solicited a lawyer, Morris Ernst, to assist Duncan in his severance.[3] But a letter from Anaïs Nin, which she described in her diary, may have been the primary impetus for Duncan to excuse himself from boot camp: "You refuse to free yourself from serving in the Army by declaring your homosexuality. And by this you will live a double lie, for you are also against war.... If you run away from it without conquering it (I say accept the homosexuality, live it out proudly, declare it), then you will remain asleep and enchanted in a lifeless neurosis."[4] Whatever the catalyst, after three weeks at Fort Knox, Duncan told his commanding officer that he was gay. He wrote Lili Fabilli about the encounter: "I walked ... into the captain's office (young, with eyes way back in his head that were perhaps gentle, certainly looking not at his men but into somewhere else) and said I want a psychological examination for a medical discharge sir or some impossible first sentence like that and he says . . . what is the matter, don't you get along? No sir, I say. I'm homosexual."[5]

Duncan was transferred to a military psychiatric ward and later released, in his words a "sexual psychopath." On June 25, 1941, he was granted a dishonorable discharge. During his few weeks as serial number 32045273, Private Robert E. Symmes, he wrote "Spring 1941," later titled "A Spring Memorandum: Fort Knox." The poem commented on the European conflict but also gave a curious glance into his army experience:

> We are weary with marching.
> Slow and deliberate, the last shelter lifts
> from the killing
> and we stand at attention in the mechanized day.
>
> The eye and the hand which trembled
> when it first took the pistol grow steady
> and directed to murder. In his two dimensions
> the flat man is easily shot.
>
> He might have been loved.
> It would have been harder. We conceive
> a small triangle with bullets
> over his heart.[6]

While detained in the psychiatric unit at Fort Knox, Duncan refined his opinions about authority:

> The eternal politicos, they are always there in the Paris commune, in the Bakersfield Chamber of Commerce, in Hitler's home town troops, in the armies and the governments and the industries of the world: this race sitting smugly, having its stupid virtue, an inward joy in ordering others in being president, or vice-president or head-sherrif [sic] . . . at every chance showing that they have the sacred right and duty to shove the others around: in the name of Democracy, in the name of Lenin, in the name of Liberté, in the name of God.[7]

It was one of his most articulate early statements of his politics, affirming the anarchist principles that would pervade his life's work. During the Viet Nam war, Duncan again called upon his readers to understand his doubts about manmade law, writing in "The Multiversity, *Passages* 21,"

In this scene   absolute authority
        the great dragon himself so confronted
        whose scales are men officized—ossified—conscience
            no longer alive in them,
        the inner law silenced,   now
    they call out their cops, police law,
        the club, the gun, the strong arm,
        gang-law of the state,
        hired sadists of installd mediocrities.[8]

When Duncan returned to his old haunts in New York that summer, he found some of his most intimate relationships strained beyond repair. Virginia Admiral had met another student of Hans Hofmann's, Robert De Niro, and the two had begun dating.[9] While Duncan was at Fort Knox, De Niro confessed to Admiral that he and Duncan had slept together before his departure. Duncan "came back to New York seeking a nest," wrote Anaïs Nin. "There was no room for him at Virginia's because he had made love to her Bob. No room in my studio for him. He ended up at Marjorie's, who had an extra room."[10] For the first time, Nin acknowledged Duncan's narcissism: "I had not noticed before that he does not feel for or with others."[11] For Admiral, the news of the affair was not entirely a surprise. She had seen Duncan attempt to wedge himself between other friends and had shared her bed with him on many occasions. Years later she mused philosophically, "Robert always had to sleep in the middle."[12]

When Admiral and De Niro moved to Provincetown, Massachusetts, that summer to continue studies with Hans Hofmann, Duncan followed, again receiving a cold reception. A poem he wrote that season, "The Encounter," likely addressed the fallout from the love triangle he had created:

His eyes are like mine so that I realize
his brain is much too bright with this, and when I move
about the room or sit as I sit now
listening while they talk, I remark
how he follows every movement . . .

The room has been disturbed by this violence
in its dimensions, and I feel, sitting apart from it,
the giddy recurrence of the speaker's distortions.
Barely listening, I see reed mats upon the floor
lean back into an inner room, into contortions

of an unseen space as mystery. I have
a private twist of the disease that lies
inside these others.[13]

Nin, also in Provincetown for the summer, reported to Henry Miller in July that "Robert came but he could not stay. Virginia threw him out, and as he had nowhere to sleep but a parked car and I could not take him in, he has returned to New York."[14]

Duncan took up residence with Marjorie McKee at 526 Grand Street in lower Manhattan. With Virginia Admiral now seeking companionship elsewhere, Duncan transferred his affections and discovered that McKee was an enchanting partner. Seven years older than Duncan, she had started her career in the Chicago theater circuit of the early 1930s. When she moved to New York and was introduced to Hans Hofmann, she became one of his students beside Admiral and De Niro. McKee's enthusiasm for life suited Duncan, and her close connection to Admiral reinforced a rivalrous drama that he found hard to resist. Admiral, who first met McKee in 1935 in Chicago, had also coveted her:

> Marjorie was my introduction to Bohemia. My mother was very shocked when she'd come in and find us sitting around on the beds or on the floor. Marjorie didn't have any chairs. . . . At this point she was very busy carrying on with two different psychiatrists and working at the B&G coffee shop to supplement her eight dollar a week allowance . . . , and I think taking some courses. She had dropped out of school and come to New York to be in the Yiddish theatre. Although she wasn't Jewish, she could pass for it.[15]

Duncan recorded his fascination with McKee in his notebooks:

> She was quick and clever. We sat in a kitchen which they [Marjorie and her third husband, Melvin] shared with another apartment while Marjorie ironed some collars and the coffee was brewing. Out of all this unsettled thing she seemed settled—removed, ironing, such a bird in a way, from the gloom and disorder of the room itself—her little order, her little domestic gesture held captive in a sense.[16]

From the sanctuary of McKee's apartment, Duncan turned again to literary pursuits. The September 1941 issue of the *Experimental Review,* edited by Sanders Russell, included Duncan's "Concerning the Maze," "A History of My Family," and "Fragment from a Journal" as well as his negative review of James Laughlin's *New Directions 1940.* Faulting Laughlin for poor editorial practices, Duncan further alienated himself from the New York literary community. Even Anaïs Nin's studio was soon off limits to him, she wrote in her diary in late fall 1941:

> Because of my vision into the inner Robert I still refused to see how his behavior crystallized into coldness and selfishness. He always came in without a greeting. He went straight to the icebox. He was never concerned whether he finished the last carton of milk, or the last slice of bread. . . . He never helped to put away the dishes. He served himself, no one else. He monologued without regard for others' work or fatigue. . . .
>
> When he rang the bell this morning I did not answer. I was in the kitchen when I heard him entering through the transom window.
>
> I told him how I felt. He left angrily.[17]

In December, Duncan tried his luck with Blanche and James Cooney, who were starting a new farming project in Ashfield, Massachusetts. It was there that Duncan and the Cooneys received news of the bombing of Pearl Harbor, and it was there that Duncan began writing poems with a renewed determination. He finished several pieces during the holidays, including "Variations upon Phrases from Milton's 'The Reason of Church Government'" (printed later in *Contour*), "Variations in Praise of Jesus Christ our Lord," "Snow on Bug Hill," "Witnesses" (published in *Death* magazine), and "From Richard Burton's *Anatomy of Melancholy*." He also made forays back to New York to spend time with Marjorie McKee, and after the New Year, he celebrated his twenty-third birthday with friends, reporting to his mother, "On my birthday last night I made a chocolate cake . . . Pauline Kael and the poet Robert Horan came over, brought me a copy of Marianne Moore's poetry and Marjorie brot [sic] Burgundy and anchovies. We all sat around and by the light of the kerosene lamp celebrated."[18]

THIRTEEN

Marriage

Marjorie was always very impractical about who she married.
VIRGINIA ADMIRAL in interview, 1998

HAVING BURNED BRIDGES ON THE EAST COAST, Duncan returned to Berkeley in early 1942, intending to take classes at the University of California. Weary of financial dependence on others and emotionally drained from his skirmish with the army, he informed his mother that he had decided to become a teacher: "I have been thinking about this course of action, seeking the advice of professors and considering all the factors. . . . The fields in education which are most open; where there is . . . the least competition and the best provisions for graduate scholarships . . . —two possibilities remain for me to choose between: theoretical math—and classical scholarship: latin and greek. It is the latter which I wish to study."[1]

Duncan reconnected with old friends, first living with Mary Fabilli and her husband, Griff Borgeson, in their garden cottage. Cecily Kramer was still in Berkeley as well, recovering from shock treatments she had received in a Bay Area psychiatric hospital during Duncan's absence. Duncan secured a job as a stockman at a Montgomery Ward mail-order house in Oakland, and he also found work in the local shipyards. He remained in Berkeley for a little less than a year, quickly losing his commitment to work or studies, and again began depending upon others for shelter.

That spring, he moved in with a newlywed couple, Hamilton (Ham) and Mary Tyler. Of the beginning of their friendship, Ham Tyler wrote,

> No one can now remember what the exact date was, or even which night of the week . . . , but a month or so after our marriage I came down the usual midnight street after a shift in the shipyards to find Mary looking for me. She seemed in the best of spirits and ran down the outside stairway . . . from our apartment . . . , greeting me with "Ham! What do you think? Robert has come to live with us!" I cocked my head back into the collar of my greasy tin-

coat and looked up the wooden stairs. At the top in the lighted porch was a young man I had known slightly as Symmes.[2]

Duncan set up quarters on an enclosed porch of the apartment and began spending his evenings with the Tylers talking about politics, listening to Mozart, and writing poetry. Ham Tyler, born in Fresno, California, in 1917, had also studied literature at Berkeley and had briefly served among Loyalist forces during the Spanish Civil War. Duncan found in him a partner for his intellectual pursuits, and the new friendship flourished:

> That summer, perhaps it was six month of 1942, I lived with Ham and Mary Tyler, the three of us working in the shipyards, and in all our social hours we read and talked about our reading. The Tylers were enamored of the English poetic tradition; Sir Walter Raleigh, John Donne, John Milton— . . . Ham identified with all three as heroes, and Mary with Raleigh's and Donne's wives. I could be a sort of Kit Marlowe (another poet of an irregular life) befriended by the noble and regular Raleigh.[3]

Unable or unwilling to register for classes because of his late arrival that semester, Duncan reported to his mother, "I have had work to do—not only Aunt Fay's giving me the gardening at her Forest St. place but I have worked several mornings other places trimming hedges and vines, etc., worked at the Unitarian Theological School putting up their library and . . . had several typing jobs."[4] Duncan's enthusiasm for gainful employment partly stemmed from his desire to establish himself as a provider for a family. Throughout that spring, he corresponded with Marjorie McKee in New York, and the two made plans to marry. Though McKee's analyst dissuaded her from relocating to California, Duncan remained committed to the idea of marriage, perhaps in response to Virginia Admiral's and Mary Fabilli's moves in that direction. Duncan described his soon-to-be wife to his mother and reinvented himself as a heterosexual: "Marjorie is petite—just five feet. Looks a little bit like Luise Rainer. Scotch on both sides and black haird with dark eyes. She makes me feel big with big hands and I like that. And she makes me feel as if I am really a responsible and capable man."[5]

Throughout the several months of separation from McKee, Duncan moved forward with his writing career. He associated the period with his first meeting with poet Kenneth Rexroth:

> [Rexroth] had marvelous and very, very crotchety and funny letters that he sent into *Partisan Review* and *View* magazine . . . , so that by the time I came

out to San Francisco in 1942 I wanted very much to meet Kenneth Rexroth and . . . wrote to him beforehand and almost the first week I was here. . . . Both Marie and Kenneth Rexroth were working sort of underground to get Japanese out of this area [to avoid incarceration in internment camps]. . . . And they were also working in the camps, . . . taking messages back and forth. So the first Kenneth I met was in his 30's, about 38, and he was a marvelous man.[6]

Rexroth, born in Indiana in 1905, had spent his early years in Chicago before moving to New York and then to California. His encyclopedic knowledge and political activism attracted Duncan, and while their relationship later became thorny, Rexroth was an important mentor in their early encounters. In *An Autobiographical Novel,* Rexroth gave a somewhat skewed account of Duncan's history: "Robert Duncan was going to school in Berkeley, where he had organized around himself a circle of Trotskyite, surrealist young women, over whom he exercised a kind of Svengali influence. . . . Duncan married one of these young women and shortly after was drafted. After a couple of months in the army, he wrote to her saying, 'Marjorie, you've got to get me out of this. If you don't, I'll kill myself.'"[7] Despite Rexroth's need to embellish Duncan's résumé, he did take the younger poet seriously and welcomed him to his Portrero Hill home, along with other young writers and antiwar activists. During the early and mid-1940s, Rexroth's circle— including Duncan, Philip Lamantia, and William Everson—set the stage for a blossoming of Bay Area poetry.

During that spring and summer, Duncan wrote "An African Elegy" and "The Years As Catches," two significant poems of his early career. Moving away from his "shaman" novel, he incorporated traces of Nin's influence as well as echoes of the surrealist art and poetry he had discovered in New York. In "An African Elegy," he romanticized the colonized continent of Africa as a metaphor for the surrealists' attention to the unconscious, as well as for the taboos of homosexuality:

> Negroes, Negroes, all those princes,
> holding cups of rhinoceros bone, make
> magic with my blood. Where beautiful Marijuana
> towers taller than the eucalyptus, turns
> within the lips of night and falls,
> falls downward, where as giant Kings we gatherd
> and devourd her burning hands and feet, O Moonbar
> there and Clarinet! Those talismans

that quickend in their sheltering leaves like thieves,
....
I know
no other continent of Africa more dark than this
dark continent of my breast.[8]

With the help of Kenneth Rexroth, Duncan began publishing his work in earnest. The poem "A Letter to Jack Johnson" appeared in the February-March 1942 issue of Charles Henri Ford's *View,* and in May, Duncan saw his first publication in Chicago's *Poetry* magazine.[9] In August, his review of Kenneth Patchen's *The Dark Kingdom* appeared in an Urbana, Illinois, journal, *Accent.* Propelled into the national poetry scene, he began to publish his work under the name Robert Duncan.[10]

In the fall, Duncan took a train east to reunite with his fiancée and Pauline Kael for Thanksgiving. Stopping first at James and Blanche Cooney's farm in Ashfield, he felt some unease. He confided to Woodstock acquaintance Doris Townsend, "The Cooneys here are continuing their farm which supplies them with vegetables and milk. They have a cow and three goats and the large farm house is furnished with a ... simple comfort and order that is a long way from Woodstock days. ... The problem here is that I have no cash, nor means of making, earning cash and whatever work I may do on the farm counts as nothing to assuage the disgrace of that factor."[11] To complicate matters, the Cooneys were receiving financial support from Duncan's ex-lover, Eduardo Sanchez. Uncomfortable with the patronage, Duncan left the farm abruptly. When he wrote to the Cooneys some months later about retrieving his possessions, he admitted, "My bad egg descent upon your household this last winter has embarrassed me so that I have not written."[12] Marjorie McKee recalled that Duncan had difficulty maintaining an equilibrium with friends during this period: "He wanted to write. He hadn't been trained ... to earn a living. A lot of times if people asked him to come to the country to visit, he'd just stay ... until they'd finally practically ask him to leave. ... He could stand chaos better than anyone I knew. ... He could have multiple feelings about people too. By the time he denounced someone there would be a lot of back and forth feelings."[13]

In February 1943, Duncan accepted a job with Dell Publishing as a traveling salesman and was soon on the road, working in and around Boston. Two months into the job, he questioned whether he was suited for such labor, complaining to Pauline Kael on March 23, "I'm going quite crazy again. The minute I face this after-business report to write I feel like running away, jumping out of a window—only this one isn't high enuf—god I feel ill— . . . I don't know why I can't just be calm about it and quit but I feel so damnd guilty—as if it were 'failing someone.'"[14] The income from his job at Dell at least took him closer to creating a stable household for his future wife. On a Saturday afternoon in May 1943, Duncan and Marjorie McKee were married in New York City. Robert De Niro and a pregnant Virginia Admiral attended the wedding, McKee's fourth.[15] The couple moved into an apartment at 114 West 11th Street.[16] Duncan again wrote to the Cooneys a week after the wedding, in a tone far from that of a happy honeymooner: "we are living on borrowed blankets and borrowed time—the down comforter of mine which you have is a necessity for us now. Can you send it to us c.o.d. as soon as possible?"[17]

The marriage was a short-lived fiasco. Years later, a discombobulated letter to Virginia Admiral gave a clue to the extent of the mismatch: "In order to apply for a passport I have to answer the following questions I was married on *don't know* to Marjorie McKee who was born at *don't know* on *don't know* who is an American citizen and who is now residing at *don't know*. Our marriage was terminated by divorce on *don't know*."[18] While it was not entirely unusual for gay men in Duncan's circle to marry, his attempt to live within a heterosexual marriage was short-circuited by the emotional dynamics with his new wife. Admiral remembered:

> They had a lot of fun together. She found him a charming companion and really was crazy about him. And she was very nice. But once they got married it was scary for him. Margie has a side . . . that would be bound to scare him, which is her mother speaking, "Well, if you really loved me, you'd take the garbage down. And the fact that you don't take the garbage down means that you don't love me." . . . She'd only pull this when she felt . . . stressed herself. . . . Robert . . . was working very hard. He had a . . . job in a publishing house and [was trying] to be a good husband and potential father . . . ; then she'd pull one of these things on him and spoil it.[19]

Duncan's poem "Marriage" gave his stark view of the relationship:

> When I love
> hate burns my right side.
> When I stop
> hate stops.
>
> Love and hate go back where you came from.
>
> I loving, hate burning my right side,
> who is the nothing on my left side
> left to face when I stop and hate stops?[20]

Retreating to his notebook, he reflected upon his relationship with Ned Fahs, in which he had fallen into the role of the clingy, insecure partner:

> Maggie's attachment to me has been, still is, a kind of necessity.... It is an ALL or NOTHING necessity.... so the image grows in her mind: as I remember the image growing in my own mind with Ned.... Love was not a torture it seemd to me finally, but the incapability to love was a torture—to be held to someone by one's very need, for protection, for affection that was a torture if one could not love that source of affection and protection.[21]

Duncan's interest in men was another decisive factor in the end of the relationship. The "figure" of a man as a sexual partner persisted in Duncan's imagination, and as he said in 1971, "In my twenties I was in a heterosexual marriage and the one thing that broke that was this figure always being there, so I was guilty before it."[22]

McKee remembered that the less-conflicted side of their relationship made it difficult to part. The two spent their weekends visiting art galleries in midtown and mingled with other artists and political activists in Greenwich Village:

> I think that was a wonderful period.... [Robert] had a recording of Stravinsky.... I remember seeing him [Stravinsky] too. And New York was an exciting place. I remember when New School opened and they had a big dance.... It was a mixture of all of the tension from the war, but still there were so many people from Europe ..., settling in New York to be away from the war. It was making New York a place it hadn't been before. [Duncan] was really interested in all that was going on.[23]

The couple's circle of acquaintances included writer Jackson Mac Low, translator Charles Glenn Wallis, and Joyce scholar Seon Givens. Wallis directed Duncan to the work of Yeats, Cocteau, and Lautréamont, and Givens introduced him to the writings of Mary Butts.[24] Mac Low joined Duncan in the New York City anarchist movement the following year, but his first meeting with Duncan and McKee came on September 12, 1943, his twenty-first birthday. Newly arrived from Chicago, Mac Low met the couple at Charles Glenn Wallis's Bedford Street apartment:

> Robert completely dominated the "conversation"—he monologized on everything under the sun, reading from his journal, telling obscure (to me then) dirty jokes, most of which seemed to end with his leaping into the air from his seat, holding his ass. He said things I thought incredible then but

later found out to be true: the only one I can now bring to mind was that Robert Frost was a "fairybaiter" (Robert's term). I'd never seen or heard anyone like Robert before. Years later I came to believe that he'd been putting on a show for the hicks from Chicago, but now I don't really think so. He was just being Robert.[25]

FOURTEEN

Divorce

BY NOVEMBER 1943, Duncan's marriage was in a deadlock: "Faced with either Maggie's alternating declarations that she cannot live without me or that she cannot live with me—I do not feel much relation to these feelings. They seem to violate my person, to be emotions and needs transferrd from other people, other areas of conflict to me."[1] At the beginning of 1944, he made a break from McKee, moving out of their apartment and beginning a relationship with painter Leslie Sherman.[2] McKee, then pregnant with Duncan's child, returned to Chicago to have an abortion, a decision that dismayed Duncan. "I had said that I *would* take care of a child—," he wrote his mother, "that was a point that I did not veer from tho I said too that a child would never be a bond between Marjorie and me—and . . . Marjorie wanted to have the child but her mother declared she would cut her off entirely if she did such a thing."[3]

In the wake of their separation, Duncan traveled to Florida by train—true to form, arriving without plans, halfheartedly seeking employment, and again asking his mother for money. Moreover, he found that the escape south did not provide the hoped-for recovery from the traumas of the previous months. He wrote to Minnehaha on February 12,"I have been in four cities looking for work, restless and almost out of my mind staring at the fact that there is—except for the Millers with whom I am staying this weekend in Orlando . . . —no one that I know in Florida."[4]

The multiweek sojourn south was later shrouded in myth. Duncan claimed that he had worked as a male escort there, albeit with little financial payoff:

When I was a gigolo in Florida, . . . I was in a schizy state, but I could explore it providing I stuffed money back. I would be given $300 at the beginning of the evening and it was taken for granted that I would keep it, but she would be so drunk I'd stuff it back in her purse. . . . So that got me caught out in my wasp middle class hypocrisy, that while I could be in this play, . . . it wasn't play money. . . . And yet I didn't mind having clothes bought for me. . . . The pleasure boy of Ancient Greece was doing fine, but cash . . . blew that whole scene.[5]

He also spoke of a pilgrimage to visit the poet Laura (Riding) Jackson, who had moved to Wabasso, Florida, with her husband the previous year. Duncan had studied her poetry in the months preceding his travels, and he likely was eager to make such a connection. Though he mentioned the encounter in later years, his correspondence from the period provides no evidence of such a meeting.[6]

In reality, Duncan's stay in Florida was largely unremarkable. By late February, having traveled through Orlando, Vero, Palm Beach, and Tampa, he found a job in the restaurant of the Gulf Stream Hotel in Lake Worth. In letters that spring, Duncan tried to persuade Leslie Sherman to join him, and he gave Pauline Kael details of his daily activity: "I am a busboy with room and good board and a little over twenty five dollars coming in cash every two weeks—and a couple of dollars in tips a week. In the evening I sneak in for a show at the town movie palace or sit and talk with bell hops. I have from 2:00 to 5:00 in the afternoon to myself. I go to the library . . . or to the beach."[7]

Almost immediately weary of the social isolation, Duncan returned to New York at the beginning of the summer. After a brief visit with Pauline Kael, he followed Leslie Sherman to Provincetown, where the couple found a cottage and Sherman settled into studies with Hans Hofmann. Duncan returned to more menial labor, reporting to his mother that he'd had a "vacation" in Provincetown working full-time as a dishwasher. Pauline Kael was again his key confidante:

There will be a long period this afternoon . . . when the dishes will fall off; the cook goes to sleep; Jennie who cuts the pies, ladles out the olives and tomato-juice, will sit down to chat with the cook's boy; and I will have a thing or two to say about Read's *Cult of Leadership,* Ciliga's *Russian Enigma,* and some notes after reading this English pamphlet *Trade Unionism or Syndicalism*— notes suggested more by my own reflections than by those of the pamphlet which seems rather thin.[8]

His summer reading of anarchist and socialist tracts accompanied the composition of "The Homosexual in Society." The essay was accepted by Dwight Macdonald, editor of *Politics* magazine: "You've written a really thoughtful and sincere piece here, and very well expressed (though your style is more rococo than my personal taste)."[9]

Duncan's pleasure in Macdonald's support and the promise of a fifteen dollar payment for his work spurred him to undertake another intellectual pursuit. He traveled to Northampton, Massachusetts, where he "held free discussions at Smith College" for the female undergraduates. He wrote his mother that they seemed only vaguely interested in his ideas: "I had hoped that in the process of the discussions I would get at least a spark of truth-sense out of them. I didn't get anything at all worth my effort and the stay was a disappointment."[10] Once again without funds, he returned to New York, where he shared an apartment with Leslie Sherman in the Hell's Kitchen neighborhood and began working at Stecharts, a book export company.

Another disappointment came in an October letter from *Kenyon Review* editor John Crowe Ransom. Ransom, who had accepted "An African Elegy" for his magazine, pulled Duncan's poem after he read "The Homosexual in Society" in the August 1944 issue of *Politics*. The two began a correspondence about their differing views of homosexuality, and as Duncan recalled in 1971, Ransom made clear that "he didn't know what the law was, but he felt that homosexuals should be 'altered' . . . to prevent breeding of that type." His response to Ransom was simple: "I would willingly take a pledge that I'm not really going to breed this year, but just leave me with my equipment, could you?"[11]

"The Homosexual in Society," a landmark document that led to a larger public recognition of the gay community in the American art world, had been inspired by James Agee's "Pseudo-Folk" in the *Partisan Review*. Agee's essay condemned the commodification of folk culture in America and black Americans' complicity in accepting stereotypes in order to entertain whites. In turn, Duncan made the unexpected move of denouncing "the cult of the homosexual" in his essay, describing gay subculture as a clique that intentionally and unnecessarily alienated others. While expressing ambivalence about the attitudes of the gay community, he also made clear that he was a homosexual active in the literary world.[12] Having witnessed the exclusivity of the avant-garde community in New York in the late 1930s and early 1940s, particularly in the circle around Charles Henri Ford, Duncan took a stand against the authority of any group bound together by an exclusive social or cultural agenda. His attraction to such anarchist ideals became clearer in the aftermath of the John Crowe Ransom incident. Toward the end of 1944, when Jackson Mac Low became involved in an anarcho-pacifist group publishing the paper *Why,* and later, *Resistance,* Duncan followed along to "discussion meetings at the Spanish anarchists' loft at 813 Broadway, between 11th and 12th Streets."[13] Others in the collective included Paul Goodman, Julian Beck, and Judith Malina. Duncan later recalled, "There were six of us. . . . Within four meetings, Paul Goodman and Jackson Mac Low, and a whole score of people were attending. Toward the end there were a hundred people or so. Actually, there were other anarchist circles, more than we ever knew. . . . These were people who were against the Second World War."[14] Duncan continued to push forward his views. In January 1945, *Politics* magazine published a letter he titled "The Politics of the Unrejected," and that winter he published "Notes on Some Painters and Poets" in Holley Cantine's *Retort* magazine. At the end of the year, with his time on the East Coast drawing to a close, Duncan returned to poetry, penning "Christmas Letter 1944" for his mother:

> Dear Mother, this by way of poem is little
> more than Christmas greeting, by way of letter
> sums more than a year, in and out, older
> than not so long ago, but short
> of the full greeting heart
>
> might give had time not tampered . . .
> This by way of Christmas greeting is little
> less than poetry;
> . . . .
> It allows
> a certain warmth to show, a pause,
> a Christmas hiatus in the midst of battle.[15]

THREE

The Enamord Mage

FIFTEEN

The End of the War

These are the fields where we enter a cold season.
The thinning moon hangs over our house.
In the early dark we move about our chores.
We turn homewards to sit in the lighted room,
to drink our wine and meditate
upon a cigarette. We have come safely
thru a war, and we face
another war.

ROBERT DUNCAN, "The End of a Year"

WHILE FRIENDS AND ACQUAINTANCES had maneuvered around the draft or waited out the conflict detained as conscientious objectors, Duncan narrowly escaped being sent to the front. In January 1945, he constructed a utopian plan for his own postwar life: "What I want is . . . a field for a house, a vegetable garden and some goats, to house my library and my beginning collection of paintings. A field in the backwoods with an eye for Northern California, for the sort of country where I lived in Woodstock—in kerosene lamp country."[1]

That spring, he ended his relationship with Leslie Sherman and left Manhattan for Bearsville, New York, drawn by an invitation to live with writer and anarchist Holley Cantine. There in the Catskills, in search of some autonomy, he began to build a log cabin in the woods with the help of a friend, Bill Humphrey. The project was short-lived. Duncan again wrote his mother to request money to "buy floor boards and finish the house" and shortly thereafter expanded his appeal:

I am asking . . . that you might send me fifty dollars a month for six months. If I finish any work and have it accepted . . . you can send me . . . the difference between the sum I make on my writing . . . and the needed fifty dollars. In that way I will not be subject to the anxiety of being stranded or being . . . a burden.[2]

Minnehaha reluctantly reinstated his allowance, and Duncan secured a studio near the Cantine property. He began work as a dishwasher at a Woodstock inn run by a young German couple, an experience he alluded to in *The Opening of the Field*'s "The Dance":

> That was my job that summer. I'd dance until three, then up to get the hall swept before nine—beer bottles, cigarette butts, paper mementos of the night before. Writing it down now, it is the aftermath, the silence, I remember, part of the dance too, an articulation of the time of dancing.[3]

During the rainy summer season in the mountains, Duncan's anxieties about events in the outside world resurfaced, prompted by the death of Franklin Roosevelt in the midst of Allied offensives in Germany and the suicides of Hitler and Eva Braun:

> The whole current of the war has profoundly distracted me. Mine is no "lost generation." We came after those disillusioned by the last war and we saw clearly and judged them and their contemporaries who did not question what they had done. . . . We discovered for ourselves belief and took the responsibility that if we accepted that murder was evil we were not to kill nor to make the weapons that kill. . . . This war . . . has been my first trial before which to such a measure I have failed. But not changed—except to be made more sure, less than ever "disillusiond." I return after all to a tradition . . . deep rooted in America's history. . . . To Thoreau's *Duty of Civil Disobedience* and to *Walden,* to Emerson, to the letters of Melville and of Vanzetti. And to the belief which Henry James had in a complex personal moral conscience.[4]

In the company of Holley Cantine and other Woodstock anarchists, Duncan stayed involved in current affairs, writing "Notes on Direct Action" for the fall issue of Dave Dellinger's *Direct Action* magazine.[5] In August 1945, upon the U.S. bombing of Hiroshima and Nagasaki, Duncan again wrote his mother:

> I cannot think of a more fiendish weapon of war—the most shameful expedient in history. . . . But what . . . can avail against the powerlust which sweeps the nation? Were the assassinists of the 19th Century right? . . . At the right moment the assassination of ten men who were working on the atom bomb might have saved the lives of . . . hundreds of thousands of civilians and might have saved what honor Americans might conceivably have left.[6]

The age of the atom coincided with Minnehaha's prediction that the world would be destroyed by fire during her son's lifetime, and the unleashing of the atom became a fixed image in Duncan's work. The words *Adam* and *atom* were twinned in his poetic vocabulary; the first man of Judeo-Christian myth and the elementary particle of matter became starting points for building his cosmology. In 1972, while teaching at Kent State University, he was still pondering the events of August 1945, giving a reading of Eliot's "The Waste Land" as an occultist's revelation of the atomic age.[7]

Amid the dire news of the late summer, Duncan undertook a short love affair with the German writer and translator Werner Vortriede. While Vortriede and Duncan spent only a few months together, Duncan credited the scholar for refining his relation to his craft as a poet and expanding his reading in European source materials:

> I received from Werner V—— a third geist out of Yeats, [Stefan] George and [Hugo von] Hofmannsthal. That young poet . . . handed on thru a story round that lasted from midnight until dawn . . . an imperative which has commanded my obedience and from which the orders of a poetry extend. I write since that night in order that a knowledge of the real and the unreal appear, and I write also that a longing (this geist from the fin de siècle) be given its fullest life.[8]

The introduction to the German poet Stefan George's work led Duncan back to Berkeley that fall and toward the study of medieval history with one of George's followers, Ernst Kantorowicz. At the end of the tourist season in Woodstock, he headed west, taking two detours on his way to the Bay Area. First visiting his Aunt Fay in Sacramento, his unkempt appearance and his reluctance to meet her circle of friends led to a showdown. Fayetta reported to her sister Minnehaha, "Robert has not changed one whit from what he was when last he was here. I do not think this is good news, at the same time it does not portend bad. It's just the truth. He has not yet grown up."[9] The destiny, and indeed hygiene, of her theosophically chosen nephew was likely on Fayetta's mind when she bought Duncan a new suit and a bar of Life Buoy soap. But Duncan's growing need for economic and emotional independence coupled with the physical exhaustion of the long trip west sent him into what he called "a complete breakdown." He wrote his mother that his aunt's needling had helped spur the crisis: "By the time I had been four days in Sacramento I was in a fever rage, trembling. . . . —You're just a baby, my aunt said smiling—winning. . . . Your mother still has to support you."[10] Duncan fled Sacramento, fearing a family plot to have him hospitalized, and sought refuge with Ham and Mary Tyler at their new home, a farm near

Guerneville, California. Ham Tyler recalled, "Robert arrived at Pond Farm looking back over his shoulder in a high state of excitement, though perfectly reasonable. Mary and I wrote letters assuring his mother that we knew his son well, that he was of sound mind though a poet, and that in any case working on a farm was a far preferable solution to any she had in mind."[11] Duncan also wrote to Minnehaha, complaining of recurring nightmares about the stay in Sacramento and pointedly describing his happiness with the Tylers, where he enjoyed a guest room decorated with crayon drawings and spent his days "feeding the chickens and the cows."[12] Though he was certain that his mother and aunt had conspired to have him institutionalized, relations were back to normal by Thanksgiving, when Minnehaha sent Duncan and his friends a box of oranges for the holidays.

The Tylers had moved to Pond Farm in July 1945, taking up residence in the midst of a pottery and ceramics camp headed by German Bauhaus School artist Marguerite Wildenhain. The arrangement was complicated, but the young couple made the most of it. Ham Tyler remembered, "Pond Farm was perched on a hilltop which was more suitable for crafts students . . . than for our herd of cows, but the fragile arrangement was that we would feed these artisans in summer, then sell cream to the buttermaker and eggs to the co-op for the remainder of the year."[13] Duncan's contributions to the operations of the farm were modest. He learned to milk cows and care for sick chickens, but he preferred to write poems. Taking advantage of the solitude of country life, he began to reflect on the war and his marriage in a series of works later published in *Heavenly City, Earthly City* and *The Years As Catches*. In "Upon Watching a Storm," he wrote:

> This is my ruind Europe; after war
> remembering you in the twilit summering rooms
> shaken and vacant in the near and far
> distance of love
>
> . . . .
>
> My heart keeps the long watch over hours of sleep.
> My heart is now like a dull bird
> struggling in water, come home to its love.
> Be still, heart. Listen. In the corridors
> tomorrow resounds its patient deep tide; and I,
> death-wedded, bride-still, will
> sometime come home.[14]

During this melancholy autumn, the Tylers proved good company and helped Duncan turn away from the failures of his early twenties. He reported some contentment to his mother, "This is so much the kind of a life I have wanted. This sunlit and happy passage coming at a time that seemd so dark is something indeed to be thankful for."[15]

When the Tylers relocated to Healdsburg, California, in January 1946, Duncan followed. Ham Tyler described their new farm, Treesbank, as "eighty acres in a nearly perfect setting, the heart of which was an open space on a gentle slope with deep woods on both sides. Around the house, at the end of a country lane, were twenty-five acres of apples and cherries while below . . . hayfields and pastures drifted into a quiet valley."[16] Freed of the obligations of the artisans community at Pond Farm, Ham tried his hand at a serious agricultural venture. Meanwhile, Duncan's poems began to take on a tone of leisure, reminiscent of his early Woodstock period. An erotic thread emerged during the winter of 1946, when a visiting student from Berkeley, Richard Moore, captured Duncan's interest. Moore joined the small community through his interest in anarchist politics and his participation in Kenneth Rexroth's Libertarian Circle discussion group.[17] Duncan had Moore in mind when he began his "Treesbank Poems," a loose sonnet sequence lamenting unrequited love. He also composed poems for two new West Coast magazines: *Ark,* edited by Sanders Russell, and *Circle,* edited by George Leite. To Russell, he confided, "I have hopes that in a year or so I should be . . . ready to tackle the literary world full force. I try here for the first time in years—since *Experimental Review* days— . . . to keep at writing daily."[18]

The Healdsburg farm became a place for writers to gather in the year following the war. Labor camps in the Pacific Northwest began releasing conscientious objectors, and resistance politics continued to infuse communities north of San Francisco. Duncan recalled, "By 1945, when I came back and Kenneth [Rexroth] began coming up to Treesbank, already the Tylers had gathered around Richard Moore. . . . and [Tom] Parkinson, who was at the time thinking of himself as possibly a poet. . . . And Philip Lamantia was back from New York."[19] A number of key activists from New York City anarchist circles, including David and Sally Coven and Audrey Goodfriend, also moved to San Francisco just after Duncan arrived, and as in Woodstock, Duncan placed himself in the center of a familial scene, encouraging friends to set up house with him on the Tylers' property. Poet William Everson gravitated toward the community in 1946 after his release from a wartime detention camp in Waldport, Oregon. Mary Fabilli spent time there, as did Sanders Russell, lured by Duncan's description of the place: "The country [is] . . . above Redwood forest . . . , high enuf that we are a kind of island above fog banks lifted up into the sunlight: it is all wildly and romantically beautiful. Forested ridges above the fog banks are like islands below us, islands in a Japanese painted screen."[20] Kenneth Rexroth made forays to both Pond Farm and Treesbank with friends of his own. Duncan related one such scene to Werner Vortriede:

> We had a lively weekend when . . . Kenneth Rexroth . . . and his wife Marie . . . arrived bringing along Richard Eberhart and wife. Eberhart has had several books of poems printed in England . . . but I have never found his poetry interesting, certainly not striking—and he was much the same: a lieutenant commander in the navy with a very specialized hobby, kite-flying. We stood up on our Pond Hill while Eberhart and his wife tried to launch an enormous kite. . . . But it was all to little avail. . . . A difficult enthusiasm.[21]

Despite his disappointing guests, Rexroth held sway over the imaginations of the younger poets visiting the Tyler homestead. Duncan wrote to Pauline Kael, "We have . . . become rabid Rexroth devotees—. . . . He has a truly amazing quantity of knowledge. We learned only this last week that he reads the *Encyclopedia Britannica* from cover to cover yearly."[22] Perhaps ready to gather his own devotees, Duncan soon decided to leave Treesbank for a more bustling scene. By the summer of 1946, he was back home in Berkeley.

SIXTEEN

The Round Table

A bright antique of sacred presences,
the windy armor grows alive with song
and in that darkend helmet
the poet's face is curious. The lonely men
about the revolutionary table sit.

ROBERT DUNCAN, "Medieval Scenes"

EARLY IN HIS CAREER Robert Duncan claimed three companions in
poetry: Mary Fabilli, Sanders Russell, and Jack Spicer. Fabilli and Russell
received little public acknowledgment for their craft. Jack Spicer seemed
destined to share an analogous fate but made a vast contribution to the San
Francisco poetry scene of the 1950s and 1960s. His influence on Duncan's
poetry was likewise formidable. Through conversation and correspondence
with Spicer, Duncan was pushed to reenvision his poetics: to study the lin-
guistic basis of poetry, arrange objects in poems as magical talismans, and
question the role of poetry and language in the world. The two writers
crossed paths several times in the spring of 1946, and when Duncan left the
Tylers' farm for Berkeley, Spicer became one of his closest friends. Duncan
later described his first impression of Spicer when he espied him across the
room at Kenneth Rexroth's apartment: "At one of the San Francisco anarchist
discussion group meetings he was there—a curious intense foreign pres-
ence—a stranger, a loner, even in that congregation that attracted those es-
tranged from the ways of the established social system."[1]

Spicer, like Duncan, had been raised in Southern California. His stories
about his childhood seemed incredible: he was part Native American, his
father was a member of the Industrial Workers of the World, a Wobbly. Bril-
liant but insecure, the young writer manifested his self-doubt in his slop-
ing shoulders, disheveled red-brown hair, and shabby, wrinkled wardrobe.
Six years Duncan's junior, Spicer initially viewed his elder colleague as a
source of titillating stories about New York City and its literary circles.
Duncan, with his connections to Anaïs Nin and Henry Miller, was already

an anomaly to the undergraduate population of Berkeley, and the fact that by twenty-seven, he had already been married, divorced, drafted, and publicly professed his homosexuality only added to his mystique. Spicer was so impressed with Duncan that he sometimes gave his birthdate as 1946, the year their friendship began.

Soon after their first meeting, Spicer introduced Duncan to his fellow undergraduate student Robin Blaser. The twenty-one-year-old Blaser, born and raised in a Catholic family in Idaho, presented a balance between the eccentric passions of Duncan and Spicer. He had spent his youth engaged in the physical demands of the Northwest and the intellectual demands of a Jesuit education. Unlike Spicer, he was meticulous about his appearance, and he won others to his side with a cheerful gap-toothed smile. The three writers formed the core of what would later be known as the Berkeley Renaissance, a precursor to the San Francisco Renaissance of the mid-1950s. They were, Spicer said, a "secret boy's club." Duncan recalled later:

> Playing poetry. [Spicer] wanted to keep us true to the game. That was always what the public meant to him— . . . the public of poetry like the public of baseball or football. We were to be champions of a new team: "Most of us are rather good poets," he writes in the *Occident* symposium of 1949. "If we were actors or singers or cartoonists of the same relative talent, a sizeable percentage of the students of this University would recognize our names and be familiar with our work."[2]

With his new status of elder poet, Duncan resumed classes in early 1948, but his initial months on the scene were spent as a poetry entrepreneur. One of the first public venues for the writers of the Berkeley Renaissance was a ramshackle Victorian house in North Berkeley, Throckmorton Manor, where he organized a series of lectures focusing on, among other works, Joyce's *Finnegans Wake,* Williams's *Paterson,* and Eliot's *Four Quartets.* The house, located at Telegraph Avenue, was owned by a philosophy professor who had plastered the dining-room walls with blackboards, making it an ideal space for Duncan's plans to offer "an off-campus seminar and a series on contemporary masters, and poetry readings."[3] Visiting scholars included Kenneth Rexroth, who lectured on William Carlos Williams; Tom Parkinson, who lectured on Yeats; and classics scholar Rosario Jimenez, who introduced the group to the work of Federico García Lorca.[4] The audiences, mostly graduate students and local poetry enthusiasts, soon formed the outer circle of the Berkeley Renaissance. James Broughton, Josephine and Fred Fredman, Ariel Reynolds, Ellen King, and Leonard Wolf all frequented the venue, planting the seeds of long-standing friendships.[5]

Sometime during 1946, Duncan met another Berkeley student who would become a lifelong friend. Hilde Burton, a German émigré who was then beginning graduate studies, recalled meeting Duncan at the White Log Tavern, an all-night coffeehouse near the campus. Duncan overheard her conversing at an adjacent booth and peeked around to ask, "You speak German, don't you?" He then introduced her to a group of Rilke enthusiasts, including Spicer and Blaser, who were in desperate need of help with their translation.[6]

Through the late summer and fall, Duncan lived at the Throckmorton house, where he returned to reading and writing. As he told his mother, his new work was influenced by "Herbert (*The Temple*), of Wyatt and Surrey, of the 20th-Century poet Rilke and of Edith Sitwell."[7] His correspondence with Minnehaha had tapered off after his return to the West Coast, and he made an effort that fall to reconnect to her, telling her that he had begun dating a student named Lester Hawkins and that the two planned to live together. Although the relationship was short-lived, partly because, as he told his mother, "his appeal is not heady," Duncan composed a poem to mark the encounter.[8] "Heavenly City, Earthly City," as much a commentary on Berkeley as on Hawkins, appeared in the book of the same title, Duncan's first collection, published by Bern Porter in 1947:

> I walk in the eclipse of my Beloved.
> but O the Earthly City remains.
> In my dismal century the Earth replenishes,
> replenishes her beauty.
> Against the Siren's monotone, the fixt accusing glare,
> your voice, Beloved, rises in praise
> of that fair spirit, my inward heaven.
> I know that my Redeemer lives.
> The light, His sun, is the radiant song
> that consumes in its focus a world I have sufferd,
> asserts, asserts, against the Siren counterfeit,
> the Earthly paradise in which I walk.
> This is the measure of my dismay:
> to know its beauty like the face of my Beloved
> that is torn in the rage of an inward flood.[9]

When Duncan turned twenty-eight in January 1947, he began writing the poems of his "middle ages," a pun on his studies of medieval history and on his anxiety about approaching thirty. Amid the activity of his new circle of friends, he hatched the idea of creating an Arthurian round table writing group, to meet at the Hearst Avenue home of newlyweds Hugh and Janie O'Neill. Duncan described the setting in his 1962 manuscript "Author's Notes to the Medieval Scenes Papers": "In January 1947, . . . Jack Spicer introduced me to '2029 Hearst' as we came to call ourselves . . . —a group of students, returning GI's and CO's, would-be Bohemians and artists. I was stranded in Berkeley after an unhappy love affair, with no money as always, making my living typing students' papers and theses. And at 2029 Hearst we all drifted, making the rent and food as we could, in a kind of cooperative house."[10] One of the Hearst Avenue regulars, Josephine Fredman Stewart, recalled that there was in fact no round table; visitors simply sat in the living room and talked and composed poems. On any given night, an assortment of young writers would descend upon the O'Neill household, including Duncan, Spicer, Dick Brown, Robin Blaser, Leonard Wolf, and Fredman and her husband, Fred, who moved to Berkeley during the summer of 1946.[11]

Out of these nightly meetings came "the serial poem," a form similar to that of a comic book, where each poem overlapped narratively to maintain continuity between episodes of writing. While Spicer later built a body of work almost exclusively in serial form, Duncan took credit for the innovation: "I had led the way toward the serial poem that was to be the governing concept of Spicer's and Blaser's later work with *Medieval Scenes* in 1946, which I wrote, making like my parents, who in their Hermetic mysteries had received messages at their séance table, setting up now a table where I proposed in ten consecutive nights to receive ten consecutive visions that were also messages in Poetry."[12] Spicer's biographers Kevin Killian and Lewis Ellingham detailed the unusual activities at the house, including "impromptu performances of Shakespeare or Gertrude Stein" and the use of "tarot cards, crystal balls, all the props of magic."[13] Fred Fredman, then a student in Oriental languages, introduced the divinatory device of the Kenkyusha, a Japanese dictionary that the group would skim through looking for answers to personal questions and found lines of poems.[14] The round table took Duncan back to the allure of the hermetic brotherhood, as well as to the shamanism of his Woodstock days. In the late 1940s, he wrote some of the first major poems of his career, much inspired by his relationships with Blaser, Spicer, and other novice writers in the Berkeley community. In many ways, Spicer's influence was the clearest:

> For the next two years, Spicer and I all but saw each other every day, days of intensive talk and study and writing toward what we thought of as a "Berkeley Renaissance." We wanted a learned poetry, learned not in the terms of the literary world but in the lore of a magic tradition and of a spiritual experience we believed to be the key to the art. This was the period of Spicer's elegies of a black Calvinism, the beginning of his life long contention with God, the Father, and of my orphic "Heavenly City, Earthly City" and of my "Medieval Scenes."[15]

SEVENTEEN

The First Poetry Festival

> At 27 I am a serious young man because seriousness is impressive to me. I cherish moments of conscious effortful dignity and I cherish what experience yields to the grave and earnest sense. I am a passionate young man because I cherish what experience hotly affords. I am a humorous young man because the lie of the seriousness, the dignity and the passion. . . . This is the journal then of a young man who concedes no god and yet lives upon his divinity and the divinity of others; who concedes no order and consequently can make bold to create his "order." ROBERT DUNCAN, notebook, August 28, 1946

WHILE THE BAY AREA WAS ALREADY saturated in literary happenings, another important moment came in April 1947 with Madeline Gleason's First Festival of Modern Poetry. A seasonal event, it eventually led to the establishment of San Francisco's Poetry Center in the mid-1950s. Gleason was born in 1903 in North Dakota and had arrived in San Francisco during the early 1930s to write for the WPA. A poet and avid organizer, she conceived her festival with the help of Duncan and James Broughton: "For two evenings twelve poets, including Kenneth Rexroth, Robert Duncan, Jack Spicer, and William Everson read to a packed room in the Lucien

Labaudt Gallery on Gough Street."[1] Duncan associated the poetry festival with new creative friendships, and he saw Gleason and Broughton as instigators of new energy for the burgeoning Bay Area poetry scene:

> In the years of the Poetry Festival, 1947–1952, I came to work in an entente with Madeline Gleason and James Broughton in which my own poetry reflected their work. . . . I sought out Madeline Gleason [in 1945] after friends had given me her first book, POEMS. . . . In the first [festival], . . . we found ourselves and began to hear our poems as belonging to a world of poets working with us, yes, but we also found that there was an audience. We had been told that modern poetry had no readers. That was the decisive message writ large in the 1930s. . . . Certainly, it was in San Francisco that the first audience began.[2]

His participation in the festival deepened Duncan's connection to Broughton, a playwright, poet, and filmmaker with whom he had a number of affinities. Broughton, born in 1913 in Modesto, California, had spent his early twenties tracing a trajectory similar to Duncan's, living on the East Coast as an aspiring writer and escaping service in the Second World War by declaring his homosexuality. Broughton's story of one of their early encounters underscores Duncan's tremendous appetite for attention:

> It was often difficult to know whether he was looking at you or at the wall behind you. Sometimes when he changed focus the discarded eye would wander off to a side wall, and he would remind one of Cyclops. When sexually attracted to anyone both eyes would come into fierce focus. His stare could be relentless.
>
> This I experienced early in our acquaintance. When I was living . . . in a Sausalito cottage I asked Robert to come to dinner and spend the night. . . . Pauline Kael was staying with me. . . . Before turning in . . . I went down [to the guest room] to take Robert a pillow. The door stood ajar. I entered to find Robert naked except for his scivvies [sic]. He came toward me focusing his greedy stare, then grabbed hold of me.
>
> "You don't want to sleep with Pauline, you know you don't. Look at me!" He moved back to drop his shorts and reveal his erect cock. "I want you! You want me, don't you? I can give you a better fuck than Pauline can!"[3]

Duncan engaged with more remote audiences that year as well, starting new correspondences with elder poets from the East. In a six-month period, he came into contact with Louis Zukofsky, Ezra Pound, and Charles Olson. Zukofsky, a New Yorker by birth and a chief theorist of objectivist poetry, responded positively to Duncan's first missive in the summer of 1947: "Since your letter makes me feel less alone as a writer (despite what you call the boldness of my social conscience) I should especially like to meet you."[4] Zukofsky's long poem *"A"* and his later book *80 Flowers* had a lasting impact on Duncan's writing, as did their correspondence, though Zukofsky's judgment in a second letter was likely disappointing to Duncan: "Your prose is much better than your verse—as you know or I wouldn't be saying it to you."[5]

Duncan next made a pilgrimage to meet with one of his modernist masters, Ezra Pound, at St. Elizabeths Hospital in Washington, D.C. The first leg of his journey took him to New York, where, on August 4, 1947, he received a telegram from Dorothy Pound: "No telephone. Bed here. Visit Wednesday or Thursday one to four. If convenient lunch with me Red Cross cafeteria midday in St. Elizabeths."[6] Duncan spent two days with the Pounds—his evenings as a guest in Dorothy's small apartment and his afternoons at St. Elizabeths, where Ezra Pound, like Zukofsky, seemed more interested in his young visitor's ideas than in his poems. Pound, arrested in Italy for treason during the spring of 1945 and sent to a United States Army prison camp near Pisa, had been returned to America later that year and incarcerated in St. Elizabeths. Judged incompetent to stand trial, he remained institutionalized for twelve years.

Unlike fellow poets Jackson Mac Low and Charles Olson, who were disappointed to find that Pound's anti-Semitism dominated personal conversations during their own visits to him, Duncan viewed his hero's prejudices philosophically: "[Pound's] anti-semitism . . . is just WASP anti-semitism as thick as my parents' or anybody else I ever knew in my childhood. . . . About the Wiles [Jewish neighbors in Bakersfield] . . . my mother said to me— 'well they prefer to be with their own people.' . . . Then I realized whenever they came to dinner they always came en famille; they never came to dinner when other people were there."[7] Duncan also relayed some of the happier particulars of his visit to Pound in his later correspondence with H.D.:

> Each day it took all of fifteen minutes for him to begin the conversation, those conversations that went on then for four hours. His life seeming to be in . . . all the talk of the past; Ford Madox Ford, Wyndham Lewis . . . the host of voices in which he lived. He said that he did not want to write any more on the CANTOS during this time "when his mind was straind"; but he works on a translation of the *Book of Odes* with a sense of appointment. "If I am imprisond for ten years and therefore have a time in which to learn Chinese, I shall be happy." The government now, through the Library of Congress, arranges that he have everything he wants to work with that is available.[8]

After some subsequent weeks in New York, Duncan hitchhiked home to the Bay Area, his trip interrupted briefly when he checked into a Denver hotel to wait out a fever and "the obliterating pain of four wisdom-teeth, infected and compacted."[9] He reached the West Coast too late to attend his sister Barbara's September 13 wedding in Bakersfield, instead focusing his sights on a family of his own.[10] While Duncan was East, Hugh O'Neill had left his wife, Janie, who was soon to give birth to their child. At the Hearst Avenue house, Duncan spent the early part of the autumn juggling the roles of surrogate husband and nursemaid. While Janie held hopes that he would become a permanent member of the household, within weeks, Duncan was swept in other directions.[11]

One perhaps welcome distraction that September came in the form of a visit from a writer who would soon join Duncan's inner circle. Scholar Charles Olson and his wife, Connie, arrived on the West Coast in July, traveling from Seattle to Sacramento to Berkeley on an extended fact-finding trip for a book on California history and the Donner party. It was on the Berkeley campus that Olson and Duncan, soon-to-be innovators of the Black Mountain school, had their initial rendezvous. Duncan, like all who met Olson, was first struck by his new acquaintance's powerful physical presence: "Charles threw himself down on the lawn, so that my first experience is of Charles (outside of this rather startling sight of this *thing* advancing at me) . . . right down on my level . . . lying flat on the ground, my maybe sitting—we talked person to person."[12] At six foot seven, Olson's height was amplified by his width. Duncan, almost a foot shorter and nearly a decade younger, was nonetheless the intellectual match of the mustachioed, bespectacled East Coast thinker. According to Olson's biographer, Tom Clark, "They talked at length on a lawn adjoining the library, with Connie as silent witness and Olson . . . basking recumbent on a sloping bank of grass like some inquisitive Gulliver as the handsome young Berkeley poet matched him move for move in the kind of intellectual acrobatics that delighted him."[13] Duncan also noticed early on that Olson was "a man filled with the things that . . . had to be done. He sat down right away: 'We've go to do this. We've got to do that.'"[14] Challenging each other to a range of topics above and beyond poetry, Duncan and Olson spent the afternoon rambling about ecology, farming, and socialist politics. While Duncan would later view his new friend as a fellow craftsman and innovator, he had yet to recognize Olson as a writer: "He had looked me up because he had read *Medieval Scenes*. . . . And I did not know that this man wanted to be a poet. . . . One of [his poems] had even gotten into the *Atlantic Monthly,* a place where I had never been caught in my life."[15] Olson's late arrival into American poetry circles was soon counterbalanced with his epic poem sequence *Maximus,* and in the wake of their first meeting, Duncan and Olson began a correspondence and friendship that would endure for more than twenty years.

EIGHTEEN

The Venice Poem

Of Desdemona:
say she was my true witness,
say I named her advocate
in whose arms I lay
virtuous therein.

ROBERT DUNCAN,
"The Venice Poem"

INSPIRED BY HIS MEETINGS with Pound and Olson, Duncan again decided to test the waters of academia. Between the spring of 1948 and the fall of 1951, he worked toward a degree in the University of California's Civilization of the Middle Ages program, studying with Paul Schaeffer and Ernst Kantorowicz. His reason for returning to classes was simple: "Most people do not go to college for an education. . . . I was going back for an education. . . . This is almost impossible to explain to a university. [It's like saying] I like banks because I want to take money home."[1] True to his word, Duncan received an education, but not a degree. Alongside Jack Spicer and Robin Blaser, he entered into the enchantment around Ernst Kantorowicz, a Jewish-German refugee from Posnan who had fled Europe during World War II. Kantorowicz, a medieval scholar mentored by the romantic poet Stefan George, had been a member of George's *kreis,* or coterie, in Germany.[2] Robin Blaser recalled that Kantorowicz's rolling accents and sophisticated knowledge of theology and history mesmerized the otherwise talkative and uninhibited group of young writers studying under him. At one party hosted by Kantorowicz, Blaser and Spicer came across their bow-tied mentor stretched out on a divan in the center of the room, making sweeping gestures with a cigarette in his hand. Startled by the extravagant display, the two fled.[3]

Kantorowicz's style as a teacher, thinker, and conversationalist became a model for Duncan, and it infused the poet's idea of himself as a "master" teacher later in his career. Emulating the meetings of the Stefan George circle, the professor held seminars in his home and served food and wine to the students during their studies. The search for community, city, or "polis" was already a driving force behind the Berkeley Renaissance, and Kantorowicz's classes provided a theoretical framework for configuring such a community.[4] Robin Blaser wrote years later, "The discovery that theology could be political and inform the polis was fundamental to our youthful gaze. And it was the beginning of the notion that one is after a world—that poetry does, beyond a singular voice, 'exhibit a world.'"[5]

The world that Duncan, Spicer, and Blaser sought was utopian, a place where poetry descended from the divine and poetic community could be assembled like a Greek city-state. Trapped within America's oppressive homophobic postwar culture, they found refuge in their studies.[6] Spicer meditated upon these ideas in a series of poems written late in his life, "A Textbook of Poetry":

> The city redefined becomes a church. A movement of poetry. Not merely a system of belief but their beliefs and their hearts living together . . .
> the city that we create in our bartalk or in our fuss and fury about each other is in an utterly mixed and mirrored way an image of the city. A return from exile.[7]

Kantorowicz's influence gave shape to the Hearst Avenue round table, but Duncan's energy fostered its growth. The eldest poet of the group, he sought to educate his peers with the texts he had studied over the previous decade, including the writings of Cambridge classicist Jane Harrison. Duncan, Blaser, and Spicer read Harrison's *Prolegomena to the Greek Religion* and *Themis* during their studies with Kantorowicz, and in 1949, when another classics scholar, E. R. Dodds, arrived in Berkeley for his lecture from his soon-to-be-published book, *The Greeks and the Irrational,* the poets submerged themselves in his complex examination of the social and religious customs of the ancient Greeks.[8] Duncan's notebooks from 1948 show the spectrum of his reading, from Charles Homer Haskins's *The Re-*

naissance of the Twelfth Century to E. Sidney Hartland's *Legend of Perseus* and J. J. M. de Groot's *The Religious System of China*. In addition, Kantorowicz's insistence that his students work with original source materials led Duncan and his peers to seek out their friend Rosario Jimenez to teach them Greek.[9]

Duncan's return to the classroom was accompanied by another pleasure, the beginning of a romance with an undergraduate named Gerald Ackerman. Ackerman had happened upon the Berkeley Renaissance group while living in a boardinghouse on McKinley Street also inhabited by Jack Spicer.[10] When Spicer issued the peculiar demand that Duncan and Blaser refrain from dropping by the house, Duncan was compelled to investigate. Soon after a November 1947 visit, he began dating Ackerman, precipitating the first serious crisis in his friendship with Spicer: "Jack was already living in that building; we shared the same shower, and so forth. And Jack was not speaking to me at all nor looking at me. . . . The reason that he didn't want us to go over there was exactly because of what happened. And that made the first real rift."[11] Ackerman remembered that after their initial meeting, Duncan had invited him to spend the night at Hearst Avenue, a place busy with activity and colored by the complex dynamics of Duncan's relationship with Janie O'Neill. Despite his apprehensions about his new lover's unconventional household, Ackerman was easily won over:

> Duncan was almost thirty, charming . . . , full of humor, his large head making his shoulders seem even more narrow than they were; . . . even without noticeable muscularity he had the suppleness of a dancer. His hair was usually in need of a haircut, one eye was slightly askew, but only enough to be noticed when you were mad at him (and were trying with desperation . . . to "look him in the eye"); or when he himself was angry, for its indirection gave a particular terror to his rage. He was also kind, loving, generous, and evidently, considering my tastes, very tolerant.[12]

A sandy-haired, athletic nineteen-year-old, Ackerman was delighted and overwhelmed by Duncan's creative energy, and Duncan was equally delighted with the boyish literature student and aspiring prose writer. The relationship promised a return to the domesticity he had found with Ned Fahs. Attending classes and working during the day, the two spent evenings together, sharing an intimacy that had not often been within Duncan's reach. He wrote about the relationship in his notebook with flourishes of language borrowed from the Kantorowicz seminars:

I held Gerald's hand; we two lying upon our backs. . . . I felt then sacramentally in embrace. The marriage envisions the final embrace of their images upon their sarcophagus; lying in a sleep of state from which they will awake together. The élan of marriage, of the grand armour, was embodied herein; when the great tomb disappeard, the marriage had already retreated from the sacrament of death from which it took its sacred quality. We are images of a third hidden thing.[13]

Infatuated with Ackerman, Duncan moved into the McKinley Street house, where his literary friends came and went, talking late into the night. Duncan read his poems to anyone who would listen, and Ackerman developed a coping mechanism to survive the din: "After I had more or less memorized the pieces, I learned to live with it as you do with television in some houses, always on."[14] While Jack Spicer took several weeks to warm to Duncan's presence, other members of the Hearst Avenue community frequented the room he shared with Ackerman, as did Pauline Kael and another boarder, future science fiction author Philip K. Dick.[15] For Ackerman, the courtship was at once gratifying and frightening:

[Duncan] was continually interested in the "new," . . . I was still exploring the past, reading classics. He had already swallowed the past; he knew everything I was reading, and even seemed to be able to form an opinion of a new book or author I was reading—whom he hadn't read—simply by looking over my shoulder occasionally. . . . Although he wanted to make . . . his life a maelstrom that drew everything into it (the act of super egocentricity necessary to his type of poetry) he allowed me to spin in my neighboring eddy. He wanted me to succeed on my own, perhaps to justify our relationship among his friends.[16]

In March 1948, when Ackerman's attention to Duncan briefly waned, Duncan began composing a testament to an encroaching psychodrama. He called it "The Venice Poem." By far his most ambitious early work, the poem was similar to Eliot's *The Waste Land* in its tone and structural complexity. Creating within the poem a grid that he called a "sonata form," Duncan delineated his floundering relationship with Ackerman.[17] Unlike his later work, "The Venice Poem" was heavily revised, constructed as a collage as well as a sonata and incorporating ideas on architecture from Sigfried Giedion's *Space, Time, and Architecture*.[18] The poem took root from the modernist practices of Pound and Eliot; its narrative was fragmented with repetitions of words and phrases, giving it the texture of a shattered cubist composition. Duncan later wrote about another structural aspect of the poem: " 'The Venice Poem' was conceived, after Jane Harrison's theory of the dithyramb in *Themis* as 'Zeus-leap-song,' the hymn of the kouretes that makes Zeus leap or beget as a ritual poem—dance bringing the daily psyche-drama, the creative preoccupations of the artist, and the creative imagination—the mythopoeic—into a common ground of activity, of in-formation."[19]

"The Venice Poem" became a memoir of the collective erotic longings of the Berkeley Renaissance participants, and it also bore their collective influence. The "Imaginary Instructions" section was a response to Landis Everson's "Green Homage."[20] The bells that rang in the poem were those of the Berkeley campanile, and much of the visual imagery came directly from Ernst Kantorowicz's spring 1948 course on medieval and renaissance architecture, The Thirteenth Century. When the professor showed slides of the Church of San Marco in Venice, Duncan inserted those images into the dramatic exposition:

> Lantern-slide visions
> of Venice repair; not happy, but splendid.
> Six-hued colord photographs
> reproduce a monument of all desire and fear[21]

Sexual innuendo was present from the opening lines:

> The lions of Venice crouch
>
> suppliant to the ringing in the air.
> The bell tower of San Marco
> shakes the gold of sound upon
> the slumbering city.[22]

In his marginalia to a published version of the poem, Duncan noted that the bell tower and lions represented a penis and testicles. Superimposing Venice on Berkeley, he also inserted references to Shakespeare's *Othello,* casting Jerry Ackerman as Desdemona, "whore of Venice," and Jack Spicer as Iago. Duncan appeared variously as the loved/unloved, genius/idiot, wretched/anointed one. He was the moody "cross-eyed king of 1000 lines," "young William Shakespeare," and Othello. In his journal, he commingled the opening lines of the poem with notes of a more personal nature: "Now I must sit in these hours listening to the clock tick. Jerry's being away with someone else fucking or wanting to fuck casts panic upon me. There is no agony like these moments or hours, these unbearable stretches of time. . . . If only Robin had come up with me to sit and talk, to divert my mind."[23]

Relegating sexual relationships to the primitive and savage, in the climax of "The Venice Poem," Duncan relied on rhythms similar to those in Vachel Lindsay's long poem "The Congo," again identifying sexual drama with an exotic vision of Africa:

> When you come to this moment there are no gods.
> In the merciless light there you are shown,
> naked and silly as the primevil bone.
> There isn't any poetry. The doggerel begins
> like the drums in the dark where the cannibals chew
> at the monotonous liver and spit their bile
> and the words in the dark go round and round.[24]

The events leading up to the first rift between Duncan and Ackerman were exaggerated in "The Venice Poem." For Ackerman, still in his late teens, six months of monogamy had already seemed like something of a commitment, and his affection for Duncan remained intact through a brief affair he had that spring.[25] By late March 1948, the turmoil had died down somewhat, and Spicer had also recovered from his petulance about Duncan's transgressions: "After four months, Jack's anger has at last abated and he has expressd a willingness to break his feud. The atmosphere in the house is somewhat relieved. His change is co-incident with the new phase between Jerry and me; these days of renewd affection and relief from the tension of the period of adultery."[26] When Duncan and Mary Fabilli began a new project, the *Berkeley Miscellany,* Spicer's work featured prominently in the first issue.[27] The second issue also included work by Fabilli and Ackerman, and a supplemental publication of Duncan's work, *Poems 1948–49,* mapped out his relation with Ackerman, opening with "Three Songs for Jerry" and including "The Venice Poem" as well as a more somber piece called "Revival," in which he mused, "Am I on the brink of happiness? / Am I on the brink of panic?"[28] While Duncan and Ackerman continued their relationship into the following year, they began to see that it had run its course.

Duncan meanwhile resumed his studies with zeal, earning As in most of his classes. That summer, he enrolled in Kantorowicz's seminar on Renaissance Italy, and the following fall he tackled a medieval history course taught by Paul Schaeffer, a course called The Principles of Politics: The Philosophical and Religious Matrix of Political Problems in the Periclean Age, and a class in Oriental languages called The Life and Times of Confucius. Close to the completion of his degree, in the spring of 1949 he returned to studies with Shaeffer and Kantorowicz, focusing on the history of the Albigensians in France and the constitutional history of England.

NINETEEN

Indian Tales

> The old man is like a city
> laid waste by war. He is noble.
> He is pathetic. He is an old nuisance
> with his fits of fury, tipping over the pisspot.
> He is a bombd house, falling away from us,
> reappearing in his own light,
> a spiritual refinement.
>
> ROBERT DUNCAN, "An Essay at War"

THE SUMMER OF 1949 brought Duncan into an educational experience of a different sort. As his relationship with Jerry Ackerman drew to a close, he moved into a cottage in the Berkeley Hills owned by anthropologist and linguist Jaime de Angulo and his wife, Nancy. While there, he assisted in the care of Jaime, who was dying of prostate cancer.[1] Duncan entered the household with an introduction from Ezra Pound, but he had been aware of de Angulo since the 1930s, intrigued by rumors of a "man who lived on the Sur, and who lived like an Indian Shaman."[2] De Angulo, born in 1887 and raised in Paris, was an acquaintance of Pound's and D. H. Lawrence's during the 1930s. A scholar of Native American traditions, he had lived among the Pit River Indians of Northern California and was attempting to finish his life's work, which included a sequence of uncollected short stories and a textbook on Native American languages.[3]

Taking a semester's leave from the university, Duncan acted as de Angulo's typist, and later as his nurse. In de Angulo, Duncan found a mentor with whom he could engage in an intensive study of linguistics, while also gaining a glimpse into the mysteries that he had attempted to explore in his novel *Toward the Shaman.* Duncan proposed that de Angulo's youthful forays into transvestism had been partly shamanic in nature, and in a 1979 interview, he recalled another factor that deepened de Angulo's mystique: "In one of the ironies of the time, in a treatment for cancer, Jaime took female hormones. And I remember coming into [the] kitchen-dining room, and Jaime was washing himself stripped to the waist, and he had female breasts . . . he had become a hermaphrodite."[4]

Duncan inhabited the bleak world of Jaime's physical decline for nearly a year. The news in the outside world was no better: in January 1950, President Truman approved plans to develop a hydrogen bomb, and the following month, Senator Joseph McCarthy warned that the State Department had fifty-seven communists in its employ. A mimeographed holiday card for the 1949–50 season from Duncan's Aunt Fay sounded a lighter note: "Dear Friends and Fellow Scientists . . . in line with previous Christmas letters, [I] will present my solution of another of the problems that have so long confronted scientists: namely, finding the fundamental cause of PERPETUAL MOTION."[5] Duncan's New Year holiday and thirty-first birthday were spent mourning the break with Jerry Ackerman, and he recorded in his notebook that he had little interest in sex as he was bereft of a lover charming enough to have "talk" or "intercourse" with: "I have not, of course, recovered myself wholly from the misery of the past two months—but yesterday morning I was in an extraordinary euphoria. I wrote Jerry (My dearest bear) etc. extravagant in affection 'this is probably the only real love letter I have ever written you'—well, it was. The thot of him still at times is a joy, abstracted somehow from the fact that seeing him is no joy unmixd: repeating as we do the scenes of rejection."[6]

In an otherwise discouraging season, Duncan at least had the promise of a new book from James Broughton's Centaur Press. To be titled *Medieval Scenes,* the collection included the poems he had written at the Hearst Avenue round table sessions. The new year also saw the publication of Charles Olson's seminal essay "Projective Verse" in *Poetry New York.* Olson's idea of "composition by field" would reverberate for years to come, and for Duncan, it not only drove his first major collection, *The Opening of the Field,* but also determined his view of the relationships between objects in the physical world. He later told a comical story of the essay's reception in the Bay Area poetry community: "'Projective Verse' we read avidly, and we totally misunderstood it.... Since we read poetry aloud everywhere and we were beginning to have audiences for the reading of poetry aloud . . . I felt very enthusiastic about it. . . . Perhaps I thought all of you out there [the audience] were the field, and you [the reader] project poems!"[7] But projective field poetics became a serious influence for him, and in the decade following the publication of the essay, he continued to experiment with the possibilities of the line and the use of the page as a field for the free movement of language.

While caring for Jaime de Angulo during the spring of 1950, Duncan returned to school, taking introductory German and a course called Symbolism: A Study of the Expressive Functioning of Signs. That year a crisis erupted at Berkeley when the board of regents, supported by President Robert Sproul, instituted a mandatory "loyalty oath" for its employees in an effort to rid the university system of potential communists and communist sympathizers. Ernst Kantorowicz refused to sign the oath and resigned, as did graduate student Jack Spicer, who left for Minnesota later that year. A larger crisis took the headlines during the early summer of 1950 when North Korean troops armed by the Soviet Union crossed the border into South Korea. On June 24, President Truman ordered the navy into action to stop the invasion, and soon after, the United Nations organized an international task force under General Douglas MacArthur. Amid rising tensions with China, U.S. involvement in the conflict continued until Eisenhower's election and declaration of a ceasefire in 1953, by which time more than thirty thousand Americans had lost their lives. Duncan wrote about the conflict in "An Essay at War," integrating scenes from the de Angulo household:

> The fire lighting up the room
> almost to a tropical heat where
> the old man is dying of cancer. "You
> do not know how to light a fire,"
> he cries. "I will teach you
> how to make a fire. So few ... nobody
> today knows how to make a fire
> with kerosene." This blaze
> is the same kind roar of flames
> that destroys in terror Korea
> and we
> do not know how to make a light
> pouring kerosene on the already burning paper.[8]

During the fall semester, Duncan engaged in a more rigorous lineup of classes, receiving As in Paul Schaeffer's Medieval Culture course, German, and French, and a B in Early Christian and Byzantine Medieval Art, taught by Walter Horn. Meanwhile, as Jaime de Angulo became weaker and more cantankerous, Nancy hired another nurse, and Duncan braced himself for the worst. He admitted a squeamishness at the sight of de Angulo, who was "withered, the head a skeleton in which mad (in all senses of the word) eyes rolled back in the sockets."[9] When de Angulo died in October, Duncan registered his shock to Dorothy Pound: "Jaime is the first person other than my father close to me to die. That he is dead, I find, as I found my father dead, utterly ununderstandable."[10] He also wrote Josephine Fredman, connecting de Angulo's death with the end of the Berkeley Renaissance:

> Your leaving and then Spicer's and the Wolfs has shaken up the intellectual balance of the scene. . . . It is as if a hurricane had swept thru the town. Old tensions, perhaps, but they were all the tensions of friendship—tense in the sense of the exact tuning of a cat-gut: one had after all a melody in mind and even, at times, heard it. And such a music rests in the community of those that love it well. . . . what Berkeley was . . . rested, for me, in the intimacies of mind. Now, I no longer think of it as Berkeley.[11]

TWENTY

The Song of the Borderguard

In the beginning there was weeping,
an inconsolable grief
I brought · the storm I came in
ROBERT DUNCAN, "These Past Years"

ENDING HIS RELATIONSHIP WITH JERRY ACKERMAN, Duncan wondered if he'd ever find a stable domestic situation, but out of the trauma described in "The Venice Poem" came an unexpected turn. One of the audience members at a 1949 reading of the poem in Berkeley was a painter and literature enthusiast named Jess Collins. Duncan was thirty when he first met the twenty-six-year-old Jess. Shy, willowy, and the epitome of tall, dark, and handsome, Jess attracted Duncan's attention immediately. With him, Duncan came into a marriage and companionship that lasted thirty-seven years.

Born Burgess Collins on August 6, 1923, in Long Beach, California, Jess spent his childhood in the southern part of the state, where his father, James Francis Collins II, was a civil engineer, and his mother, Clara, was a housewife. He was the younger of two sons, in a household he described as "Republican," where "children were to be seen and not heard."[1] In 1940, Jess graduated from Woodrow Wilson High School and spent a year at Long Beach Junior College. In 1942, he enrolled in the California Institute of Technology to study chemistry, but in February the following year, he was recruited into the army. In 1944, assigned to Oak Ridge, Tennessee's Manhattan Project site, he participated in the manufacture of plutonium.[2] Released from service three years later, he completed a bachelor's degree in chemistry and found employment with General Electric Laboratories in Richland, Washington, then under contract with the Hanford Atomic Energy Project. There, while working in the "controls" area processing uranium, his responsibility was "to make sure that there wasn't a Chernobyl."[3]

In 1949, with a growing awareness of his complicity in the war machine, Jess requested a leave of absence from Hanford, citing a desire to pursue a master's degree in chemistry at the California Institute of Technology. He headed instead for Berkeley, hoping to study in the university's art department. A professor there looked at his portfolio and encouraged him to apply to the California School of Fine Arts in San Francisco, then run by the ambitious curator Douglas MacAgy.[4] Jess soon became involved in the scene at Cal Arts, studying with MacAgy's new hires Edward Corbett, Elmer Bischoff, Clyfford Still, and Hassel Smith and befriending younger painters Brock Brockway, Harry Jacobus, Lyn Brown, and Lilly Fenichel. A self-styled "Sunday painter," he suddenly found himself in the company of artists engaged in their own Bay Area Renaissance.[5]

Jess's second encounter with Duncan was at 1350 Franklin Street, a run-down artists' flop known as "the Ghost House" where he rented a studio, as did Brock Brockway, who was then dating Duncan. The previous year's poetry reading was still fresh in Jess's mind because he had not only fallen in love with "The Venice Poem" but had fallen in love with Duncan himself.[6] Soon after their Ghost House meeting, Duncan began courting Jess, and, as a tribute to the beginning of their relationship, he began composing "The Song of the Borderguard." He later recalled, "In 1950, sitting in the studio of an artist with whom I was officially supposedly having an affair, but I was also sitting with a second artist with whom in between time I was sleeping...this poem may have been a little announcement, because the following year I was to live with the second artist and still do, for twenty years."[7] A loose translation of a poem by Jacques Prévert, "The Song of the Borderguard" conjured Jess in the image of a lion.[8] The poem also took inspiration from William Saroyan's short story "The Comic Page and Vital Statistics," in which Saroyan wrote:

> Beloved, you will live until the end: it is the tiger stalking through the night, sometimes with hate and sometimes with love: the dime squandered, the smile wasted: months and months ago.

> And I mean the heart's road: Agony Avenue: where the tiger is: lithe and supple, international.

> He turns his face from gloom of winter night to warmth of window light, and does not weep: the tiger stands before him in grace and purity, waiting for the groan or lamentation, and then they wrestle.[9]

Duncan responded to Saroyan's rhythms and subject matter, casting a spell toward the beginning of a marriage:

> I the guard because of my guitar
> believe. I am the certain guard,
> certain of the Beloved, certain of the Lion,
> certain of the Empire. I with my guitar.
> Dear, Dear, Dear, Dear, I sing.
> I, the Prize-Winner, the Poet on Guard.[10]

While visiting his mother during the Christmas holidays in 1950, Duncan decided that he and Jess should live together and that "this was the most important thing."[11] In January 1951, just after Duncan's thirty-second birthday, he and Jess took marriage vows, and Duncan moved into Jess's studio in the Ghost House. They began their domestic life together in a large, sunny renovated ballroom known as Studio 7. With limited amenities, the couple created a makeshift kitchen using an electric hot plate as a stove and shared a bathroom with the other inhabitants of the building.[12] The Ghost House, a long-standing gathering place for bohemians, is described in Rebecca Solnit's *Secret Exhibition* as "a decrepit, cavernous Gothic-Victorian ... whose three floors of rooms were rented out as studios and illegally inhabited by young writers and artists.... [Wally] Hedrick recalls it as a hangout conveniently located between North Beach and the Fillmore, a place where Thelonius Monk or Miles Davis might drop in, where drugs and parties were common."[13] Despite the wild atmosphere, the move and the beginning of the relationship with Jess cleared the way for Duncan to close doors on relationships that no longer felt emotionally satisfying. This newfound domesticity was not only appealing; it was essential to the development of his later writing projects. The physical and temporal boundaries of the household allowed both men to delve into complex creative projects that occupied their attentions for nearly forty years. As Hilde Burton recalled, "Duncan was all over the map [in the late 1940s]. Jess calmed him down, focused him."[14]

In the summer of 1951, when Jack Spicer returned to California after his father's death, he was disappointed to find that his Berkeley Renaissance comrades had dispersed. Ernst Kantorowicz had taken a position at Princeton, many of the Hearst Avenue writers had moved on, and Duncan was absorbed in his relationship with Jess. Duncan's attentions to his nascent household strained his friendships with Spicer and Blaser, but James Broughton recalled that the shift away from his Berkeley peers also had something to do with geographical distance: "They first lived together . . . on Franklin Street. . . . Robert who had discovered my children's poems was charmed and gave me a reading in their apartment and he did very amusing crayon invitations and set up a little throne in there. . . . He had local friends. Blaser and Spicer weren't there."[15]

As Duncan's East Bay relationships fell to the wayside, so did his academic pursuits. He half-heartedly continued German and art classes at Berkeley during the spring, but he withdrew from the school later that year, five credits short of his degree. Meanwhile, he was pulled in two other directions: first, toward the artists of Jess's circle, and second, toward the writers of the Black Mountain school. Brock Brockway had initially introduced Duncan to "the so-calld 'Drip' school of painting," and in correspondence with Josephine Freedman, Duncan wrote, that he had "pursued almost to exhaustion the adventure of seeing what is going on: Bischoff, Still, Edward Corbett, Hassel Smith, and Brockway—all demand one's eye."[16]

There were also forces of poetry that lured Duncan toward the East Coast and Europe. During 1952, his work was published in Cid Corman's *Origin* and in the *Black Mountain Review,* edited by a younger friend of Charles Olson's, Robert Creeley. Encouraged by Olson, Duncan and Creeley began corresponding that year. Creeley, then living in France, had his first glimpse of the San Francisco scene and of Duncan's work through Duncan's "An

African Elegy," whose ornate images immediately put him on the defensive: "So Charles [Olson] is reassuring me that it's really terrific. And I can't believe it, because that rhetoric is really displacing. And also I'm scared, not so much critical of, but I'm scared of his [Duncan's] homosexuality, that I'm going to be this square straight, which was not the problem at all, ever."[17] Notwithstanding Creeley's early hesitancies, the two writers launched into a correspondence laying the groundwork for what would later be dubbed the Black Mountain School of poetry.

After nearly a year in the Ghost House, Duncan, Jess, and their two cats, Princess and Kit Kat, moved to James Broughton's apartment at 1724 Baker Street when Broughton and his lover, Kermit Sheets, left for an extended trip to Europe. The move gave Duncan and Jess more privacy and more space, and they celebrated their new home by hosting a housewarming that doubled as a gallery opening, "with a show of Lyn Brown's paintings which filld the hall and three rooms with a plenitude of elegance."[18] During the time the couple lived on Baker Street, they turned the apartment into a salon for their coterie of poets and painters. By the end of 1952, they had transformed the place into a prototype of their later households: "Two walls in a hot tangerine orange, one wall in a soft orange-pink and one in white; ceiling in white; floor in what the paint company with poetic inspiration calls Bermuda blue; woodwork in white and gold; center medallion with canvases and smaller pieces: two Norris Embrys; the Virginia Admiral; three Lyn Browns; one Lilly Fenichel; three Jess Collins . . . and my big rug frame with my months long projected extravagant rug modeled after my crayon style. It is our Paris dateline 1927."[19]

In public, Duncan and Jess assumed contrary social roles. Jess was often painfully shy in groups, venturing into conversations selectively and sometimes retreating from the room. Mary Margaret Sloan recalled an event years later that indicated the intensity of her friend's social phobia. At a small dinner party, Sloan watched as the gathering became "more loud and animated" and "Jess was like a sea creature. He just pulled in his body. His head lowered. He stared at his plate . . . and went completely silent. . . . It was clear that he was protecting himself from energy that made him uncomfortable."[20] Duncan, in contrast, was frantic to fill the air with words: "I throw myself into the thick of any talk. If I keep a constant silly company, mere monkey that I am in this, I should become quite ill with silliness."[21] Before long, Jess had drawn up the parameters of the couple's guest list. Spicer, with his clumsy habits and morose countenance, was discouraged from visiting. Harry Jacobus, a close friend to Jess, was a regular, and other acquaintances were more selectively invited. Madeline Gleason and her lover, Barth Carpenter, took part in the Baker Street activities, as did Pauline Kael and her young daughter, Gina. The poet Philip Lamantia also sometimes visited in the company of Jaime de Angulo's daughter, Gui.[22]

Duncan meanwhile attended to Broughton's Centaur Press, tracking the inventories and sales of books by Madeline Gleason, Muriel Rukeyser, and Anaïs Nin. He also began two new projects of his own, a series of Stein derivations and a play called *Faust Foutu*. While Broughton was in London shooting one of his first films, *The Pleasure Garden,* Duncan engaged in an affectionate correspondence with him, referring to Broughton as his "little brother poet" and giving news of a ruckus in the household:

> I have imported Norris Embry who was in a state of collapse in the East and he is to stay with us until Spring; imported then is a bit of the *Third Man* Vienna and of the Dreigroschenoper Berlin. It means new paintings . . . these with as Jess says "the deadliest darks" nervous ruins of blood that shines like jewels in a carnal black drek. Norris has thoroughly known and seen one Europe; I wait for you to discover another Europe. . . . Norris is for me a meaningful and dramatic participant in failure; and I think of both of you [Broughton and Sheets] as meaningful and dramatic participants in success.[23]

Embry, a painter whom Duncan had first known in New York and Provincetown during the 1940s, became one of the models for the misfit character of Faust in the new play: "An opera in progress, a FAUST FOUTU, dedicated to Norris Embry, (Faust himself is compounded of Norris, Brock and Myself, if not other ingredients . . . and a bit of Broughton there will be mayhap) an opery for people who cannot sing (like myself)."[24] The "dramatic participant in failure" had arrived in San Francisco manifesting signs of serious mental illness. While Embry stayed at the Baker Street house periodically over the next two years, neither Jess nor Duncan had the emotional resources to manage his needs.

Around the time of Embry's first visit, Duncan signed on for a mind-bending experience of his own, volunteering for an Army Chemical Corps experiment during which he was given the hallucinogenic drug mescaline. Sponsored by two covert programs, Artichoke and MKULTRA, the tests were carried out in conjunction with the Central Intelligence Agency. The experimenters, Duncan recalled, said they were "looking for the development of schizophrenia disorder" and "they wanted to have a creative person and a non-creative person."[25] In an interview with Ekbert Faas, he described his experience: "What I saw was the world tree. It was also, however, a tree realized in jewels as well as being cosmic with lights."[26] Years later, Duncan spoke of a more humorous aspect of the experiment. Asked to write a poem while under the influence of the drug, he found himself unable even to use the tools presented to him:

> I knew that I was going to go through about eight sessions of tests with an electroencephalogram for my reactions . . . , and then . . . I would take mescaline. . . . I felt my body chemistry produced visions and images and words with a great deal of intensity . . . so I was superstitious about taking mescaline . . . they give me a paper . . . and they give a pencil, and the pencil floats . . . and I giggle, . . . and no poem comes.[27]

TWENTY-ONE

———

The Way to Shadow Garden

> I remember once at that period I thought this is so hopeless . . . I lay down in the street at the top of one of those hills . . . and stuck my feet out there with the mad idea . . . that a young woman would come along and run over my legs and she would be an heiress, and she would feel so sorry that this had happened that she would rescue me . . . and restore me to health and I would have a way to survive. . . . And I remember in the background . . . the fog horns, and there was a mist and everything. And I lay there for a long time and then I began to feel silly and then I got up and left. . . . But really that's how desperate it was, and Robert and Jess were what I had.   STAN BRAKHAGE
> in interview, 1998

STAN BRAKHAGE WAS NINETEEN YEARS old when he arrived in San Francisco in 1952. The previous year he had withdrawn from Dartmouth College after suffering a nervous breakdown two months into his first semester. Unsure that he would ever fit into a traditional academic community, he crossed the country and landed in the Bay Area, where he was introduced to Duncan and Jess by Kenneth Rexroth. Rexroth's home had long been a gathering place for younger writers, and Brakhage's high school classmate and fellow filmmaker Larry Jordan recalled that the San Francisco poetry community was generally a welcoming place: "We'd call people up and say, "Could we come over?" And they'd say, "Sure." And we'd go over see what they had to say and what they did and then we'd become involved. We'd have a film show and they'd come. . . . You sensed that everybody was very active and very creative and needed the support of the others."[1]

Brakhage was quick to make a move from Rexroth's circle to Duncan's. A chubby-faced youngster with eagle eyes, he captured the attention of both Duncan and Jess, and in 1953 he began living in their basement, where in exchange for room and board, he acted as the couple's "houseboy," cleaning the apartment and running errands.[2] His quarters were filled with James Broughton's painting collection and the Centaur Press inventory. The low-ceilinged alcove with a double door out to a garden became a playroom for his first experiments in filmmaking. Like Duncan, Brakhage had been adopted as an infant. Overweight and nearsighted, he was ridiculed by his peers throughout his adolescence. For the emotionally vulnerable young man, Baker Street became a fulfillment of a childhood fantasy of belonging, with Jess and Duncan taking the roles of surrogate parents. While Duncan spent his weekdays working as a typist in Berkeley, Jess, a decade older than the new boarder, spent afternoons drinking tea and eating gingersnaps with Brakhage and reading to him from the Oz books. For lunch, there was peanut butter bisque, a recipe Jess had found in *Gourmet* magazine.

Brakhage's attachment to the two older men was reciprocated. Duncan wrote to James Broughton that Brakhage had been "sent by Rexroth (no I mean delivered unto me, not 'sent' in the vulgar). . . . Brakhage is 'it.'"[3] Harry Jacobus visited almost every day, and Brakhage sat quietly and listened to the older men talk. Jacobus, like Jess, was painting abstract works, and at the time was experimenting with the oil crayons provided to the circle by Gui de Angulo. Such occasions fueled Brakhage's creative energies, and during one such visit, he had a revelation about nonrepresentational aesthetics:

> [Jacobus] came over and he put this painting down—it was like an assault. . . . so we all gathered around it and Jess said "hmm . . . well, there's your face." Well [Jacobus] got up and he tore the thing to pieces . . . and broke the wood and ripped the canvas and everything was so dramatic, and he stuck the whole thing in a trash bin and walked out. And that was when I first became aware that there was an ideal to not have any nameable thing . . . [in] Abstract Expressionism.[4]

Jacobus's work came to adorn the walls of Duncan and Jess's household over the years. His abstract paintings and crayon drawings, with eerie afterimages of background light, had a significant influence on Jess's early work, as well as on Brakhage's films. Brakhage turned toward filmmaking after Duncan discouraged him from continuing to write the novice poems that he brought to the elder poet for critique. But, in a letter to Duncan and Jess in the late 1950s, Brakhage also remembered the deeper emotional bond forged in the house: "The nostalgia for those warm afternoons of wonderment reading between cups of Oolong Tea in the orange room . . . and the evenings, the artichoke suppers, curried rice, the long table talks which would often last till bedtime (how often I've needed desperately the example of your creative energy, dear Robert, which used once to keep the clap-trap world of triviality beyond star's reach in an instant and hold it at bay well into my own night's sleep.)"[5]

With the household salon bursting at the seams, Duncan and Jess began a gallery venture in December 1952 with the help of Harry Jacobus. The King Ubu Gallery, at 3119 Fillmore Street, was a renovated garage with concrete floors and gutted walls and ceilings. It later became the Six Gallery of San Francisco Renaissance fame, where Allen Ginsberg gave the first public reading of his long poem "Howl." Duncan and Jess poured time and money into the project. With the help of benefactor William Roth of the Matson shipping company fortune, the Ubu curators managed the rent payments for the operation, but other expenses loomed, and Duncan told James Broughton, "Mailings, and openings, utilities and props eat into our monthly income and I am going to have to go to work again to keep things going well rather than poorly."[6]

In the long run, the effort paid off. The December 20 opening showcased works by Elmer Bischoff, Brock Brockway, Lyn Brown Brockway, Jess, Harry Jacobus, Claire Mahl, David Moore, David Park, Philip Roeber, Hassel Smith, Fred Snowden, James Weeks, and Miriam Hoffman. Exhibitions continued through December 1953 with several one-person shows for established and novice artists.[7] A precursor to the vibrant gallery scene of the mid-1950s, King Ubu was one of the first public venues to provide a view of paintings by the teachers and students Jess had met at the California School of Fine Arts. Along with Hassel Smith, Elmer Bischoff, and Edward Corbett, a host of younger painters displayed work at the gallery, including Norris Embry and Lilly Fenichel. Stan Brakhage was also involved, premiering two of his earliest films, *Interim* and *Unglassed Windows Cast a Terrible*

Reflection. Lyn Brown Brockway, who appeared in a group show alongside Jess and Harry Jacobus in April 1953, recalled the stir that the gallery created among Bay Area artists. While droves of middle-class Americans were moving to tidy new suburbs, young painters were challenging those aesthetics in the King Ubu:

> It was indeed very different from other galleries which were, and are, essentially businesses. I suppose each of us hoped to fill the place with his or her work and have the crowds standing in line to purchase [it]. But (that remote hope aside) I think our main excitement and pleasure were in seeing so many paintings and sculptures in one place instead of viewing them in the artists' usually cramped quarters. Paintings were hung whichever way the artist chose; nothing was hung in a straight, horizontal line at the King Ubu . . . and sculptures filled the floor. The idea of a casual and artist-involved gallery was certainly not new, but the King Ubu was the only one of that size and stature in San Francisco at the time.[8]

The gallery also facilitated a meeting between Duncan and Jess and a young couple from Southern California, Wallace and Shirley Berman, who visited both Baker Street and King Ubu during a 1953 trip to the Bay Area. Berman, soon to be a protagonist in the West Coast assemblage movement alongside George Herms and Bruce Conner, was born in 1926 in Staten Island, New York, and had moved to Southern California with his family during his childhood. In 1955, Berman began editing the eclectic mail-art magazine *Semina*.[9] For Jess, the relationship with Berman started a correspondence beyond his circle of San Francisco painters. The two shared a delight in collage, the art of found objects, and the art of the "salvage," all mainstays of Jess's later work.

With drafts of *Faust Foutu* still in progress, Duncan changed gears and began planning for a summer 1953 performance of Gertrude Stein's play *The Five Georges* at the Ubu Gallery, complete with his own contribution of "gorgeous crayon back drops."[10] Throughout the spring, his own series of Stein-derived poems filled a large laboratory notebook, a birthday gift from Jess. On alternating white and yellow pages of grid paper, he immersed himself in playful images and cadences, writing poems such as "1942, a Story", "A Fairy Play a Play," "Greatness, an Essay," "A Butter Machine," and "Smoking the Cigarette." He recalled later that the project became something of an obsession: "For a year, I wrote like Gertrude Stein. I wrote every day, and obliterated every possible trace of originality."[11] The poems, some of which appeared in the collections *Writing Writing* and *Derivations,* give insights into a style Duncan mastered early: "Now if we are in the evening of the world we are at home writing writing. Now if a history is beginning we are not beginning in history. Now if in Korea we hear there is continual killing, now if we rightly have no longer faith in our nations, now if we tire of futile decisions, we are at home among stranger relations."[12]

The Stein derivations led to another fruitful project: *Letters,* a series of pieces through which, in June 1953, Duncan began a correspondence with poet Denise Levertov. Levertov, then living in New York City, mistook Duncan's initial communication for a critique of her writing. The poem Duncan sent, later titled "For a Muse Ment" appeared in the *Black Mountain Review* in 1954.[13] Levertov remembered,

> Just about the time Cid Corman included some poems of Duncan's in *Origin* ('52) I received a communication from a San Francisco address signed only "R. D." It was a poem-letter that (I thought) attacked my work, apparently accusing it of brewing poems like "stinking coffee" in a "stained pot." When the letter spoke of "a great effort, straining, breaking up all the melodic line," I supposed the writer was complaining.[14]

Duncan subsequently explained to Levertov that he had written his poem in admiration, asserting that she, like Duncan, belonged in the company of "Marianne Moore—E. P.—Williams—H. D.—Stein—Zukofsky—Stevens—Perse—surrealist—dada."[15] With this clarification, the two began a correspondence that occupied them throughout the middle years of their careers. Meanwhile, Duncan's correspondence with James Broughton about the Centaur Press tapered off as he dedicated himself to the business of the Ubu Gallery. Throughout the summer, Stan Brakhage came and went and Duncan and Jess found a rhythm of social and creative life:

> The town for us is the Tylers and the Barkers with shots of Ruth Witt, Maddy and Barth, the Barys, Robin, a charming mauvaise little fellow by the name of Terzian. There are great undertakings: our famous scrapbooks—there is no way of explaining the giant dimensions of the project; and my wool rug which I work upon a very medieval seeming frame by the fireside; and our new Xmas aquarium with red and gold wagtails and black mollies and Siamese betas and a hysterical clowny inch or so of Brazilian catfish.[16]

Fall and winter saw another influx of creative energy to the Bay Area, with the arrival of composer Harry Partch and filmmaker Kenneth Anger. While

Duncan tried to wrap up the year quietly, spending a number of sunlit winter afternoons reading Virginia Woolf's diaries, visitors often interrupted his reveries. During a brief reprieve in late December, he recorded his thoughts about his upcoming thirty-fifth birthday: "I imagine fifteen years of some curious age between 35 and 50. 'The Ripening' and this another curiosity, a cultivation of that ripening."[17] After three years of married life with Jess, Duncan also noted the beginning of an emotional crisis, an instinct to rebel against the confines of the domestic and against "the damnd figments of the middle-class marriage—a sexual bargain and guarantee in bond for the security of sex."[18]

His distractions were the young and more than mildly attractive filmmakers Kenneth Anger and Stan Brakhage. The slender, dark-haired Anger, then in his mid-twenties, held a number of interests in common with Duncan and Jess. Raised in Southern California, he had entered the world of cinema as a child actor in Max Reinhardt's *Midsummer Night's Dream*.[19] In 1947, he completed his first major film, *Fireworks,* which presented a psychodramatic landscape of sadomasochistic homoerotic images previously unseen in cinema. Anger was also involved in the Order of the Temple of the East, the organization claiming descent from British satanist Aleister Crowley's legacy. Though Crowley had died in December 1947, the order continued to grow, with major satellite groups sprouting up in California. Jess and Duncan approached the black arts with caution, but they were open to Anger's work as a filmmaker and were pleased with his engagement in Victorian "fairy-lore." Stan Brakhage remembered that the couple issued social invitations to Anger with a certain wariness, as they "didn't like people leaving belongings or leaving talismans ... or sending little balls of hair in the mail."[20] Regardless, Anger added a new voice to the creative dynamics of Baker Street, collaborating with Jess and Brakhage on a film using Jess's 1951 collage *The Mouse's Tale* as a backdrop. Brakhage later recalled:

> There was a film that Kenneth made with my photographing a collage of Jess's that had cut outs of hundreds of male nudes that were ... from 19th Century engravings, [and] ... pin ups ... the only thing like it I've seen is Rodin's *Gates of Hell* ... and Kenneth ... photographed it through lit fires in an ashtray and I photographed it through the heat waves in those little matches, and we made a whole hundred feet.[21]

Throughout January of 1954, Duncan and Jess spent time with Anger and Partch as well as with the Baker Street regulars: Philip Lamantia, Gui de Angulo, Madeline Gleason, Barth Carpenter, Jack Spicer, James Keilty, and a new friend, the photographer Chester Kessler. After one outing to Lamantia's apartment, Duncan recorded in his notebook that he had encouraged Kenneth Anger to accompany him and Jess back to Baker Street, "cavalierly" creating "a rift of desire in the excitement."[22] Later that week, Anger took Jess and Duncan to Harry Partch's apartment, where Anger screened *Fireworks, Puce Moment, Aqua Barocco,* and the first sequence of an unfinished project, probably *Inauguration of the Pleasure Dome.*[23] When Norris Embry arrived in town on the evening of January 20, he too made his way to the Baker Street apartment, where he was greeted by a small roomful of friends that included Duncan, Jess, Partch, and Lamantia. A few days later, when Duncan's friends again gathered to smoke hashish at Lamantia's apartment, Duncan refrained from participating, caught up in an uncharacteristic wintertime ennui. He wrote in his notebook that the sexual overstimulation of Anger's new films, as well as Norris Embry's reappearance, had darkened his mood. By early March, Jess gave Embry an ultimatum alongside money for a bus ticket east, and Duncan penned a final verdict on his old friend: "Embry is a professional down-and-outer."[24]

Duncan's winter malaise also stemmed from the prospect of a long road of conventional employment. Throughout the early years of his marriage, he continued the work he had begun as a student at Berkeley: typing thesis manuscripts. Jess meanwhile found part-time employment as a medical laboratory technician, finally using his education in chemistry for something other than atomic research. At the end of March, the two sought a short reprieve from work: "Five days vacation . . . (with a splendid weekend with Harry [Jacobus] and the Barys; and then Carmel at Marie Short's) give just enuf of divine idleness to inspire a vague movement of ideas. All those contact points with the world of consciousness—things heard (Lou Harrison's afternoon at the Lowell House) . . . or seen (Jay DeFeo's paintings . . .) . . . or read (Malaparte's *The Skin*) are vivid enuf but must be stored away 'in the blood.'"[25]

For Duncan, the remainder of the spring brought bursts of creative activity amid social and economic obligations. He worked on the poems that would later appear in *Letters* and came closer to a final draft of *Faust Foutu.* The play had become infused with references to the recently ended Korean conflict, and as usual, his practice of writing was triggered by his practice of reading, which this time encompassed an odd assortment of texts by and about John Adams, Anton Webern, Ben Franklin, and Ezra Pound. Later Goethe's *Faust* joined the stack of books on his bedside table, and by the summer, he was diving into Olson's recently published *Maximus Poems I–X*.

TWENTY-TWO

The Workshop

> Prince of the world he is! At birth already he walks and talks pure poetry, addresses the stars as playmates, and sets up kings in imaginary realms, invents in a word the history of cities, gardens, peoples nations with likenesses, creates whole languages for speaking with himself or moontalk, devises cryptic pictures, makes animals dance, houses explode, banquets appear at his will or his wont. ROBERT DUNCAN, *Faust Foutu*

IN THE AUTUMN OF 1954, Duncan was offered a teaching position through San Francisco State's recently created Poetry Center. The center had been established that year with a grant from W. H. Auden and was first headed by Professor Ruth Witt-Diamant. Because Duncan lacked academic credentials, Witt-Diamant also asked poet Norman McLeod, "a straight-line modernist," to sign on as a moderator for the weekly workshop held at the San Francisco Public Library.[1] Titled The Writing or Reading of Poetry, the class almost immediately presented a problem for Duncan: "I have had a deep dissatisfaction . . . with the course of this Poetry Workshop— amounting to an actual illness on several occasions, . . . the question mainly before us has been the possible success or failure of poems, whether and how we liked or disliked them."[2] In an attempt to reroute the group, Duncan created a rigid framework through which the students were asked to dissect poems. Structuring most of his later teaching ventures around such plans, he emphasized the idea of the poet as a technician rather than a connoisseur: "I propose . . . that we explore the rhythmic organization of a poem, beginning with technics [techniques] but I had better say physics.... beginning with the kinds of motion and levels of motion in poetic language: accentual, syllabic, by breath phrase, periodic, by repetition, development, variation, contradiction, disassociation, etc. That rime, meaning, images, color, texture, etc. should be considered as aspects of motion in a poem."[3]

The classes were attended by a disparate group of writers, including Jack Spicer, Helen Adam, Ida Hodes, Lawrence Fixel, Paul Cox, Jack Gilbert, Michael McClure, Jim Harmon, and occasionally Stan Brakhage. Brakhage recalled Helen Adam's appearance as the stuff of legend: "One night, very near the beginning of that workshop ... Helen Adam came with her sister and I'll never forget it because everyone took turns reading, ... and when it came to Helen Adam a storm came up and was flashing lightning outside the window, and it was very spectacular, and she cut loose with one of her witchy poems and she just completely charmed Robert with this, and everyone else."[4] Adam, born in Glasgow, Scotland, had arrived in the United States in 1939 with her mother, Isabella, and sister, Pat. She had published poetry since childhood and had been deemed a prodigy by Scottish newspapers.[5] The spirited, gangly woman, a decade Duncan's senior, came to serve as a curious mentor and friend, but Duncan also sought credit for "discovering" her. She imported to San Francisco the Scottish tradition of the Border ballad, and as James Broughton remembered, "Everybody fell under her spell when she started reciting in her Scottish dialect."[6] Border ballads, while referring primarily to the geographical border country of southern Scotland, also often delve into the psychological borders of existence, especially the otherworldly—ghost stories, tragic love affairs, and great catastrophes. For Duncan, Adam's creative influence was immediate. In October 1954, he wrote "A Third Piece for Helen Adam," opening with the lines

> An imaginary woman reads by her lamplight, inclining her head slightly, listening to the words as I write them: we are there, as the poem comes into existence—she and I—losing ourselves in the otherness of what is written.... The poem she is reading reaches her, reaches out to her—just so it reached out to me; or we, reading I but she is writing, listend and saw in hearing a layer murmuring existence of its own.[7]

A number of workshop attendees would soon join Duncan and Jess's inner circle. Ida Hodes, whom Duncan had met in Chicago during the early 1940s, was one of the first to enter the household.[8] Businesslike and hardworking, the Lithuanian Jewish immigrant became a surrogate older sister to the couple and was one of the few friends unaffected over the years by Duncan's tempers and Jess's banishments. Another notable student was a twenty-one-year-old Kansan named Michael McClure, whose relationship with Duncan had a slow start:

> I brought in poems . . . like . . . perfect Petrarchan sonnets in the style of Milton. Villanelles in the manner of "Do Not Go Gentle Into That Good Night" . . . with perfect metrics, perfect rhymes. Robert was astonished and dismayed. . . . It was at least a couple meetings of the class before I brought in what I'd been writing before that: pictographic, in a sense post–William Carlos Williams, post–Ezra Pound poetry by way of the entire Modernist movement. . . . Robert was greatly relieved. . . . Then he really warmed to me.[9]

McClure and his wife, Joanna, began visiting Baker Street, in the process beginning a lifelong friendship with Stan Brakhage: "On . . . perhaps my first visit to Robert and Jess's San Francisco flat . . . , Stan came upstairs [from his basement room] to visit. . . . Stan is the same age as I am, within a few months, and also as I am, Kansas born. When I saw his huge head with dark, tousled hair and intense eyes that were simultaneously focused and staring, I recognized a kindred spirit."[10]

That fall Duncan also collaborated with Brakhage and Jess on the film *In Between*—a portrait of Jess, with brief appearances by Duncan and the household cats Pumpkin, Princess, and Kit Kat. Filmed in color, *In Between* presented images of Jess, first in various rooms at Baker Street and then outdoors in the bright sunlight of a San Francisco afternoon, running across a lawn dancing with his own shadow. Unlike Brakhage's early black-and-white psychodramas, the film captured the playfulness and attentions to magic that were integral to Jess and Duncan's early household, with images of cats in shadows and dappled sunlight, and with Jess's face variously reflecting curious glee and startled excitement at happenings just outside the camera's view.[11]

Brakhage, given free range at Baker Street, remembered visits from high school friends, including James Tenney and Larry Jordan, which transformed the basement into a crash pad for teenagers amid James Broughton's treasured collection of paintings by Clyfford Still and Hassel Smith. He also remembered a sadder event that occurred there during the late fall of 1954. By Brakhage's account, Duncan came down to the basement one afternoon, climbed into bed beside him, and began masturbating, saying to his startled protégé, "This is the way little boys do it." That evening Jess asked Brakhage to move out, implying that it was time for him to "leave the nest."[12] Effectively, it was the end of their friendship. While Brakhage remained emotionally and aesthetically attached to his mentors, at times with a nearly pathological devotion, Duncan and Jess distanced themselves, often criticizing Brakhage and his work with an equally pathological cruelty. The twenty-one-year-old packed his bags and headed for New York, with Larry Jordan following some months later. The trauma of the move was at least balanced by new opportunities, and as Jordan later recalled, "Stan and I shared a cold water flat near the Bowery in New York. But when I first arrived there, we were homeless, so Maya Deren, whom Stan had sought out, let us sleep on couches in her Greenwich Village studio. We paid her by filming a Haitian wedding she was in charge of. We hung out with Willard Maas and Marie Menken sometimes, and we also met Joseph Cornell."[13] In December 1954, Brakhage sent a postcard to Jess, pleading for a response: "Even in the midst of all this excitement, I miss you and Robert very much. To me, those months of living with you two were like a continual celebration."[14]

Brakhage's departure coincided with the busy advent year of the Poetry Center as well as the opening of the Six Gallery in the former King Ubu space. Duncan chose this venue to debut his play *Faust Foutu,* holding rehearsals through the fall and recruiting friends and students to participate. In what became a collaborative theater experience, each actor sounded out a role during rehearsals as Duncan revised and expanded the text. Ida Hodes, who played Marguerite in the production, later reflected to Duncan upon his working process:

> At the end I did understand what you wanted—but you had not said enough about what you wanted before then—and in a way that was good because it was in the nature of an experiment to say "here is one of my songs—sing it" and I believe you were really pleased with the total response to such a request. I think, Robert, that it would have been impossible for you not to have a "plan" . . . for *Faust* . . . —but . . . you also wanted even more a creative participation—and that made it exciting for all of us.[15]

The play premiered on January 20, 1955. Billed as a comic masque, it unfolded as a satire about bohemian culture during the Cold War, charting the aesthetic and sexual confusions of a painter named Faust, played by Larry Jordan. The cast also included Helen Adam, Michael McClure, Jack Spicer, Ida Hodes, Fred Snowden, Yvonne Fair, Jody James, James Keilty, and Harry

Jacobus, with Duncan and Jess making appearances as well. Michael Mc-Clure described the first performance:

> We all sat at a long table on a little dais in the large room. Self-consciously, . . . we belted out and mumbled and sang the play. Poet Spicer leaned towards the audience with his harsh voice and boyishly innocent but leering expression. Jess spoke . . . with the immense clarity and irony that we see in his collages. Faust chanted out his songs with loud, untrained voice. The whole event was held together with the thread of Duncan's presence. . . . When it ended, Duncan, trembling and cock-eyed with pleasure stood up, took off his pants and showed the nakedness of the poet. All of us knew we'd done something outrageous, something that took a little courage in the silent, cold gray, . . . chill fifties of suburban tract homes, crew cuts, war machines, and censorship.[16]

Duncan's exhibitionism was noted by a young poet present named Allen Ginsberg, who recorded in his journal what he considered to be the high point of the performance: "He took off his shirt declaiming, 'This is my body' before the audience."[17] The following year, when faced with a heckler at a reading in Los Angeles, Ginsberg disrobed and shouted, "A poet always stands naked before the world!"[18]

TWENTY-THREE

Mallorca

> Often I remember our conversation one morning riding . . . on the bus with you and Jess to Palma from Banalbufar. I listened very carefully . . . ; you were asserting that I too could hope to be usefully employed, for a reasonable income . . . —well, of course I could not believe it. ROBERT CREELEY TO ROBERT DUNCAN, 8 December 1956

ON MARCH 3, 1955, Robert Duncan was issued his first passport. The brown-haired, gray-eyed, five-foot-ten San Franciscan listed his occupation as "writer," and the laminated photograph showed him dressed in a dark suit, a grin creeping across his chubby face and waves of tousled hair styled over his broad forehead. The passport arrived in time for a springtime adventure in Europe with Jess—something of a delayed honeymoon, Duncan wrote to the Cooneys, "The last four years have been very happy ones for me—life sometimes gives us what we little deserve. And then I think I like being thirty-six more than I ever did being twenty-six."[1] The couple packed up the Baker Street house and left Kit Kat and Pumpkin in the care of Michael and Joanna McClure, and Princess with Ida Hodes. The goals of the trip were threefold: to escape the bustle of the San Francisco poetry scene, to see the sights of Europe, and to meet Robert Creeley, who was living on the Spanish island of Mallorca.

For Duncan, a transition toward Black Mountain school aesthetics began in his correspondence with Olson and continued through his meeting with Creeley that spring. The key Black Mountain poets—Olson, Creeley, Duncan, and Denise Levertov—came to form an incongruous company. Olson and Creeley, Harvard-educated New Englanders, stood in stark opposition to the "never-graduated," theosophically raised Californian, Duncan. British-born Denise Levertov, who never stepped foot on the Black Mountain College campus, brought her own exotic preoccupations: a mix of Christian and Jewish mysticism inherited from her rabbi-turned-Christian father, as well as an economic use of line and image redolent of Williams and the objectivists.

Creeley, born in Arlington, Massachusetts, in 1926, was raised by his widowed mother, an aunt, and an older sister. By his midtwenties, he had attended and dropped out of Harvard University, served in the Second World War, married, had three children, worked as a pigeon breeder, and lived in France and Spain. In 1950, he began corresponding with Charles Olson, and from 1954 through 1957, he edited the *Black Mountain Review.* In 1952, the year he began his correspondence with Duncan, his first book, *Le Fou,* was published. The friendship between Duncan and Creeley had a timid start, but by the time the two met in Mallorca, they were on the way to a rich companionship that saw few interruptions between 1955 and Duncan's death in 1988.

Duncan, Jess, and Harry Jacobus left San Francisco in February 1955, first traveling by car to the East Coast and spending three weeks there. They started the trip with the idea of "looking at things."[2] Neither Jess nor Duncan drove, which made it easier to do just that. With Harry Jacobus at the wheel, the group went first to Black Mountain College near Asheville, North Carolina. They found the school in a state of disrepair. As Jacobus recalled, "It was the first hippie place I'd ever seen, with no discipline at all. I was just amazed."[3] Duncan remembered other details of the visit years later:

It was already dark by the time we got to Asheville . . . and phoned Charles. . . . When at last we made our way to the College, driving over doubtful roads through the derelict grounds of the "old campus," which had been sold to a Summer Camp, it was nine or so. The place was frozen in, and there were no students. . . . It was a night of high intellectual excitement; we drank and talked after dinner and then, at midnight or one in the morning, under a sky blazing with stars, we were out with Charles on the way to the "Gropius" building, stopping to give Olson's stranded car a heave-to to get the dead battery to turn over. Then . . . Charles read *O'Ryan* to Jess and me as we huddled in the cold of our guest quarters.[4]

After camping out on the floor of one of the campus's semiabandoned buildings, the trio made their way to New York City. There they stayed with Stan Brakhage. Relations between Duncan and Brakhage had been strained since Duncan's clumsy attempt to seduce the young filmmaker, but Brakhage was happy to host his mentors in his downtown apartment and was eager to show Duncan and Jess his new film *The Way to Shadow Garden*, shot in the basement at Baker Street. Jess meanwhile was more concerned with surviving the cacophony of New York, reporting to Ham and Mary Tyler, "We're living in primitive N.Y. style in a little apt. of Stan Brakhage's. A bit grim but not too bad. How life in the big city is real scary outside here on the streets."[5]

The visit also allowed Duncan and Jess to meet Denise Levertov and her husband, Mitch Goodman. Levertov was greatly impressed, soon sending a note to Duncan in Europe: "I've wanted to write ever since you left but I wished to write such a special kind of letter—something befitting the effect on me of your visit—that I put it off, to save for a special day."[6] Duncan's glimpse into a new community of writers and artists in New York was not enough to appease his old gripes with the "greater madness" of the city, but the brief visit at least gave him an opportunity to catch up with old friends. He likely visited Blanche and James Cooney in Woodstock, and he and Jess spent an afternoon with Virginia Admiral and her eleven-year-old son, Bobbie, at her loft on 14th Street.[7]

Leaving New York on March 8, Duncan, Jess, and Jacobus sailed to Lisbon, Portugal, and then traveled to Barcelona. Arriving on the island of Mallorca on March 22, they were greeted by the scrawny, goateed twenty-eight-year-old Creeley. Creeley took them to his typical Mallorcan "ranch-style" house, where he lived with his first wife, Ann, and their children, David, Thomas, and Charlotte. As Creeley and his guests sat around the fireplace that evening, the host, in "trying to emphasize to Robert some absolute confusion someone had had vis-a-vis something," said, "You know it's like one of those cross-eyed sons of bitches who can't get anything right." A pause ensued, and Duncan retorted, "You mean like me." Creeley's sheepish response, "Well, you know, one-eyed, whatever," was greeted by laughter.[8] A more substantial tension arose in Duncan and Jess's relationship with Ann Creeley, as Duncan confided to Denise Levertov: "Bob we both liked very much indeed. . . . But . . . she isn't really likeable. She is embitterd—and while one can piece together why—what has that to do with it as Jess says. Plenty of unembitterd people have all the why in the world. And then she is, I am afraid, stupid."[9] Despite Duncan's hostility to his wife, or perhaps partly because of it, Creeley was delighted to have his visitors, as he later recalled in an interview with Ann Charters, "Things were very tight in my house and I was very relieved to see them. I liked Duncan in an instant. We took a trolley into the city to try to locate a pension for Duncan and Jess . . . , and I can remember . . . Robert looking at me and saying with that crazy smile, 'You're not interested in history, are you?' "[10] Duncan, pinpointing one of the differences between his work and Creeley's, nonetheless appreciated his younger peer's minimalist, emotion-driven aesthetics. In turn, Creeley, during his weeks with Duncan and Jess that spring, found the support he needed to propel himself away from his troubled marriage.

Meanwhile, the honeymooners stayed on Mallorca from March 1955 until February 1956, for the most part in Bañalbufar. Situated east of Spain in the Mediterranean, the island was as yet a fairly untouristed site, though it had served as a literary outpost for the likes of Robert Graves and Laura (Riding) Jackson. Graves had gone to Mallorca in the late 1920s on the recommendation of Gertrude Stein, and he wrote of his time there in a memoir: "I chose Deya, a small fishing and olive-producing village on the mountainous north-west coast of the island . . . where I found everything I wanted as a background to my work as a writer: sun, sea, mountains, spring-water, shady trees, no politics, and a few civilized luxuries such as electric light and a bus service to Palma, the capital."[11] Duncan and Jess likewise found that the atmosphere of Bañalbufar was conducive to their work: for Jess, a series of collages and paintings; and for Duncan, writings for *Letters* and *Caesar's Gate*. The island's landscape consumed their imaginations. High cliffs overlooking the sea shadowed Bañalbufar's cathedrals and the ruins of medieval walls and towers. Its marketplaces overflowed with seafood, olives, saffron, and local wines. Living on an allowance from Duncan's mother, the couple settled into an eight-room apartment once inhabited by the Creeleys, paying ten dollars a month—high by the standards of the region but ideal for Duncan and Jess. The space felt palatial, including a kitchen with a fireplace, dining room, living room, bedroom, and work studio all laid out in a railroad-style flat. Another common room at the end of a long hall provided a balcony view of the ocean through an arched doorway, a regular feature of Mallorcan architecture.

Duncan and Jess's correspondence with friends and family back home reflected the leisure they enjoyed in Mallorca. They swam every day, Jess painted, and Duncan spent long hours reading. The texts that later influenced the poems of *The Opening of the Field* filled Duncan's bookshelves in the Bañalbufar flat. When he began translating Cocteau's writings that spring, he mused in a notebook about "a period of virulent contagions, fevers of Blake; and the closeness of Cocteau's journals to my own designs. . . . But to give my vices a world in which to flower, and a universe for my demons to walk by night is a virtue of writing at all."[12] The haunted island atmosphere also played a role in directing his reading choices. Helen Adam sent books by Scottish fantasy writer George MacDonald, Bram Stoker's *Dracula* was a favorite for postdusk candlelit reading, and John Livingston Lowes's *The Road to Xanadu* became, as Duncan reported to Robin Blaser, his bible.[13]

Duncan also had an opportunity to think about the more immediate creative influences he had left behind in the Bay Area. His frequent letters to Helen Adam were filled with insights into his poetics: "That we found you all—the Adam family such a special revelation. It is the kinship one feels with those however and wherever that live in an enchantment of the imagination—antiques, we are, of the 19th century? It is this that I admire in the surrealists: the powers of the word rather than the power of the word. I reach for the distinction."[14] His notebooks from that summer contain a series of ballads for Helen Adam alongside a final wave of Stein derivations. In May and June, while struggling to make sense of the Spanish conversations around him, Duncan also started an essay, "Poetry Before Language," reflecting upon the mythophysiological origins of speech.[15] In a note to James Broughton, he exclaimed, "We have a splendid piso, which we furnished and are beginning to be at home in. But O Spanish—how did I ever learn English!" and to Denise Levertov he admitted the near panic he felt when out of his element: "My notebooks are becoming deformd by the 'ideas' which ordinarily I throw into talk, invaluable talk for a head like mine that no wastebasket could keep clear for a poem. I can more than understand dear old Coleridge who grew up to be a boring machine of talk. . . . And, isolated from the city of idle chatter, here, my head fills up, painfully, with insistent IMPORTANT things-to-say. I toss at night, spring out of bed to sit for hours, crouchd over a candle, writing out—ideas, ideas, ideas."[16]

Duncan did find one English speaker to descend upon that summer. Los Angeles painter John Altoon lived nearby, coming to Duncan and Jess with an introduction from the Creeleys. Altoon, the son of working-class Armenian parents, found himself on one occasion treated to a lecture on "the authority and magnificence of the Armenian empire." Robert Creeley remembered, "It took [Duncan] about two hours plus to do it, but it was just incredible . . . and [Altoon] was dazzled."[17] Altoon and Jess also settled into a friendship, finding common ground through their work. After the couple visited Altoon's Mallorcan studio, Duncan reported to James Broughton that Jess had been inspired to begin "a new phase of non-objective canvasses, the first in two years."[18]

For Jess, Europe provided inspiration in other forms as well. A June trip to Barcelona included stops at the Museum of Catalan Art and several architectural sites. While the journey began with confusing boat schedules and third-class tickets that left Duncan and Jess on the deck in the rain, they arrived in the city ready to be enchanted. The Oz-like works of architect Antoni Gaudi dotted a horizon "filld with wonders . . . with storybook fantasies of color and strange forms, grottoes, hanging terraces, arcades, dragon fountains, and little houses at the gate out of Grimm's world."[19] Jess's 1955 collage works, haunted with ornate objects stacked precariously on the sides of cliffs, point to the influence of those Spanish cityscapes.

TWENTY-FOUR

Caesar's Gate

Summer verano summer verano summer verano.
Using words from what we heard.
A little frog is a rano pequeno.

ROBERT DUNCAN, "Another ido"

ON JUNE 26, back from Barcelona, Duncan reported to Ida Hodes that he and Jess had acquired two overactive kittens, Billy and Jeoffry, offspring of a black cat belonging to the Creeleys. Hodes, who had been doting over Jess and Duncan's other black cat, Princess, responded with several letters about pet activities in San Francisco, including Princess's traumatic trip to the veterinarian after swallowing a long piece of string. Relieved that Princess had survived the ordeal, Duncan turned to writing a small book called *Ballads for Helen Adam,* which he soon abandoned for another project, *Caesar's Gate.* The limited-edition book was published by Creeley's Divers Press in the fall of 1955. It included poems Duncan had written between 1949 and 1950, a series of collages by Jess, and another layer of poems composed during the collaboration. Duncan told Helen Adam,

> The marvelous outcome is a bit of home magic. For the thirteen collages are to be a book, dispersed like the leaves of a book among thirteen holders. Once it leaves my pen and Jess's scissors and paste-pot it will come into being as it falls apart. I shall keep no copies of the poems any more than Jess can keep a copy of his collages. But the numberd copies . . . will give the sequence of the scenes. This whole mystery has made for a most excited period of work. Indeed, I have written with the sense that I too in writing am about a hidden other work that must go like seeds from the pod . . . where it is wanted.[1]

Duncan's reading practices that summer also became a grand collage. He would draw what he needed from a text, sometimes at random, and then move on to the next adventure.[2] His Mallorca notebooks are filled with passages from the multivolume *Zohar,* a work of Jewish mysticism explicating the secrets of the Old Testament, and from Darwin's *On the Origin of the Species.* Reading lists document his other scholarly explorations: "George

MacDonald *Lilith,* H. D. *By Avon River,* Shakespeare *Troilus and Cressida,* Dodds *The Greeks and the Irrational,* Emerson *On Dreams,* Freud *Civilization and Its Discontents,* Cassirer *Essay on Man,* Laura Riding *A Progress of Stories,* Blake *Songs of Innocence and Experience,* Bergson *Creative Evolution,* Sapir *Language,* Nijinsky *Diary,* Ibsen *Peer Gynt,* Jane Harrison *Themis,* Dorothy Richardson *Pilgrimage.*"[3] Sifting through the materials at hand, he arrived at thoughts about his process as a writer, confiding to Helen Adam,

> This "romantic" view that poetry comes by an inspiration, a visiting genius that may return or no—is a part-truth. . . . Another part-truth is that poetry is a practice, a love: and that one's own love for the language, one's own ardor ebbs and flows. . . . This word "practice" (which Charles Olson used in a letter to me recently) calls up the sense that just as one practices the arts of magic or medicine; so in poetry one practices life. Then there is another life—not just that poetry refers to it but that poetry is the practice of it. One of the ways of coming alive. Surely it would be wonderful enough if what Christ meant when he said "I am the Resurrection and the Life" were just this—this coming alive. Which we are all calld to by so many things: by cats, by the light in a window seat, by the disturbance of distances in views of the city, by moments of friendship.[4]

Disturbing Duncan and Jess's creative reveries were more conflicted aspects of the stay in Mallorca. While President Eisenhower was deploying U-2 spy planes over the Soviet Union, the couple was likewise watching activities in the Creeley household from a distance, including the development of an affair between Ann Creeley and a visiting Black Mountain College student named Victor Kalos. Duncan noted, "It becomes clear . . . with Kalos that we are in an untenable position in extending our hospitality. And I want the fortitude to practice the abruptness needed and long overdue. To announce as Stein had the character to do that she rescinded her invitation. As Pound was turned away after having been invited to dinner."[5]

A meeting with Robert Graves also proved uninspiring, as Robert Creeley recalled in a nostalgic letter to Duncan during the 1960s: "I thought of ourselves back in Mallorca, that time you and I went up to see him [Graves]—and you asked about Laura Riding, and also what he was reading—and G[raves] answered that he found very little of interest, to which I remember you saying, 'oh I find a lot, in fact anything that's written.'"[6]

When Kenneth Anger arrived from Paris on July 10, Duncan and Jess were happy to have familiar company. On the same day, Creeley departed for the United States, leaving his wife and children behind. Duncan limited his contact with Ann Creeley after her husband's departure, replacing that turmoil with the less complicated community afforded by Anger's visit. He delineated the pleasures of their midsummer household in a letter to Helen Adam:

> In the dark of night there is no breeze. Great moths flutter about our light and a chorus of cricket, mosquito and beetle has replaced the lusty orchestra of frogs of May and June. On such a night . . . we talk of Dracula, of cat and wolf ghosts, of the dead in Homer lapping at the blood-filled fosse. I read the strange section from Smart's *Jubilate Agno* about man's regaining his horns—ending "God be gracious this day to bees and beeves—" it is just such an evening for contemplation of the cauld that now by lamplight (electricity goes off on Saturdays at midnight) while Jess lays out cards for a game of solitaire I take up my pen to converse with you.[7]

In other correspondence that July, Duncan rallied Ida Hodes and Denise Levertov to gather American subscribers to pay for the production of *Caesar's Gate*. Meanwhile, Jess turned out a large number of artworks between swimming sessions, sunbathing, and cooking Spanish curries. As of mid-September, he had completed twenty-eight oil paintings, including *Electric Powerhouse in Bañalbufar* and *The Nasturtium That Dissolved the World (Imaginary Portrait #13: Denise Levertov)*.[8]

With Kenneth Anger in tow, the couple returned to Barcelona in early August. Duncan shared with Olson his assessment of "the Catalan romanesque frescos and sculptures," in the process deepening his evaluation of the relationships between poetry, history, and architecture:

> The epiphany (mine) is that just here a complex iconography (where all images are signs) is brought into a complex plastic knowledge (where the two dimensions of the fresco, and the symbolic many dimensions of what is represented, and the three dimensions of the architecture . . . provide spatial counterpoints with the advancing and recedings of forms and colors). You see at a glance a created space, which being drawn, draws. And—the exhilaration of the maker is so keen—see the created time of a poem and that as the plastic feeling be complex there, then needs—for this exhilaration—a like wise complex iconography. Wherever the spatial knowledge does not exist, the iconography does not exist.[9]

In correspondence with Levertov, he returned to another question about his poetics, spurred by his readings of Darwin: "What if poetry were not some realm of personal accomplishment, open field day race for critics to judge, or animal breeding show— . . . but a record of what we are, like the record of what the earth is is left in the rocks, [is] left in the language? Then what do we know of poetry . . . compared to this geology? and how silly we must look criticizing . . . as if geologists were to criticize rather than read their remains."[10]

Duncan's ongoing dialogues with Olson and Levertov served as the foundation from which his theories of poetics would mature. At the same time, as he and Jess made plans to visit Paris, important literary connections were being forged back in San Francisco. In August 1955, Allen Ginsberg met Lawrence Ferlinghetti, who two years earlier had founded City Lights bookstore, fast becoming a haven for the poets of the San Francisco Renaissance. Ferlinghetti would soon publish Ginsberg's collection *Howl and Other Poems,* and on Friday, October 7, Ginsberg read the title poem of the collection at the Six Gallery to an audience that included Jack Kerouac, Gregory Corso, and Kenneth Rexroth. A postcard advertisement for the reading, written by Ginsberg, read in part, "All sharp new straightforward writing— remarkable collection of angels on one stage reading their poetry. No charge, small collection for wine and postcards. Charming event."[11]

Neither Jack Spicer nor Duncan was in town for the reading that marked the beginning of the San Francisco Renaissance. Spicer had been in New York that autumn, and in late October, he was en route to Boston to visit another recent East Coast transplant, Robin Blaser. Duncan and Jess were meanwhile making plans to visit Paris, but the importance of the Six Gallery reading was not lost on Duncan. He reflected later to Robin Blaser, "Well, Ginsberg's *HOWL* is the San Francisco poem of all poems for 1955–6. When we were in Majorca everybody from San Francisco writing was affected by it."[12] Events at the Poetry Center further heated up the San Francisco poetry scene, as Ida Hodes reported to Jess and Duncan:

> The Poetry Center readings at the Telegraph Hill Community House have been tremendously attended. Rexroth read last Sunday to an overflow crowd— much over a hundred people, and sold books too. . . . He read from the translations of *100 Japanese Poems,* and the *Spanish Exile Poems,* and then from the *Bestiary* which was delightful. City Lights is featuring Rexroth this week, a full window. Previously they did a window on Henry Miller, and very effective.[13]

On November 4, Duncan and Jess left Spain for France and England, aided by a two hundred dollar gift from Duncan's mother. Their first stop was Paris, where they helped James Broughton celebrate his birthday and delighted in a city they had both longed to visit. Duncan wrote to Mary Tyler from an apartment on the Rue du Chateau in the 14th arrondissement, "The traffic speeds along the great avenues, and cafes are busy with talk— one can find good talkers to compete with, the kind one even stops to listen to; the food is extraordinary (and we have not been able to have but one swank meal . . .)." [14] The two explored the Luxembourg Gardens, the museums, and the neighborhoods along the Seine. With an opportunity to reflect upon one of the European centers crucial to his studies of medieval history, Duncan told Ida Hodes in a late November letter that he had become aware of a compelling aspect of the city: "Paris devours itself—it is not just that the city is self-centerd but that it is ghoul haunted. If we ever wonderd why Poe with his ghoul haunted weirds seemd so very great to Baudelaire, or if we were to wonder now why Lovecraft is translated and admired here; it is because this city rests upon its cemeteries. And bookshops are filld with books of or on the dead, . . . books on the occult, on necromancy, or on dead empires."[15]

Duncan and Jess also met New Yorker Paul Blackburn, a translator and poet then studying at the University of Toulouse on a Fulbright scholarship. Having recently read and admired Blackburn's work in the *Black Mountain Review*, Duncan was eager to make his acquaintance. After celebrating New Year's Eve with Blackburn and his wife, Winifred, Duncan and Jess began the final leg of their yearlong exploration of Europe, on January 4 traveling north to London.

FOUR

The Opening of the Field

TWENTY-FIVE

The Meadow

O Lasting Sentence,
sentence after sentence I make in your image. In the feet that
measure the dance of my pages I hear cosmic intoxications of the
man I will be.

ROBERT DUNCAN, "The Structure of Rime I"

DURING HIS STAY IN ENGLAND in January of 1956, Duncan composed a poem that would serve as the entranceway to his first major book, *The Opening of the Field*. While it would later be known as "Often I Am Permitted to Return to a Meadow," the piece was initially titled "Having Been Enraged by John Davenport," a reference to an argument Duncan had with a literary critic "at the end of an evening at G. S. Fraser's over Pound."[1] Davenport was the victim of a Duncanian lambasting in later-deleted lines of the poem:

> The besotted man as if he were dead
> Strove against each one reading
> Life! Life! You do not bring me life
> Rubbish! Bosh! Miserable stuff.
> Stumbled the length of dim hall
> To blow out—No! No! No! Each
> Poor candle ...[2]

The Opening of the Field was a creative turning point for Duncan. It was the first book he conceived of as a discrete world, a microcosm in which each poem would be related through a series of interlocking themes. It was also the first collection in which most of the pieces would go substantially unrevised. In February, he sent fragments of the new meadow poem to Helen Adam, James Broughton, and Denise Levertov. In his letter to Broughton, composed en route to London's Natural History Museum, Duncan registered his excitement about the project: "So I shall have still another book before I go down to join the Sloth, Cave Bear and Dodo to leave whatever haunts of extinction among the fruitful surviving species."[3]

The poem that first appeared in letters to friends was published without emendation in Michael McClure and James Harmon's *Ark II/Moby I*:

> Often I am permitted to return to a meadow
> that is not mine, but is a made place
> —as if the mind made it up—a poem.
>
> Often I am permitted to return to a hall
> that is a made place, created by light
> wherefrom the shadows that are forms fall.
>
> Wherefrom fall all architectures I am
> I say are likenesses of the First Beloved
> Whose flowers are flames lit to the Lady.
>
> Often I am permitted to return to a poem
> where I too stirrd may burn however poor
> and turn my face to her shadowless door.[4]

Evolving out of his reading of the *Zohar* and his meditations on the process of writing, the poem, in its later revised form, became one of Duncan's best-known compositions.

The trip to England also brought fulfilling social encounters. Duncan and Jess visited with painter Kit Barker and his wife, Ilse, who were then living in West Sussex, and during a month of sightseeing in and around London, they met the young Scottish poet and medical doctor Gael Turnbull.[5] As in Paris, the world of art beckoned. In a wistful letter to the Tylers, Duncan described financial woes that scrapped a plan for more extensive travel: "Our romance with Europa is drawing to a close. . . . If we will never see Matisse at Vence, or Picasso at Antilles, or magnificent Italy— . . . we have gorged ourselves on museums of Paris and London."[6]

Leaving London on February 10, the couple again stopped briefly in Paris en route to Mallorca, staying with a friend of James Broughton's, painter Dan "Zev" Harris, in the 14th arrondissement.[7] As they began packing for home in late February, Duncan wrote to Ida Hodes complaining of the winter weather, and he and Jess fought off the cold during their last weeks in the Bañalbufar flat, huddled in bed reading to each other. The impending return to the United States at least came with the promise of employment. Ruth Witt-Diamant had invited Duncan to work at the Poetry Center in

San Francisco during the fall of 1956, and Duncan, tired of making do with meager economic resources, was quick to accept. At Charles Olson's request, he also agreed to teach at Black Mountain College during its final spring and summer semesters. He reported the details to the Tylers: "Olson offers a house for Jess and me, a food allowance and $115 month. Which means Jess can stay on until someone in S[an] F[rancisco] finds an apartment for us. . . . Black Mountain will be going to the very center of our activities. *Black Mountain Review* #6 is loaded with selections from my notebooks, an article on Olson's poetics, and a long poem by me; and with collages and selections from Morgenstern translations by Jess."[8]

Duncan and Jess flew to Lisbon on March 7, and ten days later Duncan boarded a flight to Boston. Jess stayed behind at the Francfort Hotel to arrange shipment of a large number of new paintings home to San Francisco. The couple had not spent more than a weekend apart during their first six years of marriage, and from opposite shores of the Atlantic, their written correspondence began. The missives spanned the next three decades, becoming their primary form of communication while Duncan was away on reading tours. It was, for both men, an important extension of their lives together, and the letters clearly delineate the dynamics of their relationship. Jess acted as householder, caretaker, and nurse, while Duncan took on more traditional head-of-household work, flying from city to city on business, bringing home paychecks, and occasionally having affairs while on the road.[9] During this first separation, Duncan reflected to Jess, "It seems strange indeed to be so far from you—not the space so much as the fact that it will be eighteen days. And I am haunted by your having only to *wait*—tho I hope the library and the zoo with sketchpad may furnish diversion. Bring me back some flamingos and I would like a rhinoceros and some baboons."[10]

In the interim, Duncan created diversions for himself, renewing his relationship with Berkeley peers Jack Spicer and Robin Blaser, who greeted him in Boston. Blaser, then employed at Harvard's Widener Library, had also procured work for Spicer at the Boston Public Library that winter. Spicer, after spending the summer and fall of 1955 in New York City, found the stay in the East to be trying. But for Duncan, the first days back on home soil in the company of his itinerant round table companions was a welcome reconvening, complete with "a session of ciggrette [sic] smoking and talking like an overwound up fast-motion tik-tok!"[11] Despite a storm that had shut down the city's subway system, Duncan also explored Boston, making his way through knee-deep snow to visit Harvard University's phonograph archive on March 20, where he listened to recordings by Ezra Pound, Yeats, William Carlos Williams, Marianne Moore, Vachel Lindsay, and Jean Cocteau.

From there he was off to Black Mountain, on March 22 flying to Washington, D.C., and then taking a bus to the warmer, wetter climes of Asheville, North Carolina. From Asheville, he hitchhiked the short distance to the grounds of the college, hidden in the Black and Craggy Mountain foothills. The return to the school that had once rejected him was an emotional victory. Olson had invited him to take Robert Creeley's place as a teacher, help boost the morale of the students, and assume some administrative duties. Painter Paul Alexander remembered the almost comic state of disrepair of campus facilities by 1956, including a library building "buried in briars, briar roses, blackberries, and weeds" where "the door was permanently ajar" and "there was no librarian."[12] Duncan's correspondence from the period relayed his appreciation for the solitude afforded by the school's low-enrollment end days. He told Jess that the living quarters were hospitable enough—a well-lit painting studio with a large bedroom attached—and he was quick to liven them up with a record player left behind by Robert Creeley.[13]

Because other senior faculty members were away for Easter, Olson asked Duncan to stay at the college for the opening of the spring semester.[14] Scrapping plans to go to New York, Duncan sent student Dan Rice in his stead to meet Jess on his early April return from Mallorca. While Rice assisted Jess in transporting luggage south to Black Mountain, Duncan indulged in rounds of martinis with students Tom Field, Paul Alexander, and Jerry van de Wiele.[15] As Alexander recalled, the new teacher ran at full speed from the start: "He arrived and initiated this incredible monologue which went on and on. Since there was no official school thing happening, it was more or less the three of us and him."[16]

When Jess joined Duncan that week, the students had even more to look forward to. Jess's stay at the college was brief, but while he was there, the couple's living space became a salon. Jess unrolled the paintings he had brought from Europe, Duncan provided gossip about the San Francisco poetry scene, and, as Tom Field recalled, their openly homosexual partnership was a source of wonder: "I had only been to bed with one guy, and I didn't know much about it, and it was a big hang up. I was sort of observing these two people and their lifestyle, because one knew they were gay and a married couple. My sexual experience had been jacking off with a guy once in high school, and I thought that was all there was."[17]

While students came and went from their quarters, Jess settled into a painting routine, and Duncan extended his energy in several directions, writing new poems, developing his teaching style, and engaging in collaborative playwriting and directing. He opened the semester with "An Introductory Proposition," a lecture that invoked Dante, Rilke, Cassirer, Pound, and the *Zohar*. In an April 4 notebook entry, he pointed toward the organizing theme for his teachings: "Dante in *De Vulgare Eloquentia* writes: 'what we call the vernacular speech is that which children are accustomed by those who are about them when they first begin to distinguish words . . .' In search of the makings of poetry we are going to turn back to the very seeds of language, back to that first beginning to distinguish words which is a beginning of newly distinguishing the world."[18] He later described the range of his classes to Black Mountain scholar Mary Emma Harris: "basic techniques in poetry, which was working out things. And I gave a lecture course in the ideas and the meaning of form. And in the summer, this course in *Illuminations* and a continuation of the basic [techniques]."[19] He also had the opportunity to teach a theater workshop with Wes Huss, an activity that led the two to plan further playwriting ventures when Huss and his family moved to Stinson Beach in the fall of 1956.

The workshops on basic techniques and the lecture class Ideas of the Meaning of Form laid the foundation for the teaching Duncan did throughout his career. Years later, those pedagogical preoccupations emerged as the groundwork for a core class called Basic Elements in the master of fine arts program at New College of California. Ideas of the Meaning of Form also came into the New College curriculum during the 1980s and eventually became the title of an essay in Duncan's *Fictive Certainties*. Of the Black Mountain "basic techniques" course, Duncan said:

> We met every morning in a seminar room . . . and I'd plug in the coffee and we'd have coffee all morning long. It might have met as early as 8 o'clock. I'd run around to get people and have to wake them up because they weren't used to having a morning class. . . . We dealt first with vowel sounds and took quite a long time with that. Then consonant clusters, and then we did syllables. . . . Perhaps thinking of the work Albers had done earlier at Black Mountain, my idea was to work with the materials of poetry, when a technique applies, and everything else would be their own account.[20]

Joseph Albers's ideas about painting indeed found their way into the language work with the students. Duncan's own nontraditional education fit well with the ethos of the Black Mountain community and the Bauhaus School before it. He told interviewer Mary Harris in 1971:

> Thinking about my class [on basic techniques] before I went to Black Mountain . . . I just had what would be anybody's idea of what Albers must have been doing. You knew that they [Albers's students] had color theory, and that they did a workshop sort of approach, and that they didn't aim at a finished painting. . . . I thought, "Well, that's absolutely right". . . . I think we had five weeks of just vowels . . . and . . . syllables. . . . Numbers enter into poetry as they do in all time things, measurements. But . . . [with] Albers. . . . it's not only the color, but it's the interrelationships of space and numbers.[21]

The seminar on the meaning of form centered not so much on the particulars of language as on the larger form that a poem might take. Duncan asked the students in the class to look at the formal structures of various texts, beginning with the Old Testament book of Genesis.[22] Out of the classroom conversations, he wove together early poems of his *Structure of Rime* series with its attention to ideas of "law" or form. "The Dance" and "The Law I Love Is Major Mover" were also penned at Black Mountain, incorporating directives for an audience of a few devoted apprentice writers:

> Responsibility is to keep
>   the ability to respond.
> The myriad of spiders' eyes that Rexroth saw
>   reflecting light
> are glamorless, are testimony
>   clear and true.
>
> The shaman sends himself
> the universe is filld with eyes then, intensities,
>   with intent,
>   outflowings of good or evil,
>   benemaledictions of the dead,
>
>   but
> the witness brings self up before the Law.[23]

The influence of master educator Ernst Kantorowicz was also evident in a statement Duncan made to his students at the beginning of the semester:

> In the morning meetings, . . . we will study tekniks [techniques]. From time to time, I will read short lectures either as introductions to the work at hand, as hypotheses arising from the work we have done, or as summaries of what

we have done. . . . We will be detectives not judges. . . . Week by week we will study . . . vowels, consonants, the structure of rime,—these are the elements of tone in writing both what we call poetry and what we call prose. Then three weeks on elements of movement, what is often calld "metrics." The syllable, the word, the phrase, the line, the paragraph, and the sentence. The seventh week you will . . . read and analyse *[sic]* for the group a passage of prose and one of poetry of your own choosing; and a poem and a prose piece which you have written. . . . In the evenings I will read a series of lectures as general as the morning studies will be particular; but I want these too to be bull-sessions . . . on the concerns of the writer or the painter, or the musician, or the actor: and above all our own concern with this thing calld FORM.[24]

Throughout the spring, Duncan and Olson ran their classes as oddly opposing forces, with Olson delivering sprawling late-night lectures alongside Duncan's early-morning seminars, guaranteeing that the students were sleep deprived and overstimulated. Duncan also gave late-afternoon lectures that frequently delved into the subjects of imagism and modernism.[25] Encouraged by the college's emphasis on theater, he continued work on *Faust Foutu,* mounting a performance for which composer Stefan Wolpe wrote musical settings. Two other Duncan plays, *Medea at Kolchis* and *The Origins of Old Son,* a farce lampooning Charles Olson, were also staged at Black Mountain during Duncan's tenure there. He recalled a unique form of collaboration spawned out of limited resources: "I could get a cast of six—more than six, since some would double in a performance . . . and there were just barely more people in the audience than there would be in the play. Out of it came the idea of having a play with everybody in it in the play, no audience at all."[26]

TWENTY-SIX

New York Interlude

UNCERTAIN ABOUT THE STATUS of Black Mountain's summer session, Duncan made a brief trip to New York in early May to search for work as a freelance typist. When he returned south to wait for a head count of remaining students, he recorded the small measure of domesticity he had achieved in North Carolina: "The black kitten, Mr. Rimbaud, sleeps under the spray of azalea. Lotta Lenya sings 'Surabaya Johnny' with seductive persistence. White surfaces of an enameled pot and a willow-patterned sugar bowl are cool in the May heat."[1] Meanwhile, Jess left for San Francisco, where he first stayed with Joanna and Michael McClure at 707 Scott Street and later found an apartment for himself and Duncan on Potrero Hill's De Haro Street.[2] Throughout the summer, Duncan longed for Jess's presence, sharing his thoughts about his teaching projects and their relationship in a flood of letters: "I've got a good deal of my poor soul all mixed up with yours and it makes me absent-hearted like absent-minded. Well, I find it delicious tho thinking about you like it used to be thinking about you before we finally started living together. And here we are 'living together'—there it is."[3]

Diverting himself from the pangs of separation, Duncan took advantage of his proximity to the East Coast. On Friday June 15, he drove with Charles Olson to Charlotte, North Carolina, where he boarded a bus for Philadelphia. There he met with novelist Michael Rumaker, a 1955 graduate of Black Mountain whose thesis project he had supervised. Rumaker recorded his initial face-to-face encounter with the elder poet in his memoir *Robert Duncan in San Francisco:* "The first thing of course, were his eyes, those curious and lovely eyes that looked at me, directly, while in the same instant, with hesitancy and vulnerability, looked around me and off to the sides. . . . Voluptuously plumpish, with a coxcomb of dark hair, he stepped into the room. Shy with each other at first, he began to talk, nonstop, generating energy for a dozen people, radiant with intelligence and enthusiasm . . . overwhelming, like a force of nature."[4]

After a morning spent entertaining Rumaker, Duncan went to the Philadelphia Museum of Art to revisit his favorite works by Miró, Braque, and Picasso.[5] He then moved on for a two-week stay in New York, setting up house at Virginia Admiral's loft on 14th Street and socializing with painter Lilly Fenichel, a colleague of Jess's at the California School of Fine Arts, as well as two New York painters, Grace Hartigan and Larry Rivers. Between those meetings there was another important engagement, a visit to his old haunt, the Museum of Modern Art.[6] On June 22, during a casual afternoon with Louis and Celia Zukofsky in Brooklyn, Duncan penned a long letter to Jess complaining about financial pressures and the irritations of New York. It was a hot, humid summer, and the city still reminded him of his divorce and tattered friendships from the mid-1940s. He also pined for every luxury that New York had to offer: "There was a delicious red and blue striped . . . cotton blazer what that I ogled this morning. And white cord hiking length shorts. And uptown beautiful silk and cotton shirts with a metallic sheen—and black silk suits. . . . And what an array of red, vermillion, orange, pink, yellow, ochre, olive drab . . . finery."[7]

Duncan had an opportunity to see an alternative community established by former faculty members of Black Mountain College when he was invited to the Stony Point Colony on the weekend of June 23 and 24. North of Manhattan in Rockland County, the cooperative housing project attracted a range of creative visitors and inhabitants, including potter and painter Mary Caroline (M.C.) Richards, John Cage, Merce Cunningham, Paul Williams, Karen Karnes, and David Tudor. Duncan told James Broughton that despite his ambivalence about New York, he saw something redemptive in its more bohemian residents: "It was pleasant because of a variety of people . . . —an evening with Lilly Fenichel, movies and dinners with Nik Cernovich (who printed *The Borderguard*) and a week-end at Stony Point with M.C. Richards and some time with John Cage whom I like very much—he inspires what shreds of art I have left for such climates."[8] Returning from Stony Point on a Sunday evening, Duncan dined with Lilly Fenichel at her apartment on West 13th Street.[9] The following night he had dinner with Virginia Admiral, and later that evening he met Donald Allen for the first time. Duncan described his new acquaintance to Jess only as "a friend of Robin's," though Allen, an editor with Grove Press, would soon establish the careers of many of the writers of Duncan's generation, particularly with the publication of the 1960 anthology *The New American Poetry*.[10]

At the end of June, with income from New York typing jobs in his pocket, Duncan made a short visit to Boston to see Robin Blaser and Jack Spicer, who were having a difficult summer. Blaser, then living with James Felts but hosting Spicer as well, reported to Duncan, "Jack isn't at all well here. The total absence of his admiring juniors leaves him pink and shell-like."[11] Duncan in turn told Jess of his increasing reservations about Spicer and his worries about potential intrusions into their San Francisco household: "Robin here plays nurse-maid and companion and Jack usurps all and more of the time given . . . It will be important to keep Jack in his place. The role he takes over in Robin's life makes that only too clear."[12] Spicer's deepening alcoholism, along with a certain feeling of rivalry toward Duncan, continued a deterioration that had begun soon after Duncan met Jess and that eventually ended their friendship in the early 1960s. Robin Blaser attempted to maintain a relationship with both of his old friends, occasionally acting as a mediator and enduring Spicer's demands on his time. He recalled in a 1992 interview,

"He could be terribly mean, in Boston . . . It was essentially one room. And everything had to be put away. This gorgeous couch. . . . Jack was staying there, and . . . he dumped red wine purposely on this gray silk couch, it was unbelievable. . . . And then he would leave his dirty socks under the couch."[13]

At the beginning of July, Duncan began "A Poem Beginning Slow," in which he reflected upon his relationship with Spicer and Blaser, as well as Jess's role in rescuing him from the dramas of his Berkeley years:

> tho the lamps strung among
> > shadowy foliage are there;
> tho all earlier ravishings,
> > raptures,
> happend, and sing melodies, moving thus
> > when I touch them;
>
> such sad lines they may have been
> that now thou hast lifted to gladness.[14]

While New York's heat and Spicer's moods lessened Duncan's enthusiasm for his summer travels, he nonetheless enjoyed spending time with Blaser and Jim Felts. After the Independence Day holiday with them, he returned to New York briefly and then crossed the Hudson to meet another Black Mountain School graduate and poet, Joel Oppenheimer. Oppenheimer and his wife were then living in Westfield, New Jersey, and as Duncan told Jess, "Joel and Sis . . . I like very much: so it was a pleasant last afternoon, sitting under shade trees with beers and chatting about books and people and telling jokes."[15]

Duncan returned to Black Mountain for a summer session that had been organized after much uncertainty. There were ten remaining students, including one new face, the New England poet John Wieners. Born in 1934, Wieners had attended Boston College and subsequently studied with Charles Olson. Duncan's first report of Wieners had come some months earlier in a letter from Robin Blaser: "When I . . . saw his apartment he had 'Song of the Borderguard' nailed to the wall and lines of Pound written on the paint with frames over each."[16]

The nearly abandoned campus was not at all lifeless that summer. Throughout July, the residents made the most of their time together. When former student Jonathan Williams visited with his new edition of Olson's *Maximus II,* the resulting reading and Bastille Day party left students and faculty alike with champagne hangovers. In San Francisco, Jess was looking for a job, while Duncan found himself overworked. Teaching five days a week, he reported home that he was never sure what would happen in the classroom: "The new course on 'content,' since I am making it up as we go along, is like a double-course for me. We started out by making up nonsense sentences; and then after selecting one particularly obscure one from each in the class writing 'explanations' of what they mean."[17] As the summer wore on, Duncan felt the strain of the distance from his household in San Francisco and the frenetic energy of Black Mountain. In early August, he again wrote to Jess, "Walking home just now down the hill from Jerry's [van de Wiele] . . . I was most entirely thinking of you with me, most entirely wishing on the full moon magic. After a day and yesterday too of depression, I suppose—of the crawling into bed and reading mood that when you are not actually here is a lonely looney retreat."[18] By mid-August, Duncan was having difficulty stretching his salary to pay for food, and his apartment had become infested with fleas. Finding some solace in evenings spent with two new friends, Don and Eloise Mixon, he began composing *Medea at Kolchis,* completing it in time for a late August performance on campus. He was pleased with his cast, telling Jess, "Wes [Huss] is playing Mrs. Garrow; Don [Mixon], Jason. A new student Eric [Weinberger] is playing the Doctor (who is Jason's guardian—and "soul" in some sense)—Eloise [Mixon] has a wonderful part for her as Edna Medea's aunt, all celtic twilight and romantic talk. The old man I am playing myself—wheezing and grunting, sighing and rattling on."[19] The August 28 and 29 performances of the play were the college's final events, though Duncan, Wes Huss, and the students made plans to regroup in San Francisco and form a theater company there.[20]

When Black Mountain closed its doors, its writers and artists headed for New York and San Francisco. A number of the young painters and writers who would form a community around the San Francisco Renaissance had first been educated at Black Mountain. At the end of the summer of 1956, Duncan looked forward to returning home. After a brief visit to Denise Levertov and Mitch Goodman in New York, he boarded an August 31 flight to San Francisco to be reunited with Jess after nearly three months of separation.

TWENTY-SEVEN

The San Francisco Scene

San Francisco is a part of a boat that is sinking, and I'm not the
kind of rat who gets out of a sinking boat.   ROBERT DUN-
CAN, "The History of the Poetry Center," 1976

WHILE DUNCAN WAS AT BLACK MOUNTAIN COLLEGE, the San
Francisco poetry community was in the midst of transformation. Through-
out the early part of 1956, Duncan had received reports from both Michael
McClure and Robert Creeley about events in his home city, but he may not
have been entirely prepared for what awaited him upon his return. As a
fledgling poet, he had always been at the center of activity: "There was only
one poet here when I came back in [19]42 briefly and that was Kenneth
Rexroth, and then there was Philip Lamantia and myself and Kenneth
Rexroth. And maybe I might get [William] Everson to want to live here and
that would be a handful of poets."[1] But by mid-1956, the city had blossomed
into a meeting place for writers from all parts of the country. Two former
Black Mountain College students, Leo Krikorian and Knute Stiles, opened
a bar called The Place in North Beach that served as an informal classroom
for Jack Spicer's protégés, and the Poetry Center and Lawrence Ferlinghet-
ti's City Lights Bookstore provided more official sites for poetry business.
During the spring, Robert Creeley had visited the Bay Area and met a num-
ber of writers, including Helen Adam and Allen Ginsberg. He subsequently
became one of the key emissaries between the Black Mountain School and
Beat Generation poets. Ginsberg's *Howl and Other Poems* was published
that year by City Lights, and Creeley liked the New Jersey poet, though he
was skeptical of some parts of "Howl," telling Duncan, "[Ginsberg] has a
quick intelligence but tends to exploit it, for sensations."[2]

With the influx of poets came an influx of turmoil, as Michael McClure
observed: "Creeley got to town—a very delightful person—Creeley stayed
(stays) drunk—Creeley joins Ginsberg, Kerouac, Whalen, Snyder, Neal Cas-
sady and stays drunk, high, etc. with them."[3] That spring Creeley began an

affair with Kenneth Rexroth's wife, Marthe, and the two fled for Taos, New Mexico, sending elder poet Rexroth into a rage. Having watched Creeley's first marriage crumble in Mallorca, Duncan was not surprised to see the pattern of romantic confusion continue, and in the end, he resigned himself to it: "In the last year Creeley has made many declarations of love; and started with each only to find the default."[4]

While Duncan acted as a hesitant advisor to his younger peer that year, his main concern upon returning to San Francisco was the storm of literary activity awaiting him in his new job as assistant director of San Francisco State's Poetry Center. Anxious at the prospect of bearing the brunt of Ruth Witt-Diamant's demands, Duncan entreated Ida Hodes to quit her job and join him as an office mate. Hodes willingly complied.[5] Duncan was responsible for arranging events, writing introductions to the weekly readings, and keeping track of the center's correspondence. Witt-Diamant meanwhile negotiated the difficult ground between the academy and the writers. While Madeline Gleason's poetry festivals of the late 1940s had been designed as a tribute to the modernist movement, the Poetry Center allowed an experimental aesthetic to emerge alongside more mainstream traditions. Ida Hodes remembered Witt-Diamant's complex role:

> Ruth in some ways liked to behave like a person who is really very proper but keeps breaking the rules. . . . She was a real individual. . . . She had I think many arguments with other faculty members . . . , that the poets never knew about . . . where she was really standing up and wanting the Poetry Center to go on. . . . It was a very strange path she had to walk on. . . . She [also] had all the poets, who hated her for just even being a professor, or thinking she could run the Poetry Center.[6]

For Duncan, the job soon became a burden, and he again realized that his creative life depended on the energy of individual households. With that in mind, he began seeking to rebuild his circle of friends in San Francisco. In October 1956, he wrote to Michael Rumaker encouraging him to come west and offering to make temporary housing arrangements for him. Rumaker arrived to find Duncan and Jess living "in a large comfortable apartment in a gray framed house on Potrero Hill, the old Russian section of the city. The walls were hung with paintings by Jess and others, and lined with bookshelves built by Jess. . . . In the bathroom you could read Jess's cutup and reassembled Dick Tracy comic strips, mounted on the wall over the toilet, while you pissed. The apartment was filled with an abundance and pleasant disorder of beloved objects."[7] Other younger writers were equally inspired by visits to De Haro Street. Michael and Joanna McClure were frequent guests and found a model for their own relationship and lifestyle in the older couple. When the McClures moved from their Scott Street abode to Fillmore Street in 1956, Duncan was on hand to carry boxes and Jess took part in the renovations, rewiring the electricity in the apartment. Michael McClure pointed out another crucial aspect of Duncan and Jess's presence in San Francisco:

> They actually set the styles for us . . . their style of living and the community that grew from the earlier anarchist bohemian tradition. . . . We were all very poor. It was quite a different world. It was an enjoyable poverty too, because, I recounted once . . . watching Robert and Jess make the first bouillabaisse I'd ever seen . . . —to make such a thing was a big affair. I'd never dreamed that such a thing existed. . . . To watch them take a squid and put saffron into it and do all this, and you had a party with your friends. . . . There was great vigor and involvement in things. But then what I'm calling poverty was actually very rich. Robert and Jess were living with less money than they actually had because much of what they had went into buying art from their friends.[8]

De Haro Street became a haven for Duncan after his long stretch of travels. That fall, he wrote to Denise Levertov, "Jess and I found the best apartment we have had yet. And both Kit Kat and Pumpkin are back with us; I have a beautiful little writing desk, made for writing letters—so perhaps I shall fulfill its promise."[9]

His plans for his own writing were, however, interrupted by the demands of work at the Poetry Center. In the midst of drafting new poems toward *The Opening of the Field,* he was forced to host poets whose work he disliked. When introducing Randall Jarrell's October 3, 1956, reading, Duncan presented a barbed review, noting the poet's relationship to the New Critics and announcing, "He has no obsessions: he has been trained in psychology and his poetry never yields to unreal convictions. . . . Jarrell is both a poet and a university professor. In the latter profession, of course, a divine madness is not an asset. Daemonic inspirations such as Yeats or Lawrence sought, or discomforting convictions such as Williams or Pound have been limited by, are not compatible with the responsibilities of teaching in the humanities."[10] The thinly veiled attack provoked an antagonistic encounter between Duncan and Jarrell after the reading, which James Broughton described in *Coming Unbuttoned:* "While I was driving Randall Jarrell back to his hotel after his reading, Jarrell snickeringly remarked that Edith Sitwell's verse was as desiccated as her pussy. Duncan, who was riding with us, shouted to me: 'Stop the car! I will not ride another mile with this despicable person!' He was adamant. I had to let him out at the next corner."[11]

On October 21, Allen Ginsberg and Gregory Corso took the Poetry Center stage. Duncan wrote another ambivalent introductory statement for the writers, focusing on the abstract ideals behind their work rather than the craft of their poems: "These new poets are gang-minded, taking poetry and the angels (but we discover the angels are of the gang) with them. They challenge, and rightly, all our personal, sexual, and cultural modesty. But what is Modesty if it not be challenged."[12]

The pressures of the scene also took their toll on Jess and the De Haro Street household, as Duncan told Denise Levertov that fall:

> Jess who is more seriously alarmed by public-mindedness than I am, and by the assaults of "brotherhood," threw Ginsberg and Peter [Orlovsky] out of the house when they came to see me, and made it clear that . . . we had both decided . . . that when I took the job . . . the household would be kept for friends. I do not believe that one can close one's doors to the demand . . . without a cost in closing doors to life: but I am willing to undertake the cost in homage to the household which I worship and draw from.[13]

While Duncan had crossed paths with Ginsberg in San Francisco in 1954, his return to the city in 1956 facilitated connections to other writers of the Beat Generation. During that year, Michael McClure escorted Jess and Duncan to meet Jack Kerouac at a Potrero Hill housing project.[14] Kerouac was spending most days in Mill Valley practicing meditation and writing a long poem-novel, *Old Angel Midnight.* Duncan described the encounter to Gerald Nicosia in 1978:

> Creeley was quite close to Kerouac, and so Kerouac was looking forward to meeting me because I'm very close to Creeley. It was a non-sequitur meeting. Kerouac was soused, so his eyes were slightly out of focus, and they tried to look deep into mine, and since I'm cross-eyed, he couldn't decide which eye to look deep into. I found the meeting humorous enough . . . because there was a little mercurial character about it. You can't really look deep into my eyes, so the "window of the soul" thing doesn't quite work; and . . . he had that sort of blurry look that a drunk has, and I'm not amused by drunken effusions.[15]

Kerouac meanwhile in his 1965 novel *Desolation Angels* portrayed Duncan as Geoffrey Donald, an elegant sad-weary type who's been in Europe to Ischia and Capri and such, known the rich elegant writers . . . and had just spoken for me to a New York publisher so I am surprised (first time I meet him) and we go out on that veranda to look at the scene. . . . I wonder as I lean with sad Donald . . . what he's thinking—suddenly I notice he's turned fullface around to stare at me a long serious stare, I look away, I can't take it—I don't know how to say or how to thank him.[16]

Another social nexus for Duncan was an apartment on Buchanan Street shared by Black Mountain graduates Michael Rumaker, Tom Field, and Paul Alexander. Alexander had arrived in San Francisco first, to be joined by Tom Field in the fall of 1956.[17] Field became Duncan's main point of interest in the household, and as Michael Rumaker remembered,

Tom always had a radiant tan, his hair streaked blonde from the sun. . . . Tom was a simple heart, his generosity and good-nature often taken advantage of. He could be quickly hurt, and as quickly to forgive. His abstract paintings at the time had a dense and lyrical richness. . . . You couldn't help but respond to his earthy warmth and humor.[18]

In Rumaker's account, after a dinner party in the Buchanan Street household one evening, Field asked his roommates to allow him privacy with Duncan. When Rumaker returned home after midnight, he found the two still engaged in lovemaking. Eager to get some sleep before the next day of work, Rumaker made his presence known, much to Duncan's annoyance. Gathering up his clothing, Duncan "had a few quiet words with Tom" before brushing past Rumaker in protest of the intrusion.[19]

The affair with Field set the stage for Duncan to carry out other infidelities in the periphery of Jess's vision. Rumaker, who had looked to Duncan as a role model in his own struggles as a gay man, later conjectured, "Duncan . . . had a very powerful sexual appetite. So he was always on the make. He was making, 'the maker'— . . . I think he was much more successful because he was . . . much more bold. . . . There are not a lot of people like that . . . That liveliness, that aliveness, of being erotically alive, imaginatively alive and poetically alive, and all the things he was—an extraordinary person. . . . He couldn't have been monogamous. It was not in his nature."[20]

TWENTY-EIGHT

Olson, Whitehead, and the Magic Workshop

A living occasion is characterized by a flash of novelty among the appetitions of its mental pole. ALFRED NORTH WHITE-HEAD, *Process and Reality*

THE 1956 SEASON AT THE POETRY CENTER ended with readings by Eve Triem, Landis Everson, Richard Wilbur, Madeline Gleason, and Brother Antoninus; and the poets of San Francisco had even more to look forward to the following year. In February, Jack Spicer began teaching a workshop called Poetry as Magic at the San Francisco Public Library. The fifteen-week class was sponsored by the Poetry Center, and Duncan was a participant along with Helen Adam, Joe Dunn, Jack Gilbert, George Stanley, Sue Rosen, Robert Connor, and Joseph Kostolefsky. Spicer told his prospective students, "This is not a course in technique or 'how to write.' It will be a group exploration of the practices of the new magical school of poetry which is best represented in the work of Lorca, Artaud, Charles Olson and Robert Duncan."[1]

With a penchant for mischief, Spicer created an atmosphere in which the students were forced to reevaluate their suppositions about magic. Robin Blaser recalled, "Everyone sat around a round wooden table and Jack always sat in the East looking West. . . . Magic, it became clear, was a matter of disturbance, entrance and passion, rather than abracadabra."[2] In the first session, Spicer asked his students to fill out a questionnaire with inquiries such as "What is your favorite political song?" and "What animal do you most resemble?" He also included a history section, asking for "the approximate date of the following people or events," including figures from Plato to Joan of Arc. George Stanley remembered Spicer's warning "that anyone who answered any of the questions requiring dates, whether they were right or wrong, would be excluded from the workshop."[3]

The class set off a proliferation of community reading and discussion circles. When Spicer's tenure ended that May, Kenneth Rexroth began holding workshops at his house on Scott Street, much in the spirit of the political meetings he'd hosted during the 1940s. In the fall of 1958, Duncan began a workshop in basic techniques, which Spicer and some of his students attended. Perhaps more significantly, poets of the 1957 Spicer workshop began to congregate in bars in North Beach and in Sunday afternoon reading sessions at various apartments. The so-called Spicer Circle came into existence out of those gatherings. Tom Field recalled that the informal meetings seemed at times like an extension of the classes at Black Mountain: "I felt that education was over for me [with the end of Black Mountain]. But it continued in a way in the attic at the first East-West House, where Joanne Kyger organized a writing group. It wasn't organized except we met there religiously every Sunday. She had Spicer and Duncan coming along with [Joe] Dunn and Ebbe [Borregaard] and six or seven other poets."[4]

Meanwhile, Charles Olson made his first West Coast appearance of the San Francisco Renaissance. He arrived by train with his wife, Betty, and on the evening of February 21, 1957, gave a reading for the Poetry Center at the San Francisco Museum of Art. According to biographer Tom Clark, Olson, apprehensive about meeting with the new crop of Bay Area poets, began drinking and retreated to bed, forcing Duncan to retrieve him and sober him up for his performance.[5] That night, Olson read from the *Maximus* poems and from his *O'Ryan* series, soon to be published by White Rabbit Press with illustrations by Jess. While most visiting writers received a one-page introduction, Duncan showed his deference to Olson by composing three single-spaced pages, which included the personal recognition "For those of us who had been waiting (circa 1950) for the moment to come when the art of poetry could be turned from personal use and misuse toward a new life, Charles Olson turned the tide."[6]

Olson infused the Bay Area scene with a new source of inspiration, giving a series of talks derived from "The Special View of History" lectures he had offered at Black Mountain the previous year. His presentations, given in Duncan and Jess's living room, overflowed with references to Alfred North Whitehead's 1929 philosophical tract *Process and Reality,* and his audience consisted of two dozen inquisitive young writers, including Michael McClure, Jack Spicer, Philip Whalen, and Michael Rumaker. Olson's readings of Whitehead seemed haphazard to some audience members, but the lectures consumed Duncan's imagination. The proposal that key themes in *Process and Reality* might be integrated into a poetics held great appeal, and those themes soon crept into *The Opening of the Field.*[7] Duncan's enthusiasm was well evident when he wrote to Robin Blaser later that year: "The great thing in music for the year has been the complete Webern . . . And one such book— Whitehead's *Process and Reality* that gives that grandeur. I came to it on Olson's insistence. It sets up a craving in me for large spatial architectures at the edge of the chaos. That the primordial is always 'ahead,' 'beyond'! My mind does not grasp it; my mind is graspd by it."[8]

Many of the poems of *The Opening of the Field* came to be laced with Whitehead's language. "The Propositions," borrowing its title from a *Process and Reality* chapter heading, was partly written during one of the Olson lectures and included notes from that talk. Duncan wrote Denise Levertov on March 1 that the poem "springs into itself from the excitements, tunings up, resistance and confirmations of Olson's visit here."[9] The piece paid homage to Jess, but the kinship Duncan wrote of extended to Olson and Whitehead as well:

> When I summon intellect it is to the melody
>   of this longing. Thy hand,
> Beloved, restores
>   the chords of this longing.
> Here, in this thirst that defines Beauty,
>   I have found kin.[10]

As with much of Duncan's work, the poem began as a dialogue with another writer. Taking up where the original source left off, the poet launched into a series of reflections:

> Olson names Love one of four qualities.   What
> sensations prosper in the good?
>
> Pain, pleasure,   in this focus
> we hold to the condition.
>
> The qualities as we know them in-
> form demand.
>
> And for Love   I stand   perilously.[11]

There was a larger reading list to be culled from conversations with Olson that February, and Duncan dutifully noted the Gloucester poet's suggestions of high-priority texts: Carl Sauer's *The Morphology of Landscape,* Edgar Andersen's *Plants, Man and Life,* William Boyd's *Genetics and the Race of Man,* and archaeological reports from journals such as the *Illustrated London News* and the *Bulletin of the American Society of Oriental Research*.[12] The scope of Olson's intellect transposed against the hubbub of the San Francisco scene helped reinforce Duncan's identification with the writers of the Black Mountain School. He confided to Denise Levertov, "It's you, Creeley and Olson that always are there for me, from whom I backslide into the inner unrooted in the outer, or the outer unrooted in the inner; and whom I imagine when the best is there, when the poem turns one of its wonderful clear things for me, as sharing my joy in the thing made."[13] And while there was no doubt that San Francisco was in the midst of a poetry renaissance, Duncan wondered about the attention being paid to sociality over craft. In a notebook entry titled "A View of San Francisco Poetry 1957," he echoed the comments he had made to Levertov:

> There has been in San Francisco, as there had been in the United States at large since the work of Pound, Stein, Williams, until the advent of Charles Olson's "Projective Verse" circa 1950, no structural poetries . . . Nor is there yet any widespread concern with "form." Those explorations drawing upon the sciences of language, history and psychology—which characterize the new poetry of Olson, Creeley, Blackburn, Eigner, Levertov, which have occupied me in the last five years, have also isolated me . . . from the regional scene.[14]

With Olson's departure that spring, Duncan returned to the trials of the Poetry Center. In an April letter to Donald Allen, he announced that he was prepared to resign: "Poetry is not my stock in trade, it is my life. And I want that life to be as happy as I can live it."[15] Realizing he could still make a living typing manuscripts, he decided to limit his commitment to the work that put him in the line of poets and personalities. In a 1976 interview, he also spoke of his distaste for the Poetry Center as an academic institution: "After six months I . . . gave my six month notice. . . . I couldn't have had any say to separate [the Poetry Center] from the college, because the money was coming from there, there was no way to move that thing around."[16]

The spring's busy reading schedule left Duncan little room to carry out any immediate plans to retreat. In March and April, he facilitated a number of events, including appearances by May Sarton and Robert Lowell. In late March, Jack Spicer and Conrad Pendleton took the stage, giving Duncan the opportunity to reflect upon his reverence for Spicer and his poetry:

> Spicer disturbs. That he continues to do so is his vitality. The abortive, the solitary, the blasphemous, when they are not facetious, produce upheavals in

the real. Life throws up the disturbing demand "All is not well"—sign after sign generated of accusation manifest—which it is the daring of Spicer . . . to mimic. If you do not allow that life vomits; that the cosmos with its swollen and shrunken stars, its irruptions, vomits—you can refuse to allow only by denying fact. And, in the fullness—the image of God must contain the grotesque.[17]

Spicer's "disturbing" influence on Duncan was well evident as he completed several poems for *The Opening of the Field*. The Poetry as Magic workshop, which he continued to attend through the early summer, inspired "Four Pictures of the Real Universe," "Evocation," "Of Blasphemy," and "Nor Is the Past Pure." George Stanley recalled that the workshop was enormously generative: "Jack gave assignments . . . like 'write a poem that should create a universe' or 'write a poem in which the poet becomes a flesh-eating beast.' "[18] The workshop also launched Spicer into local notoriety. Duncan observed that in the wake of the Beat invasion, his Berkeley Renaissance companion began putting together his own "team," from which Blaser and Duncan would eventually split: "George Stanley, Harold Dull, Joe Dunn, Ebbe Borregaard, Jim Alexander, Lew Ellingham, Ron Loewinsohn, Stan Persky—there were star players, bench sitters, and water boys. Joanne Kyger could play on the team, but she was a girl. Helen Adam was team godmother. Fran Herndon would make the posters, pennants, and paint the portraits of the old guard—Spicer, Blaser, and Jess and me—and the gang would rally round."[19]

But Bay Area camaraderie went hand-in-hand with strife. In April 1956, Duncan refused Kenneth Rexroth's request to be paid fifty dollars for a free-admission reading at the Poetry Center. Duncan suggested that Rexroth either read for free or read for fifty dollars with a fifty-cent admission fee. The argument spiraled out of control, and on April 23, Duncan relayed a two-pronged message to Rexroth about the reading and an *Evergreen Review* project being planned by Rexroth and Donald Allen:

I understand that in your radio address for last week you stated that as a result of your attack on the role the Archbishop of San Francisco plays in censorship you received an abusive letter from the Poetry Center canceling your engagement to read. First: as you know very well the letter written to you by me on April 9 had nothing whatsoever to do with an action or statement of yours outside of the conditions which you had laid down for your reading. . . . Second: . . . not only does the letter not cancel your reading but it provides in case admissions are charged for paying you any amount over the expenses of the reading. . . .

Upon reflection then today after you phoned asking me to record for the *Evergreen Review* record . . . I have come to the conclusion that being associated with you at the present time is too unpleasant.[20]

On another front, Lawrence Ferlinghetti and his business partner Shigeyoshi Murao were arrested in late May for selling Allen Ginsberg's "obscene" book *Howl* at City Lights bookstore, and on June 7, the Los Angeles vice squad shut down Wallace Berman's first solo show at the Ferus Gallery.[21] Berman was fined $150 for displaying lewd art: an erotic drawing by the artist and occultist Cameron. At the end of 1957, Berman published the second issue of *Semina,* in which he announced, "I will continue to print 'Semina' from locations other than this city of degenerate angels."[22]

To mark the end of an arduous spring season, the Poetry Center hosted a June 9 reading for participants in Spicer's workshop, with performances by Duncan, Helen Adam, Bob Conner, and Ebbe Borregaard. Duncan was looking forward to a summer break from his employment and an escape to "hole in on [Potrero] hill."[23] At De Haro Street, he had pleasant relationships to attend to away from the bustle of the poetry scene. Hilde Burton and her husband, David, often visited from Berkeley, taking a genuine interest in both Duncan's poetry and Jess's paintings and contributing to the couple's income with purchases of Jess's work. Hilde Burton's career as a psychologist and her husband's as an architect gave the two couples much to talk about. Duncan, with his two-decade immersion in Freud's writings, was always eager to read the papers Hilde had presented at psychoanalytic symposiums. She recalled that he "knew what was original about Freud. I think what he liked about Freud was that he was quite a good writer."[24]

Stan Brakhage's classmate Larry Jordan also spent time with Duncan and Jess that year. Jordan had recently returned from New York and an apprenticeship with Joseph Cornell. Soon to begin a series of film projects, he acquired a new collaborator in Jess.[25] Meanwhile, with those quieter friendships at the core of his home life, Duncan was able to retire to his library. In late June, he purchased Yeats's *Autobiografies* from a British bookseller, and he continued making his way through Whitehead's *Process and Reality.* In August, he immersed himself in Gilbert Murray's *Five Stages of Greek Religion* while penning a review of H. D.'s *Selected Poems* for *Poetry* magazine. Returning to H. D.'s work, he began to gear up for a more comprehensive study of her writing that would occupy him through the early 1960s.

TWENTY-NINE

The Maidens

The poet
Robert D.
Writes poetry while we
Listen to him.
Commentary—follow
The red dog
Down the
Limit
Of possible
Quarterbacks.

JACK SPICER, "For Robert"

DURING THE FALL OF 1957, Duncan divided his energy between his Poetry Center responsibilities and more personal business. As he neared completion of *The Opening of the Field,* he also supervised the Jargon production of his book *Letters* at Banyan Press and applied for a Guggenheim Fellowship with the assistance of Louis Zukofsky and Donald Allen. The fellowship was to elude him, but the application gave him the opportunity to clarify his ideas about the structure of *The Opening of the Field* and to begin to see the book's boundaries. At least one of the interruptions to his own work that autumn was pleasant. On October 10, he served as master of ceremonies for a reading by Marianne Moore at the San Francisco Museum of Art. Duncan reported to Donald Allen, "Miss Moore's performance here was magnificent; I cannot imagine a more thorough entertainment, she removed us from any effort of appreciation into the full diversion of her charms and humors."[1]

While Duncan would soon be able to step down from the Poetry Center, he was not able to escape from the ongoing expansion of the San Francisco poetry scene. Throughout 1957, writers and artists arrived in the Bay Area at the same time that major poetry journals were zeroing in on the community. *Evergreen Review* #2 and the seventh and final issue of the *Black Mountain Review* both reflected the previous year's caucuses in San Francisco. The latter, coedited by Robert Creeley and Allen Ginsberg, collected *Black*

Mountain Review regulars alongside Ginsberg, Kerouac, and William Burroughs (writing under the pseudonym William Lee). Ginsberg's poem "America" saw print for the first time in the issue, as did excerpts of Kerouac's "October in the Railroad Earth." Joanne Kyger, who had fled college in Santa Barbara hoping to encounter like-minded young people in San Francisco, remembered that her first education in poetry came through those magazines, copies of which disappeared from her apartment when friends visited.[2]

With informal Sunday afternoon poetry meetings convening at various households around the city, Duncan remained in demand. Newcomers Kyger, Harold and Dora Dull, Joe Dunn, and David Meltzer all gravitated toward the gatherings, relying upon Spicer and Duncan to bestow wisdom, if not praise. Kyger remembered the two elder poets playing distinctly different roles, with Spicer's "more straightforward language" and Duncan's "sonorous and swooping tones" converging to create a larger sense of fellowship: "There was a big emphasis on 'truth,' finding the 'real' poem. But all away from an 'academic' environment and attitude. With an understanding of poetry as existing in a magical parallel universe. . . . The poem is a reality which invites you to enter, written by the poet in the 'office of poet' with news from another life. Nothing to do with your personal 'self.' "[3] The Sunday gatherings benefited the Berkeley Renaissance veterans as well: Spicer completed his first book, *After Lorca,* in the course of the meetings, and Duncan often sat in the center of the boisterous wine-drinking group penning poems toward *The Opening of the Field.*[4] By the end of the year, workshop regular Joe Dunn had established the White Rabbit Press and printed an edition of Spicer's *After Lorca.* Jess was recruited to design a cover for the book, and both Duncan and Jess assisted Dunn in the project's final production details.

Spicer's and Duncan's devotees began to identify themselves as a new kind of San Francisco poet, characterized by George Stanley as "antibeatnik."[5] Joanne Kyger had a similar assessment of the Bay Area's poetry politics: "Black Mountain College had just broken up when I arrived . . . ; I was meeting people like John Wieners, Michael Rumaker, Ebbe Borregaard. . . . They were closer to me as contemporaries than the Beat generation, who'd developed romantic kind of political ideals that Spicer couldn't stand, the whole sense of self propagation, self-advertising."[6]

Several factors separated Duncan, Spicer, and their students from the influence of Beat culture. While Ginsberg and Kerouac emphasized peripatetic experiential learning as a key to the craft of writing, Duncan and Spicer shared an obsessive bookishness and an erudition fueled by their studies with Ernst Kantorowicz. And though Spicer liked to drink, he found other mood-altering substances less useful, warning his followers away from the marijuana and amphetamine that had crept into the scene. Duncan, who rarely even frequented the bars of North Beach, provided a more extreme example of the old-fashioned. Alongside Madeline Gleason, Helen Adam, James Broughton, and Eve Triem, he formed "the Brotherhood of the Maiden and its Secret Six." Gatherings of the Maidens began early in 1957, conceivably as an alternative to Spicer's bar scene, and as Broughton remembered, "We had a very jolly group.... We met not only once a month, but usually on a birthday of one or the other of us, or a feast day, like Easter ... or Equinox. And they were always joint feasts at one house or another ... and we always had to write a poem for each occasion, and that was fun, because we knew we'd have a good audience."[7]

Between Sunday poetry meetings and gatherings of the Maidens, Duncan began to put the finishing touches on his work at the Poetry Center. On November 27, 1957, he submitted a formal proposal for future activities at the venue. Under "Major Spirits of the Age Who Should Be Heard Again and Again As Long As They Live," Duncan listed Robert Frost, William Carlos Williams, Ezra Pound, H. D., T. S. Eliot, Robinson Jeffers, Marianne Moore, e. e. cummings, and Charles Olson. Under "Contemporary Poets Whose Work I Find Disturbing But Whose Influence Is Apparent Upon the History of Poetry," he named Muriel Rukeyser, Kenneth Patchen, Kenneth Rexroth, Allen Ginsberg, and Jack Kerouac. After attending a reading by Patchen in early December, he told Denise Levertov that he was disturbed by the pathology of former mentors Patchen and Rexroth, who seemed tormented by "'the sons of bitches' who excluded them from publication." Of Patchen he wrote, "All emotion has died ... and the deracinated sentiments of the revolutionary poet remain: he writes for his own Noah (in whom he no longer believes) and promises world destruction of those bastards (who do not believe in him)."[8]

Duncan was able to converse with Levertov in person in January of 1958 when she and Mitch Goodman visited the Bay Area. In an appearance at the Poetry Center on January 19, a sequel to Olson's presentation the previous winter, she gave the community another entrance into the works of the Black Mountain writers. Duncan had put together a diverse itinerary for Levertov's stay, including a trip to Ham and Mary Tyler's farm on January 20 and 21 and a White Rabbit Press book party in Mill Valley to celebrate

Joe Dunn's editorial work.[9] Michael Rumaker recalled that several of the guests at the Mill Valley event gave performances in honor of Levertov's visit:

> Toward the end of the afternoon we were all lounging on the broad open-air deck overlooking the valley far below and drinking wine when Robert asked Helen Adam to read one of her new poems. With alacrity, with the most genial of grins splitting that fascinating scrawny face, twittering with quick jerky movements, she whipped her poem out of her pocketbook and hopped up on the railing. Precariously perched there on the edge . . . she commenced to read with terrific animation and energy, "I Love My Love."[10]

Rumaker, anxiously anticipating Adam's fall from the rail, noted that Duncan with "a grin on his face almost equal to the stretch of Helen's, was bobbing his body to the beat of the line and rolling his shoulders in pleasure with the ballad."[11] Jack Spicer, in his characteristic role of trickster, directed a poem toward Dunn called "For Joe," with the lines "People who don't like the smell of faggot vomit / Will never understand why men don't like women. . . . The female genital organ is hideous."[12] Levertov said little about the incident in her correspondence with Duncan later that spring, but she mused upon it in "Hypocrite Women":

> . . . And if at Mill Valley perched in the trees
> the sweet rain drifting through western air
> a white sweating bull of a poet told us
>
> our cunts are ugly—why didn't we
> admit we have thought so too? . . . [13]

After Levertov returned to New York, Duncan wrote to her about the happier aspects of her visit:

> Your reading has won the praise of all whose praise means something to me, and praise elsewhere. It enlivens all to have that Sunday group referring again and again to those poems to take measure. And perseveringly as I have read your work, eagerly, these last years; the reading for me too brought the concerted thing—together! . . . I could not imagine goodbyes. Writing to you is always so vivid for me, a solitude in which you are, that I do not lose all in your distance. Yet the reality, the company of you *you* and Mitch gives the firmer ground of actual companionship.[14]

As passionate to defend his pleasures as he was to announce his distastes, in February of 1958, Duncan placed himself at cross-purposes with James

Broughton by publishing an unenthusiastic review of his friend's collection *True and False Unicorn* in *Poetry* magazine. Duncan, perturbed that Broughton had solicited him to review the book, titled the piece "A Risk of Sympathies":

> There is a bravado when [Broughton] announces to the reader that "the poem is what it is, but it is also a great deal more," or again, that "the poem . . . is not to be defied without dire consequences." These are solemn announcements that bespeak either an intensity of purpose and vision concerning the nature of poetry or a claim to importance. But it is claim to importance, not intensity of purpose or vision, that is concerned with audience and risk.[15]

Throughout the review, Duncan kept up the complaint that Broughton had promised more than he could deliver as a poet. He closed with the statement:

> It is because his self-consciousness is a general human factor that Broughton must somewhere if not everywhere delight. It is because our desire moves toward release in a larger cosmic more-than-personality where the powers of subject and object may both increase that, if we make the critical demand, we come to a disappointment.[16]

Duncan admitted to Denise Levertov that he had approached the review with an obsessive attitude, comparing it to an experience during the 1940s in Woodstock: "hired as kitchen help in a summer hotel and ordered to kill a chicken, panickd I tore the bird to pieces."[17]

THIRTY

———

Elfmere

FREED FROM POETRY CENTER POLITICS, Duncan and Jess also freed themselves from the social obligations of San Francisco's poetry community during the spring of 1958. In mid-March, they relocated to Stinson Beach in Marin County north of San Francisco. Christening their new home "Elfmere," they remained there until early 1961. The landscape of Stinson

Beach—the fruit trees and gardens, the long stretch of Pacific coastline, and the green and gold-tinged fields along the coastal highway—flooded into the next decade of Duncan's writing. As in Mallorca, the solitude also allowed him and Jess to renew their relation to the domestic. Jess painted, Duncan began constructing stained-glass windows, and the couple came into a routine of strolling on the beach every day before lunch. Duncan detailed the joys of the seclusion in a late April letter to Denise Levertov:

> In the morning at nine I walk the two blocks down our hill to "town" which is just Airey's store and the post office; and collect the mail. Sit over coffee with Jess, stare at the sea. Then, after writing letters . . . —there's the garden. . . . Jess and I spent most of yesterday cultivating a plot for climbing peas and beans. Today I'll put more peas along a fence, if'n I can root up the briar and morninglory: both of which take over the countryside.[1]

As they cleared the yard around their new abode, Duncan cleared a space in the final poems of *The Opening of the Field* to chart the quotidian activities of Stinson Beach:

> The handsome builder, sun-swarthy, black-hair'd, has cleard
> ground at the boundary. He has torn away the purple briar-rose.
> That we could not name. He has hacked away the briar-rose, the
> purple loveliness.
>
> In the tall grass, the cat sleeps.[2]

The first poem he composed at Elfmere was occasioned by the death of one of the two household cats, Pumpkin. "A Storm of White" created a focal point for the theme of the dead that was crucial to *The Opening of the Field* alongside two other principal themes, the field and the law. Duncan had decided that each of the poems in the book would in some way address one or more of these themes, and he sought to weave the project together into a dense multilayered tapestry.[3] "A Storm of White" became an elegy to the pneumonia-stricken Pumpkin:

> O dear gray cat that died in this cold,
> you were born on my chest
> six years ago.
>
> The sea of ghosts dances. It does not
> send your little shadow to us.

I do not understand this
empty place in our happiness.[4]

The poem contained another subtext: the comfort Duncan took in his rela-
tionships with Denise Levertov and Robert Creeley. He included in the
composition an excerpt from one of Levertov's letters and referenced the final
lines of Creeley's recent poem "Heroes," "death also / can still propose the
old labors."[5] Duncan's correspondence with Levertov had been for several
months a sounding ground for his poems in progress. He wrote to her that
spring to express an appreciation for her attentions:

> I can't separate always . . . the love of everything you write and that I love you.
> There's friendship and its courtesies—you're perhaps right that we've to de-
> serve friendship. . . . Could I send you the storm that is coming up again,
> blowing in with columns of rain? Or the vine flourishing single-roses at the
> north wall of the house? . . . But wherever you find again . . . the visible na-
> ture that's yours, it is mine too. That's your continuing gift to me, or thru you
> the poem, the gift that comes to me.[6]

In late March, Robert Creeley and his second wife, Bobbie Louise Hawkins,
visited Stinson Beach with their infant daughter, Sarah, in tow.[7] Duncan
and Jess liked Hawkins, whom Creeley had begun courting in Albuquerque
the previous year, though she later remembered Duncan greeting her with
the anxious exclamation "Thank god you don't look like the photographs
Jonathan Williams took of you."[8] The gregarious, rosy-cheeked Hawkins
seemed a good mate for Creeley, with his love of talk and company, and the
newlyweds helped rouse Duncan from an uncharacteristic depression brought
on by Pumpkin's death.

While Stinson Beach was pounded by springtime rainstorms, Duncan
escorted Creeley across the bay to a Sunday meeting at Joe Dunn's apart-
ment. Creeley read several poems to the audience gathered there, and for
Duncan completed a "triumpherate [sic] of the beauty the discrete voice can
give to the poem" alongside Olson's and Levertov's recent first readings in
San Francisco. In his notebook, he reflected on the impact his Black Moun-
tain peers had had on him:

> In this period the drawing together, the informing—
>
> From which I have contemporary test: Charles Olson, Denise Levertov, Rob-
> ert Creeley. They test, they enlarge necessity.

And from which I have contemporary mixd appreciations, partial associations, among poets in San Francisco.[9]

In the wake of the Creeleys' visit, Duncan organized himself to attend to professional obligations, throughout the spring and early summer making efforts to finish a review of Edward Dahlberg's recent book *The Sorrows of Priapus*. While escaping social demands was not as simple as Duncan and Jess had expected, most of their company in Stinson Beach was welcome. Weekend visitors from San Francisco and Berkeley included David and Hilde Burton, Helen and Pat Adam, Ida Hodes, and James Broughton. Another visitor who arrived that summer was Louis Zukofsky. In May, Duncan wrote to Zukofsky proposing that he accept a teaching job at San Francisco State during the summer term. Zukofsky agreed, arriving in San Francisco on June 20 with his wife, Celia, and their teenaged son, Paul. During their first weekend in the Bay Area, they rendezvoused with Duncan and Jess at Stinson Beach, a visit that was pleasing to all, though plans for future excursions to Elfmere were scratched when Paul Zukofsky became carsick on the winding coastal highway back to San Francisco.

Duncan and Jess kept in touch with the Zukofskys as best they could throughout the summer. Zukofsky had confided in Duncan before his arrival, "There aren't many people I want to see or know for that matter—Kenneth Patchen if he's there, Kenneth Rexroth if etc., [Richard] Duerden? Maybe one or two acquaintances in Berkeley."[10] Zukofsky's social reticence became all the more clear in his relationships with the students at San Francisco State. For Duncan, a significant disappointment came in Zukofsky's disdain for fledgling writer Ebbe Borregaard's work. Shades of Black Mountain "mythos" and "aesthetic fervors" hardly appealed to the objectivist master, and Duncan lamented to Denise Levertov, "I feel sad anyway because I had imagined that there wld be a direct exchange between Zukofsky (as I have found myself thru his work an area of sympathetic contrary) and the small group of young poets here who would need a contradiction to my own doctrines and Spicer's."[11] Another student of Zukofsky's that summer was George Stanley, who later recalled, "The 'seminar,' such as it was, was very unsuccessful. . . . I remember Ebbe [Borregaard], a Chinese-American poet, . . . and possibly Elyce Edelman. The sessions were held in the Zukofskys' . . . apartment. . . . Ebbe didn't get along with Zuk at all, and I remember him at one point threatening (facetiously) to throw Zuk. out the window—we were about 12 storeys up."[12]

Duncan steered clear of Zukofsky's workshop, though he continued to play a role in Sunday poetry gatherings, then being held at George Stanley's house. With limited bus service between San Francisco and Stinson Beach, his visits called for overnight stays in the city. The blondish, bookish twenty-four-year-old Stanley was soon to discover that another motive lurked behind Duncan's appearances at the gatherings. When he was propositioned by the poet fifteen years his elder, Stanley submitted hesitantly: "I didn't much enjoy the sex, but the attention, being a favorite, yes!"[13] Throughout the time Duncan and Jess lived in Stinson Beach, Duncan's tryst with Stanley was one of his more discreet weekend entertainments, concealed from Jess under the guise of an inconvenient bus schedule.

While Duncan came and went, warm sunny days gave Jess an opportunity to work on a portrait of Helen Adam he had begun in July.[14] The couple also looked forward to entertaining a new wave of visitors later in August, including Tom Field, Helen and Pat Adam, and Joe and Carolyn Dunn. Dunn was then working on three new White Rabbit Press projects—Helen Adam's *Crow Castle,* Charles Olson's *O'Ryan,* and Duncan's *Faust Foutu*—and Jess was again called upon to act as White Rabbit's artistic consultant. In September, the Elfmere household welcomed a white kitten named Merlin and a black kitten named Miranda. With Jess sequestered in his studio and kittens climbing across tabletops, Duncan reenvisioned and revised the first poem of *The Opening of the Field.* In "Often I Am Permitted to Return to a Meadow," he strategically embedded the book's three main themes—the field, the law, and the dead—into what he later described as a "mistrusted still almost beautiful pseudo-casual opening."[15]

The field of "Often I Am Permitted to Return to a Meadow" was in essence the field of Mechpelah, described in the *Zohar* as the burial place of Adam, Eve, Abraham, and Sarah. Duncan combined that story with a personal memory, a childhood nightmare about a game "of ring a round of roses" during which he was crowned king and ascended to a throne with a sense of foreboding.[16] Interlocked between the field and the dead was a third and final theme, the law. The anarchistic poet structured his poetics around the idea that each composition abided not by a manmade law of form, but by a natural or metaphysical law of language distinct from the poet's intent. After the reworking of "Often I Am Permitted to Return to a Meadow," he decided he would no longer revise any poems; instead, the initial writing of each piece would demand a wholehearted attentiveness. The novelty of the decision was not lost on Duncan's old friend Jack Spicer. In a 1958 letter to Robin Blaser, he wrote,

The trick naturally is what Duncan learned
years ago and tried to teach us—not to search
for the perfect poem but to let your way of
writing of the moment go along its own paths,
explore and retreat but never be fully realized
(confined) within the boundaries of one poem.[17]

THIRTY-ONE

Night Scenes

IN SEPTEMBER 1958, Duncan was drawn back to the Poetry Center to
teach a workshop at the San Francisco Public Library. The class, focused on
"basic techniques," had a roster that included Mary Callaway, Katherine
Abend, Julia K. Watson, Robert Kaffka, Joanne Kyger, George Stanley,
Ebbe Borregaard, Bruce Boyd, and Jack Spicer. Duncan's syllabus hinted at
his desire to separate himself from the Spicer circle and the levity of a poetry
scene based in North Beach bars. In an entrance survey, he asked the stu-
dents a number of questions about the cosmologies of their work as writers.
The search for law that had begun with *The Opening of the Field* was now
a subject of exploration in the classroom. Using a stanza of a poem by Emily
Dickinson as a springboard, he presented a further challenge: "list the
sounds used in chronological order, making the following assumptions:
There is a certain sound at the beginning of all creation; out of which came
three primeval sounds or creators. Eight succeeding powers or angels ap-
peard as teachers and imagined approximations of these sounds—distortions
from which the elements of human speech derive."[1] Veteran workshoppers
Joanne Kyger, George Stanley, and Jack Spicer were poised to challenge
Duncan's more grandiose gestures, but Kyger recalled that the workshop
also offered a useful alternative to their Sunday meetings. They had a chance
to see Duncan in action as a teacher and were provoked to consider the intri-
cacies of language in a new light: "He presented a more formal approach. He
talked about vowels, consonants, consonant clusters, syllables, syllabic mea-
sure, pitch, stress; and to practice being aware of them in one's writing.
'Vowels the spirit, Consonants the body.'"[2]

While Duncan's regard for the role of the intellect in the creative process could feel heavy-handed to some of his young charges, he proved himself open to mischief making, at least from his favorite students. George Stanley remembered an incident when Duncan "was giving a reading on an early, warm evening, at the Telegraph Hill Neighborhood House.... The reading had already started when Joanne and I entered, half-naked, half-drunk (& I was carrying a half-empty half-gallon of cheap red wine). We were probably making some noise, too. Some of the audience expressed their disapproval of our disrespect, but RD quieted them, saying (something like)— 'Let them stay . . . ; nakedness and wine have always been a part of poetry.' "³

With the workshop in progress, during October and November Duncan returned to the pleasures of his library, immersing himself in George Trager and Henry Lee Smith's *An Outline of English Structure* and rereading Shelley's "Prometheus Unbound." Intrigued by Frank O'Hara's "In Memory of My Feelings," published in the autumn 1958 issue of the *Evergreen Review,* Duncan wrote to the New York poet suggesting that he and O'Hara might share some common ground. Irritated with Duncan's affected tone, O'Hara returned the letter via Donald Allen without a response. Duncan's miscommunications with the writers of the New York school—tempered by a friendship with John Ashbery—were never to be resolved. O'Hara expressed his view of Duncan to Jasper Johns in 1959: "Among those poets of the West Coast Robert Duncan seems to have the esthetic position that Kenneth Rexroth occupies in the press and there are several books of his poetry around which might be interesting to go into—I can't stand him myself, but he is their Charles Olson—to me he is quite flabby by comparison, but maybe because I'm on the East Coast."⁴

O'Hara's rejection was but one of Duncan's problems with the poetry world that fall. As Donald Allen made plans for a Grove Press anthology titled *The New American Poetry,* Duncan found himself bristling against editors, publishing houses, and anthologies.⁵ He also went to war with Jonathan Williams, who had published his collection *Letters* in cooperation with printer Claude Fredericks and raised the price after a miscalculation of the production cost. With some pride, Duncan reported to Denise Levertov, "I have written him I will no longer have anything at all to do with him. Neither write to nor accept letters from him."⁶

The ongoing weeding out of friendships and professional associations seemed to clear a path for creative endeavors. Late in 1958, he began to make plans for a new playwriting venture. Duncan had wanted to begin a poet's theater since his move to Potrero Hill, an idea that he had first proposed to James Broughton from Black Mountain:

> What is needed is a Writers Theater, and that means Writers—set up with control of writers whose written plays is writing plays is going to write plays; it's you and me at this point as far as I wld trust. And gradually . . . we can add to the strength of it. Only by keeping it to what we damn well know is WRITERS can we govern how much and what of the margin will go. You and I know when a play bores us. Connected with the Poetry Center . . . means the old disastrous compromise.[7]

The presence of Duncan's former theater collaborator Wes Huss and a handful of Black Mountain students allowed him to set the plan in motion. During the fall of 1958, he held rehearsals for an expanded version of his *Medea at Kolchis*. Painter Paul Alexander remembered that in the end, little came of his efforts: "We never got the theatre work going because unlike at Black Mountain where we met every morning and had nothing else to do, in San Francisco people were scattered . . . and they had to get jobs and couldn't keep appointments."[8] Alexander, Huss, Tom Field, Ann Simone, and other Black Mountaineers took part in the planning, and Duncan harnessed the energy of the rehearsals to continue his work on the script. While struggling to gather his cast, another glitch in the proposed production came when Duncan locked horns with James Broughton, who had taken the initiative to set up a writer's theater of his own called the Playhouse. Duncan eyed the project with both wariness and jealousy and wrote to Broughton on December 28 in the reproachful tone that dominated his business correspondence that winter: "I said I would 'try to write something for your opening show' but 'on the record,' . . . let me state it straight that I just don't have any interest or believe in the venture. I don't want my name associated with the thing, because then there would be some sense of approval where actually I disapprove—I would not want to be forced to a public statement of that disapproval."[9] His relationship with Broughton, increasingly becoming a roller coaster ride of wrath and reconciliation, led Duncan to turn his back on the Playhouse and scrap the production of *Medea*. Two months later, in a more cordial mood, a Valentine greeting to Broughton included a weekend invitation to Stinson Beach.

The advent of 1959 brought Duncan the satisfaction of completing *The Opening of the Field,* in time for his fortieth birthday on January 7. He spent the early spring typing copies of the manuscript and presenting them to Helen Adam, Denise Levertov, Jack Spicer, Norman O. Brown, Ida Hodes, Robin Blaser, and Robert Creeley. Just after the New Year, Creeley sent Duncan a copy of his new poem "The Door." Dedicated to Duncan and influenced by H. D., the poem again reflected the strength of the bond between the two Black Mountain veterans.[10] Jack Spicer also wrote Duncan during the first week of January with praise for his recently published *Selected Poems* from City Lights. The two men often butted heads publicly, but the letters between them during the late 1950s still radiated the playfulness that had characterized their decade-long friendship: *"Domestic Scenes* made me cry. 'Friend' was originally 'Jack' which is much stronger. Why not cut the dedication and go back to that. The original dedication was 'Upon Jack's Return.' Anyway. MS ['Medieval Scenes'] and V ['The Venice Poem'] will knock the Snyderites on their asses. I still disagree with the ending of VP but hell."[11]

The culmination of *The Opening of the Field* coincided with the end of Duncan's Workshop in Basic Techniques. On January 23, he held the final session of the class, and that spring many of the workshop's participants drifted back to Sunday household meetings.[12] Duncan continued to be an active participant in the informal sessions, and after one particularly contentious afternoon at George Stanley's house in late February, he composed a fourteen-page letter to Stanley that was later published as the White Rabbit Press chapbook *As Testimony.* The letter, which began as an apology for Duncan's petulance with the younger poets, captured the high-spirited, cliquish nature of the growing San Francisco poetry community:

> As in the scene Sunday I see Joanne Kyger kneeling. There had been a chair, but she sits always on the floor, . . . on her knees when the poem was read. As my "rank" had been in the taking of the Chair, arguing from it. As Borregaard and Stanley argued "from where they sat." . . . I sat between Jack and Arthur, which is not a Christian name but a king. "In antiquity statues tried to be men." Where we refer to antiquity, names have powers too. In the Maze poem Joanne had read—I saw the bird / on the sidewalk / his neck naked / as in prehistory; this is how I read it, reciting it to Hal and Dory today. But Hal corrected me: *prehistoric* it had said. Slowly, to discover the design we must find the exact word, the exact name. John and Joanne are the same name: Webster says it means—God is gracious. Harold is Herald from *hari,* army + *waltan,* to govern; who proclaimed war on peace. . . . Robert is Bright in fame; Duncan is Brown warrior. Joseph is Hebrew and means He shall add.

I mistake Borregaard for Beauregard which in French can mean a fair glance; it can also mean a fine scowl. George means a husband-man, a tiller of the ground. Of Dora I find only the note that the name is latin. But Brautigan's wife had said in scorn that the Door was a Freudian symbol, a cover-image for Dora.[13]

During his second year at the Elfmere cottage, Duncan began to compose works toward a new collection. Later titled *Roots and Branches,* the book reflected his efforts to move away from the dense structural considerations of *The Opening of the Field* and marked a return to the freedom of individual occasional poems. The early pieces fell into place as strands of autobiography: the opening poem, an observation of the Monarch butterflies of Stinson Beach; the second poem, a response to John Wieners's request for a piece about the Kabbalah for his magazine *Measure;* and the third, "Night Scenes," a sketch of an evening out in Berkeley. At a reading in 1964, Duncan recalled the inspiration for the book's title:

> When we had moved to Stinson Beach I had suddenly realized that I was in the presence of a series of rhythms that were all around me constantly speaking to me and that I could not understand how they could enter the poem. One was the not-repetitive nor monotonous sound of the surf.... Along about March everything has broken into the first green ... but also vast flocks—millions is the impression—of Monarch butterflies come along the coast of California, and behold, the whole vista becomes another series of rhythms: the movements of Monarch butterflies—and statistically so many of them that it is like the surf.... Right away I wrote down "roots and branches." It seemed to me that what I was seeing in the movement of these butterflies was like the entanglements of roots and branches going everywhere. Above and below, branching out, rooting out.[14]

"Night Scenes" was equally a product of quotidian occurrences. In late March of 1959, Duncan attended a Berkeley film screening organized by Pauline Kael. There he met a twenty-three-year-old classics student named Norman Austin, and the two found themselves in bed together under unusual circumstances. Austin, eventually one of Duncan's closest confidants in matters of the intellect, reminded him years later of the evening's events: "You ... had been visiting Michael Wilsie, with whom I was living at the time, in Jordan Brotman's house in Berkeley. Michael and I had had some altercation ... So I had retired, and some time later, Michael sent you upstairs to spend the night in our room.... maybe it has its own kind of fit, a premo-

nition that we were to meet much later."[15] Though the two would not recon-
nect for sixteen years, Duncan memorialized their first intimacy in "Night
Scenes," composed the following morning during his bus ride home to Stin-
son Beach:

> youth spurts, at the lip the flower
>   lifts lifewards, at the
> four o'clock in the morning, stumbling,
>   into whose arms, at whose
> mouth out of slumber sweetening,
>   so that I know I am not I
> but a spirit of the hour descending into body
>   whose tongue touches
>   myrrh of the morgenrot . . . [16]

THIRTY-TWO

H. D.

WITH A NEW BOOK IN PROGRESS, Duncan began to seek out worthy
publishers for *The Opening of the Field*. In July of 1959, he began a preface to
the book and sent the manuscript to Macmillan Press. That month, the
Creeleys were again guests at Elfmere before departing for Guatemala, where
Robert Creeley had secured a teaching job. Another young couple, Diane
and Jerome Rothenberg, also visited the cottage toward the end of July,
bringing news from the East Coast poetry scene and encouraging Duncan
to visit them in New York. Jerome Rothenberg, then the editor of *Poems
from the Floating World,* had already fielded a series of comments, questions,
and criticisms from Duncan about the first issue of the journal. The meeting
in Stinson Beach allowed the two men to continue their conversation and to
begin an association that would span three decades.

A friendship of another sort blossomed that summer when Duncan
wrote to H. D., sending her a copy of *Letters* and a manuscript of *The
Opening of the Field*. H. D., then seventy-two and in ill health, responded

graciously and maintained a correspondence with Duncan until shortly before her death in September 1961.[1] For Duncan, the connection offered an opportunity to revisit the Symmes family's hermeticism. H. D.'s own childhood had been filled with the rituals of another heretical Christian religion, the Moravian Brotherhood, and her poetry, like Duncan's, resonated with references to the occult. The Moravians, led by an eccentric theologian from Saxony named Nicholas Ludwig von Zinzendorf, arrived in Bethlehem, Pennsylvania, in the mid-1700s after being banished from Europe. The secret brotherhood incorporated séances and spirit worship into its rituals, and those preoccupations with the numinous flooded into H. D.'s poetry. From the mid-1930s when Duncan began reading her writing to the spring of 1986 when he taught a comprehensive seminar on her life and work at New College of California, he returned to her again and again as a driving force of his poetics. Duncan's disclosures to H. D. seemed to fulfill a longheld desire to confide in a poetic mentor and mother figure. He wrote in *The H. D. Book*:

> There is in the height of my fantasy, not an obsession but a thought that persists, a fancy that psychoanalysis has found entertained by many children, of an other more real mother than my mother. In the play of dates, my birth year 1919 and the death of my first mother in the complications of child-birth and the flu echoes in my mind the birth of H. D.'s child in the complications of the London flu epidemic. In the play of the initials H. D., my birth name Edward Howard Duncan—E. Howard Duncan echoes her signature.[2]

In early September, Duncan and Jess hosted Erich Heydt and his wife, Dori, at Elfmere. Heydt, a German physician and psychoanalyst who had treated H. D. during the early 1950s, took news back to Europe of the California meeting. Duncan likewise reported to H. D. that the Heydts were somewhat taken aback by Duncan's and Jess's newly grown bushy beards. He explained that he had stopped shaving as a reminder that he was now a middle-aged man, a fact he reflected upon further in the poem "Nel Mezzo Del Cammin Di Nostra Vita."[3] During September and October, he also began to compose "A Sequence of Poems for HD's 73rd Birthday," the opening section of which derived from a dream:

> A young Japanese prince falls in love with a servant boy. I bring his uncle . . . to understand that the heir of the family's tradition is homosexual. . . . But

then in his sexual relations with his lover the Japanese prince no longer is in a love affair but conducts his experiments in a laboratory. . . . In tanks or cribs in a large room . . . are deformed and or mutilated torsos, dead or alive I do not know which, but preserved; and what was a vignette of first love and sexual affair is now a dream of pervading sexual monstrosity.[4]

Duncan took the dream to be a vision of hell, incorporating it into the first section of a longer autobiographical sequence addressed to H. D., with meditations upon his adoption, the death of his birth mother, and his relationship with Minnehaha Symmes.

As *Roots and Branches* progressed, the fate of *The Opening of the Field* remained unclear. Duncan had declined an offer from Macmillan Press to publish the book as part of its *Pocket Poet* series, put off by an unpalatable design plan. While continuing to type copies for friends, he wrote to Donald Allen in November to raise the possibility of publishing the book independently: "Like Spicer, I am intrigued by the idea of deriving reputation and income eventually from my actual audience, however small, and not from the possible 'public.'"[5] The thought coincided with a new publishing venture, Enkidu Surrogate, which Duncan had initiated to fill a gap left by Joe Dunn's drug-induced retreat from White Rabbit Press. Spicer's *Billy the Kid* was published under the Enkidu Surrogate imprint in October 1959, as was *Faust Foutu*. While preparing the books for publication, Duncan and Jess spent several autumn weekends entertaining Spicer, Robin Blaser, and Hilde and David Burton. An unlikely newcomer, the poet Wendell Berry, was also added to the social circle that season. Duncan wrote Denise Levertov about his first meeting with Berry, now a neighbor in Stinson Beach: "I was hitching in to the city and he pickd me up at Tamalpais junction. Introduced himself by name and when I gave mine said that he thought he had recognized me from the picture in *Evergreen*. (I am clean-shaved again!)—we had a day then, gathering up his wife and infant girl and coming back to Elfmere for tea."[6]

By mid-December 1959, Duncan was ready for a holiday from his beach cottage hermitage. He had made a short visit to the Pacific Northwest the previous month and jumped at the opportunity for a more extended reading tour in the area, this time to Portland, Seattle, and Vancouver. A November lecture at Portland State College had been greeted with resistance, and as audience member Tolbert McCarroll recalled, "It was sad and very unfair to

Robert. The few people who were there didn't know who he was."[7] McCarroll, a twenty-eight-year-old lawyer and political activist, immediately took a liking to Duncan:

> The next week I wrote him and asked if he would like to try it again. I organized a big reading followed by a second session in my home for an interesting circle of friends.... For as long as I was in Portland this became a twice a year event. He then had a circuit of friends which went up to B[ritish] C[olumbia]. This gave him a chance to re-touch some old roots in Oregon. He was very interested in the people and had me write notes to him on what was happening in their lives.[8]

Duncan's return visit to Portland was fulfilling on several fronts. He wrote to Jess that McCarroll and his wife, Claire, were "very sweet professional-class [Law] earnest" and remarked "I like them as thoroughly as they seem to like me."[9] As the friendship blossomed, Duncan became a regular visitor to their household, giving lectures and readings for the Ethical Study Society, a nonprofit outfit created by McCarroll to gather "artists, writers, musicians, professional people, many with children and facing those issues of parenthood in the post-war years."[10] Duncan's appearances served both parties well, providing Duncan a new audience and providing his audience a new perspective. McCarroll recalled,

> Robert's focus on the human experience appealed to them, even if they did not always understand him. He tried to be straightforward and really liked the people and their children and their struggles. He was like a visiting Uncle. The topics he talked on were The Imagination of the Good, Poetry as a Vocation (like the priesthood), Sexuality, Against War etc. We would go back and forth by mail before a topic was selected. The collection from that gathering (75–100) would pay the air ticket.... We would gather at my house for a reading. Robert sat in a big swivel chair he loved. My kids would sometimes run in and out in the beginning and he would engage them. People sat on the floor, brought food, wine, etc.... Only once or twice was there a large (over 100) public reading.... Robert preferred the smaller circle of people he knew from my house.[11]

While with the McCarrolls that December, Duncan was inspired to begin another of the early poems of *Roots and Branches*. Titling it "The Law," he dedicated the poem to the couple, who had watched him compose the opening stanzas at their breakfast table. The new kinship with the community in Portland was inspiring, and Duncan told the McCarrolls upon his return to San Francisco, "The great thing for me was finding in that group of friends that you have gatherd round just such a group as I would gather . . . —your house was . . . a counter-part of my own world."[12]

From Portland, Duncan traveled to Seattle to read at the University of Washington. Housed at the Hotel Edward Meany, and wined and dined at a reception at Theodore Roethke's house, Duncan seemed pleased with the glamour of the poetry business. The readings that winter, in anticipation of the publication of *The Opening of the Field,* began a new phase in Duncan's professional life. His income came to be derived from readings and lectures at universities across the country and in Europe—a change that kept him away from home for nearly half the year throughout most of the 1960s and 1970s. Duncan's forays into the university reading circuit also put him in contact with academic poets he had previously rejected. With his boundless social energy, he created friendships in unlikely places, though usually without admitting any interest in his new acquaintances' poems. A perhaps more compelling aspect of traveling was the novelty of the journey itself, as he told Jess that December: "I . . . want to be a millionaire and fly everywhere, xcept [sic] Oakland."[13]

Completing his work in Seattle, Duncan continued north to Vancouver, where he gave a December 12 reading in the basement of Warren and Ellen Tallman's house. The Tallmans, both professors at the University of British Columbia, had first known Duncan through the Berkeley Renaissance circle.[14] In Vancouver, their home became a haven for the avant-garde, and Warren's classrooms served as a sounding ground for noncanonical poetries. Alongside Robin Blaser and Jack Spicer, Duncan facilitated the link between the writers of the Bay Area and British Columbia. Many younger poets in Vancouver were variously intrigued, influenced, and inspired by Duncan, and some, including Robert Hogg, Pauline Butling, Fred Wah, and David Bromige, became longtime friends.

Another old friend who crossed Duncan's path that winter was Jeff Rall. Duncan had last seen him in New York during the early 1940s and had assumed he was a casualty of the Second World War.[15] Rall meanwhile posted a query in *Industrial Worker* as to Duncan's whereabouts, and the two were reunited on British Columbia's North Pender Island that December.[16] Duncan told Jess, "Jeff Rall is in many ways like Ham Tyler . . . —it's a certain anarchist temper. What I had forgotten or mistaken was that he is not as tall as I am. But the continuity was more striking than the change—on the walls the reproductions of Picasso and Matisse, on the shelves stacks and stacks of pocketbooks of science fiction and weird tales, and memoirs and histories of radicalism."[17] After spending two days with Rall and his family, Duncan returned to Vancouver to record a lecture for the Canadian Broadcasting Corporation. On December 18, he and the Tallmans traveled to Seattle by train, and from there he continued to Portland to see the McCarrolls before boarding a flight to San Francisco. He had been away from home for ten days, and on Christmas Eve, comfortably settled at Elfmere, he reported to Denise Levertov that the tour had been a financial success and that "in the whole trip I found . . . new friends and renewd old friendships, more important than to success of it—that I have verification of my belief that there are kindred that a book might reach. Literary associations obscure what the soul seeks, fellow being."[18]

One of the heralds of the holidays, Fayetta Philip's annual mimeographed Christmas treatise, arrived in December with the title "Weight, Weightlessness, and 'Gravity.'" Duncan and Jess had likewise begun producing hand-drawn, handwritten Christmas cards for their friends, and the 1959 holiday was celebrated not only with correspondence but with a dinner party whose guest list included Ida Hodes, James Broughton, and Harry Jacobus. Duncan and Jess observed the New Year with Robin Blaser and Jim Felts, confined indoors by wet weather that gave rise to blue-eyed grass, a "four-foot tall evening primrose in yellow full bloom," and a wind-shaken bougainvillea looming in one of the cottage's windows.[19] Two new cats, Sybil and Tom Bombadill, entered the household that winter, as did two new creative projects. In February, Duncan began his long poem "Apprehensions," and Jess began collaborating with Larry Jordan on a film called *The 40 and 1 Nights (or Jess's Didactic Nickelodeon)*. The work, which eventually took the form of a six-minute color film, included a sequence of forty-one collages prepared by Jess and coordinated with short fragments of music.

The dawn of 1960 also brought the resolution of difficult publishing business. Early in the year, Duncan negotiated with Grove Press toward a contract for *The Opening of the Field*. Several disputes slowed the process, including a disagreement about the book's cover, which Duncan insisted be designed by Jess. A highlight of Duncan's correspondence with Grove came in a letter to editor Richard Seaver:

> I have had occasion before and shall always have to attack at its roots what art becomes when it becomes a commodity. Today painting has all but become slave to the designs of a market where Picassos DeKoonings or the New York

School are analogous as conspicuous expenditures to Jaguars, and whatever fancy cars. . . . If you think over what as a poet I come to in *The Opening of the Field* to show nature to be, you may reflect that there is an incompatibility between the content and the dominant taste in Madison Avenue Art.[20]

In the end, the press agreed to use Jess's art on the title page while retaining responsibility for the book's cover. From there, the work progressed quickly, with galleys printed in June and the first copies of the book seeing print in October.

With the tapering of winter rains, Duncan and Jess began their third year at Elfmere by indulging in leisure, gathering wild mushrooms on Mount Tamalpais and getting to know new neighbors to their east in Larkspur, Shirley and Wallace Berman. On March 18, Ebbe Borregaard, Joy Aikin, and Helen Adam joined Duncan and Jess for a hike, and the following weekend, the couple hosted the visiting Scottish poet Gael Turnbull. Duncan, weary with a head cold, continued working on the long poem "Apprehensions," embedding images of the day-to-day environment of Elfmere alongside a familiar invocation of Eros:

> Let my awe be steady
> in the rude elements of my household.
> At the window, the rose vine.
>
> Sage architect, you who awaken
> the proportions and scales of the soul's wonder
> of stars and water,
> paeans of color
> that bathe the cumulus at the horizon, yet
> direct
> discrete light
> defining the lintel,
>
> *Bells tied in the foliage ring as the wind rises.*[21]

THIRTY-THREE

Go East

BY 1960, Duncan's friendships on the East Coast were impressive in their diversity, and his appetite for travel was insatiable. In the spring, he left Stinson Beach for the beginning of a substantial northeastern reading tour during which he would spend time with Norman O. Brown, Norman Holmes Pearson, M. C. Richards, John Cage, Merce Cunningham, Jerome Rothenberg, and Denise Levertov. Making his way first to Denver by train, he admired the Rocky Mountains with their "granite extrusions and towering piles of red, rose, pink, stone" before being greeted at the terminal by his exiled protégé Stan Brakhage.[1] Brakhage, then living in Silver Spruce, Colorado, with his wife, Jane, had scraped together funds and an audience for a reading at the University of Colorado in Boulder on April 2. Still ambivalent about Brakhage, Duncan wrote to Jess, "He is in the midst of a meglomaniac [sic] movie (he himself envisioning it as such) of himself as mad 'savior' and he's let his hair grow."[2] The epic project, *Dog Star Man,* was soon to secure Brakhage a place in film history.

After a tense three-day visit with the Brakhages, Duncan continued on to Jacksonville for a reading at Illinois College, and then to Chicago, where he read on April 7. There he was hosted by poet and *Big Table* editor Paul Carroll, whom he described to Jess as a "big and sort of bouncy" Midwesterner.[3] Staying in Chicago through the weekend, Duncan indulged in a trip to the barber and a round of shoe shopping. After attending a reading by poet John Logan, he began the final leg of his journey to New York.

Manhattan's avant-garde was in the midst of transformation.[4] In the neighborhoods around Greenwich Village, where Duncan had once lived with Marjorie McKee, small cafés now hosted musicians such as Bob Dylan and Jimi Hendrix, while young poets flocked to give readings at Les Deux

Mégots and Le Metro. The city was entering a decade of intense political and creative change, and Duncan viewed it through the eyes of a curious yet exhausted visitor plagued by too many social invitations. During his first twenty-four hours in the city that April, he convened with Denise Levertov, Paul Blackburn, Jerome and Diane Rothenberg, and David Antin, and attended a piano performance by David Tudor and Toshi Ichiyanagi at the Living Theatre.

As would become his habit, he also created time for side trips to New England. On April 12, he landed in Middletown, Connecticut, to visit Norman O. Brown and to participate in the Spring Poetry Festival at Wesleyan University. Brown, whom Duncan had met the previous year in Berkeley, was a professor at Wesleyan and had recently published *Life against Death: A Psychoanalytic Meaning of History*. Both a classics scholar and a key thinker in Freudian psychoanalysis and political science, Brown was first-rate intellectual company. Welcomed into Brown's household, which included his wife, Elizabeth, and their three children, Duncan made himself at home and returned regularly. On Wednesday, April 13, he also had a first taste of the Wesleyan poetry festival, a reading by a student of Theodore Roethke's named James Wright, which Duncan gave a mixed review in a letter to Jess: "His work was well within the bounds of literary convention but it was a poet's voice working there."[5]

For the next month, Duncan enjoyed the East Coast, staying in New York with the Rothenbergs, taking an Easter weekend trip to Stony Point to celebrate Merce Cunningham's birthday and to hunt for mushrooms with John Cage, and giving poetry readings at Yale, Wesleyan, and Dartmouth. At Wesleyan, he rendezvoused with alumnus Charles Olson, who was also a participant in the poetry festival. Flanked by the energies of Olson and Norman O. Brown, Duncan had little time to rest. Continuing on to Yale, he met another star of New England academia, Norman Holmes Pearson, an advocate of H. D.'s work and an American studies scholar. Pearson had arranged Duncan's April 20 reading at Yale and also made an intriguing offer: a thousand dollar grant to prepare a treatise about H. D.'s writing as a Festschrift for her seventy-fifth birthday in 1961.[6] Soon titled *The H. D. Book,* the project became all-consuming, occupying Duncan for years and regularly luring him east to study H. D.'s papers at Yale's Beinecke Library. Conceived as a multivolume undertaking, *The H. D. Book* was meant to serve as a tribute to the women in Duncan's life, from his grandmother and Aunt Fay to his high school teacher Edna Keough, to the women writers of H. D.'s era. The book also allowed Duncan to elaborate upon his own relation to poetry while circumnavigating an academic framework. He told Denise Levertov, "Even with the H. D. where I so heartily respond to her spirit—I find the task of critical prose all but impossible. I . . . have to discard false attempt after false attempt. You know, I've long ago discarded, if I ever had it, the thot *[sic]* of whether some reader would think whatever of a poem. I live directly in that medium—and if there's any judgment then it's in the poem itself and not outside it listening to it."[7] Eventually published in fragments in literary magazines during Duncan's lifetime, *The H. D. Book* remained unfinished, partly because of his ongoing desire to expand its parameters and partly because he could not find a suitable publisher for the work.

Duncan's absence from Stinson Beach made room for the growth of his career at the same time that it left a hole in his relationship with Jess. Though their correspondence brimmed with intimacy, it increasingly became clear that Duncan preferred a roaming sociality that was well beyond Jess's emotional limits. Jess tended to the garden during his partner's absence, writing to Duncan on April 24, "I think, instead of the Rose, the Artichoke is my heraldic emblem. I don't comprehend the sweetness and the grace, rather the tastiness and the obstinancy: not angelic, demonic."[8] A few friends in the area could draw Jess out of his prickly isolation. Hilde and David Burton, Robin Blaser, and Harry Jacobus visited Elfmere during Duncan's six-week absence, and Jess continued his film collaboration with Larry Jordan. On April 26, when Sybil gave birth to a litter of kittens, he had even more company. Meanwhile, his deeper loneliness was expressed through his art, as he told Duncan in early May: "I just did a big homosexual oil panel—I've never seen a painting of this subject before, naturally—it's very Manetian paint (except I don't have his accuracy). Obviously I miss you in more ways than a million. I guess this just illustrates it."[9]

For Duncan, there was little time to be homesick. The final two weeks of his tour were centered in New York, where he directed the first East Coast performance of *Faust Foutu*. Again staying with the Rothenbergs on 163rd Street, he held rehearsals for the play in late April, with a group of actors that included former Black Mountain student Nik Cernovich and Living Theatre manager James Spicer. The abbreviated one-act performance, held at the Living Theatre on May 2, was a success. In celebration, the cast introduced Duncan to the New York jazz club the Five Spot. Predisposed toward classical music, Duncan was naively fascinated with the "ravishing jazz" of "a trumpeter (but the trumpet was a special Arabic instrument) by the name of

[Don] Cherry . . . where the aristocratic African beauty of his physical presence, his lean entirely muscular face, that then bellowd out its cheeks to blow . . . reiterated African objects seen earlier in the day in a shop on Madison Avenue."[10]

Newspaper headlines of early May meanwhile gave notice of conflicts both international and domestic. The Soviet Union's interception of a U-2 spy plane over Soviet air space seriously altered the direction of President Eisenhower's impending negotiations with Nikita Krushchev, and at home, a highly publicized domestic crime drama came to an end with the execution of Caryl Chessman on May 2 at San Quentin prison. Convicted in 1948 of kidnapping and sexual assault, Chessman maintained his innocence throughout his twelve years on death row.[11] When a rally was organized in New York in support of Chessman's appeals, Duncan made plans to join the protest in the company of a young poet and peer of Jerome Rothenberg's named Robert Kelly. Kelly remembered his first glimpse of Duncan, an excited figure pouncing upon him as he walked through the doors of the Café Figaro in the West Village. Duncan's greeting, " You *must* be the Kellys!" was an exclamation the fledgling writer later saw as an imperative— that Duncan had bestowed upon him the obligation to be Robert Kelly, the poet.[12] Kelly, born in Brooklyn in 1935, had attended college in Manhattan and had begun editing *Trobar* magazine there in 1960. His interest in Black Mountain school poetics endeared him to Duncan, though the two would find many other areas of correspondence over several years of friendship.

While Duncan was fond of many of the apprentice poets of San Francisco, the East Coast offered him conversations and convergences that were somehow more instinctive. At home with Levertov, Rothenberg, and Kelly in New York, he also had the pleasure of Olson's presence in Gloucester and the two Normans in New Haven and Middletown. But the most satisfying engagement of his East Coast tour came on Friday the thirteenth of May. Beginning the auspicious day at Grove Press where he made final editorial adjustments to *The Opening of the Field,* Duncan continued on to the Stanhope Hotel on the Upper East Side for his first meeting with H.D. The seventy-three-year-old writer, who had returned to the United States to receive the American Academy of Arts and Letters Medal, greeted Duncan warmly, though he found her "surrounded by discretions" in the form of three caretakers: her daughter Perdita, Norman Holmes Pearson, and "a beautiful Swiss girl" who was an assistant and nurse to the ailing poet. Duncan, H.D., and her overseers had a two-hour tea session that day, and Duncan was invited for a longer visit on the following Monday.[13]

In the darkened hotel room, Duncan and H. D. exchanged memories of childhood—fairy tales, séances, and astronomy—and H. D. reminisced about her half-century career as a writer. While Perdita came and went from the room, H. D. spoke to Duncan of the aspects of her work that she had intentionally obscured from public view, including her involvement in one of Britain's midcentury Roman Mithra cults. Duncan excitedly wrote home to Jess of the disclosures:

> Over a table of William Morris during the second World War there had been the first séances—and she has written a trilogy of novels as historical keys: one on William Morris and the pre-Raphaelite brotherhood, one on Count Zinzendorf and the Bohemian brethren, and a third (or a first) telling how she "went too far" with the Marshall of the Air, and came upon something she should not have known about the Mithra cult in the second World War. A vision that saw "behind the screen" a mystery of the old war cults (that no woman was to know or to see) that had been there since the Roman legions in Britain, not a British thing but the Mithraeum. Underground.[14]

The visit was monumental for Duncan, who wrote to H. D. during his flight home, "But I wanted somehow to say—what? of what my visits with you meant. . . . your presence had spoken so directly to me in your work, and freed in me some force, even *the* force, of my own work—there is a genius, a particular one attending the awakening of what a writing is—and I had that, your acknowledgement and obedience then of the genius—a benediction."[15]

With a final scramble to tie up loose ends in New York, between May 16 and May 20 Duncan made a number of outings with Denise Levertov: a trip to the Bronx Zoo, a reading at Brooklyn College, and a lunch date with H. D. at the restaurant of the Metropolitan Museum. On May 21, he flew to Chicago for another Midwest reading, and from there, was off to San Francisco on May 24 and across the bay to the Elfmere cottage in Stinson Beach. A final communication to Jess from New York had foreshadowed his return: "Dearest, the heart has strings, it would seem—yearning for you and home is like a tug of strings (do arteries and veins strain toward loved things we are separated from?) and images of your dearness, all most almost recaptured pictures of you, come to me."[16]

◀ PLATE 1. Fayetta, Dee, and
Minnehaha Harris, ca. 1900.
Courtesy Susan Gardner.

◀ PLATE 2. Edwin and Minnehaha Symmes, 1913. The Robert Duncan Collection: The
Poetry Collection of the University Libraries, University at Buffalo, The State University
of New York. Reprinted by permission.

▶ PLATE 3. Duncan with Minnehaha and Barbara, ca. 1927. The Robert Duncan
Collection: The Poetry Collection of the University Libraries, University at Buffalo, The
State University of New York. Reprinted by permission.

▲ PLATE 4. Duncan
in Bakersfield,
ca. 1935. The Robert
Duncan Collection:
The Poetry Collection
of the University
Libraries, University
at Buffalo, The State
University of New
York. Reprinted by
permission.

▶ PLATE 5. Mary
Fabilli and Duncan on
the Berkeley campus,
ca. 1938. The Robert
Duncan Collection:
The Poetry Collection
of the University
Libraries, University
at Buffalo, The State
University of New
York. Reprinted by
permission.

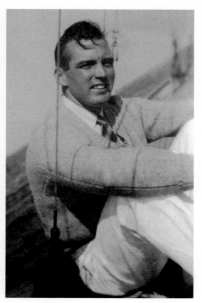

▲ PLATE 6. Duncan in New York City, ca. 1940. The *Phoenix* Collection, PCMS-017: The Poetry Collection of the University Libraries, University at Buffalo, The State University of New York. Reprinted by permission.

◥ PLATE 7. Ned Fahs, late 1930s. Courtesy Alice and Mimi Fahs.

▼ PLATE 8. Jess at Baker Street (Norris Embry seated), ca. 1953. Courtesy Kevin Killian.

PLATE 9. Helen
Adam and Jess stand
behind Duncan and
Ida Hodes, Stinson Beach,
late 1950s. The Helen
Adam Collection: The
Poetry Collection of the
University Libraries,
University at Buffalo,
The State University
of New York. Reprinted
by permission.

PLATE 10. Duncan and Jess in their garden, Stinson Beach, late 1950s. Photo by Helen
Adam. The Helen Adam Collection: The Poetry Collection of the University Libraries,
University at Buffalo, The State University of New York. Reprinted by permission.

▲ PLATE 11. Jack Spicer and Joanne Kyger (Lew Welch in background), early 1960s. Photo by Helen Adam. The Helen Adam Collection: The Poetry Collection of the University Libraries, University at Buffalo, The State University of New York. Reprinted by permission.

▼ PLATE 12. *Left to right*: David Wevill, Alberto de Lacerda, Duncan and Robert Creeley, in Austin, Texas, 1969. Photo by Frank Armstrong. Courtesy Ruth Lepson.

Ken Irby, Robert Duncan + Anne Waldman.
April 1972. Dorfman

▲ PLATE 13. Ken Irby,
Duncan, and Anne
Waldman, Cambridge,
Massachusetts, 1972.
Photo by Elsa Dorfman.
Courtesy Elsa Dorfman.

▶ PLATE 14. Exterior
photo of 3267 20th Street,
San Francisco, shortly
before Duncan purchased
it in 1967. The Robert
Duncan Collection: The
Poetry Collection of the
University Libraries,
University at Buffalo, The
State University of New
York. Reprinted by
permission.

▲ PLATE 15.   Page from Duncan's notebook: "The Soldiers: *Passages* 26." The Robert Duncan Collection: The Poetry Collection of the University Libraries, University at Buffalo, The State University of New York. Reprinted by permission.

▼ PLATE 16.   A Homer Group meeting at Aaron Shurin's apartment, early 1980s. *Clockwise from bottom left*: Susan Thackrey, Shurin, David Melnick, Steve Anker, Jim Powell, Duncan, Michael McClure, Tom Fong, and Noel Stack. Photo by David Levi Strauss.

▲ PLATE 17. Jess (broken ankle) and Duncan (broken collarbone), in recovery, 1986. Photo by Norma Cole.

▼ PLATE 18. *Left to right:* Jess, Hilde Burton, Duncan, and David Burton, ca. 1986. The Robert Duncan Collection: The Poetry Collection of the University Libraries, University at Buffalo, The State University of New York. Reprinted by permission.

THIRTY-FOUR

Apprehensions

Something must be lost, stolen.
Something must be told that should have been kept,
known by the heart. He is all but forsworn.
Home could have won.

ROBERT DUNCAN, "Four Songs the Night Nurse Sang"

DURING HIS NEW YORK SOJOURN, Duncan had a brief affair and re-corded the details of it in a letter to Robin Blaser. Blaser in turn put the let-ter into Jess's hands shortly before Duncan's return to Stinson Beach.[1] As Blaser recalled in a 1992 interview with Kevin Killian, "A letter arrived, and I picked it up, packed my bag, and left . . . to stay over the weekend with Jess. . . . The letters were always wonderful, and they were usually . . . both for me and for posterity—I rather liked my relation to posterity—and so I just gave Jess the letter, and said, you know, 'Read it.'" After a quiet evening with Jess, scavenging for mussels and preparing a pasta dinner, Blaser retired to his guest room in the attic with Duncan's letter: "I nearly died. . . . It was telling me about someone he'd met in New York, . . . and it was important, the person he'd met in New York, . . . and so I got up, and went downstairs, knocked on Jess' bedroom door, and went in to tell Jess I had not read the letter."[2] The confusions of the situation were soon doubled. Blaser and Jess, alone at Elfmere for the weekend, initiated their own sexual relationship, and Duncan arrived home faced with a crisis in his marriage. A veiled record of the discord appeared in a June 2 notebook entry, and was later incorpo-rated into the poem "Cover Images":

> I woke in the night again
> from a dream of the murderer that I am,
> A stream of hatred runs in the bough of
> life's tree. . . .
>
> seen in the dream where my beloved
> masturbated, away from me, facing
> a man, partly seen, undressing or

disclosing his
nakedness in an open window . . .

Who left the notes accusing himself
of being me? In the morning
I was relieved of what knowledge,
lifted by angels that are
rays of actual light of the sun
out of the solitary?[3]

The details of Duncan's affair and Jess's reaction to it remain undocumented, though the rift clearly occupied Duncan's mind that summer as he composed three other poems toward *Roots and Branches:* "Come, Let Me Free Myself," "Risk," and "Four Songs the Night Nurse Sang." In June, during a sweltering heat wave, Duncan made a rare visit to his mother at her ranch in Soquel, California—perhaps partly to escape from the dilemma at home. Ida Hodes remembered that Jess was loath to accompany Duncan on such journeys, as his meetings with Minnehaha invariably triggered asthma attacks.[4] At least some smaller token of happiness entered Elfmere that summer when Duncan and Jess chose to keep a cat from Sybil's litter, "a black long-haired Orlando," who would remain in their household through the mid-1970s.[5] In June and July, Duncan also immersed himself in *The H. D. Book,* though he confided to Denise Levertov that the work required great effort: "I have no more than sketchy paragraphs—I am overwhelmd at what is involved in mastering prose—in managing anything natural and direct."[6] After cobbling together pieces of the project over the summer, he hitchhiked to the Pacific Northwest with plans to continue the work while visiting friends. On August 24, he arrived in Portland to see the McCarrolls, after which he traveled to Seabeck, outside of Seattle, to stay with Ariel Reynolds Parkinson. The tensions of the early summer contributed to an emotional correspondence between Duncan and Jess, and Duncan's solo vacation again seemed like a flight from marriage. On August 30, Jess wrote Duncan that he wouldn't come see him and asked him instead to return to Stinson Beach. Duncan responded with a description of his own psychic turmoil: "I'm being baby-ish too, throwing myself out of my crib and climbing back in to prove that you are really there, risking you (as again there seems to be the problem of how to risk, what does it mean in living and work?)."[7]

Called home, Duncan complied, returning to Elfmere after two weeks and bracing himself for an autumn of poetry events in the Bay Area. Throughout the season, he chipped away at *The H. D. Book* and sent the first chapter to its subject in early September. In October, *The Opening of the Field* was published, and Duncan impatiently awaited the reviews, reporting to Toby McCarroll, "If I become famous, I'm going to go to charm school and become a snob. Of the worst sort. And cultivate the crushing manner. Except at home, where my cats won't allow it."[8] Jess also looked forward to some acknowledgment of his work, having prepared paintings for a December show at San Francisco's Dilexi Gallery. Back in the thick of conversations with their Bay Area peers, the couple ventured to events in Berkeley and San Francisco. On October 28, Duncan gave a reading at the University of California to mark the publication of *The Opening of the Field*. The next evening, he and Jess attended Helen Adam's play *San Francisco's Burning,* performed by Adam and her sister Pat at the recently christened Borregaard's Museum on Buchanan Street. Poet Ebbe Borregaard and his wife, Joy, had established the venue to showcase the creative achievements of the Spicer circle. The following year, the museum hosted a show of Jess's work as well as a series of lectures by Duncan on the history of modern poetry. Duncan's fifteen-part outline for the course mapped out a journey through symbolism, free verse, and imagism, with forays into mythology, depth psychology, and linguistics. The list of writers and thinkers he planned to discuss held no surprises: Freud, Joyce, Stein, H. D., Pound, Jane Harrison, and Whitehead.[9] Duncan's tenure at the museum began on December 15, and he reported to Denise Levertov that winter, "At present I have between twenty sure and thirty . . . at the most attending. At a dollar a lecture (one-third going to the Museum . . .), both those attending and I am *[sic]* held to a certain 'investment' or exchange."[10]

Helen Adam, who was similarly pleased with the reception of her Halloween weekend presentation of *San Francisco's Burning,* arranged a second reading of the play in early December and also made plans for a larger production of the work at James Broughton's Poet's Theatre. Anxious about this collaboration between his two old friends, Duncan wrote to Adam, complimenting her on the performance at Borregaard's Museum but expressing wariness of her plans to work with Broughton and Kermit Sheets:

> The performance, Helen, was the real magic of theater. I am the more savagely opposed to the idea of a production that will lack the information, the eloquent gesture you have thruout. Your music is an integral part of the work. It is seed, root and branching flower of the inspired creation: I am severe in my sense of its being a part of the divine wonder. That such a daemonic gift is at work . . . is a very sacred thing—I have seen the daemon, I do not want to see the impersonation.[11]

The protest was registered by Adam, but the lure of a larger staging of her play prevailed, and the Playhouse production took place at the end of 1961.

By November 1960, Duncan and Jess had resolved springtime tensions, and they planned a Thanksgiving celebration that included Blaser and Jim Felts, Pat and Helen Adam, Ida Hodes, and Hilde and David Burton. Before the holiday, they made a brief trip to Soquel to visit Minnehaha, who had suffered a heart attack in early October. In a confluence of events again related to Duncan's sense of "the mother," on December 21, 1960, the winter solstice, in the height of his correspondence with H.D., his adoptive mother died at the age of seventy-three. Duncan's sister Barbara arranged for their mother's ashes to be interred beside the urns of Edwin Symmes and Lewis Burtch at the Chapel of the Chimes Mausoleum in Oakland. When Duncan and Jess spent Christmas day with Pat and Helen Adam, Duncan did not divulge his mother's death. He wrote to H.D. in January that he had yet to fully experience Minnehaha's absence:

> I was a dependent, literally—and that also means expressively too; yet I can't locate the loss. There was immediately the residue of some me in childhood who wanted to keep her as person—and in that me a child's immediate "coming to grief," "being left behind." But in my adult years there's always been personally distance between us of mind, of aesthetic, of actual geography—and the distance of "death" seems so allied that it is hard to remember I can not, have not to, write a letter.[12]

Saying good-bye to the headstrong woman who had ushered him through childhood and had been the most important confidante of his late adolescent years, he penned "Two Presentations":

> You are gone and I send
> as I used to
>   with the salutation *Dear Mother*
> the beginning of a letter
>   as if it could reach you.
>
> Yet *Dear Mother* could catch at my heart to say
>   —and did when I was a child, as you
> now are a child among shades—
>   as if the words betrayd
> a painful nearness and separation.[13]

FIVE

———

The Nasty Aesthetician

THIRTY-FIVE

The Will

(The President
orders history
reupholstered)

ROBERT DUNCAN, "Stage Directions, *Passages* 30"

ON JANUARY 20, 1961, Robert Frost acted as the poet of ceremonies at the inauguration of John F. Kennedy. Frost recited his poem "The Gift Outright," and Kennedy spoke the now-famous lines "My fellow Americans, ask not what your country can do for you, ask what you can do for your country." Duncan felt little sympathy for the new president, whom many looked upon with hope and admiration. Kennedy's administration was confronted with major crises, including communist threats in Cuba and Viet Nam, the erection of the Berlin Wall in 1961, and growing civil unrest in the South. Early in his administration, the new president increased the defense budget 15 percent, began stockpiling intercontinental ballistic missiles, and created a counterinsurgency group to monitor suspicious political activity in Latin America and Southeast Asia. As Duncan entered middle age, his parents' prophecy of the imminent destruction of civilization took on new meaning. After a decade of mutual fear between the United States and the Soviet Union, the Viet Nam war directed the public's apprehensions to a new front. It was a war through which Duncan grieved, and it was a war that fed his imagination, inhabiting the ground of his poems for two decades.

During inauguration week, the unhappy news arrived that Duncan's friend Tom Parkinson had been shot while meeting with a student in his English Department office at the Berkeley campus of the University of California. Parkinson survived the attack but was seriously injured, and as his wife, Ariel, later remembered, the violence came at the beginning of a decade of unrest:

In 1961 *[sic]*, students protesting the McCarthy HUAC hearings asked [Parkinson], as a respected faculty member and potential witness, to monitor their demonstration outside San Francisco City Hall. His appearance there ... led to savage, scurrilous criticism in the far-right ... press. Armed with ... a sawed-off shotgun, intending to start "the third world war," a former student appeared in the doorway of Tom's office. The first shot blew off half his face. The second murdered Abner Dean, the student who was talking to him.[1]

The incident prompted Duncan to meditate upon his relationship with Parkinson, an advocate of Bay Area poetries and a peripheral member of the Berkeley Renaissance: "I realized ... the curious affection I have for Tom. ... He is a character in the fiction of my life (as he is for the Tylers or for Jack Spicer) and has in that the affection of 'belonging' that endears impossible characters in Dickens' novels—as members of cherished occasions. But back of that is my sense that Tom is earnestly a champion of the good, he strives to find the good life."[2] He wrote Toby and Claire McCarroll of his recognition that he too could be the target of a disturbed individual: "One of my public habits is to goad those whose opinions I despise into a frenzy. Next time I start letting some contemptuous smile leer up and thinking of infuriating lines to take. ... But unfortunately, challenging is an old penchant of mine."[3]

At home he attended to other troubling matters. With Minnehaha's death, he came into an inheritance, but he and his sister Barbara disagreed about certain details of the estate. Fishing for legal advice, he wrote Toby McCarroll in mid-January, citing among his grievances his sister's reluctance to hand over two coveted items: his mother's toaster and a book by Thomas Troward called *The Law and the Word*.[4] McCarroll traveled south from Portland to accompany Duncan to his mother's home in Soquel on February 1. Barbara Jones remembered her brother arriving at the ranch with someone she assumed was a book dealer: as Duncan angled volumes from the shelves, McCarroll offered discriminating nods. Having appropriated the gems in the collection, Duncan donated the rest of the books to libraries, leaving his sister to dispose of their mother's furniture and clothing.[5] For Jones, the worry arose that Duncan—a bohemian by the family's standards—would squander his inheritance. Toby McCarroll had another perspective on the conflict:

We went to the house ... to explore the will. It was a strange group which included the aunt [Fayetta] who once told a very young Robert "You are no good, you were no good in former lives and you will be no good in future lives!" ... I found the various provisions of the trust stingy but Robert, and Jess, were satisfied. I remember ... a difficult bank trust department. He finally got enough to close the gap in his living expenses. There was also $15 on

Christmas or Thanksgiving to assure he would have something to eat as the assumption was he would be a bum. I thought it was insulting but Robert and Jess again thought it was considerate.[6]

Minnehaha left Duncan her ranch in Soquel, and the proceeds from the sale of the property were converted into a trust fund stock portfolio.[7] It was an account from which Duncan and Jess drew money monthly, though usually not more than a few hundred dollars at a time.

On February 4, having completed their inquest at Soquel, Duncan and McCarroll drove to Portland, and Duncan then flew on to Vancouver, where he had been invited to read at a "festival of avant guarde [sic] arts" organized by Warren Tallman.[8] He spent a busy week meeting with Tallman's students and recording two new lectures at the studios of the Canadian Broadcasting Corporation. To Jess he reported that a "manic energy" informed the trajectory of his talks: "I realized one good passage relating Beethoven to Carlyle's inner nature of things as melody and contrasted with the concentions of music before Beethoven. And the other lecture turned out to be on uncertainty as the path between reality and our souls that Whitman thot [sic] poetry was for."[9]

Ecstatic visions of music and verse were dampened that week by a meeting with confessional poet W. D. Snodgrass, a student of Randall Jarrell's. Duncan lodged his complaints about Snodgrass's festival reading in a letter to his steadfast confidante Denise Levertov: "as stupid and ugly a bid for a place in the sub-urban conscience as I've heard. I loathe these personal problems that have no deep root but are all social currency—case history of a social worker. Wld. as soon attend divorce court."[10] A poet on the scene during Duncan's early Vancouver visits, Frank Davey, recalled the fierce competition between Duncan and Snodgrass, noting that during a party hosted by the Tallmans,

> each "held court" in different rooms. . . . After an hour or so there were only a few people listening to Snodgrass and 60 or 70 crowded around Robert. Duncan . . . extemporaneously (and loudly and hilariously) parodied several of Snodgrass's poems. A very impressive performance. He wasn't just trying to upstage Snodgrass, . . . he was also seeking to emphatically discredit his aesthetic and limit Snodgrass's possible influence on students at the party— even if this meant humiliating Snodgrass, which I think it did.[11]

Throughout the visit, personal worries were clearly on Duncan's mind. With the promise of an income from his mother's estate, he began contemplating a move from Stinson Beach back to San Francisco. There, Jess could be closer to the galleries and scavenging sites that fed his work, and the couple could be "free and independent at times that call for getting a kitty to the hospital."[12] Lurking beneath such logistical concerns was a more contentious detail of the household dynamics. Jess, still shaken by Duncan's affair the previous spring, was worried that his partner had been escaping from home to continue *The H. D. Book* in solitude. With both men engaged in their careers, they had difficulty organizing their days, a fact Duncan addressed from a distance: "Dear heart, it's not some washing of dishes or cooking a meal . . . that distracts me from work. And if you've felt your necessary involvements were a drag, I've felt more and more how you take on to do everything about the house—with me holding back from not only paragraphs but normal household work."[13]

The early part of the year gave Duncan and Jess little time to resolve domestic issues. Duncan returned to San Francisco on February 16, and a week later he delivered a lecture at the University of California, Davis. In March, at the height of their search for an apartment in San Francisco, Duncan and Jess were sideswiped by a springtime flu. Roused from his lethargy by a letter from H. D. that included a typescript of her poem sequence *Hermetic Definition,* Duncan mobilized himself to return to *The H. D. Book.*[14] Inspiration came on another front as well: on April 7, he boarded a bus to visit his father's sister Alvie in Oakland. Alvie Symmes Brumm, who had lived next door to the Symmeses on Pearl Street in Alameda, was one of the few relatives whose company Duncan enjoyed.[15] Still a member of a theosophical Christian group years after others in the Symmes family had abandoned such preoccupations, Brumm treated her visiting nephew to recitations from the Gnostic Gospel of Thomas.

As the more tangible details of economics bore down upon the household that spring, Duncan took a pause from *The H. D. Book* to deliver a series of lectures to a small clique at Borregaard's Museum. In late April, he gave two talks at a California Scholarship Federation conference in San Francisco: "Finding Life Values in Modern Poetry" and "Finding Your Way in Modern Poetry." That spring and summer, he undertook other conventional writing tasks, including an essay on the French poet Saint-John Perse for the Catholic magazine *Jubilee* edited by Thomas Merton, Edward Rice, and Robert Lax.[16] And when Denise Levertov became the poetry editor of the *Nation,* she designated Duncan as a reviewer of H. D.'s *Helen in Egypt,* a task he added to his list of projects for the year. While public attention gave Duncan some pleasure, he also bristled against it. Both *The Opening of the Field* and *The New*

American Poetry had bolstered his reputation as a writer, though, as he told Levertov, his resistance to the anthology remained strong: "My sense of outrage has been mounting thru successive reviews of Allen's anthology. That the established mediocracies seem to be setting you, me, Creeley up as 'best' or 'good'—as having then the likeness of belonging to the same world of 'poetry' as Louis Simpson, Richard Wilbur, Merwin or Snodgrass."[17]

On May 10, 1961, Duncan and Jess left Elfmere Cottage and moved to an apartment in San Francisco at 3735 20th Street. It would be the couple's home for the next six years. Abandoning the task of unpacking, Duncan returned to Vancouver for three weeks in July. A number of the students who had met him the previous winter had each donated five dollars toward his travel expenses in exchange for admission to a series of lectures culled from his research for *The H. D. Book* and his studies of Charles Olson's "Projective Verse" essay.[18] For the newly initiated, the scope of Duncan's knowledge was overwhelming. His barrage of facts and anecdotes about imagism, Pound's *Cantos,* Williams's line, H. D.'s hermeticism, and Olson's view of history set the groundwork for a new poetics curriculum at the University of British Columbia, and as he told Jess, "The first 'lecture' provided a great tangle and swarm of ideas, leaving me and everybody else sufficiently bewildered."[19] Poet David Bromige echoed Duncan's sentiment, recalling that those who attended the lectures spent the next two years puzzling over *The New American Poetry* and Olson's essay: "When Duncan came I really had no idea where he was coming from; . . . even though for Olson and the others that was all worked through material by then . . . but for us it was all new, and without a context, or much of one, [it was] hard to decode."[20]

For Duncan, the work with the students came naturally. On July 17, he again wrote Jess, reporting that his audience "seem[ed] to be opening up worlds for themselves with the interplay of Olson, Creeley and me," also noting with some satisfaction, "Warren showed me a term paper by a nineteen-year-old girl Pauline Butling on the Pindar poem that developed fully the musical picture of the work and the psyche-eros theme."[21] Butling later recalled the dramatic impact of the influx of American poets and artists on her education:

Those two years (1961–1963) proved to be as exciting as any tour of Europe. Duncan was just one of many innovative writers and artists to visit Vancouver during that time. The . . . Festival of Contemporary Arts brought in . . . John Cage, Merce Cunningham, and Robert Creeley in 1962. *TISH* magazine began in the fall of 1961; Roy Kiyooka started a poetry reading series for local poets at the Vancouver Art School; bill bissett, Gerry Gilbert and others created a lively downtown scene. And Warren and Ellen Tallman had what seemed like a continuous stream of parties where the young writers, artists, students and professors...came together and formed a community. However,...Duncan was the first and probably the one with the greatest impact.... He became an inspiration, a role model, a treasure trove of poetic techniques, and a catalyst for action.[22]

Duncan remained in Vancouver through the end of July, talking with students, spending time with the Tallmans, and finding spare moments to sculpt his essay on Saint-John Perse. Around the first of August, he departed for North Pender Island to relax with Jeff Rall and his family for "four days of sun and woods and harbours."[23] In both the Tallman and Rall households, Duncan was immersed in thriving domestic scenes. He gravitated toward such settings, expressing an appreciation for the familial and for an audience of adults and children alike. Ellen Tallman recalled:

When Duncan arrived on visits, we evolved a ritual: From the airport we went to the Valetor Cleaners where Robert would leave a suitcase full of dirty shirts—they did a better job than San Francisco, he said. Next, we'd go to the liquor store (although Robert didn't drink, we did), then to the greengrocers and the Safeway. In all of the stores we would clog up the aisles with Robert's incessant talking which gathered much attention, as the talk was loud and his appearance dramatic because he always wore the three-tiered black cape that he had brought back from ... Mallorca.[24]

Duncan's early August stay on North Pender Island brought an adventure of another sort. Jeff Rall, who had been told of a haunted house on the island, suggested that he and Duncan hold a séance there. The two men, setting off one morning to explore the site, found that they were too frightened to proceed. Duncan described the expedition to Jess: "We followed a path past the gate of a cemetery and even before we came to the porch of the house I was struck by the dreary oppressive spirit of the place. Jeff was no longer adventuresome or playing but hesitant. I found a back door open and we went into the house—in the full light of afternoon it was a dreadful little house. A woman had shot her husband there."[25] His hopes spoiled for a revival of the occultism of his Woodstock days, Duncan hopscotched from Pender Island back to Vancouver and then to Portland to see Toby and Claire McCarroll before returning home to Jess for a quiet end to summer in San Francisco.

THIRTY-SIX

The Playhouse

The Divine moves in this Comedy.
What does she know of these rites
that she did not receive from
hidden orders
of laughter and catastrophe?

ROBERT DUNCAN, "What Happened: Prelude"

WHEN H. D. DIED IN ZURICH ON SEPTEMBER 27, 1961, Duncan was in the midst of the second section of *Roots and Branches,* composing a poem called "Doves." Dedicated to H. D. and partly inspired by William Morris's fantasy novel *The Well at the World's End,* the piece evolved from a tribute into an elegy.[1] H. D. suffered a stroke and a heart attack in early June, and Duncan had followed news of her decline via his correspondence with Norman Holmes Pearson. He recorded his thoughts about her death in a September 28 letter to Pearson, including the sentiment "You will understand how even in my few meetings with her, she had become most dear."[2] *The H. D. Book* had been in progress for slightly over a year, with Duncan transitioning from handwritten texts in spiral-bound notebooks to typed manuscripts, which he shared with friends Pearson, Robin Blaser, Denise Levertov, and Donald Allen.[3]

Meanwhile, when news came that Helen Adam and James Broughton were planning a December presentation of Adam's *San Francisco's Burning,* Duncan composed a theater piece of his own, *A Play for Masques,* for a Halloween party at Paul Alexander's studio in San Francisco. A small section of the work, "A Country Wife's Song," was later included in *Roots and Branches,* and as Duncan told Denise Levertov, "This one is a horse play. With no subtleties—writ mostly in Elizabethan rhetoric. With the 'hero' referring to Bottom in *Midsummer's Night Dream.*"[4] By the early 1960s, Duncan's correspondence with Levertov had become a point around which he organized his days. His New York intimate made her second trip to San Francisco on November 7, 1961, arriving by bus from Southern California and staying in a guest room at the new apartment on 20th Street. Between readings at the Poetry Center, Mills College, and the University of California, she spent a good deal of time with Duncan and Jess. Duncan's covetous attitude toward Levertov crept into a mid-October letter: "Thinking of the almost grim array of those who will want to see you in the four days you will be here, I think it might be solved by a reception sort of thing here—just for those who have some personal claim, a real concern."[5] Levertov reciprocated the affection, writing him on her flight back to New York, "I can't say what I feel about your poems, usually, any more than I can say what I feel about you as a presence, except to say I love you. Perhaps some of it can someday be a poem for you."[6]

On the heels of Levertov's departure came the eruption of a conflict long in the making. Duncan's rejection of James Broughton's Playhouse Theater and his disapproval of Helen Adam's creative alliance with Broughton became the subject of a scathing poem, "What Happened: Prelude." Duncan, who had few qualms about censuring friends, used the occasion to condemn everyone involved in the presentation of Adam's play, beginning with Broughton, "Mr. Fair Speech," and Kermit Sheets, "Mr. By-Ends," the "false advisors" of Adam's venture.[7] In a letter to Broughton mailed the week before the play's late December opening, Duncan continued to sound his protest of the theater project: "No, James, we are not going to the Playhouse version of *San Francisco's Burning*. We have a tape of the authentic work, and have seen it done by Helen and Pat. We have only been offended and outraged by the changes Helen has made and consented to be made to convert her work into a Playhouse styled musical from what was originally a great and inspired work of poetry."[8]

After Duncan and Jess boycotted an opening-night party in the Adam household, Helen wrote to Duncan in an attempt to reconcile with him. When he subsequently suggested that she had disrupted a metaphysical order by staging the play as a contemporary musical, her anxious response revealed the extent of her belief in the occult and in Duncan's role as a magician of sorts: "I am afraid of your predictions Robert, because I feel you have power in those worlds, and when you pronounce a thing it may very well come true."[9] But Adam's personal financial difficulties had made the production of a mainstream play appealing, and her friendship with Broughton had given her further reason to proceed. The play, a dark comic story of the reveling of sailors, prostitutes, and ghosts on the eve of San Francisco's 1906 earthquake, was an instant hit. A *San Francisco Examiner* reviewer wrote in January of 1962, "The show threatens to break every Playhouse attendance record. . . . I was convinced [not only] that it is a work of infinite, haunting liveliness, but that it is a real milestone of little theater production and that it deserves to be seen elsewhere, particularly on the off-Broadway stage in New York."[10]

Seeking to remove himself from the hubbub around Adam's play, Duncan spent part of the holiday season in New Mexico, catching up with the Creeleys in Albuquerque just after Christmas and accompanying them to see friends Jorge and Barbara Fick in Santa Fe. Jorge Fick, a painter who had studied at Black Mountain College, had suggested a New Year outing to a native dance festival at the local Santo Domingo Pueblo. When a tribal dispute led to the cancellation of the event, the group made alternate plans, as Duncan told Jess: "We had anyway a New Years party, in full artists colony style—and thanks to the news that the Turtles would not dance at dawn, we did not have to last til dawn ourselves. The party was at the Sihvonens—the husband a very good disciple of Albers (Black Mountain was everywhere) and the wife in the same spirit a very good weaver."[11]

After celebrating the New Year and his birthday with the Ficks, Duncan returned to Albuquerque on January 8 to be interviewed by Robert Creeley for a local radio program called "The Single Voice." On January 12, he returned to San Francisco to find that his condemnation of *San Francisco's Burning* had not only deepened his rift with James Broughton but had contributed to Helen Adam's nervous collapse. When Adam wandered out onto the Golden Gate Bridge one night intending to jump into the bay, her sister Pat committed her to the Langley Porter Psychiatric Clinic, where she was given electric shock treatments for depression. Duncan's communications with Adam while she was hospitalized were couched in a philosophical defensiveness:

> Every dramatic life force in us rises to win the fullness of our life when Death itself challenges: I do think that, while we always have the immediate will of our own death ready, we have also the imagination of our own life that will not be done, whatever suffering, until the body itself is at last run its course. My feeling about suicide is just that we always can have that tyranny over our life; we can always make such passionate decisions, but I would choose to dream for a long time of my death—to let Death live in me for a life-time before, in the mystery of a design of me beyond my own will and passion, I come to the end.[12]

Duncan never backed down from his insistence that the new version of *San Francisco's Burning* was a travesty of a divine order, but James Broughton later conjectured that a jealousy of Adam's success may have played a larger role: "She became an idol of the whole town.... She was written up in the papers.... She was spectacular on stage, and she had written the part... that she played.... And so because I had introduced her into the theater, ... she dedicated a book to me, and she insisted on doing that, ... and Robert was furious. He never forgave her when he found out that the book was dedicated to me."[13]

On January 18, Duncan had an opportunity to pen a letter to Denise Levertov reporting that the New Year had been difficult. Already prone to ennui around his birthday and the holidays, he found Helen Adam's breakdown to be an extra burden, though he rationalized that her hospitalization was precipitated in part by "having her play produced but drastically redone by James Broughton and Kermit Sheets."[14] Unable to admit his role in alienating Adam, Duncan spent the early winter cultivating other friendships. Robin Blaser and Paul Alexander frequented the household during those months, as did two new friends, artists Liam O'Gallagher and Robert Rheem, with whom Duncan shared ideas about forming an occult group. H. D.'s death in September had likely revived Duncan's interest in theosophical teachings, and his work on *The H. D. Book* had led him back toward hermetic source materials, including the writings of Madame Blavatsky. In a journal entry of January 1962, Duncan listed potential invitees to a "Moon Society" coterie: Robin Blaser, Michael and Joanna McClure, David and Tina Meltzer, Richard Baker, and a medium named Michael Hughes.[15] Characterized by participant David Meltzer as "Full Moon Summits," the meetings occurred on Tuesdays after the new and full moon.[16] Michael McClure remembered that the gatherings were "not about magic as much as about whatever anyone's special area of information or gift or curiosity lay in." McClure's contribution was a presentation "on the active ingredient of psychedelic mushrooms."[17]

On January 21, snow fell in San Francisco for the first time since 1931. Duncan and Jess woke to find the cats wrapped around each other on a chair, and Jess likewise spent the morning curled up in bed while Duncan reflected upon the weather and household events in his journal. That afternoon, the couple greeted visitors Ramon Sender, Laurel Johnson, and Pauline Oliveros, with whom they attempted to drive to Santa Cruz for a concert by composer Lou Harrison. Turned around near Los Gatos by snow closures, the group returned to San Francisco to have dinner and late-night coffee at 20th Street.[18] The following week Duncan made his seasonal foray to Portland to visit the

McCarrolls and to speak to McCarroll's Ethical Study Society on "The Role of Homosexuality in Life Patterns and Meanings." He wrote to the couple before his arrival, "I have in mind talking about how homosexuality is used to satisfy dramatic needs—and contrast dramatic needs with ethical needs."[19] Duncan suggested that he might also host a private audience over the weekend for a reading from *The H. D. Book*. Meanwhile, at home, Helen Adam was released from the Langley Porter Clinic, and upon Duncan's return to San Francisco, he attempted to ease the tensions of the preceding months:

> What I must get across is that I do most understand how much you wanted to see the play done. And tho I think the poet in you rebelld against you when you went along with the poetic way being alterd, and that the angelic-demonic in you (your guardian angels, powers of your heaven and hell) struck when the divine was interfered with in the production . . . , it's because I am an ordinary mortal, with my own dread of offending these very powers that I have any integrity at all.[20]

The heavens took the headlines on February 20, 1962, when John Glenn became the first American to orbit the earth. In early March, Duncan wrote "A Set of Romantic Hymns" that pointed to his own interest in modern science. The poem took inspiration from James Watson and Francis Crick's efforts to map the DNA molecule, for which they received the Nobel Prize in Medicine that year. Duncan embedded an homage to their discoveries in the lines "The dancers cross over to the other side, / change places and again divide."[21] The poem, an example of Duncan's deep-rooted use of collage, wove together images of DNA mapping, a trip to the San Francisco Zoo, and New Mexican Native American rituals. When he sent a copy of the piece to Jorge and Barbara Fick, he reflected upon their contribution to the composition:

> At last 'our' Indians came in a poem, that day-after-Xmas dance at Santo Domingo pueblo and the dancing files of chromosomes (as drawn in *Scientific American* really does look like a crowded charm bracelet)—the women's black dresses and turquoise sky tiaras which I got in the beginning as blue-black (Prussian) and turquoise of the Argus peacock's eyes. With lots of rustling—We'd been to the zoo on one of those magnificent rare days San Francisco can manage . . . —and I'd been fascinated by the rattlesnake rustling of the peacock fan in full erection.[22]

THIRTY-SEVEN

The Political Machine

From what we call Poetry a cock crows
away off there at the break of something.
ROBERT DUNCAN, "A New Poem (for Jack Spicer)"

DUNCAN AND JESS HAD A RARE OPPORTUNITY to travel together during the spring of 1962, flying to Denver on Thursday March 22 to begin a longer journey to the East Coast. Though reluctant to venture far from home, Jess embarked on the trip to fulfill a commission from friend and benefactor William Matson Roth "to make . . . a 'political machine,' a construction out of objects 'found' in Washington, D.C."[1] On their first night in Denver, the couple accompanied Stan and Jane Brakhage to a performance of Duncan's 1956 play *Medea at Kolchis: The Maidenhead,* produced by a local theater group. The following evening Duncan gave a reading at the University of Denver's International House, and on Sunday the 25th, the Denver Forum held a reception for the couple. Stan Brakhage had again arranged Duncan's appearances. Still eager to mend the nearly decadelong estrangement from his "magic parents," Brakhage wrote later to thank them for their visit: "I am very much at work again, for the first time in almost a year; and the house is filled with a new growing happiness and reaching out to the sun . . . and to all becoming. And for whatever you have done to help us . . . I send you whatever joy of it I can in a letter."[2]

On March 26, Duncan and Jess began a zigzag path of travel that allowed them to visit museums in the Northeast. In Chicago, they saw an exhibition of works by Odilon Redon, Gustave Moreau, and Rodolfe Bresdin. Moving on to Washington, D.C., they stayed briefly with journalist James Truitt and his wife, Anne, who would later become a renowned minimalist sculptor. Duncan gave a reading at George Washington University before continuing east with Jess to visit both the Philadelphia and Rodin Museums. From there, Duncan departed for New York, and Jess returned to Washington to search out the materials for his commission.

Housed at the Hotel Earle in Greenwich Village, Duncan prepared for an April 8 reading at the 92nd Street YMHA Poetry Center, a venue that had hosted the likes of T. S. Eliot, Dylan Thomas, and Marianne Moore during its twenty-three-year history. The reading, introduced by Denise Levertov, was Duncan's first at the center, and as he told Jess, "Denise's introduction somehow made or transformed the reading situation into a wave I had only to ride in on, rise toward the *Apprehensions* and the *Romantic Hymns*. And in the aftermath, the audience was in the glow too. Not only the glow . . . but then a rush of people to fill up a calendar of morning, afternoon, and evening appointments."[3] Those appointments included a late-night party for Duncan at LeRoi Jones's apartment, as well as time with the Rothenbergs, Seon and Robert Manley, Marjorie McKee, Virginia Admiral, Denise Levertov, and Gael Turnbull who was also visiting the city that spring.[4] Between coffee dates with friends and fans, Duncan made time to scout around to a few galleries carrying slides of Jess's and Harry Jacobus's work, and he also squeezed in stops to a show of Norris Embry paintings and to the Guggenheim Museum to see the work of French cubist painter Fernand Léger. He reported to Jess that though he had little time to sleep, he made the most of his trip, partaking in one of his favorite rituals: exploring haute cuisine. At a farewell dinner with Seon and Robert Manley in a "vast sumptuous restaurant" serving South American fare, Duncan and his companions dined on "a pumpkin cream bisque, bocaditos of avocado, cheese and sea foods . . . and Argentinian barbequed ribs."[5]

The following day, Duncan traveled to Ithaca, New York, for another reading and talk, staying with fellow Kantorowicz student Robert Benson. Benson, a medievalist in his own right, had recently settled into the small upstate town with his wife, Joan, and two children. Seeking a moment of refuge, Duncan huddled in a cubicle in the Cornell University library to catch up with reading and correspondence. Despite his intent to recharge before the next leg of his travels, he almost immediately threw himself back into the public sphere, attending "an excellent lecture on music from the ninth to the twelfth centuries; a lunch with a handsome Pound scholar; cocktails and dinners and things said; at least one admiring young poet and a collection of interested faculty members."[6] During a short flight back to New York City on April 22, he wrote to Jess of the loneliness that lurked below his inexhaustible social energy: "I don't come into myself until I am with you. I want to save impressions until we share them. The passing things I enjoy—

but the bits of real stuff, like seeing the Léger show, I see deprived of you. What a love lorn pang, just to savor, takes over when a letter comes."[7]

Back in Manhattan on a humid Easter Sunday, Duncan visited with the New York school painter John Button before taking a train toward Bard College.[8] Greeted that evening in Poughkeepsie by Robert Kelly, Duncan walked the grounds of the private undergraduate college with his host, admiring the "lilacs already on the walled gardens."[9] Kelly, who had been appointed a professor at Bard the previous year, had arranged a reading for Duncan, the first of many appearances he would make at the college over two decades. After meeting with students and enjoying the hospitality of Kelly and his wife, Joby, Duncan returned to New York on Thursday April 26 for a day of odd poetry companionship: lunch with mainstream poet W. S. Merwin and dinner with one of his *New American Poetry* peers, LeRoi Jones. As Duncan told Jess, he liked "Bill" Merwin more than he expected to: "In photographs and in Robin's account of him, Merwin had some glamour that wouldn't have made for liking. But the Merwin I met . . . was concerned with the new poetry, eager to talk about what he'd found in *The Opening of the Field*—another person."[10]

Duncan spent that Friday in New York with Denise Levertov and Mitch Goodman before departing for Middletown, Connecticut, to again visit Norman O. Brown. Brown had offered Duncan private office space in the library on the Wesleyan campus, and Duncan bicycled between the household and the school grounds, returning each day for lunch with Brown and his family. Throughout the end of April and into early May, he worked obsessively on *The H. D. Book,* setting aside writing time from 8 A.M. to 6 P.M. and completing a dozen pages at a time. As the work came into focus, he continued to extend his stay in the East, making forays to the Beinecke Library at Yale, all the while rationalizing his absence to Jess: "I'm on page 72 now and about 2/3 the way thru section 8 which now involves, still ahead, a discussion of Plutarch's Isis and Osiris and his Delphic Oracles from Book V of the *Moralia.* I'm certain it's the source for what I've unearthed in the process of the essay on *Palimpsest.* The *Palimpsest* has a gold mine, and . . . I think my study will arouse the would-be reader to what H. D. has realized."[11] Jess in turn made another short trip to Washington to continue his assemblage work, rendezvousing with Duncan there on May 12.

Despite hopes for a quiet vacation season, Duncan became enmeshed in a web of summer antagonisms. On May 22, he wrote to Helen and Pat Adam turning down yet another invitation from them, this one for a *San Francisco's Burning* cast party. The conflict over Adam's play had now dragged on for months, with Duncan restating his misgivings about the project: "Broughton, Sheets and that 'composer' [Warner Jepson] are enemies of the poetic imagination, that stood against song, in ignorance—but also, struck out, alterd, 'improved' the authentic."[12] Stan Brakhage inadvertently stepped into the middle of the war at the peak of Duncan's hysteria. A June letter praising his San Francisco idols and making a passing reference to Broughton was greeted with Duncan's ire:

> That Jess and I might be "each incredible magicians," who together make a spell "of such majestic beauty to me as to be 'indescribable'" may be terms when your feelings tend to a depth and complexity, but there is no care in these terms for what we actually are, much less for our own effort to be truthful to what we are.[13]

That month Duncan reported to Denise Levertov that he had also faced an assault on his own work:

> "Night Scenes" in *Floating Bear* had caused a scandal at my ineptitude in North Beach poetry circles. Robin [Blaser] was distressd and could not account for the poem's possibly being other than a botched job. And on two occasions, by George Stanley and again by a Lewis Ellingham the poem had been read in ridicule, as evidence of my infatuation with my own habits and of my decline.[14]

Despite a satisfying visit from the Tallmans that summer, the season closed on a sour note. At an August dinner party hosted by Robin Blaser, Duncan and Spicer came to a final impasse. With several guests assembled, Spicer launched into a tirade against a number of poets and painters, most pointedly against Jess.[15] While Duncan and Spicer would cross paths at public events until Spicer's death in 1965, they never recovered the friendship they had shared as Berkeley Renaissance companions.

Conflict stayed on Duncan's mind into the autumn. The September 28, 1962, issue of *Life* magazine included an article about warfare among New Guinea's native Willigiman-Wallaluas and inspired "Tribal Memories," the opening poem of Duncan's *Passages* series. The *Passages* poems came to document the events of the Viet Nam war, but they also commented on the general destructive forces of humankind in the late twentieth century, tying contemporary social distress to what Duncan perceived to be an eternal battle between good and evil inherent in the human condition. He said during a reading a decade later, "We've just come to the place where we realize we're one species. Only our century's begun to admit it. In anthropological terms we've only barely begun to admit that there are not primitive men, primitive civilizations and advanced civilizations, but they're all contemporary in their ways of being the human being."[16] In "Tribal Memories," Duncan revisited the idea of the Willigiman-Wallaluas as primitive "others," blurring the boundaries between their ways and the ways of so-called civilized man:

> among tribes setting each the City where
> we Her people are
> at the end of a day's reaches   here
> the Eternal
> lamps lit, here   the wavering human
> sparks of heat and light
> glimmer, go out, and reappear.[17]

The *Passages* poems served another purpose as well. They allowed Duncan to address formal considerations that had been part of his craft from the beginning. Ezra Pound's *Cantos* stood out as a model for such a series, and as Duncan said in a lecture during the early 1960s,

> I thought if I would open up and let's say call something just "Passages" as you might call something just "fragments," try to prevent it from forming into a poem as the Pindar poem or "Apprehensions" formed into . . . the symphonic form or the sonata form, [the idea] fascinated me. I like to orchestrate a large poem, I like to have related movements . . . and poems within poems, and now I wanted to see if I could let that loose. . . . I have begun this poem in order to see if I can open up and eventually have some of these passages much more free of it.[18]

As the first of the *Passages* pieces appeared, Duncan also returned to playwriting. On October 1, the San Francisco Tape Center hosted a reading from his work in progress *A Play of Adam's Way*. The cast included Helen Adam, Lewis Brown, Robin Blaser, Peter Bailey, Paul Alexander, Deneen Brown, Ida Hodes, Fred Snowden, and Duncan. The author-actor-director reported to Denise Levertov, "In *Adam's Way* I let myself go in a free rhetoric, outside the bounds of modern taste."[19] Later published in *Roots and Branches,* the work was subtitled "A Play upon Theosophical Themes" and included the characters Adam and Erda-Eve, as well as an assortment of dragons, tree spirits, and angels. In a later evaluation of the play, Duncan wrote, *"Adam's Way* began in July 1962 [as] a masque, not for the stage but for a company of friends to perform—a show of reptile-men I had found in the curious pre-historical lore of Rudolf Steiner and sun-angels and fairies. And, in my own mind, it would be a Masque of Man."[20]

A secondary drama occurred on the outskirts of the performance when Jack Spicer and a handful of his students arrived to picket the event. Robin Blaser recalled, "[Stan] Persky . . . and . . . [George] Stanley . . . carried signs saying, 'Fuck Duncan, Fuck Jess, Fuck Chichi!'"[21] The incident cemented the bad feelings between Duncan and Spicer and ended any chance for civil relations between Duncan and the poets of North Beach. With a taste of blood, Spicer encouraged his students to taunt Duncan. Larry Fagin, a poet who joined the San Francisco circle during the early 1960s, remembered see-ing Duncan come into a North Beach poets' bar to be accosted with the barb "It's past your bedtime."[22] George Stanley also recalled the fireworks between Duncan and Spicer:

> It was a grand feud—a transcendent feud—ultimate issues were at stake. It was conducted at a distance . . . —Duncan never came to Gino and Carlo's, where the Spicer circle met, and I think Jack was persona non grata at 20th Street—not that he would have wanted to attend anyway—so the ripostes were carried back and forth by the young—like me. I recall something like this: someone told Jack that Robert had recently written a great poem. Jack said, sarcastically, "How many Egyptian gods are there in it?" That set the tone. But the great exchange was this. Jack accused Robert of having "broken the vow he had made to poetry"—this refers back to Berkeley in the 40s, I guess. I remember Robert's reply exactly: "I never made any vow to poetry except to cut its throat, if I could make someone laugh."[23]

During the first weekend of October, Duncan, groggy with a head cold and hoarse from the cigarettes he'd smoked during the staging of *Adam's Way,* retreated to bed to read Joseph Campbell's *Oriental Mythology.* He re-emerged on October 11 for a dinner and movie date with Ida Hodes. The fol-lowing week, Robert Creeley arrived from Vancouver to give readings at the University of California and at the Poetry Center. Alongside Creeley's visit came a news story that cast a shadow of gloom across the globe. U.S. recon-naissance photographs had identified Soviet missiles being constructed on the island of Cuba, and at the end of October, an American U-2 spy plane was shot down over the island. The ensuing standoff forced the Soviets to dismantle their Cuban bases, and an era of Red Scare politics began to come to a close. The crisis in many ways stood as a prelude to the surge of activism that would soon characterize the decade. Meanwhile, Duncan mused over a more personal war in his notebook:

> Of Spicer's perverted values. He has come to insist that there is only fairy gold or currency to things—love too is fairy gold; and turns to shit and dead leaves in the light of day. This is his attack and it has just that much truth as it has of value, that to hold even shit and dead leaves to his value we must fail to realize that these are the manure or return to the earth.
>
> The lie of his attack is that he despises the true gold, the cup and chasuble workd in rich gold of the artist.[24]

Brooding over the complexities of Bay Area poetry politics, Duncan made a foray south to bring income into the household for the holidays. On Sunday November 25, he flew to Santa Barbara to begin a two-week tour, staying in Ventura with recent immigrant Gael Turnbull and his family. There, he took part in the rush of a domestic scene that included children, children's books, and a new publication from Turnbull's Migrant Press: Ian Hamilton Finlay's *The Dancers Inherit the Party*. Drawn to Finlay's work, Duncan became an advocate of the Scottish poet, later visiting him at his home of Stonypath, outside of Edinburgh. During his November travels, Duncan also saw Berkeley friends David and Lloyd Bary, then living in Santa Barbara, as well as Wallace and Shirley Berman in Topanga Canyon. He wrote Jess that the Bermans' bohemian lifestyle reminded him of his Woodstock days: "The last night I was there, Tosh, Shirley and Wally were in the one double bed; Minne (the di Prima infant) and I in one single (Tosh's bed) and the floor littered with the corpses of [Alan] Marlowe, Diane [di Prima], and Dean Stockwell."[25] Amid the clamor of old and new friends, Duncan also found common ground with the Bermans' eight-year-old son, Tosh: "He is wild WILD about Oz and Oz books and changed from a shy little disappearer into a chatterbox when he found out I could tell him what happens in the Oz books he hasn't got yet.... I found him (for $1) *The Lost Princess*. He went about in a daze, clutching the book and scornd television, trying to make out words and sentences in the book."[26]

After giving a reading at San Fernando State College, Duncan flew from Los Angeles to Tucson for a four-day residency arranged by the Ruth Stephan Poetry Center. On December 5, he read at the University of Arizona and the next day he presented a lecture titled "The Image in Poetry" at the Workshop

Center for the Arts. His new acquaintances during the trip included poets Drummond Hadley and Keith and Heloise Wilson, and he told Jess that the schedule and the cottage provided by the Poetry Center afforded him a certain leisure: "It's nothing to do here outside of my program. . . . But I do have a little house to myself and time in the morning to write this letter, read Whorf on language, which I asked from the library here—and Sayers' *Gaudy Night* which was on the shelf in the house."[27] Forgoing the New Year turtle dance at the Santo Domingo Pueblo, Duncan arrived home in mid-December to spend the holidays with Jess. On December 17, the couple had dinner with Jim Felts and Robin Blaser, again trying to come to terms with a year of disquiet in San Francisco. The company was welcome, and after dinner Duncan read to the group from Ian Hamilton Finlay's *The Dancers Inherit the Party*.[28]

THIRTY-EIGHT

Knight Errant

I shall draw back
and among my sacred objects
gather the animal power back,
the force that in solitude
works in me its leases,
the night-bird's voice
in the day's verses.

ROBERT DUNCAN, "A Part-Sequence for Change"

ALFRED HITCHCOCK'S FILM *The Birds* was released on the New Year of 1963. That spring, as moviegoers shuddered to imagine the skies of San Francisco and Bodega Bay besieged by flocks of angry birds, South Vietnamese and American troops cooperated in a number of new military operations. Away from the birds and the helicopters, Duncan proceeded with *The H. D. Book* and spent the New Year rereading E. R. Dodds's *The Greeks and the Irrational*. He also spent time reflecting on a disappointment with the San

Francisco poetry scene that struck at the roots of his old Berkeley friendships. His relationship with Jack Spicer and the younger poets in Spicer's circle continued to be contentious, and Duncan suspected that Robin Blaser had an active hand in the discord. The boycott of *Adam's Way* had been just the beginning, and as Duncan told Denise Levertov, he wrote "A Part-Sequence for Change" to address the problem directly: "The effort is just to make real what was happening in the charged rejection of my work in 'North Beach.' Of . . . *Adam's Way*—that was the crisis, and it involved even Robin. But then I found it had involved Robin for some time, for Robin and Spicer and others had since the publication of *The Field* posed their poetry as a poetry of attack, against the poetry of celebration which was mostly my work. And mine became then 'just the poetry of celebration' some indulgence in itself."[1] Registering his paranoia that the Spicer circle might be conjuring black magic, Duncan invoked his own spell against the culprits:

> If they had cursed the man,
> dried back the water in the spring
> by boiling water in a frying pan
> until the thirsty sun
> feared for the songs that he once sang
> and burnd to sing,
>
> over *them* the cursed image
> over *them* the blackend thing.[2]

Interrupting these worries came news that William Carlos Williams had died on March 4. For Duncan, the poet's death arrived as "another emptiness *within* as well as in the world. For the life I've drawn from his work and from the fact that he was working. Now only Pound remains of our 'great ones,' and from that little group that were gathered in the *Egoist* . . . only two others remain—too cautious to be great—Eliot and Marianne Moore."[3] Despite naming Williams as one of his modernist masters, Duncan had distanced himself from personal interactions with the elder poet after a disappointing initial encounter with Williams in New York in 1939 or 1940: "The first time I met him was at a Gotham Book Mart party . . . and at that time I was with Virginia Admiral. And he had obviously . . . landed on that blonde head of hair and complexion, and was moving in, and suddenly was presented with a young poet who didn't look very appetizing at all to be courting this young lady. I don't know that he made any connections . . . with my existence really as a person."[4]

On April 16, partly as a reward for surviving the dreaded tax season, Duncan went on a mushroom-hunting outing with Jess near Stinson Beach. It was an adventure he reveled in after "sitting at the typewriter so many days."[5] Throughout the spring, he had been working on the "Nights and Days" section of *The H. D. Book* and on his series *The Structure of Rime,* with new pieces composed for Louise and George Herms and Shirley and Wallace Berman. The poem for the Hermses came in response to a gift that had arrived in March, an assemblage piece constructed by George Herms: "a little household altar, enshrining two photos of Garbo as enigma, beauty and woman" doubling as "a homunculus, with the woman in two phases enshrined in his heart."[6] During a season when Duncan was fending off spells, he was pleased with the guardian structure, telling Denise Levertov "How George Herms is entirely with us."[7] In "Structure of Rime XXI," he reflected on the fact that Herms, who had first met Duncan and Jess in Stinson Beach while collaborating on a film with Larry Jordan, shared the couple's pleasure in gathering materials from the detritus of urban life:

> The electric lamp in the isinglass casing. The painted shadow on the glare of the plate. The like lightness of the plate when lifted. All these things left in the design of the maze.
>
> Slowly the ear turns in time round to the sound it is listening for. The coil of thickness let fall from the table. But here there is no floor to the melody. In the broken plate arcs of higher sympathies cross actual tones and erect in the lonely herm the musician sees a window.[8]

Another gift arrived in April, a letter from the Guggenheim Foundation notifying Duncan that he would receive a grant of four thousand dollars. The award accommodated his estimate of the cost of completing *The H. D. Book,* and it relieved the household's financial burdens, allowing Duncan to plan another trip east to continue his work at Yale's Beinecke Library. In May, he took a short road trip with Helen Adam for a joint reading at the University of California, Los Angeles. The invitation came from Robert Haas, Duncan's acquaintance from his undergraduate days in Berkeley. Haas, who had once lent Duncan his cherished collection of Gertrude Stein recordings, had since become a Stein scholar and a professor in the University of California system.

Duncan and Adam had partly resolved their argument about *San Francisco's Burning* with Helen Adam's capitulation "Someday I must have a production of *San Francisco's Burning* as I really want it, and with the right music."⁹ But even with the business of the Playhouse behind them, Duncan and Jess were drawn into two other crises in the Adam household. That summer, Adam left Duncan to communicate on her behalf with Virginia Admiral, who had agreed to print Adam's book *Ballads* with illustrations by Jess. Admiral's Acacia Press, funded on her income as a painter, began to flounder as she attended to her own household and a "very expensive" twenty-year-old son. Admiral stretched out the production schedule beyond Duncan and Jess's patience, later providing various excuses for the delays: "We will just go modestly until I can get Bobby educated . . . and then I will paint. I have been doing a lot of drawings and pastels this summer and started one large canvas which isn't finished yet. Bobby is hitchhiking through Europe this summer. . . . He goes to Stella Adler during the winter and wants to become an actor, God forbid."¹⁰

Helen Adam was further distracted from *Ballads* in July when her eighty-six-year-old mother became gravely ill. Having lived her entire life with the companionship of the family matriarch, Adam entered into a state of denial, and as Duncan reported to Denise Levertov, who had also served as a New York intermediary on the book project, "It was strange in that house, with Helen entertaining in the back parlor franticly—and Pat crying at the door to her mother's room and Jess and me on that tremulous edge of saying goodbye to a most dear old woman for it may be the last time."¹¹ Contributing what emotional support they could to the troubled sisters, Duncan and Jess also prepared for a trip to Vancouver with the Burtons and Ida Hodes. Duncan had been invited to a late summer poetry conference that Warren Tallman and Robert Creeley had arranged at the University of British Columbia, and his select group of Bay Area friends was eager to use the occasion as an opportunity for a sightseeing vacation.

THIRTY-NINE
———————

The Vancouver Conference

> During one of the early Seminar sessions … Allen Ginsberg
> blithely and accurately and instantly tacked a label on the four
> poets leading the talks that morning: he himself as a "beatnik,"
> Duncan as the "nasty aesthetician," Creeley as the "maker of
> exquisite little poems," and Olson as the "father figure of us all."
> CAROL BERGÉ, *The Vancouver Report*

THE SYMPOSIUM THAT CAME TO BE REMEMBERED as the Vancouver Conference brought together poets of Duncan's generation in full force. Beginning on July 24 and continuing through August 16, 1963, its participants included the major writers of the Black Mountain school as well as San Francisco poet Philip Whalen and Canadian poet Margaret Avison. Students of poetry—from the Vancouver faithful to Drummond Hadley of Tucson to two young East Coast writers, George (Michael) Palmer and Clark Coolidge—flocked to the event from around North America.[1] Workshop meetings for the credit-based students were held three days a week, and panel discussions and readings were interspersed throughout the sessions. Duncan and his fellow teachers were a motley group, described by a young writer from New York, Carol Bergé, in a Fuck You Press chapbook titled *The Vancouver Report:*

> Charles [Olson] dominates any session he is at: whether he speaks or not: just his large, wise hulk seems to give a needed dimension to the talking. . . . Allen [Ginsberg] in jeans or the "informal" Indian attire of white jacket and loose-fitting white slacks: his hair uncut, curls to the first large spinal vertebra, is clean and has the smell of Japanese hair oil; he is bearded, is reticent at the morning sessions and more talkative when drawn-out on the lawn after sessions. . . . Denise is a white Peter Pan collar; Margaret Avison is a comfortable woolen sweater of indefinable age or color; Philip Whalen looks like a prosperous Buddha, . . . and in jeans, yet. Creeley is the crisp crow of his own poem; always in jeans + clean shirt; or the stainless steel razorblade which doesn't wear out ever: but taut, like that same blade formed into a spring.[2]

Bergé, acting as a cultural correspondent for the poets of New York City who were not represented at the conference, offered an equally humorous description of Duncan:

I came to this seminar convinced that nothing Robert Duncan has ever written is worth a damn, and that he is personally not merely a bore, but an offensively affected bore. I hate to be wrong and I hate even more to admit it: I am wrong. I still think he is not my dish of tea as a poet, but I say now that he is a vitally interesting lecturer and an unforgettable personality. He has a warmth of projection of personality which sweeps one along until one forgets to be annoyed.[3]

Duncan participated in several panel discussions and gave a July 26 reading during which he presented pieces from *The Opening of the Field* and *Roots and Branches,* closing with "A Poem Beginning with a Line by Pindar." On August 5, adopting a strategy he was to repeat two years later at the Berkeley Conference, he gave a lecture organized around "drawing the sorts"—choosing directives at random from his Japanese dictionary, or Kenkyusha. During the talk, Duncan described how the Kenkyusha had come to the 20th Street household:

> We looked two years before we found one that would agree to live in our house. That is, you would find a Kenkyusha in a bookstore, and you'd say, very politely, "Would you like to come home and kind of let me use you?" and the Kenkyusha would say, "Take a very long run to the nearest lake." Or you'd say, "Are you a truthful Kenkyusha" and Kenkyusha really would say, "Are you kidding?" This particular Kenkyusha actually was agreeable to coming home.[4]

The three phrases Duncan drew for the lecture were "go to the office," "he would go to any expense in such matters," and "throw a person off his balance, upset, bewilder." From these prompts, he mused upon the office of the poet and the childhood influences that had led him to his vocation.[5]

Unleashed in panel discussions, Duncan dominated the conversations, which was likely a relief to his copanelists Olson and Ginsberg, who were less eager to engage in chatter before noon. With many attendees well educated in modernist poetries and open field poetics, the talks provided the first public airing of key precepts of a midcentury American experimental tradition. The gathering also brought together the strange bedfellows of institution-resistant writers and members of the English department's faculty. A certain disenchantment with the classroom atmosphere spawned numerous informal meetings and late-night parties, affording novel views of the elder poets. Hilde Burton remembered one gathering during which Allen Ginsberg leaped off a high beach cliff into the bay to the amazement of his fellow revelers, and Pauline Butling remembered an unexpected intimacy with Duncan at another event:

> Mid-way through the course, my husband, Fred Wah and I had a party in our small, campus apartment. With some 80 people crammed into our tiny place, Duncan and several others ended up sitting on the double bed in the bedroom. Charles Olson was at the head of the bed with, in his words, "five women in my arms".... Duncan was at the other end, flirting with a handsome young Vancouver poet. At one point, Duncan removed his shirt to show off his "bear hair" on his back—no doubt as part of his seduction—also because the bear was a totemic figure for him—to invoke its power. In the midst of all this, he turned to me ... and said, ... "you're writing on me and I haven't even kissed you" and then immediately gave me a big, smoochy kiss. I was taken aback, but Duncan seemed nonplussed, the kiss being just one link among many in an interconnected cosmic network: Whitehead's "presentational immediacy."[6]

While Jess, the Burtons, and Ida Hodes had rented a house apart from conference activities, Duncan took little interest in such a retreat. Between readings and parties, he had opportunities to attend to old friendships and to interact with a new crop of North American poets. One Spicer circle representative, nineteen-year-old Harris Schiff, recalled his odd encounter with Duncan that summer:

> So, Jack [Spicer], for one reason or another—I think he thought it was quite a joke— ... told me to stay with Creeley and have him take me around to go to the festival. And then he said, "I'd like you to look up Robert Duncan and ask him a question for me." So I said, sure.... I was really a very innocent young man. I had no idea about poetry feuds.... There was a big ... Saturday night party, and I told Creeley that Jack had asked me to deliver a message to Robert Duncan.... I'm pretty sure I had some drinks, and ... I'm sure everyone else there was blasted. So Creeley introduced me to Duncan and said, "This is a young friend of Jack Spicer's from San Francisco." And I said hi, and I said "Jack asked me to ask you a question," and he said, ... "Oh yeah, what might that be?" And I said, "Well he wanted you to tell him if you could tell the difference between poetry and cable cars," and Duncan said—I don't remember his exact words, but what comes to me is "Why you little son of bitch, get the fuck out of my face. How can you come here and do that?" I had no idea what had just transpired. I never saw Robert Duncan again. And Jack wrote ... to apologize for the poor manners of the poets in Vancouver.[7]

Spicer, who had once said "Poetry is only for poets. Cable cars are for tourists," proved again that he could raise Duncan's hackles, even from a distance.

The weeks that followed the Vancouver Conference were filled with continued social activity for Duncan and Jess. After driving back to San Francisco with the Burtons and Ida Hodes, they were joined, at the end of August, by the Tallmans, who had decided to take a postconference vacation. Settling into the autumn at home, there were business obligations to attend to as well: Duncan negotiated with Scribners to see *Roots and Branches* into print, and Jess completed illustrations for Helen Adam's *San Francisco's Burning,* slated to be published that year by Ebbe Borregaard's Oannes Press.

On September 15, the Sixteenth Street Baptist Church in Birmingham, Alabama, was bombed, killing four black children attending Sunday school. Duncan wrote to Denise Levertov, "I am too shaken with rage or the grief of it to recover myself."[8] The South had seen increasing violence throughout the year, including the June 12 assassination of Medgar Evers, secretary of the National Association for the Advancement of Colored People. It was rare for Duncan to comment on the civil rights movement, and he was even less vocal about President Kennedy's assassination in Dallas on November 22. Reflecting upon the event later in "Stage Directions, *Passages* 30," Duncan collaged the narrative of Abraham Zapruder's home movie of the assassination with lines from Shakespeare's *Macbeth,* Hesiod's *Theogony,* and Spenser's *The Faerie Queen.* Unlike Whitman's lament for Lincoln in "When Lilacs Last in This Dooryard Bloomed," Duncan's mourning was not for the president but for the troubled American democracy:

> And from the dying body of America I see,
> or from my dying body,
>
> emerge
>
> children of a deed long before this deed,
> seed of Poseidon, depth in which the blue above
> is reflected
> released[9]

On December 11, 1963, when Duncan gave a reading for the Poetry Center at the San Francisco Museum of Art, he made no mention of the political climate in the United States. Focusing on his poetic craft—distilled through the filter of Jakob Boehme's mystical Christian writings—he composed an introductory note for his appearance:

> What I call the Divine is what I begin to divine in the poem.... The dream, the dance, the falling-in-love, and the poem seem to me of one kind. A sei-

zure, given to us, overcoming the pose of the ego, commanding us to attend the need, enthralling us in the spell of a form we must achieve. To be a poet is to be prepared for that seizure, to have learned in the hand all the command one has of language, to have a tongue that is ready and true to the heart so that speech may come when the mind is not yours.[10]

Duncan continued along those lines in a Christmastime notebook entry that found its place in one of his most important essays, "Towards an Open Universe." Again focused upon the autobiographical and attached not to the current political moment but to a larger metaphysical truth derived from readings of Alfred North Whitehead, Jakob Boehme, and Erwin Schrödinger, Duncan proposed, "To become a poet, means to be aware of creation, creature, and creator coinherent in the one event. There is not only the immanence of God, His indwelling, but there is also the immanence of God, His impending occurrence. In the expectancy of the poem, grief and fear seem necessary to the revelation of Beauty."[11]

FORTY

Bending the Bow

WITH A THREE-MONTH HIATUS from reading and lecturing responsibilities in early 1964, Duncan settled into the landscape of new poems. In January, he wrote the title piece of *Bending the Bow,* which arrived while he was penning a letter to Denise Levertov. Embedding the lines into a January 12 missive, he again demonstrated his inclination to create conversations between texts, in this case responding to Levertov's early book *The Double Image.* But the poem also expressed a deeper and nearly erotic fascination with her:

> in the course of a letter to a friend
> who comes close in to my thought so that
> the day is hers, my hand writing
> in thought shakes in the currents, of air?
> of an inner anticipation of? ghostly
> exhilarations in the thought of her

at the extremity of this
design[1]

Having fallen out with many of his San Francisco peers, Duncan continued to turn to Levertov as he composed the opening pages of *Bending the Bow*. In early February, he wrote "At the Loom," the second poem of the *Passages* series, and *Passages* 3 and 4, "What I Saw" and "Where It Appears," followed soon after. The collection reflected not only Duncan's attention to correspondences between reading materials and readers, but also presented a midlife assessment of his craft, interspersing references to his study of phonetics and his preoccupation with architectures. In the opening of "Where It Appears," he reaffirmed his commitment to a nonlinear open field poetics:

> I'd cut the warp
> to weave that web
>
> in the air
>
> and here
>
> let image perish in image,
>
> leave writer and reader
>
> up in the air
>
> to draw
>
> momentous
>
> inconclusions . . . [2]

In the early spring, Duncan went back on tour, arriving in Albuquerque, New Mexico, on March 20. Met at the airport by Robert and Bobbie Creeley, he returned with them to their mountain home in Placitas for a few days of leisure before giving two readings arranged by Creeley: on March 23, at the University of New Mexico; and on March 25, at Highlands University in Las Vegas. The Creeleys were in good cheer, enjoying income from a recent Guggenheim grant and hoping to buy a new house. Also relocated to the area were two Vancouverites, Fred Wah and Pauline Butling. On March 27, Duncan drove with Butling from Albuquerque to Tucson to take in Yaqui Easter rituals at a local pueblo "with the Jesuits the Catholic and pagan . . . woven into one." In a letter to Barbara Joseph, he recorded the trajectory of the drama: "The Fariseos hunt Christ, stalking him, killing him and then in a fiesta of dances at 2 a.m. to 3:30 a.m. Saturday morning celebrating their success; the Pascolas stalk the Deer Dancer and sometime around dawn Easter morning make their kill."[3]

Duncan remained in Tucson through the Easter holiday, housed with Drummond Hadley and his wife, whom he had met during a previous trip to the area. The weather was warm, and he was relieved to be away from the San Francisco drizzle, telling Jess, "It's been two days so crowded with impressions—when not Indians, then the little colony of Tucson 'friends.' The Hadleys and their animals, two dogs, two cats, four kittens, and a tame bobcat (whose purr is as much bigger than a cat's as he is . . . and he is as much more of a baby, leaping all over one and—alarming at first, nuzzling and nipping without breaking skin)."[4]

From Arizona, Duncan took a longer journey by train to the Midwest, arriving in Chicago, where he was met by *Big Table* editor Paul Carroll and learned of the death of Charles Olson's wife, Betty, in an upstate New York automobile accident.[5] Duncan telephoned Olson on the night of March 31 and arranged to fly to Buffalo the following day. He had been scheduled to give an April 3 poetry reading at the State University of New York, but he first attended to Olson's grief. On April 5, he wrote Barbara Joseph complaining that Stan and Jane Brakhage had assaulted Olson with their condolences. Taking the opportunity to vent his anger at Brakhage, Duncan rendered the scene with a certain viciousness: "And damn them, wldn't you know that the Brakhages would hunt him down by phone, relentless ghouls, and claw away at the possible wound until Charles broken down sobbing. It was here at Mac Hammond's that they caught up with him, during a party last night. But Charles and I were alone in the kitchen when he took the call. I held that dear hand and head, held on for the perhaps whole minute it took him to summon himself."[6]

Soon on the road again, Duncan drove from Buffalo to Rochester with Norman O. Brown, who had recently begun teaching at the University of Rochester. After a speaking engagement at the school, he headed for the University of Michigan to give a reading at Ann Arbor's Wolgamot Society on April 8. His hosts, Keith and Rosmarie Waldrop, remembered that Duncan's reading spanned three hours and that the poet's enthusiasm continued as he held forth loudly throughout a postreading reception at their house.[7] The following day, Duncan had a quieter meeting, joining Keith Waldrop on campus for tea and dinner. From there he departed for a reading at Detroit's Wayne State University on April 10. Finvola Drury, a local poet who had helped with the arrangements for Duncan's visit, wrote to him with delight after the reading, "On the way home, our small, tired son recited his memory of the last four poems you read. They were all in his head; it really *is* the child come into his world."[8]

Duncan made a stop in Buffalo to see Charles Olson before continuing on to New York City, where he gave an April 16 reading with Robert Creeley and Denise Levertov for the Guggenheim Foundation. After the event, a party was held at Denise Levertov and Mitch Goodman's apartment, and more socializing was on the calendar the following evening, recorded by Phoenix Bookstore owner Robert Wilson in his memoir *Seeing Shelley Plain:* "The party seemed to continue at the Phoenix, with a large group of the previous night's attendees converging on my shop; this time Robert Kelley and his wife Jobyna . . . Barbara Joseph, John Wieners, Gerard Malanga. . . . Over tea and cookies the conversation continued until two a.m."[9]

While Duncan had several housing options in Manhattan, he chose to spend the night of April 17 with Wilson, who recalled that the beginning of the acquaintance came with an odd request:

> Duncan . . . told me that he wanted to come see my Gertrude Stein collection. Of course I was charmed by this, and suggested that he come up in the morning. But no, to my amazement he wanted to come up immediately. . . . It was now well after two a.m., and I lived at 157th Street and Riverside Drive, a one-hour ride once the subway came along. . . . Once safely in my apartment we looked at all the Stein first editions I possessed—not a lot at this time, but apparently several things that Duncan had never seen before. He then totally astounded me by asking if I had any pornographic photos he could look at.[10]

Although initially taken aback, Wilson housed Duncan during many of his subsequent stays in Manhattan. Three years Duncan's junior, he became a fast friend not only through a shared interest in rare books but also through a companionship centered around the less visible activities of the gay community in New York City.

As usual, Duncan had a number of people to see, and a number of train journeys to make outside of town, during his short time in New York. During a brief retreat to visit Seon and Robert Manley in Bellport on Long Island, he had time to describe his surroundings to Jess: "The Manley's [sic] house is not a palace or a mansion, but a big sprawling beach house with comfortable style to have a guest suite, and servant's rooms and nursery, lawns that go out to a little country road just beyond which the Atlantic and the yacht harbor. . . . It's been a fine break in the hectic hourly schedule or attempt at schedule in New York."[11] Relying upon such sanctuaries during long tours, Duncan made certain to cultivate relationships in the world of academics and art patrons. And despite his bristling against his parents' tediously conservative household, he drew on his early experiences there, always ready to don a business suit and keep the company of those who could offer him comfortable accommodations.

Back in Manhattan, Duncan met with Virginia Admiral to try to pin down a date for the publication of Helen Adam's *Ballads* and then boarded a northbound train for an April 27 reading at Bard College. He arrived in Annandale-on-Hudson on April 24 and again stayed with Robert and Joby Kelly. Exhausted after a month of traveling, Duncan told Jess he was further worn out by "the Kellys who were insatiable talkers—on until 4 or even 5 in the morning."[12] In Duncan's absence, Jess had found equally interesting company, with visits from filmmaker Larry Jordan and painter Jasper Johns, though he admitted to Duncan, "I'd make a good hermit; I miss nobody but you."[13]

With another three weeks of professional obligations in front of him, Duncan returned to New York to spend time with more intimate friends Barbara Joseph and Denise Levertov. He reported home to Jess that he had also met a young poet named Ed Sanders at Levertov's apartment whom he "liked . . . immediately."[14] On Sunday May 3, Duncan boarded a train to New Haven, Connecticut, where he had a number of tasks to attend to. Hosted by rare book dealer Henry Wenning and his wife, Adele, at their house on York Street, "a homelike recuperation station," he had a base from which he could continue his studies of the H. D. papers at the Beinecke Library.[15] Also commissioned to carry out a three-day residency at Yale, he gave two readings and a lecture between May 5 and 7. *The Yale Daily News* advertised Duncan's visit in a front-page article on May 6, complete with a photograph of the plump, grinning poet in a suit and tie. The piece gave a view into Duncan's antagonism toward his Ivy League audience:

> "I am ignorant of Frost and almost entirely inept at Auden," boasted poet Robert Duncan before a reading of his own poetry . . . last night.

"My only advice to aspiring poets would be to get out of anything to do with English Literature." Later he added, speaking in broken sentences and jumbled thoughts which resemble his style of poetry, "Culture entirely disinterests me."[16]

On May 9, after participating in a radio broadcast for the Voice of America as his final obligation at the school, Duncan returned to the New York City area to seek more like-minded company. The weekend of May 16 and 17 found him outside of the city at Robert Wilson's house on Fire Island, a territory friendly to gay poets and artists. Engrossed in conversations on the beach, Duncan overlooked the threat of sunburn and wrote to Jess about his new expertise in applying "vitamin A & D ointment over lobster red areas."[17] Spending the rest of the month traveling back and forth between New York and New Haven, he continued to work on *The H. D. Book* and made plans to return home after a two-month absence.

FORTY-ONE

A Night Song

the bright tongues of two
languages

dance in the one light.
ROBERT DUNCAN, "Structure of Rime XXV"

IN THE SUMMER OF 1964, Duncan worked as hard at home as he had on the road, producing poems toward *Bending the Bow* and turning in his final version of *Roots and Branches* to Scribners for a September publication date.[1] The themes of household, love, and language were heavily on his mind and evident in *Passages* 9 and 10, "The Architecture" and "These Past Years." Giving views into the household and into Duncan's marriage to Jess, the poems also returned to a Steinian lyric playfulness and to the projective form of a Black Mountain aesthetic. He opened "These Past Years" with the lines

> Willingly I'll say there's been a sweet marriage
>   all the time   a ring
>   (if wishing could make it so)   a meeting
>   in mind   round   the moon
> means rain.²

With Jess working long hours toward an autumn show at the Rolf Nelson Gallery in Los Angeles, Duncan drew inspiration from his partner's work. The images in Jess's painting *Ex. 4—Trinity's Trine: Translation #5,* based on an 1887 *Scientific American* illustration of a chemist's laboratory and Bunsen burner, echoed in Duncan's midsummer *Structure of Rime* poems:

> The Fire Master waits always for me to recall him from a place in my heart that is burnd or is burning. He comes to my mind where, immediate to the thought of him, his rimes flicker and would blaze forth and take over.
>
> You too are a flame then and my soul quickening in your gaze a draft upward carrying the flame of you. From this bed of a language in compression, life now is fuel, anthracite from whose hardness the years spring . . . ³

But a more sinister thread also entered into Duncan's poems that summer. The Republican National Convention was held in San Francisco in mid-July, with ultraconservative nominee Barry Goldwater presenting a speech that emphasized America's need for vigilance in the face of communist threats. Dismayed by Goldwater's message "extremism in the defense of liberty is no vice," Duncan turned to the writings of William Blake for solace.[4] His reading notes on *The Marriage of Heaven and Hell, Visions of the Daughters of Albion,* and *America: A Prophecy* resonated throughout a poem written on the Lammas, August 1. "A Night Song," later renamed "My Mother Would Be a Falconress"—a meditation on his sexuality, his relationship with his adoptive mother, and larger themes of authority and freedom—became one of Duncan's best-known works.[5] He credited Helen Adam for inspiring the composition's dark subject matter and near-ballad form, telling her during the 1970s, "You are the true godmother of my ever writing the Falcon poem; and I remember I could hardly wait to get to your place to read it alive that first day."[6] The poem pointed beyond the autobiographical to turmoil in the "motherland" and the war in Viet Nam:

My mother would be a falconress,
and I her gerfalcon, raised at her will,
from her wrist sent flying, as if I were her own
pride, as if her pride
knew no limits, as if her mind
sought in me flight beyond the horizon.

Ah, but high, high in the air I flew.
And far, far beyond the curb of her will,
were the blue hills where the falcons nest.
And then I saw west to the dying sun—
it seemd my human soul went down in flames.[7]

Alongside poems toward *Bending the Bow,* Duncan continued work on *The H. D. Book* and on a review of John Wieners's *Ace of Pentacles* and *The Hotel Wentley Poems* for the *Nation,* an assignment he was keen to tackle, telling Denise Levertov, "The poems assert the validity of a great unhappiness and have such authenticity I am ashamed to come back with any criticism that he [Wieners] ought to live a different life. Then I find the pleasure in rimes rung out loud when there's a song to it and it dances."[8] When *Roots and Branches* was published that fall, it received a number of reviews of its own. Though Duncan straddled mainstream venues with his poetry, he was not always popular within them. One piece, by crime novelist Charles Willeford, appeared in the *Miami News* on November 15:

> Duncan has been identified with the San Francisco poets, but his work is carefully controlled and almost without emotion. Except for the rare use of a four-letter word, his songs are somewhat old-fashioned, hammered out of cold, soft metal—and his lines are rough. Duncan's poetry is concerned primarily with personal experience, but his lines are dotted heavily with literary references. Apparently, if he cannot find a connection between his personal experience and his reading he does not find the experience worth the making of a poem.[9]

An even more hostile assessment of his work was printed in the *New York Herald Tribune,* describing *Roots and Branches* as "undigested clots of autobiography, puerile incantations, improbable allusions, and insufferable arrogance in its privacy."[10]

Overshadowing poetry business came turmoil in the East Bay. In September, students at Berkeley protested a ruling by the university's administration banning the distribution of written materials related to off-campus political and social causes. In October, the student-led Free Speech Movement began. Duncan, all too familiar with the policies of the Regents of the University of California, followed the skirmishes with great interest. As a student during the 1930s, he had been obliged to participate in ROTC training exercises, and as a returning student during the late 1940s, he had seen his mentor Ernst Kantorowicz dismissed from the college after his refusal to sign a loyalty oath. His sympathy for the Free Speech Movement increased as an anarchist rhetoric began to surface within it. In December 1964, undergraduate Mario Savio issued a plea to his fellow students that formed the backbone of the movement:

> There is a time when the operation of the machine becomes so odious, makes you so sick at heart, that you can't take part; you can't even passively take part, and you've got to put your bodies upon the gears and upon the wheels, upon the levers, upon all the apparatus and you've got to make it stop. And you've got to indicate to the people who run it, to the people who own it, that unless you're free, the machines will be prevented from working at all.[11]

Duncan held no positive feelings toward "the machine" and was eager to lambaste two particular villains: Robert Sproul, who had headed the University of California system during the 1930s, and Clark Kerr, who held the post during the 1960s. He memorialized them, alongside the university's chancellor, Edward Strong, and President Kennedy's ambassador to the United Nations, Adlai Stevenson, in his twenty-first *Passages* poem, "The Multiversity":

> not men   but heads of the hydra
>
>   his false faces in which
>   authority lies
>
> hired minds of private interests
>
>   over us
>
>
>   here: Kerr (behind him, heads of the Bank of America
>   the Tribune,
>   heads of usury, heads of war)
>   the worm's   mouthpiece   spreads
>   what it wishes   its own
> false news . . . [12]

While the student movement gathered steam, a matter of personal importance also claimed Duncan and Jess's attention. In November 1964, Helen and Pat Adam moved to New York City, expecting the relocation to be temporary. When they arrived on the East Coast, they were largely unprepared for the economic and social realities they would face there, and in a December letter, Duncan attempted to ease their fears while making clear his own prejudices against New York: "I don't think that the furies pursue you: But I am willing to believe that going to New York was an expensive (both in money and effort) move that will mix its rewards with all the discomforts of that giant hive of men scrambling to propitiate Mammon."[13]

Duncan and Jess took a short autumn trip to another sprawling urban center, Los Angeles, where Duncan gave poetry readings, Jess met with gallery owner Rolf Nelson, and the couple visited museums.[14] Duncan's reading at UCLA on November 20 was part of a series organized by Lawrence Lipton titled West Coast Avant-Garde Writing: Conversations with Writers at the Edge. The trip was one of Jess's few returns to the landscape of his childhood, and he reflected on the relationship between that geography and his work as a painter, writing to Helen Adam, "I followd along to see what that jazzy city of the pop-arteries had become since boyhood days: I report that it has gone on becoming more-so. It's the blinkingest sign-world ever, a sensation! To be seen, not lived in. I expect them soon to learn how to cast most-pic-billboards onto the smog-ceiling, thus artfully integrating the major vicissitude of the land."[15]

FORTY-TWO

Anger

Death by fire, death by water.
Fireblast and flood,
the rending air, the
shaking earth.
Where the tents of the Great Assembly stand,
I used to make up my
tents, my treasuries,
my powers within powers
ROBERT DUNCAN, "Structure of Rime XXVI for Kenneth Anger"

RETURNING TO SAN FRANCISCO ON NOVEMBER 22, Duncan and Jess celebrated Thanksgiving, enjoyed a short visit from Kenneth Anger, and caught up with the news across the bay. In early December, the Berkeley campus was briefly shut down by Free Speech Movement protests, and nearly eight hundred students were arrested after they took control of the campus's main administrative building. Around the conflict, Duncan penned a series of lines into his poem in progress "The Multiversity," laying out in the clearest terms his political beliefs: "Where there is no commune, / the individual volition has no ground. / Where there is no individual freedom, the commune / is falsified."[1]

Mired in an annual winter melancholy, Duncan spent the early weeks of 1965 attempting to complete his review of John Wieners's poetry and rereading works by Jakob Boehme and Northrup Frye. While not one to linger in depression, he reported to Denise Levertov that a bout of writer's block and looming deadlines were accompanied by other bleak matters: "The rains that have brought floods north of us, . . . have brought a long dreary period, colored glower that coincided with Christmas holidays . . . haunted by its being the time of my mother's death, not grief but an oppression of mortality, of turning away from mortality and then an inertia before it."[2]

Duncan's uneasy feelings were exacerbated by an incident related to Kenneth Anger's December visit. The filmmaker had left a trunk of personal belongings in one of the closets in the 20th Street apartment. Telling Duncan and Jess that the box contained items that had belonged to occultist Aleister Crowley, Anger set Duncan's imagination to work. In late January 1965, Duncan recorded in a notebook,

> Rising about five to pee, I thought . . . that the closet had been disturbd, remembering Fran's [Herndon] picking up the small statue of the Virgin when she was looking for art magazines, knowing nothing of Kenneth's things with the banishing rod . . . still there. It seemd to me then that some influence was abroad from the closet—"Baphomet" came to mind. I cld see no activity in the room or the hall but I lookd only in passing, returning to bed and to dream.
>
> From the dream I remember the silver statue of a peacock, its tale-fan [sic] closed; then the falling of the Moon, red—as in eclipse thru dramatic torn clouds, and close upon the moon a smaller moon. "Baphomet" was first present in shadowy presentations of groups of men copulating; in the dream I was aroused to a state of satyriasis.[3]

Duncan woke in the night, certain that a smell of semen and blood had permeated the house. Tracing the scent to the closet where the trunk was stored, he phoned Anger, demanding that he come immediately to retrieve his belongings. In the following days, Duncan pored through his books on magic and spells, carrying out various makeshift rituals to evict the unwelcome spirits.[4]

In the incense-clouded household, he also moved ahead with poems of the *Passages* series. "The Multiversity" was completed on January 9, and he began "In the Place of a Passages 22" the following day, continuing his thoughts on the Free Speech Movement: "That Freedom and the Law are identical / and are the nature of Man—Paradise."[5] The tensions in Duncan's poems rose as war tensions rose overseas. On February 7, the U.S. military began systematically bombing the North Vietnamese. By early spring, American combat troops were introduced to the region, and in August, they initiated ground action. Nineteen sixty-five was in all ways a year of political discord. Malcolm X was assassinated in late February, and in April, an antiwar rally organized by Students for a Democratic Society drew twenty-five thousand protesters to Washington, D.C. The growing crisis in American politics distracted Duncan from his work:

> To write a letter or a poem or a passage of *The H. D. Book* means each time clearing away the thought of the do-nothing policy in regard to the plight of the Negro and the bomb them policy in regard to the plight of the

Vietnamese.... Blake and Boehme with their revelation of what a time of wrath means may give a key ... to the vision one must have. For these men— the Johnsons and the Stevensons and Humphries *[sic]*—are creatures of the malevolence that moves liberal and progressive men to enslave a people in the name of their freedom.[6]

Woven into his brooding over the political came a return to the study of language. That spring, he composed a translation of Victor Hugo's poem "Pleine Mer" and began teaching a graduate-level creative writing workshop on phonetics at San Francisco State. In February and March, he accumulated copious reading notes from *Outline of English Structure* by Trager and Smith and *Phonetics* by Kantner and West. A poem penned the previous year, "Spelling, *Passages* 15," had also been assembled as a collage of language-studies materials, including quotations from linguist Otto Jespersen's writings. In the piece, Duncan recorded word sounds and their phonetic notations with a certain obsessive glee, and at readings he drafted the lines onto a chalkboard:

> /k/   examples: **kan, kind, kreep, klime, kween, skin,**
> skratch, thikker, brakken, siks, kase, kure,
> kreem, klame, kwarter, skwire, konker, distinkt,
> **eksamplz**[7]

While picking away at the particulars of the English language, he caught glimpses of a work in progress by Jess. Titled *The Enamord Mage: Translation #6,* the painting showed Duncan peering out from a thick array of semi-shadowed household images rendered in equally thick paint. The inclusion of revered objects—Duncan's multivolume collection of the *Zohar,* G. R. S. Mead's books on gnosticism, candles, a stained glass lamp, and numerous semi-identifiable ceramic knickknacks—gave a view into the life that Duncan and Jess shared.[8] After a successful show in Los Angeles that winter, Jess's art dealer, Rolf Nelson, had arranged for a handful of his paintings to appear in an exhibit of California artists at Macy's New York store. Jess, ever skeptical of both traveling and the art world, asked Pat and Helen Adam to look in on the display for him: "I don't ever want to go stay in New York City. It scares and horrifies me as a place to live, let alone work in."[9]

Completing his semester of teaching at San Francisco State, on May 12, 1965, Duncan flew to Topeka, Kansas, to give a lecture called "The Psyche Myth and the Moment of Truth" for the Menninger Foundation. His talk, an early version of a lecture he gave later that summer at the Berkeley Conference, burrowed through the material of *The Opening of the Field,* lingering on "A

Poem Beginning with a Line by Pindar" and explaining the outside texts collaged into the work. Influenced by the novelty of the trip to the Midwest and reflecting upon his relation to reading, writing, and myth, he told the audience, "I know that we now have had about fifty years in which not only are we not supposed to be earnestly concerned with the home ground of our Judeo-Christian reality, but we're not supposed to be concerned with fairy tale reality at all, instead they read stories about the tractor who made it and plowed the plains. Well, no wonder we get poems about the tractor who made it and plowed the plains; that's what they're reading."[10] The following afternoon Duncan performed at the University of Kansas in Lawrence. The May 14 issue of the campus newspaper reported that he had sung sections of *Faust Foutu* and "kept the audience of some 300 people laughing as he described the life of the two main characters."[11]

The visit was the first of several he made to the University of Kansas over three decades. His 1965 appearance had been arranged by the assistant chairman of the English Department, Edwin Eigner. Eigner, a scholar of Victorian literature and a cousin to poet Larry Eigner, recalled that Duncan's visit set off a midwestern poetry mania:

> My colleague Ed Grier had met Robert . . . and suggested that I write him. A week or two before his arrival, I walked into my office and found Bob Creeley waiting to see me. He was traveling across country, was short of cash, and had heard from Robert that Kansas was paying poets to read. Thus started what was for two of three years the most active program of poetry readings in the country. [W.S.] Merwin stopped by unannounced in the middle of a reading. He was driving through Kansas and came by to see if anything was going on.[12]

For his hosts, Duncan was an exceptional visitor not only because of his performance skills but also because of his inquisitiveness about the people and places around him. During his stay, he frequented Kansas City's Nelson-Atkins Museum of Art and also quickly formed a bond with Ruth Eigner, whose husband recalled a peculiarity of Duncan's first performance: "He fixed one eye on my wife and gave the whole reading to her. He told me that overweight middle age women were his favorite audience. 'Nothing shocks them,' he said. 'They've seen everything.'"[13]

When Duncan returned to San Francisco in May, he completed "Orders, *Passages* 24," reflecting on two disparate events: the death of T.S. Eliot in January and a revolution in Santo Domingo in April, to which Lyndon

Johnson responded by strong-arming the victorious rebel forces into a provisional U.S.-approved government. At the center of the poem came a melancholy Whitmanesque catalogue that again underscored Duncan's dedication to collage techniques:

> and now that Eliot is dead, Williams and H. D. dead,
> Ezra alone of my old masters alive,   let me
>   acknowledge Eliot was one of them,   I was
>   one of his,   whose   "History has many
>   cunning passages, contrived corridors"
>
> comes into the chrestomathy.[14]

A late May trip to Los Angeles turned Duncan's attention to another modernist master, as he gave a reading of Gertrude Stein's work to celebrate an exhibition of Stein photographs and rare books at UCLA. When he returned home at the end of the month, he found the May 31 issue of the *Nation* containing his review of John Wieners's *Ace of Pentacles* and *The Hotel Wentley Poems*. The piece reiterated the positive comments Duncan had made to Denise Levertov, interspersing quotations from Jakob Boehme:

> He derives from whatever songs of unrequited and unhappy love, transient rapture, enduring tenderness—from Rimbaud or Baudelaire, but also from blues or the high speech of Elizabethan theatrical passion—all that might provide a tradition for what is most real in his own life. It is a great tradition . . . ; not only the poets but seers and prophets have reiterated the ultimate value of an ecstasy that is identified with sexual orgasm, with sight beyond sight, with divine or demonic inspiration.[15]

A less pleasurable professional task also faced Duncan that month when he was asked to serve as a judge for the University of California's 1965 Shelley Memorial Award. Preoccupied with the previous season's protests at the Berkeley campus, Duncan at first drafted a letter to university president Clark Kerr refusing the assignment: "A poet does not serve institutions . . . for he has one allegiance, to his vision of the good of humanity, and he has one responsibility, to the truth of the human spirit."[16] Duncan left the letter to Kerr tucked away in a notebook and accepted the post—only to resign from it in anger on July 2. Duncan's recommendations largely centered on Beat writers—Allen Ginsberg, Gregory Corso, and Michael McClure—but also included other poets he considered to be heirs of a Shelleyan tradition: Ezra Pound, Charles Olson, Louis Zukofsky, Denise Levertov, Robert Creeley, and

John Wieners. In a June 29 letter, fellow judge and poet Charles Angoff wrote to Duncan: "All I want to say at this time is that I am opposed to Allen Ginsberg, Ezra Pound, and Louis Zukofsky. I know their work. I think it's poor. Allen Ginsberg's is very poor."[17] Irked, Duncan dropped off the committee, leaving room for Vermont poet Ruth Stone to receive the award.

FORTY-THREE

The Berkeley Conference

> As I stand here tonight, 54½ years old, . . . drinking a bottle in front of you. Well, excuse me, as both Mr. Ginsberg and Mr. Creeley would ask you to. And I'm almost going to finish it, so we might finish earlier than you think. CHARLES OLSON, reading at the Berkeley Conference

THE BERKELEY POETRY CONFERENCE BEGAN ON JULY 12 and continued through the 24th of the month. Organized by Richard Baker, the event took place at the University of California and was sponsored by the school's extension program. Duncan and Donald Allen were Baker's key advisors on the conference focus and list of invitees, though Duncan reported to Denise Levertov in the weeks preceding the gathering, "I wanted Clayton Eshleman and Jackson Mac Low and got neither."[1] Duncan had also pushed to include LeRoi Jones but had second thoughts when Jones appeared in the Bay Area that spring espousing a newfound belief in black separatism.

The politics behind the conference were complex, but for those who congregated in Berkeley from around the country, the events provided a firsthand introduction to the writers in Donald Allen's *The New American Poetry*. The two weeks of festivities featured lectures and readings by Duncan, Jack Spicer, Gary Snyder, Charles Olson, Ed Dorn, Allen Ginsberg, and Robert Creeley. Several younger writers were also invited to present their work, and the audience included fledgling poets such as New Yorkers Lewis Warsh and Anne Waldman, who came to watch the events unfold and coincidentally found themselves on their first date. Waldman, who had recently graduated from Bennington College, remembered:

> They were a refreshing contrast to the poets I'd been hearing at Bennington—
> May Swenson, Richard Eberhart, Stanley Kunitz, John Berryman, all solid,
> but more staid and carrying the burden of English poetry on their backs.
> The New American Poetry . . . was not in the literature department's curriculum. There was an attitude about Stein, as I recall, Howard Nemerov . . .
> thought her "silly" and Ezra Pound was too controversial because of his anti-
> Semitism. I remember asking why we weren't studying them, let alone Ginsberg or Creeley. . . . The poets encountered at Berkeley were less predictable
> and less content driven, more open, expansive, performative, inter-active,
> radical, investigative. De-centered. . . . Robert Duncan's arms waved and
> danced in the air as he read . . . This was a "body poetics."[2]

Duncan made several appearances at the conference, performing his own work, presiding over seminar meetings, and emceeing performances by his peers. On July 13, he redelivered "The Psyche Myth and the Moment of Truth" lecture. Tom Parkinson introduced him, saying to the glee of the audience, "If it weren't for Robert Duncan, none of you would be here." Duncan mapped the course of the talk using three phrases chosen by Jess from the household Kenkyusha, and one audience member, David Franks, remembered the intrigue the San Francisco poet created around himself: "When he entered the lecture room, Robert Duncan was silent, smiling always like a mischievous child as if he had something up his sleeve and he always did—though he most often didn't know what it was—discovering it in the act of talking. . . . After a few moments of waiting for people to settle in, he turned his smile to face the blackboard. On cue, . . . Jess Collins entered the room and handed Duncan an envelope."[3] The audience, unaware that Duncan had prepared parts of the talk in advance, was led through a seemingly spontaneous exposition on "A Poem Beginning with a Line by Pindar," alongside digressions inspired by the Kenkyusha-drawn phrase "an ill-kept garden." Seizing upon the ill-kept garden as a metaphor for the practice of a field poetics and for the lecture itself, Duncan relaxed into a series of anecdotes:

> [John] Wieners at one point came out to Stinson Beach . . . and he said, looking at the garden, "You weed the garden; William Carlos Williams never
> would." I said, "Well we want lettuces and we just get those awful weeds out
> of there." Now, in some sense . . . you do not weed a poem, because you really
> are not producing lettuces. Well, there are some poets who produce lettuces,
> and there's nothing like having a poet give you lettuce and then the second

course is lettuce, and the third course is lettuce, and the fourth course is lettuce and there ain't no other kind of plants coming along.[4]

On July 14, the *San Francisco Examiner* ran a glib article about the conference, focusing heavily on Duncan's involvement and describing him as a "plump mephistophelean type." The piece quoted him saying of his estranged friend Jack Spicer, "We can't tell what he means, but we get a kick out of it."[5] The morning the article appeared, Spicer gave his lecture "Poetry and Politics," weaving together commentaries on the Free Speech Movement, the Viet Nam war, and the poet's relation to the social world. His health already significantly compromised by his alcoholism, the puffy-faced, nervous Spicer rallied himself to display both his brilliance and his commitment to the ideals of the Berkeley Renaissance. Extending Duncan's thought that "A Poem Beginning with a Line by Pindar" had been channeled from an outside metaphysical source, Spicer made a further proposition about the intuitive nature of poetry: "I think poems are delivered very much like a message that's delivered over a radio and the poet is a radio. . . . I think fundamentally a poem comes from the Outside. I have no idea where, I have no theological or any other . . . notion of it. Green Martians was the thing I used before. It's obviously not Martians. But I do think poems are delivered, when they're good, from the Outside, and I think they give messages to the poet, to other poets."[6]

Duncan gave a reading of the first twenty-five *Passages* poems on July 16 after having spent an afternoon at home continuing lines toward "In the Place of A Passage 22."[7] And as long days of conferencing evolved into equally long nights of socializing, he pursued another crush. At a postreading party at the Buzz Gallery in San Francisco, he singled out Spicer circle artist Bill Brodecky, who later recalled: "I allowed Duncan to seduce me, and we wound up in my bed. The next day I took his watch, which he had left on the bedside apple crate, with me to another Berkeley reading, perhaps one at which Duncan was the MC. I made a public spectacle of handing him his watch, and he was embarrassed."[8]

On July 20, Duncan introduced Charles Olson's lecture "Causal Mythology." The following day, he attended a reading by younger poets Ted Berrigan, Ed Sanders, and Leonore Kandel, after which he wrote a sonnet sequence reflecting upon his relationship to the New York School and singling out his appreciation for Berrigan's performance: "I put the coda towards the last / for friendship's sake / The audience is crowding in / To hear what we need and is lovely."[9] The final days of the conference featured readings by Robert Creeley and Charles Olson. Olson's July 23 appearance became one of the more talked-about events of the two weeks. Introduced by Duncan, the drunken elder poet lectured for slightly over three hours. While many present deferred to the bulky, podium-clutching Olson, Duncan eventually shouted out in exasperation, "Charles. Give us a break to pee." When Olson acceded to the idea, Duncan exited the proceedings along with many other members of the audience.[10] Duncan later reported to Denise Levertov that Olson's state had been enhanced by amphetamines:

> He had begun reading very badly (too drunk to get thru) his "Ode On Nativity," then he announced he was going to talk, and (belligerently) that "talk was poetry"; O.K., but nothing was moving anywhere but up and at 'em in the first part. After the break when I left, he talkt on "out of his head" until first the janitors and then the campus police arrived at midnight to remove him and the remaining audience.[11]

Younger writers such as Ed Sanders and Anne Waldman stayed to the end of Olson's talk, and as Waldman remembered,

> I took a further vow to poetry at the Charles Olson marathon event, for he . . . spoke and raged and wept more than he technically "read." But Olson was powerful that night, vulnerable, arrogant, bombastic, poignant, embarrassing. He was the poet coming apart before our eyes. . . . His friends were dismayed.[12]

While the conference continued the conversations begun in Vancouver in 1963, mobilizing younger writers to participate in the traditions established by the first generation of the Black Mountain School and the San Francisco Renaissance, it also exposed the incompatibilities between bohemia and academia. Robert Creeley later admitted to Duncan, "I came away with mixed feelings. . . . I think I went through the whole business with a resistance to the rush, and the specious professionalism of the arrangements, etc. . . . Elsewise we simply wore out . . . and on the last night I found myself screaming obscenities at a cleancut young Berkeley policeman. . . . Happily I did not go to jail."[13]

The hoopla of the gathering gave way to difficult news for the San Francisco poetry community. On July 31, Jack Spicer collapsed into an alcoholic coma in the elevator of his apartment building on Polk Street. Visited in the hospital by friends and students, and tended to by Robin Blaser, who stayed by his side as his condition deteriorated, Spicer drifted in and out of consciousness for two weeks before succumbing to internal bleeding and pneumonia on August 17. Missing from his bedside was Duncan, who received daily updates from Blaser and another Spicer circle intimate Deneen Brown. In notes delivered to the 20th Street household, Brown tried to coax Duncan to visit his dying friend: "Jack was very lucid Friday night—it's probably worth going over. He'd like to see you I'm sure, Robert."[14] Prodded to have a last glimpse of the man who had brought him both inspiration and rage, Duncan made a stealthy trip to the intensive care unit, documented by Robin Blaser in a 1983 interview: "Robert arrived at the hospital only one day, I was there. He came to the door of the ward and looked in and left. Robert wasn't easy with this kind of thing."[15]

As newspapers in the Bay Area covered the story of the Watts riots in Spicer's hometown of Los Angeles, Duncan received the news of Spicer's death at the age of forty via a message from Deneen Brown: "Tuesday. Dear Robert, Jack died at 3 o'clock this morning. Stan [Persky] asked me to drop a note by to you."[16] An obituary for Spicer appeared in the *San Francisco Chronicle* the next day: "A heavy, round-faced man with a rich mellifluous voice, Spicer occupied a paternal niche in the lives of scores of younger poets who sought him out in the North Beach intellectual saloons where he spent his evenings. . . . While Spicer's work was often compared to that of other innovators such as Charles Olsen [sic] or Robert Duncan, it was generally conceded that Spicer belonged to no school but his own."[17]

For the poets of the Spicer circle, their mentor's death was the end of an era, but the event roused less emotion in Duncan. He made a brief appearance at Spicer's wake, and he later told Denise Levertov, "His opposition to my poetics had been so fanatical, his death did not mean the loss of a friend. But even in this short time since his death, which I have accepted as certain since that Monday two weeks ago, I've been able to read his work freed of its person, the programmatic content is no longer significant of quarrels I must have with Jack, and I find much more of meaning and feeling released . . . There too, such a terrible obstruction thrown up against any fullness of life."[18]

FORTY-FOUR

The Sixties

The beautiful young men and women!
Standing against the war in their courage
Has made a green place in my heart.

ROBERT DUNCAN, "Earth's Winter Song"

BY THE EARLY 1960S, those of Duncan's generation were struggling to acclimate themselves to a youth movement that would soon radically alter the face of American life. The San Francisco Renaissance participants who had been inspired by the Beats and schooled through Jack Spicer's half-decade reign now crossed paths with another wave of adolescent energy in the form of the counterculture. Duncan weathered the changes with an active curiosity. While he was critical of young people's use of drugs, he listened to their views on politics and sympathized with their plight in relation to the Viet Nam war.[1] Seeing the activists of the New Left as heirs to the evolving democracy Whitman had championed, he expressed a hope for what was happening on the streets and in the classrooms: "Along with the flower children . . . the same generation is giving rise to a very alive college intellectual. Perhaps to say the same 'generation' is wrong—more than one genesis is at work . . . a variety of life areas being sought."[2]

In the aftermath of the summer's Berkeley Conference and the disquiet of Jack Spicer's death, Duncan immersed himself in Dante's poetry. On October 27, he appeared at Dominican College in San Rafael to speak on the seven hundredth anniversary of the Italian poet's birth. Titled "The Sweetness and Greatness of Dante's Divine Comedy," Duncan's talk focused on two topics he knew well: techniques of a "tone leading of vowels" in poetic craft and the more theoretical issue of the poet's relation to the creative imagination.[3] He wrote Denise Levertov about his readings of Dante's *Convivio,* also giving insight into the title of his later collection of essays *Fictive Certainties:*

> It seems to me that the allegorical "truth hidden in a fiction" refers to the actual life experience seen now as creative, a fiction in which a truth is to be

uncovered. This would be our sense of the story in the actual (at its most simple) or of the romance; for Dante it was a sense of the creative intent, the divine sentence moving towards its message,... and of all happening as God's expression moving toward communion.[4]

In late autumn, Richard Moore, an old acquaintance from Treesbank farm, brought a camera crew to the house on 20th Street to film Duncan for the National Educational Television series *USA: Poetry*. Aired the following spring, the segment captured Duncan reading poems from *Bending the Bow*. The series, directed by Moore, featured a number of Duncan's associates, including Frank O'Hara, Louis Zukofsky, Michael McClure, Ed Sanders, and John Wieners. Another professional opportunity arose in October, the details of which Duncan again relayed to Denise Levertov:

> I've accepted an honorary office as advisor to the Poetry Collection in the Rare Books Room at [the University of California] which brings an honorarium of only $250 a year . . . In these first months I am having to spend a full day each week getting a picture of what the Library has . . . ; but I receive also full Library privileges, which I have long wanted (extended borrowing for instance) and I will have direct effect in getting a solid collection in the stacks for open circulation, as well as a free hand in building a non-circulating collection.[5]

The position put Duncan on the inside of affairs at Berkeley's Bancroft Library, and he would continue consulting there for nearly twenty years. In other visits to the East Bay that autumn, he participated in the antiwar activities of the recently formed Viet Nam Day Committee. On November 12, 1965, in the midst of composing two of his major poems of the period, "Uprising, *Passages* 25" and "The Soldiers, *Passages* 26," Duncan appeared at a benefit for the organization. He continued to set down lines toward the latter poem through the end of the year, infusing it with intonations of Whitman:

> O you, who know nothing of the great theme of War,
> fighting because you have to, blindly, at no frontier
>   of the Truth but in-
> structed by liars and masters of the Lie, your own
>   liberty of action
>   their first victim,
>
> youth, driven from your beds of first love and
>   your tables of study to die
> in order that "free men everywhere" "have the right
>   to shape their own destiny

in free elections"—in Las Vegas, in Wall Street,
   America turns in the throws of "free enterprise",
   fevers and panics of greed and fear.[6]

Concurrent with the late *Passages* poems of *Bending the Bow* came a project of another sort, a series of translations of the *Chimeras* of Gerard de Nerval, which Duncan began in response to the publication of Robin Blaser's own translations of the work.[7] With old Spicer circle antagonisms in the air, and likely with lingering anger about Blaser's affair with Jess, Duncan made public his grievances about Blaser's reworkings of Nerval, including his conviction that Blaser had intentionally overlooked the French writer's devotion to hermetic traditions. Duncan's "corrective" translations appeared in *Audit* magazine alongside excerpts of his correspondence with Blaser. His offensive rivaled the viciousness with which he had attacked James Broughton in the early 1960s. In "A Footnote, April 1966," Duncan wrote,

> The basic misunderstanding between Blaser and myself seems to arise between his poetics in which the poem is to be authentic, i.e. an expression of what is really his own . . . and my poetics in which the poem is thought of as a process of participation in a reality larger than my own—the reality of man's experience in the terms of language and literature—a community of meanings and forms in which my work would be at once derivative and creative. So, I have taken Blake's "The authors are in eternity" as my guide. Blaser . . . aims at signature or style; I aim at meaning, both in form and content.[8]

Meanwhile, Jess had been at work on his *Translations* series for a one-man show at the Rolf Nelson Gallery in Los Angeles. After the Thanksgiving holiday, Duncan, Jess, and Hilde and David Burton drove south to attend the November 30 opening of the exhibit. A dozen of the fourteen paintings sold immediately, including the *Enamord Mage* portrait of Duncan, which found a fitting home with the Burtons.[9] Though Rolf Nelson later absconded with a portion of Jess's income from the show, the development of the *Translations* series brought satisfaction to both Duncan and Jess. Upon his return from Los Angeles, Duncan wrote to Denise Levertov of an insight into the mechanics of sound phrases in poetry:

> [Jess] has gone far ahead . . . in exploring color tones and sets (what in poetry would be vowel progressions), and . . . I can see what correlating the intuitive organization of vowels with the designing organization of numbers—so that in composing vowels might appear by progressions of three and of four, giving another more obscure source of measure . . . , particularly

as the deeper imagination begins to awake to the numbers as meanings—I can see some such development of trinities and quarternities in the patterning of the poem as opening out archetypal feelings such as Jung is fascinated by, and also organic-cosmic feelings of mathematic and algebraic relations—of music.[10]

Just after the first of the year, Duncan departed for Vancouver, where he would celebrate his forty-seventh birthday with Ellen and Warren Tallman while he prepared for an expanded presentation of *Adam's Way*. He stepped back into the rituals of his life with the Tallmans, this time greeted by a blanket of winter snow, and he wrote Jess about his arrival: "We, of course, sat up to all hours. And I slept in until eleven this morning. Now Ellen will be going out shopping and I'll be going along to mail this, to get shirts and my cords to a laundry. . . . They have arranged for me to have a work cubicle at the library so I will go in . . . with Warren or Ellen five days a week, which shld make for some work getting done."[11]

The community that Duncan had so influenced in his first visits was experiencing a metamorphosis. Poet Frank Davey described the mid-decade shift away from the "late-beatnik" atmosphere of 1960: "variously & (contradictorily) more public, marxist, psychedelic, and intermedia—'be-in's,' open-air concerts, a lot more drugs and political activism. At the parties the soundtrack changed from Miles Davis to Bob Dylan. Much more interest in film-making; the start of image-exchange art; the founding of the Western Front gallery which brought writing & performance art together."[12]

Duncan's contribution to the scene came in the form of a February staging of *Adam's Way* at the University of British Columbia. Through the end of January, he met with student actors while writing marginalia around the original script. The revisions were unwieldy, and he was forced to exercise some restraint in his rewritings. In a January 18 letter, he told Jess, "I'm not pushing for the impossible here—I'm taking the play as easy as I can imagine. . . . But with the Kafka maze or tangle of chores I've gathered . . . I get the message that just as I am trying to cut back and down the load of food I carry over from an earlier appetite, I've got to cut back the load, the taking on of tasks, that has all but taken me over."[13] While the original play read as a fairy tale of theosophical-biblical adventures, the new production included "Narrative Bridges," which offered philosophical commentary about the actions of the players on the stage. With two showings, on February 4 and 11, the performance was a highlight of that spring's Vancouver

Poetry Festival. On February 8, Jess reluctantly traveled north to join Duncan. Surviving a "wall-to-wall party swinging at the Tallmans," he at least found pleasure in conference readings by Duncan and Robin Blaser.[14] Crossing paths with Blaser in the more neutral territory of Vancouver, Duncan also expressed a sympathy for his poetry, and in private correspondence, he softened his stance on the Nerval translations:

> Robin read the entirety of *The Holy Forest*... which came as a great delight—I was struck with the poetics of the whole as a ritual of magical objects (including the individual poem itself as a magical object), to cast a wonder or spell, in and of itself, such as a fairy-persona maintains itself by, a privacy in that sense, in which the actual soul appears in the context the chimeras are most true, not to Nerval in the original, but to the Nerval who is resurrected in ... the poetic world of Robin's own things.[15]

Returning to San Francisco in mid-February to attend the marriage of poet Joanne Kyger and painter Jack Boyce, by early March, Duncan was traveling again, staying first with the Bermans in Topanga Canyon and then continuing on to Albuquerque to give a reading and visit the Creeleys. Both the Bermans and the Creeleys offered Duncan a taste of counterculture that would largely bypass his household with Jess. Topanga Canyon by the mid-1960s had become an oasis for the avant-garde artist and the acid tripper alike. Wallace and Shirley Berman's son Tosh remembered, "Topanga was going through a golden period—due that people like my father, Dean Stockwell, Russ Tamblyn, Neil Young, etc. were living there.... Although it is only 40 or 45 minutes away from Hollywood, Topanga felt like another country or planet. In the late 60's it was a mixture of artistic haven, hippiedom, low-level drug dealers, lots of community picnics ... and basically a very strong feeling of (not meaning to over-use that word) community."[16]

In Placitas, the Creeleys had an open-door policy beyond anything Jess would allow, and Duncan was particularly taken by one young apprentice of Creeley's, David Franks. Franks, a graduate student at the University of New Mexico, lived on a ranch nearby, where he was, in addition to writing a dissertation, raising doves. After dinner with the Creeleys, Franks gladly acquiesced when Duncan asked to view the doves, escorting the elder poet on a winding walk "up to the top of the Sandia mountain" and stopping for a view of the Rio Grande. Upon arriving at the ranch, the awed but nonetheless heterosexual Franks discovered Duncan's ulterior motive:

I opened one of the cages, and let two of the doves out, perched on a finger of each hand. I asked Robert Duncan to put up a hand . . . and I put one of them on his finger. He smiled his smile and said . . . , "I don't want to embarrass you, or myself either, but I'd like to spend the night with you." . . . Because of the gentle, graceful way in which he asked me—I wasn't afraid. . . . I simply said, "I'm honored, honestly, but I'm sorry, I can't." He left it at that. And I went on showing him how the male doves sit on the eggs and how both male and female feed their babies. Then I . . . walked him up the dirt road past the pink church until we were back at the Creeleys .[17]

When Duncan returned home that spring, he and Jess attended to the death of their white cat, Tom. Long-haired black Orlando became the sole feline resident of 3735 20th Street, curling up with the couple as they watched television news reports from the war front. The television had increasingly become the hearth of the household, and the slaughter that Duncan and Jess witnessed on the screen began to permeate their work. As "The Soldiers" continued to develop, Duncan collaged pieces of advertising and news into the composition alongside a suggestion that the Zoroastrian demon Ahriman was at work in the war:

> In the endless Dark   the T.V. screen,
>   the lying speech and pictures   selling its time and produce,
>   corpses of its victims burned black by napalm
>
> —Ahriman, the inner need for the salesman's pitch—
>
> the image of the mannequin, smoking, driving its car at high speed,
>   elegantly dresst, perfumed, seducing, without
>
>   odor of Man or odor of sanctity . . . [18]

Seeking distractions from the misery of the war, Duncan and Jess took refuge in friendships. At the end of May, Barbara Joseph visited San Francisco and stayed with the couple. Although only peripherally associated with the arts and poetry of the Bay Area, she, alongside the Burtons, had become part of the household's inner sanctum. Her visit prompted a trip to see Patricia and Larry Jordan in San Rafael, with the Burtons along for the ride. When plans for a Southern California vacation with Joseph fell through, Duncan and Jess resigned themselves to a foggy gray summer in San Francisco, during which the city's cultural offerings were considerable. On April 7, Russian poet Andrei Vozneskensky read at the Fillmore Auditorium, sharing the stage with Lawrence Ferlinghetti and the Jefferson Airplane. On May

27, Andy Warhol appeared at the same venue with the Velvet Underground, and on June 24, Lenny Bruce performed there with the Mothers of Invention, some six weeks before his death of a heroin overdose.[19]

By August, a personal sadness was on the horizon. Throughout 1966, Duncan's correspondence with Denise Levertov had become subtly more contentious, beginning with Levertov's disapproval of a mock-Dantean line in Duncan's "Earth's Winter Song": "Wearing the unctuous mask of Johnson from his ass-hole emerging the hed [sic] of Humphrey."[20] Avoiding a direct response to her criticism, Duncan complained instead of her editorial decisions as a consultant for Norton publishing's poetry series. In a departure from his friendly intimate banter, he peevishly offered his alternatives to Levertov's choices of poets: "God, Denny, I think of Jackson Mac Low, Gael Turnbull, Ian Hamilton Finlay.... well, it isn't that you didn't happen to publish some poet I already am keen on, but that you didn't come up with one."[21] Levertov ended her next missive with a barbed note: "I cannot believe that you really meant that the reason I liked these poets was because they were 'genteel'—you may think they are 'genteel,' but you don't really believe that's why I like them & yet in the same breath speak of my own work with love."[22]

As Levertov and Duncan aired their differences, Duncan completed "The Soldiers, *Passages* 26."[23] The war had become costly on both sides, with the United States pouring more than forty million dollars and four hundred thousand men into the effort while displacing two million South Vietnamese civilians. By the end of 1966, over five thousand Americans had been killed. Closer to home, to Duncan's dismay, Ronald Reagan claimed the governor's seat in California in early November. A December 1 raid on James Lowell's Asphodel Bookshop in Cleveland reopened a debate about the censorship of literature and also raised fears about local and federal authorities' monitoring of the activities of the Left. The "obscene" books confiscated in the Asphodel raid included *The Niagara Frontier Review,* D. A. Levy's *Marijuana Quarterly,* and Duncan's *Faust Foutu,* giving him newfound notoriety as a pornographer.

That autumn Duncan received the more positive news that he was being considered for a grant from the newly established National Endowment for the Arts. Putting aside his antipathy toward President Johnson, whose Great Society program had earmarked funding for the humanities, Duncan accepted the ten thousand dollar award and joined the first wave of NEA grantees. In late November, he had another opportunity to interact with the establishment, accepting an invitation to the Houston Council of Teachers of English Festival of Contemporary Poetry. It was the first business trip on which Duncan wore a peace button on his lapel, a gesture geared toward raising awareness of the antiwar movement.[24] Duncan wore the pin for the remainder of the Viet Nam conflict as he made appearances around the country, and that fall he and Jess also donned black armbands to mourn the dead.

In December when Denise Levertov sent Duncan her poem "Advent 1966," it widened the fissure in their relationship but also helped Duncan clarify his ideas about the separation between creative activity and protest politics. Levertov's poem catalogued the suffering of the Vietnamese and offered reflections upon her own plight as a writer, assuming a tone not unlike Duncan's in the *Passages* poems:

> infant after infant, their names forgotten,
> their sex unknown in the ashes,
> set alight, flaming but not vanishing,
> not vanishing as his vision but lingering
>
> cinders upon the earth or living on
> moaning and stinking in hospitals three abed,
>
> because of this my strong sight,
> my clear caressive sight, my poet's sight I was given
> that it might stir me to song
> is blurred.[25]

Duncan's response underscored his feelings about the sanctity of poetic craft, but it was also laced with judgment:

> Denny, the last poem brings with it an agonizing sense of how the monstrosity of this nation's War is taking over your life, and I wish that I could advance some—not consolation, there is none—wisdom of how we are to at once bear constant ... testimony to our grief for those suffering in the War ... and at the same time continue as constantly in our work (which must face and contain somehow this appalling and would-be spiritually destroying evidence of what human kind will do—for it has to do with the imagination of what is going on in Man) now, more than ever, to keep alive the immediacy of the ideal and of the eternal.[26]

While Duncan and Jess donated money to antiwar causes and Duncan participated in peace marches and rallies, he made a distinction between the writing of a poem and the activity of political dissent. In a 1976 interview, he reflected, "Protest is the way you feel. You get out and say it. You don't write a poem in protest, man; you walk. You protest at the same level that two hundred thousand people protest. . . . And when you write a poem that's not your business to protest at all. That's not what a poem does."[27] Throughout the later part of the *Passages* series, Duncan would explore further the poet's role in human conflict, and he would eventually use his work as a forum through which his disagreements with Levertov could be aired. The two continued to correspond as the war progressed, but their relationship had been altered by the outside world. As the situation in Viet Nam grew darker, Levertov and Duncan drifted apart and eventually called an end to what had been a tender and generative friendship.

SIX

Domestic Scenes

FORTY-FIVE

The Household

San Francisco is for me . . . a household. Beyond that I don't
have much of a picture of the rest of the country; it's almost as
vague as living in the rest of history, or all of time.   ROBERT
DUNCAN, "The Psyche Myth and the Moment of Truth," 1965

DUNCAN ONCE JOKED that he lived in San Francisco because it was where
his mother had been born. He saw it as Oz, a part of the imagination. For
both Duncan and Jess, the city's Mission District became a nook removed
from the responsibilities of professional life. They preferred its rough edges to
more obviously favorable parts of town such as the Castro, a traditionally gay
neighborhood, or Bernal Heights, which provided more spectacular views of
the city. Down the length of the Mission, colorful sidewalk markets displayed
fresh fish, Central American spices, and pyramids of lemons, limes, and man-
goes glistening in the sun. The festive atmosphere of the palm tree–lined
streets was complemented by cavernous barrooms piping salsa music day and
night. For Jess, the neighborhood Salvation Army store provided a rich hunt-
ing ground for assemblage materials, and for Duncan, bookstores along the
side streets became regular haunts.

The property that the couple bought in early 1967 was on the eastern end
of the crosstown thoroughfare known as Mission Block No. 53, between
Folsom Street and Treat Avenue. Nestled in a working-class enclave with
mostly Spanish-speaking residents, it was, according to Duncan, "not a real
estate agent's idea of where you want to live," a factor that worked to the
couple's economic advantage.[1] The front windows faced north toward down-
town San Francisco and the Golden Gate, though that view was obscured by
the street's low elevation. The house was the tallest on the block, a looming
three-story Victorian with ornate woodwork that had survived the earth-
quake of 1906. A garage adjoined the house, and a garden behind the house
offered a lemon tree, ornamental flowers, and two Mongolian elms. The yard
also included a carriage house, and the garage had at one time been a pas-
sageway for horses and buggies.

At 3267 20th Street, Duncan and Jess were able to amass a record of their lives together. In early December of 1966, they had their first view of the place, and they quickly made plans to buy it. The independently wealthy Barbara Joseph advanced the mortgage, which the couple returned in installments of one hundred dollars a month throughout the late 1960s and 1970s. Duncan reported the financial details to Joseph in a December 5 letter:

> Today we . . . went over the house again with Richard Eigner, the poet Larry Eigner's brother who is an investment lawyer . . . , and with David Burton who cld add an architect's eye, and found our hopes verified. The venture involves a lot (. . . and that is why we needed as much as $22,000 in mortgage, after our $4000 down, we will have to have the electrical system redone . . . , a matter of at most, we understand, $1000 and, when the rains stop, we will have a roofing job of around $400 and a painting job (outside) of around $800).[2]

Three days after Duncan's forty-eighth birthday, the couple signed a deed granting "Robert Duncan, a single man and Jess Collins, a single man . . . joint tenancy" of the real estate. They then spent several weeks moving in amid major renovations. On January 29, Duncan sent Barbara Joseph an update along with a payment on the couple's loan: "Project number one: the electrical circuits, begin the end of this week. Project number two: new flooring, walls redone, sink area, storage cabinets and stove will follow. Project three: roof and flashings will be—if not more than we can budget—the works for the first half of the year."[3] While the major structural enhancements required a team of electricians and builders, the couple also engaged in do-it-yourself renovations. Hilde Burton remembered that Duncan and Jess, with their passion for collage, stripped layers of wallpaper in the various rooms, stopping when they came to a pattern they liked.[4]

To enter the household was to begin an adventure. Museum curator Michael Auping recalled Duncan once telling him, "You can't take a piss in this house without getting hit with a myth."[5] From the house's steep front steps, the visitor was enveloped in a foyer shadowed by the staircase to the upper floors. The walls, even at the house's entrance, were arrayed with artworks by R. B. Kitaj, Wallace Berman, Harry Jacobus, and other friends, and a set of bookshelves in the hallway hosted Duncan's favorite science books, including his large collection of works by and about Charles Darwin. From the foyer, one came into a bright, high-ceilinged living room lit through a panel of tall, street-facing windows and cluttered with photographs, paintings, statuary, and vases reminiscent of the arrangement of objects in Freud's study in Vienna. Behind the living room was a darkened sitting room, outfitted with the couple's phonograph and collection of classical records, where they and their guests settled in after meals to listen to Duncan's latest musical finds.

The intellectual center of the house was a smaller rectangular room tucked in alongside the sitting room containing Duncan's reference books. Over the years, he amassed into that space the texts that were at the heart of his poetics—from the writings of Jessie Weston to those of A. E. Waite, G. R. S. Mead, Ovid, Homer, Whitehead, Freud. The library contained a breathtaking variety of key texts of the Western tradition, with each tome carefully placed, identified with Duncan and Jess's household bookplate, and catalogued in an obsessive numerical filing system invented by Duncan.[6] It was not a room designed for relaxation but rather an austere, awe-inspiring spectacle of hardcover and leather-bound books stretching up to the ceiling and filling the house with the smell of aging paper.

At the very back of the ground floor was the kitchen, another center of activity, most remarkable for the crescents and rectangles of red and orange stained glass installed by Duncan and Jess.[7] Through the quirky array of flower petal–patterned windows, sunlight streamed into the room, illuminating the kitchen table and warming the large area that included a pantry, appliances, and counters where the couple cooked together and made their morning coffee. The kitchen was Duncan's favorite writing place, and he often sat at the table looking out onto the lemon and elm trees in the yard as he gathered his thoughts.

Much of the second story of the house was given over to Jess, whose studio took up the front and north end of the floor, with Duncan and Jess's bedroom behind it. Jess, also a meticulous organizer, arranged the sunny studio to include shelves of brushes, paints, and tools as well as long file drawers filled with carefully archived images and scraps of paper cut out and categorized by subject. It was from this library of images that the intricate collages he produced during his years in the 20th Street house came into being. The bedroom next door held a treasury of books with significant symbolic value to the two men, pointing to their shared devotion to the imagination.

The Oz books and other fairy-tale tomes they each had collected since childhood filled the shelves around their bed.

Up another flight of stairs, the third-floor hallway's eastern wall was lined with Duncan's crayon drawings and with books of a darker nature by the likes of Aleister Crowley and Madame Blavatsky. Four west-facing rooms were reserved for yet more libraries. A guest room that included Duncan's collection of poetry magazines was followed by a study that housed copies of his own books and memorabilia of his youth in Berkeley and New York. One wall was adorned with Virginia Admiral's painting *Red Table #2,* another with Marjorie McKee's *Orpheus and Euridice.*[8] When he sat at his writing desk to type his poems or attend to business matters, he faced photographs of Ezra Pound, Sigmund Freud, Charles Olson, Robert Creeley, Jack Spicer, and Virginia Woolf. Next to Duncan's study was another room ringing with early influences. Dubbed "the modernist room," it housed a significant collection of works related to James Joyce and Gertrude Stein. Finally, at the very back of the third floor was "the French room," in which Duncan kept his foreign-language books and his multivolume edition of the *Zohar.*

In addition to obtaining a new house in the New Year, Duncan received a new name. On February 16, 1967, the California Supreme Court approved his request to abandon his adoptive name of Robert Edward Symmes and to conduct business under the name of Robert Edward Duncan. Amid the home renovations, he began the season's work with a reading at Cody's Bookstore in Berkeley in celebration of the publication of *The Years As Catches,* a volume of early uncollected poems published by Robert Hawley's Oyez Press. Negotiations with Scribners were also on the table, though the press expressed reservations about publishing *Bending the Bow,* noting that some of the Viet Nam war poems—"The Fire," "The Multiversity," "Up Rising," "Earth's Winter Song," and "The Soldiers"—"seemed rather didactic and shrill, without the complexity, or, broadly speaking, the fine quality of the other poems."[9] Duncan refused to omit the pieces from the collection, eventually publishing the book with New Directions instead.

That spring, he also made an appearance in a class taught by Jack Gilbert at San Francisco State. One student in the group, Berkeley native Ron Silliman, recalled the awe-inspiring visit: "Every time he made a point, Duncan literally made a point, with a blunt piece of chalk on the blackboard. By the time he finished talking, the board was . . . white with dots. It had been as much theater as lecture and I will concede to having been enchanted. It was . . . like having been visited by a creature from another dimension."[10]

While roofers and plumbers descended upon Jess and spooked Orlando the cat, Duncan set off for one of his seasonal trips to the Pacific Northwest. On Wednesday March 8, he gave a reading at Catholic Portland University, and he subsequently made appearances at Reed College and Lewis & Clark College. After a stop at home to inspect the new kitchen sink, he flew to Southern California in late March for a weeklong residency at the Pomona College Spring Arts Festival. While there, Duncan found refuge in the Berman household after long days charged with classroom enthusiasms.[11] Student Stephen Fredman recalled Duncan's artful pedagogical skills:

[He] walked into a light-filled classroom at Pomona College on an April afternoon . . . during my freshman year, shrugged the satchel from his shoulder, and began to arrange its contents on the podium. When he finished, he looked up at faces wide open to register his every movement and then swept the room with his gaze. When he looked at me I felt a wave of vertigo: his eyes were aimed about sixty degrees apart.

"Well," he said in a high, wavering voice, "we're spending this week together . . . , so let's begin by taking a look at one of your poems. . . ."

I raised my hand.

"All right. Let's see what you have."

The poem was a fractured portrait of W. C. Fields, in a style derived from e. e. cummings. Duncan read the poem aloud. He offered no judgment but instead turned to the blackboard and wrote down the first three lines:

> w. c.
> fields performs
> the unreal feat of walking

Then he filled the rest of the board with names like *commedia dell'arte, Aristophanes, Pico della Mirandola, Picasso, Einstein.* "These," he said, gesturing toward the board, "make up the lineage of this poem." He then moved back and forth in front of the blackboard, pointing out lines of derivation, constructing a cultural network.[12]

After another reading in the area at Jack Shoemaker's Unicorn Book Shop in Isla Vista, Duncan had a brief first meeting with British poet Basil Bunting, then a visiting professor at the University of California, Santa Barbara. During the trip, he also sought a closure for *Bending the Bow,* penning the final lines of "Epilogos." Brimming with the influence of the seventeenth-century metaphysical poets, the work returned to the theme of risk that had first appeared in *Roots and Branches*. Acknowledging his shortcomings, Duncan also reavowed his love for his partner of fifteen years:

> Yes, how many times I have broken word
> with you, generously, broken my word,
> with you generously understanding me
>
> . . . .
>
> I see in your eyes your sight of me
> —for you too, times
> when all that we are bound to feel
> bounds with life, leaps up,
> and your eyes shine in the shining of
>   my seeing you.   Brimfull
> the cup my heart is upon the very
>   edge
> of spilling . . . [13]

FORTY-SIX

The Summer of Love

If we cannot find a way to make our lasting own-manse, we will make it in our imagination here or wherever we must as the big wind sweeps.   JESS TO ROBERT DUNCAN, January 1966

AT HOME IN EARLY APRIL, Duncan and Jess prepared for tax day while roofers paced and pounded overhead. Abroad on the city streets, a noisy series of dramas was unfolding, including an April 15 antiwar march that drew over a hundred thousand protesters. Leaving the turmoil behind, Duncan flew to Kansas to begin a two-month Midwest and East Coast reading tour. He made his way through the opening obligations of the trip while fighting off a head cold and adjusting to an early spring heat wave. It was his second visit to Lawrence, where he gave an April 17 reading and spent time with new friends Edwin and Ruth Eigner. His lodgings were with another University of Kansas professor, Whitman scholar Ed Grier, in an environment he found "most comfortable": "a beautiful house and ample towels, lounging room, garden."[1] Such amenities offered a welcome respite from the usual vagaries of the road: unpredictable housing, late-night academic chatter, alcohol, and lack of sleep. He noted to Jess, "I weatherd the cocktail party magnificently because they were all drinking bourbon, and I stayd with ginger ale straight. If I can do that for most of the run I will come thru in fine form . . . but right ahead of me I see Paul Carroll's lethal martinis."[2]

Leaving Lawrence on the evening of April 19, Duncan was greeted in Chicago by Michael Anania, a former student of Charles Olson's and editor of *Audit* magazine.[3] In his room at Evanston's Orrington Hotel, he prepared for a day that would include a poetry reading, a view of works by Clyfford Still and Alexander Calder at Chicago's Art Institute, a scouting mission to local bookstores, and a dinner with Paul and Inara Carroll. The next stop was Madison, Wisconsin, where he was hosted by and interviewed by Larry Dembo, an English professor at the university there. Staying with Dembo and his wife, Duncan fell into the now-familiar rhythm of business travel, toiling through "official rounds of lunch, library tour, reading, cocktail party, and dinner."[4]

On April 25, as he moved on to St. Louis, his work was at least mixed with the pleasure of familiar company. Presenting a reading at Washington University alongside Robert Creeley, Duncan also met scientist and poetry enthusiast Joseph Eigner, Larry and Richard Eigner's younger brother. A tour of St. Louis with Eigner and his wife, Janet, included "the Saarinen Arch looming up over the river in the moonlight" and "Singleton Palmer and his Dixieland Band in Gaslight Square."[5] Sneaking away from his scheduled activities long enough to see the St. Louis Zoo and browse in bookstores, Duncan wrote Jess about his finds: "Ginzberg's *Legends of the Jews* for $5, an interesting looking book on fairy religion, Edward Carpenter's *Pagan Religion and Christianity,* a book of Steiner's mystery plays, and. . . . a copy of Pound's *Lustra.*"[6] As his tours increasingly extended for months rather than weeks, Duncan's letters to Jess became more detailed, filled with spontaneous reviews of restaurants and museums and with stories of friendships made and renewed. While Jess rarely left San Francisco, he toured the country vicariously through Duncan's daily missives.

From St. Louis, Duncan accompanied Robert Creeley to Buffalo. Creeley had recently accepted a teaching position in the English Department at the state university and had invited Duncan to appear at the school's spring arts festival. In the Creeleys' recently uprooted Placitas household, now relocated to Eden, New York, Duncan again succumbed to the exhaustion of travel. The Creeleys' late-night energies, the springtime Great Lakes thunderstorms, and a pounding pulse brought on by his negligence with his blood pressure medication left him sleep deprived during the first days of his stay there.[7] But as he told Jess, he also appreciated the opportunity to spend time with a steadfast group of friends gathered for the conference, including the Creeleys, Norman O. Brown, Ed Sanders, Pauline Butling, Fred Wah, and Warren Tallman: "There have been lovely times here . . . —Warren is a dear; and I feel more and more at home with Bobbie—when she is playing her guitar and singing and when she is showing her collages. . . . She is an immediate intelligence."[8] On May 4, when Stan and Jane Brakhage arrived, Duncan's reaction was less positive. Attempting to remove himself from their reach, he retreated to Pauline Butling and Fred Wah's home outside of town. His letters to Jess that week gave a deeper view into his attachment to household routines: "Warren, the Wahs and I have had a happy time indeed. With good nights of sleep, the Wah's [sic] sprawling country house . . . as quiet and resting as the Creeleys' town house is upset and uproaring and meals at the Wahs' being as regular and planned as the meals at the Creeleys' were hastily got up only when hunger overcame the scene and then . . . consisted—three of them—of beans pressure cookt up; no meat, no vegetables."[9]

With the closure of the conference in Buffalo, Duncan flew to Albany on May 8 to spend a quiet night in a hotel before boarding a train toward Poughkeepsie, New York, where he was scheduled to give a reading at Vassar College. His stay there had been arranged by Denise Levertov, then a visiting professor at the school, and his arrival intersected with the visit of another traveling scholar, Richard Ellmann. Duncan attended Ellmann's May 9 lecture on W. B. Yeats and Oscar Wilde before giving his own performance. The next morning he headed to New York, where he was hosted by two recent San Francisco émigrés, Joanne Kyger and Jack Boyce, at their loft on Greene Street. That evening, he gave a reading at the Guggenheim Museum sponsored by the Academy of American Poets. New York provided several welcome reconvenings, including a May 12 dinner with Helen and Pat Adam, Denise Levertov, and composer Al Carmines. Duncan was equally pleased to be staying with Kyger and Boyce, telling Jess, "They manage an island of almost San Francisco in the midst of things."[10] His accommodations came with one minor glitch, later recalled by Kyger: "We were baby sitting someone's ancient aristocratic cat (who had modeled a diamond necklace in a Tiffany's ad) and he was very jealous of Robert and . . . shit on his bed. I remember Robert saying, 'Is this for me?' "[11]

Another unique social matrix awaited him at Anne Waldman and Lewis Warsh's apartment on St. Mark's Place. Since meeting at the Berkeley Conference, the two native New Yorkers had placed themselves at the center of literary activity on the Lower East Side, and as Waldman recalled, "Our apartment one flight up was a smaller version—and a poetry version—of Andy Warhol's Factory. . . . Collaborations, editing projects (typing stencils for *The World* etc.). Poets coming and going, often staying. . . . Poets sitting at the window watching the action on the street. The apartment was two blocks away from the Poetry Project at St. Mark's Church. [Duncan] got into the spirit and created a little marriage poem book for me and Lewis—black ink on heavy white folded . . . paper."[12] Waldman's other memory of Duncan's visit was a party at Boyce and Kyger's loft during which the elder San Francisco poet and the twenty-two-year-old Waldman spent the evening on the dance floor together. Duncan held everyone's attention not only with his "nimble, sort of early 20th century expressive 'free rhythm'," but also with his exit from the celebration in the company of John Ashbery.[13]

On May 16, Duncan returned to business, making the trek from Manhattan to Long Island to read at the State University of New York at Stony Brook. He told Jess that he liked the community around the English Department very much, particularly for its "Duncan enthusiasts," including the young poet and teacher George Quasha.[14] Offered a future weeklong residency, Duncan would return to the school in the fall. As his tour neared its end, on May 17, he flew to Washington, D.C., for a reading and a visit with friends William and Joan Roth before continuing on to New Haven to visit Henry and Adele Wenning and Norman Holmes Pearson. Ending his trip at Yale's Beinecke Library, he immersed himself in the sprawl of the recently neglected *H. D. Book* before flying home to San Francisco.

Duncan began the Summer of Love on his hands and knees in the backyard of the new house, digging shards of glass from the garden beds. The season was filled with personal and creative undertakings that had been swept aside amid the moving and traveling. His yearly physical came with the edict from his doctor that he consume fewer eggs, and the desk in his study overflowed with paperwork. One new project, spurred on by Black Sparrow Press editor John Martin, was to prepare drawings for a limited edition of the poem "Epilogos." Having rejected the Scribners offer for a pared-down version of *Bending the Bow,* Duncan made plans to publish the book with Robert Hawley of Oyez Press. When James Laughlin at New Directions expressed interest in the project as well, Hawley worked with Laughlin and typesetter Graham Mackintosh to put the book into production. Duncan also returned to the solitude of his journals, and alongside reading notes about Whitman's poetry, he began a long essay, "The Truth and Life of Myth," in preparation for an October presentation at a theology conference in Washington, D.C.

The autumn brought the task of proofreading galleys of *Bending the Bow,* and the advent of the school season brought opportunities for readings at home and around the country. According to David Gitin, a writer and cofounder of the Poets' Theatre in the Haight-Ashbury district of San Francisco, in the early fall, a bearded Duncan "gave a reading with Brother Antoninus and Kenneth Rexroth at the amphitheater on top of Mt. Tamalpais."[15] Ron Silliman remembered another local reading of Duncan's around the same time:

> During an intermission at a marathon antiwar reading at Glide Memorial Church . . . where I was hovering . . . at the periphery of a crowd that surrounded Robert Duncan, . . . Mark Linenthal, whom I knew from his role as the director of the San Francisco Poetry Center, approached with a granite-faced man and said to Duncan, "Robert, I want you to meet George Oppen." I can recall also Oppen's first words to Duncan, "I want to speak to you about your open vowels." It was an event that seared itself into my memory because it violated one of the tenets of my imagination, that all famous writers already knew one another.[16]

On October 12, Duncan flew to Granville, Ohio, to give a reading at a liberal arts school called Denison College. The first busy day there included a lunch with three new English professors—Fred Jacobs, Bruce Bennett, and Jim Kiehl—followed by dinner with a group of students, a reading on campus, and a reception for the poet at Professor Tony Stoneburner's house. Pleased with the crisp autumn landscapes, Duncan wrote Jess that Granville was reminiscent of Mallorca with its antiquated architecture and culture: "a beautiful little town with Baptist Convention Hall, Methodist and Presbyterians, and three drugstores, four grocery stores, [with] pumpkins heapt up in front . . . and black-green acorn squashes, a coffee house, and one movie house . . . neatly collected for its two blocks of downtown."[17]

Tony Stoneburner continued along with Duncan to Washington, D.C., for the conference titled Parable, Myth, and Language, which Stoneburner had organized under the sponsorship of the Church Society for College Work at the College of Preachers. The event was held in the National Cathedral's library from October 13 to 15, convening a group of poets and theologians that included Duncan, Denise Levertov, Robert W. Funk, Stephen D. Crites, James M. Robinson, and Samuel Laeuchli. Duncan presented "The Truth and Life of Myth in Poetry" on October 14, an edited version of which later appeared in *Fictive Certainties*. The piece cast a wide net of references from Shakespeare to Pound, Homer, and St. Augustine while touching upon the autobiographical and upon the war in Viet Nam. It showed Duncan's skill in blending fluid lyrical lines of prose into revelations transcending simple commentary on poetry: "Now, I would understand sin as Man's refusal of Love Itself, his refusal of the love that strives to speak in the poem.... Our daily affections are a gentle practiced removal from a reality that threatens to overcome us. Our sexual pleasure is a protective appetite that distracts us or blinds the psyche to the primal Eros, as all the preoccupations of our poetic craft preserve a skin of consciousness in which we are not overtaken in fear of the Form that works there."[18] He wrote Barbara Joseph that the conversations spawned during the conference allowed him to rethink the relation between his work and larger theological principles:

> Theologians are theologians; they are not myth-makers or makers-with-myths. And they are not saints, those who live in the religion and become god directed. But theology is very akin to poetics. And the myth or story of what poetry is must enter any structure-theory. This is only to say that the problems that have come up in Christian theology over the last fifty years ... are related to problems we face in poetry. One thing I learnd was that the Permission, which I have been searching for in myth since the term came up in "Often I Am Permitted to Return to a Meadow" and in Structures of Rime later, is a term that has been advanced by German theology.[19]

The gathering also allowed Duncan to spend time with Levertov. Despite the cantankerous nature of their recent correspondence, they huddled together as the two poets in a sea of theologians. Tony Stoneburner recalled that "[Duncan] was full of joy in being with Denise Levertov. Old buddies, they palled around together within the larger group. Levertov was outgoing but Duncan tended to stick to her (... in those periods other than those in which the official dialogue was advancing: in it, Duncan was fully interactive)."[20]

On October 16, Duncan flew to Long Island to complete the work he had begun earlier in the year at the State University of New York at Stony Brook. During the visit, he and John Cage held a public conversation that was recorded by George Quasha, and Duncan told Jess that he had learned as much from Cage as he had from the theologians in the capital:

> In one loving correction John . . . got across to me that in my formation of love and hate, hate might be viewd as a substitute for creative forces—anger and disgust. Well, some burden I was carrying shifted with his illuminations here . . . —for surely "Up Rising" is anger and very much not hate. It was not that hate was wrong except that it was the wrong term (I mean the emotion itself the wrong term and hence destructive—where anger sweeping clear is not). This was a radiant meeting with John. He himself in the lectures before the meeting already illuminating.[21]

After a stop in New York to see Pat and Helen Adam, Duncan circled back to Washington, D.C., to participate in one of the key events of the antiwar movement: the historic October 21 March on the Pentagon organized by the National Mobilization Committee to End the War. Having begun the day supervising the teenaged daughter of William and Joan Roth in the crowd of one hundred thousand, he later found himself in the curious company of David Dellinger, Robert Lowell, Dwight Mcdonald, Barbara Deming, Dagmar Wilson, Noam Chomsky, and Benjamin Spock. Encouraged by his colleagues, Duncan decided to answer the rally organizers' call for civil disobedience. He recounted the experience in a letter to Barbara Joseph. On the road outside the Pentagon,

> one line of soldiers went thru us; and then another shock troop marcht upon us to force us to retreat. Only Dellinger, Barbara Deming and Dagmar Wilson held to their positions (but, also, only these knew clearly *how* to carry thru the action). Spock bore the full brunt of the attack in the section of the front where I was next to Mrs. Spock . . . so that what I felt was a brutal pushing, no direct blows. To my right, beyond Barbara Deming, soldiers were kicking Mrs. Wilson to force her to move, but also to get at her. Doctor Spock was, I think, concerned for his wife, tho she urged him not to be. We sought the eyes of the troops, finding the ones who did not want to do what they had to do. . . . Dr. Spock, after bearing for several minutes the assault, decided too that it was futile, and got up, lifting his wife and turning back to lift me up. At which the ranks (ours) were broken. . . . Only those the troops

physically had to drag off were arrested. At a loss, then relieved, we were sur-
rounded on three sides by troops, and wandered . . . off in the direction the
troops had come from. [22]

When Duncan returned to San Francisco in November 1967, he added an
account of the march to *Bending the Bow*. In a section of the introduction
called "The Readers," an analogy emerged:

> Standing before the advancing line of men . . . , it seemd futile at first to
> speak to them. They were under a command . . . to overcome us or to terrify
> us, a force aroused in the refusal to give even the beginnings of a hearing. . . .
> The doctor kneeling upon the earth before me bore the full shock of the hos-
> tile readers. No . . . Looking up, I saw the readers themselves bore the shock
> of what they were to encounter. Their commanders are possesst by rage, con-
> fronted by the question we raise in the heart of things, they move their men
> as if there were ranks of that rage down upon us to break that heart or to beat
> from its beats gouts of life-blood until the truth of what we mean to do, the
> faltering truth, dies and is done. . . .
>
> What would I have tried to tell them? That we were unarmd? That we were
> not the enemy, but men of their kind? In the face of an overwhelming audi-
> ence waiting for me to dare move them, I would speak to those alike in soul,
> I know not who or where they are. . . . The line of the poem itself confronts
> me where I must volunteer my love, and I saw, long before this war, wrath
> move in the music that troubles me.[23]

At the end of a year spent as much in airports as at home, Duncan found
less dramatic entertainments to appreciate. On the weekend of November 25
and 26, he and Jess hosted two visitors from Wallace Berman's circle, actor-
artist Dean Stockwell and singer-filmmaker Toni Basil. Another art-world
luminary, painter R. B. Kitaj, visited the couple that month, bringing along
curator Peter Selz of the University of California Museum to view Jess's work.
The Cleveland-born Kitaj, who had spent his early career in London, was in
the Bay Area that season as a visiting professor at the University of California,
Berkeley. He and Duncan, "instant friends," traveled to Southern California
in early December, where Duncan introduced Kitaj to Barbara Joseph, John
Martin, and Bernard Forrest.[24] With Kitaj's wife, Elsi, and their children
along on the trip, the group of travelers also made time for an expedition to
Disneyland.[25]

Duncan returned to San Francisco to spend Christmas with Jess in their
new home and to attend the December 20 marriage of Ham and Mary
Tyler's daughter Brenda. After a New Year in bed with an apparent head

cold, he wrote to Barbara Joseph admitting that he wasn't certain if he had actually been ill or had been sidelined by an anxiety attack. The respite nonetheless allowed him to get "started on a new block of poem. With reading Nerval's *Isis* and the Gospel of John with commentaries, interspersed with *Popul Vuh*."[26] The poem, "Tribunals, *Passages* 32," was later published in *Ground Work: Before the War* with a composition date of December 20, 1969, an accidental or intentional change in the chronology by Duncan.

FORTY-SEVEN

Days of Rage

Do you think I do not know what the curse of
    darkness means? the power in confusion?
Do you think I do not remember
    the tyranny of establisht religions,
the would-be annihilating cloud of lies
    and the despairing solar malevolence
that is rumored to lie back of these?
    the madness of kings?

ROBERT DUNCAN, "Circulations of the Song"

THE ASSASSINATIONS OF MARTIN LUTHER KING, JR., and Robert Kennedy, followed by riots at the 1968 Democratic National Convention, plunged the New Left into crisis. At the Olympic games in Mexico City, American medalists Tommie Smith and John Carlos caused controversy by raising their fists in a show of solidarity with the black power movement. The year had begun with the Tet offensive, a massive attack on U.S. military sites in South Viet Nam by the Viet Cong on the Vietnamese lunar New Year.

Beginning the poems that would be collected into *Ground Work: Before the War,* Duncan wove the world into his life's work as he rode the waves of change. Phasing out the business suits he had donned for readings in his early career, he had a new look in his passport photo that spring. A peace button adorned the lapel of his corduroy jacket, and his graying hair was tied into a ponytail. When criminal charges were raised against Mitch Goodman and Dwight Macdonald in January 1968 for their antiwar activities, Duncan wrote Barbara Joseph wondering whether he might be in line for investigation: "With indictments against the first ranks of the Resist signators (and I hear from George Stanley that Paul Goodman and Dwight Macdonald have come up in New York since the first six in Boston) and here against the organizers of the demonstrations in Oakland, I find myself looking forward to possible trouble. I think, if it were possible, I wld go into exile to escape prison. We could, perhaps, turn the house over to you for whatever duration."[1]

In February, while the Jimi Hendrix Experience played at the Fillmore Auditorium, Duncan kept a low profile, settling in at home and reading Merleau-Ponty's *Structure of Behavior* and Hölderlin's *Hyperion*. In March, he flew to Buffalo for the city's annual Festival of the Arts, where fellow participants included Louis Zukofsky, Robin Blaser, and Allen Ginsberg. While Blaser's presence was a source of anxiety for Duncan in the aftermath of their Nerval translation wars, Duncan told Barbara Joseph that in the end there was good cheer on all sides. An added surprise for Duncan was a newfound affection for Allen Ginsberg's work: "Robin was completely charming and agreeable, as I was. . . . Allen's chanting of mantras was most beautiful, something more, lift that to a truly moving experience. And his reading of poetry has been elevated. He no longer projects his persona, but goes with the poem. And he closed with a new work, an evocation of the holy spirits of Albion that rang out to my hearing as one of the great experiences in poetry I've ever had."[2]

As part of the festival, Duncan was interviewed by Bobbie Creeley at a Buffalo radio station on March 5. Reading "Up Rising" and "Epilogos" between comments about politics, poetry, and Dante, he prepared his listeners for a longer performance the following afternoon at the Albright-Knox Art Gallery, during which he would present two key poems of his career, "The Venice Poem" and "My Mother Would Be a Falconress." A review of the reading in the *Buffalo Evening News* noted, "Mr. Duncan spoke like a Shakespearean actor. His address was in soliloquy, full of reference and grand reference. And his gestures were like an orchestra conductor's."[3]

On Friday March 8, Duncan flew to Forth Worth to give a reading at Texas Christian University. Arriving with a cough and flu, he settled into the local Holiday Inn to sleep off his fever and woke the following morning to discover that the signboard outside the hotel read "A Texas Howdy for Poet Robert Duncan."[4] After pacing himself through a sluggish hot weekend in

Fort Worth, he flew home to San Francisco, still fighting off fatigue. Throughout that dreary spring, the forty-nine-year-old had difficulty shaking off aches and pains, but he at least looked forward to seeing the first copies of *Bending the Bow,* scheduled for a March 31 publication date. The end of the month also brought Lyndon Johnson's televised announcement that he would not run for reelection. What had begun for Duncan as a skepticism about the Kennedy administration had spilled over into an overt hatred toward Johnson. Duncan delighted in telling friends that as he watched the president announce his resignation from candidacy, he saw Satan departing from Johnson's body.

Ambivalent about melding poetry and politics, Duncan nonetheless allowed the Viet Nam war to saturate the later part of the *Passages* series, and he labored to maintain a balance between the poem's intentions and the poet's rage. In "Before the Judgment, *Passages* 35," he expressed the emotional toll of the war in a pun: "Discontent with that first draft. Where one's own / hatred enters Hell gets out of hand."[5] In essays written during the period, including "Man's Fulfillment in Order and Strife," Duncan carved out a space to more clearly articulate his feelings. He had always been interested in the art of the political essay, and his burgeoning career as a lecturer allowed him to transform his journal notes into lengthy performances. Another shift in his work came that year as well. At the same time that he began to distance himself from the increasingly strident factions of the youth movement, he took a vow in 1968 to create a fifteen-year gap between the publication of *Bending the Bow* and his next collection of writing. With the exception of two volumes of his early work from Fulcrum Press that year, it was not until 1984 that Duncan released *Ground Work: Before the War.* There was more than one reason for the fifteen-year silence. Seeing his way through *Bending the Bow* had been an arduous process for Duncan, and communicating with publishers and printers often exasperated him. Never a complacent author, he demanded perfection in the presentation of the poems on the page, and as he wrote in "A Prospectus for the Prepublication Issue of Ground Work . . ." in 1971, "I want a time and a space to work in that will be, as time and space were only in the years before others were interested in publishing me, the time and space of a life of the work itself."[6] As Duncan began the project of *Ground Work* during the late 1960s and early 1970s, he imagined an entirely different kind of book: one that he would typeset himself and allow to sprawl across the pages as was his desire.

There was little threat that Duncan's publishing hiatus would remove him from the public eye. His 1967 tour had taken him to almost twenty American cities, and in 1968, he would extend his route to Europe. With a monthlong sabbatical in preparation for traveling, he and Jess entertained guests at home. During the first week of April, while flags flew half-staff to mourn the death of Martin Luther King, Jr., the Creeleys visited San Francisco, and Charles Olson arrived the following week. On April 6, composer Lou Harrison's arrangement of Duncan's "Up Rising" was performed in Berkeley, and as Duncan wrote to Barbara Joseph, there was another social event on the horizon: "the 17th, Jess's retrospective show of collages opens at the Museum in the Civic Center. They will be gathering . . . pieces from the East and L.A. and Jess has done a magnificent new nightmare of America."[7] Interest in Jess's work also came from afar. That spring, New York art dealer Federico Quadrani and his wife, Odyssia Skouras, visited the 20th Street household, and Quadrani soon signed Jess on as one of his artists. Duncan wrote Barbara Joseph about the terms of the agreement with Quadrani's Odyssia Gallery: "The great news is . . . that now they have taken Jess over, starting at 800 a month as advance on the sales of paintings once he has finisht the present series. To start in May."[8]

Another unexpected visitor to the Bay Area that year was poet Elizabeth Bishop, who had arrived in Berkeley in January 1968. Duncan befriended her during her year and a half on the West Coast, partly encouraged by a mutual friend, British poet Thom Gunn. Gunn recalled one of the highlights of their acquaintance:

> She and Duncan got along marvelously. And I said to each of them, separately, "Well, what do you think about Elizabeth's poetry?" and "What do you think of Duncan's poetry?" But each said in almost the same terms,. . . . "Oh, I don't take any notice, I can't even read it." That didn't matter though. . . . [Duncan] had never turned onto marijuana. . . . so she decided to make him some brownies. . . . I got this story from the both of them at the time. It was delightful. Here he was sitting on the floor giggling uncontrollably. And of course it was such a wonderful reversal. . . . Here was the wild poet of the West Coast being turned on by the ladylike poet from the East Coast.[9]

Duncan's springtime vacation ended on April 14 when he flew north to attend the Seventh Annual Symposium on American Values at Central Washington State College in Ellensburg. The theme of the three-day symposium, organized by English professor David Burt, was "Language and World Order." Duncan's fellow lecturers came from the disciplines of philosophy, psychology, and anthropology, and on April 20, he gave an early version of the lecture-essay "Man's Fulfillment in Order and Strife." The piece visited the civil unrest of the 1960s with an anarchist critique. Invoking Dante and Blake, he warned the audience,

> Any group . . . as large as this audience gathered here today, if it be moved, given a crisis in political life . . . if they want to have the power a people has, want a voice to arouse them. They will feed, feed, feed, to become a demos, where the demotic speaker casts his spell, to become inspired democrats, breathing in his breathings. . . . In the complex idea of our democracy, we have not only the potentiality of free communities of interest but we have, even stronger, in times of crisis, the potentiality of giving over the individual volition with its powerlessness to move the mass, giving over the uncertain individual consciousness to the sweeping certainties of becoming one of the crowd.[10]

Duncan's enthusiastic oration led to a visiting lectureship in Ellensburg the following autumn and to new friendships with academics David and Edie Burt, Fred and Kay Stockholder, and Philip Garrison. Garrison noted years later, "I spent every hour I could with him, because, apart from producing an awesome body of work, he was a wise, kind, funny, patient guy. I . . . [was] lucky enough to be exposed, young, to Robert's vision of what a classroom ought to be."[11]

Duncan's return to San Francisco on April 21 was less than a home-coming. Two days later he would depart for his first trans-Atlantic tour. Flying to New York and then to Providence, Rhode Island, he gave a reading there on April 26. In New England during those few days, he completed one of the early poems of *Ground Work: Before the War,* "Structure of Rime XXVII: Jess's Paste-Ups." After visiting Henry and Adele Wenning in New Haven and Helen and Pat Adam in New York, he boarded an April 30 flight to London's Heathrow Airport. It was his first trip to Europe since he and Jess had been there some dozen years earlier, and he arrived prepared for whatever exhilaration was to be had. The trip was in no way a disappointment.

Stuart Montgomery of Fulcrum Press greeted Duncan upon his arrival and assisted him with the logistics of his stay. The men had begun a correspondence the previous year through which they worked out a plan for the publication of two volumes of Duncan's early poems, soon to be titled *The*

First Decade and *Derivations*. With Montgomery, Duncan attended to a key pleasure of the trip: a drive north into the Scottish border country for a weekend visit with Ian Hamilton Finlay. The forty-three-year-old Finlay, then recovering from a heart attack, greeted Duncan with a high-spirited impishness that belied his recent brush with death: "He dances around in moving, tosses himself into chairs or to stretch on the couch, and Scotch speech itself is a lilting songful thing."[12] Stonypath, the home outside of Edinburgh that Finlay shared with his wife, Sue, and their son Alec, sat amid a landscape that the couple had begun to fill with structures, sculptures, and concrete poems. Renamed Little Sparta in 1980, the place would become one of the most remarkable and visionary artist's projects of the period. Duncan reveled in the peculiarities of Finlay's work, and he was equally delighted by his host's dialect. His own Scottish ancestry could not have been far from his mind as he wrote home to Jess: "Snow along the ridges, rain today, and a wee burn running deep thru the turf of the hill side. Sheeps all round, black-faced Highlanders, and cats happily underfoot. A mass of daffodils at the window. . . . Ian's poem-sculptures: a water weathercock floating on the surface of the pond, or land weathercocks on an outdoors table, a cloud trap (a wee round pool with whatever cloud reflected within (on), bring words into the yard and the country beyond)."[13]

London held additional gratifications and more good company as Duncan made his home with curator Bryan Robertson at his flat on Barnsbury Street. Robertson, who had been influential in shaping London's Whitechapel Gallery, likely had come into Duncan's acquaintance through R. B. Kitaj, and he introduced Duncan to a number of artists and writers during his monthlong stay. On May 10, Robertson accompanied Duncan to a "hair-raising" performance of *Oedipus,* followed by dinner with a group that included the star of the production, Sir John Gielgud. Robertson had also arranged for him to meet poet Ted Hughes, Princess Margaret, and her husband, Lord Snowdon, though as Duncan told Jess, he had few illusions about his prospects for social climbing. He also had an opportunity to attend an odd gathering of the art world on May 11, "a formal lunch for Mark Tobey and his Swiss friend of some forty years—two aged cloisterd-side-of-self-centerd distinguished gentlemen. . . . The hostess Vera Russell was a once-ballet star, and the lunch, one more splendid processional of haute cuisine . . . consommé with caviar and sour cream; then cold salmon and tomatoes with mayonnaise, tosst green salad and a great flan caramel."[14]

The following day Duncan traveled to Brighton with the poet John Montague, where he spent two days getting to know the Irish writer and convened with a circle of local poets and literature enthusiasts. Back in London on May 15, Duncan entered the familiar territory of art viewing, this time at the National Gallery. Trips to the British Museum and the Victoria and Albert Museum followed, and he reported to Jess that there was one other venue of interest: "the opening of the [Graham] Sutherland show—a series of animals as bestiary—at the Marlborough."[15] The remainder of the month was spent mixing business with pleasure. Giving readings in York and London, Duncan also made time to see the zoo and visit with Gael Turnbull. On May 27, the weary poet flew home to California. The trip had come with the joy of social interaction, but it also stirred Duncan's ambivalence about career, publishing, and life on the road. As he told Jess during the last days of the tour, "I don't relish the being pusht. The main battle now will be to win back areas of free volition."[16]

FORTY-EIGHT

Ground-Work

WHILE DUNCAN OFTEN had the luxury of quiet summers in San Francisco with Jess, he was away for a good part of the season in 1968. Invited to an international poetry festival in late June at Stony Brook and to Buffalo for a six-week teaching job at the state university, he prepared for travel amid news of the June 5 assassination of Robert Kennedy.[1] Once back on the road, Duncan's concern shifted from politics to poetry, and he registered an ill temper with the business at hand. He wrote Jess that "the few real poets" in attendance at Stony Brook were Clayton Eshleman, Allen Ginsberg, and Denise Levertov, and he reflected that the seventy other writers at the festival that weekend were simply evidence that "poetry is a rare animal."[2] Duncan's irritation may have come in the fact that the American poets present had been asked to cede the stage to guests from around the world and to appear as participant-listeners rather than as readers.

In Buffalo, he was commissioned to teach two classes from June 24 through August 2: a lower-division offering called The Tradition in Poetry and a graduate seminar, Punctuation in the Modern Poem, focusing on Pound's *Cantos*. The presence of Charles Olson and Robert Creeley at the university during the previous years had lured a number of serious students, and Duncan found friends in the classroom, including Albert Glover, an Olsonite, and Robert Hogg, whom he had met in Vancouver during the early 1960s. Hogg, who worked as Duncan's assistant that summer, later recalled that a good number of the graduate seminar sessions focused on Pound's first "Canto," particularly the opening word "And" and the closing phrase "So that:" Hogg also remembered the appearance of an unkempt student from New York who seemed intent on ruffling Duncan's feathers with questions. Demanding that the young man leave the classroom, Duncan dismissed him as "unfit to be in a public forum" and warned his charges that a student should never challenge a master's authority.[3] Another odd incident was documented in a letter to Jess. On the morning of July 9 as Duncan stood at the blackboard, he found himself scrawling "The invisible punishes poets for their visibility." He superstitiously attributed the writing to the intervention of Jack Spicer's ghost, especially in light of a recent warning by Helen Adam that Spicer would remain active in the "visible" world because of his untimely death.[4]

On weekends, Duncan took the opportunity to visit friends in New York City and New England. In July, he spent Independence Day at poet Barbara Guest's house in South Hampton, and he visited Manhattan to wander through the Metropolitan Museum with Helen Adam. The summer also held welcome meetings in and around Buffalo. Painter Robert De Niro, Sr., a fellow visiting professor at the university, rendezvoused with Duncan for a July 15 dinner date, and two new acquaintances, student Duncan McNaughton and his wife, Jeanne, became dining companions on other occasions. With Albert Glover, Duncan made a trip to see Diane and Jerome Rothenberg on the Seneca Indian Reservation in the upstate town of Salamanca where the couple was conducting research. Glover remembered Duncan's excitement at the prospect of an authentic Native American experience and his disappointment when his Seneca hosts offered him a plate of potato chips.[5]

When he completed his tenure at Buffalo on August 2, Duncan flew to Maine for a weekend with Mitch Goodman and Denise Levertov at their summer house in the town of Temple. Using the stopover to decompress from teaching, Duncan also wanted to spend time with Goodman, who in July had been sentenced to two years in prison for his role in the resistance movement's antidraft activities. Though Goodman and his three codefendants' convictions were overturned the following year, the anguish of the war was far from over. By the end of 1968, there were four million homeless civilians in South Viet Nam, and thirteen thousand American soldiers had died. Meanwhile, the West Coast counterculture was mutating. In early August, Charles Manson and his young, primarily female followers moved onto Spahn Movie Ranch in the San Fernando Valley where they planned a race-riot apocalypse called Helter Skelter, and later in the year, the Zodiac killer claimed his first two victims in the town of Vallejo. Throughout the fall, domestic disturbances related to the war also continued, and Duncan looked to Blake's *The French Revolution* and Whitehead's *Process and Reality* for escape. In an election season dominated by Richard Nixon, he also decided to vote for the first time: "I couldn't stand the idea of Nixon being in and so I voted for—anything. . . . I was just chagrined ever after, I was a perfectly honest anarchist before that, never voted. Now I go ahead and vote . . . just like taking on the gambling at Las Vegas, there goes your allowance . . . I vote almost entirely negatively."[6]

After casting his ballot, Duncan traveled to the University of California at Santa Cruz to participate in a John Cage festival, where he was able to spend time with Cage, Merce Cunningham, Lou Harrison, Norman O. Brown, and philosophy professor Paul Lee. One campus insider, librarian Rita Bottoms, recalled, "They all went mushrooming. . . . A number of wonderful people went through our woods, because we are really a major mushroom environment, and an amazing thing happened: John [Cage] was overcome with this whole place and vowed he was giving his mushroom collection to the campus."[7]

Returning home pleased with the adventure but disappointed by Richard Nixon's victory, Duncan found a beginning for *Ground Work*. On December 10, he wrote a tribute to H.D. called "Achilles' Song," a poem precipitated by his wintertime readings of Walt Whitman and the book of Job. The opening of the volume in fact paid homage to the lineage of modernism central to Duncan's work. "Achilles' Song" was followed by "Ancient Questions," an address to Ezra Pound. As Duncan pondered the shape of the new group of poems, the book's place in his life's work became clear: "With the Field, the Tree, and the Bow before me, I propose to return to the Ground-Work (the title of the fourth Book then)."[8] The subtitle of the book, *Before the War,* succinctly described Duncan's vision of human conflict and his role as an observer. Departing from Denise Levertov's view of events in Viet Nam, he proposed, "You can't scold an earthquake and you can't scold a war. A war is a real state. In this I would be like Homer. Homer doesn't praise war or dispraise it. It isn't a moral question at all. It is a catastrophe."[9]

The approaching holidays put another, more personal matter on Duncan's mind. A December letter to Barbara Joseph included an invitation: "I sort of want to 'celebrate' my fiftieth birthday—which would be an almost decent event if ground rules of no—absolutely no gifts—could be establisht. Keep the seventh open. Just for a very small group of friends."[10] Two of the guests were Denise Levertov and Mitch Goodman, who arrived in the Bay Area in January when the former began a teaching job at the University of California. While both Levertov and Duncan had at various points expressed a longing to be neighbors, they would rarely cross paths during her stay. As she became absorbed in Berkeley's political community, Duncan embraced the pleasures of gardening in his backyard and worked through drafts of the long essay that would become "Changing Perspectives in Reading Whitman." Writing to Barbara Joseph at the end of March, he expressed concerns about the course of the antiwar movement:

> Last week I made the decision to refuse a reading—that originally I had understood to be for Student Defense funds; and that turned out to be for the Strike committee and the Third World Liberation Front. With the appearance of programs that include violence and racism . . . I begin to dissent anew myself. The Resist movement that . . . gave rise to the trial of Spock, Coffin, Mitch, etc. grows new horns; following the conspiracy trials, those interested in a conspiracy (including agents provocateurs) seem to be busy at work.
>   Denise and I had a talk . . . about her own conflicts, sentiments that anything against the law must be supported and furthered that "non-violence" has been a failure (those who are working for the furtherance of non-violent action are not "leaders," the young do not follow them) and that sabotage now is needed against the war.[11]

With little sense of resolution of the matter, on April 15, 1969, Duncan returned to the East Coast for an extended business trip that would include visits to Canada and the Midwest. After giving a reading at Bard College on the 16th, he spent a day in New York, where he met Marjorie McKee for dinner. The following day he was en route to Montreal, where he found a late spring dusting of snow. In addition to giving readings at Sir George Williams University and Carleton College, Duncan completed two interviews, one with poet George Bowering and former student Robert Hogg, and one with Phyllis Webb of the Canadian Broadcasting Corporation.[12] On April 21, Duncan was back in Manhattan and en route to Stony Brook, where he took part in a seminar on the writings of philosopher Louis Althusser. During his weeklong residency there, he made a side trip to a Whitman celebration at New York University, where he presented his lecture in progress "Changing Perspectives in Reading Whitman." From there, Duncan flew to Lawrence, Kansas. In a followup to his gratifying 1965 and 1967 visits, he found both good company and large audiences. Although Ed and Ruth Eigner had since relocated to Southern California, the poetry frenzy set off by Duncan's first appearance there had gained momentum. Ed Dorn was a visiting professor at the school in 1969, and several bookstores had sprung up on the edges of the campus. Dorn launched Duncan's May 7 reading with a generous introduction, and Duncan in turn treated the audience to a performance of his *Passages* poems. Graduate student Don Byrd remembered the event well: "That [was] the best poetry reading I [ever] heard. Whatever was second best wasn't even close. There were perhaps 300 people at the reading; it went on for nearly three hours. Somewhere in the midst of the apocalyptic passages, he stopped and said, 'Some times people ask me why, if I believe this, I bother to write poetry. I write poetry for the fucking stars.'"[13]

Throughout his two-week residency in Lawrence, part of yet another Walt Whitman sesquicentenary celebration, Duncan was irrepressible. Teaching a seminar to a group that included outpatients from Topeka's Menninger Clinic, he also gave readings and presented a variation of his Whitman lecture under the title "The Force of Whitman in the American Spirit." Don Byrd recalled yet another activity that consumed Duncan's time in Kansas that spring: "He would hang out in the coffee room and go teach whatever classes anyone would let him teach—Milton, Hawthorne, introduction to poetry, Jacobean drama. In one class, he went through the table of contents of *Controversy of Poets,* and gave one-line judgments on everyone."[14]

FORTY-NINE

Helter Skelter

> Reject Mae West as vulgar or Hitler as the enemy, reject them as
> fellows of our kind, and you have to go to battle against the very
> nature of Man himself, against the truth of things. Hitler can-
> not be defeated; he must be acknowledged and understood.
>
> ROBERT DUNCAN, "Man's Fulfillment in Order and Strife"

IF 1968 WAS THE SUMMER OF LOVE, 1969 was the summer of murder
and mayhem: the Stonewall Riots, Chappaquiddick, the Zodiac killings,
and the murder of Sharon Tate. On May 16, just after Duncan returned
from Kansas, Governor Reagan ordered National Guard troops to reclaim
the recently established People's Park in Berkeley as the property of the
University of California regents. The park, a plot of land liberated from
the university by community activists, became a bloody battlefield that week
as thirty thousand people clashed with guardsmen, who fired birdshot and
tear gas into the crowds. One protester, James Rector, later died of his inju-
ries. On June 2, Duncan appeared at a benefit reading for the park, though
he had doubts about the intentions of the protesters, as he told Denise
Levertov:

> I find the People's Park, . . . that in its very virtue is a confrontation and will
> reveal the nature of the Power of the University as a murderous tyranny,
> admirable. And I am certain that there were those heroically inspired who
> in the planting of the Park are fully aware and creatively determined that
> all will be exposed—and that Rector will be shot and Blanchard blinded
> ([proving] that the administrative tyranny is willing to kill and to blind).
>
> And I know . . . that there were many who did not want to believe anything
> like that . . . —but these are . . . self-deluded; hypocrites of the revolution.
> Those who thought they had *merely* "made for each other / a green place" and
> couldn't see that the green place was staked out upon a battleground. . . . This
> kind of thinking outrages me.[1]

A more personal emergency soon took precedence over turmoil in the
East Bay. At the end of June, a routine physical examination and chest X-ray

showed a small tumor on Duncan's left lung. The next week, upon Duncan and Jess's return from a stay at Ham and Mary Tyler's farm in Healdsburg, a second set of X-rays confirmed the existence of the anomaly. Duncan's doctor Sandor Burstein recommended an immediate biopsy, and on July 2, Jess and Barbara Joseph accompanied Duncan through admissions procedures at San Francisco's Mount Zion Hospital, where he was rolled into the operating room at 10:00 the next morning. The surgery was straightforward though invasive, and Duncan, rather than registering anxiety, later mused in his notebooks about his admiration for the doctors' skills. The incision started beside his left nipple and continued under his arm and around his torso "to a corresponding terminus in the back." To excise the tumor, the surgeon first removed a six-inch section of the rib cage. The growth was the size of "the end of a pencil" and encased "a deposit of grains of carbon," basic coal dust.[2] Informed that he would be in extreme pain for two days, Duncan documented the experience with meticulous detail:

> There were terrible fragments of consciousness, even the afternoon of the operation . . . : Sandor's gentle and intense regard looking deep into my eyes and telling me that "it was alright, it was not cancer." . . . And there were terrible fragments of consciousness of that pain . . . their movement of my body from the operating room cart to my bed, in which I had a knowledge of being *in* pain previous to being defined by that pain. Knowledge of the primevil *[sic]* pain was still there the second day . . . But by the third day, that abysmal pain was gone. The wound was no longer open to the abyss; the fabric of me had begun to reknit *for sure,* and the pains I knew now would be *my* pains.[3]

While Duncan was in the hospital, the international space race dominated newspaper headlines: on July 3, a Russian rocket malfunctioned and exploded, ending the Soviet Union's hope of beating American astronauts to the moon. The launch of the U.S. *Apollo 11* came on July 16, and its crew made its celebrated moon landing after a four-day trip from earth. Duncan and Jess had little interest in the event. As Stan Brakhage recalled, they expressed concern that a place in their imaginative lives had been colonized by "the real."[4] Closer to home, gloomy news came on August 9 of the murders of actress Sharon Tate and a group of her friends at Roman Polanski's home in Los Angeles. The following night a couple in a nearby neighborhood was killed in a similarly brutal fashion. The crimes, later traced to followers of Charles Manson, went unsolved through the winter.[5]

Still in recovery from his surgery, Duncan spent the week of the Manson murders reading Jerome Rothenberg's *Technicians of the Sacred* anthology and preparing to teach a fall seminar on "the individual and his totality" at Central Washington State.[6] Ten students enrolled in the four-credit offering, which revolved around readings of Dante, Milton, Blake, and Whitman. Duncan's assignment there began on September 25, and during his stay he also gave a series of public lectures, organized by David Burt and Elwin Odell. The *Campus Crier* described the first of the talks, "The Vocation of Poetry in a Democratic Society," as an autobiographical address that concluded with readings from *Medieval Scenes*. The following week, Duncan's topic was Ezra Pound. Reciting from the *Cantos* and describing Pound's influence on his own writing, Duncan gleefully dissected the opening lines of the epic, pointing out the linguistic craft involved in each turn of phrase.

Lurking behind the classroom preoccupations were the ongoing realities of the war in Viet Nam. A mid-October Moratorium Day on campus inspired Duncan to begin a canvassing campaign, which he detailed to Jess: "My class and I will be going from house to house..., talking with householders where they will, about the war—instead of marching in demonstration."[7] For Duncan, the energy of the students and the theme of democracy came together in exceptional ways. He reflected his satisfaction in a report to the school's assistant dean of arts and sciences:

> I want most personally to register that in every sense this has been an extraordinary group of students to work with.... It is an experience so far unique in my work in teaching, and it reflects not only the given intelligence of the class, but the success, I believe, of participatory rather than competitive or acquisitive learning in bringing into action such intelligence in full. In my concept of democratic action the intellect of any one member of a group cannot come to its fulfillment except to the extent that the group it works in comes to like fulfillment.[8]

Arriving home to cloudy weather, Duncan found Jess in a petulant mood as he waited for enough sunlight to return to the projects in his studio. The beginning of November remained rainy, and after a few weeks of quiet in the damp, shady house, Duncan embarked on a short business trip to an international poetry conference at the University of Texas in Austin. Organized by writers Octavio Paz and Alberto de Lacerda, the conference was ambitious in its theme and invitees. Duncan and Polish poet Czeslaw

Milosz gave a reading together on the opening day along with writers David Wevill of Canada, Dionisio Ridruejo of Spain, and Peter Rühmkorf of Germany. Intrigued by Milosz's ideas about poetry, Duncan noted afterward that the Polish writer had forced him to think about his creative biases:

> "Classicism," Milosz felt, a classicism which Polish poetry had preserved, was the poetic stance in which the secret was not profaned: here, to my mind, the secret and the sacred were one, and the term "classicism" was . . . an establisht church—i.e. Roman Catholic order—in art, preserving Poetry from the disorders of mysticism. . . . If we pose classicism as containing or incorporating, I realize I seek to evoke or to charge language with an exploding apprehension . . . to bring a panic into the containment of language.[9]

The conference also launched a friendship between Duncan and de Lacerda, then a visiting professor at the University of Texas. The Portuguese poet would remain in contact with Duncan through the 1970s, rendezvousing with him on the East Coast and in London.

The early winter in San Francisco was likewise filled with new friendships. On November 26, Duncan and Jess hosted Pauline Oliveros, who introduced them to her partner, Lynn Lonidier.[10] Lonidier, a thirty-two-year-old poet who had studied with Oliveros at San Diego, subsequently became another 20th Street insider. The two couples' discussion about "keeping the counsel of dreams" inspired Duncan to begin a new project in his notebook, a series of "dream work" entries with interpretation and self-analysis.[11]

As the holidays approached, Duncan drifted into his mid-December ritual of spending time in bed, dreaming, reading, and recuperating from his autumn tour. His New Year vacation was interrupted by word from the East Coast that Charles Olson was dying of liver cancer. Flying to New York on January 2, 1970, Duncan made his way by cab through the crisp, snowy dawn to New York Hospital. Olson had first shown signs of illness during November while teaching at the University of Connecticut at Storrs and, after a short hospitalization there, had been escorted to Manhattan by his friend and benefactor Harvey Brown, a wealthy young Clevelander whom he had met in Buffalo during the mid-1960s.[12] As friends and fans swarmed into New York to say their good-byes to Olson, Brown sought out alternative medical treatments for the dying poet and reserved a suite for the well-wishers at the posh Plaza Hotel. When Duncan arrived at the hospital, he was grateful to find Olson alone and awake, and he spent the early part of the day with his old friend, who during their conversation remarked, "It's been a great 25 years" and asked Duncan to climb into bed with him. The two talked side by side for a last time amid sheepish interruptions by an alarmed nursing staff. Despite Olson's size, his skin hung loose on a jaundiced frame bruised from needle and biopsy punctures, and, as Duncan recorded, "particularly his head magnificent, askew, beautiful finally, for one saw the tragic mask of the man who writes in October 1950 . . . 'The Present going reality is the only such soil,' come to the present-going reality of cancer of the liver, the cancer of 'other organs' indicated in the background."[13]

Leaving the hospital briefly that afternoon, Duncan returned to find a sign on the patient's door warning visitors that he was asleep. There had been a flurry of activity outside Olson's room, with students clamoring to see him, and as Ed Sanders remembered, book dealers hoping to coax the author into signing entire collections of his work. Eager to avoid the spectacle, Duncan left for New Haven that evening to visit Henry and Adele Wenning. After a weeklong stay that encompassed his fifty-first birthday, he returned to New York Hospital on January 8. Seated bedside, Duncan watched in silence as the now-unconscious Olson opened and closed his hands into the air. Realizing that there was little more he could do, Duncan spent the afternoon lending emotional support to the poet's daughter, Kate. His return to San Francisco coincided with Olson's death, marked in Duncan's notebook with "Charles dead, Friday night, Jan. 9th, as Creeley phoned Saturday."[14] Unable to return east for the Gloucester funeral, Duncan set about completing "The Feast," which he had begun in late December while reading works by Arthur Schopenhauer and Joseph Campbell. Set in projective form and including quotations from Carl Sauer's writings, the poem was haunted by Olson's ghost:

> On *this* side   Man's fortunate feast,
>   harvests of his growing mastery   over his nature,
>
> *"Antiphonal to this   the revenge of an outraged nature on man."*[15]

FIFTY

Santa Cruz Propositions

THE EARLY PART OF 1970 seemed slated for bad news. The loss of one of
Duncan's closest friends in the field of poetry was followed by the death of
Fayetta Harris Philip at the age of eighty-eight. Duncan, then in Vancouver
for a weeklong visit to the Tallmans, received the news on February 15 via a
telegram from his cousin Mercedes Gardner.[1] Returning to the Bay Area, he
attended to family obligations, driving to the funeral in Folsom, California,
with Mercedes's daughter, Susan. Staying close to home through the spring, he
also prepared for two local readings. With *Bending the Bow* in print and
Ground Work in progress, Duncan performed the complete sequence of the
Passages poems in appearances at Berkeley's Le Conte School auditorium on
March 6 and 13. One attendee, Alameda High School student Michael Franco,
remembered Duncan's celebrity status in the Bay Area:

> There was a huge audience. Robert entered in flowing robes, a long-haired
> wonder. . . . The read-through of 1–22 was followed by a standing ovation and
> an encore of "My Mother Would Be a Falconress." The event of the reading;
> the physics of it—a choreography and nothing short of it—his hand, the
> blackboard work, the dictionary and the movement between high and street
> voice . . . were in every way to my eighteen-year-old reception equal to what I
> was experiencing at the Fillmore . . . with the [Grateful] Dead and company
> as they moved from psychedelic fields of movement into old Appalachian
> folk songs and back to Merle Haggard California folk and Chicago blues . . .
> a field of discovered encounters. (The encore cinched it and I forever gave up
> my pretensions to rock and roll for Poetry.)[2]

At Duncan's primarily local appearances that spring, his audiences included
many factions of an emerging generation of writers who were about to come
into their own in a post-Beat, post-Spicer-circle world. Obliged to find their

290

relation to Duncan, some revered him, some challenged him, and others kept a cautious distance. Ron Silliman remembered,

> It was hard for me to imagine just how this character I'd seen on Telegraph Avenue in Berkeley, usually at a poetry event, always surrounded by a group of older women I'd heard referred to as "Robert's Theosophists," with wildly crossed eyes and . . . the first signs of mutton chop sideburns, made any sort of living. He didn't look like anyone I'd ever seen in an office. And he certainly was too debonair to be a beat or hippie. Maybe because he was always the center of attention, but Duncan seemed quite extravagant and that was before he began sporting the purple cape and wide-brimmed hat that [later] became [his] calling cards.[3]

At the end of April, Duncan presented a lecture to biology students at California State College in Hayward, an event arranged by professor Norman Goldstein. On May 7, at the invitation of David Bromige, he read at Sonoma State College in Santa Rosa. Bromige and Duncan had begun their friendship in the fall of 1962, and Bromige remembered the immediacy of their bond: "I never really looked back with Robert. We became good friends. He came to Berkeley, once or sometimes twice a week on the bus. . . . to use the library, and we'd meet for lunch or after lunch, and it was a marvelous education."[4] After spending time with Bromige in Santa Rosa, Duncan traveled south to read at the University of California, San Diego, where he saw poet David Antin, linguist Ed Klima, and Pauline Oliveros and Lynn Lonidier. He wrote to Jess that he had visited the San Diego Zoo, indulged in a margarita extravaganza with Klima, and encountered unconventional activities in the Oliveros household: "Their arrangements have graduated (the directive . . . was Pauline's beginning an affair with one of her students) to a foursome, with Lynn having found likewise a bedmate. The two new girls are very charming indeed. . . . Lynn . . . said there were some painful psycho-dramas along the way. Well, all four were very sweet to me."[5]

The return to San Francisco that summer came with the burden of unfinished projects. While Jess was cloistered with paintings in progress, Duncan attempted to clear his desk. The two men had arrived at a schedule that suited Jess's need for sunlight hours in the studio. They rose at 7:00 A.M., had breakfast together, and began the workday. By 10:00 P.M., they were both in bed. In July, Duncan made a list of the writing projects impinging upon his gardening season:

After the Whitman "lecture" which I struggled to bring to some consequence, I had resolved to eschew all assignments and to release prose to my own counsels. Yet over the last year I have taken on task after task that remain . . . no more than struggling, even strangling, propositions: a Preface for Oyez's volume of my Poetry Center notes, an essay on Denise's poetry, particularly to study out the meaning and effect of the War and Revolution in that context—this is a self assignment, and a series of essays for the Library Journal of U.C. to set into motion ideas back of and gathering round the special poetry collection. And there are older unfinished works—a Preface for and seeing thru the publication of the second "collected" volume for Oyez, and long overdue, after six years, to resume work on *The H. D. Book*.[6]

The psychic weight of those tasks drove Duncan in another direction entirely: by the end of July, he was deep into Norbert Wiener's *Cybernetics* and Jackson Mac Low and La Monte Young's fluxus art collection, *An Anthology*. He also prepared for a fall teaching assignment in the History of Consciousness program at the University of California, Santa Cruz, where he would lead an undergraduate seminar Reading the Modern Poem: William Carlos Williams, *Paterson,* and a graduate-level course called The Idea of Person.[7] The position, arranged with the help of Norman O. Brown, who had recently joined the school's faculty, came with a salary of five thousand dollars. Between September 28 and December 19, Duncan spent the first part of each week in Santa Cruz, returning to San Francisco on Thursday evenings to be with Jess through the weekends. The pleasure of Norman O. Brown's company filtered into "Santa Cruz Propositions," an expansive collage poem occupying the center of *Ground Work*. Sparked by a lecture of Brown's on Giambattista Vico and James Joyce, the poem soon moved in several other directions. Its title was influenced by Duncan's rereadings of Whitehead's *Process and Reality,* with its own propositions about the real, but Duncan wrote some eight years later that he also saw the poem as "so directly a student piece to William's patents in *Paterson,* in every reader's mind the relation will come up again and again and remain problematic," adding the afterthought "I fly, after all, straight into that trouble."[8]

Another reference entered the poem the week after Duncan penned its first lines: on October 19, 1970, Santa Cruz ophthalmologist Victor Ohta, his wife, two young sons, and secretary were murdered by John Linley Frazier, a delusional twenty-four-year-old with an interest in the tarot.[9] Santa Cruz had been a site for unusual occult activity during the late 1960s, and it had seen enough bloodshed during the period to briefly be dubbed "Murder

Capital of the World." The Frazier case set off a panic among the locals while giving Duncan rich material to weave into the poem. He pasted lines from newspaper accounts of the murders into the piece, much in the fashion that West Coast assemblage artists incorporated the materials of modern life and media sensationalism in their sculptures. The ominous tone and fragmented structure of the poem pointed toward strife well beyond Central California. That fall, national news networks were also reporting on the My Lai massacre trials of American soldiers accused of murdering Vietnamese civilians in the spring of 1968. "Santa Cruz Propositions" was a testing ground for Duncan's beliefs about the Viet Nam war, and in it he incorporated references to a metaphysical contest of good and evil, questions about the significance of humanity within the natural world, and a fascination with the youth movement. One of his most ambitious pieces of writing, it opened with a melancholy capitulation:

> Poetry! Would *Poetry* have sustain us? It's lovely
>   --and no more than a wave--to have rise
>   out of the debris, the stink and threat
> --even to life-- of daily speech,   the roar
>   of the giants we begin from,
> primordial Strife,   blind Opposition,
>   a current that sweeps all stagnant things up
>   into a torrent of confidence   beyond thought.[10]

By integrating lines from Plato's *Symposium*, Frazier's note at the scene of the crime, and local media reports, Duncan carried out a typographical feat that distilled the violence of the time into a cacophonous mythological landscape:

```
Junked cars line the muddy road to the
shed,  and a chicken, a rooster, a cat
and a dog
```

>   *"What do you mean, Diotoma, is Eros then evil and foul?"*

```
**
Frazier's residence was a dilapidated cowshed
behind a half-dozen larger similar structures
```

>   *"He is a great demon, and like all spirits, he is*
>   *intermediate"*

```
"as brought to you by the people of the Free
Universe"
```

> *"He   the mediator who spans the chasm which divides them
>   —the divine and the mortal"*

> "Knight of Wands, Knight of Cups,
>   Knight of Pentacles, Knight
> of Swords"

> *"and through Him   the arts of the prophet and the priest"*

> The victims, their hands tied with scarves,
> were shot and thrown into the pool of the
> $250,000 Ohta home, a half-mile from Frazier's
> ramshackle cabin[11]

The poem closed with yet another narrative: Duncan's debate with Denise Levertov about activism, poetry, and revolution. No longer able to keep private his hostility toward her, he sketched an unflattering portrait of his former confidante as Kali, the Indian goddess of war:

> She has put on her dress of murderous red.
> She has put on her mini-skirt   and the trampling begins.
> She has put on her make-up of the Mother of Hell,
>   the blue lips of Kore,   the glowering
>   pale of the flower that is black to us.
> She has put on her fashion of burning.[12]

Sending a draft of "Santa Cruz Propositions" to Levertov in late October, Duncan cheerfully directed her to her appearance in the poem. While she subsequently reported that she had misplaced the manuscript, the antagonistic characterization was on her mind when she wrote to Duncan and Jess in February 1971: "Life is too damned busy as usual, but don't, very dear friends, cut me off & condemn me to Kali category, please—I am just as human as I ever was."[13] Duncan, while intrigued by the possibility of writing about Levertov's work for a public forum, seemed little concerned with continuing their correspondence. Autumn on the West Coast allowed him to cultivate local friendships, including October and December visits to see David and Sherryl Bromige in Sebastopol, California, and a November invitation to write a ceremony for the wedding of Ebbe and Angela Borregaard.[14] When R. B. Kitaj arrived for the opening of the new University of California Art Museum in early November, he stayed with Duncan and Jess, later recalling his feeling of honor at inhabiting the top floor of the house while the couple went about their business below.[15]

As the semester drew to a close in Santa Cruz and the holidays approached, Duncan made the most of the break from travel and teaching. Again beginning new projects while unfinished essays lingered on his desk, in December he collaborated with Lou Harrison at his studio in Aptos, California. The composer and poet documented the arc of Duncan's writing career, recording the 1947 poem "Sleeping all Night," portions of his Halloween masques, and the songs of *Faust Foutu*. While the music was reserved for the entertainment of a private audience, Duncan remarked in a notebook, "The recording has at least the pleasure that it is done by a friend for a friend: we had been planning . . . the session for some years, and just that evening with the excellent conditions of Lou's studio . . . and of our after dinner mood we struck it. Lou recorded, Bill Colvig dozed, and . . . when I came to the finale of my Hallowe'en mask he joind in to do the hooting 'horn' choruses."[16]

In late December and early January, Duncan again turned to creative activities that brought immediate and unofficial pleasure. A new box of crayons inspired a drawing and an accompanying Christmas poem:

> O tree of lights! Tree of colors!
> How readily you arise to my
> designing hand, at hand
> to delite the eye, as ever
> night's branches, day's branches
> intermingling, moon and sun
> silver and gold
> or at the horizon transmuted—
> crimson. O tree
> of a million branches,
> tree of a million roots, tree
> of resources! Again,
> the treasure of fruits and presents,
> again the mosaic of many colors.[17]

FIFTY-ONE

The Torn Cloth

> When I was near the house of Circe, I met Hermes
> in the likeness of a young man, the down just
> showing on his face. He came up to me and took my
> hand, saying: "Where are you going, alone, and
> ignorant of the way?"
>
> THOM GUNN, *Moly*

AS HE REFLECTED upon his experiences in Santa Cruz that autumn, Duncan also prepared for an extensive winter and spring tour. The 1970s would see a turn in his career, with multiweek commitments becoming the norm. Jess meanwhile indulged in the solitude, content with quiet days of work in his studio. On February 9, Duncan began an epic trip across the continent with a reading at Simon Fraser University. Staying with Warren and Ellen Tallman, as had become his February ritual, he also visited Victoria for three days before taking a winding journey by train through the Canadian provinces to Toronto. Once there, he had a glimpse into another active Canadian poetry scene. He reported the Valentine's Day highlights of the last leg of his journey to Jess:

> Once I got out to Frank Davey's the remaining stay in Toronto was beautiful.... comfortable, and socially delightful. George Bowering had come down from Montreal; Victor Coleman (whose *Light Verse* I had admired) and b.p. Nichol (*GRONK*) came ... that Sunday evening. Nichol brought a color page of *Little Nemo* to be relayd to you. I hadn't realized that Nichol whose neo-Dada sound invention poems I had delighted in was the Jess-devotee who had sent the *Gronk* Little Nemo issues to you.[1]

George Bowering remembered the day's activities in another light:

> Frank and I talked with Duncan all afternoon. Then Victor Coleman and Sarah Miller came for dinner, and bp came ... later. We listened to Duncan's tape of his songs for his masque, and we were all pretty well bored.... Victor and bp missed the more interesting talk of the afternoon. We'd even been

296

discussing competitive story-telling. With bp we did get into talk about horror movies. I thought at the time that Duncan wasn't all that much interested in bp, but knew that Jess was.[2]

On February 17, Duncan was again stateside, giving a reading at Baltimore's Goucher College. His performance there was documented in the school newspaper the following week: "Duncan brought his full character to the ... campus in his reading, as well as in his long gray hair, beads, and colorful suede tunic. His voice peaked, paused, and at times even drifted into song. His hands expressively kept the rhythm which absorbed his feet and ultimately his whole body."[3]

Throughout the tour that winter, the household was in Duncan's thoughts as he prepared an essay on the *Translations* paintings for Jess's first major show at the Odyssia Gallery. Home from Canada in March, he continued to write intensive notes about the works while Jess remained in the studio finishing the twenty-sixth piece in the series, *Mort and Marge*.[4] In early April, Duncan set off for work in Ohio, New York, and New England, beginning at Kent State University, where he gave an April 7 reading and lecture alongside Allen Ginsberg for the school's Creative Arts Festival.[5] The festival's organizer, thirty-year-old English professor Robert Bertholf had become acquainted with Duncan's work as a graduate student at the University of Oregon, and he soon became one of Duncan's most ardent followers. In 1975, he would launch a small magazine called *Credences* as a sounding ground for Duncan and the younger poets influenced by him. Housed with Bertholf during his visit to Kent, Duncan described him to Jess as "the young professor here who is most concerned with what's going on."[6] Ambivalent about academia, Duncan nonetheless found Bertholf a useful supporter as he expanded his touring path to other parts of the Midwest. The following year he would return to Kent State for a lengthier residency, and Bertholf would continue to have a hand in his career for the next two decades.

From Ohio, Duncan went east, first returning to Baltimore, where he stayed with David Franks, and then to Philadelphia, where he spent the last two days of April with Stephen and Paula Prokopoff and their son Ilya. Stephen, curator of a 1969 exhibition that included pieces from Jess's *Tricky Cad* series, and Paula, later the director of the Poetry Center of Chicago, became Duncan's preferred hosts during his trips east during the 1970s. He told Jess that he found them "adorable ... with the suggestion of children, kittens and puppies. Of cheerful and whimsical humors."[7] Duncan's easy way in the household made him likewise a coveted guest, and Stephen's commitment to Jess's work opened opportunities for exhibitions in new venues.

In early May, Duncan found equally comfortable lodgings at editor James Laughlin's loft in New York and at Henry and Adele Wenning's house in New Haven. Reporting to Jess that the completion of *The H. D. Book* was again on his mind, he described a day spent in the Beinecke Library as a "blissful time with all the old excitements. It seems deepend over these . . . years during which that work has lain fallow."[8] After reading at Yale on May 4 during a janitorial strike that left the campus strewn with garbage, Duncan boarded a bus for a six-hour ride to Portland, Maine. Passing through the scenic spring landscape, he became absorbed in Thom Gunn's *Moly*, which he had procured at a New York bookstore that week. The British poet, then living in Berkeley, had struck up an amiable relationship with Duncan a few years earlier. Gunn later recalled,

> I was a favorite for a while. I was often asked to lunch, which was wonderful. . . . Robert would do the talking and I'd go away . . . wanting to fill notebooks with ideas for poems. Somebody once said to me after Robert's death, "You must have known Robert very well" or maybe "You were close to him?" . . . and I thought, well, I knew Robert well, but I don't think he knew me at all because I never had a chance to say anything.[9]

During his May 5 Greyhound journey, Duncan began notes in the pages of Gunn's book that would become "Poems from the Margins of Thom Gunn's *Moly*." One section of the new piece, "Rites of Passage I," was completed that day, and he presented the poem in progress to an audience at the University of Maine alongside "Santa Cruz Propositions" and works from *Roots and Branches*. Over the next two days, he wrote another subsection, "Near Circe's House." In addition to paying homage to Gunn's work, the poem delved into the themes of sexual awakenings, the figure of Eros, and the craft of the poem. Duncan opened "Rites of Passage I" with allusions to an erotic sensuality conjured by the metrical phrase:

> These   are
> the passages of thought
> from the light air
> into the heavy flesh
> until from the burning
> all the slumb'ring dark

matter comes alight,
the foot that has
its reason in bright rations
it would measure

hardens and beats
the trembling earth,
reaches out of measure
into the hoof that
tramples
pleasure and pain   compounded
into a further brightness.[10]

Returning to New York from Maine, Duncan looked forward to one of the central motivations for his journey east: the May 8 opening of the exhibition Translations by Jess at the Odyssia Gallery. Still phobic of New York and content to stay out of the spotlight, Jess received a written report about the event from Duncan, and Federico Quadrani supplied photographs of the installation. The opening, underattended because of a spring downpour, at least gave Duncan an opportunity to see Jess's work adorning the walls of the 57th Street gallery and to catch up with old friends Helen Adam and William Roth. There were other art world events to attend that week as well, including a cubist exhibition at the Metropolitan Museum of Art, which he viewed with Robert Bertholf, and a small display of Mayan pieces at the Grolier Club. The evening after Jess's opening, Duncan dined with Federico and Odyssia Quadrani at a Greek restaurant near James Laughlin's loft, and, after a May 11 reading at Stony Brook, he returned to New Haven for two days, continuing his work on The H. D. Book at the Beinecke Library. On May 13, he made a final foray into New York, where he again saw the Quadranis and revisited the Translations show. Flying home on May 14, he arrived late in the evening to 20th Street and to a new home telephone number rendered into narrative by Jess: "two ate five, for two won seven!"[11]

As Duncan reimmersed himself in his writings about H. D. that spring, an anonymous edition of her book Hermetic Definitions appeared in the poetry community.[12] Part of a series produced by Frontier Press editor Harvey Brown, the publication was distributed at no charge and came into existence out of Brown's fear that H. D.'s writings would remain buried in her literary estate, then run by Normal Holmes Pearson.[13] Several fabulous stories emerged about the pirated work, including the tale that in 1971, a patron at the Beinecke Library copied the entire text of H. D.'s unpublished manuscript onto his or her shirt sleeves in order to smuggle it from the archive. In 1962, Duncan had in fact given the Beinecke a copy of the manuscript that H. D. had sent to him, and he told Pearson that he suspected his donation had been used to produce the book.[14] When Pearson contemplated suing Brown for the bootleg edition, Duncan, friendly toward Pearson but also sympathetic toward Brown, asked Pearson to forgo legal action, pointing out that Serendipity Books in Berkeley had received copies of the book "as gifts for their customers who are H. D. collectors—they are not for sale."[15] Duncan, while wary of Brown's "Robin Hood" attitude toward poets' writing, told Pearson, "I am in some way not . . . morally offended but concerned to bring him to his senses, 'senses' in the largest sense. My true relation is not punitive or defensive . . . but educational."[16]

That summer, there was library business to attend to closer to home. Feeling overwhelmed by his commitment to the Bancroft Library, on June 18, Duncan requested a leave from his advisory position.[17] During a season slated for reading and writing, another interruption arose with an invitation to the University of California at San Diego's California Creative Arts Conference. As part of a two-week residency beginning on June 21, Duncan led a writing workshop, held a series of discussions titled "Sight, Vision, and Imagination," and performed alongside Fielding Dawson, Robert Creeley, James Koller, and Michael McClure.

In August and through early autumn, Duncan and Jess were content to be at home preparing for renovations that included removing the back wall of the house to extend the kitchen. With Duncan's income from readings and lectures and Jess's monthly allowance from the Odyssia Gallery, the two were able to attend to the household with greater flourish. Duncan told Barbara Joseph of his excitement about the work that would bring more light into the kitchen and highlight the stained glass windows: "The . . . extension . . . is all and more than I dreamd it would be. The room is enormous. And the proportion of the windows leads the eye up to take in the height of the room."[18] While builders occupied the kitchen, Duncan chipped away at writing projects, and Jess completed preparations for the second part of his Odyssia Gallery initiation, *Paste-Ups by Jess,* scheduled to begin on September 28. With his partner under the pressure of the gallery deadline, Duncan considered the incompatibilities between creative work and the interventions of curators and editors. As he pushed to finish *The H. D. Book,* he began to have doubts about handing the manuscript over to John Martin of Black Sparrow Press, "where the overseeing of a printer's activities and of a publisher's betrayals of one's intentions is one of the greatest distractions from the primary ground."[19]

Along with the architectural changes at 20th Street and the intensive production of paste-ups and *The H. D. Book* came the ultimate collapse of Duncan's relationship with Denise Levertov. The poets' fall correspondence overflowed with a hostility that had been foreshadowed during their previous four years of communications. While Levertov was already on edge because of Duncan's negative characterization of her in "Santa Cruz Propositions," she was hardly ready to bear the brunt of his response to "From a Notebook: October '68—May '69." The piece, in which Levertov took up war protesters' cry of "Revolution or Death," prompted Duncan to complain, "The question is the poetry and not the revolution . . . I feel that revolution, politics, making history, is one of the great falsehoods—is Orc in his burning madness—this is not to disapprove of the fire's raging. But Art has only one place in which to be and that is in our own lives right now." He told Levertov that their differences left him at wit's end: "I feel guilty or tired of my disappointment in what is clearly so important to you. And project on you some opposition to the issue of art. The art of the poem—which has fallen into disrepair—the art of long persisting and careful work. I am not talking about prisoners, blacks, children, and angry women in revolt—I am talking about those with work to do deserting their work."[20]

Levertov responded angrily to Duncan's critiques:

Yes, you have indeed "played Orpheus for me," and then I'm exalted. And you have played Virgil for me, and then I'm enlightened. I have learned so much from you!

But there are other times when you pontificate. I can see it must be hard not to, because you are full of insight and knowledge about so many things and your friends and followers naturally drink all that in, often awestruck, so that it must get hard to distinguish, for you yourself, when you get way off course. . . . [Also,] your special ability to realize puns and to give words the quick etymological X-Ray sometimes leads you into a twisty picky-ness (so that one feels one is walking on eggs in speaking/writing to you because you are waiting to trip one up (there goes a mixed metaphor!) instead of being the illuminating faculty . . . at its/your best).[21]

In November 1971, when Levertov proposed a truce, Duncan agreed to suspend his judgments of her poetry, at least in their correspondence. His journal that winter nonetheless held notes titled "Reflections upon Reading and

Re-reading Denise Levertov's *To Stay Alive*," an essay he planned to publish despite Levertov's request to the contrary.[22] In a series of poems called "A Seventeenth Century Suite in Homage to the Metaphysical Genius in English Poetry," Duncan also addressed Levertov's "Advent 1966," reclaiming the image of the burning babe as the dominion of poet Robert Southwell. On December 16, waking before dawn in a fit of anger, he wrote a further section of the suite, "*Passages* 36," in his notebook, opening with a refrain that had entered his consciousness upon waking: "*Let it go. Let it go. / Grief's its proper mode.*" The passage reflected on the Viet Nam war and sketched out a dream in which Levertov had appeared, illuminating a deeper psychological strife at work in their confrontation:

> It was about the end of an old friendship,
>   the admission of neglect rancoring,
> mine of hers, hers of what I am,
>   and festering flesh was there.
>
> . . . .
>
> I do not   as the years go by   grow tolerant
>   of what I cannot share and what
> refuses me.[23]

FIFTY-TWO

Despair in Being Tedious

I know but part of it and that   but distantly,
a catastrophe in another place,   another time,
      the mind addresses
and would erect within itself   itself,
      as Viet Nam,   itself as Bangladesh,
itself exacting revenge and suffering revenge,
      itself the Court and before the Court
where new judges disloyal to the Spirit of the Law
      are brought.   All forces conspire
            to seat them there.

ROBERT DUNCAN, "A Seventeenth Century Suite"

WHILE THE WAR in Viet Nam continued and his relationship with Den-
ise Levertov drew to a close, Duncan turned to thoughts of his career.
With his fifty-third birthday in January 1972 came the promise of another
long year of touring and writing deadlines. After participating in a February
2 memorial reading for Kenneth Patchen, who had died in early January,
Duncan traveled to Portland to give a February 17 reading there. His annual
stay with the Tallmans was punctuated by business activities, including meet-
ings with elementary school administrators in Ellensburg, Washington, who
had asked him to consult on new learning models for children.[1] The trip also
gave him the opportunity to see friends on the outskirts of the Tallman
household, including Stan Persky, Gladys Hindmarch, Robin Blaser, and
George Stanley, all familiar faces in his decadelong relationship with the Van-
couver community.[2]

With a schedule mirroring that of the previous year, he followed the
Canadian trip with a tour of the East Coast, this time planning stops in
two dozen cities. Duncan wrote to Paula Prokopoff on March 29: "As I
barely begin to admit that I leave for the East a week from today, with the
full depressive mania of income tax finals still due and a Preface to com-
plete before I leave—there is at least the lift of transcendent spring weather.
Iris swelling to bloom and wisteria at the close of its bloom—a lingering

token still enlivening the east side of the garden."[3] The preface in progress, which he had been at work on since January, was to grace a new Sand Dollar Press edition of the 1955 collection *Caesar's Gate*. The unwieldy, sprawling essay would occupy him for the rest of the year, forcing him to put aside *The H. D. Book* once again.

On April 7, Duncan reluctantly boarded a red-eye flight to New York. While he was in the air, Jess was at home watching the sitcom *Sanford & Son* when a news bulletin announced the hijacking of a plane that reportedly had departed from the San Francisco airport. Alarmed, Jess soon learned that the flight had in fact left from Newark, New Jersey, and was diverted to San Francisco by the hijacker, where the flight's passengers were released in exchange for $500,000.[4] Duncan's trip, in contrast, was so uneventful that a midflight letter to Jess reported the details of an airline dinner of stuffed shells with creamed chicken and mushrooms. After a dawn landing and bus connection to Manhattan, Duncan wrote Jess of his travel fatigue: "Me, I guess, is still with me. And bits of how impossible it seemd for me to get myself off, a tree uprooted frantic that some essential root be left behind—which it is."[5] Swept up into the rush of the city, Duncan began his stay with a stop at New Directions Publishers before having dinner with George Quasha and accompanying him to an event at New York University that must have caused him some consternation: a reading by Denise Levertov. Quasha, who introduced Levertov that evening, remembered that she and Duncan behaved cordially yet kept their distance.[6] On Sunday April 9, Duncan dined with Marguerite Cohn, proprietress of House of Books, after which he made a special phone call to Jess, who was still skittish in the wake of the hijacking scare. The next morning, regretting the two martinis and two glasses of wine of the night before, Duncan again checked in with Jess in a hastily scrawled letter: "A tremendous effort of attention over inattention to put on my trousers, to sort out my papers for the day, to comb my hair."[7] Despite the hangover, he gathered himself to meet Helen and Pat Adam at their uptown apartment and to spend the day at the Metropolitan Museum with them and writer William Packard, curator of the 92nd Street YMHA Poetry Center and founder of the *New York Quarterly*. A special show in the Egyptian collections delighted Duncan, and he also lingered in the New American rooms, viewing works by Ryder, Church, and Winslow Homer. Taking leave of the Adams, Duncan met with a new friend, composer William Hellerman, sharing a meal with Hellerman and his wife before settling into James Laughlin's loft for the evening.[8]

Monday April 10 was another day packed with work: Duncan spent the morning being interviewed by William Packard, and after a lunch break, kept appointments at Grove Press and New Directions. Briefly returning to Laughlin's apartment, he showered and shaved and prepared for the highlight of the trip, a reading at the 92nd Street Y Poetry Center. Duncan's appearance that night, also introduced by George Quasha, attracted a large audience that included the Adam sisters and the Quadranis. Fred Martin, present as a representative of New Directions, was enchanted by Duncan's energy and penned a report for the publisher's author files: "Robert reads very well and was filled with his wild stories and enthusiasms."[9]

Waking the next morning to a burst of springtime snow and flight delays, Duncan was temporarily stranded. He arrived behind schedule at his next venue of Albany, New York, giving a reading at the state university there on April 11, hosted by Don Byrd. Byrd, whom Duncan had met in Kansas in 1969, had recently begun teaching in Albany and made the campus a welcome place for the San Francisco poet through the mid-1980s. Finding an intellectual affinity at the school, Duncan spent a good part of his first visit hopping between classrooms in search of apprentices. He wrote Jess on the afternoon of April 12, "Albany has been exhilarating—a solid morning of class room demonstrations—8 AM on Whitman, 9 AM on Stein, 10–11 in the coffee lounge expounding the doctrine, 11–12 the map of the classical nucleus, 12–1 Hart Crane's BRIDGE—then lunch and here I am somewhat stunned by my own trajectory."[10]

From Albany, Duncan boarded a propeller plane to Utica, New York, en route to Colgate College in nearby Hamilton. The upstate weather was bleak, and he documented his waves of elation and exhaustion in letters to Jess, whose April 13 response extolled the more casual tempo at home: "I've got Orlando, but he's snoring in his chair here, and a beauteous sunshine with warblers and a dozen iris whanging out in the garden (one of them yellow)."[11]

Two days later, Duncan arrived in Buffalo, where he was to stay with Marvin and Thalia Feldman. The latter, a *Beowulf* scholar, became a friend who, as Albert Glover recalled, Duncan jokingly referred to as "the Muse." After reading at the State University of New York at Buffalo that weekend, he spent the rest of his stay completing his taxes. With the calendar of readings beginning to blur into one another, on Monday April 17 the venue was Kent State University, where Duncan was once again hosted by Robert Bertholf and where the two attended a party thrown by another Kent professor and Melville scholar, Howard Vincent. The gathering attracted a handful of young academics from Notre Dame, who later returned to Bertholf's house. While the group spent the night talking, smoking, and drinking, Duncan took the opportunity to sleep.

Chauffeured to Cleveland the following morning by Bertholf, Duncan spent the early afternoon with his host in the city's Salvador Dalí Museum before catching a flight to South Bend, Indiana.[12] Arriving to high winds and a midwestern spring chill, he settled in at Notre Dame University's Morris Inn, observing wearily and warily to Jess that his lodgings came with an over-sized color television and hunting prints. That day he toured the campus with Kathy Schwille, a student assigned to escort him around the area during his two-and-a-half-day visit. She later reported on the experience in the student newspaper:

> At times I fancied I was walking across the campus with Benjamin Franklin, although in mannerisms he more resembled Jack Benny. . . . One of [his] first requests was to [see] the O'Shaughnessy Art Gallery. I learned a lot about art that day. Over lunch he explained his theories on teaching the English language to ghetto children. On the shuttle to St. Mary's he discussed his dismay with the recent political poetry of his friend Denise Levertov. At the St. Mary's Coffee Shop he listened patiently to my views about racial tension in my home state of Virginia, and sang praises to peppermint ice cream after literally stealing a bite of my cone.[13]

Schwille was most likely unaware that her sentiments echoed those of the most energetic minds in the literary community when she commented, "Conversations with Duncan drained me. Attempts to keep up with his thoughts left me exhausted and sometimes dazed."[14]

Duncan was at Notre Dame for the school's Sophomore Literary Festival, a weeklong event that began on April 16. The headline draw was a concert by Jethro Tull, and more literary invitees included novelists Jerzy Kosinski and Robert Coover. On April 19, Duncan gave a lengthy reading, and the following afternoon he participated in a symposium with Allen Ginsberg and Diane Wakoski. A new face in the crowd was poet and English professor John Matthias, who made Duncan's acquaintance during the trip and invited him to speak to one of his classes. Duncan treated the students to a performance of his *Passages* poem "Spelling," during which he rendered phrases onto the chalkboard as he spoke them, leading Matthias to dub the reading "Concerto for a piece of chalk."[15]

To countermand the stress of life on the road, Duncan had made it his habit to locate middle-class sanctuary households wherever he could find them: with the Wennings in New Haven, the Truitts in Washington, D.C., the Prokopoffs in Chicago, and later the Fauchereaus in Chantilly, the Kitaj/Fishers in London, and the Sylvesters in Buffalo. Retreating to one such haven on April 21, he traveled to Oak Park, Illinois, to spend the weekend with the Prokopoffs. The family had recently moved from Philadelphia to the Chicago area, where Stephen Prokopoff had assumed the directorship of the city's Museum of Contemporary Art. Prokopoff, busy with museum business, left his wife to entertain Duncan, though Ilya Prokopoff remembered Duncan providing his own share of entertainment: "He was very active. Helping my mom stain a pattern into the carpet in our house, or up on a ladder painting something or other. Very chatty and very much someone my parents liked having around."[16] That weekend, in addition to taking an architectural tour of Chicago that included the Frank Lloyd Wright and Sullivan buildings, Duncan attended services at the Unity Universalist Temple in Oak Park, after which he had lunch with the Prokopoffs and local architect and curator Jim Speyer. With springtime lilacs blooming in the Chicago suburbs, the visit was a happy one for Duncan, though Stephen Prokopoff remembered one distressing incident: "On Sunday, Paula made a sumptuous shrimp dinner; Robert ate hugely. Later that night he was *very* ill. A few days later a card arrived thanking us both for the joys 'of the weak-end.' "[17] After an evening locked in the Prokopoffs' bathroom, Duncan rallied for a Monday flight to Hartford, Connecticut, where he was met at the airport by Norman Holmes Pearson. On April 25, he gave the Annual Wallace Stevens Memorial Reading at the University of Connecticut at Storrs, for which he had written "Structure of Rime XXVIII: In Memoriam Wallace Stevens." Friends Charles Stein and Harvey Bialy accompanied him to the reading, and Duncan also met with Olson scholar George Butterick and his wife, Collette. Given an opportunity to look at Charles Olson's manuscripts in the rare books collection of the university, he began *"Passages* 37," embedding allusions to Olson's poetics:

> Compounded Earth Milk Maker
> the sweet myth mounting
>   stems
>   that from the understuff grow
>
> in conversations with the light
>   life's laboratories[18]

Close to the end of his travels, he wrote to Jess on April 28 confessing a frustration with public life: "One of the happy conjunctions of this tour has been meeting John Seelye (who wrote that Huck Finn version for the crikits) and his wife Catherine who is head of coordinating special collections at Storrs. It has provided the promise of having a place to stay here in the future apart from Duncan enthusiasts.... The tyranny of admirers ... wears me to a jumpy edge."[19] A short trip to Boston to see old friends lent a reprieve. On April 29, he met up with Robert Creeley for a weekend conference at Tufts University. The two old friends sequestered themselves at the Cambridge home of photographer Elsa Dorfman, where poets Anne Waldman and Ken Irby also stopped in for a visit. The following day at a Sunday brunch date with Elizabeth Bishop, Duncan presented her with a copy of his Thom Gunn tribute poem. Bishop later wrote a warm thank you with the admission, "I'm sure you know that although our approach to poetry differs a lot—I have the greatest respect for your work and admiration for your life of devotion to it."[20]

Upon returning to San Francisco in May, Duncan was more than ready to resume the household tasks of cooking and gardening. Jess was again secluded in the studio, continuing the *Paste-Ups* series for an autumn show arranged by Stephen Prokopoff at Chicago's Museum of Contemporary Art. Duncan kept the Prokopoffs abreast of Jess's progress, which included "spells of jig-saw puzzles to work" and "excursions to the junk stores."[21] Cataloguing his own obligations in the same letter, Duncan ruefully commented on the impossibility of a leisurely summer in San Francisco. Having accepted an offer from Penguin Books to write a preface to an edition of Henry Vaughan's poems, he also continued drafts of his preface to *Caesar's Gate*. Except for a short trip to San Diego for a July 10 reading, he was at his desk generating new text around the original edition of the Divers Press book, and he encountered a familiar dilemma as the material grew beyond his expectations. In addition to incorporating autobiographical material and reflections upon the initial inspirations for the book, the preface included an epilogue called "The Matter of the Bees," dated Tuesday, July 11, 1972, which recounted a hypnogogic "scheduled phantasy" carried out with a meditation instructor.[22]

As the summer waned, Duncan was also able to resume composing poems. Commissioned by Albert Glover for an Olson-inspired project titled "A Plan for a Curriculum of the Soul," Duncan began a series of poems meditating upon the works of Dante. Evolving into a chapbook called *Dante Études,* the pieces began to fill a new notebook set aside for the commission.[23]

Meanwhile, in the midst of copious reading notes on Pierre Boulez's *Boulez on Music Today,* more new poems emerged in his notebooks, including "And If He Had Been Wrong for Me," and "Despair in Being Tedious." The latter piece hinted at Duncan's lingering uneasiness about his rift with Denise Levertov. Spurred by her comment about his "talking jags," Duncan mused about his struggle to control his energies:

> A long way back I look and find myself
> as I was then I am,   a circling man
> in a seizure of talk that he hears too as he goes on.
>
> . . . .
>
> I do not know if I am bound
> to run upon this wheel, wound up,
> excited in a manic spiel of wheel in wheel,
>
> or if I'm free to talk wherever they are free
> to listen.
> . . . .
>
> There is in me a weary stretch I mean to say
> Some urgency that draws the matter out
> I cannot come to,   and I want company.[24]

FIFTY-THREE

The Cult of the Gods

What thou lovest well remains,
the rest is dross
What thou lov'st well shall not be reft from thee
What thou lov'st well is thy true heritage

EZRA POUND, Canto 81

EZRA POUND DIED ON NOVEMBER 1, 1972, just as Duncan was completing a three-week residency at Kent State University. Having spent the early part of the autumn returning to Pound's work with Michael and Joanna McClure, Duncan infused his Kent course, Studies in Ideas of the Poetic Imagination, with attentions to the *Pisan Cantos,* Williams's *Paterson,* Christopher Smart's *Jubilate Agno,* Blake's *Jerusalem,* and Sir Charles Sherrington's *Man on His Nature.* The course syllabus pointed to a larger goal: "In our projected lexicon of ideas of the Imagination, we will be concerned with whether we consider the ideas to be phantastic, scientific, known, eccentric, psychotic, etc. What we can hope to 'learn' ... is some more informed and extensive idea of what is involved in the question of Imagination, and, in turn, of how ideas of Imagination in poetry relate to the fields of religion and the psychological and physiological sciences."[1]

As the campus trees offered their autumn displays of red and gold, Duncan had the additional stimulation of staying with Robert Bertholf, whose hospitality extended to breakfasts of waffles and bacon and rib roast dinners. Duncan wrote Jess that he was not only wary of "Mr. Bertholf's gourmantizing *[sic]*" but that he had also been "stocking up on soda water to avoid ... the alcoholic syndrome of the faculty world."[2] His three-week visit to Kent State was frenetic, punctuated by visits to other colleges in the area, including October 13 and 19 readings at Ohio University and John Carroll University, and an October 24 performance at Bowling Green, attended by visiting British poet Tom Raworth. Raworth, who would see Duncan again in England during the following spring, remembered his first view of Duncan in Ohio, "walking down the corridor of the English Department ... with his black cloak flying."[3]

At Kent, Duncan taught classes in the morning and spent his afternoons meeting with students and giving a series of lectures. The company of students and faculty inspired and sustained him through the workload: poet Ed Dorn and his wife, Jennifer Dunbar Dorn, were on campus that year, and Asphodel Bookstore owner Jim Lowell and his wife, Tessa, often joined the group around the English Department. Local harpsichordist Ruth Nurmi attended Duncan's class, as did Ralph La Charity, Mary McConville, Patrick Meanor, Richard Blevins, and Jerry Cooper.[4] Blevins recalled some twenty-five years later, "I was one of Robert Duncan's students in his seminar on The Imagination. . . . I date my birth as a poet from that time and place."[5]

In the classroom, and in less formal conversations, Duncan and the students compiled copious notes on the role of imagination in creative activity. His notebooks illustrated his commitment to working alongside the novices:

> Assigning two drawings—one "from life" and one from imagination "at the edge of one's capabilities"—my thought has been returning over the past two days to test my reluctance with doing them as an ordeal, as an idea of doing, as an exploration of "imagination." By the end of the evening—it was one o'clock in the morning when, the dishes from a celebrative dinner finally washed up, we got to bed—my dreaming mind was ready to rehearse *drawing.*[6]

His public lectures on October 11, 18, and 25 were likewise ambitious, spawning a storm of Duncanian verbiage. The first, "Pound, Eliot, and H.D.: The Cult of the Gods in American Poetry," touched on turn-of-the-century cult activity in London, Madame Blavatsky's writings, and M.R. James's exploration of New Testament apocrypha. Proposing that T.S. Eliot's *The Waste Land* predicted the beginning of the atomic age, Duncan in the course of his lecture said, "In the tremendous feeling of prophecy in this great poem, those of us who are direct heirs of Eliot feel this to come forward as certainly we feel Babylon was destroyed within and prophesied. That violet air we recognized when it came. 'What is the city over the mountains / Cracks and reforms and bursts in the violet air' at last was Nagasaki, the second city that was completely blasted in the violet air, the one among the mountains."[7]

With the completion of lectures, classes, and extracurricular readings, Duncan admitted to Jess that he had reached a state of exhaustion above and beyond his normal travel fatigue. Scrapping plans to continue on to New York City, he was drawn home to San Francisco with "a wanting . . . to get back to the orders-of-the-day."[8] Those orders came partly from Jess, whose letters that autumn included reminders about the clutter of manuscripts piled throughout the upper floor of the house. Help on that front came from a young scholar and poet, Michael Davidson, an Oakland native who had recently completed a dissertation on Duncan's work and who agreed to help prepare a typescript for the 1973 edition of *The Opening of the Field* for New Directions.[9] Continued work on *The H. D. Book* was also part of Duncan's agenda for the end of the year, as were two projects drawing him back into the pleasures of the visual arts. The essay "Of George Herms, His Hermses, and His Hermetic Art" came to fruition in time for a show of Herms's work at the Memorial Union Art Gallery in Davis, California. After reading alongside Michael McClure at the show's January 12 opening, Duncan also looked forward to a January 18 appearance at the Chicago Museum of Contemporary Art, where he lectured on his collaborations with Jess.

Spring 1973 in fact held two trips to Chicago, the first for the business of Jess's *Paste-Ups* exhibition and the second, in the early part of March, for a series of readings. The back-to-back trips allowed Duncan to deepen his connection to Paula Prokopoff, and the two cemented a companionship that extended beyond the literary. Duncan wrote her between visits: "Paula, I hope that by March I will see some spending money clear and can visit that Art Deco den again—What a treat that day was! And I suspect we would have found that Housewares convention an irksome adventure. What we really wanted to see—a lot of top design coffeepots, casseroles and ice-cream freezers—had better be found sorted out by a set of good buyers."[10]

Upon his return to Chicago, he took part not only in shopping excursions but also in a poetry festival at Northwestern University, where on March 1, he presented "Spelling, *Passages* 15" to a classroom audience. Local poet and professor Peter Michelson remembered Duncan performing with an uncharacteristic awkwardness, likely because he had been paired with Kenneth Rexroth.[11] On March 2, Duncan read at Chicago's Loyola University, and on March 3, Michelson drove him to Oak Park for a weekend with the Prokopoffs. Duncan and Paula made a high-priority visit to a flea market and also made their way to the Art Institute, where, while strolling through a large impressionist exhibition, Duncan "loudly proclaimed his great appreciation of Renoir's 'dripping' sensuality."[12] Amused and chagrined by the

"Renoir outburst," Prokopoff recalled that Duncan by that point had become "a wonderful companion" for her, a sentiment he reciprocated: "In every sense I have of you, you are a rare and delicious person—*my simpatico*."[13]

After a March 6 reading at the University of Illinois, Duncan returned to San Francisco with the recognition that he had impacted the Prokopoffs in more ways than one. A mid-March letter to them included the plea that they gather the books and toiletry items he had left behind in "boy's room abandon."[14] The theme of youthful impulsiveness filtered into "Childhood's Retreat," a melancholy lyric poem he wrote that spring exercising his skills in subtle variations of traditional verse forms:

> It's in the perilous boughs of the tree
> out of blue sky   the wind
> sings loudest surrounding me.
>
> And solitude,   a wild solitude
> 's reveald,   fearfully,   high   I'd climb
> into the shaking uncertainties,
>
> part out of longing, part   daring my self,
> part to see that
> widening of the world[15]

With its dense internal rhyme, the poem seemed influenced by Duncan's recent studies of Dante and Henry Vaughan. In one of the two stilted letters he wrote to Denise Levertov that year, he described the lure of such masters and his affinity for the composition of poems over commissioned critical projects: "At my workshop desk there are still pending the little Dante-Giotto fascicle for the Curriculum of the Soul series, a kind of homage to Charles Olson's project; and there also the Selected Vaughan for Penguin I've mislaid, . . . and maybe lost, the little notebook in which I was working. And have had to start all over again on the Vaughan."[16]

FIFTY-FOUR

Elm Park Road

PUTTING ASIDE HIS STUDIES OF VAUGHAN AND DANTE, Duncan
flew to London on May 3, 1973, with a copy of Octavio Paz's *Alternating
Currents* tucked into his travel bag. After a five-year hiatus, the city would
again offer engaging company and novel sights and sounds. Lodging in
Kensington with R. B. Kitaj, he installed himself "at a great octagonal table
in rosewood" to write his first letter to Jess.[1] Noting his delight in meeting
Kitaj's new companion, Sandra Fisher, Duncan also described the sanctuary
at 62 Elm Park Road: "Everything about this house . . . is comfortable and
easy. A little realm of my own on the top floor . . . with a large light room
and bath—the luxury of big old-style tubs."[2] While he had come to England
to attend a poetry conference organized by American studies scholar Eric
Mottram, he spent his first days overseas watching breaking news of the
Watergate scandal in Washington. Throughout the trip, Duncan would
pepper his letters home with tales of "the discredit of Nixon," a service for
Jess, who made it his practice to shut out television and radio during his
partner's absences.[3]

Acclimating himself to the cold English springtime, Duncan roamed
the city bundled in layers of sweatshirts. The British Museum and its neigh-
boring bookstores were immediate lures, one of the latter yielding a copy
of Rudolf Steiner's *Fifth Gospel* and a recently published tome about the
sixteenth-century court magician John Dee. On May 9, Duncan took a
train northeast to appear at the University of East Anglia in Norwich,
where he met scholar Malcolm Bradbury, who, like Eric Mottram, was in-
troducing American studies to the English academy. A young professor
present at one of his informal readings, Eric Homberger, remembered the
energy of the performance:

What came through to me [in] "Often I Am Permitted to Return to a Meadow"... which Robert had eloquently read to a student audience that afternoon, was how completely it unlocked the sense I had of R[obert] D[uncan] as a person and a poet. I can't think of another poet whose heart and emotions were ever so rawly and fully engaged in a single poem.... I thought he was a gentle person, though rather grander in manner and every bit as infused with the exalted calling.[4]

In Norwich, there were more bookstores to scour, one of them yielding a rare find: Helen Adam's *The Elfin Pedlar and Tales Told by the Pixy Pool,* written by the Scottish balladeer during her preteen years. Duncan's next letter home to Jess duly departed from Nixon news to quote at length from Adam's childhood poems.

On May 11, after a reading at the University College of Wales, Aberystwyth, and a brief view of the countryside north of London, Duncan returned to the city to rendezvous with Kenneth Anger. Anger, who was then editing his film *Lucifer Rising* in the basement of a West London Victorian mansion owned by Led Zeppelin's Jimmy Page, made time to take Duncan on a sightseeing tour. Attributing Duncan's lingering jet lag to the fact that "one's soul doesn't travel as fast as one's body," Anger further contributed to Duncan's sense of dislocation by escorting him to a museum full of medical anomalies that included the skeleton of an Irish giant, a cycloped fetus, and rows of other malformed embryos preserved in formaldehyde.[5] Duncan went on a less grisly outing with Anger the following week, visiting Sir John Soanes's house of architectural mysteries and archaeological treasures in the neighborhood of Holborn. Pleased with the adventure, Duncan treated Anger to Bloody Marys and lunch at a nearby fish restaurant, after which Anger invited him to view his lodgings and his film in progress. Having had the privilege of a private showing of *Lucifer Rising,* which he described to Jess as a sequence of "visions of Isis and Osiris with evocations and invocations of fire," Duncan made his way back from the Led Zeppelin mansion to the Kitaj household.[6]

For a good part of his stay, London afforded Duncan a certain leisure. On May 20, he had tea at Elm Park Road with American friends George Oppen, his wife, Mary, and New Yorker Ted Berrigan, who were also in town for the week's poetry festivities at the London Polytechnic. The next morning, with the promise of sun and a chorus of bird songs at the window, Duncan wrote to Jess, whose weeks alone had been filled with the supervision of house repairs, "Whiles we are about shoring up our house, the house of Nixon is still tumbling down . . . , and hordes of rats and finks and earnest young hirelings are pouring out of a vast network of tunnels—the 'honor' of the Grand Ole Party stinking from all the gaping orifices."[7]

His return to San Francisco looming, Duncan rushed through his remaining business obligations, including a May 23 reading in Newcastle and an appearance at the opening of the Polytechnic poetry gathering the following evening. Over the next four days, he attended a number of conference activities as well as late-night festivities at local pubs. The scope of the proceedings rivaled that of the previous decade's conferences in Vancouver and Berkeley. Eric Mottram's interest in experimental poetry had led him to invite a wide range of American writers, and one audience member, Pierre Joris, recalled being stunned by the final event of the week, a reading by Duncan, George Oppen, Jerome Rothenberg, and Ted Berrigan.[8] Joris was also present for an odd postconference evening at a London pub:

> I remember one absolutely hilarious Marx Brothers–like scene where all the poets—maybe twenty—had dinner in a Greek restaurant on Charlotte Street. The talk [went] on and on, and then people slowly [began] to drift off. Duncan was in great form, so he kept talking. That night I was [supposed to drive] Robert back to Ron Kitaj's house . . . so eventually it was only he and me sitting in the restaurant and he just kept on talking. . . . This waiter . . . was kind of circling around us . . . and, it seemed to me, behaving slightly weirdly. At one level I thought he was trying to get us out, but on another level it felt as if he was possibly trying to put the make on Duncan. And finally . . . I said, "Robert, we have to leave," . . . and the waiter unlocks the door and lets us out, and all the while Robert just keeps talking. I go out to . . . the car . . . , open the doors, and notice a third person—here comes the waiter. So Robert gets into the back of the car, and the waiter jumps in next to him. Robert, without interrupting his talk . . . , and without taking any notice of the waiter, gets out . . . , walks back around the car, and gets into the front seat. Meanwhile, I have gotten out of the driver's seat to chase the waiter out of the back of the car. The scene is wonderfully weird and funny—I finally get the doors closed, and we drive off, and I ask Robert, "What was going on?" and he refused to acknowledge that anyone else had been there.[9]

Leaving London on May 29, Duncan made short excursions to Paris and Chantilly, where he visited translator Serge Fauchereau and his wife, Jocelyn. The Fauchereaus, like the Kitajs, offered him a relaxing household within proximity of several sights he was eager to visit. On May 31, he went to the town of Senlis, "Nerval Country," as he told Jess, and on June 1, he spent another day in Paris before returning to San Francisco.

The early summer of 1973 provided enough quiet for Duncan to attend to work he had long neglected. On June 11, his notebook entry "Where I See *The H. D. Book*" reflected on the long unfolding of the project and his commitment to creative work as a process rather than a progress toward an end:

> As is evident in the actual composition of my poetry also—where a Structure of Rime may appear embedded in the structure of "Apprehensions" or "Passages" may come into the sequence of the Seventeenth Century Suite—and in the very increasingly composite development of my sentences, my thought and feeling—and it would follow, my sense of what Reality is—is not only unbound, so that all jointures must be conceived of as multiphasic, but populated with nests and transitory developments.[10]

That week's mail included a letter from American studies scholar Ekbert Faas, who proposed a more linear project, a biography, which would become *Young Robert Duncan: Portrait of the Poet as Homosexual in Society*. Duncan worked with Faas—though at times skeptically—throughout the second half of the 1970s to see the book into completion. Meanwhile, he traveled to the National Poetry Conference at Thomas Jefferson College in Grand Rapids, Michigan, where on June 16 and 20, he gave a two-part lecture called "Ideas on the Meaning of Form." The talk's open-ended title allowed him to spin an obsessive autobiographical tale touching on unlikely topics ranging from his participation in mid-1950s government drug experiments to his experience of being cross-eyed and his relation to the visual world. He explained his use of the phrase "back of" in his talks and essays: "As a child I used to say 'which one is there? One is there, and one is there.' They say only children can keep this, and as an adult I obliterate this co-existence . . . the one in the nearsighted eye is perceived as of course the one I touch when it's up close but the one in the farsighted eye realizes it's seeing two fields displaced . . . I used to quarrel as a child back and forth which one is real?"[11]

In Grand Rapids for a week, Duncan spent time with another diverse group of American writers, including Carl Rakosi, Charles Reznikoff, George Oppen, Allen Ginsberg, Ed Dorn, David Meltzer, Victor Hernandez Cruz, Diane di Prima, Rochelle Owens, Kenneth Rexroth, and Ted Enslin. The audience was also impressive, including younger poets and artists Helen Luster, Ken Mikolowski, Martha King, Karl Gartung, Anne Kingsbury, and Finvola Drury.[12] But with two major conferences filling out his resume for 1973, Duncan arrived at a novel decision upon his return from Michigan:

"to accept no more lectures or readings outside of this time zone—no appointments that will involve my being away from home overnight for the next two years. . . . I don't want to be away from home when our earthquake arrives. If it hasn't arrived by '75, I won't wait around for it longer."[13]

When not anticipating a major catastrophe, he was putting the finishing touches on two sets of poems that would come to grace *Ground Work:* "A Seventeenth Century Suite in Homage to the Metaphysical Genius in English Poetry" and "Dante Études."[14] In August, with the newfound freedom from touring, he took on a request from Andreas Brown of the Gotham Bookmart, beginning an introduction to a comprehensive bibliography of Jack Spicer's work. While the project never came into print, Duncan spent several months studying Spicer's poems, producing pages of criticism and memoir as well as the poem "Over There." Tinged with the influence of "A Seventeenth Century Suite," the latter piece also seemed an attempt to come to terms with Spicer's death:

> At heart you were bleeding and I refused the blood. I turnd back from the blood and withheld the cup. I withheld the question. I took back my word from the bond I found terrible. . . . Over and out. Signd again. Resignd. Tired the bird I always hear singing a nightingale. It was the Larke, the Herauld of the Morne. No Nightingale. Night's Candles are burnt out.[15]

Remaining closer to home helped to facilitate a return to writing, but it did little to dampen Duncan's busy social life. He resumed weekday trips to Berkeley, partly to see the recently relocated Barbara Joseph and partly to look in on the progress of acquisitions at the Bancroft Library. In mid-August, Duncan and Michael Davidson took a short trip along the coast to visit Robert and Bobbie Creeley, now living in the remote Northern California town of Bolinas. That autumn, Duncan also spent considerable time with Fred Wah and Pauline Butling, who were in Oakland for a three-month stay. Butling recalled, "Before we had settled in, he showed up at the door with a stream of his exuberant, excited talk that went on for hours. I never found it tiresome to listen to him. He would drop in for coffee a couple of mornings a week, usually combined with trips to Berkeley secondhand bookstores and such bargain places."[16]

Between visits with friends, book hunting, and time spent watching the televised Watergate hearings, Duncan started back into *The H. D. Book* alongside his Spicer essay and poems toward *Ground Work*. By the New Year, he would add another writing burden to the mix, accepting a commission to compose an introduction to British poet Allen Upward's 1915 study of Christianity, *The Divine Mystery*.

The end of 1973 also brought reunions with two old friends from the Baker Street household. In November, Duncan composed a poem for James Broughton's sixtieth birthday, which he read at San Francisco State. When Kenneth Anger returned from London in December, he made his way to 20th Street, eager to show Duncan and Jess two films close to completion, *Lucifer Rising* and a new edit of *Rabbit's Moon*. Duncan mused in a notebook, " 'I am always telling a story,' Kenneth said. It is not then a mereness of image or of scene, but their manifestation in their story which unfolds. . . . Lucifer was a revelation of and verification of what the *Seventeenth Century Suite* had meant, the in-tending we attended in the writing: that certain events, exactly these events, come to happen."[17]

Despite the satisfaction of community in the Bay Area, Duncan's break with Denise Levertov remained on his mind as Christmas approached, and on December 13, he made a gesture of reconciliation, to which he received no response:

> After so long a silence, and that following my adverse readings of your recent work, I would plead that you might have my trust that eventually (meaning once the sequence of events has at last been realized) I will rearrive at what I feel to be a just reading, a reading in which all the work of these years must prove good—be made good. I see the good of it but it is not full in me.[18]

FIFTY-FIVE

Riverside

I have tamed the Lion Roar.
It will no longer use me.

Orlando, felix, my little household   relative of the Lion,
I will remember to pet you;
    Death takes his time with us.

ROBERT DUNCAN, "Empedoklean Reveries"

NINETEEN SEVENTY-FOUR WOULD BE AN UNUSUAL YEAR for Duncan. Having forsworn travels, he found himself unable to escape a long list of writing tasks that had accumulated over several months. Throughout the winter and early spring, he filled his journals with notes on Allen Upward's *The Divine Mystery,* Jack Spicer's poetry, and Georges Poulet's *Trois Essais de Mythologie Romantique.* He and Jess also kept a watchful eye on American politics. January brought rumblings of impeachment, and in mid-April, the House Judiciary Committee asked Nixon to hand over audiotapes of his Watergate conversations. On May 15, Duncan returned to work, giving a reading at the San Francisco Museum of Art for a Poetry Center conference Voices of the Forties, a celebration of the April 1947 Festival of Modern Poetry. Duncan presented a number of his early poems, including his 1948 "Homage to the Brothers Grimm." Continuing the small wave of local appearances, he read at the University of California, Riverside, on May 29, enjoying the company of Edwin and Ruth Eigner while there and making tentative plans to return the following year as a visiting professor in the English Department. Ed Eigner remembered Duncan's request regarding his brief appearance that May: "An hour or so before the reading we discussed the tediously, overlong introduction Creeley had received at Kansas. Robert told me that the only thing it was proper to say at an introduction . . . was the following: 'The person who will address you when I sit down is the same one whose name appears on the poster.' And this is how I introduced him."[1]

In the midst of a summer during which Jess prepared for a reprise of his *Paste-Ups* show at the Odyssia Gallery in Rome, Duncan burrowed back into his essay on Jack Spicer and took time for what he felt to be a more leisurely pursuit, a close reading of Heidegger's *Being and Time*. An interruption to the household order came in early August, when a film crew began several days of interviews with Duncan for the public television series *The Originals: The Writer in America*. While the poet was accompanied by crews, lights, and camera; in Washington, President Nixon's life was under less flattering scrutiny. On August 8, he announced his resignation and made way for Gerald Ford to step into the presidency. Meanwhile, as the limelight of educational broadcasting descended upon the household, Jess sought to avoid the commotion, occasionally being caught on camera walking back and forth from his studio to the kitchen. Duncan, then completing "Dante Études," included a substantial discussion of his studies of the Italian poet in the filmed interviews. During October and November of 1974, he found two other opportunities to present those poems to local audiences, giving readings of the work at San Francisco's Dharma Festival and at Sand Dollar Books in Berkeley. The Dante project came to stand as a distillation of Duncan's views on war, anarchy, and institutional power, springing not only out of his close readings of *Convivio, De Monarchia,* and *De Vulgari Eloquentia,* but also out of his correspondence with Denise Levertov during the Viet Nam war. As in "Santa Cruz Propositions," the theme of rage, a particularly feminine force in Duncan's mind, rose to the surface. Dotting the poems with references to a "she" who might "arouse in us apocalypse," Duncan allowed the ominous figure to drift as the spirit of both mother and motherland.

Nineteen seventy-five would in fact mark the beginning of troubles in the motherland beyond the lingering traumas of Viet Nam and Watergate. As the country spiraled into an economic recession, Duncan imagined a life free of market forces. He observed the New Year by buying "near complete Gestetner equipment," an early version of the office photocopier.[2] He was still determined to have ultimate control over the typesetting and distribution of his work, and the purchase inspired him to move ahead with the first volume of *Ground Work*. Meanwhile, on January 8, in anticipation of the beginning of the spring semester, he headed to the University of California, Riverside, to make preparations for a ten-week creative writing workshop arranged by professors Ed Eigner and Milton Miller. Miller's wife, Darlene, recalled that Duncan's presence in the department "seemed like a major event," partly because of his nonconformist sensibility: "He hated the rooted chair-desks in the classroom assigned to him, felt the set-up wasn't right for a creative class and that it MATTERED."[3]

The job required travel to Los Angeles on Wednesday afternoons and returns to San Francisco on Thursday nights, but Duncan's enthusiasm about the class superseded the demands of air travel. Creative Writing 106X integrated the studies of phonetics and linguistics he'd begun early in his career, inspiring him to produce more reading notes on one of his favorite linguists, Otto Jespersen. The twenty students in the class agreed to forgo the presentation of emotion-driven poems, and Duncan reported to Helen Adam that he was "giving them exercises to build up a sense and ability in the musical potentialities of the language."[4] His outline for class discussions included topics such as "Sounds and Language: Vowels," "Articulation of the Language: Phonemes and Words," and "Stanzas, Parts, Sections, Cantos."

When not immersed in his work with the class, he contemplated the life changes that came with turning fifty-six. He had resumed piano lessons, and despite his full schedule, considered studying modern dance as a means of exercise. In other reminders of mortality, the elderly cat, Orlando, required dental surgery in January, and on March 11, just after completing his first stint at Riverside, Duncan succumbed to an attack of sciatica that necessitated a ten-day hospitalization. Ongoing renovations at 20th Street, including the installation of a new kitchen ceiling, only added to the ensuing chaos in Jess and Duncan's daily routine. Throughout the spring, consultations with doctors were the priority. The inflammation of Duncan's sciatic nerve, caused by a ruptured disc in his lumbar spine, created a sensation he described as akin to a violent toothache radiating from his hip down through his leg. He told friends that his first instinct was to request amputation.[5] Lacking health insurance, the couple drew upon the Symmes trust fund to cover the costs of doctors and physical therapists. Duncan, meanwhile, found himself immobilized and alone: "Second morning in the hospital in traction. Pain extreme in phases, then settling back to a comfortable ache. At times fearing anxiety—since I do not have any clear picture of consequences—if traction does not relieve the sciatica, an operation seems to be in the offing. But Dr. Burstein is evasive on the subject. And . . . I have no clear idea of the costs involved. And isolation—I will be ten days away from home."[6]

Between bouts of pain and drug-induced sleep, Duncan found small pleasures in reading. *Darwin on Man* by Howard Gruber and John Ashbery's new collection of poems, *Self-Portrait in a Convex Mirror,* were both at his bedside. Of the latter, he wrote, "Marvelous poem after marvelous poem. He has the manners of the largest weather, of a continuous coming and going in words, clear, even willing, delighting to be bland, clouds, overcast."[7] Music served as another passive entertainment during his recovery, and when Duncan returned home, he found solace in Beethoven's later work as well as in "classical potpourri from radio."[8]

Forced to postpone a second session in Riverside, Duncan maintained contact with the outside world through written correspondence, exchanging letters with the Eigners and other friends around the globe. In early April, he assured Helen Adam of his gradual recovery, and he joked in a letter to Australian poet Robert Adamson, "My 'completely' recoverd condition, of which I am assured now, will still have governing conditions—no horseback . . . , no jeep rides on rough roads or terrain . . . , no motorboats bouncing and slapping the waves, no trampolines, etc."[9]

On April 8, heeding the advice of Michael McClure, Duncan began classes in the Alexander Technique as a supplement to conventional physical therapy. By early May, with a reprieve from pain, he finished his preface for Allen Upward's *The Divine Mystery* and by midsummer he seemed well enough to travel again. A brief foray to a June 21 reading at Stanford University was followed by another attack of sciatica, and during a July 14 doctor's visit, Duncan was told to consider spinal surgery to slow the deterioration of the damaged disc.[10] Sent to bed for another ten days, he lay listening to the radio, while the responsibility of preparing meals, adjusting heating pads, and regulating doses of codeine and Valium fell to Jess. A meticulous caretaker, Jess kept a log of his partner's condition, documenting not only Duncan's emotional and physical states but also the rituals of the household. Visits with guests took place from 2:00 to 3:30 in the afternoon, and the lights were turned out nightly by 11:30.

Duncan's inactivity, including nearly a month of bed rest, drew him into a depression and sparked nightmares of physical trauma. In one dream, transcribed by Jess, "he was an insect, a bee, with other workers in the flower banks being injured and disabled, he was cast from his hive, sent down into his pain, engulfed among the flowers, on his back . . . his mind lookt down on this from the outside . . . , trying but not understanding the lesson."[11] While a late-summer round of visitors, including Harold Dull, Michael Davidson, and John Ashbery, improved Duncan's mood somewhat, he remained agitated. His movements were restricted to short walks through the hallway outside his bedroom, and he relied on house guests for opportunities to socialize. In late August, another wave of friends visited 20th Street, and Robert Bertholf arrived from Ohio to begin the ambitious project of sorting Duncan's papers to create a bibliography of his life's work.[12]

Through autumn weeks filled with the anxiety of continued back spasms, Duncan made short, selective forays into the world. The San Francisco opera season brought the pleasure of works by Wagner, and he also looked forward to continuing his teaching in Riverside. Simplifying his preparations, Duncan presented three weeks of lectures with a recycled title: "Ideas of the Meaning of Form in Poetry." By late October, he had also composed a new poem, "Empedoklean Reveries," which touched upon his health difficulties and revealed emerging tensions in his relationship with Jess. While Duncan's illness had placed a strain on the couple, a deeper crisis of intimacy was looming:

> Don't wife me,   you arouse
> that animus   the wrathful knight   who upholds
> the honor of the Lady Anima,   her token,   that handkerchief
>   to be stolen by her handmaiden.   Her confidence
>
> bridles at the touch   in touch   music
>
>   the wedding ground of Harmony   and Discordia
>
>   melody ever upon the point   of   leaving   returning
>   a turmoil of sound the center and surrounding
> begins:
>
>   Love ever contending with Hate.
>
>   Hate ever contending with Love.[13]

A new face in the household did little to smooth the rumblings of discord. In late 1975, eminent classics scholar Norman Austin, on sabbatical from the University of California, Los Angeles, wrote to Duncan to reintroduce himself, having had a fleeting encounter with Duncan in Berkeley in 1959. Poised, intelligent, and strikingly handsome, he materialized like a ghost of Ned Fahs, fulfilling Duncan's adolescent fantasies of the ideal lover. Having come north to study with Jane Brown of the Lesser Oakland Dance Theatre, Austin found that he would also act as a muse to the poet he had admired from a distance. His presence that autumn inspired the closing

sequence of poems for *Ground Work,* and Duncan was quick to mytholo-
gize their fledgling friendship in "Eidolon of the Aion":

> who are you?   Dark Star,
> coming back into my life,   arranging
> weddings thruout of
> themes and incidents [14]

Nearly two decades Duncan's junior and intrigued by the poet's "formidable
and unique" intellect, Austin remembered a more complicated reality: "At
first I was enjoying the friendship without being as infatuated as he was.
Then I realized how strong his feelings were."[15] While working to deflect
Duncan's overtures, Austin was nonetheless drawn to the good company of
weekly lunch meetings, sometimes at 20th Street and sometimes in Berke-
ley. Duncan, channeling his libidinous instincts into his work, spent the end
of the year composing "An Interlude of Winter Light," in which he conjured
an image of his first meeting with Austin some sixteen years earlier:

> Fugitive evangel of morning,
> I don't know in what sense you are *"mine".*
>   Yet I was waiting.   Were you
> barely fitting the shadow of an old desire
>   the mind would not let go,   or
> do you come as the river of fire in the poem comes
>   surpassing what the mind would *know,*
> until Life looms over my little life like a mountain,
>   the gods themselves coming forward therein
> to light the way but of a second *"ours".*
>
> . . . .
>
> A second hour,   a second time,   a second life--
>
>   I do not want to let a second go,   and
>   talking with you,
>
> oo
> I try to sow the seed of what I am throughout,
>   as if there were secreted from long ago
>   something I was   entirely *yours*[16]

Austin's critical study of Homer, *Archery at the Dark of the Moon,* was on
Duncan's reading list for the winter, perhaps inspiring him to consider a

new project of his own. That December, he proposed a prose collection, later to be titled *Fictive Certainties,* to New Directions editor Fred Martin, telling him that his fifteen-year vow of silence in the realm of poetry need not "extend to the question of essays."[17] On another front, just before the start of 1976, Ekbert Faas visited San Francisco to complete interviews toward his Duncan biography, and in a season that usually filled Duncan with dread, the week between the New Year and his birthday contained some cheer. On January 2, he began the long poem "The Presence of the Dance / The Resolution of the Music," again saturated with references to Norman Austin. The poem returned to Duncan's earlier Steinian tone and pointed toward his enthusiasm for the fantasy of sexual experience rather than the consummation of it. Seemingly content to circle around Austin and make playful gestures of affection, Duncan wrote,

> I am addressing a proposition of moving in a declaration independently of moving. He was about to be moving or he moves into being moving until an absolute stillness became possible. "Now" appeard to him in order to give him time to dance where he was moving. This lookt at first as if he could return to a place where he just now was. And he stood between simply standing and taking his stand.[18]

FIFTY-SIX

The Heart of Rime

Seven o'clock in the morning renews itself over breakfast
—the richness of coffee, the full flavor of the bread
toasted, the assorted jams and marmalades— we
initiate the naming of the day
with the institution of a choice of things
and repetitions of our way,   yet
altering minutely the course of decisions thruout
design and unalterable variations.

ROBERT DUNCAN, "An Alternate Life"

JANUARY 1976 brought an end to Duncan's two-year self-imposed morato-
rium on long-distance business travels. Giving up the hope of being at home
to witness a major earthquake, he reengaged with the world of poetry and
began one of his busiest years on the reading circuit. At the age of fifty-
seven, his public recognition as a writer allowed him to earn a reasonable
professional income from readings, though it meant spending more time
away from Jess. Having shared a household for a little over a quarter of a cen-
tury, the couple had come to recognize the complexities of the life they had
built together. At an appearance in the spring, Duncan talked about domes-
ticity and the long-term relationship: "I would rather make up love like you
make up valentines than not have it around. The real thing may be hate, but
I'm not going to tune in on the real thing. . . . I'll take the wildest pretend.
And pretend doesn't do bad over time. Now this is the twenty-fifth year of
pretend."[1]

In February, he had an opportunity to think about such matters from a
distance. Leaving San Francisco after completing dental work that included
the extraction of an incisor, he gave a February 13 reading in Seattle followed
by a brief trip to Vancouver to see Warren and Ellen Tallman. On February
17, news came from Southern California that Wallace Berman had died in
a car accident on the eve of his fiftieth birthday. With little time to grieve,
Duncan completed a series of business obligations, on February 19 reading
at the University of Santa Clara and on February 22 flying to Lawrence for a

weeklong residency at the University of Kansas. Occupied by meetings with students and meals with colleagues Ed Grier, Richard Colyer, and Edward Ruhe, Duncan made the most of the visit. Ruhe, a collector of Australian art and artifacts, provided him with a tour of his collection as well as access to his library. With plans to visit Sydney in the autumn, Duncan spent his free time browsing through Ruhe's books and reading *The Landscape of Australian Poetry* by Brian Elliot.

Upon Duncan's return home, he and Jess spent the first two weeks of March contending with business that neither of them could easily stomach. Shaken by Wallace Berman's death and well aware of their encroaching health problems, the couple asked Berkeley lawyer Michael Ferguson to draft a joint will for them. The document made clear Duncan's commitment to the Bay Area, leaving his literary papers to the Bancroft Library and his art collection to the Oakland Museum. He named three executors to his literary estate—Michael Davidson, Robert Bertholf, and Leslie Clark—and made Jess the executor of his will as a whole, to be succeeded by old friend Tolbert McCarroll. While amendments were made to it shortly before Duncan's death in 1988, the document signed in 1976 remained the only legally recognized paperwork addressing Duncan's estate.

In mid-March, after returning to the Pacific Northwest to perform at the And/Or Gallery in Seattle, Duncan was escorted by Warren Tallman to Vancouver, where he gave a March 15 reading and spoke in a class at the request of Gladys Hindmarch of Capilano College. The following week he was in Los Angeles to see George Herms, who had also been close to Wallace Berman. After meeting with Herms at his studio on March 22, Duncan dined with Norman Austin, then back at work in Southern California but would continue to visit Duncan and Jess in San Francisco that spring and summer. Traveling south to San Diego, Duncan settled into Michael Davidson's beach cottage and prepared for a March 23 reading in the University of California's New Poetry Series. San Diego would be a mainstay of Duncan's tours through the end of the 1970s, and Davidson, then the curator of the university's poetry archive, would often escort his friend and mentor to various Southern California colleges. Opening his reading in San Diego with the recently written "Childhood's Retreat," Duncan moved to assert his continued commitment to anarchist politics, taking issue with the word *gay* and with the gay studies courses then springing up in colleges around the country: "I would have questions about any of the new minority movements simply because it seems to me that the whole issue of our time is that we barely . . . hold on to . . . writing as human beings, which is the hardest thing of all to do. To write as a woman or to write as a man or to write as a black or to write as a gay poet is absolutely minor compared with 'how do we hold this new human conscience?' "[2] Perhaps the recent discord in his relationship with Jess was on his mind as he closed the reading with two poems addressing sexual desire and domestic life, "The Torso" and "These Past Years."

On March 24, Duncan gave a reading at Saddleback College in Mission Viejo, returning to San Diego two days later to present a lecture on Ezra Pound. Back home in San Francisco, his week continued with an April 1 reading alongside James Broughton and Madeline Gleason at the San Francisco Museum of Art. Again spending less than a week at home, he left in early April for a tour of Winnipeg, Toronto, Minneapolis, Washington, and New York. His duties began on April 5 with a lecture to a modern American literature class at the University of Manitoba St. John's College. Hosted there by Dennis Cooley and Dorothy Livesay, during his four-day visit, he had a few moments to return to an essay he was composing on Freud and Jung.[3] Jess wrote that week reminding him to rest, but the plea fell on deaf ears. From St. John's, Duncan headed to Toronto, where he stayed with poet and editor Victor Coleman and gave a reading at Coleman's A Space arts center. Remaining in the Toronto area until April 23, he also made an appearance at Erindale College.

Duncan's rounds during those weeks were carefully documented in his journal. In a post-tax-day frenzy, he catalogued all his tax-deductible business expenses, scrawling meal costs, book costs, and cab fares in the margins alongside reading notes and poems. In Minneapolis, he visited the Walker Art Center, bought books for Jess, and bought luggage for $56.89. In Stillwater, Minnesota, he bought a $9 bottle of liqueur for Carl and Leah Rakosi. With a micromanagerial flair, he recorded a 20-cent phone call at the Washington airport on April 24 and a $4.75 cab ride on April 25 to visit the Edelsteins in Washington. The trip to the capital came with a gratifying April 26 luncheon and reading at the Library of Congress in honor of Duncan and Jerome Rothenberg and moderated by Stanley Kunitz.

From Washington, Duncan made a happy return to New York for both business and pleasure. Between an April 28 reading at the Poetry Project on the Lower East Side and an April 29 reading at Barnard College, he spent time with Robert Wilson, Helen and Pat Adam, and Kenward Elmslie, and made an excursion to Long Island to visit friends Madeline and Bill Lufak at Great River. Home in San Francisco for most of May, he journeyed into the closing poem of *Ground Work,* "Circulations of the Song," synthesizing his thoughts about his marriage to Jess and his infatuation with Norman Austin. The composition drew from his summertime reading of the thirteenth-century Persian poet Jalal al-din Rumi, and the piece became one of the key love poems of his career. He told Barbara Joseph that it was but one of many projects to occupy him that year: "This is . . . a rich writing period for me. I have finisht the first set of a Diwan after . . . Rumi, Duncan Sufism, and am working on a long essay as part III of another poem: these all belonging to a cluster of works that . . . have been swelling on the vine. . . . Set by set coming ripe."[4] In the months during which Duncan's libidinous attentions had been divided, "Circulations of the Song" arrived at a "he" that encompassed his love for both Jess and Austin while pointing toward a larger mythological manifestation of love via the Greek Eros. But at the heart of the poem was Jess:

> How happy I am in your care, my old companion of the way!
> The long awaiting,   the sometimes bitter hope,
>   have sweetened in these years of the faith you keep.
> How completely I said "yes" when it came to me
> and continue.   Each morning awakening you set free
>   another day for me.[5]

After a brief visit in late May to see friends Robert Peters and Paul Trachtenberg in Huntington Beach, California, Duncan prepared for another business trip. The venue was Boulder, Colorado's Naropa Institute, where during a three-day residency, Duncan taught a seminar and gave a reading and lecture for the institute's recently founded Jack Kerouac School of Disembodied Poetics.[6] Established in 1974 by Tibetan lama Chögyam Trungpa Rinpoche, the institute provided a meeting ground for the Buddhist community in the Rocky Mountains. Its writing program, organized by Allen Ginsberg and Anne Waldman, with the help of San Francisco poet Diane di Prima, brought together writers of international stature with students eager to participate in a scene charged with the excitement of poetry, alternative religion, and post-1960s experiments with sex and drugs. Situated on a small grassy block of downtown Boulder at the base of the Rockies, the school had a certain charm, its classes held beneath a vista of red rock, shady evergreens, and vast blue desert skies.

Duncan arrived with some ambivalence about the community and some doubts about how he would be received. Allen Ginsberg was in all ways

Boulder's celebrity poet, and John Ashbery, recent recipient of the Pulitzer Prize, was slated to make an appearance later that summer.[7] But for the students, Duncan's visit was more than welcome, and one young New York poet, Tom Savage, considered Duncan's presence a high point: "Duncan was this amazingly graceful individual. I've never seen a person teach a class that seemed like a dance that he was putting out spontaneously . . . he would grab up ideas as if out of the air, from nowhere."[8] In the edgy bohemian environment at Naropa, Duncan presented an alternative role model, arriving, as Savage recalled, with "a kind of cool sanity in the midst of all these lunatics running around with a kind of Buddhism that totally ignored one-third of Buddhism . . . the morality of it."[9] Aware of a chemistry between himself and Duncan, the twenty-eight-year-old Savage made sexual overtures, and the two spent a night together, which Savage described in an unpublished poem called "The Interview":

> I brought you my words
> you sat working
> no words
> no strictures in open
> space
> you explained workings
> I used
> better than I understand.
> We made love.[10]

The affair with Savage gave Duncan reason to be grateful for the trip, and there were less delicate engagements to enjoy as well. Helen Adam was a fellow visiting teacher at Naropa that summer, performing alongside Duncan for a large and receptive audience on June 9. Between their official activities, Adam and Duncan hiked in the foothills and had tea with the charismatic Tibetan guru Trungpa Rinpoche. Anne Waldman recalled that Duncan donned a business suit for the meeting and mined Trungpa for information about Tibetan Buddhism: "[Duncan] was delighted by the contradictions of the hierarchal Buddhist system with the 'open system' and fields of the New American poetry. He was curious about Tibetan (Medieval) poetics . . . Milarepa. Was Trungpa re-incarnating as a poet lifetime after lifetime? He saw certain structures, myths, hierarchies in terms of the 'fairy tale.' "[11] On June 10, in an animated final lecture to a community he had begun to warm to during his brief stay, Duncan discussed the role of religious ideas in his work, touching upon the influence of Browning in his early writing and taking a whirlwind tour of ideas about Whitman, "the poet as maker," and concepts of reality.[12] Identifying himself as a distinctly non-Buddhist participant in the institute's activities, Duncan said, "I want you to remember that . . . I am solidly a spirit of that conjunction of the Jewish and the Celtic world and . . . the great idea which came down from Greece, that of making a poem, of fabricating."[13] He wrote later that he had been "fishing and baiting various Buddhist prejudices."[14] But he was also determined to establish an aesthetic niche distinct from that of the political poem:

> Our actual art is to attend where we are. Now that means precision. What do I do in a poem? . . . The only time my art comes forward is when I am actually attentive and immediately recognizing what those words are saying and bringing forward, and I work with them. I do not use language, I cooperate with language, and that is a great distinction. . . . Gary Snyder uses language to give you a message, a good one, but that's what he uses it for. [Kenneth] Rexroth preached the use of language, and at that point I was no longer related to Rexroth. . . . I have my own orders. . . . I knew that I was not to use language but to cooperate with it.[15]

The exhilaration of Boulder behind him, in mid-June Duncan settled into the sunny breakfast nook at home every morning, sipping his coffee while documenting in his journal trips to the dentist, preparations for his September travels to Australia, and outings with Jess to museums, the Salvation Army, and bookstores. The kitchen's three columns of windows gave a view of the Chinese elms in the yard, and the sun's rays flickered through stained glass panels overhead. Much of his writing was done in that space as Jess worked upstairs in his studio, completing two new pieces in the *Translations* series, *Every Night and Alle* and *The Truth Shall Be Thy Warrant,* and embarking on a series of collages for a February 1977 exhibition of his work. In mid-June, Duncan also presented a new production of *Adam's Way,* first at the San Francisco Museum of Art on June 17 and then at the Church of the Advent on June 22. The cast included actors Duncan had little experience with, and he reserved for himself the role of the Narrator.[16]

In the rainy, foggy midsummer, the house was filled with the sounds of Saint-Saens' "Concerto Number Three" and Charles Alkan's piano works. Outside of the house, Duncan took interest in an entirely different musical experience, participating in an improvisational band started by Michael McClure. Dubbed the Elegant Buffoons, the group modeled itself after "a traditional Fukanese or Taiwanese poet's band, in which poets got together and played brass drinking cups, and bells, and castanets and whatever traditional instruments they knew how to use."[17] Duncan manned the percussion section, equipped "with a rubber drum, a coffee cup, and woodblock."[18] Michael Palmer played in some of the sessions, as did Ron Silliman, who recalled, "McClure was the leader . . ., and it took place at his house. . . . A composer out of Santa Cruz . . . Chris Gaynor . . . was also key (the actual leader of events, as such). I got to participate twice, tho not with Duncan that I recall. Whalen was there once. I remember playing Koto (I have no formal music education whatsoever), using a Navajo rug as our score."[19]

Meanwhile, Norman Austin remained a presence in Duncan's life and poems. The two men met for lunch several times in August while Austin was in town preparing for a Lesser Oakland Dance Theatre production based on Shakespeare's plays. Duncan attended the company's August 7 performance, in which Austin danced the parts of Oberon, Brabantio, and Claudius. Another installment of "The Presence of the Dance / The Resolution of the Music" arrived soon after:

> My Love, for a moment you present yourself or I present you, and this Presence, this Lord of Title, for he has title to me here, is the Night upon whose reaches this morning calld to me. Oberon, you said, you were to dance.[20]

The poems celebrating Duncan's attachment to Norman Austin stood in stark contrast to the reality of his sexual life with Jess. In his notebooks, Duncan pondered Jess's physical withdrawal, and Jess also broached the subject in a letter:

> That great new poem ["The Presence of the Dance"], even from its first stanzas arriving last year, brought me again to my inadequacies and the sorrow and chagrin at failing you. Sexually, is my meaning here, but also physically just in itself as my body in its deteriorations did not give more pleasure than the aches it exacted. This Western culture will not let one age easily and condemns an inward turning of sex. I only remember two attempts to talk of this with you, at least two years ago, but it was too soon for you not to try to make light and deflect the moment, perhaps to avoid your bitter disappointment in me—and I could not find words again or opening even to try. Again, when last year you said "it's maybe I'm ugly to you," this impossibility destroyed by irony my hopes you could approve my own ugliness.[21]

Throughout their relationship, the two shared an almost Victorian attitude about intimacy. Their physical contact had always been simple, with lovemaking restricted to mutual masturbation and occasional oral sex.[22] In the aftermath of Duncan's bout of sciatica, Jess developed his own aches and pains brought on by varicose veins and phlebitis. Alone together, the partners sublimated their physical desires into other shared activities, their days spent completing jigsaw puzzles and their evenings spent watching *Star Trek, Hogan's Heroes,* and *Upstairs, Downstairs.* While the bedroom may have lost its amatory charm, it remained the center of the household, the place they curled up together at night to share readings of ghost stories and fantasy tales, as they had done for twenty-five years.

When Norman Austin returned to Southern California in late August, the forces of Eros shifted, and the entertaining at 20th Street returned to a pattern more suited to Jess's temperament. Lunch visits with Ida Hodes and Lynn Lonidier were followed by an August 22 feast with Michael Palmer and Cathy Simon at which the dinner guests faced one of Duncan and Jess's more exotic recipes with some trepidation: a heart sauté seasoned with peppers and curry.[23] Since Duncan first met Palmer in the early 1970s, the two had increasingly begun to share aesthetics. Palmer, though a generation younger than Duncan, became the elder poet's preferred audience for recitations of new work, and was frequently sought out for an exchange of ideas about translation, teaching, and local poetry politics.

Duncan kept another matrix of his social life from Jess's view, the beginnings of a relationship with the young San Francisco poet Aaron Shurin. Shurin dated his first encounter with Duncan to early 1976:

> I was riding on the street car downtown . . . and I saw Robert . . . and so I had to go up to him and introduce myself. . . . For me, it was . . . a cosmic coincidence, because the day or two days before I had had one of the great dreams of my life. I had dreamt that I was on a mountaintop and this little loop of a rainbow appeared, pulsating in the most extreme terms, and absolutely of deific power, and it . . . stormed me off my feet and almost blew me off the clifftop. The next day, I was in Berkeley, and I had just begun to read Robert's work, and I picked up *The Opening of the Field* and I opened immediately to a poem called "The Natural Doctrine," which mentions a Rabbi Aaron of Baghdad and has the last line "the actual language is written in rainbows." So I had this completely cosmic dream, I had found it addressed in a Duncan poem, and then I met Robert, all in this one fold. . . . I was . . . practically shaking from the experience, and I told it to him, and he was so completely unmoved as if to say it was completely in order . . . that it wasn't hard for him to believe at all, that such a synchronicity in poetry and personal life took place, that that was completely the way things did take place in fact.[24]

Shurin had grown up in New York and Los Angeles and had studied with Denise Levertov at Berkeley in the 1960s. His meeting with Duncan in 1976 would burgeon into an emotionally complex relationship, beginning with their first sexual encounter at Shurin's Frederick Street apartment in late August. While the twenty-nine-year-old felt some ambivalence about Duncan's advances, he also found it difficult to refuse the esteemed elder poet. Duncan became a teacher and friend through whom he found his own way into a poetics. The importance of the relationship for Duncan was evident in a gift he left with Shurin after they made love. On the title page of an Australian edition of *The Venice Poem,* he penned verses that revealed his grief about the end of his sexual life with Jess and his gratitude to Shurin for their shared intimacy:

> Upon the Hour
> the Bells ring forth
> the Lion roars,
> but Human laughter and Human tears
> dissolve the solemnities of Time
> and in the quieting of the body's fears
> the moment opens
> wide
> an Everlasting Flower
> from the heart of Rhyme.[25]

SEVEN

Troubadour

FIFTY-SEVEN

An Alternate Life

You told me that you felt like you had set a match to brittle grass.... I wish you could see the flames here now. TE-REA NOLAN TO ROBERT DUNCAN, February 5, 1977

FOR THE WRITERS OF AUSTRALIA, Robert Duncan's arrival inspired dramatic change. The poet owed his September 1976 trek to Sydney to the efforts of Robert and Cheryl Adamson, the editors of *New Poetry*. Robert Adamson later reminisced to Duncan about their initial contact some four years earlier:

> When I got your letter I was living in a small fishing village on the Hawkesbury about fifty miles from Sydney and no phone or transport—it was around ten in the morning, winter . . . , and a magic sunny day. I read your letter over and over, there was no one to share it with. I ran down to the local store and showed it to Mrs. Styles whose only contact with poetry was me. She hadn't heard of Slessor or Eliot let alone Robert Duncan. My excitement must have been infectious because she was so proud—and suggested . . . that I use her phone to ring my mother; I did and told my bewildered mother that I'd just received a letter from the most famous poet in the world![1]

Duncan's four-week stay in Australia was, from its onset, emotionally complicated—a working vacation during which he also faced the realities of aging and the beginning of a new phase in his life as a writer. With the poems of *Ground Work* almost complete, he saw uncharted territory before him that awakened a myth from his parents' theosophical tradition: one cycle of teachings was ending, and, at the age of fifty-seven, he would begin a new one.[2] The impressive landscape of the Southern Hemisphere, its brilliant night sky, and the enthusiasms of the Australian poetry community set the stage for such a passage.

With an evening departure from San Francisco on Friday August 27, Duncan flew toward Australia via Los Angeles and planned a stop in Fiji to avoid the more exhausting option of traveling straight through via a series of transfers. Landing in Nadi at dawn on August 29, he took a cross-island bus trip to Suva, viewing a novel terrain of grasslands, rainforests, and volcanic ridges. The layover also provided an opportunity for additional income: an August 30 session with a creative writing class at the University of the South Pacific in Laucala Bay.

Duncan soon flew on to Sydney, where his hosts for the first week of September were the Adamsons in nearby Lane Cove. Aware of Robert Adamson's reputation for a bacchanalian lifestyle, the visiting poet made it his first order of business to post a list of rules on the refrigerator, including the commandment that there be no drinking before the dinner hour.[3] His fear of being trapped in an unruly bohemian household was countermanded by his immediate fondness for the Adamsons and by the availability of "a real bathroom and a real kitchen, and so forth."[4] The couple was enlisted as a prime audience for Duncan's round-the-clock monologues and as coconspirators in his social plans. Robert Adamson remembered the range of Duncan's enthusiasms from the start: "He wanted to get back to the house to do an experiment. He wanted to see if water went the other way down the drain . . . of a sink in Australia. He wanted to see the southern skies at night. He wanted to see the birds, the gum trees, Sydney harbour, meet poets and painters, but more than anything to see the night sky."[5]

On September 2, Duncan gave an early-afternoon reading at Sydney University, his first public appearance on the continent. A young poet named Chris Edwards was present for that event, and their meeting set the tone for the rest of Duncan's trip. Edwards recalled

> walking across the courtyard in one of the university buildings toward the table where [Duncan] was sitting with Bob and Cheryl and a few others. He was looking right at me as I approached, and I was looking right back, except that because he was cross-eyed, I wasn't quite sure where to focus. We talked quite a bit, both before and after the reading, and a day or so later, I was invited to stay at Lane Cove while Robert was in town. I often stayed there anyway. I jumped at the chance.[6]

The blond, beach-tawny twenty-one-year-old stood out in a poetry scene dominated by older, more established writers. Still living at home and uncertain of his career path, Edwards was enchanted by the opportunity to get to know the San Francisco poet. That week, one of Duncan's letters to Jess mentioned Edwards as part of a group of students clamoring for his time. The greater truth was that Duncan would pursue Edwards during his time in Sydney and that the two would engage in what Robert Adamson later described as "a love affair of the intellect."[7]

Duncan's second evening of public appearances took place at the Watters Gallery, an event that would also remain clear in Adamson's mind: "There was none of the usual madness that attended the poetry readings of the seventies in Sydney, not one maniac or fight, no one felt the need to hurl abuse.... Duncan had managed to bring together poets from many warring factions and had dis-spelled every form of negativity."[8] While local writers reveled in Duncan's presence, their American guest fought off fatigue and jet lag, confiding to Jess that he was barely able to process the energies of a city "as thick with poets as San Francisco."[9] The Adamsons had helped him pack his schedule with public appearances, and his first week in Australia included three lectures on American poetry and an additional reading at the Wayside Chapel with Adamson, Robert Harris, and John Millett.

Duncan found a brief break from the crowds with a visit to Robert Adamson's family in the backcountry of the Hawkesbury River. While nervous about introducing the poet to a clan that included his elderly fisherman grandfather, Adamson was nevertheless impatient to share a slice of his world with Duncan. Duncan appeared from his room that morning dressed as a dandy in his black velvet jacket, ready for a drive to "the top of Mount Cola" to catch a "first glimpse of the river, the ancient mountains and gum trees."[10] Whatever doubts Adamson had about the plan melted away as he watched Duncan in action:

> We arrived at my grandfather's house and my aunt Cathy ... offered Duncan a beer, it was only nine in the morning, he declined and took the cup of tea instead. Before we had time to start talking Cathy asked me if I would change a light bulb for her.... The bulb was welded into its socket so the whole operation took a good fifteen minutes.... By the time I got back to the kitchen Duncan had gone out on to the veranda and met up with my grandfather. They were talking in a very engaged manner but the conversation had come to a pause....
>
> I was intrigued, what on earth had they been talking about for so long in such a conspiratorial manner? [Later] when we sat down on the stone jetty and looked out over the river, I asked Duncan what he thought of my grandfather. "Why he's a poet, an expert scholar of folk music, a gentleman." And what were they talking about? "Jimmy Rogers."[11]

A boat tour of the river followed, with Adamson rowing while Duncan "just kept talking," spinning stories of Ezra Pound, Anaïs Nin, Mallarmé, Mondrian, marriage, and ornithology as "the skiff slid through the tide past rows of oysterbeds on their racks" in a "prehistoric landscape."[12]

On September 9, Duncan had another view of Australia from his window seat on a flight to Melbourne. In the second stop of his multicity tour, he rendezvoused with writer Jim Hamilton before giving a reading for the Writers Society Meeting at Melbourne University. Housed with poet Barbara Giles, then in her midsixties, Duncan found like-minded company and a break from the bustle of Sydney: "a pleasant momentary change to have the conversation of an entirely other Australia."[13] Giles, who had come to writing late, engaged Duncan not with news from the poetry scene but with talk of American and Australian politics.

The five days in Melbourne were followed by a stop in Adelaide. While there, he was interviewed by poet Ian Reid on September 13, gave a reading at Flinders University on September 16, and delivered daily lectures at the University of Adelaide. Moving on to Perth, he fulfilled a three-day residency at the University of Western Australia, ultimately returning to Sydney on September 22.

As his tour drew to a close, Duncan gave a final performance at Sydney's Hogarth Gallery and then spent a weekend with the Adamsons and Chris Edwards in Lane Cove.[14] Attempting to navigate his feelings for Edwards, Duncan made an advance that his young companion was unprepared for:

> We'd had an enjoyable dinner at David Malouf's flat . . . on Sydney Harbour— ten or twelve people, . . . Bruce and Brenda Beaver were there. Robert was always in high spirits in their company, just as they were in his. . . . After dinner, back at Lane Cove, Bob and Cheryl settled down . . . in the living room and Robert took the bedroom. I slept in the *New Poetry* office. What happened next forms the basis of "An Alternate Life," which is pretty accurate . . . in its description, notwithstanding its "dangerously poetic" language. I was making my bed when Robert came in and, without a word, began "releasing" the "catches" of my shirt, kissing me. . . . I took him by the hand, told him it didn't feel right and started shaking uncontrollably. I remember asking "What about Jess?" He didn't answer . . . at the time, but he did later, in the poem. The only embellishment I can find [in the poem] is where "an old man's hand fumbles at the young man's crotch." That didn't happen. Robert was very gracious in fact. Once I'd stopped shaking, he just quietly left the room.[15]

The following morning, September 26, sitting at the Adamsons' kitchen table amid the din of breakfast talk and clattering plates, Duncan penned the opening sequence of "An Alternate Life," the first poem of *Ground Work II*. The multipart composition took root from "Circulations of the Song," continuing complex meditations on love, intimacy, and aging. The alternating landscapes of Sydney and San Francisco appeared, as did the alternating figures of Jess and Chris Edwards. Like others of Duncan's love poems, it maintained an ambiguity of subject, partly to indicate the shifting manifestations of the Eros and partly to shelter Jess from yet another infidelity. Edwards figured heavily into the piece, as an object of sexual arousal, as a soul mate, and as a messenger of Duncan's mortality. The poet's lament for Edwards came in the opening section:

> Tho you were only an incident in an alternate life,
> and there I was   as the Lover always is,
> swift, leading,   seeking to release the catches of your shirt,
> broody, sweet,   tendering the flame of hurt in the healing,
>
> here, in the one life I am leading, I am,
> as the Lover always is,   alone before a hand that holds forth
> the burning of a heart for me to eat again.[16]

Before departing the Adamsons's, Duncan tore the handwritten verses from his notebook, crept to Edwards's bedside, and left the pages for the young writer to find upon waking from an afternoon nap. The time they had spent together was important to both men for a number of reasons, and as Edwards later wrote to Duncan, it was also conflicted:

> You have asked me to confront certain aspects of what was happening...
> that I might not have otherwise confronted....I had been awaiting your
> visit...and then when you were here that kind of "master-student" relation-
> ship came quickly to seem...irrelevant. Surely I was "taught" by you—
> but...there is the pun of a tautness which is at once an attraction and a
> moving-apart—and I knew very strongly throughout September the fear of
> a planet or alternate sun which is drawn at once by a gravitational field...
> but which fears the ignition and consequent destruction...upon...moving
> too close.[17]

After completing his tour with a two-day visit to New Zealand in early October, Duncan made the long flight home to San Francisco. Throughout late autumn and into the following year, he continued composing "An

Alternate Life." With its vignettes of his intimate relationships with Jess and others, the poem was filled with mourning. Over twenty-six years of marriage, Duncan and Jess had not only built a household, they had gained weight and gone gray. "An Alternate Life" paved the way for Duncan's final volume of poems to be "the somber coda of the natural symphony."[18] During his first nights of jet-lagged insomnia after the trip, Duncan wrote a phrase in his journal that led to *Ground Work II*'s subtitle: "The second night 'in the dark' staring."[19] The poems composed between the fall of 1976 and 1985 led Duncan toward the dark of a terminal illness that eclipsed his ability to write. But as *Ground Work II* evolved, additional themes emerged. Beginning formal studies of the French language, settling into reveries of his classes with Ernst Kantorowicz, and paying specific heed to the work of the English metaphysical poets, Duncan would inflect his final poems with the world across the Atlantic. Trips to Europe during the late 1970s and early 1980s played heavily in his imagination of the book. In anticipation of a summer tour of France and Austria in 1979, Duncan wrote,

> My "appointment" with the country of the troubadours and of the 12th century alembic of revelation, cult and romance—the appointment now, I see, of a book in the heartland: that "South" and langue-d'oc— . . . I will, with my barest grasp of French, be running into Occitan (for the French an ununderstandable French)—that country between Toulouse and Carcasonne [sic] seems to me an actual ground of ground-work. The theme, dream central to the second volume begins to emerge.[20]

Throughout October of 1976, Duncan returned to Bay Area responsibilities, toward the end of the month giving a classroom lecture called "Composition by Field in Painting" at the San Francisco Art Institute followed by an evening reading. Duncan and Jess also made the most of the opera season that year with old friends David and Hilde Burton. Duncan explained his fascination with opera to an audience that spring: "This is my third year of going to the entire opera seasons. . . . The reason I go to entire opera seasons is that by the time I came to my mid-fifties I simply regressed to my parents who went to entire opera seasons."[21] Hilde Burton remembered Duncan's obsessively democratic approach to opera viewing. While critics panned or praised variations in staging and casts, Duncan wanted to see each opera from several creative perspectives, cataloguing what was unique about each production.[22] Early in November, he was home to vote in the 1976 election. At the turn of the year, Gerald Ford would cede the presidency to Jimmy Carter, and Carter would inherit a country in the midst of a historic recession and the largest peacetime budget deficit in its history. A post-Viet Nam, post-Watergate lethargy was spreading over the country, and disco was the latest rave. Duncan meanwhile participated in one of the more spectacular death knells of the period, a farewell performance of the Band on Thanksgiving night 1976 at San Francisco's Winterland Theater. He joined several other local writers in giving readings at the event, which also boasted an appearance by Bob Dylan. When Martin Scorsese released a documentary of the proceedings titled *The Last Waltz,* he left the footage of Duncan's reading on the cutting-room floor.[23]

But more than anything that winter, Duncan's thoughts returned to the Southern Hemisphere. On December 10, he received notice that the New Guinean artifacts he had purchased in Australia, including various native masks and figurines, had arrived by ship at a San Francisco customs office. The following day he made time to write to Chris Edwards again revisiting their autumn encounter: "You, Chris, now, along with Jess, who has just that distinction of . . . being my companion in a long lasting love, and but a few of my lovers, have charged the reality of the 'you' that the deepest impulse of Eros addresses; even as I have charged the reality of the 'I'—that personal charge is incident to the creative identity of the 'I' and the 'you.'"[24]

FIFTY-EIGHT

Cambridge

> Now truly the sexual Eros will have
> left me and gone on his way.
> . . . .
> At break of day and at
> midnight's time of play
> you are turned away from me.
>
> ROBERT DUNCAN, "An Alternate Life"

THE BEGINNING OF 1977 BROUGHT NEW STUDIES, with Duncan attending French classes at San Francisco's Alliance Française. Though he had learned French and Latin in high school, and muddled through Ancient Greek texts and German during his short stint as a medievalist, he was always most at home with English, and more specifically with American English. Duncan liked the grit of his "mother" tongue: he had been adopted into a pioneer family, and his Aunt Fay toward the end of her life had drifted back to the dialects and slang of her Oregon Trail upbringing. He too held fast to that sense of the American language, occasionally interjecting an "ain't" into his conversations and abbreviating words into colloquial phrasings in letters to friends. With French he faced a challenge, and he took every opportunity to test his newly acquired language skills, though his listeners sometimes recoiled in horror.

His work at the Alliance Française, preceded by sessions with a private tutor from the Sorbonne, came in preparation for springtime travels to Europe. A new vocabulary began to infiltrate the poems of *Ground Work II,* but still at the forefront of his writing that winter was an attempt to make peace with aging. A sequence composed before Christmas, "To Master Baudelaire," positioned his life with Jess within the larger history of humankind:

> And we too,
> my life companion and I,
> entertained our projects and fancies,

346

playd house and kept company
upon the edge of what we never knew then
you made clear was there
in the human condition—your *Ennui*

plus laid, plus méchant, plus immonde . . .[1]

Duncan included the melancholy three-part poem in a February 3 letter to
Chris Edwards, and later that month he wrote an autobiographical medita-
tion returning to the fears that had haunted him the previous year. "Making
It Up, Gathering What I Mean and Coming True" began,

> In this period of a threatening drought, a storm has arrived and I have awak-
> end . . . still to plunge myself into the cauldron . . . in which—it is the prom-
> ise we may read in old stories—I may come into a mind so ephemeral it is the
> very Eternal First Body and Last Body demonic powers have offered us. The
> rain, the deep purring of an ancient cat born seventeen years ago in this
> household, the everpresent background noise of certain motors—the refrig-
> erator, the furnace—the distant signal hoot of a train. . . . the night becomes
> an extension of longing and dread, of sounds long before and after.[2]

On the rainy morning of April 6, Duncan shared coffee with Jess and
Michael Palmer, reciting to them a new section of "An Alternate Life" titled
"The Quotidian."[3] That day he set off for Europe via Denver and Boston,
beginning his tour in Boulder, where he gave a reading at the University of
Colorado and met with faculty of the school's writing program, a group that
included Ron Sukenick, Alan Duggan, and Rise Axelrod. The next day he
headed to Fort Collins some two hours outside of Boulder. After dining
there with professor David Cheatham, Duncan shared the stage with Allen
Ginsberg at Colorado State University. On April 8, he boarded a noontime
flight to Boston, where he would appear at Radcliffe College and see a num-
ber of friends. Norman Austin was teaching in Amherst, and Portuguese
poet and translator Alberto de Lacerda was a visiting fellow at Boston Col-
lege. Lacerda, with whom Duncan had corresponded since their 1969 meet-
ing in Texas, showed Duncan a recently published catalogue celebrating his
work as a writer, translator, and artist. Moved by the scope of Lacerda's cre-
ative ventures, Duncan penned a prose poem titled "Pre Preface" on the
front page of the catalogue:

> There will always be for us poets opening out from the word "Paradise" this
> window into the swirling light of roses Love has set alight in our lives, of

certain days widening blue beyond the circumscription of horizon. There will always be divine causerie, talk of Heaven and talk that the heavenly verges upon. For we are children of What Is, you and I.[4]

Duncan's trip to Boston also allowed him an opportunity to see Elizabeth Bishop. The two shared a meal at the Akropolis restaurant, after which they browsed the shelves at the Harvard Bookstore. Black Mountain colleagues Don and Eloise Mixon, then living in Brookline, Massachusetts, provided Duncan with yet another satisfying reunion, accompanying him to a reading at Tufts University, his last stateside obligation before departing for London.

On April 14, Duncan was greeted at Heathrow Airport by Sandra Fisher and R. B. Kitaj, who again had offered him lodgings at their Elm Park Road flat. On this occasion, he had the additional good fortune of sharing the couple's guest quarters with Robert Creeley and his wife Penelope.[5] Both Duncan and Creeley had been invited to participate in the Second Cambridge World Poetry Conference, and Duncan commuted between the Kitaj home and Cambridge, visiting with friends in the area when not fulfilling his obligations at the festival. Penelope Creeley recalled her first meeting with "a very natty brown corduroy suited" Duncan that week in Cambridge:

> He was on one side of the street, we on the other. . . . Robert looked across, said "look, there's Duncan." His voice softened a bit, with pleasure. He often was shy about how to greet someone in circumstances like that, in fact would avoid them. But this time he smiled, . . . said "look at the walk. I'd know him anywhere." So we went over, came up on him from behind. They were so pleased to see each other I was swept up in the general warmth.[6]

On April 18, Duncan composed a prose poem for the festival first titled "A Talk to Cambridge" and later renamed "At Cambridge an Address to Young Poets Native to the Land of My Mothertongue." A reflection upon Duncan's language studies, the piece further anchored the new volume of *Ground Work* to the theme of a return to Europe:

> Did Bruno of Nola walk these streets and Marlowe in his ruddy youth run with these boys? What do they mean to do? Not here, not now. At the touch of What Is, Time undoes its holds. The giantesses of 1921 in their frocks of emerald crêpe de chine and cloth of gold have long passed into the glare of that shadow as far from what you know as William Shakespeare's sweet lips

and his phantom lover. England and America pass each other from under us into that glare.[7]

He performed the piece the following night, reading alongside Tom Raworth, Jacques Roubaud, and Charles Tomlinson. On April 21, he again took the stage, this time for a lecture titled "Current American Poetry Directions." Perhaps most important to Duncan was the opportunity to socialize with sympathetic writers from the United Kingdom, France, and America. That week he had dinner with British poet and conference organizer Richard Burns and also met with Tom Raworth, whom he had first gotten to know in the United States during the early 1970s. Black Mountain veteran Fielding Dawson was present at another social event related to the proceedings, a late-night pub gathering of conference revelers during which Duncan descended into a storm of "pathological screaming" when a woman asked him if he was interested in Carl Jung's work or the concept of the anima: "I saw just by chance he did one of those really awful freak-outs. People didn't know how . . . awful he could be, and it was . . . frightening. . . . He really let her have it. He was not so keen on Jung but everybody else was, certainly twenty years ago. She came up very nice, asked about Jung. . . . If everybody had not been so terrified, maybe . . . someone could have slapped him because he was so awful."[8]

As the Cambridge conference neared its end, Duncan gave a solo reading on April 23 at London's National Poetry Center. The rest of his stay in the United Kingdom was reserved for leisurely dinners in the Kitaj and Fisher household as well as snippets of sightseeing through various neighborhoods, including Camden Town. On the morning of April 28, en route to Paris, Duncan wrote to Chris Edwards noting with trepidation that he would soon deliver a lecture in French to a Belgian audience likely to include "the poet Denis Roche, and the theorist Derrida (at present a rage in American circles)."[9] Upon his arrival in Paris, he headed to the suburb of Chantilly to spend time with his translator, Serge Fauchereau, and his wife, Jocelyn, hoping to be coached through a rehearsal of the upcoming talk. Throughout the first week of May, Duncan shuttled between Paris and Chantilly, and on the fifth, he purchased train tickets to Brussels and Saint-Hubert, Belgium. The colloquium at Saint-Hubert, Le Récit et sa Représentation, at which he presented the talk "Son écrit d'un texte parle" (Written Sound of a Spoken Text), seemed in some ways secondary to the adventure of sightseeing in the surrounding countryside.[10] Duncan's letters home to Jess were dominated by descriptions of the region's views and the masterpieces housed in art galleries from Antwerp to Ostend to Ghent.[11]

On May 12, Duncan flew to Dover, and the following week he gave a reading at Dartington Hall in Devon. Again descending upon the Kitaj household, Duncan extended his social energies in all directions, making rounds of London's museums, dining with Eric Mottram, and seeing friends recently arrived from the United States, Alberto de Lacerda and David and Hilde Burton. The Burtons and Duncan dined together on Elm Park Road on May 28, and two days later Duncan left England from Heathrow Airport for a second stay in Paris, lodging in a Chantilly hotel close to the Fauchereaus. Another round of public appearances filled his calendar, including a June 1 reading and book signing, a June 2 interview for Radio France, and a reading and discussion at the Centre Pompidou. On Sunday June 5, Duncan took a vacation from work, meeting with Serge Fauchereau for a lunch date, and during the final days of the trip, he also was introduced to a friend of Fauchereau's, the French painter Bernard Rancillac. As had become Duncan's habit during his European tours, he sought out all opportunities to learn the landscape and to make new friends. Even a year later, in a letter to Chris Edwards, he noted the ongoing lure of contemporary French poetry:

> At Cambridge and again in Belgium and in Paris I met and saw a good deal of Michel Deguy and Marc Roubaud [sic] of the Change group. But especially I came to know the work of a set of young poets (in their early thirties) Anne-Marie Albiach, Claude Royet-Journoud, Emmanuel Hocquard (who printed by hand a very in-group edition (of 16 copies!) of a poem of mine), Mathieu Bénézet (who has out this year ... *Le Roman de la langue* and in whose own series Premier Livraison my first poem in french to be publisht appeard) and most of all as a poet for me Jean Daive whose work I read in turn as I read Baudelaire.[12]

FIFTY-NINE

The Avant-Garde

We don't know the restrictions imposed by speech pattern/
conventions, though those involving e.g. normal sentence struc-
ture thought required to "make sense" start to show, won't until
a writing clears the air.   ROBERT GRENIER, "On Speech," 1971

DUNCAN RETURNED HOME on June 9 to find Jess putting the finishing
touches on work toward *Translations, Salvages, and Paste Ups*, a retrospec-
tive that would open at the University Art Museum in Berkeley later that
summer. Duncan meanwhile dove into activities inspired by his adventures
in France and Belgium. Continuing language classes at Alliance Française,
he filled spiral-bound notebooks with grammar exercises, laboring over the
forms of French verbs and occasionally breaking into fragments of poems.
He also took heed of poetry events in the Bay Area. On July 26, he attended a
reading by poet John Taggart, with whom he had corresponded since 1973.
The following week he gave a reading of his own at Stanford University, and
on September 15, he appeared at poet Bob Perelman's 1220 Folsom Street loft
to present a talk about sound and voice in poetry, possibly a variation of his
Belgian lecture. The occasion allowed him to engage with the area's younger
writers—particularly Perelman and Ron Silliman—some of whom would
soon be linked to the Language movement. The aesthetics and influences of
the various twenty-something poets were not yet clear, but their numbers
affirmed San Francisco's reputation as a poetry town. The group had made
several overtures to Duncan before the Folsom Street event, and more fol-
lowed. In 1978, Bruce Andrews, a young East Coast editor of the recently
established $L=A=N=G=U=A=G=E$ magazine, asked Duncan to con-
tribute to his project, adding, "I've been reading your work with care for as
long as I've been writing... and so have almost all of the contemporaries
whose work I'm interested in."[1] At first, Duncan observed the clusters of
younger writers with some curiosity. Later he lashed out against aesthetics
that seemed to him barren of, if not oppositional to, the mythopoetic, roman-
tic instincts he knew and loved.

With new perspectives on poetry in the air, Duncan also began to take interest in younger writers whose ideas fell outside the Language project and aligned more clearly with traditions of the Black Mountain school. While conflict existed, there was an energetic dialogue emerging. One witness to the transformation was Mary Margaret Sloan, who recalled the charged atmosphere in San Francisco during the late 1970s:

> If you remove the animosity and look at the flow of ideas, it's just exquisite. It was a wonderful wonderful conversation. . . . I remember something Robert said that helped me . . . have some . . . sense of peace about all that. . . . that to find your way as a young poet is . . . one of the hardest things in the world. You're really working in the dark. And . . . when a young poet feels that he or she has an elementary grasp about what their work is going to be, . . . they feel agitated and angry even about guarding it. There's a way in which to try to guard it . . . that . . . can create this kind of hubristic, cranky, oppositional state of mind.[2]

Another fledgling writer on the scene, David Levi Strauss, met Duncan in 1978 during an afternoon at Diane di Prima and Sheppard Powell's house in San Francisco. Listening to Duncan and di Prima discuss the possibility of forming a poetics school in the Bay Area, Strauss realized that Duncan had been absentmindedly nibbling on a bar of hashish left on the kitchen table. While Strauss and Powell had already found the drug incapacitating, Duncan seemed largely unaffected as he spun his monologue to the woozy group.[3]

After an autumn with few business commitments, on November 2, Duncan gave short but amiable introductions to local readings by James Broughton and Helen Adam. On November 11, he traveled south to speak at one of Michael Davidson's seminars on postmodernism at the University of California, San Diego. Jess and Duncan saw a good deal of Davidson that winter, with Davidson visiting San Francisco on December 20 and Duncan planning another visit to San Diego for February. Duncan observed the Christmas holiday by revising the opening of *The H. D. Book,* and after a quiet New Year, he was on the road again to Southern California. Back home in early March, he returned to his French studies and also began notes toward a lecture he would give later that spring at a conference in Binghamton, New York, called The Bible and Secular Imagination. The larger project of the season was the continuation of a typescript of *Ground Work,* which he sent to New Directions on March 25. In accordance with his vow of a fifteen-year silence from publishing, he would wait until 1983 to see the collection into print, but as he wrote to James Laughlin, "My purpose in setting fifteen years as firmly as I could was to allow the book its own time entirely in which to gestate and realize itself. . . . As it turns out I allowed ample time—though I would still allow for the fact that two poems, 'The Eidolon of the AION' . . . and 'The Presence of the Dance, The Resolution of the Music' are still not there."[4]

While Duncan embarked on several short business trips in late March and early April to continue bringing money into the household, Jess worked on an epic collage piece called *Narkissos*. Begun in 1959, the elaborate pencil-drawn pasteup would undergo several transformations over three decades.[5] Meanwhile, Duncan arrived in Albany, New York, on March 31, staying with Don Byrd and his family at their Glendale Avenue home. The following day, Byrd accompanied Duncan on a visit to writers Bernadette Mayer and Lewis Warsh in Lenox, Massachusetts. Warsh had met Duncan in San Francisco and in New York, but the visit was Mayer's first and only encounter with him. Of particular interest to Duncan was Mayer's knowledge of herbal teas, and she recalled being surprised that he was unfamiliar with the French word for such concoctions, *tisane*. At the end of an afternoon of domestic reveries that included Duncan's amusement with the couple's children, Marie and Sophia, the group shared dinner with poet Paul Metcalf and his wife, Nancy, at a local restaurant.[6] The Metcalfs were living in Chester, Massachusetts, and Paul accompanied Byrd and Duncan back to Albany, where, as Byrd remembered, "Robert was on a talking jag. I have a photograph of Paul after dinner, looking grumpy and glazed over."[7] Metcalf's grumpiness increased when Duncan claimed the guest room for himself, leaving Metcalf, who was scheduled to fly to Alaska early the next morning, to sleep on the floor.[8]

That week while in Albany, Duncan busily read Byrd's dissertation on Charles Olson between meetings with students. On April 6, he continued on to other schools in the State University of New York system, at Oneonta and Binghamton, and on the evening of April 11, he arrived in Canton, New York, another small upstate college town consisting of little more than a strip of shops and the hilly, sprawling campus of St. Lawrence University. Greeted at the Ogdensburg airport by Albert Glover, Duncan taught classes on April 12 and 13 in addition to giving a reading as part of the school's Forum in Contemporary Thought: Lectures on Ezra Pound, Religion and Poetry. Back to

Albany briefly the following day, he spent the night with the Byrds before flying to Ohio and into the territory of yet another of his young academic benefactors, Robert Bertholf. On April 18, Duncan gave a reading and classroom lecture on science and poetry at Hiram College, and on April 19, he gave a recycled lecture at Kent State University, "Poetry and the Secular Imagination: Bible Lore in My Poetry."

Piling professional commitments one atop the next, Duncan was increasingly living out of his suitcase and making his home in hotel rooms and dormitories. On good days, he had the company of former students and old friends. On other occasions, the work was lonely. After a brief refueling trip home to San Francisco in late April, Duncan arrived in Eugene, Oregon, to take part in Poetry and the People: Art in the Community, a tour sponsored by local colleges. Giving readings around the state, he joined the ranks of a number of other contemporary writers who had recently been on the circuit, including Robert Creeley, John Ashbery, and W. S. Merwin. Shuffled from town to town, more of a carnival curiosity than a literary figure, Duncan came to the end of the work exhausted and dissatisfied. In Eugene on April 23 for an evening reading, he proceeded the next afternoon to Willamette University in Salem, where his performance was followed by dinner with local poetry fans. On April 25, he read at the Oregon College of Education in Monmouth and while there spoke to students about poetry, English literature, and philosophy. Back in Eugene on April 27, he was a guest in poet Joyce Salisbury's creative writing class at the University of Oregon, after which he gave two readings and dined with students. The following day Duncan found a brief window to meet with old acquaintance W. S. Merwin for dinner, after which he was back at work giving a reading at the Corvallis Arts Center. The final stop of the trip included an April 29 lecture at the state's Albany Arts Festival. Duncan complained to Jess that he had resorted to penning crib notes on his itinerary to recall the names of his hosts and their spouses all along the route.

In May, basking in a few weeks of household quiet and familiar routines, Duncan began composing notes about poet John Taggart's manuscript *Dodeka,* which he had received the previous year. Eventually shaping the notes into an introduction to Taggart's book, Duncan would also turn toward Taggart for a friendship that included mutual interests in Olson, Zukofsky, and the finer mechanics of the poem.[9] Meanwhile, on May 9, Duncan gave a reading alongside Robert Creeley at the Poetry Center, and at the end of the month, he appeared with Michael McClure and Diane di Prima at a symposium in the East Bay celebrating the Berkeley Poetry Conference of 1965. In late June, Duncan flew to British Columbia and spent a week with the Tallmans, giving a reading at Simon Fraser University and completing a five-day residency at the Cold Mountain Institute on nearby Cortes Island. The experience put him in contact with a novel audience, "Gestalt analyst trainees and a group of internees" who were participating in the institute's summer program Experience in Language.[10]

SIXTY

Adam, Eve, and Jahweh

I come from a long line of eccentric Buddhists. CHÖGYAM TRUNGPA RINPOCHE

DUNCAN'S HEAVY SPRING touring schedule was followed by a mid-July residency at the Naropa Institute. In an interview given while there, he joked that he agreed to the residency only because he had been blackmailed by the two Jack Kerouac School cofounders, Anne Waldman and Allen Ginsberg. In reality, he made the commitment hoping that Tom Savage, the young poet with whom he had had an affair in 1976, would also be returning to Boulder. Savage did not appear, and in a notebook entry written during his stay, Duncan reflected mournfully, "I have now been long without the full body of love making and sexuality has been reduced to a function of discharge. The intensity of my love for Jess increases in every embrace I am permitted with him, and the intensity of my sense of his reserve increases."[1]

Recognizing his interactions with students in the classroom as a form of "love-making," he was also happy to reconnect with longtime acquaintances Gregory Corso, Amiri Baraka, William Burroughs, Ted Berrigan, and Diane di Prima. Berrigan had made the trip with his wife, the poet Alice Notley, and their two young sons, Anselm and Edmund. Notley, describing the week with Duncan as "delightful," remembered, "Robert came to our room . . . one afternoon, told a lot of anecdotes, and then chased Ted about with a five-dollar bill. This had to do with a food allowance we'd been promised which had then evaporated (a very Naropa type of thing): fifteen dollars a day or something. Ted made some remarks on the subject and Robert said he would give him some money and then started chasing him: when Ted wouldn't take the five he gave it to Anselm and Edmund."[2]

The small Naropa campus was abuzz with intrigue that summer over a sordid incident that had occurred some three years earlier. In the fall of 1975, a group of American Buddhists had joined Naropa's guru, Chögyam Trungpa Rinpoche, on a retreat in Snowmass, Colorado, during which poet W. S. Merwin and his partner, Dana Naone, had been accosted and stripped naked by Trungpa's assistants at a Halloween party. The incident was one of several transgressions acted out by both Trungpa and the retreat's participants during their three months of isolation in the mountains. It was a controversy that refused to die, and rumors emerged that Trungpa's "vajra guards" had begun carrying weapons. Trungpa meanwhile was becoming a controversial figure in American poetry and spiritual communities. During the late 1970s, his method of education and enlightenment, based on his Tibetan Buddhist lineage's "crazy wisdom," came under scrutiny. *Newsweek* later picked up on the story in an article titled "Why People Join Cults": "Trungpa, . . . rumored to have a secret plan to take over Nova Scotia, is also building a multimillion-dollar kingdom in Boulder, Colo."[3]

While there was no multimillion-dollar kingdom to be seen, Naropa students from one of Ed Sanders's 1977 summer classes on investigative poetry had produced a detailed document about "the Merwin incident" titled *The Party: A Chronological Perspective on a Confrontation at a Buddhist Seminary.*[4] The publication provided a blow-by-blow account of the events of the 1975 retreat as well as detailed information about the Naropa Institute's governing body. Sanders had consulted Duncan about possible repercussions in the poetry community, but he was familiar enough with signs of cult activity—having investigated Charles Manson's circle in the late 1960s—to risk the publishing venture.[5] Duncan's own view of the Trungpa controversy may have been more lighthearted. Bobbie Louise Hawkins remembered him jokingly referring to Merwin, Naone, and Trungpa as Adam, Eve, and Jahweh.[6]

Avoiding the intrigue, Duncan settled into his lodgings at Boulder's Varsity Manor Townhouses and set about teaching, convening his first class session on Monday July 17.[7] As he later told Fred Martin of New Directions, the teaching experience at Naropa "turned out to be immensely worth it" and left him "charged for the fall season."[8] Anne Waldman remembered Duncan's ability to adapt to his environment:

> swimming in the . . . pool a lot after his classes, extremely comfortable and curious about the whole burgeoning Naropa situation (quite Bohemian in those days) . . . and also exceedingly generous with students who gathered as a kind of cult around him (as would be expected) as they investigated gnosis and other mysteries.[9]

Throughout the seven-class sessions, he worked alongside the students, completing in-class writing exercises and composing parts of "Sets of Syllables, Sets of Words, Sets of Lines, Sets of Poems Addressing: Veil, Turbine, Cord, & Bird," which was later integrated into *Groundwork II*.[10] Duncan's participation in a mathematics class at the institute also played into the poem, as did shadows of the community's spiritual preoccupations:

> If my soul craved the currents of Buddha compassion, give up my soul-suffering to what-ever washing away from being it seek, for I go swiftly and even alone to what I love. I follow the Way of Romance, a mere story of loving and the household we found in the design of the veil.[11]

Between classroom meetings and work on the "Sets" poem, Duncan shared meals with fellow faculty and found time to explore Boulder. New York poet Larry Fagin and his wife, Joan, became dinner companions, as did Anne Waldman, whom Duncan invited to his townhouse for a homemade chicken vegetable stew. On July 18, with the temperature soaring to ninety-eight degrees, he wandered the strip of bookshops and coffeehouses of downtown Boulder known as "the mall." Writing to Jess, he noted his appreciation of the sunny mountain-shadowed environment, though he also confided that he was still ill at ease with the atmosphere of reverence around Trungpa Rinpoche. Having heard Merwin's account of the Trungpa incident earlier in the year, Duncan had some sympathy for the other camp:

> I am entirely away from the Thibetan Tibetan throne and domination of "His Holiness" Rinpoche the Lama Trungpa, for I operate only within the Poetics school and attend only the mathematics seminar and steer clear of buddhist instructions. . . . I have already had my say where it had to be heard—with Allen [Ginsberg] and Anne [Waldman] who are the believers—that Merwin's going into a rage is what a free spirit and animal would do, and that the violation of their will I can only see as an evil.[12]

The issue was heavily on his mind when he was interviewed by Anne Waldman, John Oughton, and Rob Fromme on July 21, 1978.[13] Duncan talked about his "obedience" to poetry and his rejection of his parents' religious beliefs. Turning the tables on the interviewers, he took the opportunity to ask a number of questions about Trungpa Rinpoche's lineage and the organization of authority figures within it. True to his anarchist roots, Duncan proposed that "Poetry carries very powerful heresies . . . towards the powers of this world. So this [poetry] is a little power that can co-exist with it and constantly bounce off it. We love to bounce off the powers that exist."[14] Duncan's doubts about Trungpa were reinforced when he attended a ceremony heralding the academic accreditation of the institute. At the celebration, a highlight of the summer for the locals, Duncan chanced upon an ally in his skepticism, a young San Francisco poet named Lyn Hejinian, in town to visit her sister. Hejinian recalled,

> All of Naropa was in a state of hyper-excitement because an Italian film crew had arrived. . . . There was a huge assemblage . . . to hear Trungpa speak. He arrived several hours late. He said something about its being okay to eat hamburgers—i.e., vegetarianism was not a prerequisite to enlightenment. He was mischievous and, perhaps, charming, but I was too skeptical to be charmed. . . . I couldn't take any more and left the room, and Robert Duncan was bolting from the room at the same time. We went . . . to an old hotel in downtown Boulder [the Boulderado]. . . . I just remember the wooden beams, the frontier days decor, and drinking several cups of coffee while Robert ranted, expressing all my frustration at the sanctimonious, unexamined, hippy faux Buddhism but in a tirade that was fantastically ornate and formed a kind of cosmic objection.
>
> The words "throne" and "enthronement" came up often—what Robert was articulating was a critique of power. Being himself a power, he no doubt knew what he was talking about—and I paid close attention, enormously enjoying the sense of comradeship (and of rebellion).[15]

On July 26, Duncan had his own moment in the spotlight, giving a reading alongside Diane di Prima and Amiri Baraka. The following morning he had breakfast with di Prima before heading to the school's library to read more about "the Merwin incident." Later that day, news came from New York that St. Mark's Church in-the-Bowery, home to the Poetry Project since 1966, had burned to the ground. Anne Waldman, whose creative affinities were equally distributed between the St. Mark's and Naropa communities, remembered, "I was with [Duncan] in the pool when I got word about . . . St.

Mark's . . . I was out of my mind with worry. He was very comforting. No one had been hurt. 'Poetry lives in the interstices, not in structures,' he assured me."[16] Duncan, leaning back into superstition, took the fire as an omen. He wrote to Jess the next day: "It was a beautiful space for Poetry, a True Space. But as if in a dream, this destruction of the New York Center, for the accreditation celebration of the night before, was it?"[17]

Inspired by his interactions at Naropa, Duncan returned to San Francisco on the morning of August 1 to attend to household matters and to continue his own work. Concurrent with prose projects, he tinkered with the typesetting of *Ground Work,* and as always was hard-pressed to make sense of the paperwork that flowed across his desk. When Orlando the cat died at the age of eighteen, Duncan and Jess again faced the specter of death, losing a companion who had been part of their lives since Stinson Beach. Coping with the absence, they slowly settled into a renewed, if shaky, contract of domesticity and completed various projects by the year's end. For Duncan, the early autumn was a season full of correspondence. Writing to Chris Edwards on September 27, he described an essay on Louis Zukofsky he was composing for *Paideuma* magazine as well as preparations for lectures on Whitman and Charles Olson. To Paula Prokopoff he wrote that the household was consumed in Jess's work schedule and that the couple had not even found time for phone conversations with friends: "Jess more and more demands his solitude and time/space in the observance of which I tread carefully. . . . These days again of demanding work are both presst and at the same time—for beautiful things are happening in his work—with releases and realizations."[18]

On October 3, Duncan made a public appearance close to home, giving a reading for the Grand Piano series. Curated by Barrett Watten at a Haight Street coffeehouse, the program hosted a range of poets during its four years of existence, including Ron Silliman, Lyn Hejinian, Larry Eigner, Steve Benson, and Bob Grenier. Coupled with a lecture series at the New Langton Arts Center and parties at the homes of various young writers, the Grand Piano injected new creative energy into the San Francisco scene. Meanwhile, in mid-October, Duncan spent a weekend in Los Angeles, where he attended the opening of a Wallace Berman retrospective. While there, he stayed with Berman's friend Joan Simon and had a brief reunion with Berman's now-grown son Tosh, who accompanied him from the airport into town. The trip also allowed time for visits to the Getty Collection and to the studio of an old friend, Lilly Fenichel.

Home in late October, Duncan set aside morning and evening hours to write about Charles Olson's poetry in anticipation of talks in Iowa and Buffalo. He'd had difficulty keeping a routine of daily journaling, but scholarly writing and reading notes were easier to sustain. That week, he also pruned his lecture on Whitman for an upcoming symposium in Philadelphia, and on October 25, he returned to rewriting the opening of *The H. D. Book* and began to arrange the essays in *Fictive Certainties*. In the midst of these projects, Duncan sorted through an ongoing barrage of business demands. Now deep into a very public life as a writer, one of his tasks was to respond to an October 27 request from an editor named Lucky Jacobs that he contribute to an anthology of tennis poems.

On Monday October 30, Duncan flew to Chicago, where he spent a day with Paula Prokopoff and her second husband, Jim Speyer, and the three made a visit to the Art Institute of Chicago Museum. The next day, Duncan traveled to New York via Philadelphia to continue negotiations with Fred Martin at New Directions for the publication of *Fictive Certainties*. While away from home, he began the poem "In Waking," penning its first lines in his room at Philadelphia's Ben Franklin Hotel. He continued the piece on November 8 and 14. Invoking images from the first poem inspired by Jess, "The Song of the Borderguard," Duncan wrote,

> Whose lions in this stage   scent already
> our faltering steps   and will prey
>   upon the body's marches
> opening gates in night's dream enclosures
>   to the disclosures of a last day
> following in the wake of a time that was ours,
>   years in whose count we have thrived
> rip from the feast in what we are
>   a further wake of what we were.[19]

Shuttling between Philadelphia; Camden, New Jersey; and New York City during the first week of November, Duncan made time to view a Matisse show at the Museum of Modern Art with Robert Wilson. He also attended a dinner party at the home of Federico and Odyssia Quadrani, visited Helen and Pat Adam, and saw R. B. Kitaj and Sandra Fisher, who were briefly living in New York. On the morning of November 4, Duncan presented "The Adventure of Whitman's Line" at the Walt Whitman International Poetry

Center in Camden. Two days later, he was at the University of Iowa in Iowa City for a Charles Olson festival. In lectures titled "Ideas of Primordial Time in Charles Olson's Work" and "Timing and the Creation of Time in Charles Olson's Maximus," Duncan wove together sweeping insights about Olson's poetry and philosophical preoccupations. On the evening of November 9, he gave a conference reading, introduced by Duncan McNaughton, during which he ambled through the entirety of "Dante Études."

SIXTY-ONE

San Francisco's Burning

> This is the breed of the poet— . . . not just that we are bad tem-
> pered, but we are really trained to move with tremendous feel-
> ing on the least hints—and how to manage our human lives
> needs a tremendous keel. ROBERT DUNCAN, interviewed by
> Eloyde Tovey, December 1978

DUNCAN WAS HOME in San Francisco to vote in the November elections, during which California's Proposition 6 was defeated. The measure, backed by a number of conservative organizations, would have made it legal to re- move gay schoolteachers from their jobs. On November 18, the Jonestown Massacre took place in Guyana. Nearly a thousand followers of the Reverend Jim Jones, many of them former San Franciscans, died in the mass suicide, and the city's congressman, Leo Ryan, was also killed there during a fact- finding mission to the site. On November 27, yet another tragedy befell the city when Mayor George Moscone and city supervisor Harvey Milk were assassinated in City Hall by Dan White, a disgruntled district supervisor who had recently resigned. Two days later, over ten thousand people filed past the closed caskets of the murdered men at the service in City Hall. Milk, a longtime resident of the Castro district, had been San Francisco's first openly gay public official and had played a crucial role in local and national struggles for gay rights. When Dan White was tried the following year, his lawyers claimed that he had been depressed at the time of the murders, partly because of his excessive consumption of junk food. His "Twinkie defense" and the resulting sentence of six years in prison mobilized San Francisco's gay community to violent protest.[1]

Duncan left no written record of his reaction to the events of November 1978, and he steered clear of comment on the Dan White case. In the midst of the community's grief, poets gathered to go about their business. On December 8, the San Francisco Art Institute hosted "An Evening with Louis Zukofsky for a Sharing of the Out-takes." Excerpts of Zukofsky's 1965 National Educational Television interviews were screened at the event, and Duncan and Barrett Watten shared the stage to talk about the objectivist poet, who had died in May at the age of seventy-five. Ron Silliman later conjectured, "Putting Robert and Barrett . . . on the same bill discussing Louis Zukofsky was at one level a symbolic event, identifying a way in which the New American poetics and this new poetry grew out of similar concerns and sympathies. Putting Robert on stage *first* was also symbolic, and it really gave the evening an Oedipal air."[2]

After a short introduction by organizer Tom Mandel, a younger writer then directing the San Francisco Poetry Center, Duncan opened the evening on an enthusiastic talking jag, locating his own early encounters with Zukofsky and weaving together several threads in Zukofsky's life and work, from communist politics to immigrant attitudes and the influences of Henry James, Henry Adams, and the modernists. David Bromige remembered that Duncan was in top form, "playing the part to the hilt of 'The Poet.' He had his . . . Spanish hat on with the low crown and the broad brim. He had his cape on, and he was . . . swanning about there on stage."[3] The film program followed Duncan's introductory talk, after which Barrett Watten gave a presentation on Zukofsky's poetry. The thirty-year-old Watten admitted with some deference that he had been reading Zukofsky for ten years as opposed to Duncan's forty. At various points his talk was interrupted by audience members' comments and questions, with Duncan and poet Larry Eigner being the primary interjectors. Watten also competed with the noise from a neighboring venue, and at one point someone in the audience shouted "Speak into the mic; the punk rockers are drowning you out!"[4] Though Watten's scholarship on Zukofsky's poetry was meticulous, he found himself in a difficult situation, with his detailed lecture, accompanied by projected images of Zukofsky's texts, beginning to seem labored in the wake of Duncan's appearance and the showing of the film. Watten had also stirred Duncan's ire with his take on Zukofsky's statement "the words are my life," about which the younger scholar commented, "This was an incredibly difficult thing for me to understand—how are the words your life? Your words are one thing. Your life is another."[5] Duncan's interjections became more frequent as Watten continued his textual analysis of Zukofsky, driving home points that Duncan likely considered disconnected from the heart of Zukofsky's craft.

When Duncan leapt to the stage to cut short Watten's presentation, the younger poet timidly asked Duncan to step down. Duncan's exclamation "I just wanted to get some sense of fun into this" elicited applause from the audience.[6] Watten briefly continued his talk and then ceded the stage to Duncan, who read from Zukofsky's posthumous collection, *80 Flowers*. Duncan, clearly agitated, brought forward an idea that was integral to his view of the world and its poets: "it is human life that imprints itself everywhere." He also explained his own reading practices and his relation to language: "I'm so much of the generation of Freud. . . . in my generation there are no mere words."[7] Although the discussion that followed Duncan's barbed closing statements focused more on technical issues in Zukofsky's work than on the altercation, it became clear in the weeks and even years to follow that the event set off bad feelings throughout the San Francisco poetry scene, particularly between Duncan and younger members of the community and between Duncan's future New College students and the San Francisco writers who would affiliate with the Language movement. Ron Silliman recalled, "After the disaster at the Art Institute . . . I tended to steer further away from Robert—I'd been appalled at his behavior and viciousness toward Barrett, who'd been my roommate and was/is my oldest friend, dating back to high school days."[8] Bay Area poet Stephen Rodefer's letter to the editor of *Poetry Flash* some years later took a lighter perspective:

> Robert Duncan's . . . taking over the podium from Barry Watten that night was both arrogant and annoying to those in the crowd (many) listening to the connections being proposed by BW, but it was possibly necessary to keep the evening from getting boring. . . . In that sense . . . Duncan was . . . saving the evening from the kind of over-long and potentially tedious analysis Barry Watten was not so much proposing as already relentlessly enacting— one which had forceful intelligence but little scale and Duncan simply saw the need to return the evening to Zukofsky and his measure.[9]

David Bromige, for whom Duncan had been a mentor since the two met in Vancouver in 1961, found that the event drove him into a closer alliance with the Language writing movement:

Robert presented it as people getting hold of the stick at the wrong end. I remember him saying, "You can never make an art out of a medium." ... I was always surprised when Robert came up with something like that over and over again because his mind was quite various, but it had these rigidities. ... The first time I heard him say that, it was about Brakhage's work, when Brakhage was cutting up film or destroying a frame. ... Brakhage is trying to make you aware that your eyes are watching something and that light is the chief medium ..., but that film is the intermediary. ... And Robert claimed that that was not enough for an art ... so of course Language writing, which is making an art out of a medium, could not be an art. ... And I was disappointed, because Robert was capable of going into some things with great depth ..., and it seemed like he ... [stopped] short here. ... I found him very wanting in sympathy that way. And this was someone who twenty years before had been very encouraging to us about his own generation's innovations.[10]

Duncan made no reference to the San Francisco Art Institute event in his notebooks, though he did speak of it briefly during an interview by Eloyde Tovey the following week:

I dominate the scene I'm in. This meeting on Zukofsky last Friday, for example. Oy vey! ... Well, after about twenty minutes of this young guy's address—it's so stupid in my mind and still seems so appallingly stupid—I started charging in and dominated unforgivably, just blasted so he couldn't get to the end of what he was doing. And I realize I often dominate the situation because I don't want to hear stupidities. I'm really very unwilling to hear some tedious discussions. Of course, it means that often I'm not allowing for something that's not going to be stupid too.[11]

Duncan may have been initially dismissive of Watten, but Michael Franco remembered that the Zukofsky event had a lasting impact on the elder poet. When Franco later mentioned Watten with derision, Duncan chided his student, "Don't ever underestimate Barrett Watten."[12]

SIXTY-TWO

At Sea

IT WAS CHARLES OLSON'S WORK that dominated Duncan's thoughts that year above and beyond San Francisco poetry politics. Throughout the later part of 1978, he completed preparations for the lectures on Olson he was scheduled to give in Buffalo in mid-March. Meanwhile, the new year opened with social events close to home, the first a mid-January party in San Francisco's Pacific Heights neighborhood, attended by Fred Martin and his wife, Cathy, and Miriam Patchen. At home through Christmas and the New Year, Duncan had an opportunity to hold court before a sympathetic audience, dipping into long-buried memories for a *Gay Sunshine* magazine interview. In the course of his conversations with interviewers Aaron Shurin and Steve Abbott, obscure details of the Symmes household rose to the surface, as did candid reflections upon his relationships with Ned Fahs and Jerry Ackerman.[1]

Duncan had difficulty sleeping that winter, often waking in the predawn light with ideas toward *Ground Work II.* He'd turned sixty on January 7 and acknowledged the beginning of his "passage to old age."[2] In January and February, he took a rest from travels, and while at home with Jess, he reapproached the writings of Freud, read James Hillman's *Anima,* and resumed his dream notes. On February 5, he wrote the poem "Et," integrating French phrases heavily into the piece while also invoking Pound's influence on his work. Coming out of his winter retreat, on March 18 Duncan traveled to Buffalo and was retrieved from the airport by English professor Bill Sylvester. The following morning, after three and a half hours of sleep, he wrote to Jess from his lodgings at Sylvester's house, where he would stay for the duration of his visit to the area. Remarking that he enjoyed the company of Sylvester and his wife, Jean, Duncan added, "Best of all it is a very regular household whose clock is not far off ours—breakfast at seven, dinner not far off the six o'clock to 6:30 norm. And classical music on the radio."[3] For Duncan's hosts, the visit was less tranquil, beginning with the arrival of their high-energy guest:

> He started talking the moment I met him at the airport; he rushed about, picked up his suitcase, and we were the first out to the cars. He talked on the way over, discovered he had the wrong suitcase, started dialing on our phone—to California it turned out . . . told Jess he already missed him, dialed the airlines about the suitcase.[4]

After a difficult first few hours with Duncan, Bill Sylvester, a mainstay of Buffalo's literary community and a poet himself, would come to appreciate his visitor's energy as "exalting":

> At that time I was, or had been Director of Teaching Fellows, and he looked upon me pretty much as an administrative asshole. The tectonic shift in our relationship happened the next day. He was up at seven o'clock, operating at full energy, and I . . . [said] I wanted to talk about one of his poems. I remember exactly where he was seated at the table, and that I was standing, when he said: "I hope you're not going to ask what it means." I was devastated, and showed it. I slumped into the chair. He sensed that I was hurt, deeply hurt. . . . But the remarkable thing was that I knew he had changed his view about me. . . . And he loved us too, and admitted it in a strange way by saying later on "You and Jean are so hopelessly heterosexual!"—his way of saying he loved us while he was with us, but the moment he was gone, we were out of his life completely until we met again.[5]

Duncan happily burrowed into sunny nooks at the Sylvesters' house to nap and write letters to Jess, never fully aware of the impact he was having on the household. On his first full day in town, he was escorted to bookstores by graduate student Brian Caraher, an assistant to Robert Creeley who was responsible for "showing him about and keeping him out of trouble" during his stay.[6] After purchasing a multivolume *Cambridge Medieval History* on one excursion, Duncan also took a tour of the city, with a view of "downtown Buffalo manses from the last century in various stages of disrepair, repair, well-kept pride and renovation."[7] On March 20, he had a lunch date with Robert Creeley, after which the two attended a reception for the 1979 Charles Olson Memorial Lectures. The annual event had evolved from Robert Creeley's presence in the English Department at the State University of New York, where others of Olson's colleagues also taught, including poet and Blake scholar John Clarke. Duncan's first talk, "The Power of Imagining Persons: The Poem as an Interior Play," covered "incursions and excursions" on Olson's work, with the introduction of poems by Wallace Stevens and Creeley.[8] The rest of the week was filled with a frenetic stream of public appearances. On the evening of March 21, Duncan gave a poetry reading at Buffalo's Allentown Community Center, afterward being lured into a late night of chatter with local poets. The next day, in his second lecture, "The Fatefulness of Ongoing Identifications—the Poem as Recall and Adventure of Self in Projections," he talked about "incantations and impersonations" in Pound's *Cantos* and H. D.'s *Helen in Egypt*.[9] That evening, Ekbert Faas, who had traveled from Toronto to see the subject of his biography in progress, joined Duncan and the Sylvesters for dinner.

Driving to Toronto with Faas the next morning after penning a brief note to Jess, Duncan looked forward to a somewhat quieter weekend. He made a single appearance that Friday evening for the Harbourfront Reading Series run by Greg Gatenby and spent the rest of the weekend with Faas and his wife, Barbara, venturing out of the house only briefly to meet with Gwendolyn MacEwen, a poet whom he had last seen in Vancouver in the 1960s. After a March 25 audience with instructors from Trinity College, Duncan boarded a bus for a snowy two-hour journey back to Buffalo, where he returned to his quarters in the Sylvester household and prepared for further lectures at the university. On the evening of his March 27 talk, Duncan had dinner at the home of Thalia Feldman alongside locals Irving and Micky Sanes, Betty Cohen, and the Sylvesters. To the poet's mixed horror and delight, "the dessert was the Soupe-anglaise Greek style ice-cream in a huge bowl puddled with fruits, nuts, jams, dates, orange-juice, amarette, ground coffee—whatever phantasy is on hand."[10] His lecture mirrored the ambrosial sea of dessert, and Duncan wrote Jess of his excitement about the success of "Forth on the Godly Sea: The Daemonic in the Realm of Poetry":

> The talk . . . was more "at sea" than "of the gods," tho where I brought the matter of the Sea as ground of the gods was to the edge of what we can in No Way Experience, as the true proposition of an Unconscious. And of the artist as illustrating, imaging, imagining what the contents, giving content to, what that abyss in learning is. Emerging but not last night stated was the definition: The Unconscious is that which is without content. And there is a Duncan statement of that that we have both loved "Nothing inside but the inside inside."[11]

The following day, Duncan led a workshop discussion of Olson's poetry and visited the University of Buffalo's Poetry/Rare Books Collection before attending a farewell party at Bill and Jean Sylvester's house. When a power outage interrupted the festivities, Duncan and the Sylvesters said goodnight to guests and retreated to their bedrooms by candlelight. Waking to a dark rainy horizon, on March 29 Duncan spent the last day of his visit to Buffalo leading another workshop and delivering his final lecture on Olson, "The Presences of the World: As Actual; As Real—Finding The Way."

He would return home for two weeks before embarking on another round of red-eye cross-country travel with an East Coast reading tour centered in New York. On April 11, he boarded an American Airlines flight, wrote to Jess, took off his shoes, and slept through the five-hour journey. Arriving in New York just before dawn, he made his way to Robert Wilson's apartment in Manhattan, where the two men shared breakfast and caught up on household news. New York remained a hub of Duncan's social activity, as it had for nearly two decades. The presence of Wilson and the Adam sisters, complemented by R. B. Kitaj and Sandra Fisher's stay there that year, gave Duncan ample opportunity to feel at home away from home. At lunch with Kitaj and Fisher the first day, the three talked about the New York art world, into which Kitaj had been thrust through his contract with the high-powered Marlborough Gallery. That evening, Duncan went off by himself to a Sherlock Holmes movie, *Murder by Decree,* starring Christopher Plummer. In his jet lag, he dozed off through parts of the film, after which he returned to Wilson's apartment for a late-night dinner and a solid night's sleep.

The next morning, Duncan's target was the Museum of Modern Art. Taking a lunch break in the museum's restaurant, he wrote Jess about his pleasure in viewing the works he had loved as a young man on his way to a life in poetry:

> The Surrealists look more splendid than ever. Miro and DeChirico, Magritte and Duchamp have gathered so much over years that my sight comes forward immediately close to tears. *Guernica* and *The Woman at the Mirror* brought to mind how much the truly "modern" was heroic. Not only a matter of scale, but the heroic scale is proposed by and determines the size of the canvas; but *Weeping Woman With Handkerchief* from 1937 belongs too to the heroic, the epic of modern art appropriate to and appropriating the heroic struggle in Spain. Then one enters the surrealist and dada rooms with Schwitters, Picabia, Arp . . . and the mystery cult takes over in place of the heroic.[12]

There was another gratification to come in the trip east. On Saturday April 14, Duncan boarded a Trailways bus to Amherst, where he spent the snowy Easter weekend with Norman Austin, partly staying in Austin's Shutesbury, Massachusetts, home and partly sightseeing in nearby townships. Sitting in on an Episcopalian mass, Duncan decided to partake of Christian communion for the first time. Afterward, he and Austin drove to nearby Pittsfield to see Herman Melville's house before heading back to Shutesbury for a late-night discussion about "a new book on Greek homosexuality."[13] Energized by a weekend filled with both sexual tension and intellectual satisfaction, Duncan returned to New York for a Monday night reading alongside Carl Rakosi at the Poetry Center of the 92nd Street YMHA. The two poets signed books for a long line of fans before moving on to a party at Robert Wilson's apartment. On April 17, Duncan continued his tour with Rakosi, reading at the State University of New York at Stony Brook. Paul Dolan, a professor at the school, remembered,

> We met for dinner at a local restaurant before the reading and Duncan talked non-stop. It was witty and a bit catty and fun, but it was non-stop. As we left the restaurant the other poet (Rakosi) asked if he could change the sleeping arrangement. We had booked them in a double room at the local motel. He even offered to pay for the new arrangement.... He must have seen something in my face because he said: "No. No. It's that I won't get any sleep. Duncan will talk all through the night and I'll never get any sleep."[14]

On April 18, Duncan took the short flight from New York's Kennedy Airport to Albany, where he stayed with Don Byrd and spoke to Byrd's and Chuck Stein's students at the state university. Stein, who escorted Duncan from Byrd's house to the campus, remembered that while getting Duncan into the car and walking around to the driver's side, his passenger continued his stream of chatter to the dashboard.[15] The following day Duncan returned to New York for a final reading with Rakosi, this time at New York University. At the end of the week, he resumed his rush of East Coast socializing. After a lunch at the Players Club on Gramercy Square with Fred Martin and James Laughlin from New Directions and old friends Michael and Joanna McClure, he had an afternoon meeting with Frances LeFevre at her apartment on MacDougal Street, accompanied by LeFevre's daughter Anne Waldman. Waldman remembered Duncan's interest in LeFevre's translations of Greek poet Angelos Sikelianos's work:

[Duncan] was curious about her Greece years—when she had been married to the son—Glaufkos—of the Greek poet Anghelos Sikelianos and living under the aegis of the Utopian Ideal, working with restoring Euripides plays to Delphi. Weaving the costumes, handcrafting the sandals . . . I think she showed him some documents, photos, manuscripts of Sikelianos. Isadora Duncan was part of this culture. Her brother Raymond was a colorful figure. Robert knew some of this history and I think there were some over-laps—connection to the Provincetown Playhouse in New York—links to Provincetown itself where my father had also lived—also . . . the connection through the Duncan name Robert had taken.[16]

On his way back to the West Coast, Duncan stopped in Milwaukee to give a reading at the University of Wisconsin's Center for Twentieth-Century Studies. Arriving in San Francisco on the morning of April 24, he seemed already prepared to make his next departure. That week he was issued a new passport for his summer tour of Europe, appearing in the photograph smartly dressed in a suit and tie as he had been in his Mallorcan passport some thirty-four years earlier. His gray hair was trimmed short and receding, and his once rotund face had grown taut. Another indication of his status as a venerated elder came that spring with a ceremony sponsored by San Francisco's Art Commission. Honoring his sixtieth birthday of the previous January, the commission proclaimed May 7 Robert Duncan Day and presented him with a plaque inscribed with the lines "Often I Am Permitted to Return/to a Meadow/as if it were a scene made-up by the mind."[17]

SIXTY-THREE

The Cherubim

WHEN A SUMMER 1979 teaching excursion to the Midi-Pyrénées of France was scrapped due to underenrollment, Duncan accepted a position with the University of Louisiana's study abroad program in Innsbruck, Austria. On his way to the post, he stopped in New Orleans. Leaving San Francisco on June 8, he wrote an in-flight note to Jess that registered his delight with one aspect of traveling: "For a while I was curld up in the full length of the three seats. . . . Then awake as the first horizon of light appeard before us in the east. Venus brilliant. And over a sea of clouds the rosey seam grew. Venus higher and higher, dimming as the sky became more and more blue. . . . The sun-disc burns through the cloud layer."[1] Arriving in Louisiana to temperatures in the midnineties, he was escorted to a shady, foliage-entwined apartment owned by poet Richard Le Mons, and after "snuggling into the heat of the day" for a midafternoon nap, he joined his hosts and several local poets to share a meal of Louisiana-style rice and beans.[2] The weekend in New Orleans allowed him to acquaint himself with the faculty in the university's English Department, particularly Le Mons and Jack Mueller, and to overindulge in all that the city had to offer. With Mueller, he visited the New Orleans Museum of Art, and with local poet Ralph Adamo, he wandered the French Quarter and feasted on oysters. Duncan's food-finding missions culminated in a Sunday brunch of turtle soup and a dinner that he described to Jess as "another kind of New Orleans—a diner hamburger, potato salad and coffee freeze at the Camellia Grill—with black waiters in white jacket and black tie."[3]

By the end of the weekend, distracted by the heat, the food, and the long flight to Europe awaiting him, he wrote to Jess, "I still have an empty feeling in my midriff for this being away from home when not only for us but for me in myself I am away from myself away from home."[4] In fact, Duncan would be away from home for most of the summer, as he had been for most of the spring. On June 12, en route to Amsterdam, he sent a postcard to Jess from a stopping point at Gander, Newfoundland. A delayed takeoff and two refueling stops had kept him warily awake, lessening his enthusiasm for high-altitude reveries but providing him time to begin a new poem titled "The Cherubim (I)." Destined for *Ground Work II*, the piece was partly inspired by Raphael Patai's *The Hebrew Goddess*, a tract on Middle Eastern mythology. Duncan sent the opening verses to Jess, noting that the composition fell into the category of "more Eros."[5] His play on airplane and angel entered into the first stanza:

> Across the ark   the wings
> commingling
> touch in touch   until
> the will
> of each other both close
>   dark
> and dreaming eyes,
>   lion-visaged

> man-gazed rapacious bird-
> bright fire cloud
>
> rustling. . . . [6]

Later in his Amsterdam hotel room, Duncan drifted off to sleep with the assistance of a dose of Valium. Having anticipated an adventure in the city and its museums, he was disappointed to wake to rain showers. After a morning spent ducking in and out of dripping doorways en route to see Rembrandt's *The Night Watch* at the Rijksmuseum, Duncan spent the later part of the day in the Van Gogh and Stedelijk Museums. On June 14, he wrote Jess about other visual pleasures: "canals everywhere in the centrum, the old city—and Vermeer views."[7]

With free time before the beginning of classes in Innsbruck, Duncan embarked on a long-awaited weeklong tour of France that included Paris and the Albigensian countryside. First meeting with Serge and Jocelyn Fauchereau in Coye-la-Forêt, he also spent an afternoon with them at Paris's Museum of Gustave Moreau before having dinner with poet Edmond Jabès and his wife, Arlette.[8] The combined satisfactions of Moreau's apartment museum and the Fauchereaus' guest apartment in Coye-la-Forêt entered into "The Cherubim (II)." Opening the poem in French, he embedded a note of gratitude ambiguously addressed to Jess, the Fauchereaus, and Moreau: "you have made room for me here / in the opening of a door you have made a place / of rest in which I am only I only you / life declaring itself in us."[9] Sightseeing in a region that had intrigued him since his studies with Ernst Kantorowicz during the late 1940s, Duncan took a train on June 22 to Tarascon-sur-Ariège in the Pyrénées to see the prehistoric wall paintings in the Cave of Niaux. That week he also toured Montségur, Carcassonne, and Nice before catching a train through France and Italy for the beginning of his work in Austria.

He was scheduled to teach for six weeks in Innsbruck: a morning class on Greek mythology titled Pagan and Hellenistic Roots and an afternoon class on Pound's *Cantos*. During the first days of July, he attended a number of social events for the visiting faculty and began to find his way around the city, making special note of the locations of post offices so that he could easily send letters to Jess. Anxious about the length of the stay in Europe, and distressed when another member of the faculty suffered a heart attack, Duncan registered his fears in a July 1 letter home: "Dearest—bear with me gently, I pray, in this period. And most of all I pray that you are there and well. 'Love' is all I can write to convey what at the moment is an entire pang."[10]

While he found friendships with faculty members, Duncan's greater joy again came in working with fledgling poets. At the end of his first week of classes, he noted, "My circle of students and our work becomes the enclosure, the place of an in-dwelling from which the communication radiates."[11] Two of Duncan's charges in Innsbruck, Joseph Simas and Sean Killian, were from the Bay Area. Killian, a graduate student at Berkeley, had seen a poster in Cody's Bookstore about Duncan's summer teaching plans, and he jumped at the opportunity to immerse himself in an educational experience that he came to describe as an "apprenticeship." The classes gave the younger writers an overwhelming storehouse of materials to work with, and Killian recalled that Duncan came to the program with wild enthusiasm:

> I was unbelievably impressed with him as a human being and as a teacher. I think he was . . . about the most committed person I've ever met in the poetry world in terms of just twenty-four hours a day, constant, and a real love of that world and what it meant but also wrestling with it, and never self-satisfied, . . . I felt he was an incredibly humble human being . . . , because he obviously knew how bright he was, but he never pushed that.[12]

Duncan continued his habit of extending classroom sessions beyond their boundaries. In the evenings, he and the students shared meals and then met in each other's rooms to read their poetry, and Duncan made visits with them to local museums. He also continued his work on the *Ground Work* poems, returning to the unfinished "Eidolon of the Aion" and in mid-July writing "Trinity." The latter poem, soon retitled "Styx," was heavily influenced by his work in the Greek mythology class and by his readings in Hesiod's *Theogony*. Further inspiration came from his immersion in R. B. Onians's *Origins of European Thought*. Living in the heart of Europe, Duncan was barraged with the realities of a history he'd long studied in books. He told Jess in a July 14 letter,

> A Hermes turn has come into my Hellenistic class. I had talkt to them . . . about their beginning to record and wonder about the presences, shrines, and signs of . . . Innsbruck. And told them of the votary statue of St. George. We all took him to be in his Roman warrior's dress but not with dragon—the figure held a bucket, pouring water to put out the flames of a burning house. Then one saw anew that he was a protective angel in the court that was paneled in wood facings with stairs of wood.[13]

On July 13, Duncan took a train to Munich for a happy reunion with a friend from his early days as a poet, Werner Vordtriede. Since the two men's acquaintance in Woodstock, Vordtriede had found a career as a writer and translator. The two spent much of their time together in Munich's Alte Pinakothek museum, and Duncan's letters to Jess during that week included a ten-page list of the works he had seen there, including paintings by Altdorfer, Memling, Cranach, and Dürer. Back in Innsbruck after the festive weekend, Duncan continued his work with his students, some of whom were beginning to lose interest in the courses: "What does keep me going is the group who are truly following— . . . Joey Simas, Sean Killian, and Rose Mary Prosen who came here . . . to study with me. . . . Sean and Joey are taking my Pagan and Hellenistic Roots . . . —and they stand alone in the group as being prepared for and comprehending the course."[14]

With weekends free from teaching responsibilities, Duncan traveled through Europe. On Saturday July 21, the site was Venice, a trip he and Jess had been forced to forgo during their 1955 stay in Spain because of financial constraints. Duncan gave Jess a detailed description of the city that had captured his imagination during the Berkeley Renaissance and reported that even after he returned to Innsbruck, "The canals and bridges of Venice kept coming back, the labyrinth of its ways/passage-ways and bridges. The constant visual stimulation, the glaring light of squares where the sun beat down, the soft tones of terracotta, ochre, greens in the shade, almost dark, of the passages. And great paintings in rooms so huge one could step away to see a wall entire, in the half light, the figures at first barely made out, then coming clear, fugitive."[15]

The following weekend, while fighting off a cold, Duncan went to the Austrian Alps for two sunny days of mushrooming with New York friend Robert Wilson and his partner, Kenneth Doubrava. He marveled to Jess at the "sun pouring out over the land, the rust of a mountain stream somewhere off there and birds twittering busily" and "the tiny farmsteads and hamlets scatterd upon slopes and nestled in valleys below these giant granite barriers with their glacial cliff-faces and patches of snow fields in the heights."[16] Robert Wilson in his own memoir recorded another detail of Duncan's visit: "It was a delightful time, with Robert at his garrulous, discursive, witty best. . . . filling us in with such tidbits as Denise Levertov's unrequited love for Robert Creeley, as well as his sadness that he and Levertov were now estranged."[17] Sean Killian remembered his teacher returning to Innsbruck that week with a tale of an orgy in the Alps, a detail omitted from Duncan's letters home and from Wilson's memoirs.[18]

Meanwhile, Duncan struggled to prepare for a writers' conference scheduled as part of the program's closing celebration, a chore somewhat eased by his anticipation of returning to Jess at the end of the first week of August. His homecoming meanwhile coincided with several disconcerting world events. By the middle of 1979, the Carter administration was besieged on all fronts. In July, Sandinista revolutionaries in Nicaragua forced the resignation of the country's dictator, Anastasio Somoza, replacing him with Daniel Ortega, soon to become a thorn in the side of Carter's successor, Ronald Reagan. In September 1979, the Strategic Arms Limitations Talks II treaty was imperiled by evidence of Russian military aid to Cuba, and in October, a coup in El Salvador deposed General Humberto Romero. In November, protesters in Iran seized sixty-six American hostages in response to President Carter's decision to allow the deposed shah to seek medical treatment in the United States. By December, the Soviet Union had invaded Afghanistan, and the United States poured money into support for the opposing Islamic fundamentalist army that would soon be known as the Taliban.

Still processing the information of his long summer trip to Europe, Duncan kept a wary eye on the news while he returned to his study of French and accepted a few local reading invitations. On September 23, he appeared at the opening of a Wallace Berman retrospective exhibit at the Berkeley University Art Museum. A thank you note from the show's curator, David Ross, promised a private viewing of the exhibition for Jess, who had shunned the opening day crowds. The following week Duncan left the troubles of America behind him, flying to Montreal to participate in an international writers conference called Recontre québécoise internationale des écrivains. After checking into his room at the Hotel Saint-Gabriel on the city's outskirts, he met with other conference participants for dinner. Duncan not only wanted to test the conversational French he had been studying at the Alliance Française but also had the ambitious goal of delivering his conference paper in French. He wrote Jess on his first night in Montreal that he had composed the talk in a burst of enthusiasm on the flight to Canada. He also reported, "I made my way through the cocktail hour with two tall glasses of vermouth, and dinner with my wine glass filled and refilld by invisible waiters who plied the Bordeaux and strong coffee and a cigar! And brandy. Aie! My systems in chagrin have tosst me up from and out of sleep."[19]

The next morning, after groggily surveying the city's fall colors from his window, Duncan showered and headed to the conference to give his afternoon "communication," which evolved from the idea that "Memory is Herself Muse of the Universe as Creation. That it is in Memory that the Universe is reveald to be Creation, just as we in memory experience our lives as creation."[20] The conference paper that followed his "was majorly an attack on the poetry of the primordial," and he told Jess that had the proceedings been conducted in English, he would have raised objections.[21] While he was not sure how much of his talk was understood by his audience, he nonetheless was pleased with the company:

> Already I have begun to find out new friends and am reading a little stack of works by one, Fernand Ouellette, with a volume addresst to and springing from Novalis. Naim Kattan, who visited us some years ago, you would most likely not remember him tho he had dinner with us, for I too had forgotten his name, . . . and it was not until we started talking that the pieces of the jig-saw came into place and I saw who he was: the pin-point of the Canada Arts Council. And Emmanuel Hocquard who publisht me in his Orange Export series arrived yesterday: I have had chance only to greet him and shake hands.[22]

On October 4, after three days of intensive conferencing, the writers were set loose to explore Montreal, and Duncan immersed himself in the language of the city, though he again confided to Jess, "My French is described as bizarre, which is nicer than calling it miserable or frightful. But I find I have the courage of it, for the most part, tho it continues very easy to lose what is being said, even what is being said directly to me."[23] That evening he returned to the realm of the English language, arriving in Ottawa to stay in an apartment owned by Ekbert Faas and his wife. Faas, now in the midst of more complete drafts of his biography of Duncan, handed over part of the manuscript for the poet to review on his first night in town. Duncan was disappointed with the work, condemning Faas as a writer with "absolutely no sense of humor and very little insight" and telling Jess, "My urge is to set him right where he is all on the wrong foot—but I mean instead just to correct misinformations."[24] He admitted in his letter home that the manuscript forced him to meditate upon a troubling aspect of his personality:

> All this early life before we found each other dearest—all this early "me" is miserable and yet me. I can't read it without conscience of how much still I ride roughshod over even your love and a picture can be developt in the darkroom of a photographer with no sense of more than the ego structure of me living off of everyone around. I read thru the six chapters to date . . . disheartened at what I had deliverd myself over to.[25]

On Saturday October 6, Duncan had lunch with writer Wendy MacIntyre and then spent an evening fielding questions from his biographer. He again registered his frustration to Jess: "I blew up at one point that he had no imagination of the environment of finding worlds of painting and music, and no sense of the seeking for a writing that was so much also my life."[26] In the end, as Duncan had predicted, Faas's book would focus heavily on his early sexual encounters, treating Duncan's writings primarily as narratives of sexual psychodrama and overlooking the complex cultural and aesthetic worlds from which they grew.

The rest of the Ottawa weekend was spent more agreeably with former student Bob Hogg, his wife, Leslie, and their three children. Duncan found himself at ease, indulging in good food and good company. Finding parallels between Hogg's life choices and his own, he told Jess that he was reminded of his time at Treesbank Farm and that he "had loved and found amazing" Hogg's writing, particularly his first book, *The Connections*. Ending his stay in Ottawa with an October 9 lecture to one of Hogg's classes, the following day he stopped in the Midwest for a reading arranged by Robert von Hallberg at the University of Chicago before flying home to San Francisco on October 11.

SIXTY-FOUR

Alaska

AS THE 1970S CAME TO AN END, Duncan's subtitle for *Ground Work II: In the Dark* began to read as an ominous prophecy. President Carter, in his final year in office, would find no reprieve from the troubles that had hounded his administration. In the spring of 1980, he took responsibility for a failed attempt to rescue American hostages in Iran, and the ghost of the Cold War came to the front of public consciousness as Ronald Reagan campaigned for president. Duncan despaired at Reagan's November victory, and while he struggled to make sense of his strained relationship to the younger poets of San Francisco, he also looked toward a darkening of his own physical senses.

In the New Year, he returned to his French studies and spent part of each day preparing to write an introduction to a collection of Edmond Jabès's poetry translated by Keith Waldrop. When the Modern Language Association convention descended upon San Francisco that holiday season, Duncan also participated in a panel called "The Self in Postmodern Poetry." Robert Creeley and Warren Tallman were among Duncan's co-respondents, and Creeley remembered with delight, "People were pounding to get into the room; the next session was supposed to start, and Robert was extemporizing and going on."[1]

Duncan also returned to the dream notebook he had abandoned a decade earlier. He wrote a new entry on January 8: "Charles Ponce having . . . calld me to participate next Fall in a conference on Woman—to seek there in the dream world as I must also begin to search in the 'wake' world for information concerning Woman. . . . This notebook I will be keeping at my bed side (as now just before midnight, Francesca da Rimini playing on the radio, coming to its melodramatic climax.)"[2] Throughout the month of January, Duncan obsessively recorded his dreams. He had been reading James Hillman's *Underworld,* and while still wary of Carl Jung's work, began a more concentrated study of his writings. Another text of importance to him that winter was Frances Yates's *The Occult Philosophy in the Elizabethan Age,* inspiring the *Passages* sequence "The Regulators," which he began on January 19. The first part of the poem, "The Dignities," was completed on March 21, and the remaining sections arrived over the next three months.

In a late January letter to Chris Edwards in Australia, Duncan reported briefly on the American poetry scene, noting his growing discontent with Language poetry: "My ongoing concern here . . . is . . . the ignorance of Canadian and Australian and even of English in a growing . . . American insularity. Theorists have immediate translation and coinage; but in the flood of competing poetries the idea of 'foreign' products in English is rare."[3] Edwards was able to observe the landscape firsthand when he visited San Francisco in early March. Duncan met him at the airport and escorted him back to 20th Street for his first night in town. Jess, approving of the young poet, invited him to stay the whole week. Edwards recalled the particulars of the household:

> I got to know . . . that Jess kept regular working hours. He always break-fasted early and was in his workroom by 9 am, seldom coming downstairs again until lunchtime. After lunch, he'd go back upstairs and work until late afternoon . . . both Robert and Jess were excellent cooks—and amongst other novelties . . . I was introduced, by Robert one lunchtime, to the joys of

steamed artichokes with real mayonnaise, dipped and eaten one leaf at a time, right down to the heart.[4]

During Edwards's visit, Duncan gladly accompanied him to various events and introduced him to local poets. The question of "falling in love" lingered, and Edwards recalled, "He took me one day to a French restaurant . . . that was run by some . . . acquaintances. . . . We hadn't been there long when a voice from a neighboring alcove called out: 'So Duncan, where'd ya find the young fruit?' 'Australia,' Robert replied with a grin, turning toward a disheveled-looking gentleman. . . . It was Gregory Corso."[5]

Pulled from social life by the mid-April tax deadline and bedeviled by procrastination, Duncan finished his return just in time for a midnight postmark. He took little solace in the completion of the task, observing in a notebook that his own writing felt as complicated as his tax forms: "I have been 'spending' months fruitlessly in avoidance of this I-do-not-know-where-to-start tangle."[6] In a search for inspiration, he began using a new typewriter, an IBM compositor, finding its "cramped" typography disappointing. Still insistent upon typesetting *Ground Work,* he enlisted the assistance of students, including a young Bay Area poet named David Melnick.

While Jess was housebound recovering from a gash on his leg he'd incurred while moving a bookcase, on April 26, Duncan departed for Alaska. There, he participated in the state university system's Distinguished Writers Series, a program that had recently hosted Gary Snyder, Howard McCord, and Ed Dorn. The multicity tour was busy even by Duncan's standards, but the journey also allowed him to see Alaska for the first time, and he found he liked the company: untouched by big-city poetry politics, exotically isolated, and friendly.

Duncan flew first to Seattle, during the journey penning the second stanza of "Stimmung," a subsection of "The Regulators" titled after Karlheinz Stockhausen's 1968 musical composition of the same name. As the plane descended, he had a view of Mount St. Helens, which had erupted several times that spring, and during a two-hour layover, he wrote to Jess, including the new lines of "Stimmung": "So the Preacher arises again just when, exalted, we would call upon the Dignities."[7] Among the sources entering the poem were a conversation with Michael Palmer, Jess's readings of Michelangelo, and Duncan's view "of a work (Karl Worner) on Stockhausen, whose concepts of the meaning of space in music stirrd kindred ideas of the space in teaching, of the fascism, binding of each auditor to his place in the ranks."[8]

From Seattle, Duncan flew to the small fishing town of Ketchikan, whose seven thousand inhabitants were of Norse, Finnish, and Russian descent. Spending April 27 and 28 there, he was charmed by the island scenery: leaves were budding on the trees between the dark evergreens, and crooked narrow streets led to the shore of the vast subarctic Pacific. He wrote Jess that the Ketchikan audience was "mostly young women—reporters on the local newspaper, librarians, and a young woman who works at the Heritage Museum."[9] On Sunday April 27, Duncan had lunch with some of the locals and then toured the town's museum, whose artifacts from the area's Tlingit, Haida, and Tshishian tribes tapped into his interest in primitive art and his early flirtations with shamanism. Amid sightseeing and business tasks, he had time to pen a prose poem reminiscent of his early Stein derivations:

> He changed. He changed his mind. He changed his address. He changed his dress: a Tlingit hat. He changed his look: a Haida smile. He changed his way of carving meat. He changed his party. He changed his position. He changed his sentence. He changed his gendher, she changed his way of seeing things. She changed her relation to the rest of the room. They changed their meaning from world to world.[10]

Duncan's Alaskan debut was at the Ketchikan Public Library. Dressed in a thick button-down work shirt and corduroy pants, with his white tufts of sideburns framing his face, he orchestrated the poems with the swaying of his hands, and as the *Ketchikan Daily News* reported, told the audience, "You'll never get the rhythm without using your body."[11] Satisfied with the day's activities, he was in bed by 11:30 at the home of a teacher named Bill Greene. Duncan was relieved to find points of common interest with Greene and his wife, including a fondness for Wagner and Tolkien. With the assistance of half a Valium, Duncan drifted off to sleep with the sound of the Ketchikan Creek outside his window.

The following day, despite his desire to view tribal art, he was kept busy with other matters. He told Jess that he was close to exhaustion: "Except for an almost lurching forward into talk where I am cornerd here to feed the local need, my mind has closed down. At Sitka I will set some ground rules. It doesn't look here as if I will get a nap."[12] A 9:30 A.M. appearance on a local television news program gave way to an afternoon radio interview and an evening audience with the town's writers. On August 29, Duncan flew to Sitka, another Pacific island town, landing on the shortest runway in North America. Upon his arrival, he was treated to a public dinner attended by a crowd eager to talk with the visiting poet from San Francisco. On the surface, the event—held at an establishment called the Fish Factory—lacked glamor, but Duncan was impressed with the food and was happy to be housed that evening in a lodge designed by Frank Lloyd Wright. In Sitka, he also had an opportunity to visit the totem sites in the region's National Historical Park, telling Jess about "a forest walk where at last I saw/felt in their full mystery and power totems, standing carved cypress among stands of towering cypress and the silence of rain forest—coming upon the ancient battleground where the Tlingit had fought the Russians and the stones marking the boundaries of the Tlingit stockade."[13] Duncan was especially pleased to find that his own talismanic animal, the bear, was amply represented in the local Haida totems. On April 30, he continued his sightseeing, visiting Sitka's museum of native peoples and a collection of artifacts at the local college.[14] With his hard-earned reading fees, Duncan purchased several items, including an Inuit black soapstone carving of an otter and an amber necklace.[15]

His main appearance in Sitka was at Sheldon Jackson College's Stratton Memorial Library. He was pleased with the performance, opening with "The Ballad of Mrs. Noah" and continuing on to newer work, including the poem he'd written in Innsbruck, "Styx." Perhaps even more pleasing was a chance to meet members of the audience during a postreading reception, who at least carried some exotic charm. To the locals, Duncan and his vocation were equally exotic. In a May 1 *Daily Sitka Sentinel* review, staff writer Dennis Cox wrote, "Reaction of the audience to Duncan's work varied though most of it was enthusiastically in favor. . . . Comments . . . included the estimation that 'Duncan is one of the finer poets we have around.'" The article also reported that he had written a book called "New Directions," rendering his publisher as a book title. Having no choice but to adjust to such aspects of public life, Duncan seemed even to enjoy them. In Sitka he found a place to fit in, having a postreading tea party at the home of Marlys Burnett, the university's public relations director. Also present were Andrew Hope, "the young (28 year old) leader of the Kiksadi, the Frog people of the Raven Society," and his wife, Sister Goodwin, "a beautiful young Eskimo woman" whom Duncan mentioned in a letter to Jess: "[She] brought . . . the English editions of *Roots and Branches* and *Bending the Bow* for me to inscribe and then she talked about *The H. D. Book* and how much H. D.'s writing meant to her."[16] Later that night, Duncan was deposited at the home of Don and Jan Craddick, with whom he found fewer common interests. The couple left their guest on his own to rest and view their art, which Duncan described to Jess as a collection of "unremitting mediocrity," a judgment perhaps influenced by Don Craddick's decision to leave for a bear-hunting expedition on the day of Duncan's reading.[17]

The organizer of Duncan's appearance in Juneau was poet Sheila Nickerson, whose *Songs of the Pine Woman* he read with enthusiasm while en route there on May 1. He arrived to a cold wind and rain, landing at an airport with a view of the Mendenhall Glacier. Wandering Juneau's waterfront on his first day in town, he took in the collage of Russian, Tlingit, and Eskimo culture, whose myths, he told Jess, were haunting and Lovecraftian. The next morning, while watching rain sweep over the streets of a city enclosed by mountainous horizons, he wrote his daily letter home. Duncan's $1200 payment for the Alaska tour had initially seemed generous, but he told Jess that he was feeling tired and overworked, sensing that his hosts were trying to get the most they could for their money.

On the afternoon of May 3, he led a writing workshop at a high-security prison that housed Tlingit and Eskimos, and later that day he arrived at the Eaglecrest mountain lodge on Douglas Island for an evening reading at the University of Alaska at Juneau, part of a daylong festival that included an egg toss and beer chugging. His one consolation while waiting his turn to provide entertainment for the frenzied students was a spectacular view of the sea channel between Juneau and Douglas Island. To his surprise, his reading of the *Passages* poems was well received. Despite the distractions of the festival just outside the door, the students were not the "empty headed loud callow juveniles" he feared they would be.[18] The next morning, Duncan arrived in Haines for a twenty-four-hour visit that included a wild-cucumber–gathering expedition and a wedding picnic for two of the local teachers, complete with fresh salmon and a two-tiered wedding cake. His reading that evening was equally intimate, at a family home in front of a living room fireplace. The next morning before flying back to Juneau on a four-seat Piper plane, Duncan had a chance to look at more native artifacts, including Tlingit masks and Chilcat blankets. On May 6, en route to final readings in Anchorage and Nome, he described to Jess the highlight of his journey, a bird's-eye view of the icy coastline of the Pacific:

> At the North Eastern horizon the giant peaks of a range of snowy mountains looms [sic] above the clouds. It is a spectacular landscape—blue sea, cloud cover, dark. . . . In the wetlands here brilliant metallic copper ribbons wind

their way thru, and there is a rich range of copper hues in the ground cover. We circled a huge glacier that dominates the region, and in this overcast light, the glacier has a light of its own, a glow of iridescence, rainbow hues in the white broken by the blue crevasses and tumbled cliffs of ice and rifts of almost black-blue deeper crevasses.[19]

SIXTY-FIVE

Enthralled

Still the flesh sings
fresh from making love   our two bodies
stretcht upon each other   tuning
turning and returning   beyond
eucalyptus trees in one foliage dance with the wind in their branches
and your eyes shine   answering

ROBERT DUNCAN, "Enthralled"

INCREASINGLY, Duncan's trips seemed to be an attempt to escape from the confines of the household. Home for a few weeks between his tour of Alaska and a working vacation to New York, Duncan made an emotional foray away from Jess in early June, continuing the tryst he had begun with Aaron Shurin in 1976. At the close of an afternoon of lovemaking, he lingered in Shurin's Oak Street apartment to bathe before going home to compose another section of "The Regulators" titled "Enthralled."

By midsummer, Duncan was again on the East Coast. He spent the last weekend of June with Madeline and Bill Lufak in Great River, New York, and on the following Monday took a Long Island Railroad train back to Manhattan. Immediately heading to the Strand Bookstore on Broadway and 12th Street, he tracked down a number of books in French after a long search through the shelves and then walked downtown to Riemann's Art Books on Spring Street. At the peak of a hot and humid New York summer, on July 1 Duncan had dinner with Helen and Pat Adam at their 82nd Street apartment. Despite the weather and cramped quarters, the sisters decided to roast a turkey, and Duncan reported to Jess with dismay that the overabundance of food in the sweltering apartment had given him nightmares.[1] The following day he and Robert Wilson visited the Museum of Modern Art, where they received special access to a Picasso show, allowing Duncan to view an old favorite, *Guernica,* free from the crowds. That weekend, while Robert Wilson and Ken Doubrava were vacationing on Fire Island, Duncan remained in the city to care for Wilson's big white cat, Alba. On the morning of Friday the 4th of July, he wrote Jess while listening to Noel Coward and enjoying the tree-diffused light streaming through the sitting-room window in Wilson's apartment. That afternoon he viewed some of Virginia Admiral's recent paintings at her loft on Lafayette Street, enduring the tensions that still haunted the two after forty years, including "a not to be unexpected read out and pocket-psychodrama" during which Admiral questioned Duncan's commitment to their friendship.[2] In the evening, Duncan sought less contentious company, again dining with Helen and Pat Adam at their apartment. His relationship with the two sisters ran deep, and he expressed a resigned tolerance for their quirky behavior and ill-kept household:

> Along with the hazard course—which includes that there is hardly any place to perch ("sit" won't describe it) for over the years books have stackt up on the floor and under the table (our old camping table . . . ?) so that only at the corner can one get legs, one's own, . . . under—along with the increasing discomfort—there is Helen's still entertaining talk in which folklore and popular lore of today plays with memories of poems. Only now she cannot reach for the volume: it is either unfortunately among the books in storage; or it is lost in the four-deep fifty-high stacks.[3]

The other adventure for the weekend was art viewing. While Duncan was happy to have seen Picasso's work at the Museum of Modern Art, he was more eager to spend time in the well-lit galleries of the Metropolitan Museum, on this particular visit studying the works of Church and Ryder in the nineteenth-century galleries.

Returning to San Francisco on July 7, he stayed home for a week before making his way to a D. H. Lawrence Festival in Taos, New Mexico, that commemorated the fiftieth anniversary of Lawrence's death. There, he stayed with Edward Padwa and his wife, who had been classmates at Berkeley, and mingled with other conference invitees Allen Ginsberg, William Burroughs, Stephen Spender, Derek Walcott, and Thom Gunn. Gunn flew with Duncan to the conference, and although he usually delighted in Duncan's presence, he remembered finding the journey wearying: "On the way back I had to pretend to go to sleep because I was so exhausted from him."[4]

While in Taos, Duncan participated in a group reading and presented talks on two panels, titled "D.H. Lawrence: His Influence on Poetry and Criticism" and "D.H. Lawrence and Sex and Women." The conference, extravagant in its scope, also included appearances by Dustin Hoffman and Elizabeth Taylor and "a midnight cocktail party for the scholars, writers, and stars held at the home of a wealthy art dealer."[5] A review of the proceedings in the *Nation* made mention of Duncan's presence at the late-night party, at which he "slyly suggested that this was the only genuine event of the festival since the buffet . . . was the only one that had proved worthy of him."[6] To Jess, Duncan registered his excitement in having met Roger Zelazny, a friend of his 1940s Berkeley roommate Philip K. Dick and the author of *Creatures of Light and Darkness,* a book based on Egyptian mythology.[7]

Stopping home to celebrate Jess's fifty-seventh birthday on August 6, Duncan then went north to Vancouver. Arriving on August 8, he settled into the apartment of a friend of Ellen Tallman's and the following day convened with Warren Tallman to discuss the possibility of producing a book of Jack Spicer's writings. That evening, Duncan and the Tallmans saw Peter Sellers in *Being There* and afterward feasted on sushi. While the couple had divorced, Duncan reported to Jess that they were a pleasure to be around and that, to everyone's relief, Warren had been alcohol-free for two years. Duncan was also excited that some of Vancouver's broadcasting was in French, allowing him to test his comprehension of the language. On Sunday August 10, he spent several hours watching a French mass and soap operas, pulled from his preoccupations only by the promise of meetings with friends. Over twenty years, Vancouver had become Duncan's second home, and many of the relationships he cultivated there had begun in the Bay Area. During his weeklong visit, he made time for outings with both of the Tallmans as well as with former Spicer circle compatriots George Stanley and Dora Dull-Fitzgerald, before returning to San Francisco for an autumn that would bring fewer long-distance commitments.

EIGHT

The Master of Rime

SIXTY-SIX

New College

> A pious man would no more tell out his myths than he would
> dance out his mysteries. Only when the tribe is assembled after
> solemn fasting, and holy smoking, only sometimes in a strange
> archaic tongue and to initiate men or novices after long and
> arduous preparation, can the myth with safety be uttered . . . ;
> such is its sanctity; its mana. JANE HARRISON, *Themis*

ON MORE THAN ONE OCCASION, Robert Duncan told friends that
at an appointed time he would become a "master teacher," even if it meant
standing on a street corner and imparting information to passersby.[1] He had
taught at Black Mountain College in 1956 and accepted weeklong residencies
at various academic venues throughout his career, but he had never acquired
steady employment in the Bay Area. In 1980, he had the opportunity to join
the New College of California's fledgling Poetics Program alongside Louis
Patler, Duncan McNaughton, David Meltzer, and Diane di Prima.[2] Mc-
Naughton and Patler had created the school on paper hoping that it would
eventually achieve accreditation, particularly if they brought aboard an es-
teemed faculty of local writers. Duncan, who had been waiting to receive a
more prestigious offer from the University of California's English Depart-
ment, was initially ambivalent about participating in the experiment but
soon became a committed teacher in the program.[3] His position at New
College marked a transition into a new community, and it spawned new
friendships with younger Bay Area writers. Already close to Michael Palmer,
Michael Davidson, and Aaron Shurin, by the mid-1980s Duncan would be
surrounded by a number of students devoted to him personally and aestheti-
cally, even after he became too ill to continue his work in the classroom.

New College offered something more substantial than a street-corner soap-
box, though its limited budget often left the students and faculty feeling that
they had one foot out on the street. The program was housed in a defunct
mortuary building with leaded bay windows, tattered carpets, and echoing
ramshackle rooms. As one student recalled, the classroom furniture consisted
of "a circle of fold-out tables . . . and one or two portable blackboards."[4] In au-
dio recordings of classes, the rush of Valencia Street traffic rumbles in the

background. Despite its modest beginnings, New College became a space that inspired fierce allegiance for many young poets in the Bay Area. The school provided alternative routes into a creative writing curriculum, and while its attention to the ideals of Black Mountain poetics was viewed as divisive by some, the students were able to study craft and history with a handful of the brightest writers in the experimental community on the West Coast. Duncan expounded his view of the program in a recruiting brochure:

> Why "Poetics"? It's at the level of the basic elements: in oral and in written poetry alike the sounds and silences of language, telling patterning and depatternings of consonants and vowels, the articulations of syllables in measures and utterances toward and from sentences, lines, stanzas—where rime, rhythm, and ratio originate—that creativity in language works. And it is here that poetics must begin. The realized poem will be the vehicle of the poet's emotions, psychological ventures, social urgencies, political and religious vision, philosophical dispositions, and it will be the vehicle of the poet's literary taste and learning—as a work of art it may be judged, admired or rejected, for the artist's craft.[5]

During the fall of 1980, Duncan prepared variations of two courses he had taught at Black Mountain: Structure of Rime I: Basic Elements of Composition, and Ideas of Meaning & Form: The Nature of Poetry as Presented by Poets. The students in Basic Elements I spanned a range of ages and appetites. Old friend Bobbie Louise Hawkins, then living in Bolinas, attended the class, as did Aaron Shurin and Dawn Kolokithas.[6] Shurin remembered that the class's first assignment was to transcribe a section of Shakespeare's *Romeo and Juliet* using the International Phonetic Alphabet. Indifferent to traditional academic procedure, Duncan began with lists of vast constellations of writers and ideas, allowing the curriculum to take shape out of classroom conversations. Student-selected texts in Basic Elements included writings by Basho, Shakespeare's *Cymbeline,* Verlaine's "Il pleut dans mon coeur," Wallace Stevens's "Ideas of Order at Key West," and Alice Notley's "When I Was Alive." The Ideas of Meaning & Form seminar began with a reading list of Plato, Aristotle, Longinus, Dante, Vico, Ben Jonson, Samuel Johnson, Wordsworth, Coleridge, Shelley, Carlyle, and Emerson and evolved in other directions from there.

With the teaching venture came administrative responsibilities. In mid-September, Duncan found himself immersed in a world of bureaucracy, spending his days sorting out student registration problems and attending faculty meetings alongside Diane di Prima, David Meltzer, and Robert Grenier. In other professional business, on the last weekend of September, he attended Asilomar 30: The Shores of Experience, a conference in Pacific Grove arranged by the curriculum group of the Central California Council of Teachers of English.[7] On Friday evening, September 26, he gave a talk called "A Poet among Teachers," and on the following day, he participated in a series of workshops. Before returning home on Sunday, he also attended a lecture by mythology guru Joseph Campbell, after which the two met and exchanged addresses.[8]

While Duncan took no interest in a White House dinner invitation from President and Mrs. Carter to celebrate the fifteenth anniversary of the National Endowment for the Arts, he found other social events to keep him busy that autumn. On Friday October 10, he and Jess had lunch with Barbara Joseph, to whom Duncan reported his excitement about the opening of the semester at New College, where he was working with "an eager and earnest set of 'students'—fellows in pursuit of what an emergent poetics might prove to be."[9] New College sessions soon sprawled outside of their allotted hours. In the second week of November, Duncan gave an extracurricular talk at the school titled "Shakespeare: Lear and Prospero," and on the weekend of the fifteenth and sixteenth, he delivered "Eternal Persons of the Poem," a series of lectures at San Francisco's Jung Institute. In a letter to Barbara Joseph, he described the trajectory of his work at the Jung Institute, "starting out with Gassire—the African poet-king and Orpheus and then the Muse and her Muses . . . : whoever these be in psychology, who are they in Poetry where do they appear?"[10] A gathering that began in Buffalo on November 20, Anima, Animal, Animation/A Conference on the Poetic and Bestial Faces of the Soul, again plunged Duncan into the world of Carl Jung. Other invitees to the event, organized by Paul Kugler of the Analytical Psychological Society of Western New York, included Robert Creeley, James Hillman, David Miller, Patricia Berry Hillman, and Susan Pitt. Duncan presented a lecture titled "Wind and Sea, Fire and Night" and gave a reading at the local literary center Just Buffalo on that Saturday evening. Writer Jed Rasula, who also attended the proceedings, remembered the strange convergence of the "anima-animal" conference invitees and a raging pack of football fans from Pittsburgh, who went about uprooting the fixtures in the hotel restrooms while the Jungians carried on their discussions in an adjoining conference room.[11]

Back in San Francisco, the confluence of students and teachers in the first New College classes had been a success, energizing Duncan's poetry and his intellectual life. The intense studies also brought their conflicts. On December 22, Duncan woke in the middle of the night to take half a Valium, preoccupied by a disagreement with Bobbie Louise Hawkins about the scansion of Yeats's "The Second Coming." In his notebook, he recorded his annoyance when Hawkins theorized that the term "gyre" in the poem hadn't, as Duncan suggested, derived from Yeats's study of Swedenborg, a writer Duncan suspected Hawkins had not read. The feud continued into January 1981, when Hawkins and Duncan clashed about the significance of the word "falcon" in the poem.

In time for the New Year and for their thirtieth anniversary, Duncan wrote a poem for Jess titled "From the Fall of 1950 December 1980." Embedded in the celebratory piece was a hallmark Duncanian pun:

> Even in jest your name
> tenders affection's first flamey seedling
> echo to awake the life in my life
> animal delite has come to whose call
>
> and all jokey and yet deep going
> I come always from the edge of sorrow
> to seek the shore of your regard
> enduring   let day after day
>
> fall from us into place   they
> come again to rime.   In thirty years
> happy chance of a refrain yet renders
> desire more exquisite . . . [12]

Meanwhile, on January 20, Ronald Reagan's inauguration coincided with the release of American hostages held in Iran, a move carefully orchestrated by the new administration. Duncan reflected upon the relationship he saw emerging between the political climate and the generation of poets who would come of age into it:

The United States are themselves going into a reactionary decade . . . that will surely be a decade of counter-reaction / and submerged / suppresst the vital political life, the creation of polis or "city" will itself have the nature of a cocoon.
    The other end of the cocoon? . . . My immediate experience of the talented young, of their keen intelligence . . . leads to a private potentiality that projects a luminous decade within the cover of the deadening dullness.[13]

Eager to maintain his connection to "the talented young," Duncan immersed himself in the New College project. In spring 1981, he taught Nature of Persons, attended by Aaron Shurin, Carl Grundberg, Robert Kocik, John Thorpe, and others. Incorporating his knowledge of Jung and Freud, Duncan led a study of the forces that bring poet and poem into being. For Duncan, the seminars required little preparation; throughout the semester, he presented students with the data he had gathered over a lifetime, pulling together threads of autobiography, his studies of the modernist poets, and his recent readings in semiotics. As with all his classes, the students struggled to stay afloat in the avalanche of information. Carl Grundberg recalled,

> Robert's expectations of himself and of his students . . . were severe, and this attitude spilled over into the . . . classes taught by others. In Diane di Prima's class, for example, I was relieved to hear that we were expected to do "only" ten hours per week of preparatory reading. In Robert's classes, one never knew how much reading one was supposed to be doing, but . . . it never seemed to be enough. . . . For Robert, and soon for the rest of us, books were like coal being shoveled into a steam engine that was always at maximum pressure.[14]

The energy of New College classes also spawned two important extracurricular groups: the Homer Club and the Poetics Group.[15] The Homer Club, which first convened in February 1981, aimed to read the entirety of the *Iliad* in Greek during its meetings. Many of the gatherings took place at Aaron Shurin's apartment on Oak Street, and the early members included Duncan, Shurin, David Melnick, Susan Thackrey, Steve Anker, Noel Stack, Tom Fong, and David Levi Strauss. Other students and friends who drifted in and out of the meetings included Diane di Prima, Michael McClure, Dawn Kolokithas, David Doyle, Dan Blue, Edith Hartnett, and Jim Powell.[16] While only Noel Stack and Jim Powell had a good knowledge of ancient Greek, all the students scanned the meter and translated small parts of the text. David Levi Strauss remembered the evolution of the club's work: "Every week we were assigned lines, five or six in the beginning, twenty at the end. . . . We would copy out the lines, scan the dactylic hexameter, rehearse chanting and translate. In the beginning most of us had no grammar so we looked up every word in the lexicon and cribbed from existing translations. We picked up the grammar slowly, as we needed it."[17]

SIXTY-SEVEN

Five Songs

FOR DUNCAN, the spring was to bring a meeting of great import. On April 5, at the close of a reading at Bookshop Santa Cruz, he was approached by a sixty-four-year-old woman who informed him that she was his biological sister. Anne Spaulding, then living in the area, had seen an advertisement for the reading and suspected that the poet was the younger brother from whom she had been separated in 1919. The fact that Duncan used his birth name made the identification easier, and his poems in *Roots and Branches* and elsewhere had also made public the story of his adoption. The meeting placed Duncan in a predicament. While he was curious about the family and the family's medical history, Anne Spaulding opened the way for other siblings to reenter his life.[1] That month he received an enthusiastic letter from his sister Eleanor, who lived in Carson City, Nevada, and he soon learned that another sister, Marguerite, lived in North Hollywood, California. Worried that the long-lost Duncans would impose demands upon his household and intrude on Jess's solitude, he was quick to set boundaries, writing to Spaulding:

> Your sense . . . of the privacy of my own life is most sensitive, and very important for me. With my own family (for my adopted family is the only one I have known—having no memories proper of my first six months, only residues of body feeling and emotional distress . . .)— . . . I require also distance and formality. I have lived with a painter for the past thirty years . . . ; and it is a serious requirement for him not to have outside complications enter our life.[2]

Wary of becoming the little brother his sisters had never had, while he corresponded with Anne Spaulding cordially and later met a cousin in Oakland named Gladys Kennard, he chose not to contact his other surviving sisters.

Spaulding wrote Duncan throughout the early 1980s, seemingly with the hope that the relationship would blossom further. Beginning a December 1982 letter with the salutation "Dear Elusive Robert," she continued, "I miss you a lot, and would give much thought before writing to you. I awoke this morning, talking to you in my mind, trying to decide whether you would resent my crying on your shoulder. I decided that just the crying might do me good, whether you wipe away my tears or not."[3]

For Duncan, the spring and summer of 1981 introduced a number of realities that kept him from the distractions of his resurrected family. His trip to Santa Cruz had spawned other new relationships, with Nathaniel Mackey and bell hooks, two young writers who would soon look to Duncan and Jess as mentors. Mackey, then teaching at the University of California, had written about Duncan's poetry while a graduate student at Stanford; hooks, a feminist and social activist then completing her graduate degree, began to turn to Jess for creative inspiration. In the following years, hooks and Mackey would visit 20th Street on several occasions, first to see Duncan and later to meet Jess, "the mystery voice . . . on the other side," as hooks referred to him fondly in her memoir *Wounds of Passion*.[4]

After a May 6 reading at an international writing festival in Toronto and a short visit to Ekbert Faas, Duncan settled into San Francisco for a summer of teaching, leading a New College class called What Is at Issue in Poetics: Baudelaire, Dickinson & Whitman. To Robert Adamson he reported, "It's the first time I have read Dickinson in depth—some 1775 poems in the Variorum . . . —I don't know what will emerge as the experience of her transient structures / passages of configurations, that I relate to 'ideograms,' . . . she dwells on visitations and losses (thefts, weathers, loves) contrasting with the systematic structures of Whitman and Baudelaire."[5] During the six weeks of classes, he also acted as the chair of the Poetics Program, working with the other faculty members to carve a path for the recently established college.

The summer of 1981 brought ominous news of an illness beginning to spread among gay men across the country. In July, the *New York Times* reported the outbreak of a "gay cancer" affecting homosexual men in New York and California, and within a year, with two thousand reported cases, the Centers for Disease Control had named the illness acquired immune deficiency syndrome. Continuing poems for the second volume of *Ground Work*, on September 21 Duncan wrote "Seams," a piece that touched upon his own struggle with physical decline:

<pre>
       each   flower and leaf
   in me   autumnal   day   and equinox
       the coriander is in seed   swelling   a ruddy light in the green
Sight   gathers   your radiant   smile   and the ripening smell
       into natural crowns the sun and wind address their declarations.[6]
</pre>

That fall while teaching Basic Elements II, Duncan made trips south to give readings at Beyond Baroque Literary Center in Los Angeles on October 2 and the University of California, San Diego, on October 21. The reading in San Diego celebrated Duncan's new chapbook *Five Songs,* whose sequence of poems, written during the previous spring, would become the final part of the *Structure of Rime* series that he had begun during the mid-1950s. In the piece, Duncan introduced a figure previously unimaginable in his work, stirred by his meeting with Anne Spaulding:

> My sister searches the night sky,
>   its swarm upon swarm of stars,
>   and calls for me.
>
> I answering
> —how still it is out there where
>   she sees me—   stand
>
> in her recall   my song ...[7]

Aaron Shurin remembered another appearance Duncan made in 1981, at San Francisco's 544 Natoma Performance Gallery. While reciting parts of *Faust Foutu,* "to the audible gasp of a startled crowd, he slowly, tremblingly, unlayered himself. His 62-year-old nakedness had won for him a shock-of-the-new that no youth could buy: an image of The Real."[8] On October 27, a fully clothed Duncan was in the classroom teaching his Basic Elements II class, which included lectures on phonetics and linguistic sequence and a reading list with selections from Saussure, Sapir, Whorf, Jespersen, Hjelmslev, Jakobson, Barthes, Eco, Kohler, Cassirer, Heidegger, and Merleau-Ponty. With his continued participation in the Homer Club, Duncan also resumed reading Hesiod, and on November 9, he wrote "You, Muses [Passages 22]," rendering the opening lines in the original Greek out of the *Theogony.*[9]

A long-distance business trip to Shippensburg State College in Pennsylvania came later in November. John Taggart, then a professor at the school, arranged for Duncan to meet with students and give a reading during his stay, but Duncan seemed equally eager to participate in events in the Taggart household. Joining the family for dinners on November 18 and 19, he also enthusiastically volunteered to attend one of Taggart's daughter's swim-team practices. Between meetings with students and while unwinding in his room on campus at night, Duncan delighted in the reading material Taggart had presented him with upon his arrival: Taggart's 1974 dissertation on objectivist poetry and Susan Howe's recently published *The Liberties*.[10] For Taggart, Duncan's reading at Shippensburg was the highlight of the visit, during which the poet performed for nearly two hours before saying, "Let's take a short break, and then those who care for poetry can come back."[11]

Leaving Pennsylvania on November 21, Duncan returned home to burrow into reading inspired by his New College classes. In early December, he delved into Piaget, and as a New Year's celebration, he reread *Finnegans Wake* before returning to his H. D. studies. Among the happy social occasions of the 1982 New Year was a party at Don Allen's house for Ellen Tallman on January 3, the Monday night Homer Club meeting on the fourth, and from the sixth through the eighth, a stay at Ham and Mary Tyler's farm in Healdsburg to celebrate Duncan's sixty-third birthday. "The Michaels," as Duncan and Jess called them, were frequent guests to 20th Street that season. Michael Palmer and his wife, Cathy Simon, had dinner with the couple on January 15, and when Michael Davidson visited from San Diego that month, he was enlisted to watch the British television series *Brideshead Revisited,* then running on PBS. Two other welcome wintertime guests were Norman Austin and Edna Keough. Keough, retired and living in the Bay Area, still made occasional luncheon visits to the household to hear poems from her former student as she had some forty years earlier in Bakersfield.

With the beginning of the spring semester at New College, Duncan's schedule became complex. In addition to attending Monday night Homer Club meetings, he taught Nature of Persons II on Tuesdays and Thursdays, and in February began a series of Friday night lectures on Charles Olson at the school.[12] The Olson talks, less formal than those he'd given in Iowa City and in Buffalo during the late 1970s, treated the audience to Duncan's recitations of sections of the *Maximus* poems. By the second year of New College poetics classes, Duncan had found a place that fulfilled his needs as a monologist. Not only did he have his regular class schedule, but the program had also been designed with enough flexibility that he could convene eager students for extracurricular programs whenever he desired an audience.

Meanwhile on the evening of February 2, Duncan flew to New York to begin a short tour that included stops at the far ends of the country: Buffalo and San Diego. From February 4 through 7, he acted as an "Intercultural Arts Festival consultant" at Buffalo's City Honors School and presented a "sermon" titled "The Continuity of Christian Myth" at the Westminster Presbyterian Church. The lecture clarified the Christian streak in Duncan's thinking. He told the audience that he prayed to an Old Testament God, "just in case," and at a subsequent poetry reading, he explained that he didn't believe in the soul but did feel he was an event in the soul of the world. Returning to a theme from "Man's Fulfillment in Order and Strife," Duncan again made a distinction between his beliefs and those of his adoptive parents: "No question that my poetry is poetry of spirit. . . . Is it a poetry of religion, do I have one? . . . I have been described as a mystic poet. My only possible mysticism is the experience I have of language, which to me is pure spirit and to me is something more than eternal. . . . In language I encounter God."[13]

Flying from Buffalo to New York, he appeared at the Collegiate School on West 77th Street, where Odyssia and Federico Quadrani's son was a student, and after meeting with a class on contemporary poetry there, he rushed to catch a flight to San Diego. On February 10, participating in a University of California conference called The San Francisco Renaissance, he spoke on an afternoon panel titled "The Various Arts of the San Francisco Renaissance" that also included Michael Davidson, who chaired the session, and Michael McClure and David Meltzer. That evening Duncan gave a reading with William Everson and then joined his fellow conference participants at a local restaurant for margaritas. On February 17, back in San Francisco, his Olson lecture for the week was "Projective Voice." Two days later, he began one of the final poems of *Ground Work II*. "Whose" arrived while he was en route to the dry cleaner, and he completed the poem later that afternoon over a cup of coffee, reporting in the margins of his notebook, "The opening of this poem began after the morning session on 'Person,' and before receiving once I got home [James] Hillman's letter of Feb. the first ten lines had come into my head—'to head'—as I walked home."[14] Subtitling the poem "(for Jim Hillman's tribute to Henri Corbin, *The Thought of the Heart*)," he added a note in his journal after finishing the piece: "Correspondence with Hillman has most opend up the ways for me. I had been holding back from the sublimation / sublime, the subliminal inflation in which the start I knew waited. More endangered and endangering (going beyond the respect of the poetic community . . . and beyond my own trust in the art) than the proposition of how derivative I must be was."[15]

Throughout the spring, Duncan and Jess spent time with old friends, including Michael Palmer and Cathy Simon and Hilde and David Burton, and on March 21, Duncan attended a Homer Club dinner to celebrate the completion of a section of the *Iliad*. Club members were as democratic in the responsibilities for the meal as they had been with the translations of the lines of Greek, with each participant bringing elements of a feast that would include the culturally appropriate fare of moussaka, retsina, Greek salad, and dolmades. Early April held opera dates with the Burtons and an April 5 visit from Anne Spaulding. Spaulding met Jess for the first time, and Duncan and his sister joined their elderly cousin Gladys Kennard for lunch in Oakland. Kennard, the niece of Duncan's mother Marguerite Carpenter, provided Duncan with the history of his maternal family in Oakland, also telling him about his mother's resting place in nearby Mountain View Cemetery.

SIXTY-EIGHT

A Paris Visit

IN THE MIDST OF TAX SEASON, Duncan left for a trip to Europe that would take him away from home for several weeks. Arriving at JFK Airport for a brief stop in New York City on April 13, he wrote to Jess with complaints about the rigors of traveling: "I must be sixty-three years old of it, for my frame, muskculls, flash or flush, nerbs are frazzled and silently groaning."[1] His luxurious lodgings with Federico and Odyssia Quadrani provided some consolation, though Duncan also reported home that the couple had quizzed him about Jess's output in the studio, hoping he would coax their artist into increasing his production. Jess's exhibition *The Romantic Paintings* was then on display at the gallery, and Duncan spent a good deal of time viewing it. That week he also visited a Frank Auerbach show at the Marlborough Gallery before taking a train to Kingston, Rhode Island, to give the lecture "Composition by Field and Assemblage in Painting, Poetry, and Life Style" at the University of Rhode Island. After the talk, Duncan had dinner at the home of Marjorie Keller and P. Adams Sitney. Keller, an experimental filmmaker, and Sitney, a film critic who had written extensively on the works of Stan

Brakhage and Kenneth Anger, provided good company, and the group was joined by other New Englanders, Michael Franco and Janice Knight from Boston and Keith Waldrop from Providence. Duncan dutifully reported to Jess about a feast of barbecued swordfish, though Michael Franco remembered some tension emerging because Duncan had invited Franco and Knight without informing his hosts of the additional mouths to feed. Before leaving Rhode Island, Duncan made another appearance, giving a poetry reading highlighting "The Dignities" from his *Passages* series "The Regulators" in a performance that Michael Franco recalled as "sweeping and nothing short."[2] That night Duncan phoned Jess, who missed having his partner's company to celebrate a glowing review of his work by John Ashbery in the April 26 issue of *Newsweek*.

Back in New York on April 16, Duncan met Helen and Pat Adam to view a de Chirico show at the Museum of Modern Art, before catching a red-eye flight to Paris for what was to be his final journey east across the Atlantic. Hosted by R. B. Kitaj and Sandra Fisher, who had settled into an apartment complex at 59 rue Galande, Duncan had a flat of his own that included Fisher's painting studio. Ready to enjoy the best that Paris had to offer, he spent his first afternoon indulging in cheeses, patés, and truffles, and strolling past Notre Dame. One goal of the visit was to complete a collaboration that he and Kitaj had begun discussing some years earlier: a series of drawings to correspond to Duncan's poems, in this case, the sequence "Illustrative Lines."[3] On Sunday April 18, Kitaj and Duncan had their first work date, with Kitaj sketching the poet as he read aloud from "The Regulators." The sessions allowed Duncan to rehearse the performance of his poems and experiment with variations in his presentation. Having purchased a small tape recorder, he delighted in the opportunity to revisit his monologues and to fine-tune the works while using his hand to conduct or measure the beat. While he had long attended to the musicality of his poetry, his Homer Club studies of the scansion of dactylic lines had brought his attention back to the details of meter.

Between sessions with Kitaj, Duncan also began to see friends in Paris. On April 20, he had coffee with his former Innsbruck student Joey Simas, and the two proceeded to Paris's Institut de Recherche et Coordination Acoustique/Musique (IRCAM), where Duncan had been invited to give a May lecture.[4] On their stroll that morning, Duncan and Simas were accosted by a band of gypsy children, one of whom pulled Duncan's wallet from his coat, dropping it when a plainclothes detective came into sight. Slightly ruffled, the two poets nonetheless continued on to the IRCAM, where they met with Steve McAdams, a physicist conducting research at the institute, and then moved on to the rue St. Jacques to visit occultist bookstores, where Duncan bought a copy of Johann Reuchlin's *Le Kabbale: de Arte Cabalistica.* That afternoon, Duncan returned to the Kitaj household for more work in the studio, which he documented in a letter to Jess:

> From 4 to 5 another session ... to finish the drawing of the "sleeping" head: an appearance which now I read in my mirror as well as in my poetry of pain, is it?, an anguish ... from which whatever exuberance for life must rise. It is haunting that this visage is a visage of my not talking: for Kitaj working on the mouth closed needed an hour Monday and an hour yesterday—and for much of the time not looking or seeing: for he had me close my eyes.[5]

At the end of a long day of work and social events, Duncan treated himself to a lighter amusement, taking a trip to a local movie theater to see *Conan the Barbarian,* which had recently opened in Paris in its original English form. Aroused by the hyperdeveloped biceps of its protagonist, Duncan decided that the film was a magnificent anthroposophical-theosophical epic and pro-claimed, "Conan is hauntingly, sensually, powerfully presented by Schwartz-negger *[sic]*. . . . a new star emerges."[6]

Within the first days of his Paris stay, Duncan had settled into a routine of afternoon sittings with Kitaj, during which Sandra Fisher occasionally joined them to complete her own sketches of the poet. Music events at the IRCAM were another priority, and on April 23, Duncan saw a performance of Schoenberg and Bartók's work arranged by Pierre Boulez. The IRCAM neighborhood of the 5th arrondissement was, to Duncan's glee, dotted with esoteric bookstores. While he told Jess that he was restricting his purchases to books essential to the themes of the *Passages* poems, within four weeks he had collected several boxes of materials to ship home.

At the end of Duncan's first week in Paris, he met with poet Claude Royet-Journoud for an animated discussion about music, poetry, and form. Royet-Journoud explained to Duncan that the younger French poets of his circle employed a curious technique for gauging silences in their readings— by timing pauses in five- or ten-second intervals, using a clock rather than the organic pulse that Duncan was accustomed to. In his curiosity about the method, Duncan experimented with timed pauses during his April 24 sit-ting for Kitaj and Fisher. One of the disheartening revelations of the sketch-ing sessions for Duncan was the focus upon his rapidly balding skull, which gave rise to a series of anxiety dreams about his marriage to Jess. He wrote home on April 26:

> I kept dreaming of coming to you again and again in different forms pleading for recognition and your companionship and being turned away, having nothing left of what was "me" for you . . . but my merest existence. There must be a series of "me's" you have stayed by—and such a distance for me today from 1951 that the thread can seem so fragile. The dream rehearsal itself of such a . . . questioning—you are, after all, entirely you—in the dream were—tho a series of "you's" confounded by spectral possibilities derived from lovers long ago who had rejected me—yes, I miss your presence here, in the midst of the excitements and the beauty of Paris.[7]

While worried about a relationship that increasingly cast him and Jess as little more than pen pals, Duncan was equally drawn to the social opportunities afforded by his travels. Through a wintry Paris springtime, he spent his days book shopping, working with Kitaj, and meeting with writers and artists, including Emmanuel Hocquard, Edmond Jabès, and Pierre Boulez.

The second half of his trip brought additional professional responsibilities. In early May, he was with the Fauchereaus in Coye-la-Forêt, where he prepared a lecture on form and poetry for his IRCAM appearance. Again facing the challenge of speaking French to an audience, Duncan fell into an uncharacteristic panic, which he described in a letter to Jess: "a violent headache, and a sickness at the stomach—the French say ecoeure losing heart. . . . Two aspirin did not lift the state and an attempt at retreating for a nap was no good. I had a chill across my torso, could not face supper and retired."[8] After gathering himself to deliver the lecture on May 4, he again wrote to Jess: "I performed last night as I truly was—not as a master . . . but as a student relaying somehow, as best he could/I could what an instructor askt of him."[9]

During the last week of Duncan's stay, he had another chance to speak French to an audience, appearing on a radio program with Claude Royet-Journoud, Alan Veinstein, and Jean Daive. After a final reading in Paris with Veinstein, on May 15 Duncan flew to New York accompanied by Kitaj. Again housed with the Quadranis, he read on May 17 at the Museum of Modern Art and two days later appeared with New York poet John Godfrey at the Poetry Project on the Lower East Side. Duncan's reading at the museum, with Ed Dorn, was organized by local poetry diva Lita Hornick of the Kulcher Foundation. The evening was long remembered in literary circles, not for the works presented but for Duncan's antics in placing a curse on two cameramen who were filming the event. Distracted by the movements of the film crew in his line of vision, Duncan lashed out. One audience member, Reed Bye, remembered, "Duncan's philippic is mostly inaudible to me in the back of the room, a giant loft with windows all around. I do hear him comment how 'surreal' it is to denounce the cameras when it's the 'monkeys pushing them around who are to blame,' and then proceed to level a formal curse on the two. . . . 'There are two things a poet can do: praise, and curse.' This is a curse he says that will take effect within six months."[10] Duncan continued the reading with pieces from the *Passages* series, after which, as Bye also remembered, he was accosted by one of the cameramen, who turned the curse back onto the poet to the delight of some in the crowd. Duncan came away from the hubbub unscathed, leaving the reading with Michael Franco and Janice Knight for a meal at the Carnegie Deli.[11]

Turning his thoughts toward home, Duncan made a brief stop in Chicago to see Paula Prokopoff, traveling with her to Milwaukee, where he gave a reading at Woodland Pattern bookstore. Hosted by Karl Gartung and Anne Kingsbury, Duncan read from *Ground Work,* opening with "Achilles Song." He talked briefly about the subtitle of the collection, *Before the War,* describing the beginning of the atomic age as a single chapter in a long story of strife:

> It's Pan—it's the great return to the myth of Pandora's Box . . . that haunts these books. So "Before the War" is very much that, but deeper. Homer and Hesiod both know about war, and war to me is a real entity. . . . So in history I live in relation to deep dream, and . . . [it] moves constantly. I can see it coming again and again in poems. And that deep dream is not current . . . to me there's no progress in history. . . . We are not living worse than we ever did, but deep things are coming up that we were denying, and now we're beginning to see them everywhere.[12]

On June 1, the summer session began at New College, during which he taught Political Vision in Poetry. He described the class to Barbara Joseph as "six double-packt weeks, close dealing passages of Dante, Milton, Blake and Whitman in which politics is a metaphor for poetics."[13] Settling into the familiar realm of Bay Area social life, Duncan spent the summer with Jess and close friends, attending the opera with the Burtons, cooking for Michael Palmer and Cathy Simon and the Rakosis, and appearing at the early July wedding of Michael and Joanna McClure's daughter Katherine at the San Francisco Zen Center.

SIXTY-NINE

Bard

TAKING A LEAVE from his responsibilities at New College during the fall of 1982, Duncan traveled east to teach at Bard College, where he had been appointed a Distinguished Visiting Professor in the Division of Languages and Literature. On September 23, he flew east, first giving a reading at Radcliffe College in Cambridge and then making his way to Bard to teach the first of two four-week terms. Duncan's class, Poetics I: Segmentation of the Poem, would include "lectures and discussions concerning the structures in Poetry: the sensorimotor grounds of intelligence; phone, phoneme, sememe as projecting formal meaning; coordinations—rime and reason (ration), syllable, word, line/sentence, stanza/paragraph, part/movement/'book.' Studies in the field theory of composition in relation to other approaches."[1]

Upon arriving at the school, he settled into a quiet apartment "in the midst of the woods" where "sunlight filtered down thru layers of foliage for a green radiance."[2] Robert Kelly, then twenty years into his tenure at Bard, recalled the building as "a wooden elegant modern structure, one of perhaps eight 'Ravine Houses' built in the late 60's or early 70's along the rim of the ravine beyond the art buildings. Robert would have had an apartment reached by a wooden bridge. . . . The buildings . . . were on stilts on the hillside, like Berkeley houses in the hills. They swayed in strong wind a little—and were intended to do so."[3]

The school, established in 1860, had evolved into a private liberal undergraduate institution catering primarily to middle-class East Coast youngsters with an interest in the arts. Two hours from New York City by train, and another fifteen minutes by car along the Hudson, the Bard community depended on its own cultural resources to thrive. During Duncan's stay, he found himself in the thick of an active intellectual scene. After quiet mornings in the solitude of his lodgings, he spent his afternoons with friends and evenings in the classroom. Robert Kelly, Station Hill press editors George and Susan Quasha, and local writer Chuck Stein were all part of Duncan's social circle that fall. Another visiting professor, Ephraim Isaac, was housed near Duncan and quickly became a dinner companion. The Ethiopian-born Isaac, an expert in ancient Semitic language, had attended Harvard Divinity School, and Duncan reported to Jess that he was excited about his interesting new friend and "entertaining neighbor," whom he could hear . . . in the apartment overhead "sing[ing] in Hebrew to himself and bounc[ing] . . . about."[4]

On September 29, Duncan began teaching, finding his thirty-five students shy at first but also eager to work with the visiting poet. One of his students was poet Susan Howe's daughter, Rebecca Quaytman, and others, including Elio Schneeman, Leonard Schwartz, and Elizabeth Robinson, would go on to have careers as poets. Though the students were undergraduates, Duncan continued the intensive teaching practices he'd developed at Black Mountain and New College. He told Jess, "Tomorrow night they will be working with phones—and I can lecture on the oral/aural system pre-letters and where visual/gestural signals enterd into the imagined complex of a series of possible poetries from expressions to songs and lullabies, to epics and shamanistic trance utterances."[5] As was Duncan's habit, he quickly became interested in the students' activities and ideas, interacting with them as peers and integrating their thoughts about writing into his own work. His meetings with Ephraim Isaac also entered a poem he wrote at Bard. Titled "At the Door," the piece included meditations on "Powers of ancient Africa" with references to the African trickster god Papa Legba.

Duncan enjoyed the novelty of the small Hudson Valley campus in autumn, telling Jess after his first week, "My little apartment house in the ravine . . . is in shadow and cold in the morning. I sat huddled in sweaters and my lined raincoat to read. In the plaza outside the dining hall, in the coffee bar room of which I have found my table by a sunny window, on the terrace the students spread out books for sale."[6] On the first weekend of October, Duncan made progress on an afterword for Edmond Jabès's *Selected Poems,* soon to be published by Station Hill Press, and he had an outing to the home of writer David Matlin in Saugerties, New York, with Don Byrd joining them from Albany. Matlin remembered a happy visit, on "a beautiful fall Sunday" at the old farmhouse he shared with his wife, Gail Schneider. Schneider cooked soup while Duncan kept her company, and as the group sat on the porch after dinner admiring the autumn colors, Duncan proclaimed it "a sacred day." For Matlin, the weekend made clear Duncan's desired place in the world: at the confluence of human relation, food, and the cycles of nature.[7]

On Tuesday October 5, Duncan gave a reading of poems from *Ground Work* at Bard. That Thursday evening, he traveled to New York by train for a weekend visit with friends, including Helen and Pat Adam and the Quadranis. Ida Hodes was visiting the Adam sisters that week, and she and Duncan had a Saturday lunch with a friend from Santa Cruz, Madeline Burnside, after which the three headed out to the galleries of Soho. Duncan told Jess that his survey of New York's contemporary art had been a disappointment: "Madeline was right, one would have to see it to believe it. The 'sensation' (in quotes because the whole show was drab) of the 'year' is Schnabel. The *N.Y. Times* seriously discusses—could he be the latest thing. That is exactly what it was—as going for broke as Reaganomics. Out not to impress but in a competition to depress."[8]

Returning to Bard, Duncan gave two more readings on campus on October 10 and 11, presenting the whole of the *Passages* series to his students. The second reading was followed by a dinner party at the Quashas' house, where he met Fluxus artist Dick Higgins for the first time and saw old friend Pauline Oliveros. While he took some pleasure in such gatherings, his main enthusiasm that autumn was for teaching. On October 12, he gave a lecture on Emily Dickinson, and he also began to expand his Bard talks beyond the scheduled Monday and Wednesday evening sessions. After a busy week in the classroom, Duncan departed for Albany to see Don Byrd and his family. While there, he moved on from his weeklong presentation of *Passages* to read *Mother Goose* and *Winnie-the-Pooh* to Byrd's seven-year-old daughter, Anne. Don Byrd also gave his visitor a tour of Albany's architecture and bookstores and, to Duncan's delight, took him to visit "a Barn Depot in the country apple orchard land, coming home . . . at lunch time loaded with bosc pears, Macs, and a new Japanese hybrid apple, stilton cheese and N.Y. cheddar."[9] After a further visit to a museum in Williamstown to see paintings by Sargent, Renoir, and Winslow Homer, Duncan spent the following week hopscotching between Bard and the State University of New York at Albany, giving readings at both schools and spending time with Don Byrd and Ed Sanders. As the four-week residency at Bard came to an end, Duncan reflected upon his tenure at the school: "In this month the magic feel of what is potential in this place has begun to ripen. There is a core of students in the class whose psyches are resonant; they carry their own currents of information and takes on each session among themselves. . . . They are a sweet batch of grandchildren."[10]

A frenzy of activity awaited Duncan during the end of October and early November in San Francisco. On Monday evenings, he attended meetings of the Homer Club, and on Tuesdays, he returned to Poetics Group meetings. His calendar was also dotted with social obligations: lunches with Edna Keough, dinners with the Burtons and Michael Palmer and Cathy Simon, a rare meeting with his nephew Bruce from Bakersfield, and dates with gallery owner Paule Anglim, librarian James Hart, Boulder poets Anne Waldman and Reed Bye, and old friends Carl Rakosi and Tom Parkinson.[11] After a Christmas season with visits from Michael Davidson and David Melnick, Duncan was bedridden with a birthday flu and in a panic about the obligations of the coming year.

During the spring of 1983, he would complete his work at Bard and make a series of trips that marked the end of his work as a traveling poet. On February 28, he spent time in Lawrence, Kansas, with Ed Grier and Ken Irby and gave a lecture for the university's Mellon Faculty Development Seminar. Returning to Jungian themes, he titled the talk "Creativity in the Dream, Creativity in the Poem." The following evening he gave a reading of *Passages* poems before returning home for two weeks of rest. In mid-March, he participated in the Symposium of the Whole: Toward a Human Poetics at the University of Southern California, joining Edmond Jabès, Paula Gunn Allen, Clayton Eshleman, Jed Rasula, Nathaniel Tarn, and Dennis Tedlock in a reading on March 19. The following day he presented a talk called "The Place of Spiritual and Occult Traditions in a New Poetics" as part of a conference panel.

Home at the end of March to see Ronald Reagan's televised speech outlining plans for a "Star Wars" defensive missile system, Duncan took up the more urgent business of gathering information for his 1982 tax returns. A trip to the East Coast in late March included a three-day visit to Orono, Maine, where his host was Burt Hatlen, followed by an Easter weekend in Boston, where he stayed with former student Michael Franco. Franco recalled the highlights of the holiday time with Duncan:

> We went to The Gardner [Museum] and he gave me a wonderful lecture on Titian and Genius (for once I asked the right question . . . "why is this a work of genius?") covering what genius was and how it was present in The Rape of Europa. . . . Thwarted from a picnic by a rainy Easter day we made Ukrainian Easter eggs with Roman and Mary Kay Martynuk. (I broke Robert's [egg]

trying to polish it to which he said, "You know there are no accidents, you've broken my world egg.")[12]

From there Duncan returned to Bard College to complete the second half of his residency, this time focusing talks not on his *Passages* poems but on his work for *The H. D. Book.* In the midst of his travels came news of Jess's older brother's death, an event that Duncan could make little sense of from a distance, particularly given Jess's reticence to discuss family matters even with his lover of thirty years:

> It seems always you have something to face alone—like your father's death— that I would want to be with you to share. The Quadranis have always re- markt how friendly and enthusiastic your brother's visits to your shows have been—And he too . . . must have had some of the difficulties you had with your parents. I've always wondered about your silent psycho-drama there, for there seemed no way to work it out, until at last death wrote its conclusion.[13]

Duncan too faced a troubling reality. He'd been ill since the New Year with a flu and colds, and his trips through the spring had exacerbated his symptoms. His time at Bard was marked by long days of headaches and coughing. While he pushed forward with his obligations, including readings in upstate New York, on April 15, he wrote to Jess from Rochester, "Squares of cheese and plastic demi-glasses of wine become a kind of Pavlovian signal for a wave of fatigue."[14] In Rochester to give a talk on H. D. at the Conference on Women Writers of the 20th Century Modern Era, Duncan experienced an irritation of another sort when he crossed paths with old friend Robert Bertholf, who had left his teaching position at Kent State to oversee the Po- etry/Rare Books Collection of the State University of New York at Buffalo: "Bertholf is so self-driven now in his struggles for dominance—not only in his and through his . . . position viz a viz the S.U.N.Y. [Buffalo] library itself; but also on a host of contingent fronts. . . . He was mainly busy back of the Rochester scene to force the resignation of the President (Emily Wallace) be- cause she let the Society Bulletin languish."[15] On April 19, back at Bard in time for a spring snowstorm, Duncan attended to teaching duties before de- parting for a weekend in New York, where he visited the offices of New Di- rections and then had lunch with Helen Adam, who feasted on ice cream and light beer, much to his bemusement.

The second semester of teaching had taken its toll on an ailing Duncan: "In accepting Bard College's offer . . . , I already found how out of order that vanity was. There was, I discoverd in myself, no 'leave' from the Poetics teaching, the Homer group, the continuities of our household."[16] After a May 3 reading at the Walker Art Center in Minneapolis, Duncan flew back to San Francisco. With the weight of his responsibilities in the Bay Area, obligations in an international poetry community, and strains on his health, Duncan reflected upon the anxieties generated by others' expectations of him, commenting in a notebook about various requests for essays and poems: "The editors of these magazines, with all the social blackmail of a charity organization or a cultural project that must take place, see writing as a contribution."[17] The fall brought more work. In addition to coteaching Field Theory as a Poetics with Michael Palmer, Duncan found his schedule cluttered with "Poetics teach-ins," which were held at the school on Mondays and Tuesdays and with visits to David Meltzer's Kabbalah classes on Friday afternoons. As he wrote to Barbara Joseph, "the tyranny of the Calendar begins to take over," and in an attempt to stave off further stress, Duncan began weekly massage sessions on Thursday mornings.[18]

The Field Theory class sustained Duncan throughout that fall, and as Michael Palmer remembered, Duncan showed no signs of slowing down, entering the classroom as "a verbal storm" and leading his younger colleague to reflect, "To co-teach with him was to hold on for dear life."[19] Integrating poetry and science, Palmer and Duncan presented a series of lectures about Olsonian ideas of projective verse alongside Michael Faraday's nineteenth-century theories of electromagnetic fields. In addition to trying to digest the information barreling toward them in class, students read Kohler's *Gestalt Psychology* and *The Place of Value in a World of Facts,* Piaget's *Construction of Reality in the Child,* Jung's *Memories, Dreams, Reflections,* Whitehead's *The Function of Reason,* the third volume of Cassirer's *The Philosophy of Symbolic Forms,* and Cassirer's *The Phenomenology of Knowledge.*

A fresh addition to the New College community that fall was Toronto poet Norma Cole. Though she was not a registered student, Cole had spent time on the periphery of the Valencia Street campus and introduced herself to Duncan, who soon invited her to visit him at 20th Street. Like many of the younger writers who flocked around Duncan in the early 1980s, she found herself drawn to daily life within the household, and with Jess's approval, she became a regular guest. As both Duncan and Jess struggled with health problems, they increasingly depended on New College students to assist them at home. In the late fall and early winter of 1983, Duncan continued to complain of fatigue, and after a series of medical tests, adjustments were made to his blood pressure medication. He reasoned that the "dumb inertia of mid-winter depression" was a side effect of the new medication as well as the result of a busy semester at New College.[20] More troublingly, he was having difficulty focusing his thoughts, and as he proofread *Fictive Certainties* for New Directions, a seemingly minor event would prove indicative of a larger problem. He told Peter Glassgold on December 13, "I could not figure out, I thought, how I had justified the paragraphs in the copy. Then, finally, yesterday it all came back to me and was simple."[21]

SEVENTY

The Baptism of the Blood

No faculty not   ill at ease
                 lets us
                 begin where I must

from the failure of systems
ROBERT DUNCAN, "After a Long Illness"

IN JANUARY 1984, Ronald Reagan won reelection, and Duncan turned sixty-five. Robert Glück arranged a birthday party for him, recalling Duncan's request that he invite "only family": "I wondered if he was using the old term, meaning only gay people, or if he meant the family he had created for himself. In any case, it was only gay people, so perhaps the former. Just for fun I got out some party hats, and Robert wore a pointed hat on his forehead, like a unicorn."[1]

New College student Dawn Kolokithas recalled a darker aspect of Duncan's affect during early 1984:

> Before he fell ill, . . . he ranted on about the nature of the blood, the blood this, the blood that, etc. All those gestures. And then one night [David] Levi [Strauss] and I were playing pool and drinking too much at a rough bar near the school. Tinker Greene was with us. . . . And this girl came in, covered in blood. Her mother had been stabbed to death by her father, and the girl had escaped. . . . The whole thing was rather traumatic . . . and then the next day Robert spoke to Levi and I about the baptism of the blood.[2]

In Christian theology, the baptism of blood, or *baptismus sanguinis,* refers to the martyrdom of the unbaptized: unbaptized persons murdered in the service of Christ are said to have been baptized at death in their own blood. It was a concept Duncan would have come across in Tertullian's writings, where references to such a *lavacrum sanguinis* abound. David Levi Strauss remembered the relationship between his experience in the bar and his studies at New College: "We grabbed pool cues and went to the apartment across the street to find the ax murderer sitting in a chair by the bed, ax in lap. Everything that happened to us during that time became incorporated into the 'curriculum.' Blood baptism."[3]

During the following months, Duncan's references to the blood became even more significant to his students. In February 1984, there were signs that a medical crisis was around the corner. Duncan was weary when he attended a conference on Mary Butts at the University of California, Davis, on February 23, speaking alongside Robin Blaser, Robert Byington, Kenneth Irby, and Barbara Wagstaff. He subsequently canceled an April reading in Charlottesville, Virginia, writing to Peter Glassgold, "I have to cut back" and telling Richard Jones of the University of Virginia on March 1, "My doctor has made the whole question one of my health, for during this period . . . my blood pressure has gone up to about 200."[4]

At a spring conference at Louisiana State University, Duncan became ill. Scheduled to give a reading on March 8, he had arrived in Baton Rouge complaining of symptoms that seemed indicative of a heart problem. Another conference participant, Alice Notley, remembered, "Robert arrived . . . in a state of physical distress. This was the first intimation of his kidney disease. . . . He performed very well but was of course worried, and also emotional. I read the first night, with Andrei Codrescu; he read on the second with Carolyn Kizer."[5] Making her first public appearance since the death of her husband, Ted Berrigan, the previous year, Notley recalled that Duncan approached her to express appreciation for her performance, remarking "There's so little tenderness in American poetry."[6] After his own reading, he returned to his lodgings with Rodger Kamenetz, where, as his host recalled, "It seems the battery ran out on his blood pressure monitor. It turned out he was in heart failure. The LSU student health folks advised him that if he fell asleep he might die so I stayed up all night with him while he regaled me with stories about his unique take on Cain and Abel and of course on Sodom and Gomorrah. It was all quite fascinating."[7] At a hospital in Baton Rouge, doctors initially diagnosed Duncan with heart failure. He returned to San

Francisco, accompanied by poet Carolyn Kizer and her husband, and checked into St. Mary's Hospital on Stanyan Street. There, doctors recognized his need for renal dialysis. Further tests made clear the nature of Duncan's health problems, which his doctor, Philip Hertz, later described in a medical report:

> Mr. Duncan has end stage kidney failure secondary to an unusual type of kidney disease called kappa chain deposition.... These kappa chains in a sense plug up the filtering units of the kidney and lead to end stage kidney failure. Mr. Duncan has also had hypertension and in the past, had some heart failure from hypertensive heart disease.... [He] started hemodialysis therapy in 3/84. He was switched eventually from hemodialysis to Chronic Ambulatory Peritoneal Dialysis.[8]

On March 20, still sequestered in room 804 at Saint Mary's, Duncan missed a ceremony at which he was to be presented that year's Shelley Memorial Award. In a letter to his long-estranged friend Denise Levertov, he elaborated on his condition:

> A note to let you know that I've made considerable progress since the ten hospital days. Your note meant a lot to me.
> "Heart failure," as it was diagnosed in Baton Rouge, meant ... that my heart and lungs were swampt with retaind water, so that to climb stairs and even to walk had become a heavy labor. I got back home on Saturday March 12 and by 11 o'clock Sunday I was in St. Mary's Hospital, where a crew of doctors and technicians ... saw me thru blood and urine analyses, the diagnosis of kidney failure as the underlying condition ..., then the operation to prepare my arm for hemodialysis, blood transfusions, a biopsy of my kidney and a bone-marrow tap.[9]

It was as if his childhood dream had been a harbinger, "a game of imminent disaster ... a great Deluge, in inward bursting doors under the pressure of overwhelming waters."[10] It seemed possible to blame Duncan's grueling travel schedule or his high blood pressure for his illness, but in fact the more rare kidney condition of renal kappa chain disease was responsible. Unusually large proteins produced by Duncan's kidneys "crammed up the kidney and destroyed it."[11] The disease necessitated chronic ambulatory peritoneal dialysis, or CAPD, which allowed Duncan to receive treatment at home. After resting and recovering through April, he required surgery in May to prepare for the CAPD treatment, a procedure that called for implanting a tube into his peritoneal cavity through an opening cut into his lower stomach.

Through a daily "exchange" of internal fluids, CAPD took over the natural activities of the kidneys. Required four times a day—at 6 A.M., 11 A.M., 5 P.M., and 11 P.M.—the thirty-minute procedure interrupted other household rituals. Waste fluids, essentially urine, were emptied out into one bag, and another bag of dialysis fluid was warmed in a microwave oven and then introduced into Duncan's stomach cavity through the surgical aperture in his abdomen. Cloudy waste fluids signaled an infection and required a trip to the dialysis center to sterilize the dialysis lines and to introduce antibiotic treatments. Duncan told Denise Levertov that the spring's events had attuned him to simple pleasures: "The garden is splendid with masses of bright yellow oxalis and smaller-flowerd pale lavender to white, magenta mesembri anthemum and rose impatiens. I mean to spend more time with the plant world."[12] To Barbara Joseph, he reported at the end of May that his blood pressure was low and he could not yet think of crossing the bay to Berkeley: "But I have got out—to the movies ("The White City"—a Portuguese film), to the Grant Wood show at the de Young, which lead [sic] to an excellent exhibition of Mayan painted ceramics I know you would enjoy. . . . And I've resumed sessions with students working on their theses."[13]

In the midst of Duncan's health crisis, Bay Area poets revisited an old controversy. On Sunday June 3, 1984, the San Francisco Cinematheque presented the 1965–66 National Educational Television documentaries about Duncan and Louis Zukofsky. In that month's issue of *Poetry Flash,* David Levi Strauss wrote about the December 1978 showing of Zukofsky's NET outtakes at which Duncan and Barrett Watten had quarreled. Strauss's article, with its comment that "Watten's talk was perhaps well-meaning but so tediously tendentious and closed that it did do real violence to the work at hand," set off a round of angry letters to the editor from writers on both sides of the controversy.[14] In the journal's July issue, Ron Silliman blamed the editors for "valorizing censorship" and stated incorrectly that "Watten was never permitted to give this talk. Duncan's seizure of the stage prevented that."[15] Silliman pointed to what he saw as a larger problem extending as far as New York:

I have become disturbed for the past year or so at a game which is rapidly becoming the pastime of the poetry scene. It's called Bash the Language Poets, and Levi Strauss' swipe at Watten is only the most recent example. Kenneth Warren has a piece in *Contact II,* the *Village Voice* did an omnibus thing called "Meaningless Relationship," Andrei Codrescu and Darrell Gray have each taken turns at bat, and Laurie Price blames us (if there is an "us") for there being no good readings in San Francisco in a piece the *Poetry Project Newsletter* saw fit to print.[16]

While *Poetry Flash* published a flurry of angry letters about Duncan, Watten, Silliman, Strauss, and Language poetry, another blow came to the San Francisco community with George Oppen's death on July 7 at the age of seventy-six. That month, Duncan also made his first public appearance since the beginning of his illness, a book signing for the recently released *Ground Work* at Black Oak Books in Berkeley. Still adjusting to his daily dialysis routine, he reported to Barbara Joseph that he had successfully carried off the reading that afternoon, completed the dialysis procedure afterward, and made his way to dinner with Jess and the Burtons. Language poetry wars seemed far from his consciousness, as he told Joseph: "My 'mind' is back with me. Applied currently to Homer, Milton (with a Tuesday afternoon reading group) and Joyce (re-reading *Ulysses* in the newly establisht text) but no writing yet."[17]

The publication of *Ground Work* lifted Duncan's spirits in an otherwise trying period of rehabilitation. Further good news came when Peter Glassgold of New Directions visited 20th Street in August 1984 and told Duncan that the press "felt . . . committed not only to the second volume of *Ground Work* but also to the comprehensive 'Collected Earlier.' "[18] By the fall, a weak but optimistic Duncan was back teaching at New College. And at the close of a combative summer, the editors of *Poetry Flash* called a moratorium on letters about the Language poetry controversy, publishing the final words on the matter by New College student Carl Grundberg and poet Andrei Codrescu in their September issue. Grundberg concluded that the dialogue had perhaps been useful for all involved, adding, "Duncan's perennial concern has been to invoke an inspired community in which we'll constantly be interrupting each other and flying higher and further—constantly returning to the poem rather than our own pet theories or grudges or personalities. Since Duncan is a lightning cloud, his methods have sometimes lacked finesse, but his commitment has been clear."[19]

SEVENTY-ONE

Hekatombe

For him there wasn't any difference between the world and the poem—there was a seamlessness.... It was like the world was passing through him, and it emerged as a poem. MARY MARGARET SLOAN on Robert Duncan

TODD BARON WAS TWENTY-EIGHT YEARS OLD when he first stepped through the doors of New College in early September 1984. Every Monday at 9:00 A.M., he made his way to the Basic Elements course, taught by a revolving cast of faculty members. He enjoyed studying with Michael Palmer and Duncan McNaughton, but most of all he enjoyed Robert Duncan's classes. Duncan usually arrived wearing his favorite corduroy coat with a sweater underneath and a scarf wrapped around his neck. For Baron, the excitement of Duncan's presence was twinned with an anxiety that increased as Duncan surveyed the room with one eye roving.[1] Another student, Judith Roche, remembered,

> Because of [Duncan's] eyes, he never looked directly at you but apparently at someone two or three seats away. It took a while to realize he was speaking to you and that you were expected to answer. I remember that specifically when he started going on and on about the concept of ghosts, which, with his spiritualist background, was not an unusual topic (or tangent) for him. It took a while before I realized he was speaking to me directly and responding to my then-new book, entitled *Ghosts.*[2]

For his students, Duncan became a mythological being, and they studied him as much as they studied with him. Norma Cole noted that though Duncan never wore cologne, he exuded a smell of exotic spices. Aaron Shurin recalled the intensity of his presence:

> It was scary.... He had so much energy that at rest he was shaking like something with an electric current coursing through it. And that was at rest. So you literally felt—and I suppose he did too actually—that if he were ... of a mind he could hurl a bolt at you and incinerate you. And ... he [could make]

people feel that that had happened to them, but you also weren't too sure that he couldn't actually effect it in the physical world.[3]

That fall, in addition to teaching sessions of Basic Elements, Duncan began a new course called Linguistic Approaches to Poetics with a roster that included Grant Fisher, Michael Kronebusch, Mary Margaret Sloan, Judith Roche, and Julia Van Cleve. When his strict dialysis schedule intersected with class time, he performed the procedure in the classroom, donning a surgical mask, emptying a bag of liquid waste, and refilling his peritoneal cavity with dialysis fluid through the surgically implanted tubing in his lower abdomen. Students remembered that he swung the dialysis bag over a closet door or blackboard before sitting down to begin each day's lecture. Susan Friedland recalled Duncan saying, "I'm not going to hide this. This is what I do," and Mary Margaret Sloan remembered her initiation into Duncan's dialysis routine on her first day in class: "In the middle of a sentence he just stood up and dropped his trousers and there was all this fumbling and people would jump up and help. It was quite dramatic, and I was just staring baffled."[4]

Duncan also managed several public appearances in the larger poetry community that fall. On September 22, he gave a reading at the Valencia Rose Café in San Francisco, and on a Saturday in late October, he appeared at Intersection for the Arts, after which the fledgling experimental novelist Kathy Acker sent him a postcard announcing gratefully that she had been "overwhelmed" by his performance. Also attending to private friendships, Duncan spent time with Steve Abbott, editor of *Soup* magazine and *Poetry Flash,* and in November he and Jess received a visit from Michael Davidson, in town for a meeting of the New College accreditation committee. During December, John Ashbery visited 20th Street, later mailing Jess a Winchester House picture puzzle as a holiday gift.[5]

The early days of 1985 saw a renewed optimism in the household: Duncan had the energy to entertain interviewers Burt Hatlen and Michael Andre Bernstein, who visited on January 7, Duncan's sixty-sixth birthday.[6] *Fictive Certainties* was also in production with New Directions that winter, and Duncan wrote to Peter Glassgold on January 8, "I am encouraged about this project in that it will not be carried in a period of kidney failure with its attendant confusions and loss of heart. The psychic dread of that period is gone, thanks to dialysis."[7] At the same time, Duncan was thinking about a more ambitious venture: a two-volume collection of his complete works. He had begun negotiations with New Directions, envisioning the first volume as containing work written between 1939 and 1956, some of which had been published by Fulcrum Press in the United Kingdom as *The First Decade* and *Derivations*.[8] After organizing a rough draft of the manuscript, at the end of January he again wrote to Glassgold: "The point . . . is to have available that early work for serious readers. Since I design serious reading I can only rejoice as studious readers appear and clamor for early poems."[9] Meanwhile, Ekbert Faas's biography of Duncan, which had arrived before the New Year, seemed designed for less serious reading. David Meltzer remembered, "Robert found it so funny and so totally wrong that he brought copies to give to New College Poetics faculty and students."[10]

In the whirl of activity between the new publishing projects, during the predawn hours of January 17, Duncan wrote "Hekatombe." Partly inspired by his study of Greek with the Homer Club and partly emerging from a dream, the poem opened awkwardly, "The guy on my right fell face forward in the gun-fire." The piece, which marked the closure of his life's work, revealed an apocalypse where "the ultimate hundred is Hecate's host. / They fall for Hekate not of the cross roads now / but of the waste lands without roads and swift / as the flitting bat races forth from its cover / they fly to the corrals of Hecate's devotees to wait there to attend the End of the Universe."[11] Duncan envisioned the piece as part of *Ground Work II,* though it came too late to fit into the book. Written in a curiously informal voice, it also pointed to a subject matter that could not have escaped his consciousness, as Aaron Shurin has suggested:

> Though it has to be inflected by Homer, to my mind . . . right from the beginning, . . . more so the poem is infected by AIDS. Though . . . Robert was painfully slow to realize the depth of the epidemic, the period of composition places it deep in the upward arc of mortality, and to me the tenor, the puns such as "hecatomboyos," and "a hundred chose to fall for Apollo" and the agony/ecstasy of "slaughtered for the gift to Helios" all register San Francisco in full epidemic crisis. I just don't see any way AIDS is not part of the central matter here (even, I'd dare suggest, if Robert wasn't aware of it.)[12]

On January 19, Duncan wrote to Robert Creeley, enclosing "Hekatombe" along with his last-published poem "After a Long Illness" and explaining that he had been unable to complete any other writing in the fatigue of the previous two years. The letter marked the end of his correspondence with his old Black Mountain peer.

In the spring of 1985, returning to New College, Duncan taught a course on the poetics of William Carlos Williams and Ezra Pound.[13] Throughout the semester, he was weak, and despite his relief from the "attendant confusions" of kidney failure, a life that included dialysis was in no way easy. Norma Cole remembered Duncan's resistance to the treatments: at home, he kept the dialysis paraphernalia out of his line of vision, moving it to the basement landing at the back of the house and completing the exchange on the unheated stairwell looking out into the garden. When Cole carried the equipment upstairs and left it outside the bedroom door, Duncan protested, and in a "grotesquely comic" gesture, dragged it back downstairs, keeping it there until he was too ill to navigate the house's steep steps.[14]

His kidney ailment progressed in phases, each with a new crisis more threatening than the last. As Duncan's body's metabolism shifted in response to medications and dialysis, he struggled with bouts of hypotension that precipitated fainting spells. He and Jess had been monitoring his bodily systems in a daily medical journal since the beginning of the dialysis treatments, recording the fluctuations of his pulse, blood pressure, temperature, and weight. As Duncan's health declined, notes appeared more frequently in Jess's hand in the journal's margins: coughing fits, occurrences of peritonitis, insomnia, and difficulty walking.

Intent on continuing his travels, Duncan made plans to give an April 1985 reading at Bryn Mawr College outside of New York City. Arriving in New York, he checked into a local hospital for assistance with the dialysis treatment. On this final trip to the East Coast, he stayed with Federico and Odyssia Quadrani, saw Helen Adam briefly for the last time, and was escorted to Bryn Mawr by George and Susan Quasha and Don Byrd. The Quashas also accompanied Duncan to a Rousseau retrospective at the Metropolitan Museum during his short visit, and Susan Quasha remembered pushing him in a wheelchair from painting to painting, the exhausted poet rousing himself briefly to peer up at each work as if waking from a dream.[15] Duncan managed to get to Baltimore for an April 11 reading that was part of a multiweek celebration of the Black Mountain school. His appearance, captured on videotape, revealed the extent of his exhaustion. Ambling from the podium to sit at a table for the second half of his reading, Duncan told the audience that he no longer had the strength to "steamroll" over his listeners.[16]

In early May, Australian poet John Tranter visited 20th Street, recording a conversation and photographing the weary Duncan as he rested in a lawn chair under the lemon tree in the backyard. The two talked about Duncan's

1976 trip to Australia, his work at New College, his parents' hermeticism, and the American, Canadian, and Australian poetry scenes. Duncan briefly mentioned the two poems he had composed the previous year, "Hekatombe" and "After a Long Illness." Describing the dreams that inspired them, he also considered the nature of human consciousness:

I realised that there was a level before any subconscious level . . . , a level that I could know only by rumour, or be *told* about it, in the dream, that was absolute darkness, and in that absolute darkness I was black stone. And that's come over and over again in poems. . . . Some people . . . have taken an approach of how much my childhood folklore enters my poetry, and found over and over again, it may be a fantasy of being Merlin, but another guy suggested that it was . . . those figures that were turned to stone, and a stone that doesn't feel, that doesn't hear, that doesn't see— . . . A voice came and said, 'I've given you a cat in the dark,' and I realised that meant that all along the top of my body, this stone body of mine, was a huge cat, and its electric purring was the only feeling that was entering the stone.[17]

Duncan was invited to dinner with Griselda Ohannessian of New Directions on Saturday May 25 and attended an awards ceremony at the American Booksellers Association conference held in San Francisco on the following night. *Ground Work* had won the Before Columbus Foundation's National Book Award, and Duncan wrote to Ohannessian on June 30, expressing awe that he had managed to type the entire manuscript and compose the design during the difficult period preceding his illness: "How I did that I still wonder, but I can tell you . . . in my hidden advancing condition of toxicity with my kidneys winding down to the terminus of their functions I wanted most of all to crawl into a corner and sleep it off." [18] Overwhelmingly, Duncan's activities became more curtailed. Thom Gunn remembered,

He still conversed— He was as brilliant a conversationalist as ever . . . He had a lot of adoring students, but he couldn't concentrate enough to read. So . . . as a kind of practice, he was reading all the Oz books— . . . he had all of them. And I said, "What comes next?" And he said, "Next, . . . I'm going to be reading all of Kipling's short stories." . . . I said, "Well, what after that?" And he said, "Then I think I'll re-read *Finnegans Wake*." Of course he didn't. He didn't even get to Kipling.[19]

Too, Duncan stopped writing poems, arriving at the answer to a question he had asked in "After Passage": "Will I outlive the end of the rime I meant to come to?"[20] As his life's work ended, his libido also ebbed, and he playfully told Raymond Foye that his penis was "purely for ornamental purposes," impotence being a common side effect of kidney disease and dialysis.[21]

Making a final gesture in another realm of human relations, Duncan attended a Symmes family reunion in Yosemite National Park in July 1985, accompanied by Jess. Barbara Jones was impressed with her long-estranged older brother, remarking on his determination to lead a normal life despite the difficulties of the dialysis treatments. Later that summer, Duncan received another invitation, which he declined, to his fiftieth high school reunion. With the energy he could muster, he tended to activities closer to home, accepting an offer from Bill Berkson to teach a class and give a reading at the San Francisco Art Institute on July 16 and preparing for another semester of classes at New College.

That fall when Ronald Reagan and Mikhail Gorbachev began a dialogue on world security in Geneva, Reagan joked with Gorbachev that someday their two countries might have to unite to fight alien forces like in the Hollywood movie *The Day the Earth Stood Still.* Duncan and Jess, for whom television viewing had become a comforting shared activity, chose to retreat into the Reagan-free world of *The Smurfs,* a cartoon starring animated small blue creatures who could have as easily populated an Oz book. Scheduled to teach a New College course on Emily Dickinson, Duncan became too ill to continue beyond the first session, troubled again by blood pressure fluctuations that blurred his concentration and led to blackouts.[22] For his caretakers, the episodes were alarming. Norma Cole recalled driving Duncan to a medical appointment one afternoon and watching him slump forward in the passenger's seat unconscious. With Jess and Duncan's commitment to their home as a stronghold of the imagination, the idea of interventions from the "real" world of professional health care workers was unthinkable. Throughout the four years of dialysis and decline, Duncan's students and friends stepped in to help Jess maintain the household and, to the extent possible, to maintain Duncan's emotional and physical well-being. Mary Margaret Sloan recalled the atmosphere: "Everybody was in a tizzy and . . . would . . . be swerving . . . between feeling like they wanted to . . . take care of [Duncan and Jess] and [feeling] 'What can I do? What can I do?' "[23]

During the first week of September, Jess noticed new signs of Duncan's deteriorating condition: a confusion about the steps of the dialysis procedure and a complaint of "gut pains" during the draining of the dialysis solution. That fall, the couple tried to continue some few aspects of social life. On September 28, they attended the opera in San Francisco with the Burtons, though Hilde Burton remembered fearing that Duncan was dead as he slouched quietly in his opera seat.[24] A few professional possibilities remained as well; on the morning of October 16, Duncan was interviewed for the BBC by Roberta Berke.[25] Two weeks later, he wrote a letter to Griselda Ohannessian and Peter Glassgold of New Directions in which he reported optimistically, "I've had almost two weeks of normal blood pressure. I'd like to think that the terrible doldrums of low B.P. have passt. I had [been] deprived of having the full resources of learning and research."[26] Meanwhile, Duncan was pleased when the first copies of *Fictive Certainties* arrived, ensuring the preservation of two and a half decades of talks at universities and literary conferences.

On November 6, Duncan was well enough to travel to San Jose, California, for a one-day poetry conference, but toward the end of the month, a cold kept him housebound again, triggering nosebleeds and, by early December, coughing fits that caused his blood pressure to rise. On Wednesday December 4, he woke up "feeling fluish" and was ushered off to his doctor. The notebooks so critical to his writing life—filled with meticulous reading notes and complex, sprawling poems—had given way to a thin yellow spiral notebook of vital statistics titled simply in Jess's hand "1985 August 16–1986 September 30." Jess recorded Duncan's physical triumphs alongside his setbacks: on December 13, he was able to dine with friends in Berkeley and afterward participated in a group reading for David Levi Strauss's magazine *Acts* at New College with Norma Cole, Michael Palmer, Benjamin Hollander, Aaron Shurin, David Levi Strauss, and Duncan McNaughton. Shortly thereafter, on December 23, Duncan developed peritonitis and required a brief but anxiety-provoking hospitalization. Treated at his dialysis center with intravenous drugs, he was home and recovering by Christmas day.

For the New Year of 1986, Duncan and Jess again took refuge in television, watching one of their favorite programs, *Brideshead Revisited*. Returning to another familiar engagement, on January 14, Duncan met with the administrators of the Bancroft Library—along with Thom Gunn, Ron Loewinsohn, James Hart, and Anthony Bliss—to discuss the library's future acquisitions.

SEVENTY-TWO

The Year of Duncan

> Duncan was not afraid of Death. He went into it willingly, curi-
> ous, with remarkable courage and humor. There were many
> times . . . when it was clear that he was passing back and forth
> between worlds, preparing the way, doing the work.   DAVID
> LEVI STRAUSS

THROUGHOUT ITS COURSE, Duncan's illness coincided with the San
Francisco community's growing AIDS epidemic. In 1984, the city closed its
bathhouses in an effort to limit opportunities for gay men to congregate, and
Gaetan Dugas, the man who was assumed to have brought AIDS to North
America, died of the disease. The crisis took on a more public face in 1985 with
actor Rock Hudson's death, but not until two years later did Ronald Reagan
make his first public comments about the disease, announcing a new national
commission to study it. For Duncan, focusing on the emergency was difficult
in the midst of his own health worries, though he and Jess supported several
AIDS charities. Toby McCarroll remembered,

> The overlap time between when I became very involved in the pandemic
> and when Robert died was short. But he was very concerned and very criti-
> cal of our government's lack of response. My good friend the late Paul
> Monette (AIDS activist and writer . . .) called Robert a pioneer in poetry
> AND the coming of age of . . . "The Tribe" of gay and lesbian people. Robert
> contributed . . . to our programs for children with AIDS . . . and Jess con-
> tinued that.[1]

Aaron Shurin recalled that his mentor, born into a pre-Stonewall era of
gay politics, had a very different perspective from that of his younger gay
friends:

> Even if you look at "The Homosexual in Society," it's really disinterested in
> a self-identified gay society. . . . Whereas, . . . for me, that was a fundamental
> social identity and a [very] different kind of political enactment. Being
> around for Stonewall, and instantly articulating all of those ideas, . . . was a
> fundamental social, aesthetic, moral identity for me in a politicized way.

And I don't know that he had that.... That's not to deny the courage of coming out in "The Homosexual in Society," but he parsed the territory so carefully.[2]

Duncan meanwhile made one last foray into the classroom during the spring semester of 1986. On January 21, he began teaching the Tuesday afternoon seminar The Later Poetry of H. D.: Occult Readings.[3] The course was his final intellectual offering to the New College community, and the subject was a fitting choice, focusing on a poet whom he had studied for almost half a century. On February 4, after one of the H. D. classes, Duncan crossed the bay to give a reading in Berkeley. Audience member Francisco Aragón recalled that even at low energy, Duncan was a spectacular performer:

> Up until that point, I had only read him.... I had no expectation ... (I'd had my share of famous poets reading horribly.).... What I enjoyed was how playful he was, the richness of the voice, the bantering between the poems, which was nearly as enriching—and then almost without warning he would launch into a voice performance (his illness, I suppose, did not allow for any sweeping arm gestures ... just the voice) of one of his poems, the most memorable—not surprisingly—"My Mother Would Be a Falconress." [His] recitation ... of that poem remains one of the high points of my experience with poetry.[4]

After the reading, Duncan fainted while walking down a flight of stairs on the Berkeley campus. Thom Gunn caught him in his fall, and as Duncan regained consciousness, he said, "I've always wanted to fall into Thom Gunn's arms."[5] Gunn remembered the incident in another way:

> That is Duncan's romantic version of it. The story is exactly this: He had taught a three-hour seminar in San Francisco that day and then come over to give a reading.... which he delivered sitting down.... I was walking him back to the car, and we were walking down the steps of Wheeler Hall, and I suddenly looked over and he had fallen down the steps, so I lifted him up. He ... passed out so close that he had [practically] fallen into my hands, and it was romantic enough, true.... I think it was his desire to mythologize it. I think he was thinking of how H. D. stumbled on the platform when she was getting some award.... Saint-John Perse leapt forward and prevented her from falling.[6]

On Valentine's Day 1986, Duncan woke with a cold, and the following week, another health problem arose. On February 19, he fell down the stairs at home, breaking his collarbone and cutting open his scalp. Michael Franco arrived at the house that day, expecting to meet with Duncan to discuss a joint talk they would give to a group of teachers in Oakland later that week. After ringing the doorbell and waiting for someone to answer the door, he decided to call the house from a nearby pay phone:

> After an interminable amount of time, Robert answered. I announced myself and he said yes yes with a rather strange tone and I said OK I will be right there. . . . I returned and sat down and waited. When the door opened, there was Jess dripping wet with a fever, a couple of EMT's, and Robert bloodied and in pain . . . An explanation was offered to me and they said he had to go to a hospital; he didn't want to go, and then he decided he would, and I offered to drive and avoid the cost of an ambulance . . . He quickly accepted. [7]

Duncan spent the day in the emergency room and was released after receiving a tetanus shot and stitches. When Franco returned him to 20th Street that evening, the elder poet was irrepressible as ever, carrying on a monologue about H. D. during the drive home.

Duncan had been having trouble walking, and the stairs of the house were beginning to prove too much for him as his muscle weakness increased. In the days after his fall, he experienced bouts of nausea and pain, and he found it difficult to sleep. At the end of March, in a further complication, Jess was briefly hospitalized after breaking his ankle in a tumble off the backyard fence while throwing a stray ball back to the neighbors. With both men disabled throughout April, they had to rely on others to help with the household tasks and dialysis procedures. Plans were made to install an elevator in the house so that Duncan could move more easily between the bedroom on the second floor and the kitchen below it. Amid the medical emergencies, Norma Cole asked fellow New College student Mary Margaret Sloan to join the household support network, suggesting that Sloan's husband, Larry Casalino, also help out. Upon meeting the handsome young doctor, Duncan and Jess agreed that he would be welcome in the household, and Casalino transitioned into a vital role, conveying information to the couple's various health care workers and explaining to Duncan and Jess the more technical aspects of Duncan's condition and treatment options. Mary Margaret Sloan remembered her first visit to the house: when she climbed the stairs to Duncan and Jess's room where the two were laid up in bed, Duncan remarked, "Thank god they sent one of the quiet ones."[8]

As Duncan recovered from his fall, Larry Casalino recommended that he integrate moderate exercise into his routine, and Mary Margaret Sloan devised a schedule for the loosely organized support network to visit Duncan and take him for walks. The mainstays of the group were Michael Palmer and Cathy Simon, Joanna McClure, Thom Gunn, Bob Glück, Norma Cole, Susan Thackrey, and Sloan. Walks with Duncan usually included a good deal of prodding, and the outings also yielded revelations about the terminally ill poet's state of mind. Sloan recalled one foray into the neighborhood of Bernal Heights:

> He said, "I want to go into that little park" . . . It was just a little round circle in the middle of a bunch of streets . . . and then he said, "I want to lie down," so he laid down in the grass. . . . and I remember him saying . . . something like "I am so tired of being Robert. I'm so tired of having to be what I have to be to all these people. . . ." And then we just lay there together silently kind of looking at the clouds and it was so peaceful. It was sort of like he was taking a vacation.[9]

Another sadness visited the household when Helen Adam sent a frantic letter in early May announcing that she was "cracking up." Faced with overwhelming financial difficulties, Adam looked back to Duncan's 1961 prophecy about the Playhouse production of *San Francisco's Burning:* "Why did we ever leave San Francisco? This is where the 'Worm Queen' has led us, and the offended and unforgiving gods, Puss & Anubis."[10]

While Duncan's health continued to deteriorate, he at least was surrounded by students and publishers who could help him continue his work. Robert Bertholf volunteered to assist with Duncan's literary estate, eventually taking control of it after Duncan's death. George Quasha reprinted *Faust Foutu* through Station Hill Press, and Aaron Shurin reviewed it in the *San Francisco Chronicle* on March 2, 1986: "This has been something of the Year of Duncan, having seen the publication of his long-awaited 'Ground Work: Before the War' and his collection of prose, 'Fictive Certainties.' 'Faust Foutu' broadens the territory, refreshes it."[11]

With Duncan on the sidelines, by May the Homer Group was halfway through Book XXIII of the *Iliad,* and Dan Blue reported to the ailing poet, "Diomedes has just won the chariot race."[12] When Warren Tallman visited Duncan on July 7, he found his old friend weary and weak. The springtime crisis had passed, but another arose during the middle of July, when Duncan had trouble moving out of bed and began to hallucinate, speaking of "phantom personages." Subsequent tests at Seton Medical Center in Daly City revealed that the long-term dialysis had created chemical imbalances in his blood that caused his delirium, clinically described as "a metabolic encephalopathy secondary to hypercalcemia."[13] On July 21, he was visited throughout the day by David Levi Strauss, Joanna McClure, Susan Thackrey, and Jess. Strauss documented the course of the delirium in his notebooks, writing of his and Susan Thackrey's experience in the hospital room: "[Robert] said that he'd been travelling in Russia, land of 'stalwart young men on trains.' He picked up a cup from his table, examined it, and said, 'This is certainly an American cup.' When Susan picked up a cellophane-wrapped package of candies on his bedside table and asked if they were his, he replied, 'what would a jackass have on his table?' "[14] On July 25, unable to visit Duncan because he had contracted a cold, Jess wrote a note to his partner registering the toll that the illness had taken on both men: "I know it's painful and a hardship, but please dearest do go on with this dialysis. I wish I could do it for you. And we'll be together again here with friends who have lovingly offered to come to our house as when you were laid up in bed before."[15]

After two years of dialysis, there was little doubt that Duncan was losing his will to live. Norma Cole remembered moments during which he was near death and Jess would say to him, "Not yet; don't go yet." Duncan, no longer able to write or to remain lucid for long periods of time, seemed by 1986 to rally from crises primarily for Jess's sake.[16] Leaving the hospital on July 29, he returned home complaining of a sore throat and the beginnings of a cold he'd contracted in the hospital. By August 6, Jess's sixty-third birthday, Duncan was feeling better, despite lingering throat problems, which lasted another week; on August 12, a test for tuberculosis showed no sign of the disease.

Another pressing issue was Jess's future well-being, and Duncan attempted to make financial provisions for his partner as his own health declined. One option was to sell his literary estate to the University of California's Bancroft Library, though despite his longstanding association with the administrators there, no offer came forward. While Mary Margaret Sloan and others had tried to secure health insurance for Duncan and Jess through a group called Media Alliance, in the end the responsibilities for the complex series of medical transactions fell to Robert Bertholf and the University at Buffalo Foundation of the State University of New York. Duncan's 1976 will had promised his manuscripts to the Bancroft Library and his artworks to the Oakland Museum, but in 1986, he arranged to reallocate all of his materials to the Poetry/Rare Books Collection at the State University of

New York at Buffalo, of which Bertholf was curator.[17] With little mental or physical energy left and with little interest in the logistics of estate matters, Duncan signed on to the plan that Bertholf proposed, relieved that Jess would be provided for and that their estates would be managed by professionals. In November 1986, the couple received a letter from Joseph Mansfield, the vice president for University Development at the school, sketching out the basic points of the agreement. Duncan's dialysis supplies and equipment would continue to be paid for by Medicare, and the university would pay for supplementary health insurance as well as for Jess's Blue Cross health insurance; in exchange, Duncan would sign over his manuscripts, library, and "other works of art" to be housed in the university's collection.[18]

The fall of 1986 brought more complications from the dialysis. During November, blood crusted around the aperture in Duncan's abdomen, and he became sensitive to some foods, including two of his spicier favorites, pickles and salsa. Early in December, he was in a good deal of pain, and Larry Casalino recommended that he be admitted to the hospital for tests. After a series of neck aches during the first week of the month, he was taken to the emergency room of Seton Medical Center and released later that day with instructions to drink more water and ingest more salt. By mid-December, he had begun taking Valium and Tylenol routinely to help him sleep, and in mid-January 1987, Jess recorded an anomaly in Duncan's blood pressure readings. On January 16, Jess had difficulty reading Duncan's pulse at all, and the following day he noted the same phenomenon, with the normal pulse rate of about ninety dropping to sixty. On January 19, Robert Bertholf arrived to visit Duncan and Jess hoping to obtain the manuscript of *Ground Work II*. Duncan had been quite ill that week, and on January 21, after taking a bath and being unable to lift himself from the tub, he was sent to Seton hospital for observation in the event of heart failure. A two-day hospital stay was followed by a week during which he was able to venture outdoors briefly, though Jess noted in a journal that Duncan's body stooped to the right when he walked.

During the spring, *Ground Work II* entered production, partly due to Robert Bertholf's editorial interventions. Though Bertholf had not officially been appointed Duncan's executor, he assumed the role and began to handle the business correspondence that came across Duncan's desk.

On April 14, Duncan returned home from a visit to Stinson Beach in a state of exhaustion. Becoming increasingly disoriented, in May he again experienced confusion about the dialysis procedures, placing additional stress on his helpers. Nightmares and hallucinations haunted his attempts at sleep, and coughing spells and muscle spasms placed his body under even greater stress. By the end of May, he was sometimes too weak to walk down the stairs for breakfast. On other days, he took short strolls with friends, though he still tried to beg off the physical activity by telling stories and distracting his companion from the task at hand. Thom Gunn remembered one occasion when he and one of Duncan's students arrived at the same time to take Duncan for a walk: "[Duncan] was tickled to death, and we took him to this park and we walked all around. And he forgot to bring anything to keep up his pants. . . . So we walked on either side of him with our fingers through the belt loop and he thought that was so sexy, and actually it was. . . . This is one of the important things about Duncan. He was fun to be around."[19] George Stanley also remembered Duncan's ability to keep his sense of humor in the midst of the crisis: "Around the last year of Duncan's life, at his and Jess's place . . . , Duncan was reading Jane Austen. I commented, pointlessly, that I preferred George Eliot. Duncan said, 'That's because you are a disciplinarian, and I am a society lady.'"[20]

On June 20, Robert Bertholf arrived as a houseguest, and on the following day he took Duncan for a walk in Golden Gate Park. On June 27, Duncan and Jess had dinner in Berkeley, but the next morning Duncan was overtired and slept through most of the day. Norma Cole also spent a good deal of time in the household during the summer of 1987, driving Duncan to his appointments and taking her turn at cooking meals. On some days, Cole sat with the ailing poet as he rested in bed after a trip to the hospital. She remembered one occasion when she looked around the room while he seemed to be asleep, at which point he opened his eyes and said, "You should come back here . . . and make use of all of this."[21]

Duncan's final public appearance was an October 4 memorial reading in San Francisco for Ruth Witt-Diamant. James Broughton recalled the occasion: "The last time I saw Duncan, a short time before he died, Robert Glück was pushing his wheelchair into the auditorium at San Francisco State where Ruth Witt-Diamant's friends were gathering. . . . When I expressed compassion for his failing health, Duncan sneered angrily: 'I suppose you will live to be ninety.'"[22] Robert Glück also recalled Duncan's petulant mood at the event: "He rambled for an amazingly long time. He was pretty much out of it. . . . Well, it was horrible. About half way through, he said, 'I have come to the end of the good I can say about Ruth Witt,' but really the only positive thing he had said was that she was good at finding parking places."²³

In late December 1987, the Modern Language Association Conference took place in San Francisco, and Robert Bertholf arrived in town to see Duncan briefly, returning the following month with a gift for Duncan's sixty-ninth birthday, a hardbound copy of *Ground Work II: In the Dark*. During Bertholf's January visit, he persuaded Jess to amend his own will granting the University at Buffalo Foundation his entire estate and naming Bertholf and Federico Quadrani his executors.²⁴

SEVENTY-THREE

The Circulation of the Blood

When I come to Death's customs,
    to the surrender of my nativities,
that office of the dark too I picture
    as if there were a crossing over,
a going thru a door, in obliteration
—at last, my destination Time will not undo—
ROBERT DUNCAN, "To Master Baudelaire"

ON JANUARY 14, 1988, David Levi Strauss accompanied Duncan to a doctor's appointment during which Duncan "was actually in fine high spirits . . . cutting up with the receptionist, reinventing the wheelchair, groaning loudly when the form he was given to fill out asked for his 'Occupation.'"¹After an initial exam, the cardiologist arranged for Duncan to have his heart analyzed via more conclusive procedures at St. Mary's Hospital the next day. Strauss was with Duncan and Jess at St. Mary's when the cardiologist delivered the test results: "He said that Duncan now had virtually no blood pressure, that blood was no longer getting through his heart. . . . [Duncan] had only two choices: open-heart surgery or angioplasty. Duncan replied, 'I'm glad there are so few choices left. I dislike choices. I prefer inevitabilities.'"² Strauss remembered the young doctor being "shocked" by Duncan's reaction to the news, as Larry Casalino was also struck by Duncan's tendency throughout his illness to respond to his body's failures with an active curiosity rather than any outward manifestations of panic.[3]

Over the days that followed, Duncan was subjected to numerous medical interventions. He was immediately admitted into an intensive care ward in anticipation of a cardiac catheterization scan and angioplasty treatment, and that night Jess brought him a dinner of tripe soup, one of his favorite meals.[4] Jess reported briefly in his notebook that night, "Robert is courageous, in full understanding of his condition, and showing a cheerful attitude."[5] The following day, January 16, Duncan spent the afternoon undergoing a coronary angiography, which called for lacing a catheter through a vein in his thigh into his heart to enable X rays. Mary Margaret Sloan accompanied Jess to the hospital, and the two waited until six that night to see a groggy, unhappy Duncan after the procedure. The several doctors who convened over Duncan's files concurred that the heart muscle was substantially damaged and his aortic valve was not functioning correctly. He had likely suffered a series of small heart attacks since he had begun dialysis, causing further damage to the organ. The most serious issue at hand, however, was the condition of his aortic valve. In medical terms, Duncan was suffering from a "severe aortic stenosis," a constriction of the valve that generally requires valve-replacement surgery, with an otherwise short life expectancy. More tests were planned for the following day, though the doctors conceded that surgery would be of little use given the damage to Duncan's heart muscle as a whole.[6]

On January 17, Lynn Lonidier accompanied Jess to the hospital, where the two found Duncan in slightly better spirits as he awaited another set of heart scans. That evening, Jess, Mary Margaret Sloan, and Larry Casalino convened with Duncan's doctors, and Casalino explained to Jess that it was still unclear what the next step should be. Jess spent an hour at Duncan's bedside while he slept, before returning home to 20th Street. On Monday the eighteenth, Jess again arrived at St. Mary's accompanied by Lynn Lonidier and brought along another meal of tripe soup. He made a second trip to the hospital later that day with David Levi Strauss to see that Duncan had eaten. Meanwhile, doctors had agreed that Duncan should receive an angioplasty treatment, though Duncan expressed doubts, calling Jess in the early hours of Tuesday and asking to be brought home. When Jess encouraged him to complete the treatment, Duncan complied, spending the afternoon in a haze of morphine as doctors ran a small balloon through his aortic valve, attempting to open a pathway for the flow of blood. Jess recorded in a notebook that in the aftermath of the procedure, Duncan's blood pressure had risen slightly and that his face seemed brighter.

On January 20, Duncan suffered a setback. He was unable to eat and had difficulty managing the painful aftereffects of the catheterization and muscle spasms brought on by bed rest. Jess spent the morning with his partner, who, in a haze of morphine and Valium, had begun to hallucinate. Throughout the day, Duncan's condition remained unchanged, and after an evening visit to the hospital with Ida Hodes, Jess returned home. On January 21, David Levi Strauss drove Jess to the hospital, and by the next day, after a week of invasive medical procedures, Duncan's condition had stabilized, but as Jess reported, "He is exasperated with his pains, his food, his being forced to drink water (he's dehydrated), and still has remnants of morphine hallucinations occasionally. He is short on patience."[7]

Meanwhile, Robert Bertholf flew to San Francisco on January 23 to attend a memorial reading for the poet John Logan and to see Duncan and Jess. Between visits to the couple, Bertholf was negotiating with the University of California Press to publish several volumes of Duncan's work, including *The H. D. Book,* prose writings, and Duncan's collected poems in two volumes. On January 24, Duncan had another disappointing day in the hospital and was still unable to rise from bed, though doctors encouraged him to try to do so. That Monday, Jess arrived for his daily visit to find Duncan depressed. Jess fed him tripe soup, pickles, and pears, and that evening returned for a second visit, accompanied by Norma Cole. On the twenty-fifth, Robert Bertholf accompanied Jess to the hospital and helped Duncan walk across the room. That evening, Duncan had visits from Jess, Bertholf, and Julia Connor. He remained in the hospital for two more days before being sent home.

SEVENTY-FOUR

In the Dark

It came to me in passing that when I die, "my" death is not mine at all: for it is those who have cared for my life who must suffer the death. In dying, one is incapable of inheriting the act. In this unlike writing, in which one may be among the readers of the writing.   ROBERT DUNCAN, Notebook, 21 October 1981

DUNCAN NEVER RECOVERED from the rigors of his final hospital stay, nor did the angioplasty treatment resolve the serious narrowing of his aortic valve. With little more to be done, on the afternoon of Thursday January 28, he returned home from St. Mary's Hospital. He died six days later. In the week leading up to his death, Jess and those around the couple tried to fall back into the routine of caretaking that had kept the household on track the previous three years. On January 29, Duncan received physical therapy at home and had lunch and dinner in a wheelchair at the kitchen table. Throughout that weekend, Jess performed Duncan's dialysis and attempted to help him move about the house, though Duncan had dinner in bed. His blood pressure continued to drop in the days after he left the hospital, he had coughing fits, and he had little energy to move from room to room.

On February 1, Duncan complained of pain in his neck and chest, accompanied by a stomachache. The following day he received physical therapy at home and had lunch and dinner seated in his wheelchair. Larry Casalino visited to check up on Duncan's condition, and that afternoon, Norma Cole drove Jess to Daly City to fill a prescription for nitroglycerin to ease Duncan's chest pains. Casalino recalled that even on the day before his death, Duncan possessed a clarity about the various adventures of life. Sitting in his chair in the kitchen with his physical therapist standing in front of him, Duncan flexed his arm forward in slow repeated motions, fully engaged in a study of his musculature as he quietly complied with the therapist's instructions.[1]

On Wednesday February 3, Duncan and Jess woke on schedule at 6:30 A.M. for the morning dialysis session. Duncan was weak and had difficulty making his way to the bathroom. As Jess led him back toward the bed, Duncan began to wheeze and he fainted. Jess took him into his arms, waiting for the spasms to subside, and the two men shared what was to be their final embrace crouched on the floor beneath the shelves bearing their collection of Oz books. As Duncan's breathing became more labored, Jess phoned for an ambulance. Paramedics arrived quickly, stretched Duncan out on the floor, and applied intravenous stimulants, oxygen, and electric shocks to his frail frame as Jess watched. The paramedics' monitors showed Duncan's heart rhythm briefly regularizing and then fluttering back into an erratic pattern as Duncan was lifted onto a gurney and carried out to the waiting ambulance. Later that day, Jess returned home alone and penned the final note in the medical journal that he had kept throughout his partner's illness: "The ambulance took him to S.F. City and County Hospital Emergency, where the doctor workt to save him for at least ½ hr., to no avail. He died there, never having regained consciousness. When will I?"[2]

Mary Margaret Sloan and Larry Casalino met Jess at the hospital on 22nd Street and Potrero Avenue on the day of Duncan's death. Missing Jess's first call when the paramedics were at the house, they received his second call from the emergency room, and Sloan recorded the events in her journal:

> We threw on our clothes and rushed to General. He was already dead. Poor Jess, sitting alone in the "family room" with Robert's CAPD paraphernalia. The resident came in and explained to [Larry]—in technical terms Jess and I could not follow—what they had done for Robert, fifty-five minutes in all trying to resuscitate him. Then [Larry] asked Jess if he wanted to see Robert one more time, and Jess nodded silently that he would and asked me to come with him. We were led down a long hall by a nurse, Jess holding my hand, and there in an entirely empty room, more a closet than a room, was a gurney with a sheeted form heaped into the corner, face disarranged on a pillow, with a tube in the corner of his mouth pulling it grotesquely askew. Jess flinched as the door opened. . . . [He] put his hands on Robert's face for a moment, and then he fell apart.[3]

Sloan and Casalino drove Jess home, sharing coffee with him in the quiet sunlit kitchen at 20th Street. When Casalino left for work, Sloan stayed to drive Jess to the mortuary, where he answered the mortician's questions "with extreme calm and reserve, pulling documents from his pockets as needed, and said that he and Robert had always agreed on cremation."[4] That night, Sloan and Casalino, David Levi Strauss, Julia Von Cleve, Michael Kronenbusch, Norma Cole, and Michael Palmer and Cathy Simon congregated at the house to have dinner with Jess. Federico Quadrani, who had boarded a plane from New York expecting that Jess would be distraught and alone, arrived to the comforting sight of the gathered party. After dinner, a few people drifted off together to talk and drink whiskey at a local bar.

During the following weeks, friends arrived at 20th Street to answer the phone, to cook, and to help Jess sort through Duncan's possessions.[5] Michael Palmer, who helped man the phones, recalled an exchange with someone at the *San Francisco Chronicle:* "Their 'morgue' had only a few clippings about Robert, and I had to convince them that he was an important SF poet, then put them in contact with various sources."[6] Norma Cole remembered that Jess made small aesthetic changes to the household almost immediately, gestures toward processing the loss: "Jess got rid of all the furniture that had been bugging him all those years, and bought things like a set of six simple white coffee mugs."[7] On one of Mary Margaret Sloan's visits to the house, Jess led her to the kitchen, where "Robert had had a chair. . . . On the back of the chair was . . . the cape that Robert wore for readings, and . . . hung across the top of [the cape] was this beautiful amber necklace that Robert also wore for readings that he had gotten in Alaska and [Jess] had put them there in this beautiful ceremonial way and he said 'I want you to have these.'"[8]

For the community, the loss was buffered in the haven of the work Duncan had left behind, and in the recently published final collection of *Ground Work II,* in which the poet reminded his readers:

> This is my first and final place,
>   in the outlands of the sun's decline,
>   this dark of the sexual moon,
>   this cold and shadow
>   home   in Time.
>
>   And I, ardent and would-be
>   artful talker,   of
>   wingéd words,   birds or arrows
>   sing thru the air,   soar up
>
>   not for song alone
>   this war and this return
>
>   but for their end in Time.[9]

NOTES

Many of the Duncan papers at various libraries are uncatalogued or loosely cata-
logued, including those in the Poetry and Rare Books Collection at the University
at Buffalo, the State University of New York (UAB). In addition, most of Duncan's
notebook pages are unnumbered, and some are undated. I've attempted here to de-
scribe the locations of these manuscripts and quotations from unpublished materials
as precisely as possible. With published materials, I have referenced the first editions
of all major books rather than include original publication information from small
magazines, chapbooks, and obscure print runs. I have also generally avoided use of
Duncan's *Selected Poems* and *Selected Prose* as source materials because these posthu-
mous editions depart from Duncan's intentions for the presentation of the work. Ci-
tations for *The H.D. Book* come from the readily available online version of the text.

Letters from Robert Duncan to Minnehaha Symmes are in my collection, cour-
tesy of Barbara Jones. All other letters to and from Duncan are housed at UAB
unless otherwise noted.

I conducted interviews with many of Duncan's family members and friends,
which I cite here by name and date.

Libraries and manuscript collections are abbreviated as follows: KSU, Special Col-
lections, Kent State University; NDir, New Directions Publishers Archive; STORRS,
Thomas J. Dodd Research Center, University of Connecticut, Storrs; UAB, Poetry
Collection, University at Buffalo, the State University of New York; UC, University
of Chicago; UCB, Special Collections, Bancroft Library, University of California,
Berkeley; UCD, Special Collections, University of California, Davis; UCSD,
Mandeville Special Collections, University of California, San Diego.

FOREWORD

1. Robert Duncan, "Two Chapters from *H.D.*," *Tri-Quarterly* (Spring 1968): 67.
2. Robert Duncan, *The Opening of the Field* (New York: Grove Press, 1960).
Duncan discusses his Atlantis dream in "*The H.D. Book*. Part I: Beginnings. Chap-
ter 5, Occult Matters," *Stony Brook Review* 1/2 (Fall 1968): 18.

3. Ibid.

4. Charles Olson, "Against Wisdom as Such," in *Collected Prose,* ed. Donald Allen and Benjamin Friedlander (Berkeley: University of California Press, 1997), 260.

5. Robert Duncan, "Sonnet 3," *Roots and Branches* (New York: Scribners, 1964), 124.

6. Robert Duncan, "These Past Years, *Passages* 10," *Bending the Bow* (New York: New Directions, 1968), 29.

7. *The Letters of Robert Duncan and Denise Levertov,* ed. Robert J. Bertholf and Albert Gelpi (Stanford, CA: Stanford University Press, 2004), 669.

8. Ibid., 666.

9. I have discussed Duncan's response to Levertov in "A Cold War Correspondence: The Letters of Robert Duncan and Denise Levertov," *Contemporary Literature* 45, no. 3 (Fall 2004): 538–56.

10. Robert Duncan, "To Master Baudelaire," *Ground Work: Before the War/In the Dark,* ed. Robert J. Bertholf and James Maynard (New York: New Directions, 2006), 198.

11. Ibid., 271.

12. Duncan, *Bending the Bow,* v.

13. Robert Duncan, "Often I Am Permitted to Return to a Meadow," *The Opening of the Field,* 7.

CHAPTER ONE: THE ANTEDILUVIAN WORLD

1. Duncan's adoption certificate records his middle name as Howard. A 1935 letter by Edward Duncan, Sr. gives his middle name as Howe (Gladys Kennard [Duncan's biological cousin], 14 January 1998).

2. Accounts of Robert Duncan's birth come from Faas, *Young Robert Duncan;* unpublished notes of Minnehaha Symmes, UAB; and Gladys Kennard, 14 January 1998. Apocryphal stories about the birth held that the premature Duncan, at six and a half pounds, had a wide head, further complicating the birth.

3. Faas, *Young Robert Duncan,* 290. Faas writes that Duncan was delivered by a Dr. Adams at 1110 East 22nd Street. This information contradicts adoption notes kept by Minnehaha Symmes, as well as the address on Marguerite Duncan's interment papers. Minnehaha recorded the time of birth as 6:30 A.M. Uncertainty about the exact time of birth became significant in later renderings of Duncan's astrological chart. A birth time of 6:20 A.M. put Duncan's ascendant in Sagittarius, but a time of 6:30 A.M. put it in Capricorn.

4. David Howard, the owner of 2532 12th Avenue, provided information about the San Antonio neighborhood (2 October 1998). Oaklanders hold to the myth that Stein's "There is no there there" refers to the disappearance of open spaces in her old neighborhood. In fact, she was referring to her childhood home, which had been demolished.

5. Anne Spaulding [Doris Anne Duncan] to Robert Duncan, 11 April 1981. Duncan's older siblings included Edna, George, Marguerite, Douglas, Eleanor, Florence, and Doris Anne, all born between 1901 and 1916. During the early 1980s, Duncan made contact with Eleanor and Anne Spaulding.

6. Eleanor Duncan to Robert Duncan, 16 April 1981.

7. The 1920 California Census names Marguerite, Douglas, Eleanor, and Florence as residents of the orphanage of the Ladies Relief Society on 45th Street in Oakland. A 1930 census report reveals that Edward Duncan married Mae and moved to Alameda.

8. Duncan, *Roots and Branches*, 13.

9. Anne Spaulding to Duncan, 11 April 1981.

10. Carpenter, *The Carpenter Memorial*.

11. Gladys Kennard, 14 and 16 January 1998.

CHAPTER TWO: NATIVE SON OF THE GOLDEN WEST

1. Mercedes Gardner, *The Lady Alchemist,* and Fayetta Harris Philip, *Biographical Sketch of Fayetta Harris Philip* and *Notes to Finish Biographical Sketch,* Fayetta Harris Philip Papers, Special Collections, UCD. Two of Philip's theories, "Everything is created out of units of light" and "Light is a flow of individual Units-of-Kinetic-Energy," are outlined in autobiographical manuscripts written between the 1940s and 1960s.

2. Duncan, *The Opening of the Field,* 66.

3. Gardner, *The Lady Alchemist;* and Barbara Jones, 17 January 1998.

4. Duncan to Anne Spaulding, 16 April 1981.

5. Gladys Kennard recounted this meeting of Myrtle Carpenter and Fayetta Harris Philip on 14 January 1998.

6. John Chinworth, Yoko Eishima, and William Stickevers provided interpretations of Duncan's birth chart.

7. Robert Duncan talked about his adoption and early childhood in an interview with Joseph Cardarelli in April 1985 in Baltimore as part of a "Black Mountain Revisited" series of lectures and readings organized by Cardarelli at the Maryland Institute College of Art. Cardarelli and Jim Skipper produced a video documentary of the events, *Black Mountain Revisited,* in 1990.

8. Both "Dream Data" (1959), in *Roots and Branches,* 10, and "A Lammas Tiding" (1964), in *Bending the Bow,* 51, contain references to the Lammas and explore the poet's dreams during the early hours of August 1. Ancient harvest celebrations were festivals of the dead, but Duncan also intentionally confused the Celtic "lammas" day with the malevolent "lamias" in Greek mythology.

9. Faas, *Young Robert Duncan,* 17; and Duncan, "A Sequence of Poems for H. D.'s Birthday," *Roots and Branches,* 14.

10. In 1939, a local Bakersfield newspaper named Minnehaha Harris "Socialite of the Week."

11. Duncan, *The H.D. Book,* 74. This critical volume presents Duncan's research on his own life, the work and life of H.D. (Hilda Doolittle), and the modernist movement of the early twentieth century. Chapters of the book appeared in various small magazines from the 1960s through the 1980s.

12. Simms Genealogy Page, http://users.rcn.com/lsimms21/simms1.html.

13. Notebook 46, 2 April [1978], UAB. Duncan sometimes referred to the Symmeses as his stepmother and stepfather rather than as his adoptive parents.

14. Passenger list for the *Griffin* 1634, www.packrat-pro.com/ships/griffin.htm.

15. Notebook 4, UCB.

16. Unpublished notes of Minnehaha Symmes, unlabeled folder, UAB.

17. Barbara Jones, 17 January 1998; "Former Alamedan's Funeral to Be Held," unidentified newspaper, courtesy Chapel of the Chimes Mausoleum, Oakland, California.

18. Barbara Jones speculated that Minnehaha found her "true love" when she married her second husband, Lewis Burtch, in 1938 (17 January 1998).

19. Notebook 4, UCB.

20. Duncan, *Bending the Bow,* 52.

21. Several books from the Symmes family library are now in the possession of Barbara Jones's three children.

22. Although people described Duncan as "cross-eyed," his left eye wandered and he sometimes appeared wall-eyed as well. In their introduction to a 1979 interview with Duncan in *Gay Sunshine,* Aaron Shurin and Steve Abbott ("Interview: Robert Duncan") noted that the poet always had "one eye holding you down and one eye roving." The medical term is *strabismus*—an eye-muscle disorder that prevents both eyes from focusing on an object simultaneously.

23. Duncan, *Roots and Branches,* 14. See Faas, *Young Robert Duncan,* 19, for more on the effect of this accident on Duncan's early development. Duncan often used the phrase "back of" to describe layers of information ("back of this is another thing"), which ties in with the distortions in his vision: images appeared "back of" one another. Similarly, his poems stack references on top or in back of each other, sometimes in the form of puns.

CHAPTER THREE: THE ARCHITECTURE

1. Duncan, *The H.D. Book,* 72.

2. Barbara Jones, 17 January 1998.

3. "Interview with Robert Duncan" by Joseph Cardarelli, April 1985, unpublished ms, courtesy of Anselm Hollo.

4. Duncan, *Ground Work,* 37.

5. "Interview with Robert Duncan" (Cardarelli).

6. Fayetta Harris Philip, "FHP Childhood. No. 4," unpublished transcript, UCD. More information on the Cooley and Harris clans is available in Mercedes Gardner's self-published *Family History,* UCD. Mitch Harris said that Minnehaha

Harris may have received her name via a more direct family connection. Gamaliel Harris had a cousin named Minne Ha Ha Fullenwider, born in 1862 in Kentucky (e-mail, 21 December 2007).

7. Duncan, *The H. D. Book*, 85.

8. Barbara Jones, 17 January 1998.

9. Duncan, *The H. D. Book*, 71.

10. Duncan, "The Truth and Life of Myth," *Fictive Certainties*, 7. For Duncan, the mysteries of the "inner chamber" also blurred into his curiosity about the feminine and the female sex organs. During the 1940s, when he experimented with heterosexual sex, he described the clitoris as "a ring of bone like jaw—it would be wonderful to be equipped with teeth for this machine" (quoted in Faas, *Young Robert Duncan*, 109). This "mystery" is echoed in "As in the Old Days" (*Bending the Bow*, 24), which touches upon the architecture of Moravian churches whose doors simultaneously represented the clitoris and the wound in Christ's side.

11. Fayetta Harris Philip, "No. 1, 10 May 1966," unpublished transcript, UCD.

12. The Symmes and Harris families seem not to have belonged to the Oriental Templar Order (Ordo Templi Orientis), but the OTO had widespread influence in American hermetic societies. Founded in 1905 by Carl Kellner, Franz Hartmann, Heinrich Klein, and Theodor Reuss, the OTO is a Masonic occult group still active in the United States and Europe. It was headed by poet and magician Aleister Crowley from 1922 until his death in 1947. In the 1950s, Robert Duncan befriended filmmaker Kenneth Anger, who was an OTO member and a student of Aleister Crowley's writings.

13. The Hermetic Order of the Golden Dawn was absorbed into the Oriental Templar Order in 1903.

14. Robert Duncan, "Pound, Eliot, and H. D.: The Cult of the Gods in American Poetry," Kent State University, 11 October 1972, audiocassette, UAB. Reluctant to engage in any organized religious practice, Duncan nonetheless enjoyed maintaining a peripheral relationship to occult groups throughout his life. In a course called Nature of Person that he taught at the New College of California, Duncan entertained his students with the following story:

> I remember at a table when I was trying to explain . . . that Kenneth Anger is a satanist, . . . to people who appreciate everything. . . . I said "But Kenneth is a serious satanist" and they said "Oh, how interesting" and they said "why are you so disturbed?" and I said "Well I find it pretty disturbing that he's called to a mass in Switzerland where they're going to eat the baby." And they say "Ah!!!! Eat the baby?!!" But what in the world do you think you do? If the bread is the substitution for the baby, the baby is the substitution for the bread. (Lecture, 21 April 1981, audiocassette, UAB)

15. In a 1965 lecture, Duncan used the phrase "pot and pantheism" to describe the collage technique of H. P. Blavatsky's writings. He conjectured that her addiction to hashish facilitated the clutter and creativity of her spiritual proclamations. Duncan, "The Psyche Myth and the Moment of Truth," University of California, Berkeley, 13 July 1965, audiocassette, UAB.

16. Notebook 46, 2 April 1978, UAB.

17. "In my childhood there were still mediums who talked in Indian voices among those meeting in the other room" (Duncan, *The H. D. Book,* 74). Duncan began his own study of shamanism in the early 1940s while living in Woodstock, New York.

18. Ojai's main theosophical organization exists today as the Krishnamurti Foundation of America.

19. Olson, "Against Wisdom as Such," *Collected Prose;* and Duncan, "From A Notebook," *Fictive Certainties,* 65.

20. Duncan saved some of Fayetta's Christmas newsletters, which are now with his papers at UAB. The pamphlets cover varied topics such as "There is No Gravity" (1953), "Vitamins Belong to the Living Soul" (1961), and "What Caused the Electrical Black Out in the New York Area?"(1965).

21. Quoted in Helen Adam, "A Few Notes on Robert Duncan," in Bertholf and Reid, eds., *Robert Duncan: Scales of the Marvelous,* 36.

22. Duncan, *Bending the Bow,* 27.

23. Duncan, "The Psyche Myth."

CHAPTER FOUR: A PART IN THE FABULOUS

1. Duncan, *The H. D. Book,* 87.

2. Notebook A, UCB.

3. Ibid.

4. Plato, *Timaeus,* Internet Classics Archive, http://classics.mit.edu/Plato /timaeus.html.

5. Notebook 46, 111, UAB.

6. Duncan, *The H. D. Book,* 87.

7. Duncan, *The Opening of the Field,* 7.

8. For example, during the late 1940s, Duncan took to the idea that certain Japanese dictionaries might be used as oracles. He often designed lectures around phrases he randomly found in his "Kenkyusha" (the dictionary's publisher).

9. Duncan, "The Psyche Myth."

10. Fayetta Philip to Duncan, 12 October 1964.

11. Duncan, "The Truth and Life of Myth," 10.

12. Duncan, "The Psyche Myth."

13. Duncan, *The H. D. Book,* 27.

14. Duncan's curiosity about disasters extended into the realm of geology. He worried that he would "miss out on" a major California earthquake while he was away on a reading tour (Jess Collins, June 1989).

15. Duncan, *The Opening of the Field,* 62.

16. Notebook 41, 7 August 1969, UAB. Bernice Symmes to Duncan, 7 June 1979. Duncan was learning to read during the era of the 1925 Scopes "Monkey Trial" and the battle over Darwinism. His "organic" process of poetic composition paid homage

to Darwin's theory of evolution. "The most real, the truth, the beauty of the poem is a configuration, but also a happening in language, that leads back into or on toward the beauty of the universe itself." (Duncan, "Toward an Open Universe," *Fictive Certainties,* 79).

17. Baum, *Ozma of Oz,* 72.

18. Duncan, "A Life in Poetry," Vancouver Poetry Conference, 5 August 1963, audiocassette, UAB. A transcript of this lecture is available in *W* magazine, 2005, www.kswnet.org/editables/pdfsANDscans-WMAG/w10.pdf; and audio recordings of panel discussions from the conference are available at the Slought Foundation website, www.slought.org.

19. Ibid. Duncan said in the same lecture, "I do know in my family rumor I learned to talk late and never stopped after that." Fayetta could match Duncan's chattiness. After visiting Duncan and Jess in August 1964, his then elderly aunt sent a note apologizing for dominating the conversation. With Charles Olson, another obsessive monologuist, Duncan arrived at a compromise: "We talked at the same time." "On Olson," New College of California, San Francisco, 17 February 1982, audiocassette, UAB.

20. Duncan, "The Erotic History of Don Juan de Bakersfield," unpublished ms, UAB.

21. Bobbie Louise Hawkins, December 1998.

22. Barbara Jones, 16 January 1998.

23. Pierre Joris remembers Duncan's chatter in this way: "At the worst it was a speed rap, at the best it was brilliant" (16 March 1998). In his 1965 lecture "The Psyche Myth," Duncan told this story: "I remember . . . kindly Phil Whalen came up to me and said 'well, there's good old fatuous Duncan.' . . . I looked up the word fatuous; I tried to search out a rather elevated meaning from it—dictionaries kept digging me deeper and I kept saying. . . . god, you open the box and there it said 'Hi fatuous, now try to get to Eros.'"

CHAPTER FIVE: THE WASTELAND

1. Duncan, "Poems from the Margins of Thom Gunn's *Moly*: Preface to the Suite," *Ground Work,* 63.

2. "A Conversation with Robert Duncan (1976)," 87. Robert Duncan's lifelong fastidious record keeping seemed to be more an exercise in numerology than the work of an accountant's mind. Despite his obsession with inventories (purchases of books, razors, and toothpaste), little distressed him more than balancing his bankbook and filing his taxes. "Household" matters came into focus with Minnehaha's death in 1961, when one of Duncan's first priorities was to claim his adoptive mother's kitchen appliances. Barbara Jones recalled that Minnehaha had also shown a compulsive interest in the kitchen gadgets of the 1930s.

3. Duncan, "Lecture on Field Theory at New College with Michael Palmer," 13 September 1983, audiocassette, UAB.

4. Barbara Jones, 16 January 1998. Jones also remembered her mother giving food to homeless men who wandered into the yard off the railroad lines.

5. Duncan, *The H. D. Book,* 86.

6. Barbara Jones, 16 January 1998. If Duncan remembered this, he chose not to talk about it.

7. Notebook 3, UCB.

8. Duncan, *The H. D. Book,* 87.

9. The cigar box is now in storage at UAB.

10. "Spring," unpublished ms, UAB. These poems were likely provided by a teacher and transcribed by the students.

11. Barbara Jones, 16 January 1998.

12. Ibid. Barbara Jones said that her brother created this illusion for her on more than one occasion during their childhood. His students at the New College also ascribed various supernatural phenomena to Duncan's presence, including electrical disturbances.

13. Unpublished notes of Minnehaha Symmes, UAB.

14. See Faas, *Young Robert Duncan,* for an in-depth exploration of Duncan's junior high school career and early journalistic writing.

15. Barbara Jones, 16 January 1998.

16. Duncan, *The H. D. Book,* 86.

17. Duncan, *Ground Work,* 47.

18. Duncan, "A Life in Poetry."

19. Ibid.

20. Duncan's use of sexual metaphor is most evident in "The Venice Poem" (1947), "Night Scenes" (1959), and in later pieces such as "Poems from the Margins of Thom Gunn's *Moly,*" "Circulations of the Song" (*Ground Work I: Before the War*), and "An Alternate Life" (*Ground Work II: In the Dark*). When necessary, Duncan also concealed his infidelities (or potential infidelities) from Jess by obscuring the identity of a new "beloved," and merging it with an unnamed divine incarnation of Eros.

21. Duncan, "A Life in Poetry."

22. Duncan, "His Body," unpublished ms, UAB.

23. Lili Fabilli, 1 October 1998.

24. Robert W. Sheldon to the author, 15 April 1998.

25. Duncan, "My Mother Would Be a Falconress," *Bending the Bow,* 52; Robert Kelly, 22 April 1999.

26. Duncan kept both stories alive well into his adult life. While, outwardly, he dismissed his adoptive mother as a critic and nag, he had internalized her cunning and feminine charm; and he harnessed these tools to court quiet, bookish men, many of them conspicuously like Edwin Symmes in physique and character.

27. Barbara Jones, 16 January 1998.

28. Notebook 2, UCB.

29. "Interview with Robert Duncan" (Cardarelli).

30. Duncan, *Ground Work,* 174.

31. "Interview with Robert Duncan" (Cardarelli).

CHAPTER SIX: THE FATHERING DREAM

1. Notebook 4, 22, UCB.
2. "Masonic Services Held for Symmes," *Bakersfield Californian,* 13 September 1935.
3. Duncan, unpublished ms, UAB.
4. Notebook 52, 19 January 1976, UAB.
5. Duncan, *Ground Work,* 64.
6. Barbara Jones had no memory of either of these events taking place while she was in the household.
7. Briefly described in Faas, *Young Robert Duncan,* 47; see also "Interview: Robert Duncan" (Abbott and Shurin).
8. "Interview: Robert Duncan" (Abbott and Shurin).
9. Duncan, *The First Decade,* 90.
10. For more on Duncan's high school years, see Faas, *Young Robert Duncan.*
11. Barbara Jones, 16 January 1998. Jones reflected that childhood friends and neighbors generally thought that her brother, while charismatic, was an "oddball."
12. Duncan, unpublished ms, UAB.
13. Ibid.
14. "Interview with Robert Duncan, 1986," BBC Radio, transcript at UAB.
15. Duncan, unpublished ms, UAB.
16. Duncan, *The H. D. Book,* 7.
17. Duncan claimed that Keough had been one of D. H. Lawrence's circle of admirers in Taos, New Mexico. Keough's teaching records show that she visited Taos in 1933, three years after Lawrence's death.
18. Duncan, "A Life in Poetry."
19. Ibid.
20. Ibid.
21. Duncan, *The H. D. Book,* 25. Duncan described *The H. D. Book* as a tribute to the women in his life including Edna Keough, his women friends at Berkeley, and literary heroes such as H. D. (Jess Collins, June 1989).
22. Duncan, "A Life in Poetry." Duncan's friendship with Keough was one of his longest and most consistently maintained. During the early 1980s, after Keough retired to San Francisco, she met Duncan and Jess monthly for lunch.

CHAPTER SEVEN: THE LITTLE FRESHMAN YES

1. Faas, *Young Robert Duncan,* says that in February 1937 Duncan moved out of the fraternity house, but this date was actually when he was initiated. The fraternity house was at 2340 Piedmont Avenue in Oakland.
2. "Interview: Robert Duncan" (Abbot and Shurin), 4.
3. Mentioned in passing to Helen Adam, 23 January 1962.

4. Duncan to Minnehaha Symmes [spring 1937]. Duncan's letters to his mother between 1937 and 1946 reveal a deep emotional tie. Virginia Admiral said (8 April 1998), "I imagine that he and his mother had a great deal in common as he was growing up and that she must have spent a great deal of time with him for him to develop as he did and to be so precocious."

5. Ibid. "[I have] valiant hopes for B in English (A?)—B in history (it will take a good final) C in Philosophy (after E with midterm—I will do my best to send you the report of an A final paper tho) C in geology (oddly enough Geology is no worse than last semester—a little more hopeful if anything.) (if your little boy tries very hard) a C in German." Duncan actually earned As in his two semesters of German.

6. Ibid. Ella Young was a friend of Edna Keough's who came to the United States from Ireland in 1925 to teach Celtic studies at Berkeley. Born in 1867, she was a political activist who had been close to Maud Gonne and William Butler Yeats in her younger days. The Courvoisier Gallery of San Francisco specialized in fine arts until 1937, when it took on animation marketing for the Disney Corporation. Duncan's intellectual curiosities also drew him into psychoanalytic theory, a discipline that held sway over his poetic imagination throughout his career. Friends remembered his keen interest in Melanie Klein's psychoanalytic work with children, and Duncan sometimes discussed such matters with his Aunt Fay, who then lived in Oakland. She reported to Minnehaha in March 1938, "He had been here a couple of hours and had taken most of the time to read me Freud."

7. Duncan, *The Years As Catches,* i.

8. The *Occident* was discontinued the following year and temporarily replaced by the *Grizzly,* where Duncan also served on the staff in 1938.

9. Duncan, "Lecture on Ezra Pound," Central Washington State University, 8 October 1969, audiocassette, UAB. At the *Occident,* Duncan also befriended writer and future film critic Pauline Kael, a fellow undergraduate student at Berkeley.

10. Duncan to Minnehaha Symmes [1937]. Robert Bartlett Haas (b. 1916) went on to be a professor at the University of California, Los Angeles, and an editor of Gertrude Stein's writings.

11. Duncan, *The H. D. Book,* 22, Duncan told this story again in a 1985 interview with Burton Hatlen and Michael Andre Bernstein in *Sagetrieb* ("Interview with Robert Duncan").

12. Duncan, "Lecture on Ezra Pound." Duncan also told a variation of this anecdote at the Vancouver Poetry Conference, 5 August 1963.

13. "Interview with Robert Duncan" (Hatlen and Bernstein), 101.

14. Enclosed in letter to Minnehaha Symmes [1937].

15. Duncan to Minnehaha Symmes [1937]. Duncan's obsessive reading habits contributed to his inability to excel in the classroom. His college friend HamiltonTyler described the problem: "Robert and I shared a common fault—if we had read an example of Milton's prose, such as the assigned *Areopagitica,* why not then . . . find out what else he had to say on church and state, and then perhaps why? If that approach is multiplied by the number of important writers, past and present, it is easy to drop out

of phase with requirements" (Hamilton Tyler and Mary Tyler, "In the beginning, or recatching the years as catches with Robert Duncan, in the years 1942 and 1945–46," in Bertholf and Reid, eds., *Robert Duncan: Scales of the Marvelous,* 4).

16. Duncan, "The Lasting Contribution of Ezra Pound," 25.

17. Ibid. Pound's phrase "the tone leading of vowels" occurs in Dallam Simpson's *Four Pages* magazine, March 1948, 3.

CHAPTER EIGHT: A COMPANY OF WOMEN

1. Virginia Admiral, 8 April 1998.

2. Duncan, "Lecture on Field Theory at New College w/Michael Palmer," 13 September 1983, audiocassette, UAB. Duncan's mid-1940s "round table" poetry meetings with Jack Spicer, Robin Blaser, and others were similarly cultish.

3. Ibid. Spanish poet Federico García Lorca's death at the hands of Nationalist soldiers in August 1936 also would have been in Duncan's consciousness at this point.

4. Duncan to Minnehaha Symmes [1937].

5. Ibid.

6. Ibid. Duncan was the editor of the ASU's bulletin in 1937 and 1938. In one issue, he published a poem of his own, appropriately titled "Proletarian Song."

7. Thomas Thurston and Robert Cohen, "The American Student Movement of the 1930s," http://newdeal.feri.org/students/index.htm. During the 1960s, Duncan also took great interest in the Free Speech Movement at Berkeley.

8. Heirich, *The Beginning: Berkeley 1964,* 27.

9. Duncan to Minnehaha Symmes, 4 October 1937.

10. Duncan, *The H. D. Book,* 17, 19. According to his college transcripts, Duncan was suspended from the university on 17 March 1938 for his refusal to participate in military classes, though his registration for two summer classes was later approved.

11. Duncan's "The Homosexual in Society" is reproduced in Faas, *Young Robert Duncan,* 322, and in Duncan, *Selected Prose.* The essay clearly echoed the ideas of the Fabilli sisters and Virginia Admiral. When I met with Lili Fabilli in October 1998, she spoke of "the fellowship of mankind" in the same terms that Duncan had written about it during the 1940s. For Duncan, the ideas he expressed in the essay led him into a series of contradictions. While throughout his life he possessed an insatiable curiosity about humankind's variousness and sociopolitical evolution, he also sometimes became petulant about "special interest groups." He was quick to dismiss the efforts of the black nationalist movement of the 1960s as well as the gay rights movement of the 1970s.

12. Mary Fabilli, 12 January 1998.

13. Mary Fabilli, unpublished ms, 1991, UAB.

14. That semester, Duncan enrolled in German, an art class, two English classes, and philosophy.

15. Mary Fabilli. *Aurora Bligh and Early Poems,* 3.

16. Virginia Admiral, 8 April 1998.

17. Ibid.

18. Ibid.

19. Duncan, "Relativity, A Love Letter, and Relative to What; A Love Letter," *Epitaph*, no. 1 (Spring 1938): 21.

20. Virginia Admiral, 8 April 1998.

21. Wagstaff, *Robert Duncan: Drawings and Decorated Books*, 9.

CHAPTER NINE: THE DANCE

1. Mary Fabilli, 12 January 1998.

2. Virginia Admiral, 8 April 1998.

3. Duncan to Lily Fabilli [1940].

4. Mary Fabilli, 12 January 1998. During the early 1940s, Anaïs Nin had a similar insight about Duncan: "My femininity annoys him. He loves me, but he would like me to be a boy" *(Diary of Anaïs Nin: 1939–1944,* 170).

5. Mary Fabilli recalled that Elgrin sent Duncan on his way when he came home one night to discover him picking crabs out of his pubic hair and burning them in a candle flame (12 January 1998).

6. "Interview: Robert Duncan" (Abbot and Shurin), 4.

7. Ibid.

8. Virginia Admiral, 8 April 1998. In *Young Robert Duncan,* Faas says that Duncan met Fahs in 1937, which is probably not correct.

9. Duncan, *The Opening of the Field,* 73. "The first poem" refers to an early poem about Fahs, "Passage over Water" *(The Years As Catches,* 5).

10. "Interview: Robert Duncan" (Abbot and Shurin), 3. Both Duncan and Fahs had also experienced early losses. Fahs's father committed suicide in 1930. Duncan alludes to this event in "Witnesses," *The Years As Catches,* 29.

11. Virginia Admiral, 8 April 1998.

12. Duncan to Minnehaha Symmes, 11 September 1938. Fahs's thesis was "The Image du Monde by Gossouin (A.D. 1246): Latin Sources on Geography, Meteorology, and Natural History."

13. Duncan to Russell [5 October 1938], UCB.

14. In *Young Robert Duncan,* Faas gives a detailed account of the turbulence of Duncan's life in New York City.

15. Duncan to Sanders Russell [December 1938], UCB.

16. The WPA, instituted by Franklin Roosevelt in 1935, became a meeting ground for young politically minded artists during the Second World War. It provided educational programs as well as commissions for public art projects.

17. Duncan to Russell [December 1938], UCB.

18. Duncan to Minnehaha Symmes [spring 1939].

19. *Diary of Anaïs Nin,* 14. In my interviews with them, Virginia Admiral and Stan Brakhage also mentioned Duncan's disappointment with the unyieldingness of New York gay community during the early 1940s.

20. Duncan to Lili Fabilli, spring 1939. Alice Fahs conjectures that Duncan and Fahs shared an apartment at 75 Bedford Street in New York City during the summer of 1939. Fahs told his daughters that he lived in New York for a summer at the age of twenty-eight [e-mail, 10 September 2008].

21. Duncan to Lili Fabilli, spring 1939.

22. Duncan to Lili Fabilli and Cecily Kramer [1939].

23. Laughlin, preface to *New Directions in Prose and Poetry.*

24. Breton's presence in New York lured a teenaged protégé named Philip Lamantia from the West Coast in 1944. It's not clear whether Duncan met Lamantia in New York at that time, or if their first contact came later in San Francisco.

25. Duncan to Minnehaha Symmes [September 1939].

26. Virginia Admiral wrote one of Duncan's letters of recommendation.

27. Duncan to Minnehaha Symmes [October 1939]. Duncan also said at one point that he believed he'd been rejected by the school after arguing with a teacher about the Spanish Civil War.

28. Ibid. [September 1939].

29. Ibid., 16 November 1939.

30. Ibid. [December 1939].

31. Duncan to Kael, 3 February 1940, Bancroft Library, UCB. Duncan's letters to Kael also offer valuable insights into Duncan's thoughts on socialist politics in New York and Berkeley during the early 1940s. Jeff Rall was born in Canada in 1915 and spent part of his childhood in Kansas City, Missouri.

32. Duncan to Minnehaha Symmes [October 1939]. Pavel Tchelitchew, a Russian painter, had moved to New York in 1934 and later became romantically involved with Charles Henri Ford. Parts of Duncan's research may have contributed to the essay "Notes on some Painters and Poets," published in *Retort* magazine in winter 1945.

CHAPTER TEN: FROM ROMANCE TO RITUAL

1. Duncan to James Cooney, 15 April 1939. Duncan seems to have met the Cooneys briefly for the first time in early summer 1939.

2. *Diary of Anaïs Nin,* 16. Nin's diaries were eventually collected in seven published volumes.

3. Duncan to Minnehaha Symmes and Lewis Burtch [December 1939 or January 1940]. Deirdre Bair in *Anaïs Nin: A Biography,* asserts, incorrectly, that the first meeting with Duncan took place in February 1940.

4. *Diary of Anaïs Nin,* 16.

5. Ibid., 159.

6. Ibid., 72. Admiral lived in the building through the 1950s. It was later torn down.

7. Hofmann, a German immigrant, had moved to New York in 1932 to become one of the central painters and teachers of the abstract expressionist movement.

Admiral and her soon-to-be-husband Robert De Niro both studied with Hofmann through the early 1940s.

8. *Diary of Anaïs Nin,* 18.

9. Duncan, *The Years As Catches,* 4.

10. Duncan to Minnehaha Symmes [1940].

11. Duncan to Kael, 3 February 1940.

12. Ibid.

13. Duncan to Minnehaha Symmes [1939].

14. Duncan, *The Years As Catches,* 5. The poem seems to have been important to Duncan. He made a studio recording of the piece in December 1961, and he made multiple revisions—in 1962, June 1964, and 1965.

15. Duncan to Minnehaha Symmes, 27 August 1940. Duncan commented that Fahs sailed to South America in June 1940, but no immigration record exists of such a trip. Ned Fahs later cut off contact with Duncan. He married in August 1941, had two children, and died in July 1997.

16. Notebook 4 [1941], UCB.

17. Notebook 2 [1941], 109, UCB. After his relationship with Duncan, Fahs chose a route very similar to that of Duncan's father. He found success not only in his academic career but also as a program director for the W. K. Kellogg Foundation. He never revealed his homosexuality to his family.

18. Duncan to Russell, 13 June 1940.

19. Ibid. [summer 1940].

20. Blanche Cooney, *In My Own Sweet Time,* 21.

21. Duncan to Minnehaha Symmes, 27 August 1940.

22. Cooney, *In My Own Sweet Time,* 23.

23. Duncan enclosed the text of his sermon in a letter to Minnehaha Symmes on 21 August 1940.

24. Duncan to Minnehaha Symmes [autumn 1940].

25. Ibid. Minnehaha Symmes's stance on the draft is unknown. Duncan did, however, make note of a letter from his stepfather, Lew Burch: "We are all wondering when your number is in the draft and when we can expect a fine soldier in the family!" (Notebook 2, 3 December 1940, UCB).

26. United States Army Draft Questionnaire. Filed by Duncan on 8 December 1940, UAB.

27. Ibid.

CHAPTER ELEVEN: QUEEN OF THE WHORES

1. Alvin Schwartz later married Marjorie McKee, and Marguerite Schwartz became romantically involved with poet Jackson Mac Low. Duncan referred to Marguerite Schwartz as Margaret Schwartz in his notebooks.

2. Duncan, *The Years As Catches,* iv. Russell was born in 1913 in Southern California.

3. Notebook B, 1944, UCB.

4. Alvin Schwartz, 16 April 2006.

5. Duncan to Minnehaha Symmes, 27 August 1940.

6. Notebook 2, 12 December 1940, UCB.

7. Ibid., 6 December 1940.

8. Duncan, *The Opening of the Field,* 67.

9. Duncan, "A Life in Poetry," Vancouver Poetry Conference, 5 August 1963, audiocassette, UAB.

10. This publication, labeled "issue two" to account for its previous incarnation as *Ritual* magazine, included an insert copy of its precursor.

11. *Experimental Review,* November 1940. In January 1941, an *Experimental Review* supplement included three of Duncan's poems—"Poem," "An Ark for Lawrence Durrell," and "The Awakening into Dream, Love There: Out of the Dream, and Our Beautiful Child"—alongside works by Virginia Admiral, Harvey Breit, Jack Johnson, and Sanders Russell.

12. Notebook 2, 2 December 1940, UCB. Duncan said in a lecture in 1963, "What I remember of dancing in the Catskills is very much what the poem became for me"("A Life in Poetry").

13. Sanchez to Duncan, 3 December 1940.

14. Duncan to Blanche Cooney [December 1940].

15. Notebook 2, 26 December 1940, 102, UCB.

16. Ibid., 28 December 1940, 109.

17. Virginia Admiral, 8 April 1998. Schweitzer was fifty-one when he arrived in New York in January 1940.

18. Notebook 2, 9 February 1941, 283, UCB. Virginia Admiral thought that Duncan may have halted the treatment because Schweitzer asked him to stop writing in his journals during the time he worked with him.

19. Duncan to Minnehaha Symmes, 1 January 1941.

20. Duncan first met Miller in mid-February 1941.

21. Duncan, untitled typed ms, UCB.

22. *Diary of Anaïs Nin,* 34.

23. Notebook 3, 86, UCB.

24. *Diary of Anaïs Nin,* 70. Nin named George Barker and Virginia Admiral as other writers.

25. Christopher Edwards, e-mail, 7 February 2006.

26. In her diary, Anaïs Nin also mentions Duncan's relationship with an unidentified individual named Paul during the winter of 1941.

27. Griffith Borgeson later made a name for himself as an automobile historian. Borgeson and Fabilli's marriage ended in 1945.

28. Virginia Admiral, 8 April 1998.

29. Notebook 2, 11 January 1941, 166, UCB.

30. These notebooks are now in the Bancroft Library, UCB.

31. *Diary of Anaïs Nin,* 97.

32. Ibid., 85.

33. Notebook 3, 8 March 1941, 59–62, UCB. Upon his arrival in Kansas City, Duncan apparently spent time with Jeff Rall's brother Louis but seemed to have avoided a meeting with Jeff Rall. When I spoke with Alvin Schwartz in April 2006, he speculated that Duncan and Jeff Rall had been lovers.

CHAPTER TWELVE: ENLISTED

1. Duncan. *The Originals: The Writer in America,* PBS Documentary, 1974, audiocassette, UAB.

2. Duncan to James and Blanche Cooney [April or May 1941]. Duncan's service records were destroyed in a fire in an army archive building. One enrollment form still exists, listing his potential wartime contributions: "Airplane engine mechanic or film editor, motion picture (motion picture cutter.) or public relations man or playwright (motion picture writer.) or reporter."

3. Smith, *Kenneth Patchen: Rebel Poet in America,* 153. Ernst had defended James Joyce in his *Ulysses* censorship case. He also helped establish the American Civil Liberties Union. Duncan makes no mention of Ernst in his correspondence from the period.

4. *Diary of Anaïs Nin,* 115.

5. Duncan to Lili Fabilli [May/June 1941].

6. Duncan, *The Years As Catches,* 17. This poem was first published in *Poetry* magazine.

7. Duncan to Lili Fabilli, May 1941.

8. Duncan, *Bending the Bow,* 70.

9. De Niro, born in Syracuse, New York, in 1922, studied painting at Black Mountain College with Josef Albers before moving to New York.

10. *Diary of Anaïs Nin,* 125.

11. Ibid.

12. Virginia Admiral, 17 July 1998.

13. Duncan, *The Years As Catches,* 22.

14. Stuhlmann, ed., *A Literate Passion: Letters of Anaïs Nin & Henry Miller, 1932–1953,* 337. In her diary, Nin also recalled an odder event that in Provincetown that month: "Robert came and brought a friend. He tells me that this friend writes the most beautiful short stories. His name is Tennessee Williams. We sat under the overhanging fishing nets and I cooked lunch" (*Diary of Anaïs Nin,* 132). No other records exist of Duncan's friendship with Williams.

15. Virginia Admiral, 8 April 1998.

16. Notebook B, 26 December 1941, UCB.

17. *Diary of Anaïs Nin,* 169. James Broughton in his memoir, *Coming Unbuttoned,* noted that Duncan was often too distracted by the workings of his own mind to greet people upon entering a room. Robert Glück recalled that Duncan

disposed of the customary "good-bye" at the end of phone calls, simply hanging up when he was done talking.

18. Duncan to Minnehaha Symmes, 8 January 1942.

CHAPTER THIRTEEN: MARRIAGE

1. Duncan to Minnehaha Symmes [December 1941 or January 1942].
2. Bertholf and Reid, eds., *Robert Duncan: Scales of the Marvelous*, 3.
3. Notebook 27 [1950s], UAB.
4. Duncan to Minnehaha Symmes [spring 1942].
5. Ibid., 8 January 1942.
6. "Robert Duncan Interview" (Saunders), 16. In February 1942, President Roosevelt had issued executive order 9066, allowing for the removal of Japanese Americans from their homes to temporary detainment camps. By August, the first refugees were being herded into camps throughout the western United States.
7. Rexroth, *An Autobiographical Novel*, 509.
8. Duncan, *The Years As Catches*, 34. Duncan's preoccupation with Africa recurs in a late poem, "At the Door," in *Ground Work II*. Like "The Venice Poem" (1947), "An African Elegy" seems inflected by Vachel Lindsay's "The Congo."
9. "A Spring Memorandum" and "A Pair of Uranian Garters for Aurora Bligh" appeared in the May 1942 issue of *Poetry*. Duncan had a voluminous correspondence with the editors of the magazine over the years, most centrally with Henry Rago. See Duncan Papers, Business Files, box 11, UAB.
10. Duncan associated the name change with his "coming out" to the military. Not until 1967 did he made the decision legal.
11. Duncan to Townsend [October 1942].
12. Duncan to James and Blanche Cooney [May 1943].
13. Marjorie McKee, 23 September 1998.
14. Duncan to Kael, 23 March 1943.
15. De Niro and Admiral's only child, Robert De Niro, Jr., was born in August 1943.
16. Faas *(Young Robert Duncan)* says that the newlyweds lived on West 13th Street, near University Avenue, not far from where Anaïs Nin lived. They seem to have moved there from 11th Street at some point during their marriage.
17. Duncan to James and Blanche Cooney [May 1943].
18. Duncan to Admiral [1955].
19. Virginia Admiral, 17 July 1998.
20. Duncan, *The Years As Catches*, 47.
21. Notebook B, November 1943, UCB.
22. Robert Duncan, Gay Liberation Day Poetry Reading, San Francisco, 2 March 1971, audiocassette, UAB.

23. Marjorie McKee, 23 September 1998. Ekbert Faas, *Young Robert Duncan,* wrote that Duncan was suicidal during and after his relationship with McKee. McKee disagreed with this. Except for occasional lows during his final years because of illness, Duncan seemed untouched by depression. He could be intolerant of the emotional instability of others, particularly when that instability was accompanied by chemical addiction. As he wrote to James Broughton in fall 1952, "When one gradually more and more wholly sees life as an adventure; one's sympathys *[sic]* die out tho ones *[sic]* interests may go on in people who see life as predicament." Duncan to James Broughton [autumn 1952], KSU.

24. The friendship with Wallis was brief. Wallis died in 1944 after falling out of a window during a party at Seon Givens's apartment on St. Luke's Place. Duncan remained in contact with Givens through the 1960s, describing her as "a friend and confidant, but more—and that in the midst of our Bohemian dedications—a spiritual mentor." Notebook 73, 3 February 1984, 40, UAB.

25. Jackson Mac Low, e-mail, 10 February 1988.

CHAPTER FOURTEEN: DIVORCE

1. Notebook B, 15 November 1943, UCB.

2. Ekbert Faas, *Young Robert Duncan,* mistakenly records Leslie Sherman's name as Leslie Herman. Sherman was a book illustrator for Vanguard Press.

3. Duncan to Minnehaha Symmes, 3 February 1944.

4. Ibid., 12 February 1943. Duncan may be referring to Henry Miller, though Miller most likely was in California at the time.

5. "Interview: Robert Duncan" (Abbot and Shurin), 5.

6. Riding scholar Jeff Hamilton suspects that if the meeting took place, it may have been disappointing to Duncan (e-mail, 1 January 2004).

7. Duncan to Kael, 24 February 1944.

8. Ibid., 24 June 1944.

9. Quoted in ibid.

10. Duncan to Minnehaha Symmes [spring 1945].

11. Duncan, Gay Liberation Day Poetry Reading. Jeff Hamilton discusses Duncan's correspondence with John Crowe Ransom in "Wrath Moves in the Music: Robert Duncan, Laura Riding, Craft and Force in Cold War Poetics," *Jacket,* no. 26 (October 2004), http://jacketmagazine.com/26/dunc-hami.html#fnB15.

12. Unlike many of his homosexual peers, Duncan rarely spoke of being discriminated against as a homosexual, nor did he express anxieties about the way he was perceived. The reasonable fears that went along with a homosexual lifestyle during the 1940s and 1950s seemed to be absent or deeply repressed for Duncan. Michael Rumaker wrote about gay life in San Francisco during the 1950s in his memoir *Robert Duncan in San Francisco:* "There was, in spite of the extraordinary quality of light over the city, a heavy climate of fear, not so much from the violence which occurred, although there was enough of that, but rather from the activities and pres-

ence of the police. . . . The Morals Squad was everywhere, and the entrapment of gay males in the streets, the parks and in numerous public places was a constant fear and common occurrence" (13).

13. Jacskon Mac Low, e-mail, 10 February 1998.

14. "Robert Duncan Interview" (Saunders), 20.

15. Duncan, *The Years As Catches,* 54.

CHAPTER FIFTEEN: THE END OF THE WAR

1. Duncan to Minnehaha Symmes [January 1945].

2. Ibid., two letters [spring 1945].

3. Duncan, *The Opening of the Field,* 8.

4. Duncan to Minnehaha Symmes [August 1945].

5. Duncan sold the press that he had bought from the Cooneys to Dellinger for the printing of *Direct Action.*

6. Duncan to Minnehaha Symmes [August 1945].

7. Duncan, "Pound, Eliot, and the Cult of the Gods," Kent State University, 11 October 1972, audiocassette, UAB.

8. Notebook 20, UAB.

9. Fayetta Philip to Minnehaha Symmes, 17 October 1945.

10. Duncan to Minnehaha Symmes [October 1945].

11. Bertholf and Reid, eds., *Robert Duncan: Scales of the Marvelous,* 8.

12. Duncan to Minnehaha Symmes [October 1945].

13. Bertholf and Reid, eds., *Robert Duncan,* 7.

14. Duncan, *The Years As Catches,* 56.

15. Duncan to Minnehaha Symmes [November 1945].

16. Bertholf and Reid, eds., *Robert Duncan,* 10.

17. Richard Moore later worked for Pacifica Radio, an alternative radio station founded in Berkeley in 1946.

18. Duncan to Russell [late 1945].

19. "Robert Duncan Interview" (Saunders), 18.

20. Duncan to Russell [late 1945].

21. Duncan to Vortriede, 24 January 1946, UCB.

22. Duncan to Kael, 14 February 1946.

CHAPTER SIXTEEN: THE ROUND TABLE

1. Notebook 51 [spring 1974], UAB.

2. Duncan, "Introduction to a Bibliography of the Works of Jack Spicer," UAB.

3. "Robert Duncan Interview" (Saunders), 21.

4. Jimenez later became a Greek tutor for Blaser, Duncan, and Spicer during their studies with Kantorowicz.

5. Ellen King later married Warren Tallman, and Ariel Reynolds later married Tom Parkinson.

6. Hilde Burton, 18 February 2006.

7. Duncan to Minnehaha Symmes [autumn 1946].

8. Hawkins (1915–85) later became a journalist and horticulturalist in Northern California.

9. Duncan, *The Years As Catches*, 86.

10. Duncan, "Author's Notes September 1962 to the Medieval Scenes Papers," UAB. Duncan and Spicer enthusiasts often mistakenly refer to Hearst Avenue as Hearst Street.

11. Also see Ellingham and Killian, *Poet Be Like God;* Kevin Killian, interview with Josephine Fredman Stewart, 8 March 1992, private archive.

12. Duncan, "Introduction to a Bibliography," UAB.

13. Ellingham and Killian, *Poet Be Like God,* 12. Robin Blaser recalled once seeing Duncan misread someone's tarot cards in an act of retribution.

14. Duncan and Jess owned a Kenkyusha, which they sometimes used to gather themes for Duncan's lectures.

15. Duncan, "Introduction to a Bibliography," UAB.

CHAPTER SEVENTEEN: THE POETRY FESTIVAL

1. Gleason, *Collected Poems 1919–1979,* xiii.

2. Duncan, "Voices of the '40's: A Recreation of the 'Festival of Modern Poetry—April 1947,'" 1974, audiocassette, UAB.

3. Broughton, *Coming Unbuttoned,* 62.

4. Zukofsky to Duncan, 30 July 1947.

5. Ibid., 7 August 1947.

6. Dorothy Pound to Duncan, 4 August 1947.

7. Duncan, "Lecture on Ezra Pound," Central Washington State University, 8 October 1969, audiocassette, UAB.

8. H. D. and Duncan. *A Great Admiration,* 3.

9. Duncan, *Caesar's Gate,* xiii.

10. Barbara married Stanley Edwin Jones, a World War II veteran who worked in Bakersfield as an insurance salesman.

11. For more on Duncan's relationship with O'Neill, see Ekbert Faas's *Young Robert Duncan.*

12. *Robert Duncan: An Interview by George Bowering and Robert Hogg,* 4.

13. Clark, *Charles Olson,* 126.

14. Duncan, "Ideas of Primordial Time in Charles Olson's Work," University of Iowa, 7 November 1978, audiocassette, UAB.

15. Duncan, untitled lecture, Vancouver, 23 July 1961, audiocassette, UAB.

1. Duncan, "A Life in Poetry," Vancouver Poetry Conference, 5 August 1963, audiocassette, UAB.

2. *Kreis* can be roughly translated as "cult," though George's group was not a religious cult. George was born in 1868 in Budesheim, Germany. The Georgekreis was a model for Blaser, Spicer, and Duncan in another way: George and many of his followers, including Kantorowicz, were homosexual.

3. Robin Blaser, 18 June 1999.

4. Ibid.

5. Spicer, *Collected Books,* 361.

6. For more on this and other aspects of the Berkeley Renaissance, see Davidson, *The San Francisco Renaissance.*

7. Spicer, *Collected Books,* 176.

8. Dodds's lectures were published in 1951. Two other pivotal books for Duncan appeared in 1948: Robert Graves's *The White Goddess* and Gertrude Levy's *The Gate of Horn.*

9. Duncan also took an introductory ancient Greek class during the spring 1948 semester.

10. Ellingham and Killian, *Poet Be Like God,* 21. Spicer had begun graduate studies in the English department that fall.

11. "Robert Duncan Interview" (Saunders), 18.

12. Gerald Ackerman, unpublished memoir, 9, UAB; and e-mail, 26 February 2006.

13. Notebook D, 1 March 1948, UCB.

14. Gerald Ackerman to the author, 4 July 1998.

15. Lewis Ellingham and Kevin Killian's *Poet Be Like God* includes an anecdote Duncan related to Thom Gunn: "One day . . . Dick arrived on his threshold as Robert sat on his bed. . . . Dick arched his back and masturbated in front of an astonished Duncan. 'I was the only one he could have shown this side to,' [Duncan] told Thom Gunn" (22).

16. Ackerman, unpublished memoir, 9, UAB. Barbara Jones also recalled Duncan's childhood ability to announce the contents of a book before reading it.

17. The standard sonata form has three major parts: exposition, development, and recapitulation. Some pieces have a fourth section or coda. Duncan's interest in Stravinsky's work stemmed partly from the composer's published lectures, *The Poetics of Music,* which he reviewed in the spring 1948 issue of *Occident.* For more on the form of the poem, see Berthol "Robert Duncan's 'The Venice Poem' and Symphonic Form."

18. Faas, in *Young Robert Duncan,* says that "The Venice Poem" exists in Duncan's notebook virtually unrevised, but this is inaccurate. As Duncan said at the Berkeley Conference in 1965, "When I was a young poet I used to slave with lines

that would unfold a melody without my feeling them all the way through this thing that's got to unfold all the way through you."

19. Notebook 10, 50, UAB.

20. Everson's poem was retrieved by scholar Ben Mazer and published in *Fulcrum: An Annual of Poetry and Aesthetics,* no. 5 (2006): 77–80.

21. Duncan, *Poems 1948–49,* 25.

22. Ibid., 21.

23. Notebook D, 12 March 1948, UCB.

24. Duncan, *Poems 1948–49,* 45.

25. Ackerman, unpublished memoir, note 3, UAB.

26. Notebook D, 21 March 1948, UCB.

27. Fabilli was at the time married to poet William Everson, whom she had met at the Tylers' Treesbank Farm in 1946.

28. Duncan, *Poems 1948–49,* 64. This collection also included one of Duncan's first plays, *A Poet's Masque,* which Jerry Ackerman remembered seeing performed in several households in Berkeley during the fall of 1948.

CHAPTER NINETEEN: INDIAN TALES

1. Duncan, *Poems 1948–49,* 24: Ackerman later moved to New York City, where he became romantically involved with writer Paul Goodman.

2. Callahan, "The World of Jaime de Angulo," 1. Janie O'Neill's ex-husband Hugh had also been a friend of de Angulo's in Big Sur.

3. Duncan may have typed the manuscript for de Angulo's book *Indian Tales,* which was published posthumously in 1953.

4. "The World of Jaime de Angulo [an interview with Robert Duncan]" 1. See also Gui de Angulo's *The Life of Jaime de Angulo.*

5. Fayetta's card is in the collection at UAB.

6. Notebook 11, UAB. In the notebook entry, titled "Memoir," Duncan mentioned that Virginia Admiral's (and briefly his) analyst Dr. Schweitzer had suggested a relationship between his talk and his libido, that Duncan could fall into a panic when "left at a loss for conversation—for intercourse." "Bear" was Duncan and Ackerman's pet name for each other.

7. Duncan, lecture, Vancouver, 23 July 1961.

8. Duncan, *Derivations,* 12.

9. Duncan to Josephine Fredman [October 1950].

10. Duncan to Dorothy Pound, 31 October 1950.

11. Duncan to Fredman [October 1950].

1. Jess Collins, October 1998.
2. Jess's draft registration card listed his potential occupations as "Carpenter, General or Dental Laboratory Technician (Dental technician.) or Physics Laboratory Assistant or X- Ray Technician (X-ray photographer.) or Dental Hygienist or Medical Technician or Chemical Laboratory Assistant."
3. Jess Collins, October 1998.
4. The California School of Fine Arts was later renamed the San Francisco Art Institute.
5. Jess Collins, October 1998. Michael Auping also provides biographical material in his introduction to *Jess: Grand Collage: 1951–1993*.
6. Ibid.
7. Duncan, Gay Liberation Day Poetry Reading, San Francisco, 2 March 1971, audiocassette, UAB.
8. Jess's astrological sign was Leo, thus the lion. Throughout Duncan's poems, there are references to the relationship between the bear (Duncan) and the lion (Jess).
9. Fielding Dawson, 13 July 1999. The Saroyan short story appeared in *Hairenik Weekly,* 12 August 1938. Duncan may have been working with a piece from Prévert's 1947 *Le Petit Lion.*
10. Duncan, *Selected Poems,* 28.
11. Duncan to Jess, 1 July 1956.
12. Jess Collins, October 1998.
13. Solnit, *Secret Exhibition,* 34.
14. Hilde Burton, 19 February 2006.
15. James Broughton, 26 September 1998.
16. Duncan to Fredman, 9 November 1950. Duncan likely wrote this letter shortly before he met Jess at the Ghost House.
17. Robert Creeley, 20 December 1997.
18. Duncan to Broughton [spring 1952], KSU.
19. Ibid. [fall 1952], KSU. Duncan had begun rug making during the early 1950s. He spoke about the project in a 10 June 1976 lecture at the Naropa Institute, www.archive.org/details/naropa_robert_duncan_lecture_warp_and:

This Duncan here makes rugs. None of them are complete. . . . I think you can guess that I do not have any pre-plans, so I simply have designs moving out of designs moving out of designs. Then I lapse from them. As a spider I'd look like—they did some experiments on LSD spiders. They lose track of the web. . . . They can see it before they do it and then they get bored and walk away. In my imaginary world of art there would be enough time that anybody coming along, an archaeologist, can see that this belongs to a design somewhere.

20. Mary Margaret Sloan, 17 February 2006.
21. Notebook 14 [1954], UAB.

22. Gui de Angulo was a photographer who also provided Duncan with the oil crayons that he used for his drawings. Kael's daughter, Gina James, was born in 1948. Her father was James Broughton.

23. Duncan to Broughton [September 1952], KSU.

24. Ibid. [fall 1952].

25. Duncan, "Ideas on the Meaning of Form," National Poetry Festival, Allendale, Michigan Conference, 16 June 1973, audiocassette, courtesy of Karl Gartung. The U.S. government conducted mind control experiments with a variety of hallucinogenic drugs during the 1950s under the code names Project ARTICHOKE and Project MKULTRA. It's likely that Duncan was recruited to participate in the tests carried out in Stanford, California, where writer Ken Kesey was also a volunteer. Selected documents from the project now reside at Stanford University's Department of Special Collections, http://www.oac.cdlib.org/findaid/ark:/13030/kt4b69s0bj/entire_text/.

26. Faas, "Interview with Robert Duncan," in *Towards a New American Poetics,* 55–85.

27. Duncan, "Ideas on the Meaning of Form," National Poetry Festival, Allendale, Michigan Conference, 16 June 1973, audiocassette.

CHAPTER TWENTY-ONE: THE WAY TO SHADOW GARDEN

1. Paul Karlstrom, "Interview with Larry Jordan," 19 December 1995, Smithsonian Archive of American Art, www.aaa.si.edu/collections/oralhistories/transcripts/jordan95.htm. Known as Larry Jordan during his early career, the filmmaker now uses the name Lawrence Jordan.

2. During a February 2000 conversation, Jess recalled with amusement that Brakhage never did any house cleaning.

3. Duncan to Broughton [spring 1953], KSU.

4. Stan Brakhage, 24 December 1998.

5. Brakhage to Duncan and Jess, 27 June 1957.

6. Duncan to Broughton [May 1953], KSU.

7. For more information on the gallery, see Howard, *The Beat Generation Galleries and Beyond.*

8. Wagstaff, ed., *Lyn Brockway, Harry Jacobus, and Jess.* Christopher Wagstaff also prepared the catalogue *The King Ubu Gallery: 1952–1953.*

9. Between 1955 and 1964, Berman published nine issues of *Semina.* Both Duncan and Jess participated in the eighth issue printed in 1963, which included one of Duncan's early Stein derivation poems, "Increasing," along with a photograph of Duncan swimming in the nude.

10. Duncan to Broughton [October 1953], KSU.

11. Quoted in "Poet Entertains with Song, Verse in Semester's Last Poetry Hour," *University Daily Kansan,* 14 May 1965.

12. Duncan, *Derivations,* 52.

13. For more on the relationship between Levertov and Duncan, see *The Letters of Robert Duncan and Denise Levertov.*

14. Bertholf and Reid, eds., *Robert Duncan,* 90.

15. Duncan, *Derivations,* 95.

16. Duncan to Broughton [April 1953], KSU. Kit and Ilse Barker were visiting San Francisco from the United Kingdom. David and Lloyd Bary were friends of Duncan's from Berkeley. Terzian is probably the Bay Area sculptor Jacques Terzian.

17. Notebook 14 [January 1954], UAB.

18. Ibid.

19. Anger played the role of the changeling in the film. He likely landed the part through his grandmother, a Hollywood costume designer.

20. Stan Brakhage, 24 December 1998. Brakhage also noted, "That has a lot to do with their difficult relationship with Jack Spicer. . . . Spicer was always being too personal. . . . He'd leave a trail of cigarette butts . . . , and Jess was always cleaning up after such things." Hilde Burton remembered Duncan and Jess being disturbed when they found that Anger during one of his visits had made subtle, seemingly ritualistic rearrangements of objects in the house.

21. Ibid. The film was never completed or titled and is now lost.

22. Notebook 14 [January 1954], UAB.

23. Anger shot *Aqua Barocco,* later titled *Eaux d'artifice,* in Italy in 1953.

24. Notebook 14 [spring 1954], UAB. Duncan and Jess apparently banned Embry from the household after this point. In June 1962, he tried to reestablish contact while an inpatient at New York's Manhattan State Hospital.

25. Ibid. Marie Short was a friend of Robinson Jeffers's widow, Uma. Composer Lou Harrison (1917–2003) met Duncan in New York in the 1940s. Visual artist Jay DeFeo (1929–89) likely met Duncan when she was a student at Berkeley in the late 1940s.

CHAPTER TWENTY-TWO: THE WORKSHOP

1. Duncan, "Interview: The History of the Poetry Center," 1 December 1976, audiocassette, UAB. McLeod's contribution to the workshop is undocumented.

2. Notebook 15, August 1954, UAB.

3. Ibid.

4. Stan Brakhage, 24 December 1998.

5. For more on Adam's life and work, see *Fire Brackled Bones: Selected Poems and Collages of Helen Adam,* edited by Kristin Prevallet. See also Prevallet's writing on Helen Adam at www.heelstone.com/meridian/adam4.html.

6. James Broughton, 26 September 1998.

7. Notebook 15, 29 October 1954, UAB.

8. Hodes dates her first meeting with Duncan at 1938, but it more likely took place after Duncan met Anaïs Nin at the end of 1939. Hodes recalled in April 2006:

I was an avid reader and I . . . met Emil [White] because I was always hanging around second-hand bookshops. . . . Emil had been telling me about Robert's involvement with Anaïs Nin and Henry [Miller]. Henry said, if Robert wants to stop in Chicago, would you put him up. Emil said to me, let's have a party for him; he said I can't do parties but you can, . . . and I said O.K.

9. Michael McClure, 14 January 1998.

10. In Memory: Stan Brakhage 1933–2003: "Realm Buster: Stan Brakhage, Michael McClure & Steve Anker in Conversation," http://mcclure-manzarek.com/brakhage.html.

11. In 1954, Brakhage also shot a short film in the basement at Baker Street called *The Way to Shadow Garden,* part of his series of early psychodramas, starring Walter Newcomb as a young man in the midst of a nervous breakdown. In the climax of the eleven-minute film, Newcomb's character gouges out his eyes with his fingers and wanders into the garden beyond the swinging doors of the Baker Street basement.

12. Stan Brakhage, 24 December 1998.

13. Lawrence Jordan. "My Travels with Stan," http://mfj-online.org/journal Pages/MFJ41/jordanpage.html 16 Jan. 2006. Jordan later worked with Joseph Cornell in Flushing, Queens, assisting him in the construction of some of his artworks.

14. Brakhage to Jess, 15 December 1954, STORRS. Brakhage, later philosophical about his break with Duncan and Jess, felt that Jess "endured" Duncan's "falling in love" with various people throughout their marriage. Duncan said during a poetry reading in 1971, "When you live twenty years with a person, you fall in love quite a number of times with other people. . . . unfortunately I have a proclivity for it."

15. Hodes to Duncan and Jess, 19 April 1955.

16. Howard, *The Beat Generation Galleries and Beyond,* 68.

17. Ginsberg, *Journals Mid-fifties 1954–1958,* 105.

18. Schumacher, *Dharma Lion.*

CHAPTER TWENTY-THREE: MALLORCA

1. Duncan to James and Blanche Cooney, 22 February 1955 [misdated as 22 March 1955].

2. *The Originals: The Writer In America,* PBS, 1974, audiocassette, UAB.

3. Wagstaff with Jacobus, "Interview with Paul Alexander."

4. Duncan, "Black Mountain College," *Jacket* 28, http://jacketmagazine.com /28/dunc-bert-10prose.html#x7.

5. Jess to Ham and Mary Tyler, 20 February 1955.

6. Levertov to Duncan, 31 March 1955.

7. Virginia Admiral, 17 July 1998. "Bobbie" became the Hollywood actor Robert De Niro, Jr. Admiral's main memory of the meeting was Jess's effort to procure

an ointment for her son's dog, which had a skin rash. Duncan wrote to the Cooneys on 22 February 1955 asking if he might visit them in Woodstock, but there is no record of the visit. In the letter, Duncan wrote of New York and New Yorkers, "How brutally unaware one wld. have to be to last."

8. Robert Creeley, 20 December 1997. Creeley had lost an eye in a car accident as a child.

9. Duncan to Levertov, 16 April 1955.

10. Olson, *The Special View of History*, 6.

11. Graves and Hogarth, *Majorca Observed*, 7.

12. Notebook 15, 3 May 1955, UAB.

13. Robin Blaser, 18 June 1999. Lowes's book is a study of Coleridge's notebooks leading up to the composition of "The Rime of the Ancient Mariner" and "Kubla Khan."

14. Duncan to Adam, 8 April 1955.

15. The essay appears in Duncan's *Fictive Certainties*.

16. Duncan to Broughton, 4 June 1955; Duncan to Denise Levertov [early June 1955].

17. Robert Creeley, 20 December 1997.

18. Duncan to Broughton, 11 July 1955.

19. Duncan to Ida Hodes, 26 June 1955.

CHAPTER TWENTY-FOUR: CAESAR'S GATE

1. Duncan to Adam, 26 August 1955.

2. Berkeley friend Hilde Burton speculated, "I doubt he finished any book—a month later he had integrated it. It was as if it had become his" [18 February 2006]. Duncan's reading notes do show a focus on the opening chapters of books rather than the books as a whole.

3. Notebook 15 [June 1955], UAB.

4. Duncan to Adam, 17 September 1955.

5. Notebook 15 [June 1955], UAB. Duncan's feelings about Robert and Ann Creeley's relationship are recorded in Faas's *Robert Creeley: A Biography, The Letters of Robert Duncan and Denise Levertov,* and in Duncan's unpublished letters to Robert Creeley, housed at Stanford University's Department of Special Collections. Gertrude Stein, who once referred to Ezra Pound derisively as "a village explainer," discontinued her association with Pound after he broke a chair during a visit to her home.

6. Creeley to Duncan, 4 April 1965 (written after another encounter with Graves).

7. Duncan to Adam, 20 August 1955.

8. Reproductions of these paintings appear in Christopher Wagstaff's catalogue *Lyn Brockway, Harry Jacobus, and Jess: The Romantic Paintings.*

9. Duncan to Charles Olson, 14 August 1955, *Jacket* 28, http://jacketmagazine.com/28/dunc-bert-10letters.html#fnx6.

10. Duncan to Levertov [late November 1955].

11. Howard, *The Beat Generation Galleries and Beyond,* 76. Other readers on the night of the Six Gallery reading were Philip Lamantia, Michael McClure, Philip Whalen, and Gary Snyder. Kenneth Rexroth was the master of ceremonies.

12. Duncan to Blaser, 18 June 1957.

13. Hodes to Duncan and Jess, 16 December 1955.

14. Duncan to Mary Tyler, 27 November 1955.

15. Duncan to Hodes, 29 November 1955. Duncan returned to the French language and to the theme of death in his final collection of poems, *Ground Work II.*

CHAPTER TWENTY-FIVE: THE MEADOW

1. Duncan to Levertov, 3 February 1956.

2. Notebook 13 [January 1956], UAB.

3. Duncan to Broughton, 5 February 1956.

4. *Ark II/Moby I,* 1956–1957, eds. Michael McClure and James Harmon, San Francisco, 10.

5. Duncan and Jess had met the Barkers in San Francisco in 1955. Kit Barker was the brother of poet George Barker.

6. Duncan and Jess to Ham and Mary Tyler, 8 February 1956. In a 1976 interview, Duncan said that money he had expected from his mother was stopped in Algiers during a French embargo of Africa.

7. Harris, originally part of the San Francisco painting circle during the 1940s, had moved to Europe in 1953.

8. Duncan to Ham and Mary Tyler, 26 February 1956. Duncan's poem was "An Owl Is an Only Bird of Poetry (Another Vale for James Broughton)." The issue also included poems by Louis Zukofsky, Lorine Niedecker, Robert Creeley, Charles Olson, and Denise Levertov.

9. Early in their relationship, Duncan's fees for readings and lectures made up the greater part of the couple's income. By the mid-1970s, Jess's advances from the Odyssia Gallery equaled Duncan's income.

10. Duncan to Jess, 19 March 1956.

11. Ibid. Tik-tok refers to a character in the Oz books.

12. Wagstaff with Jacobus, "Interview with Paul Alexander," 8.

13. Duncan to Jess, 23 March 1956.

14. The stripped-down faculty included "Wes Huss and his wife, Huss taught drama. And Charles and Betty [Olson]. [Joseph] Fiore taught painting. And [Stefan] Volpe *[sic]*—he taught music—and Hilda Volpe *[sic]*. . . . Huss's drama group was . . . the core of the college" (Duncan quoted in Olson, *The Special View of History,* 8).

15. Duncan had an affair with Tom Field in San Francisco in 1956. It's unclear whether he began the relationship at Black Mountain, though Martin Duberman, in *Black Mountain,* wrote, "Sometimes when Jess was away—and sometimes when he wasn't—Duncan would go on binges that challenged Black Mountain's usual

definition of *machismo*" (431). Field and Alexander, Indianans who had been friends since high school, both pursued artistic careers in the Bay Area.

16. Wagstaff with Jacobus, "Interview with Paul Alexander," 6.

17. Wagstaff, "Interview with Tom Field," 3.

18. Notebook 19, April 1956, UAB.

19. Mary Emma Harris, "Robert Duncan Interview," 27 December 1971, UAB. In *Black Mountain,* Martin Duberman reported incorrectly that Duncan taught a class on Persian history at the college. Duncan told Denise Levertov that Reading in French: Rimbaud, Les Illuminations, might more aptly be called "How to make one's way as an amateur in the French language" (18 July 1956).

20. Olson, *The Special View of History,* 8.

21. Harris, "Robert Duncan Interview."

22. "There were about fifteen students. Of these, the G.I.s were the paying students—most of them painters: Tom Field, Paul Alexander, Jerry van de Wiele, Ann Simone (who was to play Medea in *Medea in Kolchis* . . .). There were six in my basic techniques course in poetry, of whom Joe Dunn (first editor of the White Rabbit series), Eloise Mixon, and John Wieners were to become friends" (Duncan, "Ten Prose Pieces").

23. Duncan, *The Opening of the Field,* 10. "The Law I Love Is Major Mover" was first titled "Her Voice across the Water Comes" and written during the late spring or early summer of 1956.

24. Notebook 19, April 1956, UAB. Kantorowicz's directive to his students at Berkeley had been "A historian is a detective, not a judge."

25. Notebook 19 at UAB includes some of Duncan's lecture notes from Black Mountain.

26. Olson, *The Special View of History,* 8.

CHAPTER TWENTY-SIX: NEW YORK INTERLUDE

1. Notebook 18, 10 May 1956, UAB.

2. The Scott Street house was a haven for poets during the late 1950s, memorialized in John Wiener's diaries, *707 Scott Street.*

3. Duncan to Jess [June 1956].

4. Rumaker, *Robert Duncan in San Francisco,* 1.

5. Duncan had first viewed the Gallatin Collection of modernist art when it was housed at New York University between 1938 and 1942.

6. Duncan to Jess, [16] June 1956. Other acquaintances in New York that summer included Al Novac, Ray Johnson, Ernst Kantorowicz protégé Robert Benson, and Nik Cernovich.

7. Ibid., 22 June 1956.

8. Duncan to Broughton, 16 July 1956. M. C. (Mary Caroline) Richards had been a student at the University of California during the early 1940s and later taught at Black Mountain.

9. Fenichel had secured Duncan a typing job, primarily preparing manuscripts for writers.

10. Duncan to Jess, 25 June 1956.

11. Blaser to Duncan [1956], UCB.

12. Duncan to Jess, 1 July 1956.

13. Kevin Killian, interview with Robin Blaser, 22 May 1992, archive of Kevin Killian.

14. Duncan, *The Opening of the Field,* 15.

15. Duncan to Jess, 8 July 1956.

16. Blaser to Duncan [1956], UCB.

17. Duncan to Jess [20 July] 1956.

18. Ibid. [August] 1956.

19. Ibid., 7 August 1956. In Duncan's chapbook *Medea at Kolchis,* published by Oyez in 1965, he acknowledged the following cast: Garrow: Wesley Huss, Jason: Donald Mixon, the Doctor: Erik Weir [Weinberger], Medea: Ann Simone, Arthur: Louis Marbury (first night) and John Wieners (second night), Edna: Eloise Mixon.

20. Duberman, in *Black Mountain,* dates these performances on August 29 and 30.

CHAPTER TWENTY-SEVEN: THE SAN FRANCISCO SCENE

1. Duncan, "Interview: The History of the Poetry Center," 1 December 1976, audiocassette, UAB.

2. Creeley to Duncan [spring 1956].

3. McClure to Duncan [spring 1956].

4. Duncan to Levertov, 3 June 1956.

5. Ida Hodes, 6 April 2006.

6. Kevin Killian, interview with Ida Hodes, February 1991, archive of Kevin Killian.

7. Rumaker, *Robert Duncan in San Francisco,* 16.

8. Michael McClure, 14 January 1998.

9. Duncan to Levertov, 8 October 1956. Ida Hodes kept Jess and Duncan's cat Princess.

10. Duncan, "Program Notes: on Randall Jarrell, The Poetry Center, 3 Oct 1956," UAB. Randall Jarrell had been a student of John Crowe Ransom's at Vanderbilt University. Duncan's animosity doubtless also stemmed from his own falling out with Ransom during the 1940s.

11. Broughton, *Coming Unbuttoned,* 66.

12. Duncan, "Program Notes: on Allen Ginsberg and Gregory Corso, The Poetry Center, 21 Oct 1956," UAB.

13. Duncan to Levertov, 15 November 1956. Duncan and Jess often used each other as foils—explaining that they couldn't have visitors because one or the other of them objected, or was busy working.

14. McClure has no memory of this meeting.

15. "'The Closeness of Mind': An Interview with Robert Duncan," 13. Despite the awkward encounter, Duncan and Jess read Kerouac's work with some interest, and Duncan was especially fond of Kerouac's "October in the Railroad Earth," sensing William Saroyan's influence.

16. Kerouac, *Desolation Angels,* 165.

17. Paul Alexander documented his memories of 1950s San Francisco in a letter to Lewis Ellingham, 28 August 1982, UAB.

18. Rumaker, *Robert Duncan in San Francisco,* 23.

19. Ibid., 25.

20. Michael Rumaker, 4 May 1998. By the late 1950s, Duncan had developed a reputation in the Bay Area literary community as a hustler of sorts. N. A. Diaman's coming-of-age novel *Second Crossing* gave another unflattering picture in his thinly disguised character "Robert Dawson":

> I walk over to City Lights. Here I unexpectedly run into Robert Dawson who has been living in Stinson Beach.
>
> Are you coming to the big poetry reading at Fugazi Hall? I ask him.
>
> Yes. . . . Can I stay with you then?
>
> . . . I don't know how comfortable that would be. Isn't there anywhere else you can stay?
>
> There are quite a few places, he answers.
>
> Oh! I reply realizing it is a matter of sex rather than accommodations. . . .
> How could he do such a thing? . . . How could he when I respect him so much as a poet? . . . While the incident doesn't diminish my appreciation of his work, I feel I must be more cautious around him so he will not misinterpret anything I say or do as an indication of sexual interest in him.

CHAPTER TWENTY-EIGHT: OLSON, WHITEHEAD, AND THE MAGIC WORKSHOP

1. Poetry Center announcement, "A Note on the Spring 1957 Program," UAB.

2. Spicer, *Collected Books,* 353. For detailed documentation of his workshop, see the "Poems and Documents" section.

3. Lewis Ellingham, George Stanley interview, 24 June 1982, Spicer Circle Papers, UAB.

4. Wagstaff, "Interview with Tom Field," 11. Residents of the communal East-West House, on California Street, included Joanne Kyger, Lew Welch, and Philip Whalen.

5. Clark, *Charles Olson,* 263.

6. Duncan, "Introductory Notes to Charles Olson, Poetry Center, 21 February 1957," UAB. Olson gave a second reading on February 26 at San Francisco State.

7. Michael McClure and Philip Whalen were among those who challenged Olson's readings of Whitehead. The San Franciscans also had their own habits of entertaining guests. At the opening of one session, in an attempt either to woo the giant Gloucester poet or to fluster him, Jack Spicer dealt a deck of tarot cards at Olson's feet.

8. Duncan to Blaser, 19 December 1957.

9. Duncan to Levertov, 1 March 1958.

10. Duncan, *The Opening of the Field*, 36. "Thy hand / Beloved": Jess spent February and March 1957 with a bandaged infected hand after being bitten by Harry Jacobus's cat.

11. Ibid., 34.

12. Notebook 6 [1957], UAB.

13. Duncan to Levertov, 7 October 1957.

14. Notebook 6 [1957], UAB.

15. Duncan to Allen, 23 April 1957, UCSD.

16. Duncan, "Interview: The History of the Poetry Center," 1 December 1976, audiocassette, UAB.

17. Duncan, "Notes on Spicer/Pendleton, The Poetry Center, 17 March 1957," UAB.

18. Lewis Ellingham, interview with George Stanley, 24 June 1982, Spicer Circle Papers, UAB. During the workshop, Stanley wrote *Flowers* (San Francisco: White Rabbit Press, 1965).

19. Duncan, "Introduction to a Bibliography of the Works of Jack Spicer," UAB.

20. Duncan to Rexroth, 23 April 1957, UCSD. Rexroth's radio addresses were broadcast by Pacifica Radio in Berkeley. In *A Life of Kenneth Rexroth*, Linda Hamalian says that Rexroth ended the relationship before Duncan did: "(Across the back of an April 9, 1957, letter from Duncan, Rexroth scrawled 'This represents the end of relationship with Duncan)" (274). The *Evergreen Review* record was released with Grove Press's "San Francisco Scene" edition of the journal, which contained work by Duncan (including "This Place Rumord to Have Been Sodom"), Spicer, Ginsberg, Rexroth, and Kerouac.

21. On October 3, Allen Ginsberg and Lawrence Ferlinghetti were acquitted in the *Howl* obscenity trial. They were defended by the ACLU, and Duncan testified on their behalf.

22. Wallace Berman, *Semina* 2, December 1957. Cameron's drawing had appeared in *Semina* 1. The Bermans soon moved to San Francisco.

23. Duncan to Blaser, 4 June 1957.

24. Hilde Burton, 19 February 2006.

25. Jordan and Jess collaborated on two films: The *40 and 1 Nights (or Jess's Didactic Nickelodeon)* (1961) and *Finds of the Fortenight* (1980). In 1959, Jordan married Patricia Topalian, a photographer who was also close to Duncan and Jess during the 1950s.

CHAPTER TWENTY-NINE: THE MAIDENS

1. Duncan to Allen, 12 October 1957, UCSD. Duncan's introductory notes to Moore's reading are in *Selected Prose,* 94–96.

2. Joanne Kyger, e-mail, 11 May 2006.

3. Ibid., 27 March 2006.

4. Duncan speaks about these meetings in "Interview: The History of the Poetry Center." See also Ellingham and Killian's *Poet Be Like God.*

5. Lewis Ellingham, interview with George Stanley, 24 June 1982, Spicer Circle Papers, UAB.

6. Linda Russo, "Particularizing People's Lives" (conversation with Joanne Kyger, 27 February 1999), *Jacket* 11, http://jacketmagazine.com/11/kyger-iv-by-russo.html.

7. James Broughton, 26 September 1998.

8. Duncan to Levertov, 10/11 December 1957.

9. In addition to Spicer's *After Lorca,* Dunn had printed Stephen Jonas's *Love, the Poem, the Sea & Other Pieces Examined.*

10. Rumaker, *Robert Duncan in San Francisco,* 36.

11. Ibid.

12. Spicer, *Collected Books,* 62.

13. Levertov, "Hypocrite Women," *O Taste and See,* 70.

14. Duncan to Levertov, 4 February 1958.

15. Duncan, "A Risk of Sympathies."

16. Ibid.

17. Duncan to Levertov, 15 October 1957. Broughton in his memoir *Coming Unbuttoned* commented on Duncan's review: "I am not easily disposed of when my heartstrings have been attached to another's. . . . Despite dismissal I held on to the long ties of kinship."

CHAPTER THIRTY: ELFMERE

1. Duncan to Levertov, 28/29 April 1958.

2. Duncan, *The Opening of the Field,* 82.

3. Duncan outlined the compositional considerations of *The Opening of the Field* in his 1958 Guggenheim grant application and in a lecture on 18 May 1959 at San Francisco State. Both are at UAB.

4. Duncan, *The Opening of the Field,* 74.

5. Creeley, "Heroes," *For Love,* 94. A line from Levertov's 18 March 1958 letter to Duncan also appears in the poem.

6. Duncan to Levertov, 1 April 1958.

7. Duncan incorrectly recorded the baby's name as Susan in a letter to Denise Levertov.

8. Bobbie Louise Hawkins, 19 December 1998.

9. Notebook 20 [spring 1958], UAB. A photograph of Creeley's reading appears on the cover of David Ossman's *The Sullen Art.*

10. Zukofsky to Duncan, 14 May 1958.

11. Duncan to Levertov, 9 July 1958.

12. George Stanley to Lewis Ellingham, 19 December 1982, UAB.

13. George Stanley, e-mail, 3 February 2006.

14. *The Adam Family in Nesbittland: Imaginary Portrait #18: Helen Adam.*

15. Duncan to Blaser, 6 August 1958.

16. In his Guggenheim application, Duncan explained that "the field" was of a threefold nature: "known intimately as the given field of my own life, intellectually as the field of language (or spirit), and imaginatively as the field given to Man (of many languages)."

17. *Manroot,* no. 10 (1974/1975): 114.

CHAPTER THIRTY-ONE: NIGHT SCENES

1. Duncan, "Workshop in Basic Techniques" questionnaire, UAB.

2. Joanne Kyger, e-mail, 27 March 2006.

3. George Stanley, e-mail, 30 January 2006.

4. Frank O'Hara to Jasper Johns, 15 July 1959, Spicer Circle Papers, UAB.

5. Duncan at first refused to appear in the anthology but later capitulated to Allen's request.

6. Duncan to Levertov, 20 November 1958.

7. Duncan to Broughton, 3 June 1956.

8. Wagstaff with Jacobus, "Interview with Paul Alexander," 9.

9. Duncan to Broughton, 28 December 1958. This conflict later did become public when Duncan denounced the 1961 Playhouse production of Helen Adam's *San Francisco's Burning.*

10. Duncan likewise responded to Creeley's work in "A Dancing Concerning a Form of Women" in *Roots and Branches.*

11. Spicer to Duncan, 2 January 1959.

12. Kevin Killian reconstructed the final meeting of Duncan's workshop in "The Carola Letters of Joanne Kyger and George Stanley," *Jacket* 11, http://jacket magazine.com/11/kyger-killian.html.

13. Duncan, *As Testimony,* 13.

14. Duncan, Poetry Reading, Slought Foundation, Albuquerque, New Mexico, 29 February 1964, www.slought.org/content/11123/.

15. Norman Austin to Duncan, 14 March 1976. Norman Austin's lover, Michael Wilsie, was the projectionist at Kael's film series.

16. Duncan, *Roots and Branches,* 7.

CHAPTER THIRTY-TWO: H. D.

1. Duncan had previously made contact with H. D. in the early part of 1950.

2. Duncan, *The H. D. Book,* 184. H. D.'s daughter Perdita (Schaffner) was born in March 1919.

3. Duncan, *Roots and Branches,* 23. The beards Duncan and Jess sported that year were similar to one worn by the recently victorious Fidel Castro. Jess later said he grew the beard not out of homage to Castro, but out of a desire to fully engage in his Stinson Beach hermitage.

4. Notebook A, 1 August 1959, UCB. The dream occurred on the Lammas Tide, as did a later dream that entered into "My Mother Would Be a Falconress." H. D.'s seventy-third birthday was on September 10, 1959.

5. Duncan to Allen, 5 November 1959, UCSD. Duncan had similar fantasies about his later books *Ground Work* and *Ground Work II,* typesetting the manuscript himself and proposing an edition to be purchased directly from him.

6. Duncan to Levertov, 16 October 1959.

7. Tolbert McCarroll, e-mail, 11 January 2006.

8. Ibid.

9. Duncan to Jess, 10 December 1959.

10. Tolbert McCarroll, e-mail, 7 February 2006.

11. Ibid.

12. Duncan to McCarroll, 4 January 1960. Duncan also met poet William Stafford during the visit, finding him too "school-teacherish" for his taste (Duncan to Jess, 10 December 1959).

13. Duncan to Jess, 10 December 1959.

14. Ellen King married Warren Tallman in 1951.

15. Duncan eulogized Rall in "Under Ground" in *The Opening of the Field.*

16. Duncan related this story in a letter to Denise Levertov, 16 October 1959.

17. Duncan to Jess, 17 December 1959.

18. Duncan to Levertov, 24 December 1959.

19. Ibid., 1 January 1960.

20. Duncan to Seaver, 23 February 1960.

21. Duncan, *Roots and Branches,* 34.

CHAPTER THIRTY-THREE: GO EAST

1. Duncan to Jess, 4 April 1960.

2. Ibid.

3. Ibid., 6 April 1960. Duncan's initial positive experience with Paul Carroll was marred later that year by one of Duncan's tantrums about editors and publishing. On July 23, 1960, he wrote a gruff letter to Carroll [UC] after reviewing galley proofs for an issue of *Big Table* that included three sections of Duncan's "Apprehensions."

Duncan had forgotten that he had given Carroll permission to use the pieces. Carroll responded four days later, apologizing for the misunderstanding and telling Duncan: "Frankly, Robert, I feel hurt you thought I was trying to con you or pull a fast one. I remember with affection...my meeting with you last spring. I had thought we had become friends—at least had begun a friendship. I have always admired your work. Once I got to know you I came to admire you as a man; your intellectual gifts and clear honesty impressed me deeply."

4. For more on the New York avant-garde, see Kane, *All Poets Welcome.*

5. Duncan to Jess, 13 April 1960. Duncan included a draft of "Sonneries of the Rose Cross" in this letter.

6. Ibid., 21 April 1960.

7. Duncan to Levertov, 28 May 1959.

8. Jess to Duncan, 24 April 1960.

9. Ibid., 5 May 1960. This painting remains unidentified.

10. Duncan to Jess, 30 April 1960.

11. For an excellent essay on California culture, the Chessman execution, and the work of artist Bruce Conner, see James Boaden, "San Francisco, Ruin of the Nineteenth Century: The Assemblage Work of Bruce Conner," www.surrealismcen tre.ac.uk/papersofsurrealism/journal2/index.htm.

12. Robert Kelly, 22 April 1999.

13. Duncan to Jess, 13 May 1960.

14. Ibid., 17 May 1960. In studying the mystery cults, the modernist literati also relied on Jane Harrison's *Prolegomena* (1903) and *Themis* (1912) and Cook's *Zeus* (1914). Duncan's parents had read the writings of G. R. S. Mead, a secretary to Madame Blavatsky, and Duncan kept the handed-down books prominent on his bookshelves.

15. Duncan to H. D., 27 May 1960.

16. Duncan to Jess, 17 May 1960.

CHAPTER THIRTY-FOUR: APPREHENSIONS

1. This letter was either destroyed or lost. The story comes directly from Robin Blaser, who admitted to me and to Spicer biographer Kevin Killian that he may have read Duncan's letter before giving it to Jess.

2. Kevin Killian, interview with Robin Blaser, 22 May 1992, private archive. Duncan's love interest remains unidentified.

3. Notebook 28, 2 June 1960, UAB.

4. Ida Hodes, 6 April 2006. Duncan's visit may have also been precipitated by the death of Minnehaha's second husband, Lewis Burtch, in late February 1960.

5. Duncan to Jerome Rothenberg, 20 June 1960, UCSD. This cat seems to have briefly been called "Mary Butts." See also Duncan to Levertov, 6 December 1960.

6. Duncan to Levertov, 22 June 1960.

7. Duncan to Jess, 29 August 1960.

8. Duncan to Tolbert and Claire McCarroll, 23 November 1960.

9. Duncan, "Plan of Lectures for A History of Modern Poetry, Its Sources, Its Achievements—Ideas and Forms," UAB.

10. Duncan to Levertov, 12 January 1961.

11. Duncan to Adam, 31 October 1960.

12. Duncan to H. D., 2 January 1961.

13. Duncan, *Roots and Branches,* 74.

CHAPTER THIRTY-FIVE: THE WILL

1. Ariel Parkinson, letter to the editor, *California Alumni,* June 2002. The San Francisco House Un-American Activities Committee hearings took place in May 1960.

2. Duncan to Levertov, 25 January 1961.

3. Duncan to Tolbert and Claire McCarroll, 30 April 1961.

4. The book echoed some of the key ideas of Whitehead's *Process and Reality.* Troward, a British theosophist born in India, was an expert in "mental science."

5. In the midst of the process, Jones threw out her parents' papers on the hermetic brotherhood. She remembered that her brother was disappointed but philosophical about the loss. And despite Duncan's seeming estrangement from the family, he kept in touch with Barbara, occasionally visiting her in Bakersfield and sending toys to his nieces and nephew.

6. Tolbert McCarroll, e-mail, 11 January 2006.

7. By 1982, the trust fund was valued at one hundred thousand dollars, though Minnehaha's will stipulated that Duncan's estate would revert to Barbara's children upon his death. Duncan discussed the details of the trust in a 1976 interview: "My mother very conveniently died in 1961 and left me . . . at the low end of a . . . totem pole of a trust fund that started off after three years of clearing all probate, . . . delivering me four hundred a month at the present time" ("Interview: The History of the Poetry Center," 1 December 1976, audiocassette, UAB).

8. Duncan to Toby McCarroll, 23 November 1960.

9. Duncan to Jess, 9 February 1961.

10. Duncan to Levertov, 9 March 1961.

11. Frank Davey, e-mails, 1 and 2 August 2007.

12. Duncan to Jess, 11 February 1961.

13. Ibid.

14. Duncan's copy of the *Hermetic Definition* manuscript is in the H. D. Papers, box 34, folder 887, Beinecke Library, Yale University. Another version of the typescript, heavily annotated with Norman Holmes Pearson's notes on the composition of the poem, is also at Beinecke, box 34, folder 898.

15. Alvie Brumm's stepson, Leo, and her children, Carol and Dick, had been Duncan and his sister's playmates in Alameda.

16. "The Poetic Vocation: A Study of St.-John Perse," appeared in the November 1961 issue of the magazine.

17. Duncan to Levertov, 9 March 1961.

18. David Bromige, 6 May 1988. The students Duncan spent time with that summer included Pauline Butling, David Bromige, George Bowering, Daphne Marlatt, Jamie Reed, Robert Hogg, David Dawson, Lionel Kearns, and Frank Davey.

19. Duncan to Jess, 24 July 1961. Duncan's lectures from this period are available through the Slought Foundation archive, www.slought.org.

20. David Bromige, 6 May 1998.

21. Duncan to Jess, 17 July 1961.

22. Butling, "Robert Duncan in Vancouver," 10, www.kswnet.org/w/ten/w10 .pdf.

23. Duncan to Toby and Claire McCarroll, 1 August 1961.

24. Tallman, "My Stories with Robert Duncan," 66. Robert Creeley conjured another image of Duncan's need for company: "Ellen Tallman spoke of one time when she and . . . Warren had driven Robert down to Seattle. He was . . . going to be picked up by his bus or . . . by other friends there at a particular street corner. . . . And so they left with warm goodbyes, and hugs, 'what a pleasant visit,' and they go down the street, turn around . . . unbeknownst to Robert who's now standing there waiting. And she said the look of bereftness on his face was heartbreaking. His forlornness, the waifishness was just immensely moving" (Robert Creeley, 20 December 1997).

25. Duncan to Jess, 3 August 1961.

CHAPTER THIRTY-SIX: THE PLAYHOUSE

1. Duncan to Pearson, 28 September 1961.

2. Ibid.

3. Duncan scholar Robert J. Bertholf conjectures that Duncan conceived of the project as a three-volume book, and while several notebooks exist in which Duncan expounds on H.D. (including a UAB notebook titled "Generative Orders"), it is not clear that he ever planned a specific length for the project. See also *The H.D. Book,* 23.

4. Duncan to Levertov, 31 October 1961. Duncan had written another Halloween masque in 1948 for a party in Berkeley. He included the piece in *Poems 1948–49.*

5. Duncan to Levertov, 16 October 1961.

6. Levertov to Duncan, 13 November 1961.

7. Duncan borrows "Fair-Speech" and "By-Ends" from Bunyan's *The Pilgrim's Progress.*

8. Duncan to Broughton, 12 December 1961.

9. Adam to Duncan [December 1961]. Duncan warned Adam that she had offended Anubis.

10. Stanley Eichelbaum, theater review, *San Francisco Examiner,* 21 January 1962, quoted in "Works of Warner Jepson 1996,"www.o-art.org/history/LongDur /Jepson/WorksOfWJ.html.

11. Duncan to Jess, 2 January 1962. Oli and Joan Sihvonen (later Joan Potter Loveless) had moved to New Mexico in 1956. Barbara Fick, the heiress to a Chicago shoe store fortune, later reverted to her maiden name, Barbara Joseph.

12. Duncan to Adam, 23 January 1962.

13. James Broughton, 26 September 1998.

14. Duncan to Levertov, 18 January 1962.

15. Notebook 31, 30 January 1962, UAB. Richard Baker later became Baker Roshi of the San Francisco Zen Center.

16. David Meltzer, e-mail, 20 February 2006.

17. Michael McClure, 14 January 1998.

18. Oliveros first met Duncan at the Poetry Center during the mid-1950s. She collaborated with him on *Three Songs for Soprano and Piano,* setting poems by Duncan and Charles Olson to music, including Duncan's "Spider Song." She and Ramon Sender were founding members of the new performance venue and sound studio the San Francisco Tape Center, where Duncan presented *Adam's Way* in autumn 1962. See also Pauline Oliveros, "Improvisation, Deep Listening, and Flummoxing the Hierarchy," interviewed by Caroline Crawford, 2000, Regional Oral History Office, Bancroft Library, University of California, Berkeley, http://digitalassets.lib.berkeley .edu/roho/ucb/text/oliveros_pauline.pdf.

19. Duncan to the McCarrolls [January 1962].

20. Duncan to Adam, 6 February 1962.

21. Duncan, *Roots and Branches,* 113.

22. Duncan to Jorge and Barbara Fick, 8 March 1962. Duncan, the Ficks, and the Creeleys apparently attended a December 26, 1961, dance at the Santo Domingo Pueblo. Duncan also refers to it in "Thank You for Love" (*Roots and Branches,* 115), dedicated to Creeley.

CHAPTER THIRTY-SEVEN: THE POLITICAL MACHINE

1. Duncan to Jorge and Barbara Fick, 8 March 1962. This assemblage remains unidentified.

2. Brakhage to Duncan and Jess, 8 June 1962.

3. Duncan to Jess, 10 April 1962.

4. Duncan first met Seon (Givens) Manley, a Joyce scholar, in New York around 1943.

5. Duncan to Jess, 16 April 1962.

6. Ibid., 20 April 1962.

7. Ibid. [17] April 1962.

8. Button, part of a circle of artists and poets that included Larry Rivers, James Schuyler, and Frank O'Hara, had spent his childhood in San Francisco and had developed relationships in the Bay Area poetry scene during the 1950s.

9. Robert Kelly, e-mail, 24 December 2005.

10. Duncan to Jess, 28 April 1962.

11. Ibid., 5 May 1962.

12. Duncan to Adam, 22 May 1962.

13. Duncan to Stan and Jane Brakhage, 14 June 1962.

14. Duncan to Levertov, 13 June 1962. *Floating Bear* magazine was edited by LeRoi Jones and Diane di Prima.

15. For a detailed account of this incident, see Ellingham and Killian, *Poet Be Like God,* 232.

16. Duncan, Poetry Reading, University of California, San Diego, 23 March 1976, audiocassette, UAB.

17. Duncan, *Bending the Bow,* 9.

18. Duncan, Poetry Reading, Albuquerque, New Mexico, 23 March 1964, Slought Foundation, www.slought.org/content/11123/.

19. Duncan to Levertov, 3 October 1965.

20. Duncan, announcement of *Adam's Way* performance, 17 June 1976, UAB.

21. Lewis Ellingham, interview with Robin Blaser, 2 January 1983, Spicer Circle Papers, UAB. See also Ellingham and Killian, *Poet Be Like God,* 239. In *The Letters of Robert Duncan and Denise Levertov,* editors Albert Gelpi and Robert Bertholf report incorrectly that Joanne Kyger was one of the protesters.

22. Larry Fagin, 14 September 1997.

23. George Stanley, e-mail, 18 February 2006.

24. Notebook 33, 19 October 1962, UAB.

25. Duncan to Jess, 5 December 1962.

26. Ibid., 3 December 1962.

27. Ibid., 5 December 1962.

28. Duncan to Levertov, 16–17 December 1962.

CHAPTER THIRTY-EIGHT: KNIGHT ERRANT

1. Duncan to Levertov, 6 March 1963.

2. Duncan, *Roots and Branches,* 167.

3. Duncan to Levertov, 6 March 1963.

4. *Robert Duncan: An Interview by George Bowering and Robert Hogg.* Duncan and Jackson Mac Low also attended a William Carlos Williams reading in 1945 at the 92nd Street Poetry Center and spoke to Williams afterward.

5. Duncan to Levertov, 17 April 1963.

6. Ibid., 15 March 1963.

7. Ibid. Herms was equally fond of Duncan and Jess, remembering, "They took me in as a young practically unformed artist and I began to emulate [them]." In 1962, Duncan and Jess presented Herms with the "Servant of Holy Beauty Award," a household accolade that the couple usually reserved for each other. The award came with a hand-drawn certificate of appreciation and twenty-five dollars. (George Herms, 20 July 2006).

8. Duncan, *Roots and Branches,* 171.

9. Adam to Duncan [1962].

10. Admiral to Jess, 7 October 1963. "Bobby" is Robert De Niro, Jr.

11. Duncan to Levertov, 19 July 1963. Isabella "Mother" Adam died on 27 September 1963.

CHAPTER THIRTY-NINE: THE VANCOUVER CONFERENCE

1. Michael Palmer would become better acquainted with Duncan in the early 1970s, and he and his wife, the architect Cathy Simon, would become two of Duncan and Jess's closest friends in San Francisco.

2. Bergé, *The Vancouver Report,* 2.

3. Ibid.

4. Duncan, "A Life in Poetry," Vancouver Poetry Conference, 5 August 1963, audiocassette, UAB.

5. Ibid.

6. Butling, "Robert Duncan in Vancouver," 17. The "handsome young Vancouver poet" was David Dawson.

7. Harris Schiff, 25 August 1997.

8. Duncan to Levertov, 16 September 1963.

9. Duncan, *Bending the Bow,* 132.

10. Duncan, "Concerning the Art. This December 1963," mimeograph page for Poetry Center reading, 11 December 1963, UAB.

11. Duncan, *Fictive Certainties,* 81.

CHAPTER FORTY: BENDING THE BOW

1. Duncan to Levertov, 12 January 1964.

2. Duncan, *Bending the Bow,* 15.

3. Duncan to Joseph, 31 March 1964. Barbara Joseph, formerly Barbara Fick, maintained a friendship with Duncan and Jess after her separation from Jorge Fick.

4. Duncan to Jess, 29 March 1964.

5. Olson became a visiting professor at the University of Buffalo in 1963. His students there included Michael Anania, Charles Boer, Charles Doria, Henry Lesnick, Charles Brover, Joe Keough, and Albert Glover.

6. Duncan to Joseph, 5 April 1964. Mac Hammond, with whom Duncan was staying, was also part of the English Department faculty.

7. Keith and Rosmarie Waldrop, 1999. Tony Stoneburner, then a graduate student at the University of Michigan, had a different memory: "While I was at the party, Duncan primarily sat alone.... He seemed so close to abject ... that I found courage to speak to him." (8 June 2006).

8. Drury to Duncan, 11 April 1964.

9. Wilson, *Seeing Shelley Plain,* 93.

10. Ibid., 94.

11. Duncan to Jess, 23 April 1964.

12. Ibid., 1 May 1964.

13. Jess to Duncan, 10 May 1964.

14. Duncan to Jess, 3 May 1964. Sanders, then in his midtwenties, had moved to New York to study at New York University, later opening a bookstore on the Lower East Side and editing *Fuck You/A Magazine of the Arts.* Sanders remembered first meeting Duncan at Wilson's Phoenix Bookstore.

15. Duncan to Joseph, 4 May 1964.

16. James W. Rouse, Jr., "Duncan, Leader of Poetry Renaissance, Reads, Reminisces during Visit Here," *Yale Daily News,* 6 May 1964, 1.

17. Duncan to Jess, 18 May 1964.

CHAPTER FORTY-ONE: A NIGHT SONG

1. Duncan's correspondence with Scribners resides in the Robert Duncan Papers, box 12 of the business correspondence, UAB.

2. Duncan, *Bending the Bow,* 29.

3. Ibid., 37.

4. Goldwater, "Speech Accepting the Republican Presidential Nomination," *American Rhetoric,* www.americanrhetoric.com/speeches/barrygoldwater1964rnc .htm.

5. Duncan often transcribed long passages of texts into his notebooks, sometimes copying several pages of words verbatim without comment. This practice seemed to serve as an alternative to filling his books with marginalia. The first version of his Lammas poem arrived with the refrain "My Mother Would Be a Falconer." For another useful reading of this poem, see Peter O'Leary's *Gnostic Contagion,* 114–33.

6. Duncan to Adam, 9 January 1975.

7. Duncan, *Bending the Bow,* 53.

8. Duncan to Levertov and Goodman, 7 September 1964.

9. Charles Willeford, *Miami News,* November 15, 1964.

10. Quoted in a letter from Duncan to Toby McCarroll, 23 June 1965. Favorable reviews by Hayden Carruth in the *Nation* and X.J. Kennedy in the *New York Times* created a balance in the publicity.

11. Mario Savio, "Mario Savio's Speech before the FSM Sit-in," 2 December 1964, www.fsm-a.org/stacks/mario/mario_speech.html.

12. Duncan, *Bending the Bow,* 70.

13. Duncan and Jess to Helen and Pat Adam, 7 December 1964.

14. Jess's work had appeared in a group show at the Rolf Nelson Gallery in late September.

15. Duncan and Jess to Helen and Pat Adam, 7 December 1964. Paula Gianinni remembered Jess saying that he didn't like to travel because he couldn't "digest the images" (27 January 2006).

CHAPTER FORTY-TWO: ANGER

1. Duncan, *Bending the Bow,* 70.

2. Duncan to Levertov and Goodman, 6 January 1965. *The Letters of Robert Duncan and Denise Levertov* misdates this letter as 6 January 1964.

3. Notebook 33, 27 January 1965, UAB.

4. Jess Collins, 1989. Dion Fortune's books on magic and magic spells were prominent in Duncan's library. During that winter, Jess was completing the collage *Untitled (From Maeterlinck's Bluebird)* for Kenneth Anger, and Duncan dedicated "Structure of Rime XXVI" to him.

5. Duncan, *Bending the Bow,* 74.

6. Duncan to Levertov, 26 February 1965.

7. Duncan, *Bending the Bow,* 49. Duncan began studying phonetics in the 1940s and often conversed with Jack Spicer about the topic. In a letter to Duncan in the late 1950s, Spicer displayed his complex knowledge of the field: "The phoneme (or rather the Bloomfield or Block and Trager system of phonemes) is not enough. Example— the trilled r's that Pound uses in reading his Cantos are, of course, not phonemically distinct, but they change the entire *sound* of large sections. Example—no system of phonemes includes sounds that do not occur in combinations with other sounds, e.g. the click of 'tsk,' the m [with o under it] of 'um hum' etc. These sounds are important to the poet" (ca. 1959, Spicer Circle Papers, UAB).

8. Jess took his inspiration from a 1958 photograph of Duncan at Stinson Beach. While the work is often catalogued as *The Enamored Mage,* Jess's true title, *The Enamord Mage,* adhered to Duncan's idiosyncrasies of spelling.

9. Jess to Helen and Pat Adam, 28 March 1965.

10. Duncan, "The Psyche Myth and the Moment of Truth," 12 May 1965, Topeka, Kansas, audiocassette, UAB.

11. Mary Dunlap, "Poet Entertains with Song, Verse in Semester's Last Poetry Hour," *University Daily Kansan,* May 14, 1965, 9.

12. Edwin Eigner, e-mail, 25 January 2006.

13. Ibid.

14. Duncan, *Bending the Bow,* 78.

15. Duncan, "Taking Away from God His Sound," 596.

16. Notebook 6 [May 1965], UAB.

17. Angoff to Duncan, 29 June 1965.

CHAPTER FORTY-THREE: THE BERKELEY CONFERENCE

1. Duncan to Levertov, 18 May 1965. Duncan had also suggested Scottish poet Ian Hamilton Finlay, though Finlay was severely agoraphobic and unable to travel.

2. Anne Waldman, "Autobiography: Berkeley Poetry Conference," Museum of American Poets, www.poetspath.com/waldmanimages/file3.html.

3. David Franks, e-mail, 25 September 2006.

4. Duncan, "The Psyche Myth and the Moment of Truth."

5. Phil Peters, "The Beat's the Thing at Big Poetry Powwow," *San Francisco Examiner,* 14 July 1965, 16.

6. This lecture is transcribed in Gizzi, *The House That Jack Built,* 168.

7. Duncan had been reading a new book by Australian journalist Wilfred Burchett called *Vietnam: Inside Story of the Guerilla War,* and it also influenced the poems of *Bending the Bow.*

8. Bill Brodecky Moore, "Buzz Gallery," *Big Bridge* #9, www.bigbridge.org/issue9/bgpage4.htm.

9. Duncan, "At the Poetry Conference: Berkeley after the New York Style," *Jacket* 16, March 2002, http://jacketmagazine.com/16/ah-dunc.html. Ted Berrigan commented on his own role in the Berkeley Poetry Conference in an interview by Anne Waldman and Jim Cohn in Waldman, *Nice to See You.*

10. For a full transcript of Olson's reading, see *Charles Olson Reading at Berkeley.*

11. Duncan to Levertov, 9 August 1965.

12. Waldman, "Autobiography: Berkeley Poetry Conference."

13. Creeley to Duncan, 1 August 1965.

14. Brown to Duncan [August 1965].

15. Lewis Ellingham, interview with Robin Blaser, 17 November 1983, Spicer Circle Papers, UAB.

16. Brown to Duncan, 17 August 1965.

17. "Jack Spicer Dies at 40," *San Francisco Chronicle,* 18 August 1965, 22.

18. Duncan to Levertov, 23 August 1965.

CHAPTER FORTY-FOUR: THE SIXTIES

1. In "Man's Fulfillment in Order and Strife," Duncan wrote, "Today, many use marijuana or LSD in order to come into a reality larger than their own personality or case history or their one family or one city or one nation or one species. But I do it in language. Words send me" (*Fictive Certainties,* 121).

2. Duncan to Joseph, 29 October 1967.

3. This lecture appears in *Fictive Certainties,* 142–61.

4. Duncan to Levertov, 15 October 1965.

5. Ibid., 23 August 1965.

6. Duncan, *Bending the Bow,* 114.

7. Blaser's Nerval translations, which he performed at the Berkeley Poetry Conference, appeared in *Open Space* magazine and were also collected in *The Holy Forest.* Duncan's appeared in *Bending the Bow.*

8. Robert Duncan issue, *Audit* 4, no. 3 (1967): 48.

9. The painting is now at San Francisco's de Young Museum.

10. Duncan to Levertov, 3 December 1965.

11. Duncan to Jess, 6 January 1966.

12. Frank Davey, e-mail, 1 August 2007.

13. Duncan to Jess, 18 January 1966.

14. Jess to Joseph, 11 February 1966.

15. Duncan to Levertov [February] 1966, misdated in *The Letters of Denise Levertov and Robert Duncan* as 9 August 1965, 501. Duncan's comments here came prior to the 1967 *Audit* magazine critique of Blaser. The thoroughness of the linguistic and historical research behind Duncan's attack gave Blaser little room to respond, and Blaser, like James Broughton, continued to maintain a wary friendship with Duncan.

16. Tosh Berman, e-mail, 20 January 2006.

17. David Franks, e-mail, 25 September 2006.

18. Duncan, *Bending the Bow,* 115.

19. Another death that sent shock waves through the poetry community came on July 25 when Frank O'Hara was struck by a dune buggy on Fire Island. Duncan left no mention of it in his notebooks or letters.

20. Duncan, *Bending the Bow,* 93.

21. Duncan to Levertov, 17 August 1966.

22. Levertov to Duncan, 19–20 August 1966. Among the poets Levertov introduced to Norton were Joel Sloman, Helen Wolfert, and Jim Harrison.

23. Duncan included detailed notes about the composition of "Up Rising" and "The Soldiers" in a 13 July 1966 letter to Levertov.

24. A published recording of readings from the conference excludes Duncan but includes all other participants. See *Twelve Contemporary Poets* (Champaign, IL: NCTE, 1966).

25. Levertov to Duncan, December 1966.

26. Duncan to Levertov, December 1966.

27. Duncan, "Interview: The History of the Poetry Center." In this interview, Duncan also said, "Writing goes deeper than response and reaction. . . . My quarrel with Denise Levertov is, go into your reaction, don't discard it, but go in and find out what it is, what's working there. Go in below, because that's what we have to know."

CHAPTER FORTY-FIVE. THE HOUSEHOLD

1. *The Originals: The Writer in America,* PBS Documentary, 1974, audiocassette, UAB.
2. Duncan to Joseph, 5 December 1966. Hilde Burton recalled that sometime in the late 1970s or early 1980s, Barbara Joseph forgave Duncan and Jess the remainder of the home loan (Burton, 18 February 2006).
3. Duncan to Joseph, 29 January 1967.
4. Hilde Burton, 18 February 2006. One of the builders was David Coven, whom Duncan had known in 1940s New York anarchist circles.
5. Quoted in Auping, "Solar Systems: Michael Auping on Jess," *Artforum,* 1 April2004,www.thefreelibrary.com/Solar+systems%3a+Michael+Auping+on+Jess -a0116144955.
6. Duncan was meticulous about the details of his library, cataloguing the volumes into lists in the back of notebooks and arranging and rearranging the order of the books as the library grew. Like his father, he designed the bookplates that he pasted into each book. He then created a numbering system that Jess described as so complex that it almost ceased being a system. Even his phonograph collection was carefully catalogued on a set of index cards, with cross-references to compositions by different conductors and arrangers.
7. These windows were added when the kitchen was expanded in November 1971.
8. Duncan purchased Marjorie McKee's *Orpheus and Euridice* while visiting her in New York in May 1960.
9. Quoted in Duncan and Jess to Joseph [February or March 1967].
10. Ron Silliman, 9 September 2004, Sillimanblog, http://ronsilliman.blogspot .com/2004_09_01_archive.html.
11. Stephen Fredman had a theory about Duncan's decision to stay with the Bermans: "The guy who picked Duncan up at the airport thought he was a short story writer. He was taken over to Barnes' (the hip English prof.) house & talking w/ his wife mentioned D.H. Lawrence. She said Dick (Barnes) didn't like Lawrence, thought he was a queer. When Barnes arrived Duncan was stalking & raging" (Fredman, e-mail quoting from his notebook from the period, 22 June 2006).
12. Fredman, e-mail, 7 June 2006.
13. Duncan, *Bending the Bow,* 134.

CHAPTER FORTY-SIX. THE SUMMER OF LOVE

1. Duncan to Jess, 19 April 1967.
2. Ibid.
3. Michael Anania, e-mail, 25 November 2005. Anania, who hosted Duncan several times, recalled, "On one of these visits I put Robert together with Richard

Ellmann, the Yeats scholar and biographer of James Joyce. Ellmann asked me if he could talk to him about homosexuality. He was beginning work on the [Oscar] Wilde biography and was trying to find his way into Wilde's psyche, so it was a rather deliberate, serious inquiry."

4. Duncan to Jess, 24 April 1967.

5. Ibid., 27 April 1967.

6. Ibid.

7. Duncan began taking blood pressure medication during the mid-1960s. He sometimes skipped doses because it made him sluggish. The title "Up Rising" puns on this health condition.

8. Duncan to Jess, 8 May 1967.

9. Ibid., 6 May 1967.

10. Ibid., 13 May 1967.

11. Joanne Kyger, e-mail, 8 June 2006.

12. Anne Waldman, e-mail, 15 January 2006.

13. Ibid., 25 January 2006; and Kyger, e-mail, 8 June 2006. Kyger had further insights into the Ashbery incident: "According to my letter to Philip Whalen—'Ed Sanders said they [Duncan and Ashbery] only French kissed.'" Sanders's source was likely Phoenix bookstore owner Robert Wilson. Duncan later revealed his fascination with Ashbery in a letter to Australian poet Robert Adamson on 1 April 1975: "Ashbery is truly wonderful—and wonder should verge everywhere upon 'I wonder'—Most important he is never vague.... He talks about 'beautiful lines'; so there is some aesthetic pose. And a transformation of high camp (as if starting there gave the permission needed for the transcendent speech).... He is civilized, which I am not. (This is still the difference between Upstate New York stock and third generation Westerner (which means one's parents and grandparents were 'pioneers' or 1850 beatniks).) In my perspective Ashbery is a major contemporary, which I don't see Merwin or Bly as."

14. Duncan to Jess, 17 May 1967.

15. David Gitlin, e-mail, 2 February 1998. Gitlin met Duncan for the first time after the reading, and the two men stayed in touch for the next decade.

16. Ron Silliman, Silliman's Blog, 7 April 2008, http://ronsilliman.blogspot .com/2008/04/i-was-somewhere-in-vicinity-of-20-to-22.html. Oppen and his wife, Mary, were subsequently frequent guests to the 20th Street household.

17. Duncan to Jess, 12 October 1967.

18. Duncan, "The Truth and Life of Myth in Poetry," 39. This essay varies slightly from the version published in *Fictive Certainties*.

19. Duncan to Joseph, 29 October 1967.

20. Tony Stoneburner, e-mail, 10 June 2006.

21. Duncan to Jess, 17 October 1967.

22. Duncan to Joseph, 29 October 1967.

23. Duncan, *Bending the Bow,* ii.

24. R. B. Kitaj, 6 February 2006.

25. Kitaj remembered visiting Disneyland with Duncan but did not recall any details of the day.

26. Duncan to Joseph, 2 January 1968.

CHAPTER FORTY-SEVEN. DAYS OF RAGE

1. Duncan to Joseph, 30 January 1968.

2. Ibid., 29 March 1968. The Ginsberg poem was likely "Wales Visitation."

3. Karen Brady, "Poet Tantalizes Intrepid Critic," *Buffalo Evening News,* 7 March 1968. Duncan had begun "orchestrating" his poems by this time, using hand gestures in a four-count to keep the time of phrases and pauses.

4. Duncan to Joseph, 29 March 1968.

5. Duncan, *Ground Work,* 28. Duncan inserted these lines into the second draft of the poem.

6. Duncan, "A Prospectus for the Prepublication Issue of GROUND WORK to Certain Friends of the Poet," Jan. 31, 1971, ms, PS3507.U629 P7, UCSD.

7. Duncan to Joseph, 29 March 1968. This piece remains unidentified.

8. Ibid., 1 March 1968.

9. Thom Gunn, 9 November 1999.

10. Duncan, *Fictive Certainties,* 127.

11. Philip Garrison to Clelia Scala, e-mail, 20 September 2005.

12. Duncan to Jess, 5 May 1968.

13. Ibid.

14. Ibid., 11 May 1968.

15. Ibid. [May 1968].

16. Ibid., 25 May 1968.

CHAPTER FORTY-EIGHT. GROUND-WORK

1. Duncan wrote of Robert Kennedy's assassination in a notebook:

In the shot that blasted Kennedy's brain, the murder of some Arab peasants (I think here of Yitzach [Rabin] telling years ago of mowing down with machine gun fire an Arab wedding party in a border incident) at last comes home; for Kennedy in announcing that the U.S. must keep its commitments to the state of Israel (as in the Far East, the U.S. keeps "commitments" to states) in the face of higher commitments to humanity was guilty of hubris. "The Wanderer" then was a Fury, an inspired or possesst man. (Notebook 40, 6 June 1968, UAB).

2. Duncan to Jess, 25 June 1968.

3. Robert Hogg, e-mail, 28 October 1998.

4. Duncan to Jess, 9 July 1968.

5. Albert Glover, April 1999.

6. "Robert Duncan: Table Talk," 36.

7. Irene Reti, "Rita Bottoms: Polyartist Librarian. UC Santa Cruz 1965–2003," 165, http://digitalcollections.ucsc.edu/cdm4/document.php?CISO ROOT=/p265101coll13&CISOPTR=3650&REC=13.

8. Notebook 41, 20 December 1970, UAB.

9. "Interview with Robert Duncan" (Bernstein and Hatlen), 132.

10. Duncan to Joseph, 30 December 1968.

11. Ibid., 31 March 1969.

12. Sir George Williams University is now Concordia University. Bowering and Hogg later published a transcript of parts of the talk as *Robert Duncan: An Interview by George Bowering and Robert Hogg: April 16, 1969.*

13. Don Byrd, e-mail, 13 January 2006.

14. Ibid.

CHAPTER FORTY-NINE. HELTER SKELTER

1. Duncan to Levertov, 19 October 1971. Poet Aaron Shurin wrote about the People's Park clashes in "The People's P***k: A Dialectical Tale" in Gelpi and Bertholf, *Robert Duncan and Denise Levertov*, 71.

2. Notebook 41, 13 July 1969, UAB.

3. Ibid. Hilde Burton remembered that Duncan refused painkillers in the hospital in order to more fully participate in the experience (Burton, 18 February 2006).

4. Stan Brakhage, 24 December 1998.

5. Manson follower Bobby Beausoleil had starred in Kenneth Anger's *Invocation of my Demon Brother.*

6. The course's official title was 499A: Democratic Ideas.

7. Duncan to Jess, 9 and 10 October 1969.

8. Duncan to Anthony Canedo, 20 October 1969.

9. Notebook 39, 28 November 1969, UAB.

10. Jess designed the cover for Lonidier's *A Lesbian Estate: Poems, 1970–1973* (San Francisco: ManRoot, 1977).

11. Notebook 62, 27 November 1969, UAB. Notebook 62 contains several such dream entries from 1969. Duncan returned to the notebook briefly in 1980 to continue the project.

12. Brown was the heir to a family fortune acquired through the invention of Great Lakes shipping machinery. In addition to funding indigent poets, Brown edited Frontier Press, which made available a variety of out-of-print texts and collections of poetry by Ed Dorn, Ed Sanders, Robert Kelly, and Albert Glover.

13. Notebook 62, 12 January 1970, UAB.

14. Ibid.

15. Duncan, *Ground Work*, 26.

1. Philip had suffered a stroke early in 1968, after which Duncan's sister Barbara Jones urged him to be in touch with his elderly aunt, reminding him, "You know that you are her 'pride and joy' and I've always felt that she believes that she is somewhat responsible for your talents and successes."

2. Michael Franco, e-mail, 23 July 2006.

3. Ron Silliman, 9 September 2004, Sillimanblog, http://ronsilliman.blogspot .com/2004_09_01_archive.html. Another poet of San Francisco's Language School, Carla Harryman, described her first encounter with Duncan in 1978:

> I was standing at a streetcar stop in Noe Valley. . . . There was a cold, blustery wind, and I was standing next to a man in a black cape, Robert Duncan. I was crossing the street to catch a bus up to his reading at the Grand Piano in the Haight. He . . . [was] just standing there. I greeted him and told him I was looking forward to his reading. He just looked at me, . . . one of those peering looks, but different from how I remember Creeley's, not drunken but undecodable. I didn't like it and it wasn't meant to be liked. (Carla Harryman, *The Grand Piano Part 3*. Detroit: Mode A, 2007, 48).

4. The London-born Bromige, who had studied at the University of California as well as the University of British Columbia, came to rely on Duncan as a model for his own work as a poet, but he also reflected that in the early part of his career, he "assumed a lot of [Duncan's] prejudices . . . It's very hard now to remember the gap that was felt between Black Mountaineers—between their writing and the writing of the Beats and the writing of the New York School." (6 May 1998).

5. Duncan to Jess, 21 May 1970.

6. Notebook 40, 9 July 1970, UAB.

7. Duncan later revisited "The Idea of Person" while teaching at New College of California during the early 1980s.

8. Duncan to James Laughlin, 26 March 1978, NDir.

9. Duncan dated the poem 1968, though it was clearly written in 1970. Scholar Michael Davidson conjectures that Duncan felt the poem fit the mood of 1968.

10. Duncan, *Ground Work*, 36.

11. Ibid., 40.

12. Ibid., 45.

13. Levertov to Duncan, 9 February 1971.

14. Duncan's draft toward this "Ring Ceremony" is in Notebook 42 [November 1970], UAB.

15. R. B. Kitaj, 6 February 2006. Duncan gave a reading at the museum's opening celebration on November 7.

16. Notebook 42 [March 1971], UAB.

17. Notebook 41, 21 December 1970, UAB.

1. Duncan to Jess, 17 February 1971.
2. George Bowering, e-mail, 2 August 2007.
3. Karen Steenhof, "Ayre of the Music Carries," *Goucher Weekly,* 26 February 1971, 5.
4. The essay was published as an introduction to Jess [Collins], *Translations.*
5. Duncan's talk was published as "Statement of Beginnings" in Ginsberg, *Allen Verbatim.*
6. Duncan to Jess, 9 April 1971. Writer Richard Grossinger was also at the conference, and Duncan introduced his reading.
7. Ibid., 1 May 1971.
8. Ibid., 4 May 1971.
9. Thom Gunn, 9 November 1999.
10. Duncan, *Ground Work,* 66.
11. Jess to Duncan [April 1971].
12. The book was later reprinted by New Directions as *Hermetic Definition.* Harvey Brown said he chose his pluralized title because he saw more than one definition at work in the manuscript (Brown, 1988).
13. Pearson's reputation as a World War II–era spy for the Office of Strategic Services made him anathema to Olson's counterculture followers.
14. Alastair Johnston, in *Zephyrus Image,* credits Duncan with stealing the manuscript, but this scenario is unlikely. Stan Brakhage also claimed to have smuggled the manuscript from the library.
15. Duncan to Pearson, 2 June 1972.
16. Ibid.
17. The letter was likely a threat more than a resignation. Duncan continued consulting with the Bancroft staff through the mid-1980s.
18. Ibid., 31 October 1971.
19. Notebook 42, 18 June 1971, UAB.
20. Duncan to Levertov, 4 October 1971.
21. Levertov to Duncan, 25 October 1971.
22. This uncollected essay appears in Notebook 43, UAB.
23. Duncan, *Ground Work,* 82.

CHAPTER FIFTY-TWO: DESPAIR IN BEING TEDIOUS

1. Duncan to Jess, 28 February 1972.
2. In a 3 February 2006 e-mail, George Stanley recalled a particular incident of Duncan's visit: "I was having a bad time, emotionally, etc., and one evening, . . . I was exhausted and began crying. Duncan held me and comforted me, and he said something like, 'At last you are becoming human.'"

3. Duncan to Paula Prokopoff, 29 March 1972.

4. The remaining crew was instructed to take off from San Francisco on an eastern flight path while the hijacker donned a parachute and exited the plane over Utah. Two days later, a Viet Nam helicopter pilot named Richard Floyd Mc Coy, Jr., was arrested for the crime.

5. Duncan to Jess, 7–8 April 1972.

6. George Quasha, 19 March 2008. Levertov read that night with Fanny Howe, who was giving her first public reading.

7. Duncan to Jess, 9 April 1972.

8. Hellerman later composed a setting of "The Fire, *Passages* 13 for Trumpet and Tape."

9. Fred Martin to James Laughlin, 11 April 1972.

10. Duncan to Jess, 12 April 1972.

11. Jess to Duncan, 13 April 1972.

12. The Dalí collection, originally owned by A. Reynolds and Eleanor R. Morse, was relocated to St. Petersburg, Florida, in 1982.

13. Kathy Schwille, "Oh, To Be a Sophomore Now That the Festival Is Here," *Observer,* 30 January 1974. This article was printed two years after Duncan's visit, likely to publicize the February 1974 conference.

14. Ibid.

15. John Matthias, e-mail, 6 November 2005. According to Matthias, "The Winter 1980 *Boundary 2,* included a photograph of Duncan on the cover, directing . . . Passages 15, 'Spelling.' This happened as well during the Notre Dame visit, in my classroom. . . . [The photos] are not by Gerard Malanga, like the other photos in that issue (including the one of Duncan). They are by David Lenfest."

16. Ilya Prokopoff, e-mail, 22 January 2006.

17. Stephen Prokopoff to the author, 16 November 1999. Prokopoff was the director of Chicago's Museum of Contemporary Art from 1971 to 1976.

18. Duncan, *Ground Work,* 51.

19. Duncan to Jess, 28 April 1972.

20. Bishop to Duncan, 22 April 1972.

21. Duncan to Stephen and Paula Prokopoff, 17 May 1972.

22. Duncan left no record of the instructor or location of this meditation session, but it may have taken place at the Cold Mountain Institute on British Columbia's Cortes Island, where Duncan taught in June 1978.

23. The chapbook was part of a series published by Glover's Institute of Further Studies in 1974 that included prose and verse ruminations on subjects close to Olson's heart, including Homer, Bach, Egyptian hieroglyphics, and sacred mushrooms.

24. Duncan, *Ground Work,* 9.

CHAPTER FIFTY-THREE: THE CULT OF THE GODS

1. Duncan, "Studies in Ideas of the Poetic Imagination," syllabus, UAB.
2. Duncan to Jess, 8 October 1972.
3. Tom Raworth, e-mail, 9 November 1997.
4. Richard Blevins, 15 January 1998.
5. Richard Blevins, e-mail, 2 November 1997.
6. Notebook 42, 9 October 1972, UAB.
7. Duncan, "Pound, Eliot, and H.D.: The Cult of the Gods in American Poetry," 11 October 1972, Kent State University, audiocassette, UAB.
8. Duncan to Fred Martin, 29 October 1972, NDir.
9. Davidson began corresponding with Duncan in December 1969 and completed his dissertation, "Disorders of the Net: The Poetry of Robert Duncan," at the State University of New York at Buffalo in 1973.
10. Duncan to Paula and Stephen Prokopoff, 25 January 1973.
11. Peter Michelson, 25 January 2000.
12. Paula [Prokopoff] Giannini, e-mail, 16 February 2006.
13. Paula [Prokopoff] Giannini, 27 January 2006; Duncan to Stephen and Paula Prokopoff, 16 March 1973.
14. Duncan to Stephen and Paula Prokopoff, 16 March 1973. Duncan often reported to Jess on his housekeeping skills in his various lodgings. Norma Cole also recalled that while Duncan tolerated clutter, Jess tidied the house while Duncan was away.
15. Duncan, *Ground Work,* 49.
16. Duncan to Levertov, 2 April 1973.

CHAPTER FIFTY-FOUR: ELM PARK ROAD

1. Duncan to Jess, 5 May 1973.
2. Ibid.
3. Ibid., 8 May 1973.
4. Eric Homberger, e-mail, 23 January 2006. Homberger first met Duncan in Washington, D.C., in 1962.
5. Duncan to Jess, 11 May 1973. The specimens were likely from London's Royal College of Surgeons.
6. Ibid., 18 May 1973.
7. Ibid., 21 May 1973.
8. Pierre Joris, 16 March 1998. For more on Duncan's friendship with Eric Mottram, see Evans and Zamir, *The Unruly Garden.*
9. Pierre Joris, 16 March 1998.
10. Notebook 52, 11 June 1973, UAB.

11. Duncan, "Ideas on the Meaning of Form," June 1973, National Poetry Conference, Thomas Jefferson College, Grand Rapids, Michigan, audiocassette, private collection, courtesy Karl Gartung.

12. Linda Hamalian, in *A Life of Kenneth Rexroth*, says that Rexroth refused to speak to Duncan, the Rakosis, or the Oppens during the conference.

13. Unmailed letter to Jess, Notebook 48, UAB.

14. Duncan relegated "Dante Études" to a special notebook (Notebook 50, UAB). He wrote a majority of the poems of this sequence between April and October of 1973 with two supplementary pieces composed on 25 and 26 August 1974.

15. Duncan, *Ground Work*, 57.

16. Pauline Butling, e-mail, 19 March 2008.

17. Notebook 47, 13 December 1973, UAB.

18. Duncan to Levertov, 13 December 1973.

CHAPTER FIFTY-FIVE: RIVERSIDE

1. Edwin Eigner, e-mail, 28 January 2006.

2. Duncan to Joseph, 3 February 1975.

3. Darlene Miller to Edwin Eigner, 7 March 2006.

4. Duncan to Adam, 17 January 1975. This syllabus is a prototype for the Basic Elements course Duncan taught at New College in the early 1980s.

5. Duncan, Poetry Reading, UCSD, 23 March 1976, audiocassette, UAB.

6. Notebook 53, 12 March 1975, UAB.

7. Ibid., 14 March 1975.

8. Duncan to Joseph, 31 March 1975.

9. Duncan to Adamson, 31 March 1975.

10. During an August 4 consultation, an orthopedist at the University of California Medical Center told Duncan that he should forgo surgery and retire to bed during sciatic episodes.

11. Jess, uncatalogued notebook, 1975, UAB.

12. Later published as Bertholf, ed., *Robert Duncan: A Descriptive Bibliography*.

13. Duncan, *Ground Work*, 142.

14. Ibid., 155. From the Greek, *eidolon*, "image," and *aion*, "wily, spangled, or gleaming": a shape-shifting image. Austin had mentioned the phrase, out of Pindar, in a November 1975 letter to Duncan.

15. Norman Austin, e-mail, 2002.

16. Duncan, *Ground Work*, 149. Duncan had also written of his first encounter with Austin in "Night Scenes" (*Roots and Branches*, 5).

17. Duncan to Martin, 18 December 1975, NDir.

18. Duncan, *Ground Work*, 159. Parts of the poem address Norman Austin's August 1976 performance as a member of Jane Brown's Lesser Oakland Dance Theatre company.

1. Robert Duncan, Poetry Reading, UCSD.
2. Ibid.
3. Notebook 52, UAB. This essay is unpublished.
4. Duncan to Joseph, 30 July 1976. The other "essay" poem Duncan refers to is "The Presence of the Dance / The Resolution of the Music."
5. Duncan, *Ground Work,* 157.
6. On 29 May 1976, Peters and Trachtenberg interviewed Duncan, and the piece was published as "A Conversation with Robert Duncan (1976)" in the *Chicago Review.*
7. Tom Savage provided insights about the dynamics of the community; 5 January 1998.
8. Ibid.
9. Ibid.
10. Tom Savage, unpublished ms, 1976.
11. Anne Waldman, e-mail, 15 January 2006.
12. An excerpt of the lecture was published as "Warp and Woof: Notes from A Talk" in *Talking Poetics from Naropa Institute.*
13. Ibid., 3.
14. Ibid., 1.
15. Duncan, Naropa Institute Lecture, 10 June 1976, www.archive.org/details /naropa_robert_duncan_lecture_warp_and2.
16. The players included Lewis Brown, Caroline Stone, Claude Duvall, Joel Clark, Sam Matthews, Deneen Peckinpah, Denise Kessler, Peter Bailey, and Ray Rice.
17. Michael McClure, 14 January 1998.
18. Notebook 52, 15 August 1976, UAB.
19. Ron Silliman, e-mail, 29 August 2005. Jack Foley thought the group began in 1981, but it was formed earlier.
20. Duncan, *Ground Work,* 60.
21. Jess to Duncan, 12 May 1977.
22. Notebook 52, August 1976, UAB.
23. Duncan and Jess's fondness for animal organs was not often shared by their guests. Lewis Warsh recalled vomiting a meal of beef tongue into Duncan and Jess's kitchen sink (Warsh, 1997).
24. Aaron Shurin, 15 January 1998. Shurin's older brother Isak had also known Duncan when the two participated in a gay poets group around 1970.
25. The chapbook edition of *The Venice Poem* had been published in 1975 by the Poetry Society of Australia's *New Poetry.* The fragment also includes the reminder that Jess (the lion) is calling Duncan home.

CHAPTER FIFTY-SEVEN: AN ALTERNATE LIFE

1. Adamson to Duncan [March 1976]. Duncan was unaware that his plane fare had been paid for by Cheryl Adamson's income tax refund.
2. Duncan posited that another phase of hermetic teachings would begin in 1982 when he turned sixty-three.
3. Robert Creeley described Adamson as "the Bob Dylan of Australian poetry."
4. John Tranter, Interview with Robert Duncan, 4 May 1985, *Jacket* 26, http://jacketmagazine.com/26/dunc-tran-iv.html.
5. Robert Adamson, e-mail, 17 March 1999.
6. Chris Edwards, e-mail, 17 August 2006.
7. Robert Adamson, e-mail, 21 April 1998.
8. Ibid., 17 March 1999.
9. Duncan to Jess, 6 September 1976.
10. Robert Adamson, e-mail, 17 March 1999.
11. Ibid.
12. Ibid.
13. Notebook 55, 9 September 1976, UAB.
14. Robert Adamson lists Dorothy Hewett, David Malouf, J.S. Harry, Robert Harris, Nigel Roberts, Dorothy Porter, and Bruce Beaver as key figures around Duncan that month.
15. Chris Edwards, e-mail, 17 August 2006.
16. Duncan, *Ground Work II*, 2.
17. Edwards to Duncan, 9 January 1977.
18. Duncan, *Ground Work II*, 1.
19. Notebook 55, 4 October 1976, UAB.
20. Duncan to Jess, 13 April 1979.
21. Duncan, "And/Or Poetry Reading," Seattle, Washington, [14] March 1976, audiocassette, UAB.
22. Hilde Burton, 19 February 2006.
23. Michael McClure and Lawrence Ferlinghetti appear in the film. Diane di Prima's reading was also edited out. Duncan's performance is available at www.wolfgangsvault.com/the-band/video/transgressing-the-real-robert-duncan_1000044.html.
24. Duncan to Edwards, 11 December 1976.

CHAPTER FIFTY-EIGHT: CAMBRIDGE

1. Duncan, *Ground Work II*, 17.
2. Notebook 56, 22/23 February 1977, UAB.
3. Duncan began "The Quotidian" section on March 31, and he wrote Chris Edwards on April 28 that its title came "out of my sessions in French conversation,

where I have to project 'La vie quotidienne,' which I hear also as a French transla-
tion of Freud's title: 'La Psychopathologie de la vie quotidienne'—I mean to find in
the close of the things of my daily life the presence of the alternate, in the daily light
the alternate shadow; in the daily shadow the alternate light."

4. Unpublished ms, 9 April 1977, courtesy Alberto de Lacerda.

5. Kitaj's portrait of Duncan and Creeley, *A Visit to London,* was composed
during this trip.

6. Penelope Highton Creeley, e-mail, 17 March 2008.

7. Duncan, *Ground Work II,* 21.

8. Fielding Dawson, 13 July 1999. Duncan alludes to "frequently hostile interest
in Jung" in a 30 May 1978 letter to Chris Edwards.

9. Duncan to Edwards, 28 April 1977.

10. For more on this conference and on Duncan's interest in French poetry, see
Clément Oudart's "Genreading and Underwriting: A Few Soundings and Probes
into Duncan's Ground Work," *Jacket* 32, April 2007, http://jacketmagazine.com
/32/oudart-genreading.shtml.

11. Notebook 55, UAB, includes Duncan's meticulous list of the artworks he
saw during this trip.

12. Duncan to Edwards, 31 May 1978. Duncan is likely referring to Jacques
Roubaud.

CHAPTER FIFTY-NINE: THE AVANT-GARDE

1. Andrews to Duncan, 31 July 1978. Ron Silliman recalled, "In 1978, langpo
[Language poetry] was still fairly new to the broader community of poets—to
those of us doing it, it was anywhere between 4 & 8 years old. The term language
poetry had yet to be assigned to the group . . . —that didn't come about until '79.
Tom Mandel becoming the head of the SF Poetry Center that fall was a huge deal
in terms of recognizing this new writing & everyone in the poetry scene in SF rec-
ognized it as such (consider, for example, that Charles [Bernstein] & Bruce [An-
drews] did not start . . . L = A = N = G = U = A = G = E until that year)" (e-mail. 21
March 2006).

2. Mary Margaret Sloan, 17 February 2006.

3. David Levi Strauss [April 1998].

4. Duncan to James Laughlin, 26 March 1978, NDir.

5. See also Michael Palmer's "On Jess's *Narkissos*" in *Jess: A Grand Collage.*

6. Lewis Warsh, 1997; Bernadette Mayer, 1999.

7. Don Byrd, e-mail, 21 January 2006.

8. Don Byrd points out Metcalf's reference to this incident in his *Collected
Works* vol. 2, 201.

9. "An Introduction: John Taggart's *Dodeka*" also appears in *Fictive Certainties.*

10. Duncan to Martin, 29 September 1978.

CHAPTER SIXTY: ADAM, EVE, AND JAHWEH

1. Notebook 55 [July 1978], UAB.

2. Alice Notley, e-mail [1998].

3. Steven Strasser and Pamela Abramson, "Why People Join Cults," *Newsweek,* 3 December 1984, 36. Disagreements about the hierarchical nature of Tibetan Buddhism spawned the "Naropa Poetry Wars." See Clark, *The Great Naropa Poetry Wars.*

4. *The Party: A Chronological Perspective on a Confrontation at a Buddhist Seminary,* written by the Investigative Poetry Group, was published in 1978 by Poetry, Crime, & Culture Press in Woodstock, New York.

5. Sanders to Duncan, 24 September 1978. Sanders covered the Manson family trial for the *Los Angeles Free Press* and wrote *The Family* (first published in 1971 by Blank Press), the rival to Vincent Bugliosi's *Helter Skelter.*

6. Bobbie Louise Hawkins [1998].

7. Duncan's students included Arnold Arias, Linda Bryant, Kirpal Singh Gordon, Virginia Martin, Roberta Lefkowitz and John Oughton, with Charles Palau, Michael Saunders, Lorna Smedman, Simon Pettet, and Helen Luster flocking around the periphery of the sessions.

8. Duncan to Martin [September 1978], NDir.

9. Anne Waldman, e-mail, 15 January 2006.

10. Larry Fagin [1997]. Fagin remembered that Duncan began this poem in one of his classes.

11. Duncan, *Ground Work II,* 30.

12. Duncan to Jess, 20 and 21 July 1978.

13. This interview was published as the chapbook *A Little Endarkenment and in My Poetry You Find Me.*

14. Ibid., 36.

15. Lyn Hejinian, e-mail, 8 July 1999.

16. Anne Waldman, e-mail, 15 January 2006.

17. Duncan to Jess, 28 July 1978.

18. Duncan to Paula Prokopoff, 27 September 1978.

19. Duncan, *Ground Work II,* 50.

CHAPTER SIXTY-ONE: SAN FRANCISCO'S BURNING

1. White was released from Soledad prison on 6 January 6, 1984, after serving a five-year sentence. He committed suicide on 21 October 1985.

2. Silliman, e-mail, 21 March 2006.

3. David Bromige, 6 May 1998.

4. "An Evening with Louis Zukofsky," San Francisco Art Institute, 8 December 1978, audiocassette, UAB.

5. David Levi Strauss, "On Duncan & Zukofsky On Film Traces Now and Then," *Poetry Flash,* no. 135 (June 1984): 10. Watten refused permission for other excerpts of his talk to be included here. I've corrected Strauss's quotation to reflect the exact wording used by Watten. Two recordings of the event exist in public archives, one at UAB and one at the Poetry Center at San Francisco State University.

6. "An Evening with Louis Zukofsky."

7. Ibid. Duncan's 1976 lecture "Warp and Woof" at the Naropa Institute touched upon similar issues.

8. Ron Silliman, e-mail, 11 September 1998. David Levi Strauss's mention of the event in his June 1984 article in *Poetry Flash* later reignited the controversy. Even these six years later, "On Duncan & Zukofsky On Film" set off a flurry of angry letter writing among San Francisco poets. Silliman related another aspect of the Language wars in a 21 March 2006 e-mail: "There were other langpo-identified poets with whom Robert had far greater sympathies than he did Watten. Palmer, Melnick, myself. Even *after* this event, for example, Robert deliberately put me and Richard Baker-roshi, the head of the SF Zen Center, together; that led to Bob Perelman & I starting the reading series at the Tassajara Bakery in late '79 (this was the successor to the Grand Piano). That could not have happened without Robert's intervention."

9. *Poetry Flash,* no. 137 (August 1984): 7.

10. David Bromige, 6 May 1998.

11. Eloyde Tovey, "Conversations with Robert Duncan, Dec. 1978," unpublished ms, UCB.

12. Michael Franco, 1 August 2006.

CHAPTER SIXTY-TWO: AT SEA

1. "Interview: Robert Duncan" (Abbott and Shurin).

2. Notebook 52, 17 January 1979, UAB. Duncan also composed "In Wonder" (*Ground Work II*) on this day.

3. Duncan to Jess, 20 March 1979.

4. Bill Sylvester, e-mail, 5 August 2005.

5. Ibid.

6. Brian Caraher, e-mail, 21 January 2006. At the end of Duncan's visit, he signed Caraher's copy of *The Truth & Life of Myth: An Essay In Essential Autobiography* with a "playful comment on the circled word 'autobiography': 'whose bio is not clear and who cant besides drive an auto but is great at graffy.'"

7. Duncan to Jess, 20 March 1979.

8. Ibid., 21 March 1979.

9. Ibid., 22 March 1979.

10. Ibid., 28 March 1979.

11. Ibid.

12. Ibid., 13 April 1979.

13. Ibid., 16 April 1979.

14. Paul Dolan, e-mail, 10 March 2006.

15. Chuck Stein, 19 March 2008.

16. Anne Waldman, e-mail, 15 January 2006.

17. Lewis MacAdams, "The Enamord Mage," *Poetry Flash,* June 1979, 1.

CHAPTER SIXTY-THREE: THE CHERUBIM

1. Duncan to Jess, 8 June 1979.

2. Ibid., 9 June 1979.

3. Ibid., 11 June 1979.

4. Ibid.

5. Ibid., 15 June 1979.

6. Duncan, *Ground Work II,* 33.

7. Duncan to Jess, 14 June 1979.

8. Duncan's letters to Jess from this week make no mention of the meeting with Jabès. He may not have had time to document it in his correspondence home because it fell between several museum trips and a tour of historic sites in the French countryside.

9. Duncan, *Ground Work II,* 35.

10. Duncan to Jess, 1 July 1979.

11. Ibid., 8 July 1979.

12. Sean Killian, 1 March 2006.

13. Duncan to Jess, 14 July 1979.

14. Ibid., 18 July, 1979.

15. Ibid., [23] July 1979.

16. Ibid., 27 July 1979.

17. Wilson, *Seeing Shelley Plain,* 99.

18. Sean Killian, 1 March 2006.

19. Duncan to Jess, 1 October 1979.

20. Ibid.

21. Ibid., 2 October 1979.

22. Ibid.

23. Ibid., 4 October 1979.

24. Ibid.

25. Ibid. Jess was equally concerned about the potential emotional intrusions of the biography. He insisted that Faas restrict his narrative to Duncan's early life, excluding from the book any details of their marriage.

26. Duncan to Jess, 9 October 1979.

1. Robert Creeley, 20 December 1997.
2. Notebook 62, 8 January 1980, UAB. The conference was likely one held at the California Institute of Integral Studies titled Feminine Spirituality: God and the Goddess in Judaism.
3. Duncan to Edwards, 28 January 1980.
4. Edwards, e-mail, 7 October 2005.
5. Ibid.
6. Notebook 62, 16 April 1980, UAB.
7. Duncan, *Ground Work II,* 62.
8. Notebook 62, 19 April 1980, UAB. This notebook contains extensive notes about Stockhausen.
9. Duncan to Jess, 27 April 1980.
10. Notebook 62, 27 April 1980, UAB.
11. Nikki Murray Jones, "Poet Duncan Intoxicated with the Music of Words, Ideas, Reality and Unreality," *Ketchikan Daily News,* 2 May 1980.
12. Duncan to Jess, 28 April 1980.
13. Ibid., 30 April 1980.
14. The museum was probably at Sheldon Jackson College.
15. Duncan may have purchased two amber necklaces during this trip. He later gave one to New College student Todd Baron on the occasion of his marriage, and Jess also presented one to Mary Margaret Sloan after Duncan's death.
16. Duncan to Jess, 1 May 1980.
17. Ibid.
18. Ibid., 4 May 1980.
19. Ibid., 6 May 1980.

CHAPTER SIXTY-FIVE: ENTHRALLED

1. Duncan to Jess, 1 July 1980.
2. Ibid., 4 July 1980.
3. Ibid.
4. Thom Gunn, 9 November 1999.
5. Frederick Turner, "With the Lawrentians in New Mexico," *Nation,* 30 August–6 September 1980, 190.
6. Ibid.
7. Duncan to Jess [July 1980].

CHAPTER SIXTY-SIX: NEW COLLEGE

1. Susan Friedland, 13 September 1997; and *The Originals: The Writer In America,* PBS Documentary, 1974, audiocassette, UAB.

2. Duncan McNaughton provided insights about the beginnings of New College in a 14 January 2001 e-mail. Other teachers making appearances during the program's first year were Martin Epstein, Robert Grenier, Lynn Luria-Sukenick, and David Doty. Michael Palmer joined the faculty in 1982.

3. The University of California never acted on a proposal to bring Duncan there.

4. Todd Baron, e-mail, 8 November 1997.

5. Dawn Kolokithas changed her name to Dawn-Michelle Baude in 1992.

6. Poetics Program brochure, 1983, uncatalogued file, UAB.

7. Duncan had been invited to the conference by Fran Claggett, a teacher at Alameda High School whom Duncan had known since the 1960s.

8. While there are no records of further meetings between Duncan and Campbell, Duncan did form deeper associations with another thinker in Campbell's circle, James Hillman.

9. Duncan to Joseph, 3 October 1980.

10. Ibid.

11. Jed Rasula, April 2005. The journal *Spring* devoted issue 59 to Duncan's conference appearance.

12. Duncan, *Ground Work II,* 52.

13. Duncan to Robert Adamson, 20 July 1981.

14. Carl Grundberg to author, 25 October 1998.

15. The two clubs used the terms "Group" and "Club" interchangeably in their names.

16. David Levi Strauss, "Homer Letter," unpublished ms; and Aaron Shurin, April 2006.

17. Strauss, "Homer Letter."

CHAPTER SIXTY-SEVEN: FIVE SONGS

1. Hypertension ran in Duncan's family, but his relatives had no history of diabetes or cancer.

2. Duncan to Spaulding, 16 April 1981.

3. Spaulding to Duncan, 7 December 1982.

4. Hooks talks about her relationship with Duncan and Jess on pages 232–44 of the memoir.

5. Duncan to Adamson, 21 July 1981.

6. Duncan, *Ground Work II,* 72.

7. Ibid., 77.

8. Shurin, "Quite a Bit More Duncan Exposure," 8.

9. The numbering of the *Passages* series falls out of sequence with "In the Place of a Passage 22" appearing in *Bending the Bow* and "You, Muses [Passages 22]" appearing in *Ground Work II* nearly twenty years later.

10. In his interview with Michael Andre Bernstein and Burton Hatlen in 1985, Duncan names Taggart and Howe as two of his favorite younger poets (121).

11. John Taggart, 2 March 2006.

12. Duncan had several new students in 1982, including Julia Connor, Ken Pertrelli, Steve Klingaman, John Thorpe, Adam Shaw, Jeff Gardner, and Tim Kennedy.

13. Duncan, "Lecture on the Continuity of Christian Myth," February 1982, Buffalo, New York, audiocassette, UAB.

14. Notebook 68, 19 February 1982, UAB.

15. Ibid.

CHAPTER SIXTY-EIGHT: A PARIS VISIT

1. Duncan to Jess, 13 April 1982.

2. Michael Franco, e-mail, 23 July 2006.

3. Kitaj didn't recall Duncan ever being quiet during the sessions (6 February 2006). Ten of these drawings later appeared with Duncan's five-poem "Illustrative Lines" in *A Paris Visit,* published by Grenfell Press. Raymond Foye, who worked with Duncan on the editing of the Grenfell project, remembered, "Kitaj did many portraits of RD and RD submitted a long section from *Ground Work*. It really didn't make for an exciting book. So I went to see RD and shyly asked if he would consider sitting in front of the drawings . . . and write poems. He readily agreed" (24 January 2010).

4. The IRCAM, founded in 1970 under the directorship of composer Pierre Boulez, was a state-sponsored research center specializing in music and sound experiments and offering performances of avant-garde work to the public.

5. Duncan to Jess, 21 April 1982.

6. Ibid., 22 April 1982.

7. Ibid., 26 April 1982.

8. Ibid., 2 May 1982.

9. Ibid., 5 May 1982.

10. Bye, "A Reading in New York: 1980," 440. Bye misdates the reading.

11. Michael Franco, e-mail, 23 July 2006.

12. Duncan, unpublished ms, courtesy Stacy Szymaszek, Woodland Patterns Bookstore.

13. Duncan to Joseph, 28 May 1982.

CHAPTER SIXTY-NINE: BARD

1. Bard College Course Catalog, 1982–83.
2. Duncan to Jess, 28 September 1982.
3. Robert Kelly, e-mail, 29 January 2006.
4. Duncan to Jess, 28 September 1982.
5. Ibid., 30 September 1982.
6. Ibid., 1 October 1982.
7. David Matlin, 17 February 2006.
8. Duncan to Jess, 10 October 1982.
9. Ibid., 16 October 1982.
10. Ibid., 18 October 1982.
11. Anne Waldman taught a class on Gertrude Stein at New College during the fall of 1982.
12. Michael Franco, e-mail, 23 July 2006.
13. Duncan to Jess, 7 April 1983. James Francis Collins, Jr., was born in Tacoma, Washington, on 26 February 1918.
14. Duncan to Jess, 15 April 1983.
15. Ibid., 18 April 1983.
16. Unnumbered notebook, 13 August 1983, UAB.
17. Ibid.
18. Duncan to Joseph, 30 November 1983.
19. Michael Palmer, 15 January 1998. The class included Judith Roche, Eloise Sterling, Douglas Lowell, Richard Sides, Rebecca Ward, Ron Meyers, Julia Connor, Grant Fisher, and John Thorpe.
20. Duncan to Peter Glassgold, 13 December 1983, NDir.
21. Ibid.

CHAPTER SEVENTY: THE BAPTISM OF THE BLOOD

1. Bob Glück, e-mail, 15 March 2006.
2. Dawn-Michelle Baude, e-mail, 14 December 1997.
3. David Levi Strauss. e-mail, 25 February 1998.
4. Duncan to Glassgold, 8 February 1984, NDir; Duncan to Jones, 1 March 1984.
5. Alice Notley, e-mail [1997].
6. Alice Notley, April 1998.
7. Rodger Kamenetz, e-mail, 4 July 2007.
8. Philip Hertz to Robert J. Bertholf, 12 August 1986, UAB.
9. Duncan to Levertov, 20 April 1984.
10. Notebook A, UCB.
11. Larry Casalino, 11 March 2006.

12. Duncan to Levertov, 20 April 1984.

13. Duncan to Joseph, 31 May 1984.

14. Strauss, "On Duncan & Zukofsky on Film."

15. Silliman, "Re David Levi Strauss on Duncan & Zukofsky on Film," 7.

16. Ibid.

17. Duncan to Joseph, 30 July 1984. Duncan seems to have had some hand in continuing the controversy. According to Strauss, "*Poetry Flash* was scared to death to publish the thing and begged me to retract it. They knew that it would set off a firestorm, and it did, beginning with Silliman's diatribe.... If Duncan hadn't supported me, I don't know what I would have done. When he did, I was able to write my letter in reply to Silliman (published in August 1984), and I . . . still stand by every word of that" (Strauss, e-mail, 31 January 2006).

18. New Directions interoffice memo, 8 January 1988, NDir.

19. Grundberg, "Re: Ron Silliman's letter in #136," 9.

CHAPTER SEVENTY-ONE: HEKATOMBE

1. Todd Baron, e-mail, 8 November 1997.

2. Judith Roche to author, 4 January 1998.

3. Aaron Shurin, 15 January 1998.

4. Susan Friedland, 13 September 1997; Mary Margaret Sloan, 17 February 2006.

5. The puzzle may have depicted the Winchester Mystery House in San Jose, which Jess and Ashbery had visited together. Jess had rendered a "translation" of Sarah Winchester in his 1966 painting *Translation #17*.

6. "An Interview with Robert Duncan" (Bernstein and Hatlen).

7. Duncan to Glassgold, 8 January 1985, NDir.

8. This volume will be published by the University of California Press.

9. Duncan to Glassgold [1985], NDir.

10. David Meltzer, e-mail, 30 January 2006.

11. Unpublished poem, uncatalogued manuscript file, UAB. The variations of the spelling of Hecate and Hekate occur in the original manuscript.

12. Aaron Shurin, e-mail to Michael Palmer, forwarded to the author, 20 February 2006.

13. The class included Todd Baron, Grant Fisher, Matthew Haug, Scott Thompson, Michael Kronebusch, Mary Margaret Sloan, Julia Van Cleve, and Jill Elizabeth Duerr.

14. Norma Cole, 15, January 1998.

15. Susan Quasha, 19 March 2008.

16. Joe Cardarelli and Jim Skipper, *Black Mountain Revisited,* videocassette, Maryland Institute, College of Art, and Viridian Productions, 1990.

17. "Interview with Robert Duncan" (Tranter).

18. Duncan to Ohannessian, 30 June 1985.

19. Thom Gunn, 9 November 1999.

20. Duncan, *Ground Work II,* 70.

21. Raymond Foye, 24 January 2010.

22. Aaron Shurin took over Duncan's Emily Dickinson class, and Todd Baron recalled, "Aaron was an amazing teacher—a 'little' Robert if you will" (Todd Baron, e-mail, 8 November 1997). Shurin invited Susan Howe to present talks to the group based around her recently published *My Emily Dickinson.*

23. Mary Margaret Sloan, 17 February 2006.

24. Hilde Burton, 18 February 2006.

25. This interview may have been conducted in two parts. The interviewer mentions a visit to the household during the following spring.

26. Duncan to Ohannessian and Glassgold, 31 October 1985, NDir.

CHAPTER SEVENTY-TWO: THE YEAR OF DUNCAN

1. Tolbert McCarroll, e-mail, 11 January 2006.

2. Aaron Shurin, 15 January 1998.

3. Attendees included Todd Baron, Grant Fisher, Anne Fitzpatrick, Martin Fulton, Helen Hampton, Christopher Romero, John Evans, Carolyn Kemp, Jill Duerr, Douglas Lowell, Julia Conner, and Lisa Hawes.

4. Francisco Aragón, e-mail to the Buffalo Poetics List, 17 January 2006.

5. Stephen Rodefer, who also attended the reading, related this anecdote, December 1997.

6. Thom Gunn, 9 November 1999. H. D. wrote about the Saint-John Perse incident in *Hermetic Definition.* She also referred to Lionel Durand, a younger acquaintance who inspired the opening of the poem sequence.

7. Michael Franco, e-mail, 23 July 2006.

8. Mary Margaret Sloan, 17 February 2006.

9. Ibid.

10. Adam to Duncan, 1 May 1986. There is no record of a response from Duncan and Jess. Pat Adam died in late 1986, and Helen Adam's physical and emotional condition deteriorated further. She wrote to Lewis Ellingham on 7 March 1987, "My life, since my poor darling Pat's death, has been a prolonged night-mare and owing to a mixture of degrading physical ailments I am confined to a few blocks of this apartment, or sometimes Central Park." Helen Adam died in 1993.

11. Shurin, "Quite a Bit More Duncan Exposure," 8.

12. Blue to Duncan, 28 May 1986. A year later, the group would also include Norma Cole, Mary Margaret Sloan, and Alison and Edwin Frank.

13. Philip Hertz to Robert J. Bertholf, 12 August 1986, UAB.

14. David Levi Strauss. "Hosephat & the Wooden Shoes," 134.

15. Jess to Duncan, 25 July 1986.

16. Norma Cole, 15 January 1998.

17. In his 1976 will, Duncan also set aside Jess's painting *A Castle Spun from Yarn* for Tolbert McCarroll and Elmer Bischoff's *Late Afternoon* for William Matson Roth.

18. Coincidentally, in 1950 and again in 1960, Duncan had received letters from curators in Buffalo (Eugene Magner 1950 and David Posner 1960) asking him to donate works to the collection. On both occasions, he had declined.

19. Thom Gunn, 9 November 1999.

20. George Stanley, e-mail, 3 February 2006.

21. Norma Cole, 15 January 1998.

22. Broughton, *Coming Unbuttoned, 66.* Broughton died in 1999 at the age of eighty-five.

23. Glück, e-mail, 15 March 2006.

24. These revisions of Jess's will fell short of legality, and Jess later revised his will to assign his and Duncan's estate to a new group of beneficiaries.

CHAPTER SEVENTY-THREE: THE CIRCULATION
OF THE BLOOD

1. David Levi Strauss, untitled note on Robert Duncan, *American Poetry* 6, no. 1: 74.

2. Ibid.

3. Larry Casalino, 11 March 2006.

4. According to Michael Palmer, "Before he became ill, Robert would often make a traditional stew of honeycomb tripe with tomatoes, or some variation. After he became ill, and that was too burdensome, he would buy menudo (tripe soup) at one of the Mexican neighborhood restaurants in the Mission. They traditionally prepare it on Saturdays" (e-mail, 8 March 2006).

5. Jess, Notebook, 15 January 1988, UAB.

6. Larry Casalino, 11 March 2006.

7. Jess, Notebook, 22 January 1988, UAB.

CHAPTER SEVENTY-FOUR: IN THE DARK

1. Larry Casalino, 11 March 2006.

2. Jess, Notebook, 3 February 1988.

3. Mary Margaret Sloan, e-mail, 29 January 2006.

4. Ibid., 4 February 2006.

5. One of Duncan's students, Michael Kronebusch, was at the house when Robert Bertholf came to gather his own share of Duncan's personal property. Bertholf left with two pairs of Duncan's eyeglasses, his passports, his wallet, a gold-colored canvas book bag, a hat pin with an Arabic inscription, an ornate hairpin,

and a bee-shaped pin that Duncan had purchased at the Metropolitan Museum of Art. Bertholf later told his employees that he had collected the relics much in the spirit that previous curators of the Rare Books Collection had acquired James Joyce's cane and eyeglasses.

6. Michael Palmer, e-mail, 14 March 2006.
7. Norma Cole, e-mail, 6 February 2006.
8. Mary Margaret Sloan, 17 February 2006.
9. Duncan, *Ground Work II,* 6.

WORKS CITED

BY ROBERT DUNCAN

Poetry

Bending the Bow. New York: New Directions, 1968.
Caesar's Gate. Berkeley: Sand Dollar, 1972.
Derivations. London: Fulcrum Press, 1968.
Faust Foutu. Barrytown, NY: Station Hill Press, 1985.
The First Decade. London: Fulcrum Press, 1968.
Ground Work: Before the War. New York: New Directions, 1984.
Ground Work II: In the Dark. New York: New Directions, 1987.
Heavenly City, Earthly City. Berkeley: Bern Porter, 1947.
The Opening of the Field. New York: Grove Press, 1960.
A Paris Visit. Illustrations by R. B. Kitaj. New York: Grenfell Press, 1985.
Poems 1948–49. Berkeley: Berkeley Miscellany Editions, 1949.
Roots and Branches. New York: Scribner's, 1964.
Selected Poems. Edited by Robert J. Bertholf. New York: New Directions, 1997.
The Years As Catches. Berkeley: Oyez, 1966.

Prose

As Testimony. San Francisco: White Rabbit Press, 1964.
Fictive Certainties. New York: New Directions, 1985.
The H. D. Book, www.ccca.ca/history/ozz/english/books/hd_book/HD_Book_by
    _Robert_Duncan.pdf.
"The Lasting Contribution of Ezra Pound." *Agenda* 4, no. 2 (October-November
    1965): 23–26.
"A Risk of Sympathies." *Poetry* 91, no. 5 (February 1958): 328–32.
A Selected Prose. Edited by Robert Bertholf. New York: New Directions, 1995.

"Taking Away from God His Sound." *Nation,* 31 May 1965.
"Ten Prose Pieces." Edited by Robert J. Bertholf. *Jacket* 28, http://jacketmagazine
.com/28/dunc-bert-10prose.html#x7.
"The Truth and Life of Myth in Poetry." *A Meeting of Poets and Theologians to Discuss Parable, Myth, and Language.* Cambridge, MA: Church Society for College Work, 1968.
"Warp and Woof: Notes from A Talk." In *Talking Poetics from Naropa Institute: Annals of the Jack Kerouac School of Disembodied Poetics.* Vol. 1, 1–10. Edited by Anne Waldman and Marilyn Webb. Boulder, CO: Shambala, 1978.

Correspondence

A Great Admiration: H. D./Robert Duncan Correspondence 1950–1961. Edited by Robert J. Bertholf. Venice, CA: Lapis Press, 1992.
The Letters of Robert Duncan and Denise Levertov. Edited by Robert J. Bertholf and Albert Gelpi. Stanford, CA: Stanford University Press, 2004.
The Unruly Garden: Robert Duncan and Eric Mottram, Letters and Essays. Edited by Amy Evans and Shamoon Zamir. Oxford: Peter Lang, 2007.

Lectures and Readings

"And/Or Poetry Reading." Seattle, [14] March 1976. Audiocassette, UAB.
"The Continuity of Christian Myth." Buffalo, New York, February 1982. Audiocassette, UAB.
"Gay Liberation Day Poetry Reading." San Francisco, 2 March 1971. Audiocassette, UAB.
"Ideas of Primordial Time in Charles Olson's Work." University of Iowa, 7 November 1978. Audiocassette, UAB.
"Ideas on the Meaning of Form." National Poetry Festival, Allendale, Michigan Conference, 16 June 1973. Audiocassette. Courtesy Karl Gartung.
"Lecture on Ezra Pound." Central Washington State University, 8 October 1969. Audiocassette, UAB.
"Lecture on Field Theory at New College with Michael Palmer." 13 September 1983. Audiocassette, UAB.
"A Life in Poetry." Vancouver Poetry Conference, 5 August 1963. Audiocassette, UAB.
"Naropa Institute Lecture." 10 June 1976, www.archive.org/details/naropa_robert
_duncan_lecture_warp_and2.
"On Olson." New College of California, San Francisco, 17 February 1982. Audiocassette, UAB.
"Poetry Reading." University of California, San Diego, 23 March 1976. Audiocassette, UAB.

"Pound, Eliot, and H. D.: The Cult of the Gods in American Poetry." Kent State University, 11 October 1972. Audiocassette, UAB.

"The Psyche Myth and the Moment of Truth." Topeka, Kansas, 12 May 1965. Audiocassette, UAB.

"The Psyche Myth and the Moment of Truth." University of California, Berkeley, 13 July 1965. Audiocassette, UAB.

"Robert Duncan. Poetry Reading." Albuquerque, New Mexico, 23 March 1964. Slought Foundation, www.slought.org/content/11123/.

Untitled lecture. Vancouver, 23 July 1961. Audiocassette, UAB.

Unititled lecture for Nature of Person course. New College, 21 April 1981. Audiocassette, UAB.

Interviews

"'The Closeness of Mind': An Interview with Robert Duncan." Interviewed by Gerald Nicosia. In *Unspeakable Visions of the Individual: Beat Angels,* edited by Arthur Knight and Kit Knight, 13–27. CA: 1982.

"A Conversation with Robert Duncan, 1976." Interviewed by Robert Peters and Paul Trachtenberg. *Chicago Review* 43, no. 4 (Fall 1997): 83–105, and 44, no. 1 (Winter 1998): 92–116.

"Interview: Robert Duncan." Interviewed by Steve Abbott and Aaron Shurin. *Gay Sunshine,* no. 40–41 (Summer/Fall 1979): 1–8.

"Interview: The History of the Poetry Center," 1 December 1976. Audiocassette, UAB.

"Interview with Robert Duncan." Interviewed by Michael Andre Bernstein and Burton Hatlen. *Sagetrieb* 4, nos. 2 and 3 (Fall and Winter 1985): 87–135.

"Interview with Robert Duncan." Interviewed by John Tranter. *Jacket* 26, http://jacketmagazine.com/26/dunc-tran-iv.html.

"Interview with Robert Duncan, 1986." Interviewed by Roberta Berke. BBC Radio transcript, UAB.

A Little Endarkenment and in My Poetry You Find Me: The Naropa Institute Interview with Robert Duncan. Boulder, CO: Erudite Fangs Editions, 1996.

The Originals: The Writer in America. PBS Documentary, 1974. Audiocassette, UAB.

Robert Duncan: An Interview by George Bowering and Robert Hogg: April 19, 1969. Toronto: A Beaver Kosmos Folio, 1971.

"Robert Duncan Interview." Interviewed by Colin Saunders. *Beat Scene,* Summer 2005.

"Robert Duncan: Table Talk at a Dinner with Norman and Virginia Goldstein, September 4, 1970." *Poetry USA,* nos. 25 and 26 (1993): 34–38.

"The World of Jaime de Angulo [an interview with Robert Duncan]." Interviewed by Bob Callahan. *Netzahualcoyotl News* 1, Summer 1979: 5, 14–16.

Adam, Helen. *Fire Brackled Bones: Selected Poems and Collages of Helen Adam.* Edited by Kristin Prevallet. Orono, ME: National Poetry Foundation, 2007.

Auping, Michael, ed. *Jess: A Grand Collage: 1951–1993.* Buffalo, NY: Albright–Knox Art Gallery, 1993.

Bair, Deirdre. *Anaïs Nin: A Biography.* New York: Putnam, 1995.

Baum, L. Frank. *Ozma of Oz.* Mineola, NY: Dover, 1985.

Bergé, Carol. *The Vancouver Report.* New York: Fuck You Press, 1964.

Bertholf, Robert J. *Robert Duncan: A Descriptive Bibliography.* Santa Rosa, CA: Black Sparrow Press, 1986.

———. "Robert Duncan's 'The Venice Poem' and Symphonic Form." *Jacket 28,* http://jacketmagazine.com/28/dunc-bert-vpessay.html.

———, and Ian Reid, eds. *Robert Duncan: Scales of the Marvelous.* New York: New Directions, 1979.

Black Mountain Revisited. Edited by Joseph Cardarelli and Jim Skipper. Viridian Video Productions, Maryland Institute, College of Art, 1990.

Blaser, Robin. *The Holy Forest: Collected Poems of Robin Blaser.* Toronto: Coach House Press, 1993.

Broughton, James. *Coming Unbuttoned.* San Francisco: City Lights, 1993.

Butling, Pauline. "Robert Duncan in Vancouver: On Reading, Writing and Non-upmanship." *W Magazine,* 2005, 10, www.kswnet.org/w/ten/w10.pdf.

Bye, Reed. "A Reading in New York: 1980." In *Out of This World: An Anthology of the St. Mark's Poetry Project, 1966–1991,* edited by Anne Waldman, 440–41. New York: Crown Publishing Group, 1991.

Candida Smith, Richard. *Utopia and Dissent: Art, Poetry, and Politics in California.* Berkeley: University of California Press, 1996.

Carpenter, Amos B. *The Carpenter Memorial.* Amherst, MA: Press of Carpenter and Morehouse, 1896.

Clark, Tom. *Charles Olson: The Allegory of a Poet's Life.* New York: Norton, 1991.

———. *The Great Naropa Poetry Wars.* Santa Barbara, CA: Cadmus, 1980.

[Collins], Jess. *Translations.* New York: Odyssia Gallery, 1971.

Cooney, Blanche. *In My Own Sweet Time: An Autobiography.* Athens, OH: Swallow Press, 1993.

Creeley, Robert. *For Love.* New York: Scribner's, 1962.

Davidson, Michael. "A Cold War Correspondence: The Letters of Robert Duncan and Denise Levertov." *Contemporary Literature* 45, no. 3 (Fall 2004): 538–56.

———. *The San Francisco Renaissance: Poetics and Community at Mid-Century.* Cambridge: Cambridge University Press, 1991.

de Angulo, Gui. *The Life of Jaime de Angulo: The Old Coyote of Big Sur.* Big Sur, CA: Henry Miller Memorial Library, 1995.

Diaman, N. A. *Second Crossing.* San Francisco: Persona Press, 1982.

Duberman, Martin. *Black Mountain: An Exploration in Community*. Garden City, NY: Anchor Books, 1973.

Ellingham, Lewis, and Kevin Killian. *Poet Be Like God: Jack Spicer and the San Francisco Renaissance*. Middletown, CT: Wesleyan University Press, 1998.

Faas, Ekbert. *Towards a New American Poetics*. Santa Barbara, CA: Black Sparrow Press, 1979.

———. *Young Robert Duncan: Portrait of the Poet as Homosexual in Society*. Santa Barbara, CA: Black Sparrow Press, 1983.

Fabilli, Mary. *Aurora Bligh and Early Poems*. Berkeley: Oyez, 1968.

Gelpi, Albert, and Robert J. Bertholf. *Robert Duncan and Denise Levertov: The Poetry of Politics, the Politics of Poetry*. Stanford, CA: Stanford University Press, 2006.

Ginsberg, Allen. *Allen Verbatim: Lectures on Poetry, Politics, Consciousness*. Edited by Gordon Ball. New York: McGraw-Hill, 1974.

———. *Journals Mid-fifties 1954–1958*. New York: HarperCollins, 1995.

Gleason, Madeline. *Collected Poems 1919–1979*. Edited by Christopher Wagstaff. Hoboken, NJ: Talisman House Publishers, 1999.

Graves, Robert, and Paul Hogarth. *Majorca Observed*. New York: Doubleday, 1965.

Grundberg, Carl. "Re: Ron Silliman's Letter in #136, Responding to David Levi Strauss's 'On Duncan & Zukofsky on Film,' #135, June 1984." *Poetry Flash,* September 1984.

Hamalian, Linda. *A Life of Kenneth Rexroth*. New York: Norton, 1991.

Hamilton, Jeff. "Wrath Moves in the Music: Robert Duncan, Laura Riding, Craft and Force in Cold War Poetics." *Jacket* 26, http://jacketmagazine.com/26/dunc-hami.html#fnB15.

Heirich, Max. *The Beginning: Berkeley 1964*. New York: Columbia University Press, 1971.

hooks, bell. *Wounds of Passion: A Writing Life*. New York: Holt, 1997.

Howard, Seymour. *The Beat Generation Galleries and Beyond*. Davis, CA: John Natsoulas Press, 1996.

Johnston, Devin. *Precipitations: Contemporary American Poetry as Occult Practice*. Middletown, CT: Wesleyan University Press, 2002.

Kane, Daniel. *All Poets Welcome: The Lower East Side Poetry Scene in the 1960s*. Berkeley: University of California Press, 2003.

Kerouac, Jack. *Desolation Angels*. New York: Penguin, 1965.

Laughlin, James. Preface to *New Directions in Prose and Poetry*. Norfolk, CT: New Directions, 1936.

Levertov, Denise. *O Taste and See*. New York: New Directions, 1964.

McClure, Michael. *Lighting the Corners: On Art, Nature, and the Visionary: Essays and Interviews*. Albuquerque: University of New Mexico College of Arts, 1993.

Metcalf, Paul. *Collected Works*. Vol. 2. Minneapolis: Coffee House Press, 1997.

Nin, Anaïs. *The Diary of Anaïs Nin*. Vol. 3, *1939–1944*. New York: Harcourt Brace, 1969.

———, and Henry Miller. *A Literate Passion: Letters of Anaïs Nin & Henry Miller, 1932–1953*. Edited by Gunther Stuhlmann. New York: Harcourt Brace, 1987.

O'Leary, Peter. *Gnostic Contagion: Robert Duncan and the Poetry of Illness*. Middletown, CT: Wesleyan University Press, 2002.

Olson, Charles. *Charles Olson Reading at Berkeley*. Edited by Zoe Brown. San Francisco: Coyote Press, 1966.

———. *Collected Prose*. Edited by Donald Allen and Benjamin Friedlander. Berkeley: University of California Press, 1997.

———. *The Special View of History*. Edited by Ann Charters. Berkeley: Oyez, 1970.

Rexroth, Kenneth. *An Autobiographical Novel*. New York: New Directions, 1991.

"Robert Duncan Issue." *Audit* 4, no. 3 (1967).

Rumaker, Michael. *Robert Duncan in San Francisco*. San Francisco: Grey Fox Press, 1996.

Schumacher, Michael. *Dharma Lion: A Biography of Allen Ginsberg*. New York: St. Martin's Press, 1994.

Shurin, Aaron. "Quite a Bit More Duncan Exposure: Review of *Faust Foutu*. Station Hill Press." *San Francisco Chronicle,* 2 March 1986.

Silliman, Ron. "Letter to the Editor re: David Levi Strauss on Duncan & Zukofsky on Film #135 June 1984." *Poetry Flash,* July 1984.

Smith, Larry. *Kenneth Patchen: Rebel Poet in America*. Huron, OH: Bottom Dog Press, 2000.

Solnit, Rebecca. *Secret Exhibition: Six California Artists of the Cold War Era*. San Francisco: City Lights, 1990.

Spicer, Jack. *The Collected Books of Jack Spicer*. Edited by Robin Blaser. Santa Barbara, CA: Black Sparrow Press, 1980.

———. *The House That Jack Built: The Collected Lectures of Jack Spicer*. Edited by Peter Gizzi. Middletown, CT: Wesleyan University Press, 1998.

Strauss, David Levi. "Hosephat & the Wooden Shoes: Duncan and Délire." *Edinburgh Review,* Spring 1997.

———. "On Duncan & Zukofsky on Film: Traces Now and Then." *Poetry Flash,* June 1984.

———. Untitled note on Robert Duncan. *American Poetry* 6, no. 1 (Fall 1988): 74–75.

Tallman, Ellen. "My Stories with Robert Duncan." In *Robert Duncan and Denise Levertov: The Poetry of Politics, the Politics of Poetry,* edited by Albert Gelpi and Robert J. Bertholf. Stanford, CA: Stanford University Press, 2006.

Tallman, Warren. *In the Midst: Writings 1962–1992*. Vancouver: Talonbooks, 1992.

Wagstaff, Christopher. "Interview with Tom Field." *Painters of the San Francisco Renaissance, No. 2*. March 18 and 25, 1986.

———, ed. *Lyn Brockway, Harry Jacobus, and Jess: The Romantic Paintings*. Palo Alto, CA: Palo Alto Cultural Center, 1990.

———. *Robert Duncan: Drawings and Decorated Books*. Berkeley: Rose Books, 1992.

Wagstaff, Christopher, with Harry Jacobus. "Interview with Paul Alexander." *Painters of the San Francisco Renaissance, No. 3*. May 15 and 20, June 10, 1986.

Waldman, Anne, ed. *Nice to See You: Homage to Ted Berrigan*. Minneapolis: Coffee House Press, 1991.

Wieners, John. *707 Scott Street*. Los Angeles: Sun and Moon, 1996.

Wilson, Robert. *Seeing Shelley Plain: Memories of New York's Legendary Phoenix Book Shop*. New Castle, DE: Oak Knoll Press, 2001.

CREDITS

Grateful acknowledgment for permission to print or reproduce material is made for the following:

Various excerpts by Robert Duncan, from *Bending the Bow,* copyright © 1968 by Robert Duncan. Reprinted by permission of New Directions Publishing Corp.

Various excerpts by Robert Duncan, from *Fictive Certainties,* copyright © 1985 by New Directions Publishing Corp. Reprinted by permission of New Directions Publishing Corp.

Various excerpts by Robert Duncan, from *Ground Work: Before the war / In the Dark,* copyright © 1987 by Robert Duncan. Reprinted by permission of New Directions Publishing Corp.

Various excerpts by Robert Duncan, from *Roots and Branches,* copyright © 1964 by Robert Duncan. Reprinted by permission of New Directions Publishing Corp.

Various excerpts by Robert Duncan, from *The Opening of the Field,* copyright © 1960 by Robert Duncan. Reprinted by permission of New Directions Publishing Corp.

"O Taste and See" by Denise Levertov, from *Poems 1960–1967,* copyright © 1964 by Denise Levertov. Reprinted by permission of New Directions Publishing Corp.

Excerpt by Ezra Pound, from *The Cantos of Ezra Pound,* copyright © 1934, 1937, 1940, 1948, 1950, 1956, 1959, 1962, 1963, 1965, 1966, 1968, 1970, and 1971 by Ezra Pound. Reprinted by permission of New Directions Publishing Corp.

Excerpts of Frank O'Hara's letters courtesy Maureen O'Hara.

Excerpts of Dorothy Shakespeare Pound's letters courtesy Omar Pound.

Excerpts of Louis Zukofsky's letters courtesy Paul Zukofsky.

All unpublished Robert Duncan and Jess Collins materials courtesy the Jess Collins Trust and the various special collections that house them: Special Collections,

Kent State University; Thomas J. Dodd Research Center, University of Connecticut, Storrs; Poetry Collection, University at Buffalo, the State University of New York; Special Collections, University of Chicago; Bancroft Library, University of California, Berkeley; Special Collections, University of California, Davis; Mandeville Special Collections, University of California, San Diego.

Brown Brockway, Lyn, 119, 122, 126–27
Browning, Robert, 332
Bruce, Lenny, 255
Brumm, Alvie, 14, 56, 206
Brumm, Carol, 14, 471n15
Brumm, Dick, 471n15
Brumm, Leo, 14, 471n15
Bruno, Giordano, 348
Bunting, Basil, 265
Burnett, Marlys, 381
Burnside, Madeline, 406
Burroughs, William, 172, 355, 384
Burt, David, 278, 287
Burt, Edie, 278
Burtch, Lewis Andrew, 34, 56, 200
Burton, David, 170, 178, 187, 194, 200, 224, 226–28, 251, 254, 262, 344, 350, 399, 403, 407, 414, 420
Burton, Hilde, 103, 121, 170, 178, 187, 194, 200, 224, 226–28, 251, 254, 262, 344, 350, 399, 403, 407, 414, 420–21
Butling, Pauline, 189, 207, 227, 230, 268, 318
Butterick, Collette, 307
Butterick, George, 307
Button, John, 216
Butts, Mary, 87, 411
Bye, Reed, 403, 407
Byington, Robert, 411
Byrd, Anne, 406
Byrd, Don, 284, 305, 353–54, 369, 405–6, 418

Cage, John, 157, 192, 193, 207, 272, 282
Calas, Nicholas, 75
Callaway, Mary, 180
Cameron, 170
Campbell, Joseph, 219, 289, 391
Cantine, Holley, 91, 95–96
Caraher, Brian, 366
Carmines, Al, 268
Carpenter, Abigal, 5
Carpenter, Barth, 123, 128, 130
Carpenter, Isabelle, 5
Carpenter, Lewis, 5
Carpenter, Marguerite Pearl. See Duncan, Marguerite Pearl Carpenter
Carpenter, Milton, 5
Carpenter, Myrtle, 8
Carpenter, Wesley, 4

Carpenter, William, 5
Carpenter, Whipple, 5
Carroll, Inara, 267
Carroll, Paul, 192, 231, 469n3
Carter, Jimmy, 345, 375, 377, 391
Carter, Rosalynn, 391
Casalino, Larry, 424–25, 427, 430, 432–33
Cassady, Neal, 160
Cassirer, Ernst, 142, 153, 396, 409
Centaur Press, 116, 123, 125, 128
Cernovich, Nik, 157
Cheatham, David, 347
Cherry, Don, 195
Chessman, Caryl, 195
Chomsky, Noam, 272
Circle, 99
Clark, Leslie, 328
Clark, Tom, 108, 166
Clarke, John, 367
Cocteau, Jean, 58, 76, 87, 139, 152
Cohen, Betty, 367
Cohn, Marguerite, 304
Cole, Norma, 409, 415, 418, 420–21, 424–26, 428, 431–34
Coleman, Victor, 296
Coleridge, Samuel Taylor, 140, 390
Collins, Clara, 119
Collins, James Francis II, 119
Collins, Jess: childhood of, 119; collaborations with Duncan, 141, 312; collaborations with Lawrence Jordan, 190, 194, 223; education of, 119; exhibitions, 126, 199, 235, 238, 241, 251, 297, 308, 299–300, 320; health problems of, 334, 424; marriage to Duncan, 119–20; Narkissos, 353; Paste-Ups, 300–1, 308, 312, 320, 351; reclusiveness of, 122, 163, 194, 299, 375; Salvages, 351; sex life of, 197, 333–34; Translations, 251, 297, 299, 332, 351
Colvig, Bill, 295
Conner, Bruce, 127
Conner, Robert, 165, 170
Cooley, Mary Elizabeth. See Harris, Mary Elizabeth Cooley
Cooney, Blanche, 61–63, 66, 67, 69, 72, 77, 81, 85–86, 136–37

Jones, Stanley, 454n10
Jonson, Ben, 390
Jordan, Lawrence, 125, 133–34, 170, 190, 194, 223, 233, 254
Jordan, Patricia, 254
Joris, Pierre, 316, 441
Joseph, Barbara, 211, 213, 230–34, 254, 262, 271–75, 277, 283, 286, 300, 318, 330, 391, 403, 409, 413–14
Joyce, James, 11, 50, 64, 102, 199, 264, 292, 414
Jung, Carl, 252, 329, 349, 378, 391, 393, 409

Kael, Pauline, 48, 60, 64, 81, 85, 89, 100, 106, 112, 123, 184
Kaffka, Robert, 180
Kafka, Franz, 71
Kalos, Victor, 142
Kamenetz, Rodger, 411
Kandel, Leonore, 246
Kandinsky, Wassily, 58
Kantner and West, 241
Kantorowicz, Ernst, 56, 97, 109–11, 113–15, 117, 121, 154, 173, 215, 237, 344, 372, 455n2, 463n24
Karloff, Boris, 18
Karnes, Karen, 157
Kattan, Naim, 376
Keats, John, 67
Keilty, James, 130, 134
Keller, Marjorie, 399
Kelly, Jobyna, 232–33
Kelly, Robert, 32, 195, 216, 233, 404–5
Kennedy, John F., 203, 228, 237, 276
Kennedy, Robert, 274, 280
Kennard, Gladys, 394, 399
Kenyon Review, 90
Keough, Edna, 38–39, 50, 193, 397, 407
Kerouac, Jack, 144, 163, 173
Kerr, Clark, 237, 243
Kessler, Chester, 130
Kiehl, Jim, 270
Killian, Kevin, 197
Killian, Sean, 373, 374
King, Martha, 317
King, Martin Luther, Jr., 274, 277
Kingsbury, Anne, 317
Kipling, Rudyard, 29

Kitaj, R.B., 262, 273, 279, 294, 307, 314–16, 348–50, 360, 368, 400–2, 497n3
Kiyooka, Roy, 208
Kizer, Carolyn, 411–412
Klein, Melanie, 444n6
Klima, Ed, 291
Knight, Janice, 400, 403
Kocik, Robert, 393
Köhler, Wolgang, 396, 409
Kostolefsky, Joseph, 165
Kramer, Cecily, 47, 50, 51, 53, 82
Krause, Louise Antoinette, 45–46, 52
Krikorian, Leo, 160
Krishnamurti, Jiddu, 19
Kronebusch, Michael, 433
Krushchev, Nikita, 195
Kunitz, Stanley, 245
Kyger, Joanne, 166, 169, 172, 180, 183, 253, 268–69

La Charity, Ralph, 311
Laeuchli, Samuel, 271
Lamantia, Philip, 84, 99, 123, 129, 160
Laughlin, James, 58, 80, 270, 298–99, 304–5, 353, 369
Lawrence, D.H., 31, 38, 115, 162, 384–85, 480n11
Lax, Robert, 206
Lee, Paul, 282
LeFevre, Frances, 369
Léger, Fernand, 215–16
Leite, George, 99
Le Mons, Richard, 371
Lenya, Lotte, 156
Levertov, Denise, 128, 136–39, 143–44, 149, 159, 162–63, 167–68, 173–78, 181, 183, 187, 190, 192–96, 198–99, 205–7, 209–10, 212, 215–18, 222–24, 228–30, 232–33, 236, 239, 243–44, 247–51, 268, 271, 280–81, 304, 306, 309, 313, 319, 335, 374, 412–13; political argument with, 255–57, 283, 285, 294, 301–3, 321
Levy, D.A., 255
Lindsay, Vachel, 114, 152
Linenthal, Mark, 270
Lipton, Lawrence, 238
Livesay, Dorothy, 329
Loewinsohn, Ron, 169, 421

TEXT
11/14 Adobe Garamond Premier Pro
DISPLAY
Adobe Garamond Premier Pro
COMPOSITOR
Westchester
PRINTER AND BINDER
Thomson-Shore